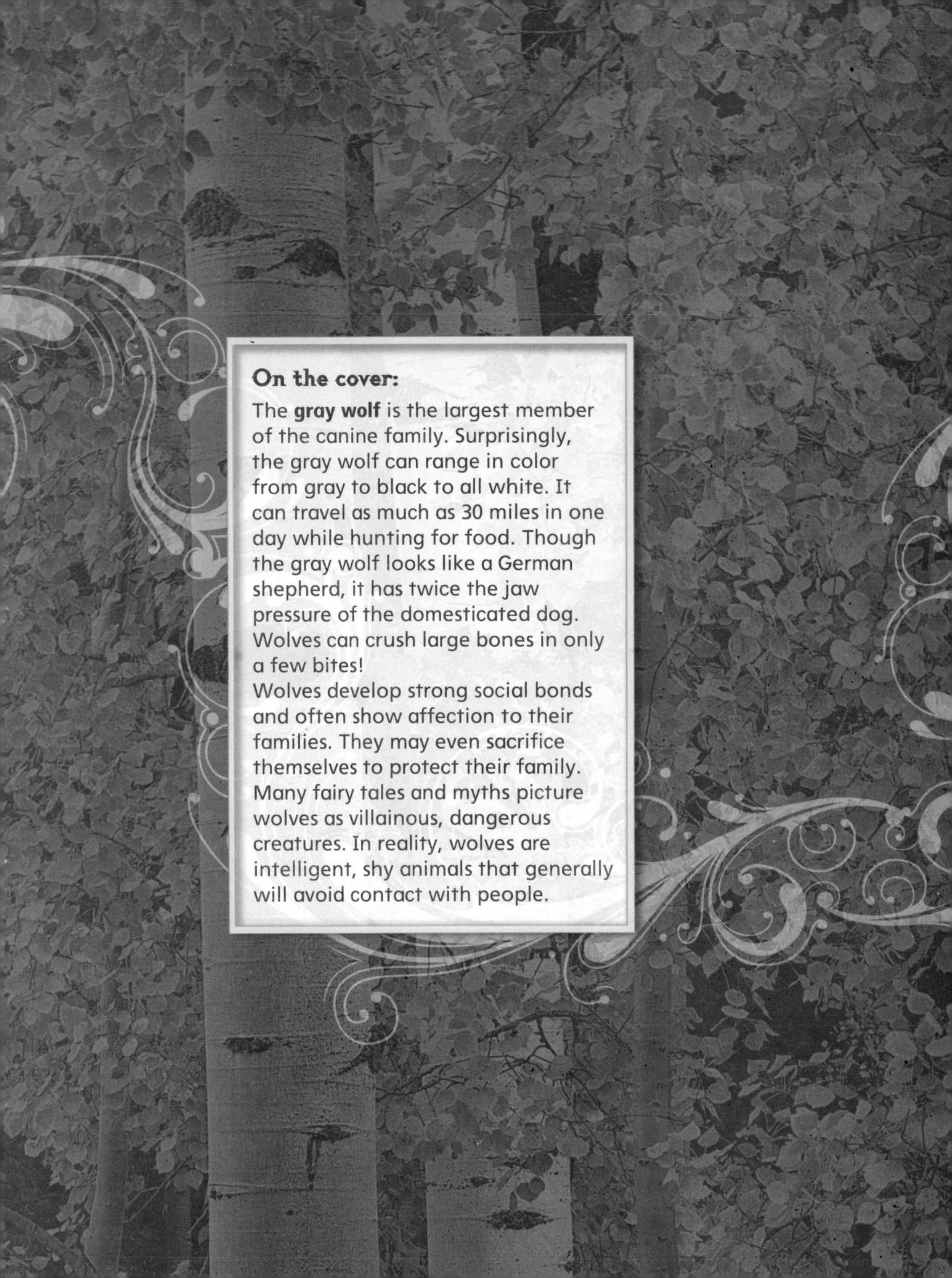

On the cover:

The **gray wolf** is the largest member of the canine family. Surprisingly, the gray wolf can range in color from gray to black to all white. It can travel as much as 30 miles in one day while hunting for food. Though the gray wolf looks like a German shepherd, it has twice the jaw pressure of the domesticated dog. Wolves can crush large bones in only a few bites!

Wolves develop strong social bonds and often show affection to their families. They may even sacrifice themselves to protect their family. Many fairy tales and myths picture wolves as villainous, dangerous creatures. In reality, wolves are intelligent, shy animals that generally will avoid contact with people.

California Treasures

A Reading/Language Arts Program

Program Authors

Diane August
Donald R. Bear
Janice A. Dole
Jana Echevarria
Douglas Fisher
David Francis
Vicki Gibson
Jan E. Hasbrouck
Scott G. Paris
Timothy Shanahan
Josefina V. Tinajero

Macmillan/McGraw-Hill

Contributors

Time Magazine, The Writers' Express, Accelerated Reader

Immediate Impact. Lasting Transformation. wex.org

learning through listening

Students with print disabilities may be eligible to obtain an accessible, audio version of the pupil edition of this textbook. Please call Recording for the Blind & Dyslexic at 1-800-221-4792 for complete information.

B

The McGraw·Hill Companies

 Macmillan/McGraw-Hill

Published by Macmillan/McGraw-Hill, of McGraw-Hill Education, a division of The McGraw-Hill Companies, Inc., Two Penn Plaza, New York, New York 10121.

Printed in the United States of America

ISBN: 978-0-02-199971-2/5
MHID: 0-02-199971-6/5

6 7 8 9 (RJE/LEH) 11

Welcome to
California *Treasures*

Imagine taking a close-up look at a rattlesnake's rattle, learning what life was *really* like in the early West, or reading about a boy who creates a new civilization in his backyard. Your **Student Book** contains these and other award-winning fiction and nonfiction selections.

Treasures Meets California Standards

The instruction provided with each reading selection in your **Student Book** will ensure that you meet all the **California Reading/Language Arts Standards** for your grade. Throughout the book, special symbols (such as) and codes (such as **R 1.1.2**) have been added to show where and how these standards are being met. They will help you know *what* you are learning and *why*.

What do these symbols mean?

CA = Tested Standards in California

 = Skill or Strategy that will appear on your test

R = Reading Standards

W = Writing Standards

LC = Language Conventions Standards

LAS = Listening and Speaking Standards

Macmillan/McGraw-Hill

Unit 1

Personal Experiences

Taking a Stand

Coretta Scott King Award

Newbery Medal

The American West

Unit 3

Creative Expression

Using Your Wits

Unit 4

Teamwork

Team Up to Survive

x

Science
Investigations

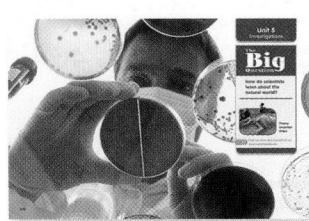

THE BIG QUESTION

THEME: Scientists at Work

THEME: Slithery Snakes

Unit 6

We're in Grade 5 Now
Changes

The Big Question

Why do people take action to support what they believe in?

Theme Launcher Video

LOG ON ▶ Find out more about people taking a stand at www.macmillanmh.com.

3

Sometimes conditions or situations cause people to take action.

If a company does not provide a safe work environment, for example, its workers might go on strike until the company installs fire alarms, easy escape routes, and a sprinkler system. The workers have that right because everyone is entitled to a safe workplace. If the employees did not take a stand, the unsafe and unlawful conditions might end up causing someone to be seriously hurt.

Learning about important issues and why people fight to support them will help you better understand why it is important to be an active citizen.

Research Activities

Throughout the unit, you will be gathering information about injustices that have made people speak up or take action. Research a cause that a person or group has chosen to take a stand. Focus your research on and create a pamphlet about it.

Keep Track of Ideas

As you read, keep track of what you are learning about people who take a stand. Use the Layered Book Foldable to organize your ideas. On the top section, write the unit theme: Taking a Stand. On each layer of the book, write facts you learn each week.

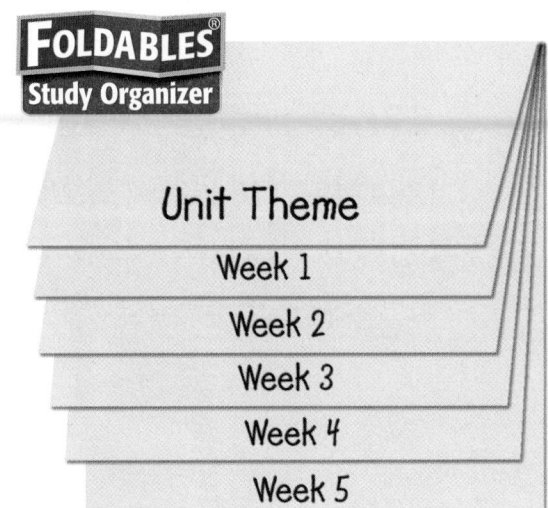

FOLDABLES®
Study Organizer

Unit Theme
Week 1
Week 2
Week 3
Week 4
Week 5

Research Toolkit

Conduct Your Unit 1 Research Online with:

Research Roadmap
Follow step-by-step guide to complete your research project.

Online Resources
- Topic Finder and other Research Tools
- Videos and Virtual Fieldtrips
- Photos and Drawings for Presentations
- Related Articles and Web Resources

California Web Site Links

LOG ON ▶ Go to www.macmillanmh.com for more information.

California People

Clara Shortridge Foltz Lawyer and Suffragette
Fought for the state bar to accept women. She was a successful lawyer, editor of a magazine and newspaper, and a force in Republican Party politics.

FIGHTING BACK

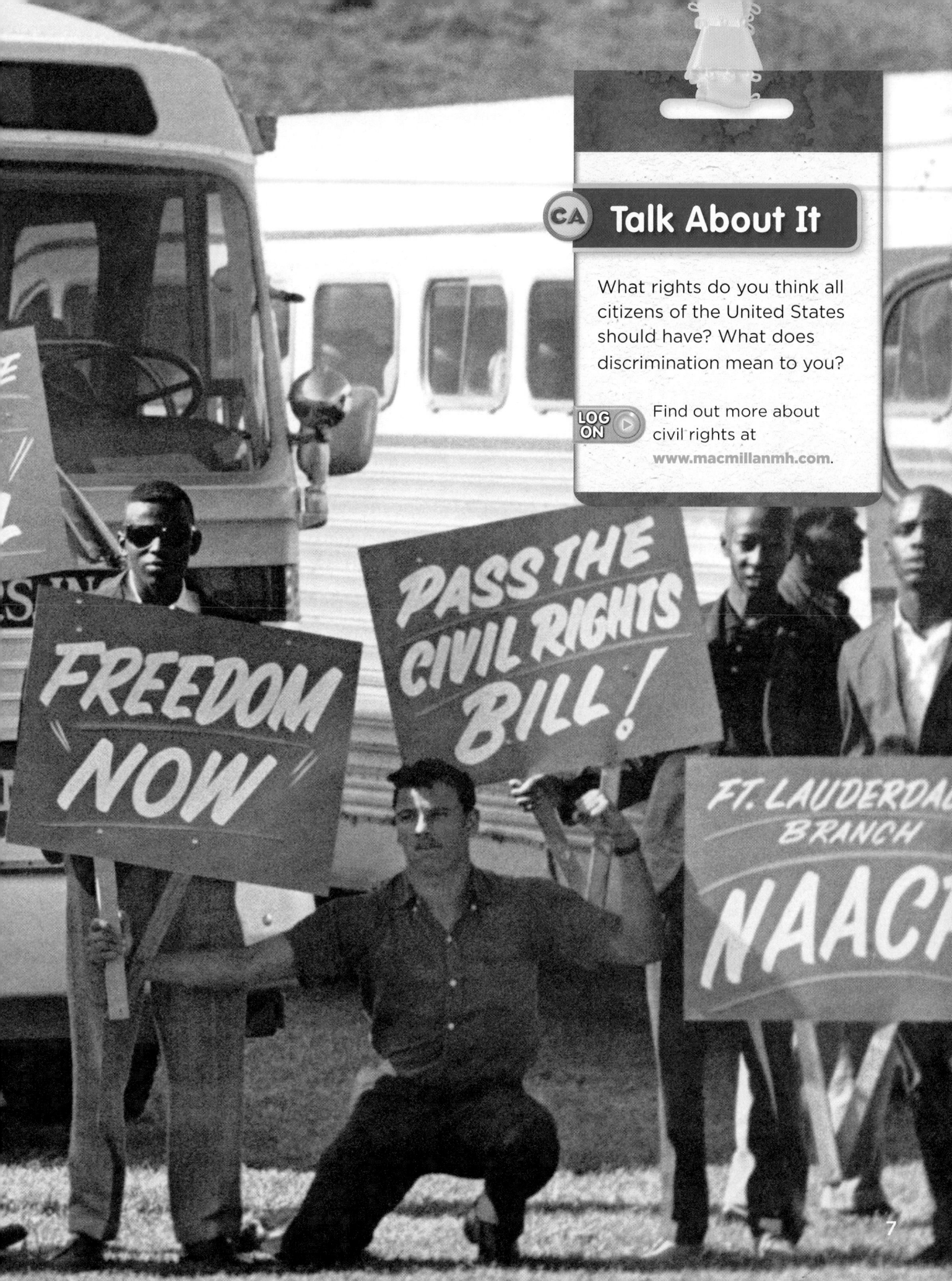

What rights do you think all citizens of the United States should have? What does discrimination mean to you?

LOG ON ▶ Find out more about civil rights at **www.macmillanmh.com**.

FREEDOM NOW

PASS THE CIVIL RIGHTS BILL !

FT. LAUDERDA BRANCH

NAAC

7

Lunch Counter Encounter

by Ilysa Samuelson

Best buddies Joe and Paul loved to play baseball. They spent the morning of June 23, 1963, working on their swings and working up a sweat. It was a humid day and the Mississippi sun felt hot enough to **scald** water. At about noon Paul started feeling hungry. He wanted to grab a burger from the drugstore on Center Street with Joe.

"Ummm, I'll ask my mom if I can go. I need her **permission**," Joe said. The situation was complicated for Joe. There were rules that would keep him from sitting with his friend because of the color of his skin.

Joe's parents and many other people were trying to change those rules. They listened to the speeches of Dr. Martin Luther King, Jr., a famous preacher who was trying to change unfair practices in many southern states. In Joe's house there was a picture of Dr. King with his **autograph** on the bottom.

"It's mighty hot," Joe's mother said. "Why don't you boys take the bus to the drugstore? I've got the bus **fare** right here."

"No, ma'am," Paul **blurted** out suddenly. "Bikes are fine!" He hated riding the bus with Joe. They would be forced to sit in the back.

When the boys reached Center Street, Joe started to get nervous.

"Dad told me about some trouble here last week," Joe said sadly. "I'll just wait outside."

"Not happening!" Paul said, as he grabbed Joe's arm and the two boys marched through the door. Paul's hand was **clenched** in a fist as they headed for two empty stools.

A scowling man suddenly **approached** them and blocked their way. "Go around back if you're with *him*," he said pointing at Joe.

Before the boys could respond, a woman's voice interrupted the discussion.

"These boys will be joining me," the soft voice said. The man and the boys turned to see a woman in a wheelchair beside them. "Excuse us," she said smiling, as she moved her chair toward the man, intending to go forward.

Not wanting to appear rude to the woman, the man stepped aside.

Joe and Paul followed the woman to the stools. She parked beside them and talked steadily as they ordered and ate their lunch.

After the boys finished, the woman met them on the sidewalk outside. "Have a **spectacular** afternoon," she said. "Two friends like you, *that* shouldn't be a problem." Then she wheeled away. Joe and Paul never got her name, but they never forgot her either.

Reread for Comprehension

Story Structure

Character and Setting Authors include details about **character** and **setting** that will enrich the story and help develop the plot. Character traits are special qualities of a story character's personality. The setting is where and when the story takes place. Use your Character and Setting Chart as you reread the selection to figure out the character's traits and information about when and where the story takes place.

Character	Setting

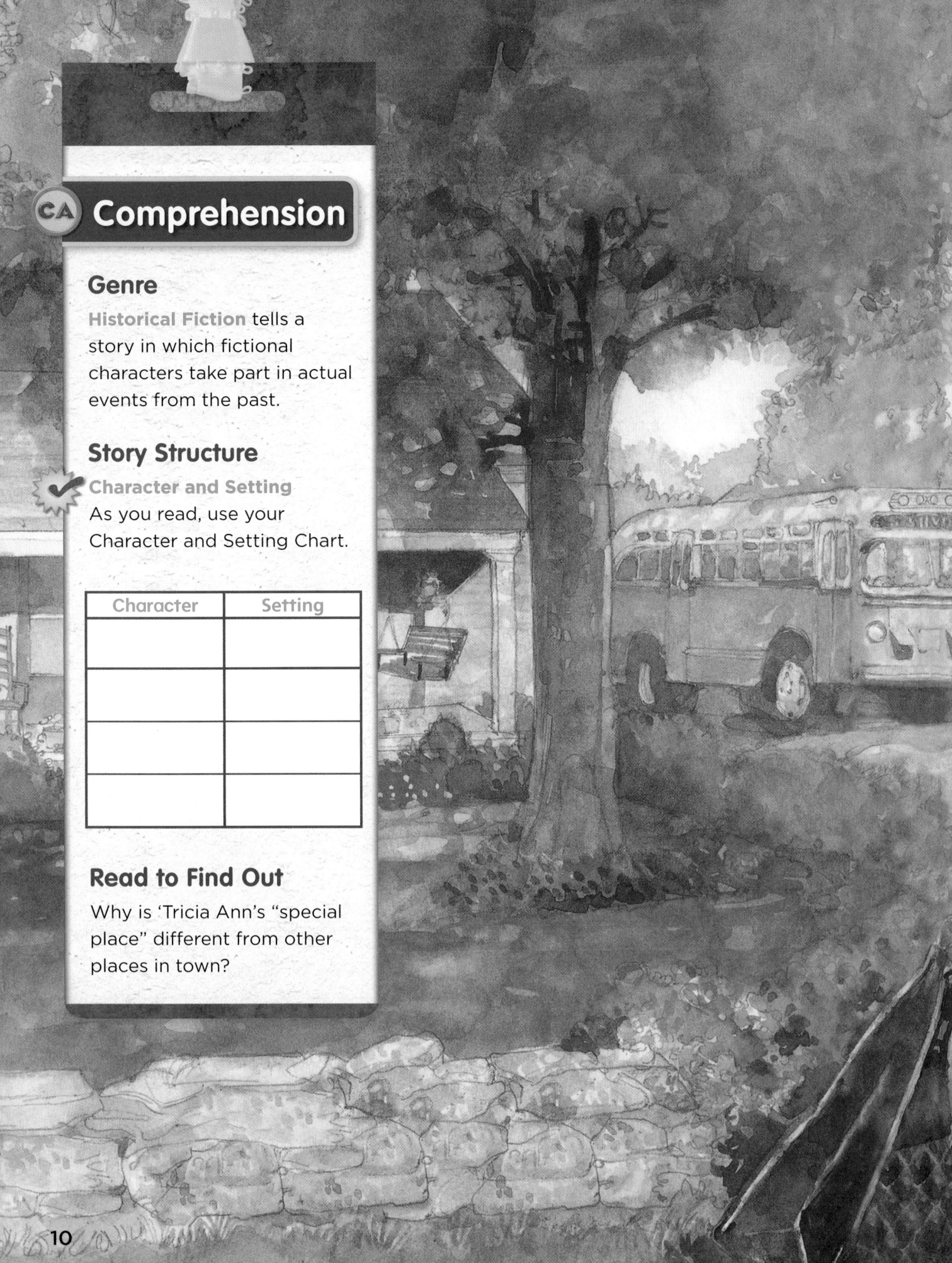

CA Comprehension

Genre

Historical Fiction tells a story in which fictional characters take part in actual events from the past.

Story Structure

Character and Setting
As you read, use your Character and Setting Chart.

Character	Setting

Read to Find Out

Why is 'Tricia Ann's "special place" different from other places in town?

Goin' Someplace Special

by Patricia C. McKissack
illustrated by Jerry Pinkney

'Tricia Ann was about to burst with excitement. Crossing her fingers and closing her eyes, she **blurted** out her question. "Mama Frances, may I go to Someplace Special by myself, today? Pretty please? I know where to go get off the bus and what streets to take and all."

Although it had another name, 'Tricia Ann always called it Someplace Special because it was her favorite spot in the world.

"Please may I go? Pretty please with marshmallows on top?"

"I don't know if I'm ready to turn you loose in the world," Mama Frances answered, tying the sash of 'Tricia Ann's dress. "Goin' off alone is a mighty big step."

"I'm ready," the girl said, taking a giant leap across the floor. "See what a big step I can make?"

Mama Frances chuckled, all the time studying her granddaughter's face. "I trust you'll be particular, and remember everything I've told you."

"I will, I will," 'Tricia Ann said, real confident-like. Suddenly, her smile grew into a full grin. "So you're saying I can go?"

"I reckon . . . But you best hurry on 'fore I change my mind."

Pulling her pocketbook up on her shoulder, 'Tricia Ann blew her grandmother a thank-you kiss. Then she rushed out the door and down the sidewalk.

"And no matter what," Mama Frances called after her, "hold yo' head up and act like you b'long to somebody."

At the corner a green and white bus came to a jerky stop and hissed. When the doors folded back, 'Tricia Ann bounded up the steps and dropped in the **fare** same as when Mama Frances was with her.

The girl squared her shoulders, walked to the back, and took a seat behind the Jim Crow sign that said: COLORED SECTION.

'Tricia Ann had seen such signs all her life. She recalled the first time she and Mama Frances had taken this bus ride, and her grandmother had told her, "Those signs can tell us where to sit, but they can't tell us what to think."

"I'm gon' think about Someplace Special." 'Tricia Ann said to herself and turned to look out the window.

Stop by stop the bus began to fill. At the Farmer's Market, people crowded on, carrying bags of fruit and vegetables. Mrs. Grannell, Mama Frances' friend from sewing club, climbed on board. As she inched her way toward the back, 'Tricia Ann noticed that there were no seats left behind the Jim Crow sign. So she stood up and gave Mrs. Grannell hers.

"It's not fair," she said glaring at the empty seats up front.

"No, but that's the way it is, honey," said Mrs. Grannell.

"I don't understand why—" she began. But by now the bus had reached 'Tricia Ann's stop in front of Capitol Square in the heart of downtown. The doors swung open and she hurried off.

"Carry yo'self proud," Mrs. Grannell called out the window as the bus pulled away.

> **Character and Setting**
> What does Mama Frances tell 'Tricia Ann about the sign on the bus? What does this tell you about the character of Mama Frances?

Holding her hat, 'Tricia Ann leaned back as far as she could to see Peace Fountain's magnificent water show. It made her dizzy to watch the sprays that shot into the air, but she liked the feeling and turned 'round and 'round with her arms outstretched. Then, giggling, she staggered on wobbly legs to a nearby bench.

Instantly, 'Tricia Ann leaped to her feet. On the bench was a sign that said: FOR WHITES ONLY.

Her face fell, and she wished for Mama Frances's strong hand to hold. "Silly signs," she muttered as she strutted away on sober legs.

At the edge of the square, she greeted Jimmy Lee, a street vendor. "What's got yo' face all clouded up like a stormy day?" he asked, handing 'Tricia Ann a free pretzel.

"Jim Crow makes me so mad!" she said. "My grandfather was a stonemason on Peace Fountain. Why can't I sit down and enjoy it?"

Jimmy Lee pointed to a sign in Monroe's Restaurant window. He said, "My brother cooks all the food they serve, but do you think we can sit at one of their tables and have a BLT and a cup of coffee together?" Then with a chuckle he whispered, "Not that I'd want to eat anything Jesse cooks. That man can't even now **scald** water."

The light changed and 'Tricia Ann carefully started across the street. "Don't let those signs steal yo' happiness," Jimmy Lee called after her.

'Tricia Ann pulled her shoulders back and fixed her thoughts on being inside that warm and welcoming place where there were no signs. Hurrying up Tenth Avenue, she passed the filling station, and stopped to buy a pop to wash down Jimmy Lee's pretzel.

At the second light, the Southland Hotel rose up in front of her, as **spectacular** as a palace. Mr. John Willis, the hotel's doorman, saw her. "I b'lieve an angel done slipped 'way from heaven," he said, smiling.

'Tricia Ann managed to smile back. Mr. John Willis always said the nicest things. "No, sir. It's just me."

"Your mouth is smiling, but your eyes aren't," he said. Just then a long white car with two police escorts pulled up in front of the hotel. A man with black shiny hair and shy eyes stepped out. Suddenly people were everywhere, screaming and begging for his **autograph**. 'Tricia Ann got caught in the crowd and swept inside.

Character and Setting
What is the time and place of the story? What clues tell you this?

19

So often she'd wondered what it would feel like to walk on the royal carpet that covered the double-winding staircase, or to stand in the light of the chandelier that looked like a million diamonds strung together. Now, there she was—smack in the middle of the Southland Hotel's grand lobby.

Somebody pointed at her. "What is *she* doing in here?

It seemed as if the whole world had stopped talking, stopped moving, and was staring at her. The manager pushed his way to the front of the crowd. "What makes you think you can come inside? No colored people are allowed!" And he shooed the girl away with his arms.

'Tricia Ann backed out, shaking her head. "I-I didn't mean . . . ," She said, trying hard not to cry.

Hurrying past Mr. John Willis, 'Tricia Ann ran straight into the Mission Church ruins where Mama Frances often stopped to rest. There in the protection of the walled garden, the girl let the tears come. "Getting to Someplace Special isn't worth it," she sobbed. "I'm going home."

"My flowers have been watered already," came a voice above her. It was Blooming Mary, an elderly woman who took care of the garden with neither **permission** nor pay. Everybody said she was addled, but Mama Frances didn't agree. "Blooming Mary is a kind and gentle soul," she'd told 'Tricia Ann.

"You lost, child?" The woman asked.

Trying to steady her voice, 'Tricia Ann answered. "No, ma'am, I just wish my grandmother was here to help me get to Someplace Special."

"You can't get there by yourself?"

"It's too hard. I need my grandmother."

Blooming Mary nodded and thought on the matter.

Then she said, "I believe your granny *is* here, just as my granny is here with me even as I speak. Listen close. Tell me what you hear."

All 'Tricia Ann heard was the distant buzz of a bumblebee. What was Blooming Mary talking about?

But as she listened closer, she began to hear her grandmother's steady voice. "You are somebody, a human being—no better, no worse than anybody else in this world. Gettin' someplace special is not an easy route. But don't study on quittin', just keep walking straight ahead—and you'll make it."

'Tricia Ann recalled these words from many conversations they'd had in this quiet place. They were so comforting, she didn't feel alone anymore. She wiped her eyes and straightened her hat. "You were right, ma'am," the girl told Blooming Mary. "Mama Frances is here. And she wouldn't want me to turn back."

"So, you aren't lost after all," said Blooming Mary, giving 'Tricia Ann a bright orange zinnia.

"No, ma'am, I'm not." And saying good-bye, she headed, real determined-like, on her way.

Two blocks later 'Tricia Ann came to the Grand Music Palace, where a group had gathered for the matinee performance. As the girl **approached**, a little boy spoke to her. "Howdy, I'm Hickey and I'm six years old today. You comin' in?"

Before 'Tricia Ann could answer, an older girl grabbed his hand. "Hush, boy," she said through **clenched** teeth. "Colored people can't come in the front door. They got to go 'round back and sit up in the Buzzard's Roost. Don't you know nothing?" his sister whispered harshly.

Hickey looked at 'Tricia Ann with wide, wondering eyes. "Are you going to sit up there?"

"In the last three rows of the balcony? Why, I wouldn't sit up there even if watermelons bloomed in January. Besides, I'm going to someplace very, very special," she answered, and then 'Tricia Ann skipped away.

"I want to go where she's goin'" she heard Hickey say as his sister pulled him through the door.

At the corner 'Tricia Ann saw a building rising above all that surrounded it, looking proud in the summer sun. It was much more than bricks and stone. It was an idea. Mama Frances called it a doorway to freedom. When she looked at it, she didn't feel angry or hurt or embarrassed. "At last," she whispered, "I've made it to Someplace Special."

Before bounding up the steps and through the front door, 'Tricia Ann stopped to look up at the message chiseled in stone across the front facing:

PUBLIC LIBRARY: ALL ARE WELCOME.

PUBLIC LIBRARY: ALL ARE WELCOME.

25

Visit Someplace Special with
Patricia C. McKissack and Jerry Pinkney

Patricia C. McKissack based this story on her life growing up in Nashville, Tennessee. Like 'Tricia Ann, she couldn't go many places, but she could always go to the public library. Patricia wanted children to know that even though life sometimes seems unfair, love and determination often make things turn out all right. It was her teachers, she says, who started her on the road to books, reading, and the public library.

Jerry Pinkney started drawing by copying from comic books and magazines, just like his two older brothers. In junior high school, he sketched people he saw on the street, and has been drawing and painting ever since. Jerry has even drawn eleven postage stamps for the U.S. Postal Service. "I'd rather draw than do anything else!" he says.

Another book by Patricia C. McKissack and Jerry Pinkney:
Mirandy and Brother Wind

 **LOG ON** ▶ Find out more about Patricia C. McKissack and Jerry Pinkney at **www.macmillanmh.com**.

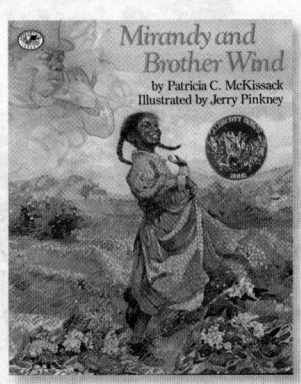

CA ## Author's Purpose
The author shares information about the past as she entertains. Identify historic details.

CA Critical Thinking

Summarize

Use your Character and Setting Chart to help you summarize *Goin' Someplace Special*. Be sure your summary includes the most important information from the story.

Character	Setting

Think and Compare

1. If the author changed the **setting** of the story to the present, how would the story be different? Use story details to support your answer. **Analyze Story Structure: Character and Setting**

2. Reread page 24. Why would the **character** Mama Frances refer to the library as "a doorway to freedom"? Use details from the story in your answer. **Synthesis**

3. How would you react to a law that denied you **permission** to sit in the front of a bus or enter a hotel lobby? **Analyze**

4. Explain what Mama Frances meant when she said that getting someplace special is not always easy. Do you agree or disagree with her? Explain your answer. **Evaluate**

5. Reread "Lunch Counter Encounter" on pages 8–9. Compare Joe's experience at the drugstore to 'Tricia Ann's experience on the bus and in the hotel lobby. How are their situations the same? How are they different? Use evidence from both stories to support your answer. **Reading/Writing Across Texts**

Through My Eyes

Genre
An **Autobiography** is an account of events in a person's life that is written in that person's own words.

Text Feature
A **Time Line** is a diagram of several events arranged in the order in which they took place. A time line helps to organize information in an easy, visual way.

Content Vocabulary
unconstitutional

banned

boycott

segregation

by Ruby Bridges

Ruby Bridges was six years old in November 1960, and she was about to make history. A judge had recently ruled that it was unconstitutional for African American students to be banned from attending the same school as white students. Ruby Bridges was the first black student to attend William Frantz Elementary School in New Orleans. Here's an account in her own words of her first day at her new school and of the events that followed:

Once we were inside the building, the marshals walked us up a flight of stairs. The school office was at the top. My mother and I went in and were told to sit in the principal's office. The marshals sat outside. There were windows in the room where we waited. That meant everybody passing by could see us. I remember noticing everyone was white.

The artist Norman Rockwell showed the event in his painting called *The Problem We All Live With.*

All day long white parents rushed into the office. They were upset. They were arguing and pointing at us. When they took their children to school that morning, the parents hadn't been sure whether William Frantz would be integrated that day or not. After my mother and I arrived, they ran into classrooms and dragged their children out of the school. From behind the windows in the office, all I saw was confusion. I told myself that this must be the way it is in a big school.

That whole first day, my mother and I just sat and waited. We didn't talk to anybody. I remember watching a big, round clock on the wall. When it was 3:00 and time to go home, I was glad. I had thought my new school would be hard, but the first day was easy.

When we left school that first day, the crowd outside was even bigger and louder than it had been in the morning. There were reporters and film cameras and people everywhere. I guess the police couldn't keep them behind the barricades. It seemed to take us a long time to get to the marshals' car.

Entering the school with U.S. Marshals

Marching Through History

CA Reading a Time Line

One way to review events from history is to organize them on a time line.

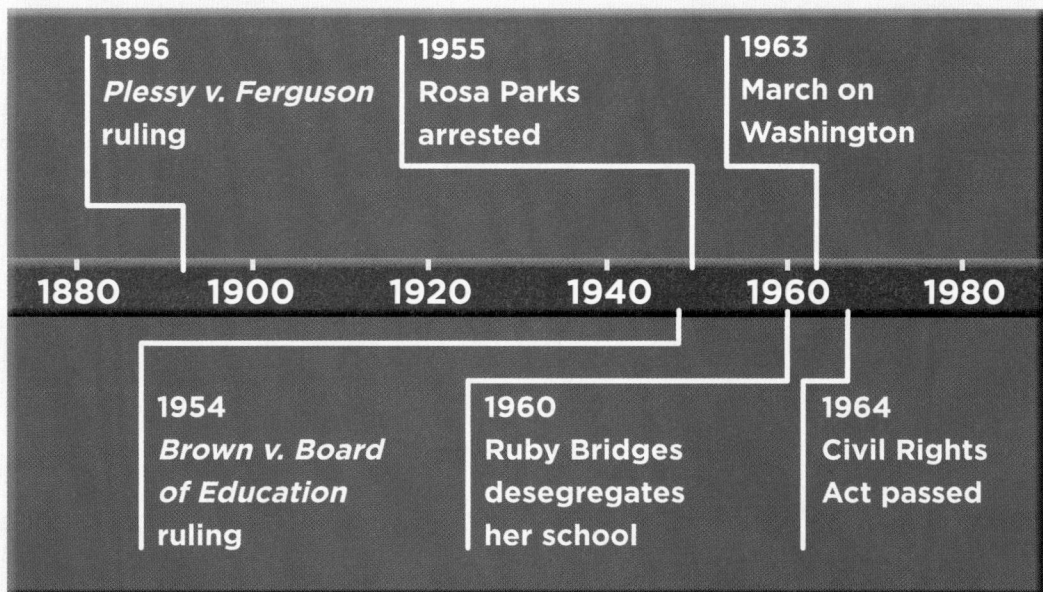

1896
Plessy v. Ferguson ruling

1955
Rosa Parks arrested

1963
March on Washington

1880   1900   1920   1940   1960   1980

1954
Brown v. Board of Education ruling

1960
Ruby Bridges desegregates her school

1964
Civil Rights Act passed

Later on I learned there had been protestors in front of the integrated schools the whole day. They wanted to be sure white parents would **boycott** the school and not let their children attend. Groups of high school boys, joining the protestors, paraded up and down the street and sang new verses to old hymns. Their favorite was "Battle Hymn of the Republic," in which they changed the chorus to "Glory, glory, **segregation**, the South will rise again." Many of the boys carried signs and said awful things, but most of all I remember seeing a black doll in a coffin, which frightened me more than anything else.

After the first day, I was glad to get home. I wanted to change my clothes and go outside to find my friends. My mother wasn't too worried about me because the police had set up barricades at each end of the block. Only local residents were allowed on our street. That afternoon I taught a friend the chant I had learned: "Two, four, six, eight, we don't want to integrate." My friend and I didn't know what the words meant, but we would jump rope to it every day after school.

My father heard about the trouble at school. That night when he came home from work, he said I was his "brave little Ruby."

The next day brave Ruby and her mother drove to school with the marshals. Here's more of Ruby's amazing story, in her own words:

When we finally got into the building, my new teacher was there to meet us. Her name was Mrs. Henry. She was young and white. I had not spent time with a white person before, so I was uneasy at first. Mrs. Henry led us upstairs to the second floor. As we went up, we hardly saw anyone else in the building. The white students were not coming to class. The halls were so quiet, I could hear the noise the marshals' shoes made on the shiny hardwood floors.

Mrs. Henry took us into a classroom and said to have a seat. When I looked around, the room was empty. There were rows of desks, but no children. I thought we were too early, but Mrs. Henry said we were right on time. My mother sat down at the back of the room. I took a seat up front, and Mrs. Henry began to teach.

I spent the whole first day with Mrs. Henry in the classroom. I wasn't allowed to have lunch in the cafeteria or go outside for recess, so we just stayed in our room. The marshals sat outside. If I had to go to the bathroom, the marshals walked me down the hall.

On the steps of William Frantz Elementary School

My mother sat in the classroom that day, but not the next. When the marshals came to the house on Wednesday morning, my mother said, "Ruby, I can't go to school with you today, but don't be afraid. The marshals will take care of you. Be good now, and don't cry."

I started to cry anyway, but before I knew it, I was off to school by myself.

Ruby Bridges finished the school year, and she returned in the fall. As years passed and Ruby continued in school, the fight for civil rights continued as well. In 1995 Ruby and Mrs. Henry decided to work together. Now they visit classrooms around the country, sharing what they have learned.

Ruby tells students that schools can bring people together. Ruby and Mrs. Henry are no longer a class of two.

Mrs. Henry and Ruby Bridges

 Critical Thinking

1. Use the time line on page 29 to find how many years separate the arrest of Rosa Parks and the Civil Rights Act. **Reading a Time Line**

2. How is reading Ruby Bridges's own words different from reading about her experience from a secondary source? **Evaluate**

3. Think about "Through My Eyes" and *Goin' Someplace Special*. How are the experiences that Ruby Bridges and 'Tricia Ann went through similar? How are they different? Explain. **Reading/Writing Across Texts**

 History/Social Science Activity

Research a person involved in the civil rights movement. Write a summary of his or her life. Include a time line of important events in the life of this person.

 Find out more about civil rights at **www.macmillanmh.com**.

Writing

✔ Moment

Good writers focus on a **moment**. They include details of sight, sound, and smell to help readers share that moment.

Reading and Writing Connection

Read the passage below. Notice how the author Patricia C. McKissack focuses on a moment in her story.

An excerpt from
Goin' Someplace Special

The author focuses on the moment when people are getting onto the bus. It lasts only a short time, but details in that moment help us picture what happened.

Stop by stop the bus began to fill. At the Farmer's Market, people crowded on, carrying bags of fruit and vegetables. Mrs. Grannell, Mama Frances' friend from sewing club, climbed on board. As she inched her way toward the back, 'Tricia Ann noticed that there were no seats left behind the Jim Crow sign. So she stood up and gave Mrs. Grannell hers.

Goin' Someplace Special
by Patricia C. McKissack
Illustrated by Jerry Pinkney

Read and Find

Read Jane's writing below. What did she do to focus on a moment? Use the checklist below to help you.

At the Aquarium

by Jane L.

I peeked into the glass cage. Where was the frog? I could just imagine the moist, brown soil smelling like my basement. Just when I was about to give up, there it was. It was about the size of the tip of my thumb. It had a blue and black swirled pattern on its back and a set of bright green eyes staring right back at me.

Read about the moment when I discovered a wonderful frog!

Writer's Checklist

 Does the writer pick a short amount of time and write a lot about it?

 Does the writer use specific details about her experience?

 Can you picture the **moment** the way Jane experienced it?

Stand Up For What's Right

CA **Talk About It**

What do you think the people in this photograph are doing? How are they taking a stand?

LOG ON ▶ Find out more about people taking a stand at **www.macmillanmh.com**.

35

Vocabulary

injury
couple
mournful
sympathy
delivering
shrieks
decency

Idioms

An **Idiom** is a phrase that cannot be understood from the meanings of the separate words in it. *To pull a person's leg* is an idiom that means "to trick or tease." You sometimes find idioms in a dictionary.

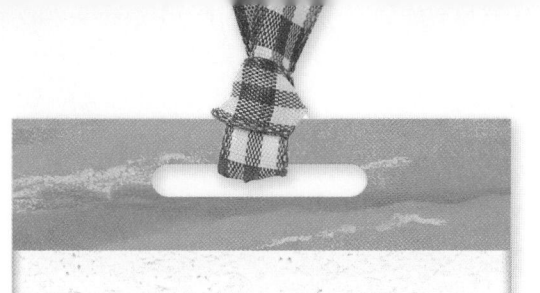

A REAL SURVIVOR

by Todd Sampson

"What was that?" Mom gasped as she suddenly stepped on the brakes of the van. "I think a big bird just hit our windshield," she said. "We've got to go look for it! I bet it has an **injury** that might be causing it some pain."

At first I thought she was pulling my leg. Then Mom pulled off to the side of the road, and I found the bird in a **couple** of minutes. It was a **mournful** sight, lying there with its sad eyes and broken wings.

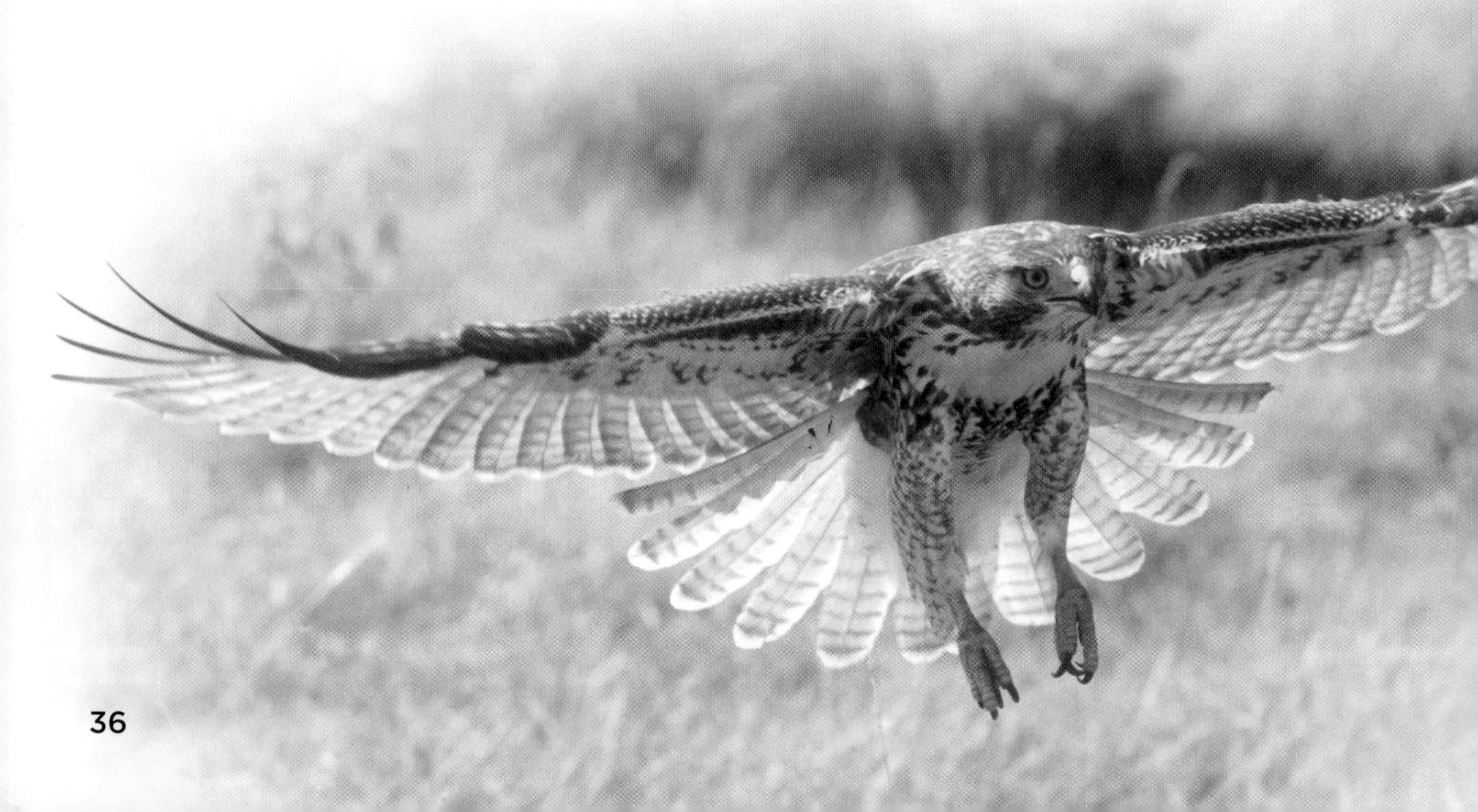

"Do you think it's going to make it?" I whispered to Mom.

Mom's face was full of caring and **sympathy**. She checked that the bird was breathing and then said we should get help. "There's a place about an hour away from here called the Raptor Trust. The people there know how to care for injured birds," she said.

"Let's go!" I said excitedly. Both of us were intent on **delivering** the bird to the people at the Raptor Trust.

The hawk didn't make a sound during our drive. Mom and I didn't say much either. All we did was slurp the icy smoothies we bought with lunch as we hoped for the best.

When we finally found the place, I was amazed. So many beautiful birds lived there—hawks, owls, falcons, and eagles. Their loud **shrieks** filled the air. The knowledgeable workers told us the bird we had rescued was a female red-tailed hawk. They explained that sometimes injured birds can be set free. Although I had become very attached to her, I hoped that would be the case with our hawk.

A veterinarian checked our bird and assured us that she would recover. When it was time to leave, I thanked all the workers for their kindness and **decency** in helping the birds. I took a picture of my hawk for the bulletin board in my room, and I promised her we'd be back to visit. That's when I knew I had chosen the perfect name for her: Survivor.

Reread for Comprehension

Monitor Comprehension

Make Inferences Writers do not always tell readers everything that takes place in a story, but they do give readers clues to help them figure out missing information. When you make **inferences,** you take clues the author gives you and combine them with information you already know. Use your Inferences Chart to make inferences about characters and plot events.

Text Clues	What You Know	Inferences

CA Comprehension

Genre

Realistic Fiction tells an invented story that could have happened in real life.

Monitor Comprehension

✔ **Make Inferences**
As you read, use your Inferences Chart.

Text Clues	What You Know	Inferences

Read to Find Out

Why does Marty take such good care of Shiloh?

Shiloh

written by Phyllis Reynolds Naylor

illustrated by Joel Spector

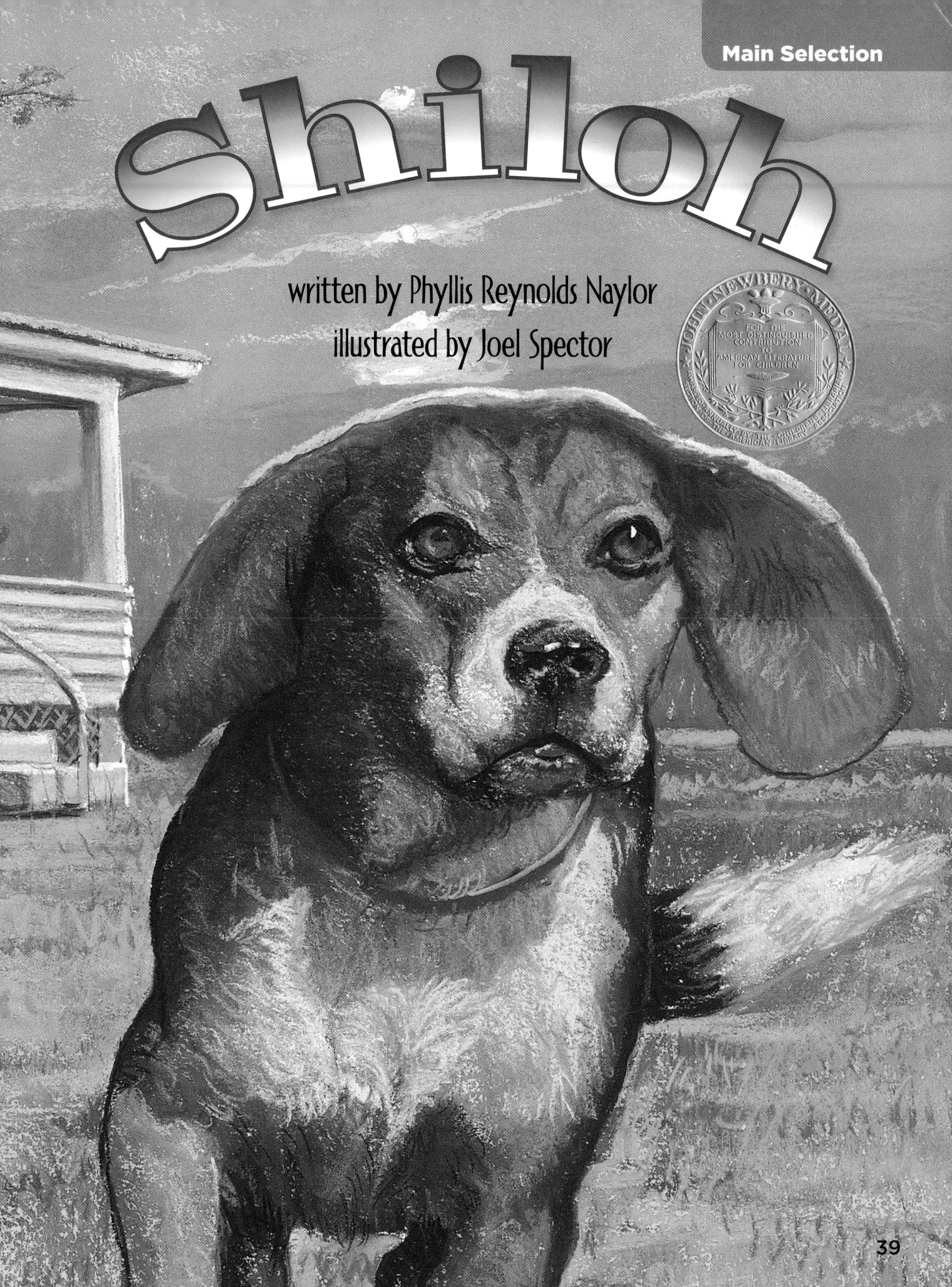

Marty Preston is faced with a dilemma when a young beagle turns up at his home near Friendly, West Virginia. Marty feels sure the dog is being abused by his owner but Marty's parents say he must take him back. It hurts Marty to return the runaway dog to his cruel master. That's when Marty secretly decides he'll do anything to save the dog he names Shiloh.

Sure seems strange having Shiloh in the house that night, after trying so hard to keep him secret. Strange, too, the way Ma takes to him. Seems like she can't hardly pass his box next to the stove without reaching down to pet him, making low **sympathy** noises in her throat, way she does when Dara Lynn or Becky or me gets sick.

Dad don't say much. He come home to find Shiloh there, he just stands off to one side, listening to what Doc Murphy said about him; he don't get close enough for Shiloh to take a lick.

But when supper's over and I go off to the bathroom to brush my teeth, I peek back through the doorway, and Dad's over by Shiloh's box, letting him lick his plate clean. Dad crouches there a minute or two, scratching all down Shiloh's back and up again.

What I'm figuring, see, is by the time Shiloh's better, everybody will love him so much they just can't let him go—even Dad. I'm hoping Dad will go over to see Judd Travers, make him an offer for Shiloh, and then he'll be ours. The trouble with this kind of thinking, though, is we don't have the money.

I'll probably be through junior high school, almost, before I earn enough to pay Doc Murphy's bill. To buy Shiloh from Judd, even if Judd's willing to sell, I'd have to collect aluminum cans all through high school, too. Can't make very much with cans. I try to think about what other kind of work I can do that would pay me more, but except for **delivering** the county paper on Friday afternoons, nothing else comes to mind. And somebody's got that job already.

> **Make Inferences**
> How does Marty's dad feel about Shiloh?
> What clues tell you how he feels?

It's sort of like Shiloh's there and he's not. In the next **couple** of days, everybody's pettin' him every chance they get. Becky feeds him the crusts off her toast—breaks off little bits, and **shrieks** every time she feels Shiloh's mouth slurp them out of her fingers.

Ma's putting up beans in jars, and all the while she hums to Shiloh like he's a baby in a cradle, not a dog in a box. Dara Lynn's got an old hairbrush, and she just can't seem to brush that dog enough. Even Dad sits down one evening and gets out every tick Shiloh's got on him. Takes a little dab of turpentine and rubs it on the tick's rear end, and the tick backs out of Shiloh's skin mighty quick.

The thing that makes it seem like Shiloh's *not* there is that nobody except me and Dara Lynn and Becky talks about him. Ma and Dad don't even once mention his name out loud, as though saying it makes him ours, which he ain't. As though if you don't talk about him, maybe he'll disappear as quietly as he come that day in the rain.

What everyone's waiting for, I guess, is something to happen. Every day Shiloh's getting a little stronger. Two days after Doc Murphy brought him here, Shiloh's up limping around on his bad leg. Ma puts some papers beside his box for him to do his business on, but he won't, so for the first couple days I pick him up, carry him out to the yard, and after he's done his business there, I bring him in again. But now he's pushing open the back screen himself and going down into the yard, then comin' back and tapping on the screen with one paw, so we'll let him in. Somebody, sometime, is bound to see him. Becky, sometime, bound to say something. Even David Howard, when his ma came to pick him up the other day, opens his mouth right off and says something about Shiloh.

43

"Who's Shiloh?" she asks, and David realizes he's let it slip.

"Old stray cat," he says, and now I've got David lying.

Worse part about having Shiloh here in the house where I can play with him anytime I like is that it's hard to leave him when I go out collecting cans. But I've got to earn money now more than ever, so each day, when Shiloh takes his long nap, I set out with my plastic garbage bag hanging out one jeans' pocket.

One day I walk all the way to Friendly and ask at the grocery, where the county paper is dropped, if they'll put in my name as a carrier. Mr. Wallace says he'll turn my name in, but he's already got six names ahead of me, and one of 'em is a grown man with a car. Don't see how I can match that.

I study the bulletin board at the back of the store where people put up notices. Stand on one foot and then the other reading the whole danged board, and seems like everybody got something to sell, or want to be hired, nobody wants to buy. Only two jobs listed, one for an appliance salesman and some woman who wants her house painted.

Mr. Wallace sees me looking at the board, and he comes over and takes down the notice about a woman wanting her house painted.

"That's already taken," he tells me.

That night, while we finish supper, Shiloh's going around the table, putting his nose in everyone's lap, looking **mournful**, waiting for somebody to slip him something to eat. I can tell Ma and Dad's trying their best not to laugh. Ma won't let us feed him at the table.

What I'm dying to ask Dad is did he tell Judd Travers about his dog being here. Dad won't mention it so I don't ask. Maybe I don't want to know, I tell myself.

And then, just as Ma's dishing up a peach cobbler that we're going to eat with hot milk, I hear a sound outside that makes my bones feel like icicles inside me.

44

Shiloh hears it, too, and I know right away it's what I think it is, because Shiloh sticks his tail between his legs, puts his belly low to the floor, and climbs back into his box.

Ma and Dad look at Shiloh. They look at each other. Then there's the slam of a truck door outside, footsteps on the ground, footsteps on the porch, and a *rap, rap, rap* at the back door. Everybody stops eating, like we was all froze to death in our chairs.

Dad gets up and turns on the porch light, and there he is, Judd Travers, looking as mean and nasty as I ever seen him look. He don't even ask can he come in; just opens the screen and steps inside.

"Ray Preston," he says, "somebody told me you got my dog."

Dad's looking serious. He nods and points toward the box by the stove. "Over there, Judd, but he's hurt, and we've been taking care of him for you."

Judd stares at Shiloh and then at Dad. "Well, I'll be danged," he says, almost softly. "Somebody knows my dog is missing, takes him in, and don't even have the decency to tell me?"

"We *were* going to tell you," Dad says, and he's looking straight at Judd. "Nobody wants to hear his dog's been hurt, though, and we wanted to make sure he was going to pull through." Then he turns to me. "Marty," he says, "you want to tell Mr. Travers how his dog come to be here?"

He knows I don't. He knows I'd rather swim a river full of crocodiles than face Judd Travers. But it's my story to tell, not Dad's, and he always did make us face up to what we'd done.

"Your dog come over here twice because you been mistreatin' it," I say, and my voice don't sound near as strong as Dad's. Sort of quavery. I clear my throat and go on: "So second time it come over, I built it a pen up in the woods and Dad didn't know it, and that German shepherd of Baker's got in and fought Shiloh."

> **Make Inferences**
> What are some of the ways Marty shows his concern for Shiloh?

"Fought who?"

"The beagle. Shiloh, that's what I've been callin' him. And Shiloh got hurt bad. It was my fault for not making the fence higher. We took him to Doc Murphy and he patched him up."

Judd Travers is still staring around the room like he never saw the likes of us before. Finally he lets out his breath through his teeth and slowly shakes his head: "And I got to find out all this from Doc Murphy?"

I couldn't believe Doc would go tell him.

"Somebody goes to the doc the other day and sees a beagle lying out on his back porch. Tells me about it later. Says he thinks maybe the dog's mine. So I ride over to Doc's this evening, and he tells me it was you who brought him in."

Judd walks across the kitchen, and at the thud of each footstep, Shiloh huddles down farther and farther in the box, like maybe he can make himself disappear. His whole body is shaking. Ma sees it, I know, because she watches for a minute, then turns her face away quick.

Judd stares down at Shiloh—at his bandage and the shaved place where he's all stitched up—the rip on his ear. "Look what you done to my *dog*!" he yells at me, eyes big and angry. I swallow. Nothin' I can say to that.

Travers squats down by the box. He puts out his hand, and Shiloh leans away, like he's going to be hit. If that don't prove the way he treats 'em, I don't know what would, but Judd's saying, "I never mistreated my dogs. This one was shy when I got him, that's all. I sure never caused him an **injury** like this one. Wouldn't never have happened if you'd brought him back like I told you." I close my eyes.

49

When I open 'em again, Judd's putting his hand on Shiloh's head, roughlike, sort of patting him, and you can tell he ain't got much practice being kind. Still, hard to prove Shiloh was mistreated *before* he got to Judd's. How do you go about proving something like that?

"It was wrong of Marty to pen up your dog, Judd, and we've already talked about that," Dad says. "He's the one who's going to pay Doc Murphy for patching him up, and soon as the dog is strong, we'll drive him over to your place. Why don't you let us keep him until then, in case he needs more care?"

Judd stands up again and looks at me. I stare back, but I don't say nothing.

And then Ma can't take it anymore. She says, "Judd, Marty's got awful attached to that dog, and we'd like to know how much you want for it. Maybe we can scrape up the money to buy him."

Judd looks at her like she's talking some kind of nonsense, like we are all getting crazier by the minute.

"That dog's not for sale," he says. "Paid good money to get me a hunting dog, and he could be one of the best I've had. You want to keep and feed him till he's better, okay with me. It's you that got him all tore up, and you paying the bill. But I want him back by Sunday."

Screen door slams again, truck starts up, and then he's gone.

51

Walk Along with Phyllis Reynolds Naylor

Phyllis Reynolds Naylor may look as if she is walking, swimming, or playing the piano, but often she is really thinking about her next book. "I'm always listening," she says. "I look at what kids are doing, and listen to what they are talking about. I am thinking back to when I was that age, and I discover that feelings don't change over the years."

Phyllis kept up with the story of the real Shiloh as years passed. Thankfully, his life has changed for the best. The once-abused dog has even become a celebrity in the town of Shiloh, West Virginia. Fans from as far away as Canada come to visit and see the dog, people, and places that inspired Phyllis to write this story.

Other books by Phyllis Reynolds Naylor:
Saving Shiloh and Shiloh Season

 Find out more about Phyllis Reynolds Naylor at **www.macmillanmh.com**.

CA Author's Purpose
Authors of fiction often write to entertain. Why do you think Phyllis Reynolds Naylor wrote *Shiloh*?

CA Critical Thinking

Summarize

Use your Inferences Chart to help you summarize *Shiloh*. Include only important information from the excerpt you read.

Text Clues	What You Know	Inferences

Think and Compare

1. Marty is supposed to return Shiloh to Judd on Sunday. **Make an inference** about what Marty will do using story details and knowledge from personal experience in your answer. **Monitor Comprehension: Make Inferences**

2. Reread page 46. Why does Marty's father make Marty explain to Judd what caused Shiloh's **injury**? What does Marty's explanation reveal about his character? Use story details to support your answer. **Analyze**

3. Marty considers many ways to earn money to take care of Shiloh. What would you do to earn money for something that you really wanted? **Analyze**

4. Marty rescues Shiloh by hiding him. In what other ways do people try to save animals from harm? **Evaluate**

5. Reread "A Real Survivor" on pages 36–37. Compare and contrast the experiences the injured hawk and Shiloh have with people who offered them help. Use details from both stories to explain your answer. **Reading/Writing Across Texts**

Genre

Nonfiction Articles present facts about real people, living things, places, or events.

✔ Text Features

Photographs and Captions give more information about the topic of an article.

Content Vocabulary

**veterinarian diagnose
fractures   contamination
anatomy**

Love at First Sight

by Amy Yin

At age 14 Rexanne Struve fell in love during a visit to a dairy farm. No, Rexanne did not fall in love with a boy on the trip but with a cow. Right then she knew she wanted to work with animals and become a **veterinarian**. To achieve her goal, she had to finish high school, college, and veterinary school. Struve eventually became the first woman veterinarian in Carroll County, Iowa.

As a teenager Struve started preparing for her future. Science was not her favorite subject in high school, but she took as many courses as she could. During the summers she worked as a horseback-riding instructor.

When Struve finished high school, she attended a university in Kansas. Struve says that her high school courses and summer job helped prepare her for her college studies. Struve took more science courses in college. These courses helped her better understand animals and how their bodies work. After college Struve went to veterinary school for four more years. Finally, she graduated and was ready to begin her career as an animal doctor.

In the beginning it was not easy being a female veterinarian. In fact, Struve's grandfather told her that being a vet was not a job for a woman. Even some of her clients felt uneasy around her as she took care of their large animals.

Today, however, Struve has a busy practice where she treats both small and large animals. The farmers with whom she works no longer question her or wonder whether she can do the work. She has proven herself to be the right person for the job.

Animal owners in far-off places rely on mobile veterinary units like the one Dr. Struve uses.

When animals are sick or hurt, Dr. Struve works to make them better. Each year she sees about 800 small animals, such as birds and cats, in her office. She also has about 300 farm clients, including many who own large animals. It is difficult for farmers to bring large animals to Dr. Struve's office, so she brings her office to them. Dr. Struve drives a special truck that holds medicines, equipment, and supplies for surgery. Sometimes Dr. Struve has to operate on animals. She also treats **fractures**, or broken bones, and gives medicine to sick animals.

Dr. Struve sees many different breeds of animals. Once she saw 16 different kinds in one day! Many days start with Dr. Struve traveling in her truck to farms where she treats sheep, hogs, horses, and cattle. Sometimes she even cares for llamas and ostriches. Then she comes back to her office to deal with people's pets.

This variety poses a challenge because Dr. Struve must know the **anatomy** of every animal in order to care for their injuries. She feels rewarded when she can **diagnose** and then treat an illness that is hard to recognize.

Like all veterinarians Dr. Struve does not just take care of sick animals. She also works to keep healthy animals well. She helps bring baby animals into the world. Another big part of her job is to give vaccinations, or shots of medicine, to animals to prevent disease.

This cattle chute holds the cattle still and in the right position. It allows a veterinarian to work safely.

Dr. Struve must be very careful not to spread disease. She does not want germs from one farm to spread to another farm and cause **contamination**. To prevent the spread of disease, Dr. Struve wears coveralls. After she treats a sick animal she takes off her coveralls and washes her boots, too.

Dr. Struve has a tough job. She is on call around the clock, so people often call her late at night. She often works 80 to 90 hours in one week. Dr. Struve also faces danger from some of the animals she works with. They can weigh as much as 1,000 pounds. She has been kicked and bitten by some of her patients. She has even had bones broken. Even so, it was love that led Rexanne Struve to choose her job, and it is love that keeps her there.

 Critical Thinking

1. Look at the photograph of the cattle chute on page 56. How does the chute help the vet work safely?
Photographs and Captions

2. Why is Dr. Struve's job important to farmers? **Evaluate**

3. Think about "Love at First Sight" and *Shiloh*. How could someone like Dr. Struve have helped Marty? **Reading/Writing Across Texts**

 History/Social Science Activity

Through research, find a photograph of someone doing a job that you might like to do someday. Find out facts about what the job requires. Write a caption, explaining what training the person needed to get this job.

Find out more about careers at
www.macmillanmh.com.

Reading and Writing Connection

✓ **Moment**

When you focus on a **moment**, you give readers details of sight and sound to help them experience the moment you are describing.

Read the passage below. Notice how the author Phyllis Reynolds Naylor focuses on a moment in her story.

An excerpt from *Shiloh*

It takes only a moment for Judd to walk across the kitchen. The details describing that moment help us imagine exactly what happened and how everyone felt.

Judd walks across the kitchen, and at the thud of each footstep, Shiloh huddles down farther and farther in the box, like maybe he can make himself disappear. His whole body is shaking. Ma sees it, I know, because she watches for a minute, then turns her face away quickly.

Shiloh
Written by Phyllis Reynolds Naylor
Illustrated by Tod Spector

Read and Find

Read Jen's writing below. What did she do to focus on the moment? Use the checklist below to help you.

The First Day

by Jen C.

I didn't know what to make of this new place. I unbuttoned my jacket and opened up my locker. It was still full of some kid's stuff from last year. That did not make me feel welcome! I put my jacket in my locker and emptied out my brand new pencil box and pink notepad.

Read about the moment I arrived at my new school.

Writer's Checklist

 Does the writer describe a short amount of time and write a lot about it?

 Does the writer use specific details about her experience?

 Can you picture the **moment** the way Jen experienced it?

Talk About It

How do we pay tribute to those who stand up for what they believe?

LOG ON ▶ Find out more about memorials at **www.macmillanmh.com**.

REMEMBERING THE PAST

This illustration depicts a stop on the Underground Railroad.

Toward FREEDOM

The National Underground Railroad Freedom Center was **dedicated** in August 2004. The museum is located in Cincinnati, Ohio, and sits just across the river from Kentucky, a former slave state.

Journey to a Better Life

In the mid-1800s, there were more than 4 million slaves in the United States. They were denied **equality** with other people. Under the law, slaves had no civil rights, including such basic rights as owning property.

The Underground Railroad was the name for a series of places where slaves could stay during their journey north

Slave pens like the one below held imprisoned slaves for days or even months until they were sold.

to escape slavery in the South. Code words were used to protect slaves on their trip. The places they stopped were called "stations," the people being guided toward freedom were called "packages," and the guides were called "conductors."

Preserving the Past

Artifacts—human-made objects from the past—and lectures at the museum teach about slavery and the trail to freedom. One of the **exhibits** is a slave pen where a slave dealer once locked up slaves. Visitors can enter the small building and imagine what it was like to be locked up in a cramped space with dozens of other people.

In the Hall of Everyday Heroes, museum visitors learn about people who stood up for what they believed. These heroes helped bring the basic right of freedom to many people. Visitors might learn that they, too, can stand up and make a difference.

Senator Ben Nighthorse Campbell

In September 2004 the Smithsonian Institution's National Museum of the American Indian in Washington, D.C., opened. What is the museum's goal? "To show and tell the world who and what we really are, and to use our own voices in the telling," says museum director Rick West. West is a member of the Southern Cheyenne tribe.

Senator Ben Nighthorse Campbell of Colorado, a Northern Cheyenne, helped get the project started. Exhibits represent more than 1,000 tribes. The sad chapters of the Native American story, in which millions died at the hands of settlers, are part of the museum's message. Native Americans insisted that Indian art and modern culture be key features of the museum.

Before the building was constructed, Chief Billy Redwing Tayac blessed the **site**. His tribe, the Piscataway, lived in the Washington, D.C., area. "The water is still here. The Earth is still here. And we are still here," he said. "We're very proud that Indian people today have a place to remember our ancestors."

TOP 5 MOST VISITED NATIONAL MONUMENTS

In 1906 President Theodore Roosevelt established Devils Tower in Wyoming as the first national monument in the United States. Today there are more than 60. Here are the 5 most popular ones.

		VISITORS A YEAR
1	**Statue of Liberty (New York)**	5,200,633
2	**Castle Clinton (New York)**	4,390,268
3	**Cabrillo National Monument (California)**	1,095,638
4	**Muir Woods National Monument (California)**	860,378
5	**Montezuma Castle (Arizona)**	853,821

(Source: National Park Service)

 **LOG ON** Find out more about national monuments at **www.macmillanmh.com.**

MAYA LIN
ARCHITECT OF MEMORY

How did one architect create two of the most powerful memorials in the United States?

Maya Lin

As is her habit, architect Maya Lin stayed away from the crowds—and the limelight. She stood behind the tinted windows of the Southern Poverty Law Center in Montgomery, Alabama. Outside, hundreds of visitors arrived at the **site** for the opening of the Civil Rights Memorial, which Lin designed. "I like standing back quietly," Lin said. "You create your message, and then it is out there on its own."

Lin's message can be found in the memorial's **exhibits**. This memorial honors those who died fighting for **equality** during the civil rights movement. Some visitors reached out to touch the names of loved ones carved into a black granite disk. Their faces were wet with tears. "I'm so thankful," said Sarah Salter, whose husband, Willie Edwards, Jr., was killed in Montgomery in 1957. "At last he's being recognized."

The Vietnam Veteran's Memorial is on the Mall with other visited places like the Washington Monument.

Remembering Vietnam Veterans

Nine years before the opening of the Civil Rights Memorial, Lin had been a senior at Yale University. She sent in the winning design for the Vietnam Veterans Memorial in Washington, D.C. After it was **dedicated**, angry veterans at first called the stark, V-shaped granite wall a "black gash of shame." Yet the memorial soon became the most visited monument in the capital. Millions of Americans touched—and were touched by—the more than 58,000 names carved into the stone. They are the names of Americans who died in Vietnam.

Lin's Vietnam Memorial does not present any **artifacts** of the Vietnam era. It is just a wall. This simple wall, however, helped the United States begin the long process of healing after years of bad feelings over the war. The memorial made it possible for the country to come together and honor those who had served.

A Different Way of Looking

"I'm an architect, I'm an artist, I make things," Lin said. "I just love the fact that I can make a work and put it out there and walk away from it and then look at it like everyone else."

As Lin grew up in her hometown of Athens, Ohio, one of the subjects she did well in was mathematics. That skill first led her toward architecture and now shapes her outlook on work. "If you present me with a problem, and if I like it and think I can work with it, I'll do it." In fact, Lin finds herself driven to solve a problem immediately.

Visitors who pay respects often leave mementos.

65

Throughout Lin's career, she has shown her range as an architect. Her other projects include the design of a stage set in Philadelphia; an open-air gathering place at Juniata College in Pennsylvania; a "playful park" outside the Charlotte Coliseum in North Carolina (with trees shaped like spheres); and a 38-foot clock for a New York City train station that has moving rays of light instead of hands.

Lin's work shows a thoughtful approach to building design. "It's the kind of thing," Lin said, "that requires patience, awareness, and added sensitivity."

Inspiration from a Great Leader

Too young to remember the civil rights movement firsthand, Lin researched it for months while working on the design for the Civil Rights Memorial. She was struck by a line from Martin Luther King, Jr.'s "I Have a Dream" speech. That line said, "We will not be satisfied until justice rolls down like waters and righteousness like a mighty stream." Lin thought the calm, soothing quality of water

...UNTIL JUSTICE ROLLS DOWN LIKE WATE
AND RIGHTEOUSNESS LIKE A MIGHTY STRE

MARTIN LUTHE

The words of Martin Luther King, Jr., carved on the wall in the background, inspired Lin's design.

At the Civil Rights Memorial, Sarah Salter touches the name of her husband, who was killed during the civil rights movement.

and its quiet, constant sound would be perfect for the area in front of the center. This is a place "to appreciate how far the country has come in its quest for equality and to consider how far it has to go."

Using King's quote as her theme, Lin designed a granite disk that is 12 feet in diameter. Inscribed on it are the names of 40 freedom fighters and landmark events of the civil rights movement. Behind it she designed a black granite wall nearly 9 feet high and 39 feet long, also covered by water. King's words were carved into the rock of this wall. "I'm trying to make people become involved with the piece on all levels," Lin said, "with the touch and sound of the water, with the words, with the memories."

Memories of the past are very important to Lin. After all, she asked, "If you don't remember history accurately, how can you learn?"

CA Critical Thinking

1. What does Maya Lin love about her work?

2. What is the main idea of this article?

3. What people and events are honored with statues and monuments in your city or town?

4. What are some things the National Underground Railroad Freedom Center, the National Museum of the American Indian, the Civil Rights Memorial, and the Vietnam Veterans Memorial all have in common?

67

Show What You Know

Author and Me

The answer is not directly stated. Think about what you have read to figure it out.

It took many years for women in the armed forces to receive recognition.

A Salute to SERVICEWOMEN

Throughout our nation's history, nearly 2 million women have served in the armed forces. Their brave work is remembered at the Women in Military Service for America Memorial. The memorial opened in Arlington National Cemetery in Virginia in 1997. The Vice President at the time, Al Gore, helped dedicate the memorial. He thanked servicewomen for "their countless acts of bravery and sacrifice."

The memorial covers more than four acres and is surrounded by a semicircular stone wall 30 feet tall. In front of the memorial are a fountain and a reflecting pool. The use of light and water symbolizes life. Two hundred jets of water create a sound that represents the voices of women blended together in one purpose. The reflecting pool is a symbol that these women's lives and stories are unified, or brought together, into one history.

The memorial's mission is to "let the generations know that women in uniform also guaranteed their freedom." To accomplish this, the outreach program provides information kits for elementary, middle, and high schools, as well as a Web site full of information. As a result 200,000 people on average visit the memorial each year to read about and honor these brave women.

Another source of information for visitors is the memorial roof, which is an arc of curved glass, 250 feet in diameter. Quotations by and about servicewomen are etched on it. Like diary entries, they give a voice to women who have served their country honorably.

Go on

Now answer numbers 1 through 5. Base your answers on the selection "A Salute to Servicewomen."

1. **This nonfiction passage mainly**

   A   describes the Arlington National Cemetery.
   B   tells about a speech given to dedicate a memorial.
   C   tells how a memorial honors American servicewomen.
   D   shows the progress women have made in gaining rights.

2. **The purpose of the quotations etched on the memorial is**

   A   to explain the monument more clearly.
   B   to describe the effects of war on women.
   C   to express thanks for the contributions of women.
   D   to provide first-hand descriptions of the experiences of servicewomen.

> **Tip**
> You have to think about the entire passage to choose the best answer.

3. **Based on the passage, which statement *best* expresses the gratitude shown by the government toward servicewomen?**

   A   The fountain and reflecting pool symbolize life.
   B   Two million women have served in the armed forces.
   C   Vice President Gore thanked all servicewomen for their bravery.
   D   A four-acre memorial was built in Arlington National Cemetery to honor servicewomen.

4. **Use details from the article, photograph, and caption to explain why it is important to learn of the achievements of American servicewomen.**

5. **Describe the features of the memorial. Use details and information from the article to explain:**
   • why these features are appropriate to honor women in the military, and
   • why the author included these facts in the article.

Write on Demand

CA

People who do good things for others are often honored.

Think about a time when you or someone you know was honored.

Now <u>tell about a time</u> when you or someone you know was honored.

Narrative writing tells a story about a personal or fictional experience.

To figure out if a writing prompt asks for narrative writing, look for clue words such as <u>tell about a time</u> or <u>write a story about</u>.

Below, see how one student begins a response to the prompt above.

In response to the prompt, the writer told about a special event.

Last Friday we had an assembly for all the classes in school. Ms. Jones, the principal, stood beside a big oval plot filled with flowers planted in three circles of red, blue, and gold. She said, "This is a special occasion." We were dedicating our new school flower garden.

Our fifth-grade class had worked on the garden after school every day for weeks. This was our project to give something to our school community before we left Tyler School behind forever.

Then Ms. Jones surprised us. She called our class up to stand with her. "We will not forget what you did for us," she said.

Writing Prompt

Respond in writing to the prompt below. Write for 5 minutes. Write as much as you can, as well as you can. Review the hints before and after you write.

People who do special things for others deserve thanks.

Think about a person who did something special and deserved thanks.

Now write a story that tells about a time a person did something special and deserved thanks.

Writing Hints for Prompts

- ☑ Carefully read the prompt.
- ☑ Organize your ideas to plan your writing.
- ☑ Support your writing by focusing on the theme.
- ☑ Write in complete sentences with a variety of sentence structures.
- ☑ Choose words that help readers understand your ideas.
- ☑ Review your writing and edit as needed.

CA **Talk About It**

What are some ways friends can help one another?

LOG ON ▶ Find out more about helping others at www.macmillanmh.com.

Helping A Friend

by Katy Morales

Vocabulary

purchased	irresistible
forbidden	elegant
reluctant	mischievous
gossiped	hesitation

Word Parts

Suffixes are word parts added to the end of a base word or root to change its meaning. The suffix *–ous* means "full of" so *mischievous* means "full of mischief."

e-mail

Inbox

TO: Ron@example.com

Subject: The Jamaican Festival

Hi Ron:

Mama and Papa have **purchased** my ticket to Jamaica, but they have not decided if I can go to the Mermaid Festival when I'm there visiting my grandparents. My parents have always refused to let me go. They said it was **forbidden** for me to go until I could swim well.

Last month when I started asking Papa if I could go, he was **reluctant** to answer me. He was unwilling to make a decision. Mama said that I should show him that I was a strong swimmer. She also said I should prove to him that I was responsible enough to go.

Here's what I did. Last Sunday at the pool, I showed my father that I could swim ten laps in a row. Then when he was relaxing on the deck, I didn't interrupt him once.

What a long afternoon that was! Everyone in my family **gossiped** about who was going to be the Queen Mermaid at the festival. I heard so many rumors!

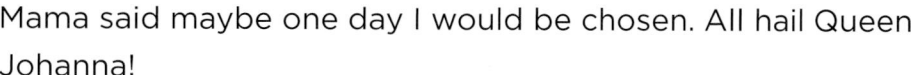

e-mail

Mama said maybe one day I would be chosen. All hail Queen Johanna!

I wanted to join in the noisy conversation. Chatting with my sisters about being queen one day was very tempting, almost **irresistible**. I wanted to describe how **elegant** I would look, dressed in a shimmering costume and glittering crown. I stayed quiet because I knew I'd get too excited and the noise might wake my father, who had fallen asleep.

Do you remember how the music blared from speakers on the beach during the festival last year? We could hear it all the way in town. With my eyes closed, I pretended that I was on the beach celebrating with everyone. I'm excited that this year I might actually take part in the festivities.

Today Mama warned me to stay on my best behavior. If I'm **mischievous** or naughty, Papa will not let me go. I will follow her advice without **hesitation** because I am so anxious to go. Wish me luck!

Hope to see you at the festival,

Johanna

Reread for **Comprehension**

Summarize

Problem and Solution

The main character in a story usually has one or two problems, or conflicts, that need to be solved. A Story Map helps you summarize information about the problems that characters encounter and how they solve them. Use your Story Map as you reread the selection to identify problems and solutions.

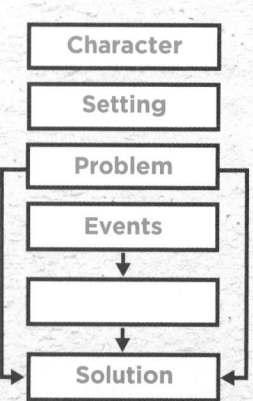

75

Comprehension

Genre

Fiction tells a story about characters and events that are not real.

Summarize

Problem and Solution
As you read, use your Story Map.

Character

Setting

Problem

Events

Solution

Read to Find Out

How do the sisters help their friend José Manuel?

The Night of San Juan

written by Lulu Delacre
illustrated by Edel Rodriguez

Award Winning Selection

Back in the 1940s, in Puerto Rico's walled city of Old San Juan, everybody knew everybody else. We neighborhood children played freely together on the narrow streets, while from windows and balconies adults kept a watchful eye on us. It was only my lonely friend José Manuel who was **forbidden** from joining us.

"Look, Evelyn," whispered Amalia. "He's up there again, watching us play."

Aitza and I looked up. There he was, sitting on his balcony floor. He peered sadly down at us through the wrought iron railing, while his grandma's soap opera blared from the radio inside. No matter how hard José Manuel tried, he could not convince his grandma to let him play out on the street.

"Too many crazy drivers! Too hard, the cobblestones! *¡Muy peligroso!*" His grandma would shake her head and say, "Too dangerous!"

77

Besides her fear of danger on the street, José Manuel's grandma kept to herself and never smiled, so most of us were afraid of her. That is, until my sisters and I changed all that.

"One day," Amalia suddenly announced, "I'm going to ask his grandma to let him come down and play." If anyone would have the courage to do that, it was my little sister Amalia. Even though she was only seven, she was also the most daring of the three of us.

We never knew what she would do next. In fact, at that very moment I could see a **mischievous** grin spreading across her freckled face as two **elegant** women turned the corner of Calle Sol. Once they strolled down the street in front of us, Amalia swiftly snuck up behind them and flipped their skirts up to expose their lace-trimmed slips.

"*¡Sinvergüenza!*" the women cried out. "Little rascal!"

We could hardly hold our laughter in. We all looked up to make sure none of the neighbors had seen her. If anyone had, we would surely have been scolded as soon as we got home. News traveled fast in our neighborhood.

Luckily, only José Manuel was watching us with amusement in his wistful eyes. Grateful for an audience, Amalia smiled at him, curtsied, and ran down the street toward the old cathedral with us chasing after her. I couldn't help but feel sorry for my friend as we left him behind.

Problem and Solution
How do you think Aitza, Amalia, and Evelyn will try and solve José Manuel's problem?

There was hardly any sea breeze that day, and running in the humidity made us quite hot.

"Let's get some coconut sherbet," said Amalia, peeling her damp red curls away from her sweaty neck.

"*Sí, sí!*" we agreed, and we chattered excitedly about our plans for that night all the way to the ice-cream vendor's wooden cart by the harbor.

It was June twenty-third, and that night was the Night of San Juan. For this holiday, the tradition was to go to the beach, and at exactly midnight, everyone would walk backward into the sea. People say that doing this three times on the Night of San Juan brings good luck. I thought of my friend José Manuel. Perhaps if he did this with us, his luck would change, and his grandma would allow him to play with us outside on the street.

I thought about this as we bought our coconut sherbet and then ate it perched on the knobby roots of the ancient tree above the port. Excitement stirred in me while the distant ships disappeared over the horizon.

"How can we get José Manuel to go to the beach tonight?" I asked my sisters.

"Evelyn, you know very well his grandma will never let him go," Aitza said. "You know what she will say—"

"*¡Muy peligroso!*" Aitza and Amalia teased at once. "Too dangerous!"

It was getting close to dinnertime, and we knew we had to be home soon if we wanted our parents to take us to the beach that night. So we took the shortcut back across the main square. In the plaza, groups of men played dominoes while the women sat by the fountain and **gossiped**. Back on the street we heard the vegetable vendor chanting:

"*¡Vendo yuca, plátanos, tomates!*"

He came around every evening to sell his fresh cassava, plantains, tomatoes, and other fruits and vegetables.

Leaning from her balcony, a big woman lowered a basket that was tied by a cord to the rail. In it was the money that the vendor replaced with two green plantains. As we approached our street I saw José Manuel and his grandma on the second floor. She gave José Manuel money and went back inside. He was about to lower his basket when I had an idea. Maybe there was a way we could ask him to join us.

"What if we send José Manuel a note in his grandma's basket inviting him to go to the beach with us tonight?" I offered.

"It will never work," Aitza said. "His grandma will not like it. We could get into trouble."

"Then we could ask her personally," I said.

"But what excuse could we use to go up there?" said Aitza. "Nobody ever shows up uninvited at José Manuel's house."

"Wait! I know what we can do," Amalia said, jumping up and down. "We'll tell him to drop something. Then we'll go up to return it."

Even though Aitza was very **reluctant**, we convinced her to try our plan. We wrote the note and asked the vegetable vendor to please place it in José Manuel's basket next to the vegetables. We impatiently waited on the corner as we watched. When he opened the note, he looked puzzled. He took the tomatoes he had **purchased** in to his grandmother. Soon he returned with his little red ball. He had just sat down to play when suddenly the ball fell from the balcony. It bounced several times, rolled down the hill, and bumped into a wall. Amalia flew after it. "I got it!" she called triumphantly, offering me her find.

With José Manuel's ball in my hand we climbed up the worn stairs of his pink apartment house. And while Aitza and I stood nervously outside his apartment trying to catch our breath, Amalia knocked loudly on the wooden door. With a squeaking sound it slowly opened, and there stood José Manuel's grandma wearing a frown as grim as her black widow's dress.

"¿*Sí?*" she said. "How can I help you?"

Aitza and I looked at each other. She looked as afraid as I felt. But without **hesitation**, Amalia took the little ball from my hand and proudly showed it to José Manuel's grandma. I wanted to run, but a glimpse of José Manuel's hopeful expression made me stay.

"This belongs to José Manuel," Amalia declared. "We came to return it." Amalia took a deep breath, then took a step forward. "We also wanted to know if he could come to the beach tonight with our family."

Aitza and I meekly stood behind Amalia.

"The beach?" José Manuel's grandma asked, surprised, as she took the little ball from Amalia's palm.

"Y-y-yes," I stuttered. "Tonight is the Night of San Juan, and our parents take us to the beach every year."

José Manuel's grandma scowled at us. How silly to think she would ever let him go. I suddenly felt embarrassed and turned to leave, pulling both sisters with me by their arms.

"Wait," we heard her raspy voice behind us. "Come inside for a *surullito de maíz.*"

It was then that I smelled the aroma of the corn fritters that was escaping from the kitchen. José Manuel's grandma was making *surullitos* for dinner.

"Oh, yes!" Amalia followed her in without a thought. And before we knew it, we were all seated in the living room rocking chairs next to José Manuel, eating the most delicious corn fritters that we dipped in garlicky sauce. Somehow, sitting there with José Manuel, his grandma seemed less scary. After we finished, José Manuel's grandma thanked us for our invitation and said she would let us know.

José Manuel smiled.

When we got home we found Mami waiting with her hands on her hips. She had just hung up the phone with José Manuel's grandma. She had reason to be upset. Not only were we late for supper, but in our excitement we had forgotten to ask for permission before inviting José Manuel to the beach. We all looked down, not knowing what to do or say.

"It wasn't my fault. It was Evelyn and Amalia's idea," volunteered Aitza, the coward.

"*Bendito*, Mami," I said. "Don't punish us, we forgot."

"Forgot?" Mami asked.

"*Sí*, Mami," we all said at once. "We are sorry."

"Actually it was very nice of you girls to invite him," said Mami. "But please remember to ask me first next time."

> **Problem and Solution**
> What is the problem the girls face when they return home? How is it solved?

Late that night the whole family went to the beach as was our tradition on the Night of San Juan. But this time was special, for we had José Manuel with us.

The full moon shone against the velvet sky. The tide was high, and the beach swarmed with young revelers who, like us, had waited all year for this night's **irresistible** dip in the dark ocean. The moment we reached the water we all turned around, held hands, and jumped backward into the rushing waves. Amalia stumbled forward, Aitza joyfully splashed back, and so did I as I let go of my sister's hand. But my other hand remained tightly clasped to José Manuel's. When my friend and I took our third plunge into the sea, I wished good luck would come to him, and that from then on, his grandma would allow him to play with us out on the street. And as a wave lifted us high in the water, I suddenly knew this wish would come true.

Travel with Lulu Delacre

Lulu Delacre was born in Puerto Rico. While her parents were at work, she stayed with her grandmother in an old pink house. She drew pictures on sheets of white paper, and saved them in the corner of her closet. When Lulu was ten, she had her first real art lesson, and she has been writing and drawing ever since. Lulu is happiest when she is telling stories about growing up on an island of blazing sunshine, and of warm summer nights surrounded by friends, family, and traditions.

Other books by Lulu Delacre: *The Bossy Gallito* and *Golden Tales: Myths, Legends, and Folktales from Latin America*

 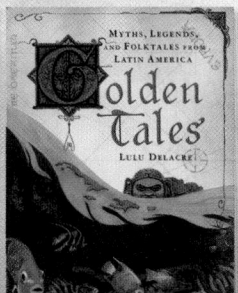

LOG ON ▶ Find out more about Lulu Delacre at **www.macmillanmh.com**.

CA Author's Purpose

What was the author's purpose for writing this story? Do you think Lulu Delacre wanted to entertain readers or inform them about the Night of San Juan and its traditions?

# CA Critical Thinking

Summarize

Use your Story Map to create a summary of *The Night of San Juan*. Explain Evelyn's problem and the steps she and her sisters took to solve it.

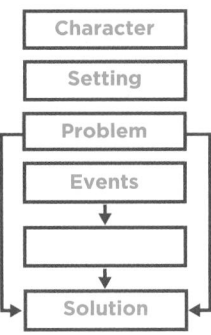

| Character |
| Setting |
| Problem |
| Events |
| |
| Solution |

Think and Compare

1. What was the biggest **problem** Evelyn had to overcome to get José Manuel to join her and her sisters? What was the **solution**? Use story details to explain your answers. **Summarize: Problem and Solution**

2. Reread page 87. Why does Evelyn hold onto José Manuel's hand during their **irresistible** dip in the ocean? Include details from the story to support your answer. **Analyze**

3. Would you choose a person like Evelyn to be your friend? Why or why not? Explain your answer. **Evaluate**

4. Amalia and the other children fear José Manuel's grandmother, yet Amalia finds the courage to ask her an important question. Describe why sometimes it is important to speak up in a difficult situation. **Analyze**

5. Reread "Johanna in Jamaica" on pages 74-75. Both Evelyn and Johanna want to change an adult's mind about something. Compare the strategies each of them uses. Use details from both selections. **Reading/Writing Across Texts**

CATCH A WAVE

By Kai-nalu Ferry

Today many people enjoy **surfing** California's waves, but do you know how this popular sport began?

Birth of the Surf

The first written account of surfing appeared in the ship's log of a British lieutenant, James King, in 1779. Although King's description of Hawaiian surfers was the first to appear in European writing, the sport had been practiced and perfected for thousands of years along the Pacific Ocean. Both Peruvians and Polynesians claim that their ancestors invented the skill of riding a wave. However, most historians agree that the first surfers were probably fishers who rode waves in order to return their catch to shore more quickly. By the time Captain James Cook and James King reached Hawaii in 1778, surfing was an important part of daily life and deeply rooted in Hawaiian culture.

The Tide Turns

By the dawn of the twentieth century, the number of surfers in Hawaii had dwindled. Yet, around this time, surfing found its way to the California coast. Traveling Hawaiian sailors are believed to have been the first to ride California's waves. However, a man named George Freeth earned the title of "the first man to surf in California" in 1907. Olympic athlete Duke Kahanamoku and surf photographers Tom Blake and John "Doc" Ball helped to popularize the sport. In the early 1960s, the founding of a surfing magazine by Californian LeRoy Grannis and the environmental organization Save Our Surf by John Kelly illustrated surfing's growing influence.

Surfing Today

In the last forty years, surfing has exploded into a sport, industry, and most recently, a science. Today a surf **forecaster** uses the same **satellites** as a weather forecaster to find the biggest waves. Surf forecasters can identify the exact time and location of ideal surfing conditions by using space technology, which gives them information and views of the ocean. Then they compare this information with data from wave charts and buoys.

Reading a Diagram

This diagram shows the exact locations of swells and their heights along the Southern California coast.

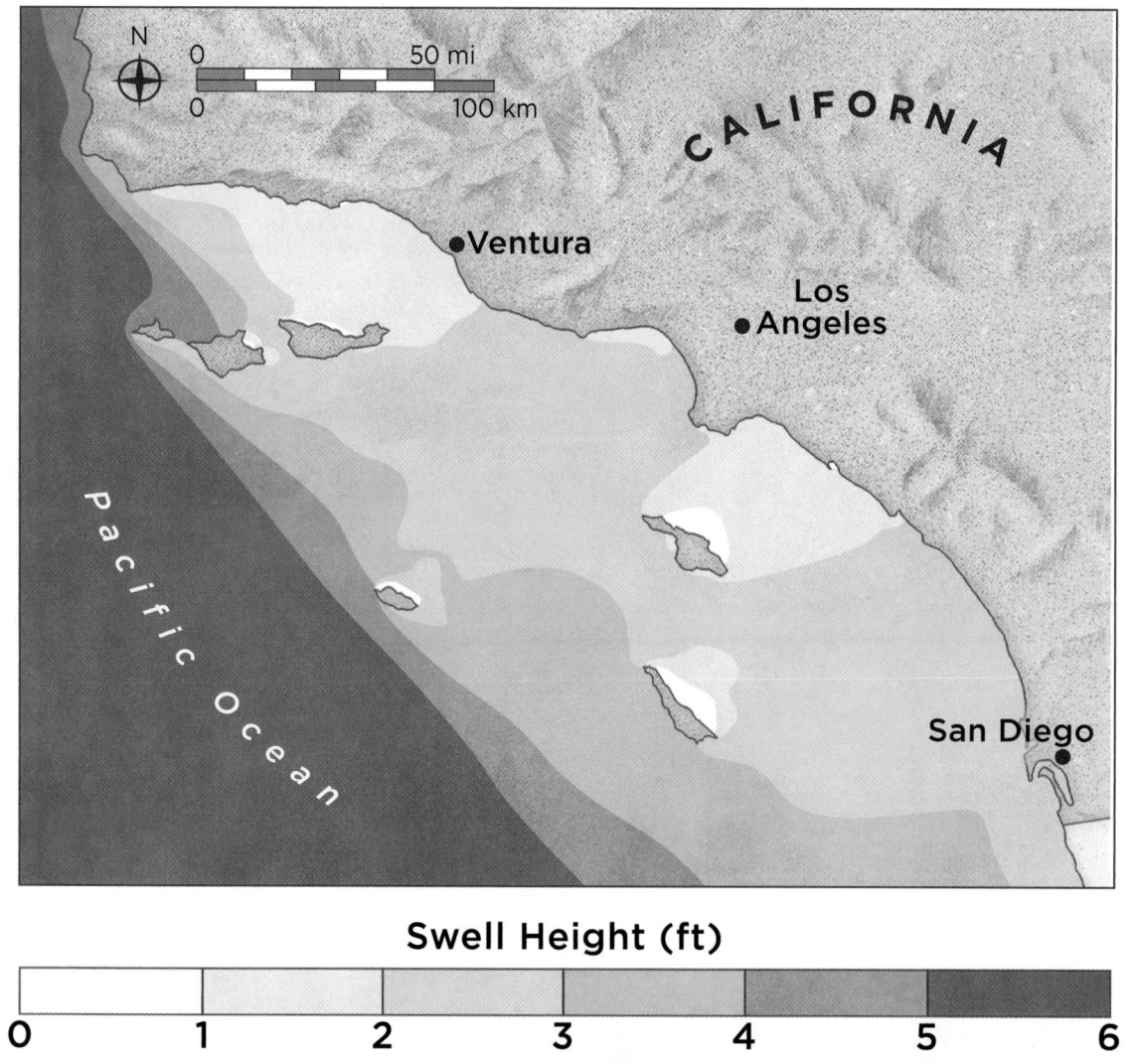

Swell Height (ft)

0   1   2   3   4   5   6

Science and Surfing

Forecasters at Internet sites, such as San Francisco-based Mavericks, use data to track which growing weather systems, such as hurricanes and storms, will create the biggest waves.

Such weather systems generate heavy winds. When these winds blow for a long time, they create heavy waves that crash into each other. The right amount of energy behind these waves results in a large **swell**. This swell travels faster and farther than the smaller waves. A large swell powers what some surfers consider the ideal wave. Fast-moving waves can be as tall as 60 feet. Often they move so quickly that surfers need to be towed-in on jet skis to ride them. Serious surfers track and will travel anywhere to catch the perfect wave.

CA Critical Thinking

1. According to the diagram, what does the dark blue area indicate? **Reading a Diagram**

2. How has science changed surfing? **Evaluate**

3. Think about "Catch A Wave" and *The Night of San Juan*. What does each selection tell you about people's feelings about ocean waves? **Reading/Writing Across Texts**

Science Activity

Research to find out how the ocean can affect the weather. Draw a diagram that shows how the water cycle affects weather.

 Find out more about surfing at **www.macmillanmh.com**.

Reading and Writing Connection

✓ Focus on Theme

The **theme** is the overall idea or message of a story. Sometimes the theme is stated. At other times, you must use details to find the theme.

Read the passage below. Notice how the author Lulu Delacre focuses on the theme of her story.

An excerpt from
The Night of San Juan

The author focuses on the theme of friendship by including details of what the girl wishes for her new friend José Manuel. We can feel her excitement about her new friendship.

. . . But my other hand remained tightly clasped to José Manuel's. When my friend and I took our third plunge into the sea, I wished good luck would come to him, and that from then on his grandma would allow him to play with us out on the street. And as a wave lifted us high in the water, I suddenly knew this wish would come true.

The Night of San Juan

Read and Find

Read Shayna's writing below. What did she do to focus on the theme of standing up for what you believe in? Use the checklist below to help you.

Recycling

by Shayna R.

I couldn't believe it! My school was throwing away mounds of paper every day. That's when my friend Liz and I took action. We wrote a letter to our principal. To our surprise, she was really excited about our idea. We got on the phone with a recycling company almost immediately.

The theme of my paragraph is standing up for something important— recycling.

Writer's Checklist

 Does the writer pick one **theme** and write a lot about it?

 Does the writer include specific details about her theme?

 Do you feel you can picture Shayna's plan to start recycling in her school?

HEROES
Young
And
Old

What do you know about the American Revolution? Why did the colonists decide to fight the British?

LOG ON ▶ Find out more about the American Revolution at **www.macmillanmh.com**.

Vocabulary

navigation   stark
instruct   governor
patriots   inspect
tyrant

Word Families

Knowing about **Word Families** can increase your vocabulary. A prefix or suffix added to a base word can change its meaning. For example, *unpatriotic* and *patriotism* have *patriot* as a base word but each word means something different.

Letters from the Revolution

by Aryeh Gross

London, England
July 1, 1772

Dear Richard,

    We were shocked to hear about the British ship, the *Gaspee* that sank off the coast of Rhode Island. Is it close to where you live? Do you know anyone who was aboard? It is hard to believe that the *Gaspee* was sunk by the tricky **navigation** of a colonist's boat. This smaller boat was able to steer the *Gaspee* into some hidden rocks. Then it quickly turned to attack the sinking ship.

    Who would be bold enough to **instruct** the colonists to act like this? It could only be their rebel leader. I have heard that he walks with a swagger and is too proud for his own good. They are hiding him and calling him one of the best **patriots** because he loves Rhode Island more than England. It is not good that so many colonists have turned against King George. We should all be his loyal subjects. Please come home to England.

Sincerely,

Thomas

Rhode Island

September 10, 1772

Dear Thomas,

Thank you for your letter, but you are wrong about the *Gaspee*. The British commander in the colonies was a cruel **tyrant** who ruled as he pleased. People who once had plenty of food stored in their homes now have cupboards that are **stark** and bare. When our leader, the **governor** of Rhode Island complained, the British commander paid no attention. The colonists took matters into their own hands. I think it shows spunk and courage for our small colonies to fight the mighty England.

I disagree with the comments in your letter. We do take pride in our act of revolt on the open seas and against England. This is patriotism. I am in Rhode Island to stay and I will take part in the coming revolution. I invite you to come and **inspect** the situation yourself.

My best wishes to you, my aunt and uncle.

Yours truly,

Richard

Reread for **Comprehension**

Make Inferences and Analyze

Draw Conclusions

To draw conclusions, you make inferences about two or more pieces of information from a story and arrive at a new understanding of a character or an event. A Conclusions Chart can help you use information in the story to draw a conclusion. Use your Conclusions Chart as you reread the selection.

Text Clues	Conclusion

Comprehension

Genre

Historical Fiction tells a story in which fictional characters take part in actual historical events with real people from the past.

Make Inferences and Analyze

Draw Conclusions
As you read, use your Conclusions Chart.

Text Clues	Conclusion

Read to Find Out

What was it like to be a child in Boston at the time of the Revolutionary War?

SLEDS on BOSTON COMMON

A Story from the American Revolution

Award Winning Selection

written by LOUISE BORDEN
illustrated by ROBERT ANDREW PARKER

In December of 1774, times were hard for all of us in Boston. Few good folk had coins to spare when they walked past the window of my father's shop on King Street . . . the best place to buy English and Dutch toys, spectacles, flutes, or the maps that my father drew with his own hand.

Sometimes he let me color the maps with his paints and his pens. "In a few years, Henry, your steady hand will be better than mine." That's what my father, William Price, said.

Months ago, on the first day of June, the British closed our harbor

By order of the King of England, George III.

King George wanted to punish those in Boston who spoke against his laws that were made across the sea: **patriots** like Sam Adams and John Hancock and other town leaders . . . and patriots like my father and my friends' fathers . . . All over Boston, south and north, people were not happy with King George III.

Or with our new royal **governor**, General Thomas Gage. General Gage was King George's top general, the commander of every British soldier in North America. Since May, he had lived in one of the biggest, tallest houses in all of Boston. Whenever my brothers and I walked to school, we passed by the redbrick front of Province House. I always looked up at the weather vane high on the cupola: a gold Indian archer that shone in the sun. Thomas Gage was a powerful man indeed.

> **Draw Conclusions**
> Why would the closing of Boston Harbor lead to hard times for the people of Boston?

On the day he closed our harbor, church bells rang in every colony in America. Other patriots in other towns said: "We will stand beside Boston in these hard times. We are all Americans together."

Now only the king's ships could enter or leave our harbor. And so there was no trade. There was little work for the men on Long Wharf, once the busiest dock in New England, filled with the tall masts of ships that had sailed to China and to Spain, to the West Indies and back. Now there was only the salt smell of the sea and the cry of gulls in an empty port.

Every day, there were more and more of the king's soldiers marching on Boston Common. Or walking with a swagger in their bright red coats along the streets of our town. Or cutting down our fences and our trees for their firewood. King George wanted General Gage to make sure that we kept his new laws and that we paid our taxes to England. Every penny. My father said that by now there was one British soldier for every five of us in Boston. People called them "lobster backs" because of their coats. Most of us didn't like General Gage's troops in our town. Most of them didn't like us either.

But King George's laws hadn't closed the South Writing School on West Street. No one had told our schoolmaster, Mr. Andrews, to stay home and not teach. So my brothers, Colin and Ben, and I still had to study our lessons each day: first reading, then writing, then arithmetic and **navigation**.

One thing His Majesty King George couldn't stop was the winter snow in the colony of Massachusetts.

After days of hard frost and ice, the snow fell for three nights in a row, fine and thick.

Then, on my ninth birthday, the gray clouds blew out to sea, and the sun shone above the steeples of our town.

It was the best kind of New England day: a day for coasting on Boston Common for any boy or girl who had a sled. And now I had my very own. It was small but it was mine, made by my father's strong, steady hands, with slick beef bones for runners and a wood plank seat . . . a present to me at breakfast in a year of hard times.

That morning at school, we practiced our handwriting in our copybooks. I had written the day's date five times for Mr. Andrews:

22 December, 1774

Then, just before noon, I tucked my copybook, pen, and ink pot under the back bench of our schoolroom. I grabbed my wool coat from a high hook. Other students at the South Writing School tramped home through the snow for hot bean porridge. But not Colin or Ben or I. We had brought our sleds to school. Our sister, Kate, was waiting for us outside the school door with three slabs of corn bread and apple jam. Some girls were afraid to go to the Common because of General Gage's troops. But my sister loved to sled ride.

We had to hurry. Mr. Andrews would expect all boys back for lessons at two o'clock sharp.

We pulled our sleds along the icy ruts of West Street. The December wind was cold, and I was glad to be wearing Kate's old mittens and Ben's patched leather boots.

We crossed to the Common, a wide, hilly field with fine new snow and a frame of blue sky. We hurried on past the **stark** row of lime trees that John Hancock had given as a gift to the town . . . and past the town's Wishing Stone, but we had no time to stop and wish that King George would change his harsh laws.

For over a hundred years the Common had belonged to *everyone* in Boston. Now it was covered by the barracks of General Gage's troops. And they were everywhere, these troops, officers and soldiers, drummers and cooks. Three thousand of them, here on Boston Common, setting up their tents, carrying letters and orders, polishing boots and bayonets, drilling, marching.

Everywhere across the Common, my brothers and Kate and I heard the shouted orders of officers and the constant *tramp-tramp* of British boots.

Our father had told us to listen with our eyes and with our ears every time we went to the Common. "Look sharp but don't look like you're looking." Every patriot who thought King George was wrong helped out the Sons of Liberty* in his own small way.

Suddenly, I stopped and pulled on Colin's sleeve. Some of General Gage's soldiers had placed their tents and their cooking fires right in the middle of our sled runs. They had broken the ice on the Common's ponds so no one could skate. And they had knocked down the snow forts the town boys had worked yesterday to build.

We were steaming mad, all four of us. This was *our* Common. These were *our* ponds to skate on. And there were no better hills to sled on anywhere in Boston. It seemed as if the British troops had made it *their* Common.

Now there was no open run to sled on. So instead, we walked among the barracks, and listened with our eyes and with our ears. Ben began to count new sheds and tents and horses. Kate and I counted kegs of powder and barrels of fish. Colin counted officers.

*A group of local Boston patriots who opposed the actions of the British. They often met in secret to discuss plans for independence.

Kate and I saw General Gage. He was right there in front of us, almost close enough to touch. He looked like a general, and he stood like a general.

But he didn't look mean. Not like a **tyrant** who would close our harbor. Not like a bully for King George. And not like an old woman, as some Boston newspapers called him. He had slate-blue eyes and was speaking kindly to his soldiers who were setting up a tent. General Gage looked like a man who would listen, a good man, a man like my father.

If I could just speak to General Gage for a few minutes, maybe he would help us. Maybe he would let us sled on our Common. But I was just a town boy. General Gage was the royal governor. I'd have to be as brave as the Boston patriots who told the king of England that his taxes were not fair.

I held on to my sled tightly and took a deep breath. "Hurry," I whispered to Kate. "Go find Colin and Ben. We're going to talk to General Gage."

And so we did, right there in the middle of the Common, with British soldiers all about us.

I walked up to General Gage, tugged hard on his scarlet sleeve, and asked if he would hear a town boy's complaint. Some of his officers glared at me sternly and began to order us away. But the tall general turned and held up his hand to still them. Then he said, "Let this boy have his words."

And so I talked. And General Gage listened.

I told him that the Boston Common belonged to all of us, not just his soldiers. I told him his troops had knocked down our snow forts, and ruined our ponds for skating, and that they had built their cook fires in the middle of the best sled runs.

Then, with Colin and Ben and Kate right beside me, I said: "And it's my birthday, sir, and I wish to use my new sled on the steepest hill in our town. But I can't, you see, because of your men. And we have to be back at our school by two o'clock for our lessons."

General Gage crossed his arms and looked out across the snowy Common. His officers stood nearby with stony faces. No one spoke a word.

Then the general put his hand on my shoulder. He told me I had a fine sled and asked who had made it. "My father," I said proudly.

He leaned down to **inspect** the other sleds. Then he stood up and said in a general's voice: "I'm a father as well as a soldier for my king . . . I have sons, and daughters, too," he added, nodding at Kate. "And I know my own children would like to sled this hill if they were here. But they're back in England in school."

Then General Gage asked me my name. "Henry, sir," I said, standing as tall as I could. "Henry Price."

"Henry." The general nodded. "That's a good name, indeed." He shook my hand, man to man. "My oldest son is named Henry."

"I'm the youngest in our house," I said.

"You may be the youngest," said General Gage, "but you have the courage of a good soldier as well as the spunk of your local rebels." He turned swiftly on his heel to one of his officers.

Draw Conclusions
General Gage has children of his own. How might this influence his decision to let the children sled?

"**Instruct** all troops that they are to allow the town children to sled where they wish. And keep the ice unbroken in one of those ponds. Tell the men they are to clear a good run. And be quick about it. It's my young friend's birthday, and he needs to try out a new sled before two o'clock this day."

I'll never forget the first time I came down that hill on a sled I could call my own: down, down, down the snowy path beneath my runners, the tents and barrels blurring past, the red coats of soldiers rushing past, the wind on my face and in my eyes, faster, faster, over bumps and more bumps, straight through the sprawling camp of British troops till I reached the bottom of the Common, then slower, slower, slow, till I slid to a stop, never wanting that ride to end.

Again and again, my brothers and my sister and I sledded down the best hill in Boston and then dragged our sleds to the top, until it was time to hurry back to the South Writing School for Mr. Andrews's afternoon lessons.

And from December 22 on, Colin and Ben and Kate and I had other days of good sledding on the Common. And skating, too. Because General Thomas Gage was a man of his word.

Spring came, and in April of 1775, the War for Independence began after General Gage ordered his troops to Lexington and Concord. Our new country was at war, and the lobster backs in our town would soon be under siege. The next October, the good folk of Boston were glad when King George sent orders for his top general to return to England. Thomas Gage was the last royal governor of a colony that wanted to choose its own.

On the night that his ship left Boston Harbor and set sail for England, I stood on Long Wharf with my brothers and Kate. We were Americans now, my family and I. We were Boston patriots hoping to win a war against a king. But we'd never forget the tall British general that we'd met on my birthday. General Gage had given us back a pond and our sled runs on Boston Common because he had children of his own. Indeed, he was a good man.

Go Back in Time with
Louise Borden & Robert Andrew Parker

Louise Borden's stories often start with a compelling image. She found the idea for this story while reading a magazine article about children wanting to sled on Boston Common during the Revolutionary War. Louise followed that lead and tracked down the story. She even corresponded with people in England about General Gage.

Robert Andrew Parker lives in an old house in a valley surrounded by wooded hills. Inside the house he keeps his collection of miniature soldiers, which inspired him to create the images for Louise's book. His studio is out back, next to a garden. It holds his paintings, and a six-foot model airplane he built. When he is not working on a painting or illustration, he can be found tubing down the river that runs in front of his house.

Another book by Louise Borden:
A. Lincoln and Me

 Author's Purpose

Do you think the author wrote only to inform readers about the events that took place in Boston in the winter of 1774? Explain your answer.

LOG ON ▶ Find out more about Louise Borden and Robert Andrew Parker at **www.macmillanmh.com**.

CA Critical Thinking

Summarize

Use your Conclusions Chart to help you summarize *Sleds on Boston Common* in your own words.

Text Clues	Conclusion

Think and Compare

1. Draw a **conclusion** about General Thomas Gage's abilities as a leader. Use story details to explain why your conclusion is logical. **Make Inferences and Analyze: Draw Conclusions**

2. Reread the first paragraph on page 102. How did the closing of Boston Harbor affect Henry and his family? Use details from the story in your answer. **Analyze**

3. Pretend you were one of many **patriots** who had been listening carefully as you walked through the soldiers' camp on Boston Common. What might you have seen and heard? **Evaluate**

4. As Henry finds out, first impressions about others can be misleading or inaccurate. Do you agree with this statement? Why or why not? Explain your answer. **Analyze**

5. Reread "Letters from the Revolution" on pages 98–99. Which letter would Henry and his family agree with? Why? Use evidence from both selections to support your answer. **Reading/Writing Across Texts**

Poetry

Poetry that tells a story or gives an account of events is narrative poetry.

Literary Elements

Meter is the regular arrangement of accented and unaccented syllables in a line of poetry.

Alliteration is the repetition of the same first consonant letter or sound in a series of words.

"Paul Revere's Ride"

*an excerpt from the poem by
Henry Wadsworth Longfellow*

Paul Revere was a hero of the American Revolution. With two other patriots, he rode across the countryside to warn the colonists of a British attack.

Listen, my children, and you shall hear
Of the midnight ride of Paul Revere,
On the eighteenth of April, in seventy-five;
Hardly a man is now alive
Who remembers that famous day and year.
He said to his friend, "If the British march
By land or sea from the town tonight,
Hang a lantern aloft in the belfry arch
Of the North Church tower as a signal light—
One, if by land, and two, if by sea:
And I on the opposite shore will be,
Ready to ride and spread the alarm
Through every Middlesex village and farm,
For the country folk to be up and to arm."
Then he said, "Good night!" and with muffled oar
Silently rowed to the Charlestown shore,
Just as the moon rose over the bay,
Where swinging wide at her moorings lay
The *Somerset*, British man-of-war;
A phantom ship, with each mast and spar
Across the moon like a prison bar,
And a huge black hulk, that was magnified
By its own reflection in the tide.
Meanwhile, his friend, through alley and street,
Wanders and watches, with eager ears,
Till in the silence around him he hears
The muster of men at the barrack door,
And the measured tread of the grenadiers,
Marching down to their boats on the shore.

The repetition of the initial "w" sound in this line is an example of *alliteration*.

121

Then he climbed to the tower of
Old North Church
By the wooden stairs, with stealthy tread,
To the belfry-chamber overhead,
And startled the pigeons from their perch
On the somber rafters, that round him made
Masses and moving shapes of shade—
By the trembling ladder, steep and tall,
To the highest window in the wall,
Where he paused to listen and look down
A moment on the roofs of the town,
And the moonlight flowing over all. . . .
You know the rest in the books you have read
How the British Regulars fired and fled,—
How the farmers gave them ball for ball,
From behind each fence and farmyard wall,
Chasing the red-coats down the lane,
Then crossing the fields to emerge again
Under the trees at the turn of the road,
And only pausing to fire and load.
So through the night rode Paul Revere;
And so through the night went his cry of alarm
To every Middlesex village and farm,
A cry of defiance and not of fear,
A voice in the darkness, a knock at the door,
And a word that shall echo forevermore!
For, borne on the night-wind of the Past,
Through all our history, to the last,
In the hour of darkness and peril and need,
The people will waken and listen to hear
The hurrying hoof-beats of that steed,
And the midnight message of Paul Revere.

There are four accented syllables in this line. The arrangement of these syllables with unaccented syllables is an example of *meter*.

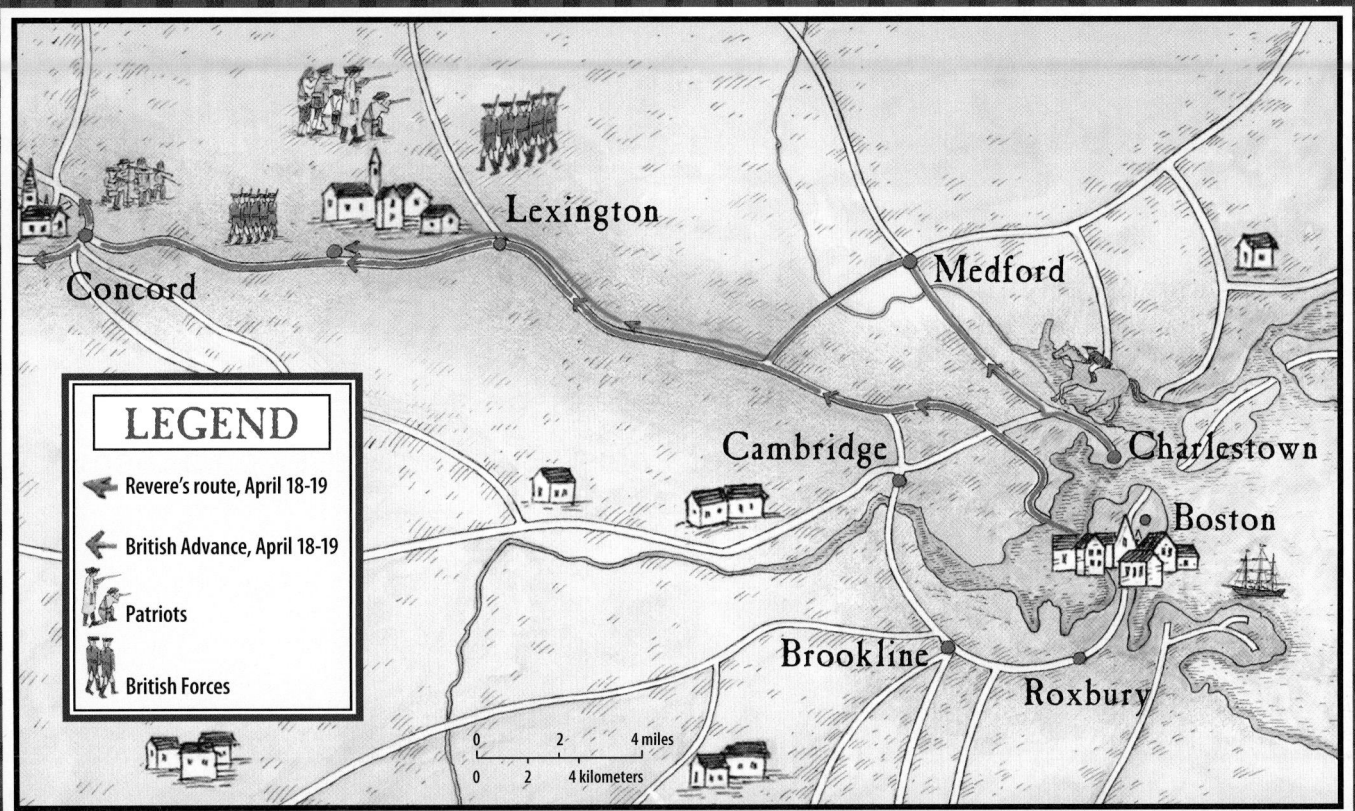

The first battle between the patriots and the British took place at Lexington. They fought again at Concord.

 Critical Thinking

1. What is another example of alliteration in this poem? **Alliteration**

2. Read the poem aloud. How might the meter help you memorize the poem? **Analyze**

3. Compare this poem with *Sleds on Boston Common*. In both the poem and the story, the authors describe the British. How are the descriptions similar? How are they different?
Reading/Writing Across Texts

LOG ON ▶ Find out more about narrative poetry at
www.macmillanmh.com.

CA Writing

✔ Theme

Good writers choose a **theme**, or main message, for their writing. Story details support the theme.

Reading and Writing Connection

Read the passage below. Notice how the author Louise Borden focuses on a theme in her story.

An excerpt from
Sleds on Boston Common

The author's theme is important changes in daily life. From the author's details, we can imagine how daily life changes with soldiers around.

Every day, there were more and more of the king's soldiers marching on Boston Common. Or walking with a swagger in their bright red coats along the streets of our town. Or cutting down our fences and our trees for their firewood. . . . Most of us didn't like General Gage's troops in our town. Most of them didn't like us either.

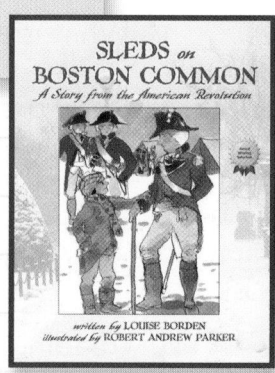

SLEDS on
BOSTON COMMON
A Story from the American Revolution

written by LOUISE BORDEN
illustrated by ROBERT ANDREW PARKER

124

Read and Find

Read Molly's writing below. How did she focus her writing on the theme of friendship? Use the checklist below to help you.

My Friend Seth

by Molly F.

Even when I was the new kid in the class, it didn't bother Seth to show me around and introduce me to his friends. I knew he was special when he didn't make fun of my limp. Not only that, but he always stuck up for me if anyone else did.

I wanted to write about the theme of friendship—and my friend Seth.

Writer's Checklist

 Does the writer pick one **theme** and write a lot about it?

 Does the writer include specific details that tell you about her friendship with Seth?

 Do you have an idea of what Seth and Molly's friendship is like?

a VOICE in the DARK

✔ **Review**

Character and Setting
Main Idea and Details
Problem and Solution
Suffixes
Photos and Captions

Marco had been dreading this day. He usually walked to school with a spring in his step. Today, he just slogged along. His friend Brianna walked beside him. "Why does Mr. Crawford have to call it a field trip?" Brianna asked at one point. "We're going to a cave, not a field!"

Just hearing the word "cave" gave Marco chills. Mr. Crawford had described the class outing as a grand adventure. "We'll learn more about Earth's history while becoming spelunkers!" he told the students. "Cave explorers discover all kinds of strange things."

Marco liked science, but the idea of being underground in the dark terrified him.

"I wonder how far down we'll go," Brianna said. "Do you think we'll see bats? What if there are monsters?" She raised her hands and stomped on the ground, her mouth open in a terrifying snarl.

"Why do you have to be so dramatic?" Marco asked.

Brianna stopped on the sidewalk. "Don't you want to go?"

"Well, to be honest..." After a pause, Marco explained his feelings to Brianna.

"Don't worry," she said. "Just stay near me and you'll be fine."

Marco thought about that all the way to the cave site. It was a crisp autumn day, dry and sunny. The air outside had warmed up by the time the students' bus arrived. Even so, Mr. Crawford advised them to bring their jackets. "Things will feel a little different underground," he said.

A tour guide greeted the class and handed each student a flashlight. He instructed them to stay together on the path, and then stepped toward the mouth of the cave. Brianna grabbed Marco's hand. "This is so exciting!" she said.

Inside the cave, darkness engulfed the class. The air was much cooler. Brianna told Marco that it felt like the frozen food section of the local grocery store.

One by one the students flicked on their flashlights. Whenever the guide stopped to explain a strange rock formation, Brianna would whisper something humorous in Marco's ear. As they walked, she told him all about her first pet, described in detail a beach trip she had taken that summer, and offered her lengthy opinion of a movie her family had rented.

Marco thought about telling her to be quiet, but in a wonderful way her voice calmed him. It made him forget about how dark and cold the cave was. It made him feel warm and safe. He listened more closely to what the guide was telling them, and even laughed with fearless glee when Mr. Crawford let out a roar to scare the class.

Near the end of the tour, Marco realized that Brianna had been quiet for quite a while. He stopped and turned to look at her. She smiled. "I told you there was nothing to worry about," she said.

"Thanks," Marco said. "I owe you one." They laughed together, then dashed ahead to join their classmates as they stepped out of the cave into the sunlight.

127

THE STORY OF RADIO

You probably listen to it in the car or at home. You push a button or turn the dial, then sound fills the air. Right away you can hear the latest song or a message about a snow day at your school. That little radio is an amazing device.

How It Works

Every radio has two parts: a transmitter and a receiver. First, sound is changed into radio waves. Then, those waves are transmitted. The signals can go through solid objects like walls or trees and are turned back into sounds once they are received.

About 150 years ago, J.C. Maxwell discovered that radio waves were possible. People used this idea to figure out how to send radio signals. The Italian scientist Guglielmo Marconi was the first to send a radio signal across the ocean. In 1901 he sent messages between England and Canada. These first messages were sounds that stood for letters, not music or talking.

The first time people heard voices and music over the radio was on December 24, 1906. A man in Massachusetts sent out a three-part broadcast. Ships picked up the signal. They heard a man speaking, then a woman singing. Finally, they heard a person playing a violin.

In the early 1920s, the first radio station, KDKA, started broadcasting in Pittsburgh. Within a few years, people eagerly sought radio sets to hear news and music. In 1930 the first broadcast was heard "around the world." Radio signals traveled from tower to tower across the globe. The golden age of radio had begun.

In the days leading up to World War II, the President's important speeches were broadcast on the radio. The whole world tuned in to listen to the news of the war overseas. Radios became even more important once the United States joined World War II.

Soldiers and sailors were able to use two-way radios to communicate with one another.

Radio was also a great source of entertainment then, much as television is today. Families and friends gathered around the radio to listen to music, comedy programs, quiz shows, and serious dramas. Companies that made laundry and cleaning products sponsored some of these dramas, which were called "soap operas."

Radio Today

By the beginning of the 1950s, television took over as the leading form of home entertainment. That did not mean that people turned off their radios.

Your parents might have a favorite radio station that plays music from their teen years. You, on the other hand, might enjoy a different station that plays the latest hits. Push a button or turn a dial. It's easy to find something you like!

During the golden age of radio, families frequently gathered around the radio. People would stop what they were doing to listen to a favorite program.

CA Critical Thinking

Now answer numbers 1 through 4. Base your answers on the story "A Voice in the Dark."

1. **How do Marco and Brianna feel about going into the cave?**

   A They are both afraid.
   B They are both excited.
   C Marco is afraid, but Brianna is excited.
   D Marco is excited, but Brianna is afraid.

2. **What is Marco's main problem in the story?**

   A He has to go into a cave, and he is afraid of the dark.
   B Brianna is mad at him and won't talk to him.
   C His teacher, Mr. Crawford, roars at him.
   D His flashlight goes dead when he's in the cave.

3. **Which word from the story has a suffix that means "without"?**

   A fearless
   B terrifying
   C wonderful
   D humorous

4. **How does Brianna solve Marco's problem? Use details and information from the story to support your answer.**

Now answer numbers 1 through 4. Base your answers on the article "The Story of Radio."

1. **Which statement *best* summarizes Guglielmo Marconi's role in radio?**

   A   He transmitted sounds that stood for letters.
   B   He worked on sending radio signals in 1901.
   C   He sent messages between England and Canada.
   D   He was the first to send a signal across the ocean.

2. **The golden age of radio began**

   A   in the early 1920s.
   B   in the early 1930s.
   C   about 150 years ago.
   D   in the beginning of the 1950s.

3. **The people in the photograph are most likely listening to**

   A   a comedy program.
   B   a serious news program.
   C   the first radio broadcast.
   D   two-way radio transmissions.

4. **How did radio solve a problem during World War II?**

   A   Companies sponsored soap operas.
   B   Two-way radios helped soldiers communicate during battle.
   C   The President spoke on the radio.
   D   The United States entered the war in 1941.

Write on Demand

PROMPT Why were radios important during World War II? Use details from the article to support your answer. Write for 5 minutes. Write as much as you can as well as you can.

The Big Question

How did the American West change during our country's early years?

Theme Launcher Video

LOG ON ▶ Find out more about the American West at **www.macmillanmh.com**.

Big
Question

How did the American West change during our country's early years?

In 1848, the population of California was under 15,000. California was a remote and wild territory far away from everything. But after gold was discovered, the population exploded with U.S. citizens, as well as immigrants from Europe and Asia.

The Gold Rush changed the state forever, making it an economic powerhouse. Then in the early 20th century, the entertainment industry, located in Los Angeles, continued to ensure that California was the most populous and one of the wealthiest states in the Union.

Learning about your state's early history will help you better understand the role it played and continues to play in the United States as a whole. See what you can discover about other western states and their development, too.

Research Activities

Throughout the unit, you will be gathering information about the American West. Research an important event that shaped the American West. Write an article explaining why that event was important.

Keep Track of Ideas

As you read, keep track of what you are learning about the American West and how it changed over time. Use the Accordion Book to organize your ideas. Across the top write the unit theme, **The American West**. In each section write what you learn about the American West in your reading throughout the week.

FOLDABLES®
Study Organizer

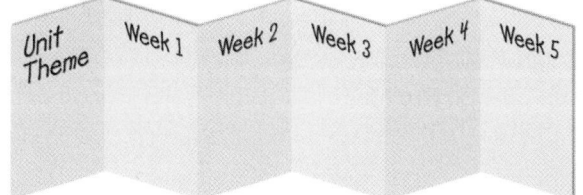

Unit Theme | Week 1 | Week 2 | Week 3 | Week 4 | Week 5

Research Toolkit

Conduct Your Unit 2 Research Online with:

Research Roadmap
Follow step-by-step guide to complete your research project.

Online Resources
- Topic Finder and other Research Tools
- Videos and Virtual Fieldtrips
- Photos and Drawings for Presentations
- Related Articles and Web Resources

California Web Site Links

Go to **www.macmillanmh.com** for more information.

California People

Ina Coolbrith
Pioneer
Ina came to California from Missouri in 1851. She later became California's first poet laureate in 1915.

THE SPANISH IN EARLY CALIFORNIA

What do you think life was like for the early Spanish settlers of California?

LOG ON ▶ Find out more about early California at **www.macmillanmh.com**.

To California

by Steven Ruiz

Vocabulary

refuge
obvious
ignored
detested
projects
obedience
depicts
eldest

Thesaurus

A **Thesaurus** is a tool that can help you find synonyms for a particular word. The word *depicts* may have the following synonyms listed: *pictures, illustrates,* or *represents.*

July 5, 1846

Dear Sara,

After months of traveling, and almost freezing to death on the way, I finally made it to the territory of California. I have found **refuge** at a rancho here run by a businesswoman named Juana Briones.

It is **obvious** to me that she is a kind woman. When I came to ask her for a job, I could barely stand, I was so sick from fever and hunger. Others had **ignored** me, because I looked too weak to work. One man walked right by me when I spoke to him. How I **detested** having to beg for work from those people.

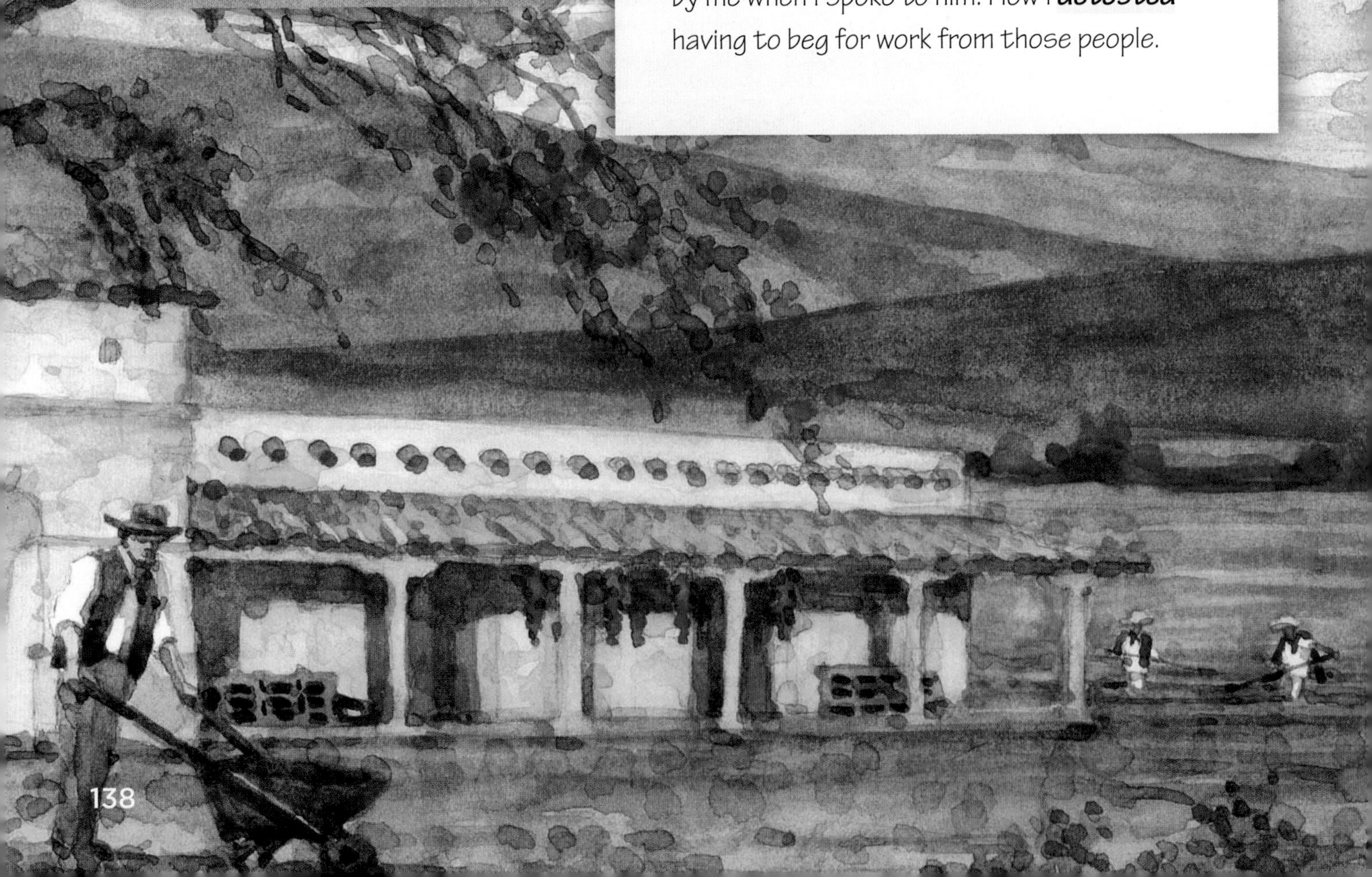

Señora Briones was different. First, she had her cook give me a thick bowl of vegetable soup and a large hunk of bread. After I had eaten, she asked me about my skills.

I explained about the different **projects** I had done at home. I told her that I could build barns, sheds, and houses. And of course, after traveling across the country, I now know how to fix a wagon.

Señora Briones owns 4,400 acres. She has given me a job and a place to live. For this reason, I will reward her kindness with hard work and **obedience**.

I am enclosing a sketch with this letter. It **depicts** me and some of the Indians who work here.

I miss you and our family. As you are the **eldest** now, please watch over the little ones.

Your brother,

Paul

Reread for **Comprehension**

Monitor Comprehension

Cause and Effect

A cause is an event or action that makes something happen. An effect is what happens because of an event or action. Readers can monitor their comprehension by thinking about how one event or action can lead to another. Use your Cause and Effect Chart to record important effects and their causes.

Cause → Effect	
→	
→	
→	
→	

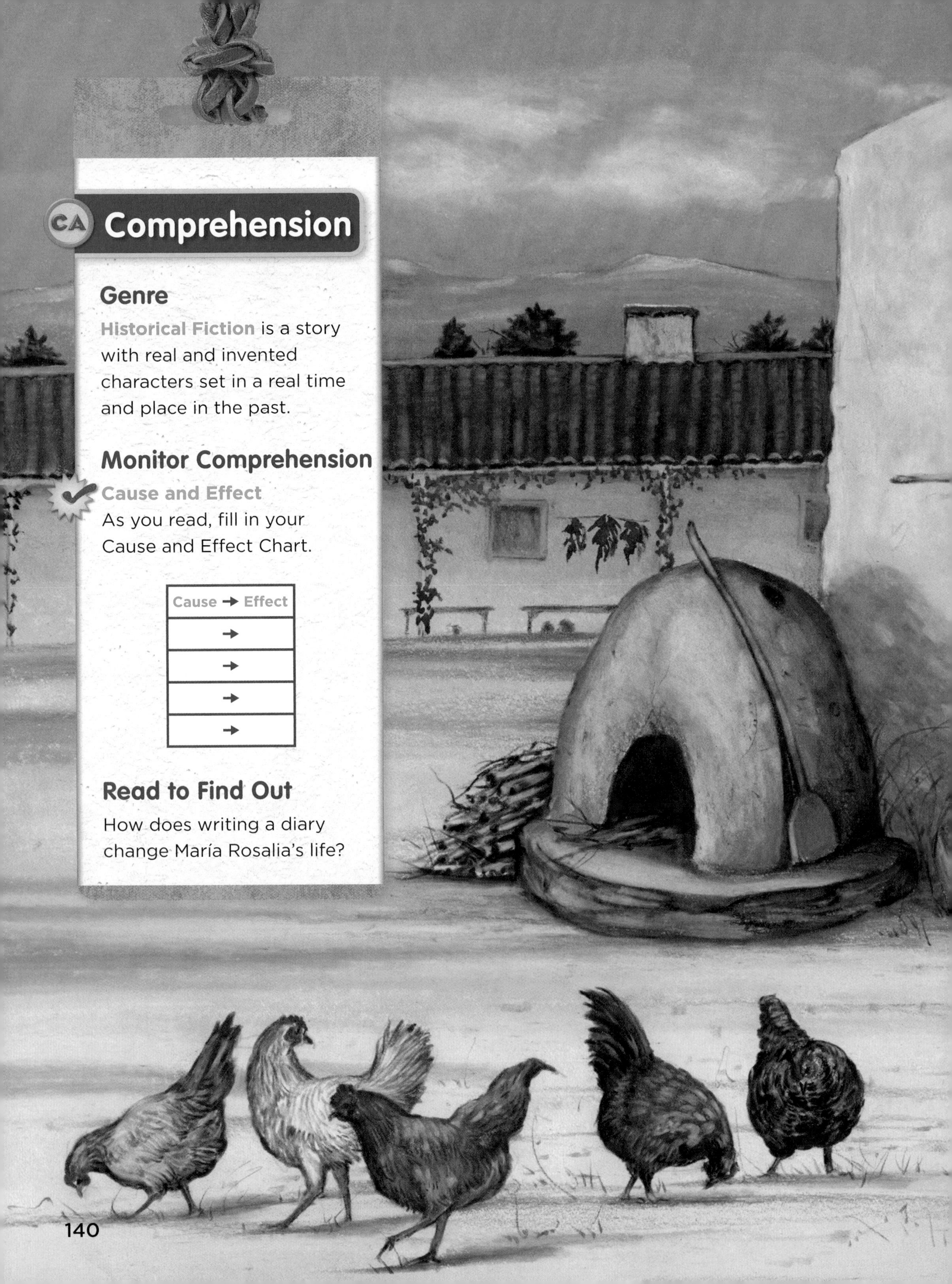

CA Comprehension

Genre

Historical Fiction is a story with real and invented characters set in a real time and place in the past.

Monitor Comprehension

Cause and Effect
As you read, fill in your Cause and Effect Chart.

Cause → Effect
→
→
→
→

Read to Find Out

How does writing a diary change María Rosalia's life?

140

Valley of the Moon

by Sherry Garland
illustrated by Kristina Rodanas

Orphaned at an early age, María Rosalia and her younger brother, Domingo, were raised by Padre Ygnacio at the Mission Rafael in Alta California. Now the children have become servants at the Medina Rancho. Taught to read and write by Padre Ygnacio, María Rosalia has recently started keeping a diary about her life at the rancho.

October 10, 1845

Tonight I begin my first diary. The Medina family is asleep, and all is quiet throughout the rancho. Only the wind racing around the corners of the adobe house and the distant yelp of coyotes break the night silence. I am snuggled in a corner of the kitchen surrounded by baskets of dried corn waiting to be ground. The tile floors feel cold on my bare feet, but I do not mind, for I know no one will find me here.

This diary is mine because the **eldest** of the Medina daughters, Miguela, tossed it over her balcony into the courtyard. My fingers quickly rescued it from a watery death in the fountain. Señorita Miguela threw it away in a fit of resentment after it was given to her by an American suitor, Señor Henry Johnston. With flashing black eyes she cried out that a girl has no more use for reading and writing than a snake has for gold earrings. She said the diary was an insult to her beauty and charm, then tossed Señor Johnston out, too.

I feel sorry for Señor Johnston, or for any man who has the misfortune of courting headstrong Miguela, but I am not sorry that I now hold her discarded diary in my hands. I must not let anyone see me writing, for I am a servant, a half-Indian orphan, a girl. I am supposed to know nothing but work and **obedience**. How amazed the Medinas would be if they knew I learned to read and write from a kind old padre at Mission Rafael, many miles from here. Maybe someday I will tell them.

> **Cause and Effect**
> Why does María Rosalia have to hide the fact that she knows how to read and write?

143

October 11

I've been thinking about Padre Ygnacio all day. It was he who found Domingo and me eight years ago beside our dying mother in the rose garden of Mission Rafael near San Francisco Bay. Her body was ravaged with smallpox, and I had placed roses over her face. I think I was about five years old and my brother was about two, but no one knows our ages for sure.

Padre Ygnacio named me María Rosalia — after the Blessed Virgin and because of the roses. He named my brother Domingo because it was a Sunday morning. For a last name he called us Milagros — for it was a miracle indeed that we did not die of the horrible plague that claimed the lives of so many Indians in Alta California. They say that out of forty thousand Suisun people, only two hundred lived. Some smaller tribes lost everyone. How Domingo and I survived is one of the many mysteries of my life.

When Padre Ygnacio found us, we did not speak much Spanish and he did not know our Indian dialect. But of one thing he was sure: Though our mother had the bronze skin of an Indian, our skin was the light brown of *mestizos* — half-Indian and half-Spanish. It was **obvious** that our father had been a white man. Whether he was a wealthy Spanish landowner, a Spanish soldier from the *presidio* at San Francisco, a Russian fur trapper, or an American merchant sailor, no one knows.

Lupita, the cook, is the closest thing to a mother I have. Her husband, Gregorio, is the head *vaquero* on the ranch. He oversees the men who tend the cattle and horses. It was Gregorio who found me and Domingo at Mission Rafael four years ago and brought us to live at the Medina ranch — Rancho Agua Verde. Lupita and Gregorio have no children of their own but have raised several orphans. I know they care about me, yet my heart feels empty. If I do not know my past, how can I plot my future? I must stop thinking such things and get back to work. If I don't finish grinding this corn, there will be no *tortillas* tomorrow.

Sunday, October 12

I have no place to hide this diary. My room in the servants' quarters is so tiny that I can hardly turn around. I share it with Ramona, the seamstress. We sleep on woven straw pallets on the floor and roll them up each morning. We take turns sitting on the one chair at the one tiny table. Whoever doesn't get the chair sits on an overturned wooden bucket. The adobe walls and ceiling are stained with black soot from the fireplace and tallow candles.

But our quarters are not as bleak as some. Ramona saves scraps of cloth from the sewing **projects**. Our walls are alive with color — a wool tapestry, one finely embroidered hanging that **depicts** the Holy Virgin, and another hanging that shimmers with flowers. Even our floor has a wool rug made of remnants from the spring sheepshearing. Pegs line the walls for our sparse clothing. Baskets hang from the heavy timber beams for food and miscellaneous items. It is better than the room I shared with four other orphans at Mission Rafael.

October 13

The Medina daughters saw me in the courtyard today carrying the diary. Miguela was amused and said I could keep it. "Perhaps you might use it for fire kindling, Rosa," she said with a toss of her black curls. Miguela is seventeen and has been available for marriage for two years. She is a great beauty but has **ignored** all the men who call on her and has refused several proposals. If I were rich, I would pay a man every *peso* I owned to take her away from this ranch.

Rafaela, the middle daughter, who is aged fifteen, is gentle and sweet but very sickly. She coughs often, and her skin is paler than white lilies. She told Miguela not to be so unkind because I am more like family than a servant. Bless her soul, how I wish her words were true.

Gabriela, who is eleven and like a little sister to me, said to just ignore Miguela. Everyone knows how Miguela is, but her words stung.

October 14

I am in the goat pen seizing a moment to write in my diary. I milked the goats faster than lightning so that I might have a free moment. I carry the diary with me all the time, tied to my waist with a sash and hidden under my skirt. I dare not write at night in my room for Ramona is a light sleeper.

I have no ink, so I am using beet juice. It leaves an uneven red color, but it must do until I find real ink. For a pen, I am using a sharpened black feather from the tail of Paladin, Señor Medina's favorite fighting rooster. Domingo stole the feather from the chicken coop and gave it to me. All I think of while doing chores is the moment I will open this diary and write. It is my island of **refuge** in a sea of work.

October 15

Señor Johnston is here again. I like him very much. He speaks to me kindly and does not order me around. He owns a merchant business in the small town of Yerba Buena on San Francisco Bay south of here. Being twenty-eight years of age and settled, he is now looking for a wife. He has decided upon Señorita Miguela (may Heaven help him!) and has visited Rancho Agua Verde many times this year.

Señor Johnston is waiting for his brother and family who are coming by wagon train from Missouri to join him in California. They will arrive first at Sutter's Fort in the Sacramento Valley, where Johnston will go to meet them. A few years ago there were very few foreigners in Alta California, just some sailors and fur trappers. Now they come in a steady stream — mostly farmers from Missouri. There are hundreds of them, especially in the Sacramento Vally northeast of here.

> **Cause and Effect**
> Why are so many farmers coming to Alta California?

Lupita does not trust the *norteamericanos*. She says they are supposed to become loyal Mexican citizens, learn to speak Spanish, and become Catholics in exchange for land. But not all of them do as they agreed. She especially dislikes the foreigner Johann Sutter, who encourages other foreigners to come to California illegally without permission from the Mexican government. There are already squatters on Señor Medina's lands. Lupita thinks they will take over Alta California before long.

I do not care what Lupita says. I like Señor Johnston, even if he is an *americano*. He is beside himself with excitement about his brother's arrival. But he is worried. The snows will soon start to fall on top of the Sierra Nevada mountains to the east, causing deep drifts and icy rocks that make the passes treacherous to cross. If the Johnston family does not clear the mountains by the end of this month, they are surely doomed.

October 16

Spent a pleasant morning working in the courtyard that is surrounded by the thick walls of the *casa grande* on four sides. I wonder if the Medina house will ever be completed. Every year, the Indian workers add a bit more. When the main house was first built, it was a simple one-story structure like nearly all the *ranchos* in northern Alta California. But after Señora Medina and Miguela saw the grand *rancho* that General Vallejo was building at Petaluma a few miles away, they insisted on having a second story with balconies and rambling rose vines. At the moment, only the Medina family has upstairs bedrooms with balconies. Everyone else, servants and guests alike, sleeps downstairs. I do not mind for walking up and down stairs makes my legs ache.

Drew ten buckets of water from the well to tend the herbs, beans, squash, pumpkins, melons, onions, and hot chiles in the garden near the kitchen door. Swept the veranda that is roofed with brown clay tiles. Pruned the rambling Castilian roses that climb up the posts to the upstairs bedroom balconies. Picked late maturing pears from Señor Medina's cherished fruit trees. I am

tired, but am writing during *siesta* while everyone else rests. Writing brings me more joy than sleep! Nothing would make me happier than to write all day and night.

October 17

¡Madre mía! My secret is uncovered! While I was in the courtyard writing in my diary today, Señor Johnston appeared out of nowhere. I was afraid he would be angry that I had it, but his large blue eyes grew wide like an owl's. He said to me in his best Spanish (which I am sorry to say is not very good): "Rosalia! I cannot believe you are writing! How did you learn such skills?"

I begged Johnston not to tell anyone, for it would only mean trouble for me. I explained how Padre Ygnacio taught the Indian boys at Mission Rafael to read and write. He let me sit quietly at the back of the room and I helped Domingo, who **detested** lessons and being indoors. The California missions were closing down, anyway, and the padre did not care if the rules said girls did not need an education. He said if a girl wanted to read and write, he would not stop her. He was very generous and tolerant when it came to the mission *indios*.

Johnston was so astonished that he dug into his leather saddlebag and handed me a bottle of ink, a very nice brass point, and two turkey quills. Now the ink flows onto the pages almost as fast as I think of words.

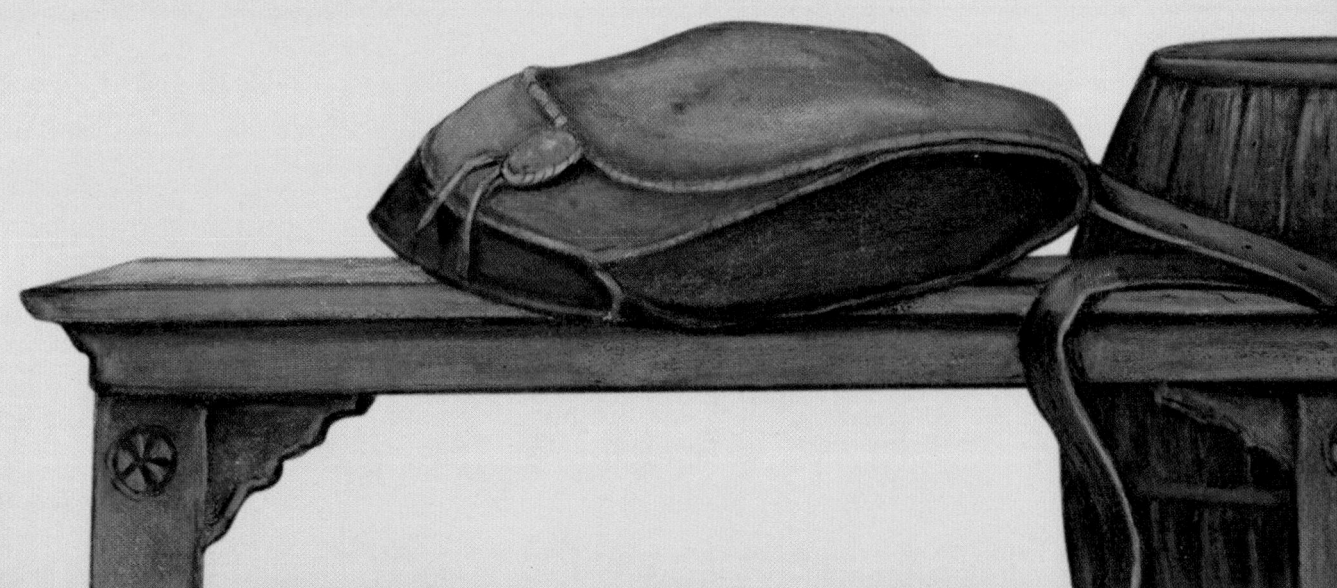

Looking at the Past with
Sherry Garland and Kristina Rodanas

Sherry Garland grew up in Texas, the youngest of nine children. She started writing in high school and had her first book published in 1982. She loves to do research and enjoys traveling to different places to find information about a topic. It usually takes her about a year to research a new book. Sherry says that she "gets ideas from real events, things that appear in newspapers, on TV, or things that really happened years ago."

Kristina Rodanas enjoys writing and illustrating. She has written and illustrated a number of Native American folktales and likes learning about different cultures. She lives in Orleans, Massachusetts.

Author's Purpose

What is Sherry Garland's purpose in writing *Valley of the Moon*? Explain your answer using examples from the story.

Other books by Sherry Garland and Kristina Rodanas.

Find out more about Sherry Garland and Kristina Rodanas at **www.macmillanmh.com**.

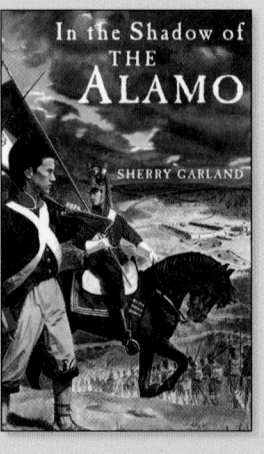

154

CA Critical Thinking

Summarize

Use your Cause and Effect Chart to help you summarize *Valley of the Moon*. In your summary, include the effect the diary has on the life of María Rosalia.

Cause → Effect
→
→
→
→

Think and Compare

1. Reread page 146. What **effect** did Miguela's words about the diary have on María Rosalia? What did her words **cause** her sisters to do? **Monitor Comprehension: Cause and Effect**

2. Think about the words and actions of Miguela and Señor Johnston. How are they different? How do these differences in their characters affect the plot of the story? **Analyze**

3. María Rosalia has to write in her diary in secret. How would you feel if you had to hide the fact that you knew how to read and write? **Apply**

4. The author uses diary entries to tell the story of María Rosalia. Why is this technique effective as it **depicts** life in California in the 1800s? **Apply**

5. Reread "To California" and *Valley of the Moon*. Describe the similarities and differences between Paul and María Rosalia. What character traits do they share? Use details from both texts to support your answer. **Reading/Writing Across Texts**

Genre

Nonfiction, such as nonfiction articles, present facts and information about a topic.

✔ Text Feature

A Time Line is a diagram of events arranged in the order in which they took place.

Content Vocabulary

independence
border
rebellion
territory

The Settlement of the WEST

In 1821 Mexico won its independence from Spain. At that time, Mexico was a much larger country than it is today. It included the present-day states of Texas, New Mexico, Arizona, Utah, Nevada, and California. These lands were far from the Mexican government in Mexico City, and few Mexicans wanted to settle there.

INDEPENDENCE FOR TEXAS

The Mexican government decided to offer land in Texas that was practically free. However, new settlers had to make several promises. They had to become Mexican citizens, They also had to become Roman Catholic, since this was the religion of most Mexicans. In addition, slavery was illegal in Mexico, so the new settlers could not bring enslaved African workers to Texas.

Most of the new settlers came from the United States. By 1835, 25,000 Americans had settled in Texas. Many of these Americans had never planned to become citizens of Mexico. They also refused to become Roman Catholics. They complained about Mexican laws, and criticized the actions of the Mexican government. They also wanted slavery to be legal.

On March 2, 1836, settlers in Texas declared their **independence** from Mexico. The Texans were defeated at the Alamo, but soon they defeated the Mexican ruler, Antonio López de Santa Anna. They forced Santa Anna to agree to independence for Texas. The

southern **border** of Texas would be the cause of continued fighting.

The new citizens of Texas wanted to be a part of the United States. However, the American government was afraid that this might lead to war with Mexico. In addition, people in northern states did not want another slave state in the Union.

This map from the mid-1800s shows the American West divided into territories.

WAR WITH MEXICO

Texas and Mexico continued to argue about their border for years. In April 1846, fighting broke out. President James K. Polk wanted to capture Mexico's northern lands so that the United States would stretch from the Atlantic to the Pacific. The United States declared war on Mexico.

When war broke out, Americans in California organized a **rebellion** and declared independence. American troops quickly made California a part of the United States.

The Mexican-American War ended in 1848. Mexico was forced to accept the Rio Grande as its border with the United States. Mexico was also forced to sell lands that are now California, Nevada, Utah, and parts of New Mexico, Arizona, Colorado and Wyoming to the United States.

OREGON OR BUST!

The United States also had lands to the north. This **territory** extended from southern Alaska to northern California. It was included in the Louisiana Purchase, but this land was also claimed by Spain, Russia, and Great Britain.

Lewis and Clark explored this area between 1804 and 1806. Later American settlers sent letters back to friends and family in the United States. Their descriptions of the rich soil and the mild climate attracted so many Americans that the nation was said to have "Oregon Fever."

Between 1841 and 1846, the number of Americans in the Oregon Territory grew from 400 to 6,000. The new settlers wanted the Oregon territory to be part of the United States. Much of this land was still claimed by Great Britain. President Polk did not want a war with Great Britain, so he suggested a conference to work out a division of the Oregon Territory. The result is the modern border between the United States and Canada. The American section was later divided into the states of Washington and Oregon.

Pioneers filled covered wagons with all the supplies they would need for their new lives.

Reading a Time Line

Read the time line starting at left and continuing to the right, in time order.

Important Events in the Settlement of the West

| 1800 | 1810 | 1820 | 1830 | 1840 | 1850 |

1804
Lewis and Clark expedition sets out.

1821
Mexico gains independence.

1836
Texas gains independence.

1846
Mexican-American War begins.

1848
Mexican-American War ends.

 **Critical Thinking**

1. According to the time line, what important event occurred in 1846? **Reading a Time Line**

2. How did the Mexican-American War change the size of the United States? **Analyze**

3. Think about *Valley of the Moon: The Diary of María Rosalia de Milagros*. How might María Rosalia's diary differ if it was written after California became a state, as described in "The Settlement of the West"? **Reading/Writing Across Texts**

 History/Social Science Activity

Research important events in the history of California. Create a time line that describes and illustrates those events.

 Find out more about settling the West at **www.macmillanmh.com**.

159

Writing

✓ **Point of View**

Good writers use **point of view** to show readers what the characters see, hear, and notice during a specific moment in their stories.

Reading and Writing Connection

Read the passage below. Notice how the author Sherry Garland showed Maria Rosalia's point of view in her story.

An excerpt from
Valley of the Moon

The author shows us what Maria Rosalia notices as she writes. By including Maria Rosalia's unique observations about the night, we see the moment through her eyes and ears.

The Medina family is asleep, and all is quiet throughout the rancho. Only the wind racing around the corners of the adobe house and the distant yelp of coyotes break the night silence. I am snuggled in a corner of the kitchen surrounded by baskets of dried corn waiting to be ground. The tile floors feel cold on my bare feet, but I do not mind, for I know no one will find me here.

Valley of the Moon
by Sherry Garland
Illustrated by Kristina Rodanas

160

Read and Find

Read Anand's writing below. How did he show us his point of view? Use the checklist to help you.

Class Trip

by Anand U.

The best exhibit at the aquarium was the giant coral reef tank. It was shaped like a tall, skinny rectangle, two stories high. The fish swam around and around inside. The crazy thing was, almost all the fish kept swimming in the same direction. From the little orange clown fish to the massive sharks, everyone swam counterclockwise.

Read about my favorite exhibit at the aquarium.

Writer's Checklist

 Does the writer show his point of view about this moment?

 Does the writer show you details about what caught his eye and his attention?

☑ Do you feel the writer is showing **point of view** through his own unique observation?

CA **Talk About It**

What can be gained by exploring new places?

LOG ON ▶ Find out more about exploring new places at www.macmillanmh.com.

162

Exploring New Places

Paul Cox collects a vine from high up in a banyan tree in Samoa.

Vocabulary

instill
combined
naturalist
vacant
diverse

The Healing Power of Plants

Even as a kid in Utah, Paul Cox was wild about plants. He built a greenhouse and collected weird, insect-eating plants.

Cox studied to become an ethnobotanist (eth•no•BOT•uh•nist). This, he explains, "is someone who loves plants and people and studies the relationship between them." Cox is most interested in how to use plants for healing.

When he won an important science award, Cox decided to use the money to "go live with native healers to learn from them." He, his wife, and their four kids moved to a remote village in Samoa, an island nation in the South Pacific. They lived for a year in a hut without running water or electricity.

Cox studied how the people of Samoa use plants to treat illness. One tree he learned about from a native healer could someday be used to make a valuable drug. If so, "the [native healer's] whole village will share the riches," says Cox. The leafy kingdom of plants is full of such treasures. Cox's work and the knowledge of native healers may ultimately lead to medicines that save many lives.

164

Teaching "EARTHKEEPING"

For more than 27 years, Joseph Andrews has tried to **instill** a love of nature in his students. "I try to tie nature into every subject," he explains. Andrews teaches a **combined** fourth- and fifth-grade class at Jones Lane Elementary School in Gaithersburg, Maryland.

One year his students helped build an outdoor classroom for the school. There students can enjoy a view of a meadow and stream while they learn. Language Arts, Social Studies, and Earth Science all come to life in the outdoor classroom. Sometimes the students read poetry and Native American tales. At other times they simply listen to the sounds of nature and hope to catch a glimpse of the deer and foxes that make their homes near the school.

"Mr. Andrews calls us his earthkeepers," says fifth-grader Emmanuel Maru. Andrews says giving students that title helps them understand that they have an important role in helping to protect the environment.

All the earthkeepers pitched in to help build an outdoor seating area and nature trails.

THE "BIODIVERSITY" MAN

Edward Osborne Wilson was a naturalist from the start. As a child growing up in Alabama and northern Florida, he loved to study nature. He made his first important scientific discovery when he was 13. In a vacant lot in Mobile, Alabama, he found the first known U.S. colonies of fire ants. Starting as an entomologist—a scientist who studies insects—E.O. Wilson went on to become one of the most respected scientists in the world. He is most well known for making the world aware of the importance of biodiversity. *Bio* means "life." *Diversity* comes from the word *diverse*, which means "different from one another." Biodiversity describes the complex web of life, with many different plant and animal species, that is necessary to keep Earth healthy.

LOG ON Find out more about biodiversity at www.macmillanmh.com.

A Historic Journey

CA Comprehension

Genre

A **Nonfiction Article** in a newspaper or magazine presents facts and information about real people, places, and events.

Make Inferences and Analyze

✓ **Cause and Effect**

A cause is what makes something happen. An effect is the thing that happens.

How did the leaders of the Lewis and Clark expedition make history as both explorers and scientists?

IN 1803, President Thomas Jefferson asked Captain Meriwether Lewis to explore a huge area of North America known as the Louisiana Purchase. The United States was about to buy this land from France. The effect of this purchase was to double the size of the United States territory, but very little was known about it. Jefferson hoped it included a water route between the Mississippi River and the Pacific Ocean that would help U.S. trade.

Besides learning about the geography of the Louisiana Purchase, Lewis was ordered to report on the people, plants, and animals that inhabited this vast territory.

Meriwether Lewis

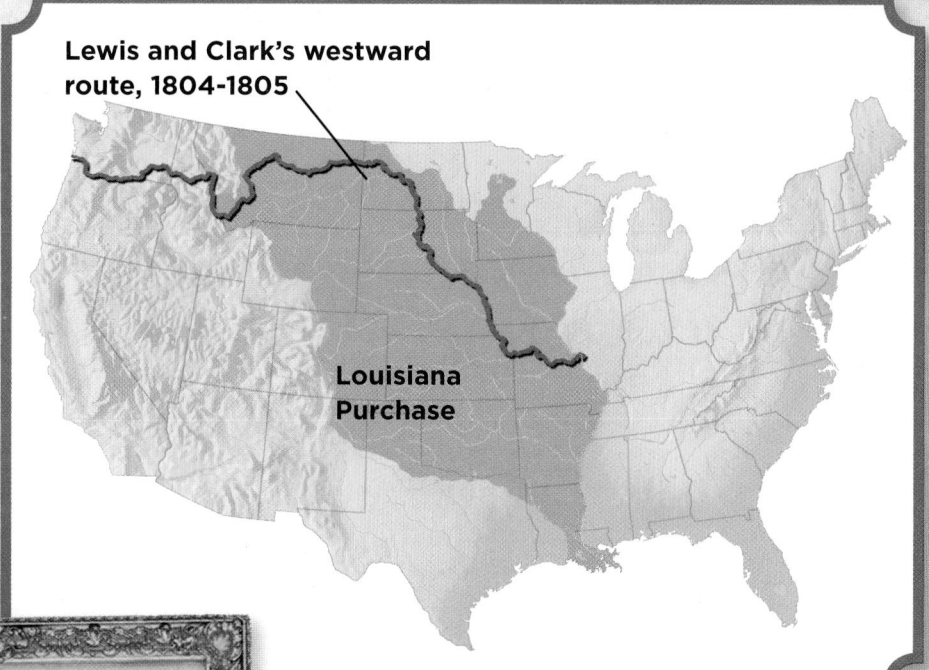

Lewis and Clark's westward route, 1804-1805

Louisiana Purchase

William Clark

Accompanying Lewis on this adventure was Captain William Clark, Lewis's best friend. During their historic journey, each of these two army captains would prove to be an excellent **naturalist**. They kept superb maps and diaries of everything they saw and learned. They were the first to write about many Native American tribes who lived in the territory. Their **combined** efforts produced descriptions of the **diverse** plant and animal life in the territory—122 kinds of animals and 178 kinds of plants.

Barking Squirrels or Ground Rats?

The expedition started in May 1804. Lewis and Clark led a 33-member team out of St. Louis, Missouri. That September, the team set eyes on an endless sea of little animals that French members of the team called *petite chiens*—French for "little dogs." Plans for future travel were halted until these creatures could be thoroughly investigated. Lewis called them "barking squirrels." Clark preferred to call them "ground rats." The name we now know—"prairie dogs"— came later. The team even captured a live prairie dog and sent it back to President Jefferson in Washington.

prairie dog

William Clark's diagram of the Handsom Falls on the Missouri River

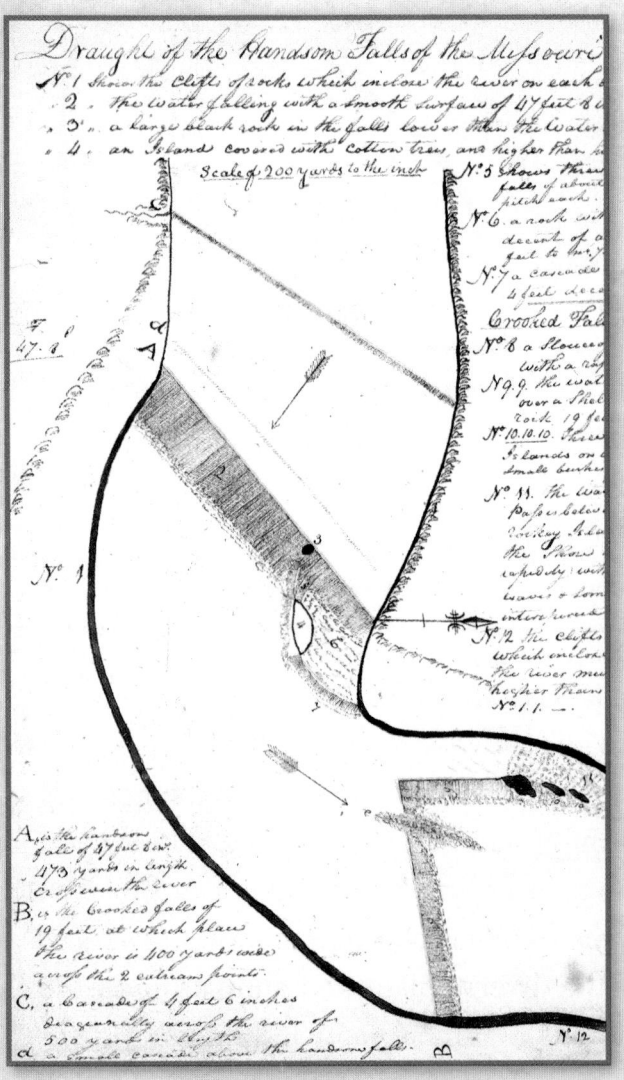

Where Do the Buffalo Roam?

The Missouri River from St. Louis to what is now North Dakota was already well-traveled by trappers and traders. But Lewis and Clark collected a trove of new plant and animal specimens from the area. They also created a detailed map of the route.

The farther north Lewis and Clark and their team traveled in the summer of 1804, the more buffalo they saw. By fall, however, the immense herds were starting to move south toward their wintering grounds. A few months later, feasts of fresh buffalo were just pleasant memories. Thankfully, the explorers enjoyed the hospitality of two Native American tribes, the Mandan and Hidatsa. Mule deer replaced buffalo as a source of meat for the explorers.

In 1805 the expedition paddled northwest on the Missouri River toward Montana. There Lewis and Clark found less open prairie. The land was broken up by shallow gullies and streams. It was dotted

with bushes and scrubby trees. The rugged landscape of western North Dakota amazed and challenged the expedition. They crossed the Badlands—a harsh, nearly **vacant** area of rolling hills and little vegetation—and moved onto the plains. Here the explorers spotted wondrous sights. Meriwether Lewis wrote this in his journal on September 16, 1805: ". . . vast herds of buffalo, deer, elk, and antelopes were seen feeding in every direction as far as the eye of the observer could reach."

Keeping Track While Making Tracks

More than 500 days and 4,000 miles after they had set out, Lewis and Clark reached the Pacific. Clark—who was a horrible speller—wrote in his journal "Ocian view! O! the joy!"

Lewis and Clark never found the water route that Jefferson hoped they would, but they became the first U.S. citizens to explore the Midwest and West—the endless Great Plains, the jagged Rocky Mountains, and the glittering Pacific. They took the time to write down in their journals everything they saw each day.

Perhaps the greatest effect of the Lewis and Clark expedition was the opening of U.S. territory west of the Mississippi River to other explorers and to settlers. Thanks to the courage, endurance, and keen observation skills of Lewis and Clark, we can look back today and see the land as it was then. The record of their journey helps to **instill** in Americans today the same sense of wonder and adventure they must have felt more than two hundred years ago.

 **Critical Thinking**

1. What caused President Jefferson to send Lewis and Clark on their expedition?

2. According to this selection, what was the most important result of the Lewis and Clark expedition?

3. Do you think you would have liked to have been part of the Lewis and Clark expedition? Why or why not?

4. What common theme can you find among all of these selections? What are the individuals in each selection interested in?

Lewis and Clark camped near here in what is now Montana. The Rocky Mountains are in the distance.

CA Show What You Know

Author and Me
The answer is not directly stated. Think about what you have read to figure it out.

Compare the shapes of these seagulls to the shape of an airplane.

Designed by Nature

What makes birds able to fly? Is the secret in their feathers? Is it in their wing shapes or in their tails? Since ancient times man has had the dream of flight. Scientists and engineers have studied birds in order to help man fly.

It is no surprise then, that like birds, airplanes have wings and tails that are necessary for flight. It seems natural that the design of airplanes would be inspired by the bodies of birds. Engineers are still trying to make airplanes do as many things in flight as birds can do.

Just spend a little time on a beach watching seagulls and you'll see the challenge. A seagull swoops over the sand, suddenly changes direction, pauses in midair, drops earthward, lands, and takes off again—all in just a few seconds. An airplane can't do that. Scientists don't yet know how birds are able to make certain movements in the air.

Understanding how birds perform their aerial feats is one step in the effort to improve the design of aircraft. The designs of planes have changed a great deal over the years. Engineers have based the shapes of aircraft on many kinds of birds, making additions to allow for pilots and passengers. Designs also depend on available materials and fuels.

The hope is to make aircraft safer as well as more efficient and maneuverable— able to change direction easily. Someday this research may produce an airplane with wings that are dramatically different from the wings we see today. Another possibility is airplane wings that can actually morph, or change shape, in flight.

Go on ▶

Now answer numbers 1 through 5. Base your answers on the selection "Designed by Nature."

1. Engineers who design airplanes are inspired by birds because

   A   they want to design sturdier wings for aircraft.

   B   migrating birds can sometimes interfere with air travel.

   C   they want to build airplanes that make similar movements.

   D   they want to find a way to keep birds away from certain areas.

2. **Among the things a seagull can do that an airplane can't do are**

   A   fly fast and carry cargo.

   B   take off and land on a runway.

   C   raise and lower landing gear in flight.

   D   pause in midair and change direction suddenly.

3. Scientists and engineers work to help man fly because

   A   they like to watch birds in flight.

   B   they enjoy testing new materials and fuels.

   C   helping people fly safely and quickly is important.

   D   someday people may not need to use aircraft to fly.

4. **Use information and details from the article, photograph, and caption to explain how observing birds helps engineers design airplanes.**

5. **Airplanes have changed over the years, from ones with simple, box-shaped wings to supersonic jets. Should airplanes continue to change? Use information and details from the article to explain your answer.**

> **Tip**
> You have to think about the entire passage to choose the best answer.

STOP

Write on Demand

CA Many new technologies have models in nature.

Think of a new technology that has a model in nature.

Now write to <u>tell how</u> a new technology has a model in nature.

> Expository writing explains, defines, or tells how to do something.

> To figure out if a writing prompt asks for expository writing, look for clue words such as <u>explain what</u> or <u>tell how</u>.

Below, see how one student begins a response to the prompt above.

> The writer uses details that support her response to the prompt.

Doctors keep trying new medicines to help sick people get well. Many new medicines begin with models found in nature. With time and more research, doctors and other scientists are trying to help sick people heal by improving on nature.

Before modern medicine, people relied on native healers and medicines found in nature. Ancient Greek healers, for example, used to prescribe willow bark to chew on. That might sound strange, but it turns out that the chemicals in the tree bark are the same ones found in today's aspirin.

Writing Prompt

Respond in writing to the prompt below. Write for 8 minutes. Write as much as you can, as well as you can. Review the hints below before and after you write.

 Many people believe it is important to learn by observing nature.

Think of something you have learned by observing nature.

Now write to explain what you have learned by observing nature.

Writing Hints for Prompts

- ☑ Carefully read the prompt.
- ☑ Organize your ideas to plan your writing.
- ☑ Support your ideas by giving reasons or using more details.
- ☑ Combine sentences to add variety and show emotions.
- ☑ Choose words that help readers understand your ideas.
- ☑ Review your writing and edit as needed.

COWBOYS

CA **Talk About It**

What do you know about the history of cowboys?

LOG ON ▶ To find out more about cowboys go to www.macmillanmh.com.

175

Vocabulary

vastness
enthusiasm
horizon
ravine
presence
swerved
distinct
suspended

Analogies

Analogies compare two pairs of words. Sometimes analogies use *antonyms*, words with opposite or nearly opposite meanings. For example, *presence* is to *absence* as *strong* is to *weak*.

The LIFE of a COWBOY

by Nancy Vilelli

The cowboy lifestyle became popular in America in the middle 1800s. One group that affected the rise of the professional American cowboy was the *vaquero* (vah KAYR oh). Vaqueros were cattle workers from Mexico. They knew how to keep animals together in the **vastness** of wide, open countryside. The American cowboys were eager to learn this skill. They accepted the vaqueros' ways with **enthusiasm** and excitement.

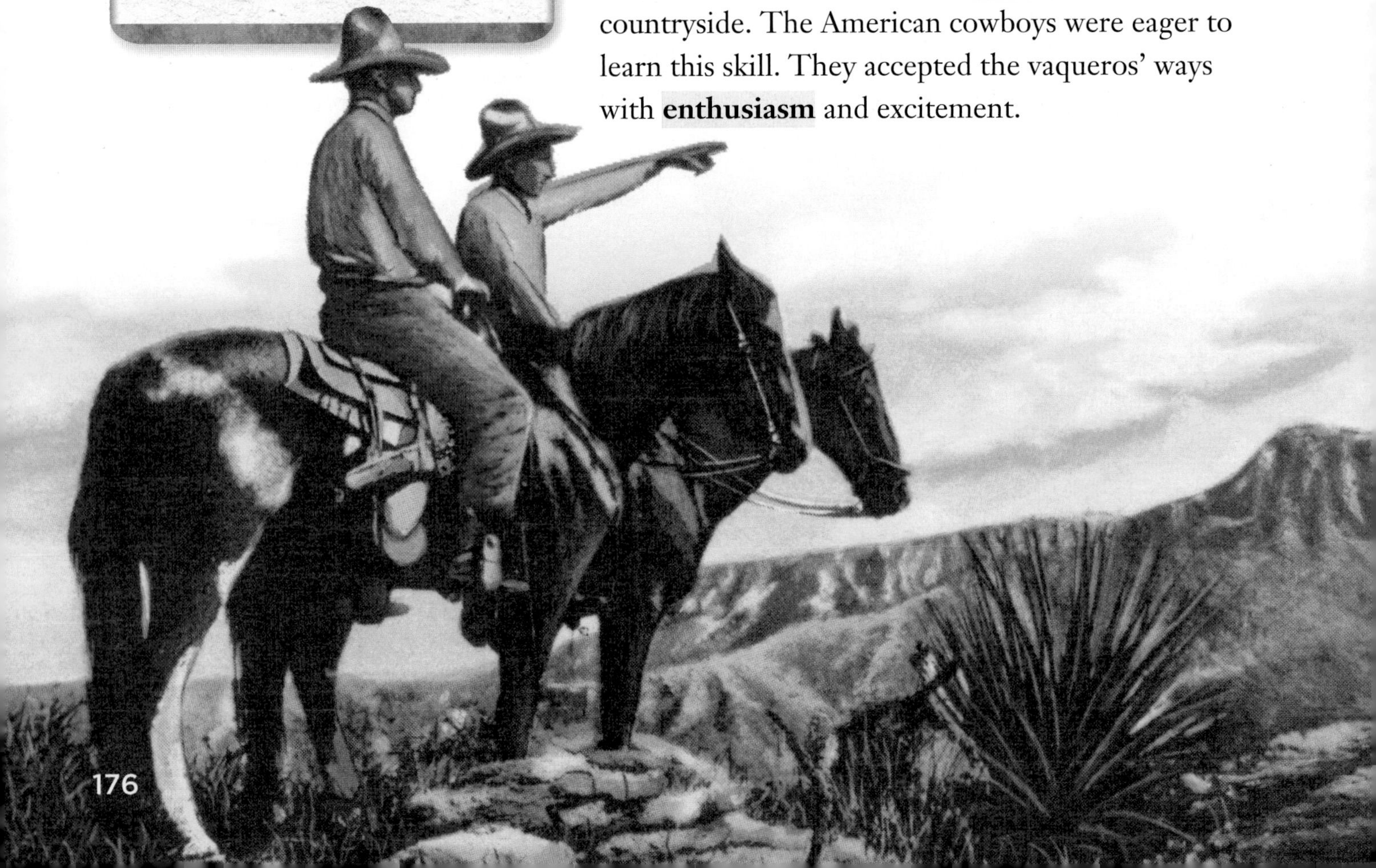

Soon cattle ranches sprang up from Texas to the Dakotas. It was hard work to keep track of hundreds of cows. Cows spread out as far as the **horizon**, where land meets the sky. No fences held them in. The cowboys rode their horses for miles every day to watch over the cattle.

There were many dangers in the open fields. A cow could fall into a **ravine** and hurt itself in the deep, narrow valley. Or a cow could be frightened by the **presence** of another animal nearby. One frightened cow can cause a stampede.

When spring came the cattle were rounded up to be counted. Afterwards the cowboys would move the cattle across the plains during the summer. Cowboys would ride inside the herd. They **swerved** as they rode, turning in and out, to move the cattle in the right direction.

A cowboy's job was tiring, so he would need a good place to set up camp, eat, and rest. After the cook fixed dinner, cowboys would sit around a campfire and listen to the **distinct** sounds of the wild. Like the vaqueros, they would tell stories or sing songs. Eventually, all but one would fall asleep as the moon hung **suspended** in the huge, dark sky. As with vaqueros' tradition, one cowboy always remained awake because the safety of the herd came first.

Reread for **Comprehension**

Monitor Comprehension

Make Inferences

When you make inferences, you take clues the author gives you and combine them with information you already know. This will help you understand why characters behave in a certain way, and how the author develops the plot. Use your Inferences Chart as you reread the selection to make inferences about characters and plot events.

Text Clues	What You Know	Inferences

CA Comprehension

Genre
A **Biography** is an account of an actual person's life told by another person.

Monitor Comprehension
Make Inferences
As you read, fill in your Inferences Chart.

Text Clues	What You Know	Inferences

Read to Find Out
Why is Bob Lemmons good at his job as a cowboy?

BLACK COWBOY
WILD HORSES
A TRUE STORY

BY
JULIUS LESTER

ILLUSTRATED BY
JERRY PINKNEY

Award Winning Author and Illustrator

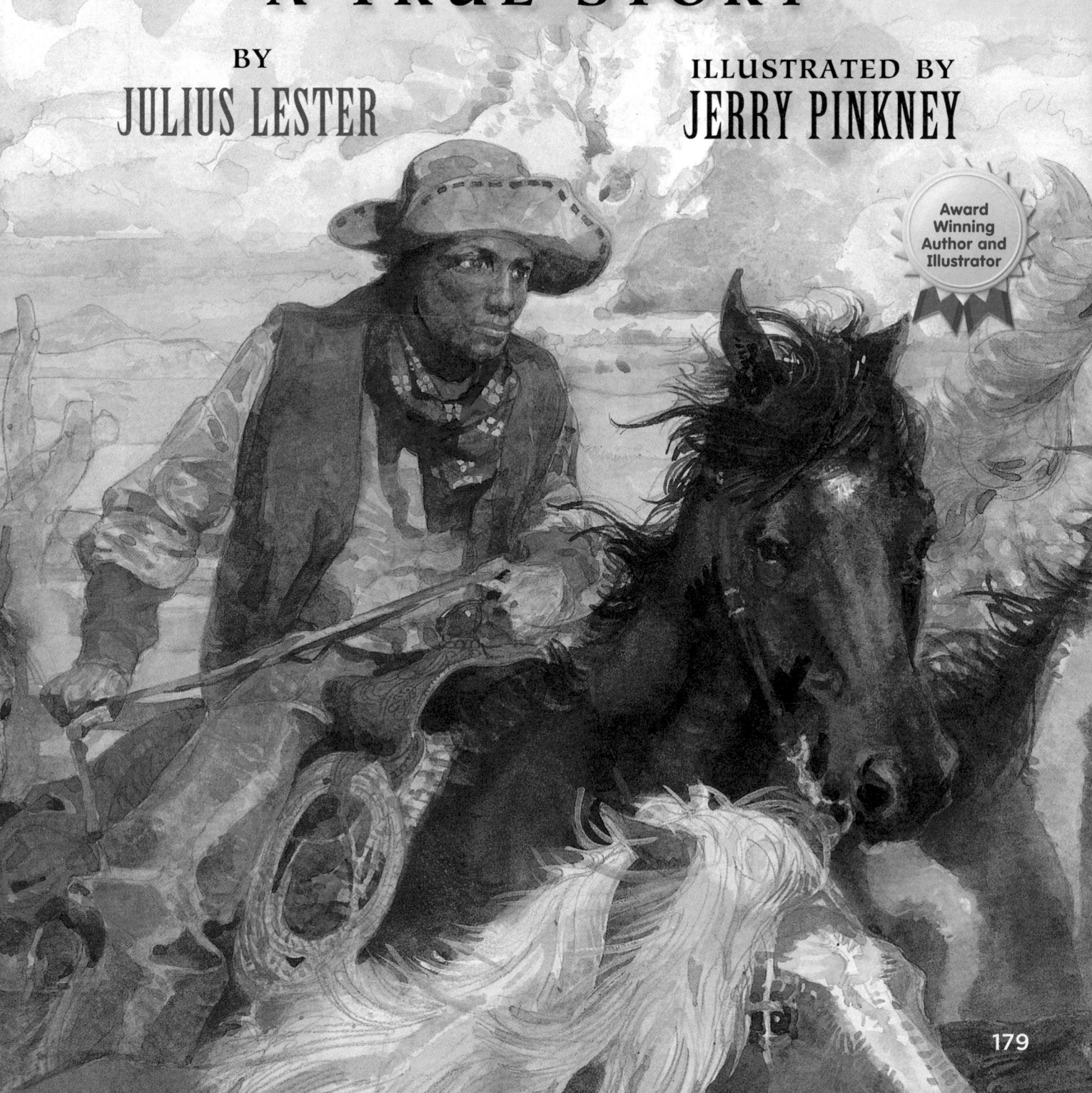

FIRST LIGHT. Bob Lemmons rode his horse slowly up the rise. When he reached the top, he stopped at the edge of the bluff. He looked down at the corral where the other cowboys were beginning the morning chores, then turned away and stared at the land stretching as wide as love in every direction. The sky was curved as if it were a lap on which the earth lay napping like a curled cat. High above, a hawk was **suspended** on cold threads of unseen winds. Far, far away, at what looked to be the edge of the world, land and sky kissed.

He guided Warrior, his black stallion, slowly down the bluff. When they reached the bottom, the horse reared, eager to run across the **vastness** of the plains until he reached forever. Bob smiled and patted him gently on the neck. "Easy. Easy," he whispered. "We'll have time for that. But not yet."

He let the horse trot for a while, then slowed him and began peering intently at the ground as if looking for the answer to a question he scarcely understood.

It was late afternoon when he saw them—hoofprints of mustangs, the wild horses that lived on the plains. He stopped, dismounted and walked around carefully until he had seen all the prints. Then he got down on his hands and knees to examine them more closely.

Some people learned from books. Bob had been a slave and never learned to read words. But he could look at the ground and read what animals had walked on it, their size and weight, when they had passed by, and where they were going. No one he knew could bring in mustangs by themselves, but Bob could make horses think he was one of them— because he was.

He stood, reached into his saddlebag, took out an apple, and gave it to Warrior, who chewed with noisy **enthusiasm**. It was a herd of eight mares, a colt, and a stallion. They had passed there two days ago. He would see them soon. But he needed to smell of sun, moon, stars, and wind before the mustangs would accept him.

> **Make Inferences**
> What clues in the story help you know when it takes place?

183

The sun went down and the chilly night air came quickly. Bob took the saddle, saddlebag, and blanket off Warrior. He was cold, but could not make a fire. The mustangs would smell the smoke in his clothes from miles away. He draped a thick blanket around himself, then took the cotton sack of dried fruit, beef jerky, and nuts from his saddlebag and ate. When he was done, he lay his head on his saddle and was quickly asleep. Warrior grazed in the tall, sweet grasses.

As soon as the sun's round shoulders came over the **horizon**, Bob awoke. He ate, filled his canteen, and saddling Warrior, rode away. All day he followed the tracks without hurrying.

Near dusk, clouds appeared, piled atop each other like mountains made of fear. Lightning flickered from within them like candle flames shivering in a breeze. Bob heard the faint but **distinct** rumbling of thunder. Suddenly lightning vaulted from cloud to cloud across the curved heavens.

Warrior reared, his front hooves pawing as if trying to knock the white streaks of fire from the night sky. Bob raced Warrior to a nearby **ravine** as the sky exploded sheets of light. And there, in the distance, beneath the ghostly light, Bob saw the herd of mustangs. As if sensing their **presence**, Warrior rose into the air once again, this time not challenging the heavens but almost in greeting. Bob thought he saw the mustang stallion rise in response as the earth shuddered from the sound of thunder.

Then the rain came as hard and stinging as remorse. Quickly Bob put on his poncho, and turning Warrior away from the wind and the rain, waited. The storm would pass soon. Or it wouldn't. There was nothing to do but wait.

Finally the rain slowed and then stopped. The clouds thinned, and there, high in the sky, the moon appeared as white as grief. Bob slept in the saddle while Warrior grazed on the wet grasses.

The sun rose into a clear sky and Bob was awake immediately. The storm would have washed away the tracks, but they had been going toward the big river. He would go there and wait.

By mid-afternoon he could see the ribbon of river shining in the distance. He stopped, needing only to be close enough to see the horses when they came to drink. Toward evening he saw a trail of rolling, dusty clouds.

In front was the mustang herd. As it reached water, the stallion slowed and stopped. He looked around, his head raised, nostrils flared, smelling the air. He turned in Bob's direction and sniffed the air again.

Bob tensed. Had he come too close too soon? If the stallion smelled anything new, he and the herd would be gone and Bob would never find them again. The stallion seemed to be looking directly at him. Bob was too far away to be seen, but he did not even blink his eyes, afraid the stallion would hear the sound. Finally the stallion began drinking and the other horses followed. Bob let his breath out slowly. He had been accepted.

The next morning he crossed the river and picked up the herd's trail. He moved Warrior slowly, without sound, without dust. Soon he saw them grazing. He stopped. The horses did not notice him. After a while he moved forward, slowly, quietly. The stallion raised his head. Bob stopped.

When the stallion went back to grazing, Bob moved forward again. All day Bob watched the herd, moving only when it moved but always coming closer. The mustangs sensed his presence. They thought he was a horse.

So did he.

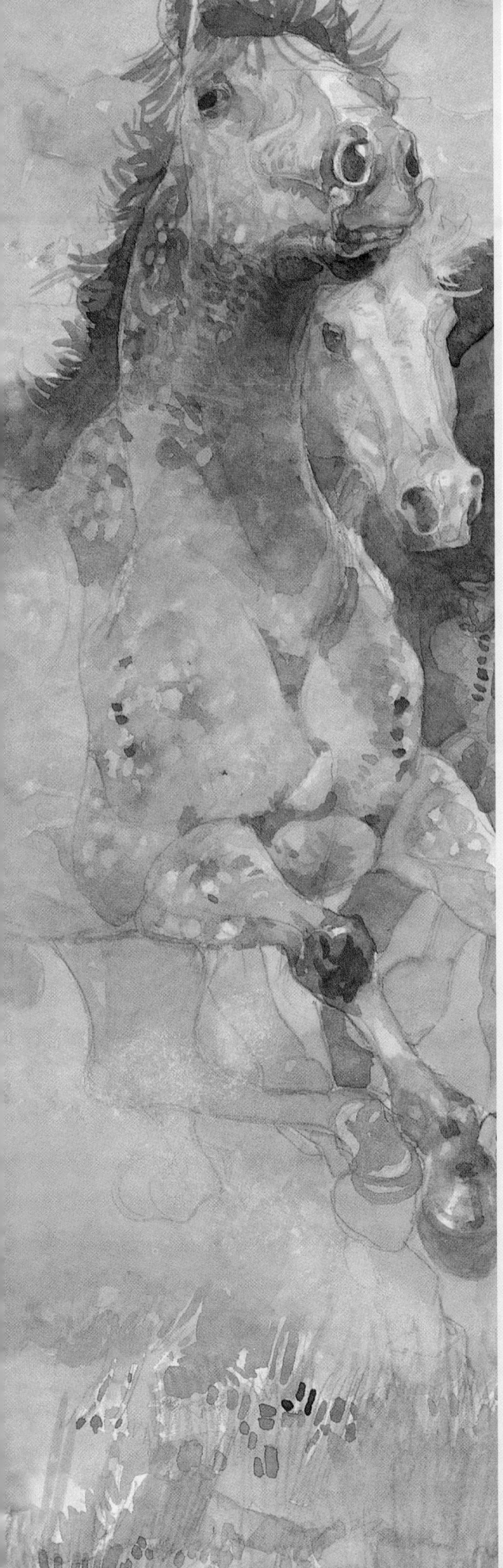

The following morning Bob and Warrior walked into the herd. The stallion eyed them for a moment. Then, as if to test this newcomer, he led the herd off in a gallop. Bob lay flat across Warrior's back and moved with the herd. If anyone had been watching, they would not have noticed a man among the horses.

When the herd set out early the next day, it was moving slowly. If the horses had been going faster, it would not have happened.

The colt fell to the ground as if she had stepped into a hole and broken her leg. Bob and the horses heard the chilling sound of the rattles. Rattlesnakes didn't always give a warning before they struck. Sometimes, when someone or something came too close, they bit with the fury of fear.

The horses whinnied and pranced nervously, smelling the snake and death among them. Bob saw the rattler, as beautiful as a necklace, sliding silently through the tall grasses. He made no move to kill it. Everything in nature had the right to protect itself, especially when it was afraid.

The stallion galloped to the colt. He pushed at her. The colt struggled to get up, but fell to her side, shivering and kicking feebly with her thin legs. Quickly she was dead.

> **Make Inferences**
> What clues in the story point to the fact that Bob respects nature?

191

Already vultures circled high in the sky. The mustangs milled aimlessly. The colt's mother whinnied, refusing to leave the side of her colt. The stallion wanted to move the herd from there, and pushed the mare with his head. She refused to budge, and he nipped her on the rump. She skittered away. Before she could return to the colt, the stallion bit her again, this time harder. She ran toward the herd. He bit her a third time, and the herd was off. As they galloped away, Bob looked back. The vultures were descending from the sky as gracefully as dusk.

It was time to take over the herd. The stallion would not have the heart to fight fiercely so soon after the death of the colt. Bob galloped Warrior to the front and wheeled around, forcing the stallion to stop quickly. The herd, confused, slowed and stopped also.

Bob raised Warrior to stand high on his back legs, fetlocks pawing and kicking the air. The stallion's eyes widened. He snorted and pawed the ground, surprised and uncertain. Bob charged at the stallion.

Both horses rose on hind legs, teeth bared as they kicked at each other. When they came down, Bob charged Warrior at the stallion again, pushing him backward. Bob rushed yet again.

The stallion neighed loudly, and nipped Warrior on the neck. Warrior snorted angrily, reared, and kicked out with his forelegs, striking the stallion on the nose. Still maintaining his balance, Warrior struck again and again. The mustang stallion cried out in pain. Warrior pushed hard against the stallion. The stallion lost his footing and fell to the earth. Warrior rose, neighing triumphantly, his front legs pawing as if seeking for the rungs on which he could climb a ladder into the sky.

The mustang scrambled to his feet, beaten. He snorted weakly. When Warrior made as if to attack again, the stallion turned, whinnied weakly and trotted away.

Bob was now the herd's leader, but would they follow him? He rode slowly at first, then faster and faster. The mustangs followed as if being led on ropes.

Throughout that day and the next he rode with the horses. For Bob there was only the bulging of the horses' dark eyes, the quivering of their flesh, the rippling of muscles and bending of bones in their bodies. He was now sky and plains and grass and river and horse.

When his food was almost gone, Bob led the horses on one last ride, a dark surge of flesh flashing across the plains like black lightning. Toward evening he led the herd up the steep hillside, onto the bluff, and down the slope toward the big corral. The cowboys heard him coming and opened the corral gate. Bob led the herd, but at the last moment he **swerved** Warrior aside, and the mustangs flowed into the fenced enclosure. The cowboys leaped and shouted as they quickly closed the gate.

Bob rode away from them and back up to the bluff. He stopped and stared out onto the plains. Warrior reared and whinnied loudly.

"I know," Bob whispered. "I know. Maybe someday."

Maybe someday they would ride with the mustangs, ride to that forever place where land and sky kissed, and then ride on. Maybe someday.

RIDE ALONG WITH
JULIUS LESTER AND JERRY PINKNEY

Julius Lester was a musician before he wrote books. He even recorded two albums and hosted a radio show. When an editor asked him to write a children's book, he found he loved doing it. Julius believes it is important to be the voice for people who can't tell their own stories, people like Bob Lemmons. His advice to young writers is read, read, read. He should know—he has about 15,000 books!

Jerry Pinkney started drawing by copying from comic books and magazines, just like his two older brothers. In junior high school, he sketched people he saw on the street. He's been drawing and painting ever since. Jerry has even drawn eleven postage stamps for the U.S. Postal Service. "I'd rather draw than do anything else!" he says.

 Find out more about Julius Lester and Jerry Pinkney at **www.macmillanmh.com**.

Another book by Julius Lester and Jerry Pinkney: *John Henry*

CA **Author's Purpose**
What was the author's purpose in writing this biography?

196

 **Critical Thinking**

Summarize

Summarize the story of Bob Lemmons and the mustangs in *Black Cowboy, Wild Horses.* Use your Inference Chart to help you include important information about the story.

Text Clues	What You Know	Inferences

Think and Compare

1. Warrior rears at the beginning of the story and once at the end. What **inference** can you make about Warrior? Use details from the story in your answer. **Monitor Comprehension: Make Inferences**

2. Make a list of descriptive words and phrases that the author uses to describe the **vastness** of the plains. Why does the author begin the story by using imagery? Use story details in your answer. **Analyze**

3. Would you want to ride with the wild mustangs? Explain why or why not. **Evaluate**

4. Bob says that everything in nature has a right to protect itself. Do you agree or disagree with this opinion? Explain your answer. **Evaluate**

5. Reread "The Life of A Cowboy" on pages 176–177. How was Bob Lemmons's life similar to the life described in the article? How was it different? Give examples using both selections. **Reading/Writing Across Texts**

Poetry

Song Lyrics are the written words of a song. Long ago poems were not just recited but were often sung.

Literary Elements

Repetition means that a line or sequence of lines appears more than once. In a song this repetition is often called the *chorus*.

Assonance means the same or similar vowel sounds occur in a series of words. The long "o" sound in *oh, home, buffalo* and *roam* is an example of assonance.

Home on the Range

words by John A. Lomax
music by Daniel Kelley

Oh, give me a home where the buffalo roam,
Where the deer and the antelope play,
Where seldom is heard a discouraging word
And the skies are not cloudy all day.

Home, home on the range,
Where the deer and the antelope play
Where seldom is heard a discouraging word
And the skies are not cloudy all day.

This line is an example of *repetition*.

Oh, give me a land where the bright diamond sand

Flows leisurely down the stream,

Where a graceful white swan goes gliding along

Like a maid in a heavenly dream.

> The short "a" sound in *land* and *sand* is an example of *assonance*.

Home, home on the range,

Where the deer and the antelope play

Where seldom is heard a discouraging word

And the skies are not cloudy all day.

Where the air is so pure, the zephyrs so free,

The breezes so balmy and light,

That I would not exchange my home on the range

For all the cities so bright.

Home, home on the range,

Where the deer and the antelope play

Where seldom is heard a discouraging word

And the skies are not cloudy all day.

CA Critical Thinking

1. What are some other examples of repeating lines or words in this song? **Repetition**

2. Read the poem aloud. How does assonance help you read the poem more smoothly? **Apply**

3. Compare "Home on the Range" to *Black Cowboy, Wild Horses.* What are some differences between the range described in the song and the land described in the story?
   Reading/Writing Across Texts

 **LOG ON** Find out more about song lyrics at **www.macmillanmh.com**.

Writing

CA

✓ Point of View

Point of view is the perspective of the writer.

This helps the reader understand where the writer is coming from.

Read the passage below. Notice how the author Julius Lester shows us the point of view of Warrior, Bob Lemmons's horse.

An excerpt from
Black Cowboy Wild Horses

The author uses showing to describe what Warrior is feeling instead of telling us how Warrior feels. We are sharing the horse's point of view as we read.

. . . Bob raced Warrior to a nearby ravine as the sky exploded sheets of light. And there in the distance, beneath the ghostly light, Bob saw the herd of mustangs. As if sensing their presence, Warrior rose into the air once again, this time not challenging the heavens but almost in greeting. Bob thought he saw the mustang stallion rise in response as the earth shuddered from the sound of thunder.

Read and Find

Read Dakaja's writing below. What did she do to show you her point of view? Use the checklist below to help you.

Embarrassed
by Dakaja C.

After the teacher told me I was wrong in front of the whole class, I slunk into my chair. My head hung in between my folded arms and I wouldn't make eye contact with anyone, not even my best friend Anasia. She knew it wasn't a good time to talk.

Read what I thought about someone pointing out my mistake in front of others.

Writer's Checklist

 Does the writer show what he or she does and feels?

 Does the writer avoid telling you what the emotion is?

 Are you able to experience the **point of view** of Dakaja?

CA **Talk About It**

Who are some of the legendary figures of the American West? What qualities must a person have to become a legend?

LOG ON ▶ Find out more about tall tales at **www.macmillanmh.com**.

Tall Tales

203

Vocabulary ✓

posed   commenced
original   impress
wring   elected
advertisement sauntered

Word Parts ✓

Compound Words combine two smaller words. Often you can figure out the meaning of a compound word by looking at its word parts. For example, *fireball* is made up of *fire* and *ball* and means "a ball of fire."

Grandma's Tales

by Daniel Fritz

My grandma lives in a town in Tennessee near the place Davy Crockett was born. She is a distant relative of his and even has a painting of him **posed** next to his cabin in Tennessee. She thinks people should get all the **original** facts about this American legend straight. She is determined to **wring** the truth from all those wild stories about him. She feels those stories are like the words in an **advertisement**: they exaggerate and try to convince readers that Davy Crockett could accomplish impossible feats! My grandma

agrees he was a man full of energy and enthusiasm. But she wants people to remember he was a talented human being—not a superhero.

It was a cold, snowy night the last time Grandma told me Davy Crockett's life story. We were sitting on the couch, sipping hot chocolate when she **commenced** telling me facts about Davy's early life. "Davy Crockett was born in 1786," she began. "The woods around here were beautiful then, but life wasn't easy. His family moved around a lot."

"Was Davy a boy when he caught a flaming fireball with his bare hands?" I asked. "Is that when he picked up a rattlesnake and used it for a lasso?" I continued, trying to **impress** Grandma with my knowledge. She didn't smile or laugh.

"Davy got married and had children. He farmed, hunted, and joined the army. He got interested in politics and was **elected** to Congress. He lived by the rule: 'Be sure you are right. Then go ahead,'" Grandma said.

"When he left politics, Davy decided to explore Texas," she continued. "That was where he had his last great adventure."

"Yes!" I said. "That's where he died a hero in the famous battle at the Alamo."

That statement of fact brought a huge smile to Grandma's face. "You got THAT right," she said, happily. Then she **sauntered** slowly over to the coonskin cap sitting on her mantel and plopped it on my head.

Reread for **Comprehension**

Analyze Story Structure

Plot and Setting

The plot is the series of events that take place in a story. The setting is where and when a story takes place. Use your Plot and Setting Chart as you reread the selection. This will help you understand how details about time and place influence the story's structure and the development of the plot.

Plot	Setting

CA Comprehension

Genre

Folklore/Tall Tale A **Tall Tale** has a larger-than-life character whose actions are exaggerated for humor.

Analyze Story Structure

Plot and Setting
As you read, fill in your Plot and Setting Chart.

Plot	Setting

Read to Find Out

What problem does Davy Crockett try to solve?

DAVY CROCKETT SAVES the WORLD

BY ROSALYN SCHANZER

I reckon by now you've heard of Davy Crockett, the greatest woodsman who ever lived. Why, Davy could whip ten times his weight in wildcats and drink the Mississippi River dry. He combed his hair with a rake, shaved his beard with an ax, and could run so fast that, whenever he went out, the trees had to step aside to keep from getting knocked down.

208

Folks always crow about the deeds of Davy Crockett, but the biggest thing he ever did was to save the world. This here story tells exactly how he did it, and every single word is true, unless it is false.

Plot and Setting
Where and when does the story take place? What clues help you to identify the setting?

209

About the time our tale begins, the world was in a heap of trouble. A way past the clouds and far beyond all the stars and planets in outer space, scientists with telescopes had discovered the biggest, baddest ball of fire and ice and brimstone ever to light up the heavens.

Its name was Halley's Comet, and it was hurling itself lickety-split straight toward America. Why, its tail alone was two million miles long. If it were to hit the earth, everyone would be blown to smithereens!

The President of the United States started getting big piles of letters telling him to stop Halley's Comet before it was too late. He made a law telling the comet it couldn't crash into the earth, but the comet paid no attention. It just kept speeding toward America and growing bigger every day.

Finally the President had an idea. He had heard of a brave man named Davy Crockett, who lived somewhere in the mountains far away. He put an **advertisement** in all the newspapers in America that said:

> # WANTED
> ## BY THE PRESIDENT
> ## OF THE UNITED STATES
> ## DAVY CROCKETT
> ## TO PULL THE TAIL OFF OF
> ## *HALLEY'S COMET*

Meanwhile, Davy Crockett didn't know a thing about any comet. He had no idea that the earth was even in danger. Davy was off in the forest with his pet bear, Death Hug. He was teaching himself to dance so that he could **impress** a real purty gal named Sally Sugartree, who could dance a hole through a double oak floor. He was not reading any newspapers.

It took two whole weeks, but once Davy had learned all the latest dances, he combed his hair nice and slow with his rake, shaved his face real careful-like with his ax, and **sauntered** off toward Sally Sugartree's cabin just as easy as you please.

All this time, of course, Halley's Comet was getting closer and closer to the earth and moving faster by the minute.

Now, Sally Sugartree was not just purty, but she was right smart too. Sally read the newspaper front to back every day, and she knew all about Halley's Comet. She had also seen the advertisement from the President.

Sally climbed up a fifty-foot hickory tree and commenced to look for Davy Crockett. Before long, she spotted him a way far off in the forest. Sally grabbed up her newspaper and waved it around just as hard as she could. When Davy saw her, he grinned and started to walk a mite faster.

As soon as Davy got close enough, Sally jumped right out of that tree. Davy caught her in his arms and gave her such a hug that her tongue stuck out half a foot and her eyes popped out like a lobster's. Then she showed Davy the want ad from the President.

Davy still didn't know what Halley's Comet was, but if the President of the United States wanted to see him, he would waste no time getting to Washington. He bridled up Death Hug and set out like a high-powered hurrycane. He could dance with Sally later.

Death Hug was so fast that rocks and trees and cows and snakes and other varmints all flew out behind him.

> **Plot and Setting**
> Why is Davy's decision to go to Washington an important event in the plot?

215

By the time they reached the White House, Halley's Comet was getting so close that there wasn't a minute to lose.

The President told Davy to climb the highest mountain he could find right away, and to **wring** that comet's tail off before it could destroy the earth. Then the President **posed** with Davy for pictures and pretended to look calm.

Davy combed his hair with his rake, rolled up his sleeves, and ate a big plateful of pickled rattlesnake brains fried by lightning to give him energy. Then he **commenced** to climb all the way to the top of Eagle Eye Peak in the Great Smoky Mountains.

Eagle Eye Peak was so high you could see every state and river and mountain in a whole geography book.

You could also look a way far off into outer space. By the time Davy reached the top, it was night.

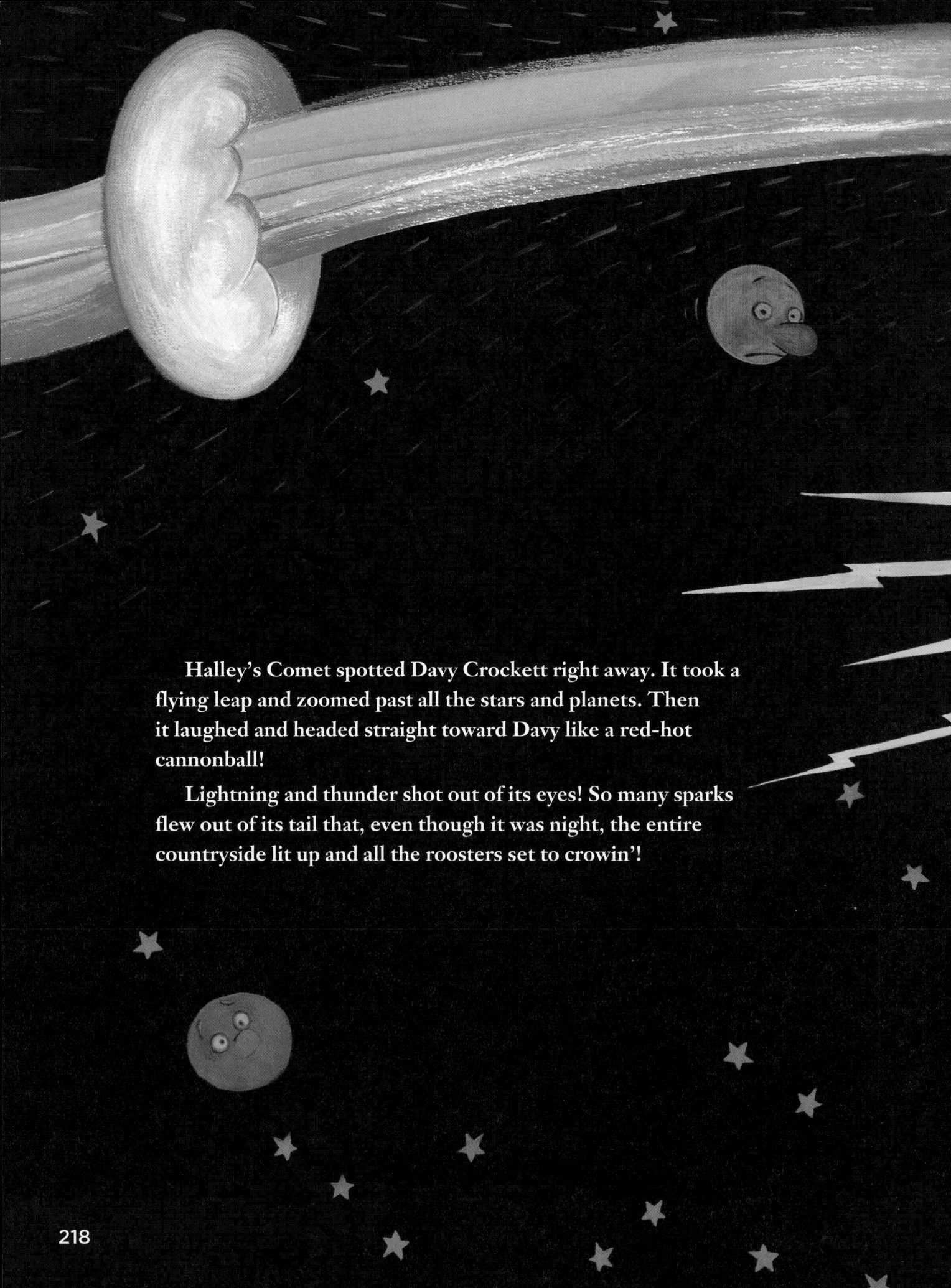

Halley's Comet spotted Davy Crockett right away. It took a flying leap and zoomed past all the stars and planets. Then it laughed and headed straight toward Davy like a red-hot cannonball!

Lightning and thunder shot out of its eyes! So many sparks flew out of its tail that, even though it was night, the entire countryside lit up and all the roosters set to crowin'!

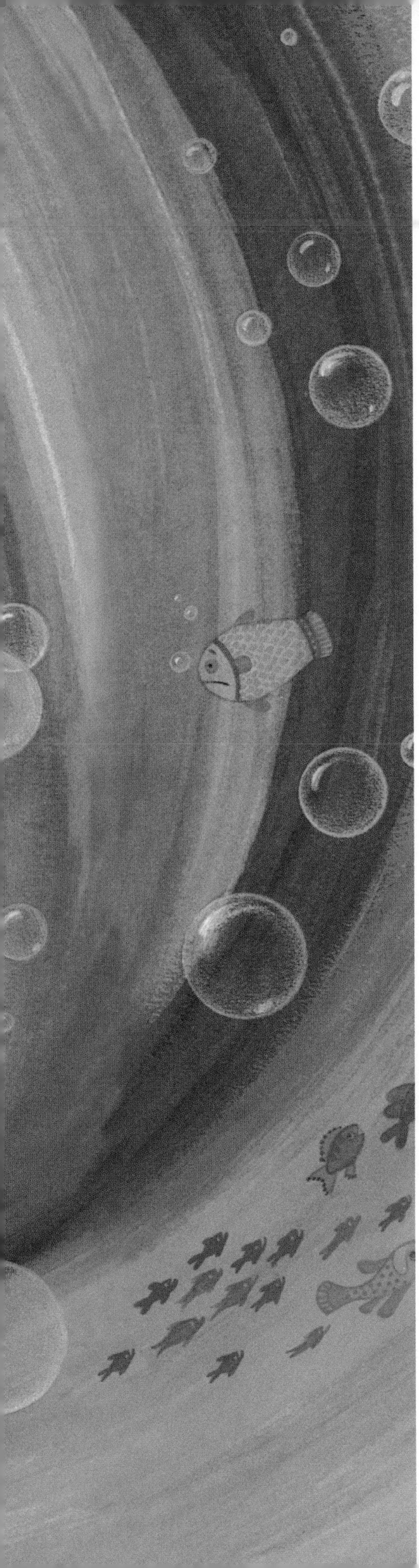

That comet must have thought Davy looked mighty tender, for it licked its chops, howled louder than a hundred tornadoes, and roared toward him with its mouth wide open!

This made Davy so mad that he jumped right over its shoulders and onto its back. Then he planted his teeth around the comet's neck and hung on. Halley's Comet spun around and around like a whirlwind trying to throw Davy off, but it couldn't.

Next off, that comet tried to drown Davy by diving into the Atlantic Ocean. The water got so all-fired hot that it boiled! The whole world was covered with steam, and the sun didn't shine as bright as usual for a month.

Just in time, the ocean put out that comet's fire and melted all its ice. It washed up on an island, and before it could grow back to its **original** size, Davy grabbed what was left of Halley's tail, spun around seventeen times, and hurled the comet back into outer space. It was so discombobulated that the next time it ever came in this direction, it missed the earth by 39 million miles.

That's how Davy Crockett saved the world. In fact, he did such a
good job that there was a huge parade in his honor, he got to marry
Sally Sugartree, and he was even **elected** to Congress.

Of course, that infernal fireball singed the hair right off Davy's head. A whole new crop grew back in tufts like grass and kept in such a snarl that he couldn't even comb it without breaking his rake.

That's why these days Davy Crockett always wears a coonskin cap.

Go Exploring with
Rosalyn Schanzer

Rosalyn Schanzer loves adventure just as much as Davy Crockett. She swam with sharks in Belize; kayaked with whales in Alaska; fished for piranhas in South America; and even sailed a boat through the Bermuda Triangle. When Rosalyn wants to create a new story, she treks to a different part of the globe to seek an unusual adventure.

Before words ever hit the page, Rosalyn illustrates her books. While traveling she asks questions, snaps pictures, and researches facts that can be used for artistic inspiration. After Rosalyn illustrates her new ideas and adventures, she brings the story to life with words. It seems only fitting that Rosalyn, who has gone on such unique adventures, takes such an unusual and adventurous approach to creating books.

Other books by Rosalyn Schanzer:
Gold Fever: Tales of the California Gold Rush and *How Ben Franklin Stole the Lightning*

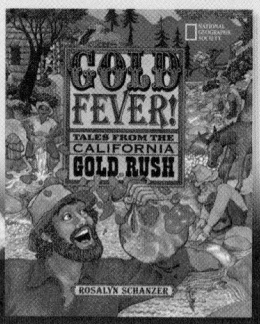

 Author's Purpose

What other purpose might Rosalyn Schanzer have for writing a tall tale other than wanting to explain Halley's Comet?

 Find out more about Rosalyn Schanzer at **www.macmillanmh.com**.

CA Critical Thinking

Summarize

Use your Plot and Setting Chart to help you summarize *Davy Crockett Saves the World.* When preparing your summary, be sure to include only important events and characters.

Plot	Setting

Think and Compare

1. How does the **setting** of the Atlantic Ocean add to the development of the **plot**? **Analyze Story Structure: Plot and Setting**

2. Reread page 208. What details do you learn about Davy Crockett? Are you meant to believe them? Why or why not? Use story details to support your answer. **Analyze**

3. If you were President, whom would you ask to save the world? Explain your answer. **Evaluate**

4. How would the President's **advertisement** to Davy Crockett be different if the story took place now? Explain. **Analyze**

5. Reread "Grandma's Tales" on pages 204–205. Describe how Grandma would react to *Davy Crockett Saves the World*. Use details from both stories to explain your answer. **Reading/Writing Across Texts**

History/ Social Science

Genre

Nonfiction: An online article has facts about people, things, places, and events.

✔ Text Features

A **Toolbar** is a strip of icons, or symbols, on a computer screen showing different features on the Web page.

A **Link** is an electronic connection on a Web page.

Content Vocabulary

exaggerating   features

superhuman

by Kyle Seulen

Links related to this topic

Related Articles

▶ Paul Bunyan

▶ John Henry

▶ Davy Crockett

▶ Pecos Bill

Have you ever visited or seen pictures of Puget Sound in Washington State or the Black Hills of South Dakota? If so, you have seen some of Paul Bunyan's greatest work. One time, when Paul was headed out West, he dragged his giant pickax behind him, and the ditch he made with it was the Grand Canyon. This statement may be **exaggerating** the facts just a little. Paul Bunyan really did not make these beautiful places, but the stories we like to tell about him make him one of the heroes of American tall tales.

✔ This is a link to more information about Pecos Bill.

Home   **Browse**   **Search** | Tall Tales

This strip of icons is called a toolbar.

Paul Bunyan and Babe

Pecos Bill

David Crockett

John Henry

Old Stormalong

Tall-tale heroes and the regions where they were born

What is a tall tale? Four **features** make a story a tall tale. First, the hero must seem larger than life and have **superhuman** skills. Second, the hero usually has a certain job that he does better than anyone else. The hero might be a lumberjack or a cowhand, for example. Third, the hero must solve a problem in a way that surprises the reader or makes the audience laugh. Fourth, the details of the tale are exaggerated to be made greater than they really are. Often, the hero is bursting with courage and ready to conquer any difficulty. As a rule, the heroes would be a little rough on the outside. Still, they had tender hearts and souls and possessed the most admirable qualities. They were helpful, always available to solve problems, and determined to create a better world for their neighbors and friends.

How did the tradition of inventing tales starring characters that were larger-than-life begin? Tall tales probably started as settlers moved into America's wilderness areas. Life on the American frontier was difficult, exhausting, dangerous, and uncertain. For the most part, the future was unknown and scary. When the day was done, pioneers gathered around the fire in search of relaxation and entertainment. Telling stories became a favorite pastime. It was a handy art form that could not only entertain but inspire as well. The tales that were told helped the people feel they could overcome danger, just as their favorite heroes had.

As the tales were repeated, they somehow took on a life of their own and grew bigger and better. For example, if someone roped a fierce bear and swung it across town, then in the retelling he

roped the same bear and swung it across the country. In the next telling of the story, the hero would have swung the bear so far it landed on the moon. Even though no one believed a bear landed on the moon, people certainly enjoyed listening to the story as much as the storyteller enjoyed telling it.

A brand-new tall tale often had the fellow who told it or somebody from the "neighborhood" as its hero. But as the tale became more famous, people began to feel it wasn't "right" that such a wonderful story be told about an ordinary man. The pioneers decided that larger-than-life stories needed to feature larger-than-life heroes. So, they began putting famous characters in the leading roles of the stories they would tell. Some were real heroes of the day, such as Davy Crockett or Jim Bridger. Others, like Paul Bunyan and Pecos Bill, were products of the imaginations of good storytellers.

A particular tall tale might also be influenced by events in the region where it was born. People who made their living from the sea liked to hear stories about the adventures of Old Stormalong and his ship. Railroad workers liked to hear stories about John Henry, who could hammer railroad spikes faster than anyone else. Ranchers and cowboys enjoyed hearing about Pecos Bill, who roped a mountain

lion and rode it a hundred feet at a step. They also enjoyed hearing about Slue-foot Sue, who rode a catfish down the Rio Grande.

Speaking of roping, if you feel up to it, you might try to catch a ride to the lumber camp on Paul Bunyan's blue ox, Babe. It shouldn't be too hard to catch him. The distance between Babe's horns is just a little over seven ax handles. Once you rope him and he takes you to the camp, relax by the campfire. The lumberjacks there will probably have another tale or two to share with you!

CA Critical Thinking

1. If you were on this Web page, what feature would you select to help you find out more information about Babe, Paul Bunyan's ox? **Using Toolbars and Links**

2. If you were to write a tall tale, who would be the hero? Explain your answer. **Synthesize**

3. Think about "The Tales Are Getting Taller" and *Davy Crockett Saves the World.* How do you know that *Davy Crockett Saves the World* is a tall tale? **Reading/Writing Across Texts**

History/Social Science Activity

Use an online encyclopedia to learn more about one hero on the map on page 227. Write a tall tale about the person you choose. Remember to exaggerate the tale.

 Find out more about tall tales at **www.macmillanmh.com**.

229

✔ **Supporting Details**

Supporting details tell more about the theme of the writing. Writers use supporting details to help readers understand the theme.

Reading and Writing Connection

Read the passage below. Notice how the author Rosalyn Schanzer uses details to support the theme of her tall tale.

An excerpt from
Davy Crockett Saves the World

The author selects details about Davy Crockett. The details are exaggerated, but they show how the author wants us to imagine him.

I reckon by now you've heard of Davy Crockett, the greatest woodsman who ever lived. Why, Davy could whip ten times his weight in wildcats and drink the Mississippi River dry. He combed his hair with a rake, shaved his beard with an ax, and could run so fast that, whenever he went out, the trees had to step aside to keep from getting knocked down.

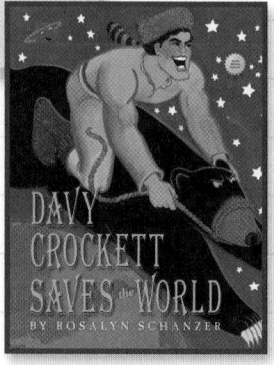

Read and Find

Read Rotem's writing below. How did she use details to help you imagine the moment? Use the checklist below to help you.

Cafeteria Chaos

by Rotem M.

The cafeteria at our school is like the Wild West—totally lawless. At lunchtime, all the classes have to walk in straight, silent lines. Once they get through the cafeteria doors, though, everyone dashes for a table and starts jabbering away with their friends. Kids make trades by sliding food across the tables or even steal food right off each other's trays!

See how I used details to show how wild my cafeteria can get!

Writer's Checklist

 Does the writer choose **supporting details** for her main idea?

 Do these details seem to have something in common?

 Do the details in the piece make you understand that the writer sees chaos in the cafeteria?

THE RIGHT TO VOTE

CA Talk About It

Why should people vote? Why do you think it took women so long to win the vote in the United States?

LOG ON ▶ Find out more about women's suffrage at www.macmillanmh.com.

MRS. PANKHURST LEADER of the ENGLISH SUFFRAGETTES

VOTES FOR WOMEN

233

U.S. Capitol Building in Washington, D.C.

YOUR VOTE YOUR VOICE

by Wyatt Thatcher

The word *democracy* comes from two Greek words which, when combined, mean "the people rule." The **notion**, or belief, behind any democracy is that the people make the laws.

In the United States, everyone could not possibly gather and vote on every law. That's why the Founding Fathers set up a special type of democracy in which people elect a **representative** who will speak for them.

Each person plays an important part in a representative democracy. One of their main responsibilities is to vote during an election. All people, from a teacher to an army **colonel**, have the right to vote as long as they are citizens.

Before the 1970s you had to be 21 years old to vote. Some people thought the age should be lowered to 18 years old, so an **attorney** challenged the law in court. Lawyers argued their case all the way to the Supreme Court. Finally, the debate was settled when Congress passed a new law that lowered the voting age to 18 years old for all elections.

Unfortunately, in recent years fewer and fewer Americans are voting. As the twenty-first century began, only one-third of those who **qualify** and are eligible to vote were registered to do so. Younger voters have the worst turnout of any age group.

People who are old enough to vote should not **postpone** signing up or they might find they will need to **submit** to laws they don't agree with. In Washington, D.C., and every state capital, the legislature decides about future laws. These laws might not be **satisfactory** for your needs. By voting, your voice can be heard in our governments. In this way, YOU can make a difference.

Reread for **Comprehension**

Evaluate

Fact and Opinion

A Fact and Opinion Chart helps you decide which statements can be proven true (facts) and which statements are somebody's personal feelings or beliefs (opinions). Use your Fact and Opinion Chart to evaluate what is fact and what is opinion in the selection.

Fact	Opinion

235

Genre

A **Biography** tells the story of a person's life and is written by another person.

Evaluate

✔ **Fact and Opinion**

As you read, use your Fact and Opinion Chart.

Fact	Opinion

Read to Find Out

What opinions does the author give about Esther Morris?

When Esther Morris Headed West

BY CONNIE NORDHIELM WOOLDRIDGE
ILLUSTRATED BY JACQUELINE ROGERS

Award
Winning
Selection

Her name was Esther Mae Hobart McQuigg Slack Morris, and in 1869 she headed out to South Pass City in the Wyoming Territory. She was fifty-five years old.

South Pass City was a place that sprouted out of nearly nothing at the mention of the word "gold." The space around it was large and wide open. That was a good thing because Mrs. Morris was a large woman with wide-open ideas that needed more room than could be had in New York or Illinois, where she'd come from. You see, she thought a woman should be able to vote and hold office, the same as a man.

Fact and Opinion
Find one example of a fact and one example of an opinion on this page.

238

After she got herself settled in South Pass City, she paid a call on a man who had already argued hard for the same new and crazy-sounding idea she was bringing in from the East. That man was **Colonel** William Bright, and he thought women's being able to vote and hold office made all kinds of sense. Since he was an elected member of the Wyoming Territory Council, he proposed An Act to Grant to the Women of the Wyoming Territory the Right of Suffrage and to Hold Office.

Colonel Bright was opposed by a feisty young lawyer named Benjamin Sheeks, another **representative** from South Pass City, who thought the idea was hogwash. His plan was to keep the thing from ever being voted on at all. He made a motion to **postpone** discussion until July Fourth, which any fool knew was a holiday.

But Mr. Ben Sheeks lost the day, and the heretofore unheard-of up and happened. In the closing months of 1869, a legislature full of men voted to give the women of Wyoming rights no other women in the world had: They could vote and hold office the same as men.

"The Deed Is Done," read one newspaper. "Ladies, Prepare Your Ballots!" read another. "Reckless Copperheads!" read a third, referring to the legislators who'd voted in such a fool thing. Back in South Pass City, the justice of the peace resigned.

Fact and Opinion
One newspaper called the legislators "Reckless Copperheads!" Is this a fact or only an opinion? How do you know?

Now that women had the right to vote, it was time to prove they could hold office just as well. Mrs. Morris had no hankering for power or highfalutin titles. But she knew an idea—even one voted into law—wasn't worth a hill of beans as long as it stayed words on a page. Her boys were grown and it was time to step away from her cooking and gardening for a spell and do a thing that might help women coming along later on. So Mrs. Morris applied for the position of South Pass City Justice of the Peace. The whole Wyoming Territory let out a gasp. But the only fellow who opposed her for the position failed to **qualify**. So there she was: a judge. And that made her the first female in the United States to hold a public office.

A test of her ability came early on from the very man she was replacing. He refused to hand over the court docket. He didn't think Mrs. Morris should have it. He didn't think any woman should have it.

"You can keep your dirty docket," Mrs. Morris told him, and got herself a nice clean one.

Then there was the time young Ben Sheeks, back to lawyering, argued a case in her court. The opposing **attorney** was having a heyday picking at every little thing and getting Mr. Sheeks's dander up real good. After he'd had about all he could take, Mr. Sheeks escorted his opponent out of the room when it didn't appear the fellow was of a mind to go.

When Mr. Sheeks came back into the courtroom, he knew he'd gone and done it. His views on the woman question were no secret and here he'd misbehaved in front of the first woman judge in the country. The situation called for humbleness and that was not a thing that came easy to Ben Sheeks.

"Your honor," he said, "I apologize for my behavior and I **submit** to any punishment you might inflict. I was in contempt."

Mrs. Morris was not educated in the fine points of the law. But she'd raised three sons in rough-and-tumble places, and she knew a thing or two about common-sense fairness. "Your behavior was justified, Mr. Sheeks," was all she said. And that was an end to it.

Along with seven other South Pass City women, the judge cast her vote for the very first time on September 6, 1870. She later claimed she had her personal physician by her side, and he determined the operation of voting had no ill effects on a woman's health.

Her term ended the following month. "My position as justice of the peace was a test to woman's ability to hold public office," she said, "and I feel that my work has been **satisfactory**, although I have often regretted I was not better qualified to fill the position. Like all pioneers, I have labored more in faith and hope." When she stepped down from the bench, Mrs. Morris handed the court docket over to the same judge who wouldn't turn his loose eight months before.

The gold fever that had brought three thousand people to South Pass City died down. Colonel Bright moved to Denver and then finished out his days in Washington, D.C.

Ben Sheeks headed for Salt Lake City and then west to Washington State. Somewhere along the way he took up the crazy **notion** that women should be able to vote and hold office the same as men.

Mrs. Morris moved to Laramie, Wyoming, and then on to Cheyenne. She was close to ninety when she died.

In the summer of 1920, a professor from the University of Wyoming made her way out to what was left of South Pass City. She got herself a wheelbarrow and took a stone from the broken-down home of William Bright, who once had the courage to propose a crazy new idea.

She took another stone from the home of Esther Morris, who had the courage to show how the idea looked in the living of it. She took a third from the home of Ben Sheeks, who hated the idea, saw how it looked in the living, and had the courage to change his way of thinking.

The professor piled the stones into a monument and invited the remaining inhabitants of South Pass City to a dedication ceremony. As the sun sank behind the mountains, nineteen human beings, two dogs, and a cow remembered for a moment that once in time a thing bigger and better than gold had happened here.

In Washington, D.C., later that same summer of 1920, the Secretary of State announced a change to the United States Constitution. He said women in all states were now allowed to vote, the same as men.

It wasn't a new idea for the state of Wyoming. The folks back East just took a little longer getting to it is all.

HEADING WEST WITH
CONNIE NORDHIELM WOOLDRIDGE
AND JACQUELINE ROGERS

Connie Nordhielm Wooldridge tried a lot of things before she started writing. She studied Greek culture and archaeology in Greece, worked as a flight attendant, and taught school in Korea. But when Connie started writing, she knew she found the right job. She loves writing stories that tell children what life was like before they were born and how much life has changed.

Jacqueline Rogers grew up as the youngest child in a family of artists. While growing up she followed her mom to her sculpture class and her sisters to their drawing classes. When Jacqueline started drawing on her own, she focused on horses. Today she illustrates children's books because it allows her to be most creative. "It pushes me and scares me and that makes my work more exciting," she says.

Other books by Connie Nordhielm Wooldridge: *Wicked Jack* and *The Legend of Strap Buckner*

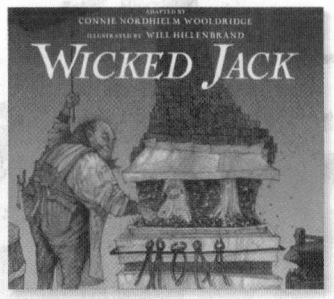

 Author's Purpose

Did Connie Nordhielm Wooldridge want to inform you or entertain you with her story about Esther Morris? How do you know?

 Find out more about Connie Nordhielm Wooldridge and Jacqueline Rogers at www.macmillanmh.com.

248

Critical Thinking

Summarize

Use your Fact and Opinion Chart to help you write a summary of *When Esther Morris Headed West*. Opinions you have about events in the selection should not appear in your summary.

Fact	Opinion

Think and Compare

1. Identify two **facts** in the story about Esther Morris's term as a judge. Then identify two **opinions** that she had about herself. Use story details to explain whether the facts support the opinions. **Evaluate: Fact and Opinion**

2. Reread page 247. What is the "thing bigger and better than gold" that happened? Explain why the author compares this event to gold. **Analyze**

3. Why do you think some people thought the idea of women voting was a crazy **notion**? What would you have done to help women get the right to vote? **Evaluate**

4. Explain why it takes courage to change people's way of thinking. When is the effort worth the risk? **Synthesize**

5. Reread "Your Vote, Your Voice" on pages 234–235. Compare and contrast women's desire to vote in Wyoming in 1869 with the decrease in voting in recent years. Find evidence from both selections to support your answer. **Reading/Writing Across Texts**

Genre

Nonfiction Textbooks present facts and ideas about nonfiction topics.

Text Feature

A Time Line is a diagram of several events arranged in the order in which they took place. A time line helps to organize information in an easy, visual way.

Content Vocabulary

suffrage   polling

amendment   media

Suffrage for Women

by Maria Chan

After more than 50 years of struggle and hard work, women finally won the right to vote in national elections in 1920.

The fight for **suffrage**, or the right to vote, began with the Seneca Falls Convention in New York state in 1848. As voting rights pioneer Susan B. Anthony argued, suffrage was "the pivotal right, the one that underlies all other rights." Suffragist leaders gained strength in 1870 when an **amendment** to the U.S. Constitution granted African American men the right to vote. Why not award the vote to all citizens?

250

In 1872 Anthony and a group of women marched into a **polling** place in Rochester, New York, and cast their votes in a presidential election. The women were arrested and fined. Finally, in 1878 after six more years of protests, a women's suffrage amendment was introduced in Congress.

Congress did not pass the women's suffrage amendment in 1878. Still, the amendment was reintroduced in every session of Congress for the next 40 years.

Suffragist leaders, such as Carrie Chapman Catt, traveled across the country giving speeches and organizing workers. Catt led a "suffrage army" of 1 million volunteers. She used the **media** to spread her arguments. Newspapers and magazines were able to reach a large number of people.

In 1920 these efforts paid off. Congress passed the Nineteenth Amendment, which guarantees every adult woman the right to vote. On August 26, 1920, the states approved this amendment. Here is what the Nineteenth Amendment to the Constitution says:

"The right of citizens of the United States to vote shall not be denied or abridged [limited] by the United States or by any state on account of sex." After a half-century of struggle, women finally won the right to have their voices heard in governing this country.

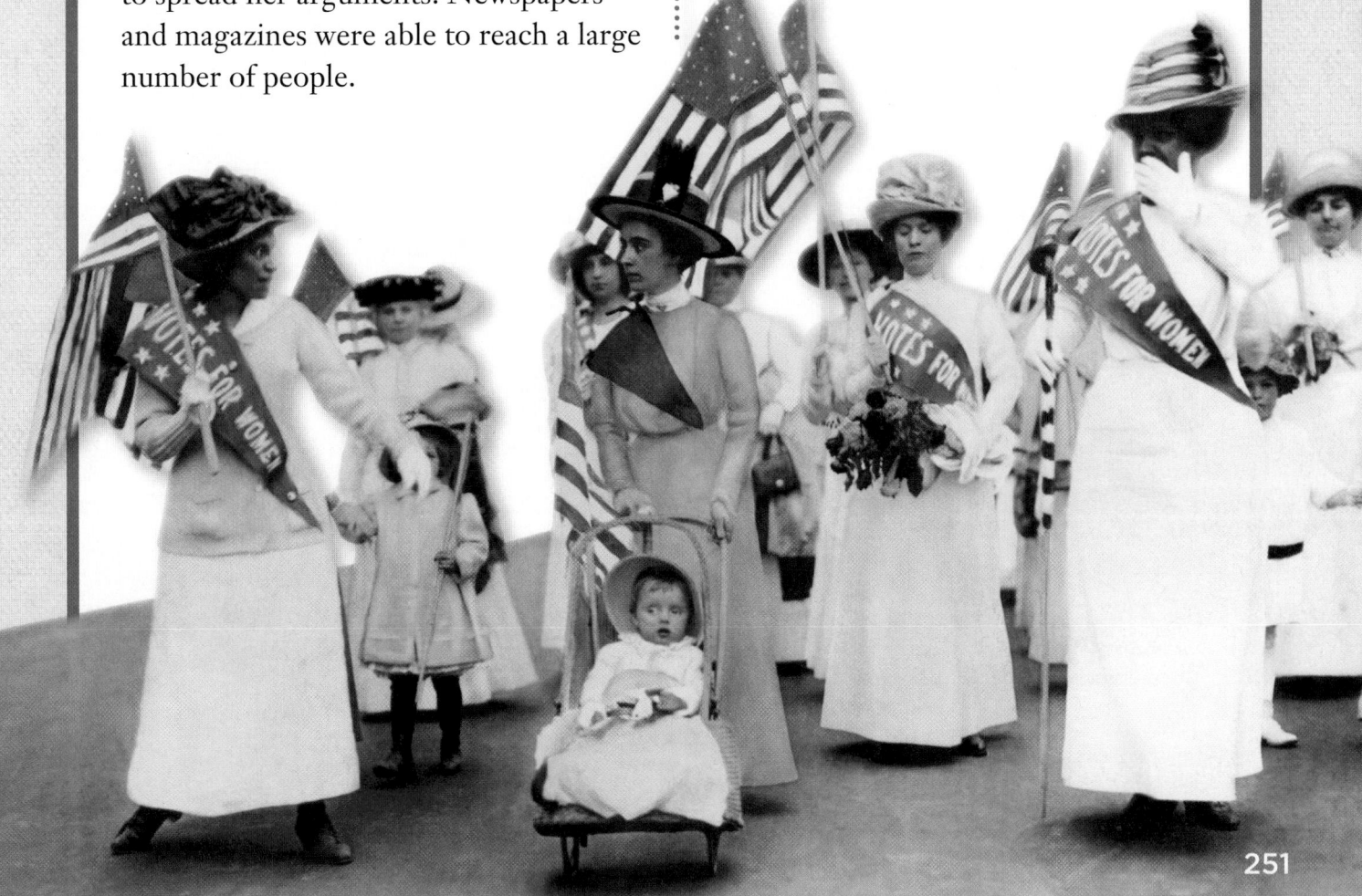

Biography

Carrie Chapman Catt was born Carrie Lane in Ripon, Wisconsin, in 1859. After college she became a teacher in Mason City, Iowa, and then the superintendent of schools in 1883. Around that time Catt became involved in fighting for the right to vote.

Over time Catt supervised thousands of volunteers and gave hundreds of speeches in favor of women's right to vote. She was elected president of the National American Woman Suffrage Association from 1900 to 1904, and again from 1915 to 1920.

Catt worked against great odds but held firm to her beliefs. "There will never be a true democracy until every responsible and law-abiding adult in it has his or her own voice in government." When American women won the right to vote in 1920, it was largely because of Catt's work.

That year Catt founded the League of Women Voters, which still exists today. She also founded the National Committee on the Cause and Cure of War in 1925. She died in 1947.

 Reading a Time Line

One way to review major historical events is to look at them on a time line. Here are some of the major events of the women's suffrage movement:

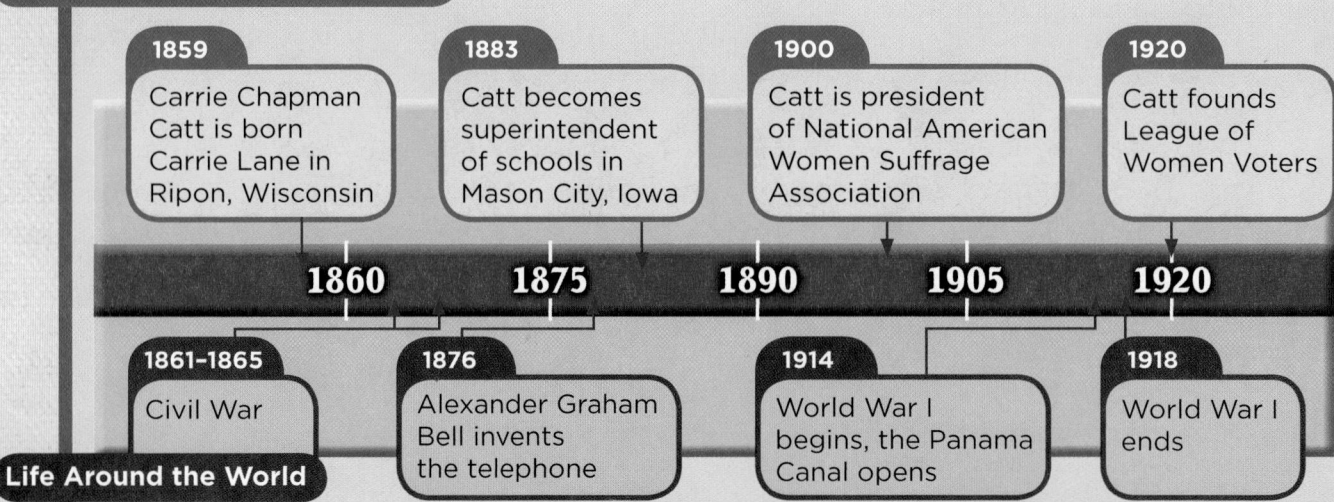

The Life of Carrie Chapman Catt

1859 Carrie Chapman Catt is born Carrie Lane in Ripon, Wisconsin

1883 Catt becomes superintendent of schools in Mason City, Iowa

1900 Catt is president of National American Women Suffrage Association

1920 Catt founds League of Women Voters

1860 · 1875 · 1890 · 1905 · 1920

1861–1865 Civil War

1876 Alexander Graham Bell invents the telephone

1914 World War I begins, the Panama Canal opens

1918 World War I ends

Life Around the World

CA Critical Thinking

1. Read the **time line** on page 252. How old was Carrie Chapman Catt when she founded the League of Women Voters? **Reading a Time Line**

2. How did Carrie Chapman Catt help women win the vote? **Analyze**

3. Compare *When Esther Morris Headed West* with this article about women's suffrage. How are the two selections similar? How are they different? **Reading/Writing Across Texts**

History/Social Science Activity

Research another suffragist leader, such as Lucretia Mott, Elizabeth Cady Stanton, or Lucy Stone. Write a summary of her life. Include a time line that shows the main events in the life of the person you choose.

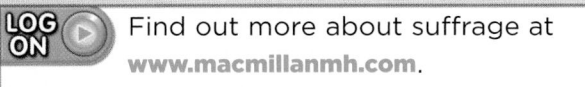

LOG ON Find out more about suffrage at
www.macmillanmh.com.

Reading and Writing Connection

✔ Supporting Details

Supporting details tell readers more about the theme or main message of a story. Details show readers what a character thought or felt at a moment in time.

Read the passage below. Notice how the author Connie Nordhielm Wooldridge used showing details in her story.

An excerpt from
When Esther Morris Headed West

The author includes details about newspaper headlines and how one judge reacted to the news. She chose details she thought would best help us understand what people thought about the decision to let women vote.

"The Deed Is Done," read one newspaper. "Ladies, Prepare Your Ballots!" read another. "Reckless Copperheads!" read a third, referring to the legislators who'd voted in such a fool thing. Back in South Pass City, the justice of the peace resigned.

Read and Find

Read Darryl's writing below. How did he use strong details to help you imagine the moment? Use the checklist below to help you.

Are You Scared Yet?

by Darryl D.

The hinges of the door creaked loudly as I eased open the door. A freezing draft blew behind me and the hairs on the back of my neck stood up. Even though the house was supposed to be deserted, I thought I heard slow, heavy footsteps walking across the floor over my head. After taking two steps into the room, the door crashed shut behind me.

Read how I show you what I saw and felt as I entered the old house.

Writer's Checklist

 Does the writer choose **supporting details** that show you how he felt at the time of the event?

 Do the details seem to have something in common?

 Do the details show you something about the house?

Review

Plot and Setting
Make Inferences
Main Idea and Details
Antonyms
Map

A Twist in the Trail

Halle and Joel Braden bickered for the first three miles of their hiking trip. Halle accused Joel of wearing smelly old shoes. Joel blamed Halle for using all of the bug spray. Halle told Joel he smelled like a skunk. Joel called Halle a weakling.

"Will the two of you just quiet down and enjoy our hike together?" their father said. "You're missing all of the beautiful scenery!"

It was true. Neither Joel nor Halle had taken notice of the bear their father had spied at the start of their trip. They hadn't looked up at the eagle he pointed out overhead. Worst of all, they hadn't paid any attention to the turns and twists in the trail while they continued their squabbling.

"Joel threw a stick at me!" Halle screamed.

"That's not true!" Joel shouted back.

Mr. Braden could no longer keep his anger suppressed. "And both of you need to stop arguing!" he erupted. As he turned to face them, his left foot caught on a root. He stumbled backward and slipped down a muddy bank. With a splash, he fell into the river that ran alongside the path.

Halle and Joel raced to their father's assistance. They helped him up out of the water, then dragged his soaked backpack up onto land.

"I think I'm OK. But my glasses," Mr. Braden said. "They came off when I fell in the water."

Halle and Joel waded back into the river. Twigs and leaves swirled around their ankles before floating away on the current. "I think they may have been swept downstream," Halle said.

"I can't see without my glasses," Mr. Braden said. "Everything's a blur. How will we get home?"

"Oh great! Now we're lost," said Joel, "and it might be days before someone finds us!"

"No thanks to you," Halle said.

"Kids, kids!" Mr. Braden shouted. "Just calm down. We'll be fine. We just need to work together to find our way out of here. Now bring me my backpack."

Mr. Braden fumbled through his soggy belongings and pulled a map wrapped in plastic and a compass from the backpack. "Now Joel," he said. "You like books about explorers and know how to read a map, right?" Joel nodded. "And Halle, you know how to use a compass from your hiking club, right?" Halle nodded. "And I remember some of the landmarks from when we came in. We should have no trouble retracing our steps."

Joel looked down at the map. "If we keep the river to our right, we'll be OK until up to here," he said.

Halle looked to where Joel was pointing. "And from there, we just take the southeast trail until it crosses that stream, then head due south."

Mr. Braden smiled. "You see? The two of you will end up saving the day," he said. "I guess you're pretty good hiking partners after all!"

THE · WORK · OF
GIANTS

The Transcontinental Railroad

Today you can board a plane in St. Louis and arrive in San Francisco about four hours later. You might even enjoy a movie while traveling. However, two hundred years ago, that same trip took many weeks. The journey was uncomfortable and often dangerous. Many people dreamed of ways to build a railroad connecting East and West. Not everyone shared that dream, however. The difficulties in building a transcontinental railroad seemed too great.

The Dream Takes Shape

The dreamers won over those who doubted, and plans were drawn for a railway that connected the railroads of the East Coast with the West Coast. The first problem was deciding on the route. Senators from the North and South argued for the railway to pass through their states. When the Civil War began, however, the Southern senators left Congress and the Northerners took charge of the plan.

Getting from There to Here

Before anyone could begin laying tracks, materials had to be shipped from New York, around South America, to San Francisco. From there all materials had to be put on smaller boats for the 120-mile trip to Sacramento, California.

Once the materials and machines were in place, workers had to be hired. The California Gold Rush and then the Civil War had taken many men away from their jobs. They were not available to build the railroad. If not for workers from China, the railroad would never have been built.

The Work Begins

In 1863 work on the railroad finally began. The Union Pacific started building west from the Mississippi. The Central Pacific moved east from Sacramento. Construction was slow. Crews had to drill through solid rock in places. They had to build bridges across rivers and ravines.

While some workers finished the track, other workers were building the rail cars. One news reporter wrote from the Union Pacific Railroad shop in Omaha, Nebraska:

The lumber used is . . . all brought from Chicago and cut into proper lengths and thicknesses. . . . When the car is finished, it is transferred to the painting department, receives its different coats and stripes, and is then run back to the drying room. In this department there are three hundred and fifty hands employed . . . and the average wages of the men is about $3.50 each per day. . . .

All the problems were finally solved. Six years later the two crews met in Promontory, Utah. A railroad linking the East and West coasts of North America became a reality.

Building the Transcontinental Railroad truly was a heroic effort. William Tecumseh Sherman, a famous Civil War general, wrote in a letter to his brother: "If it is ever built, it will be the work of giants."

CA Critical Thinking

Now answer numbers 1 through 4. Base your answers on the story "A Twist in the Trail."

1. **What is the main problem in the plot of the story?**

A   Halle and Joel will not stop arguing.

B   Halle and Joel do not see the eagle or the bear.

C   Mr. Braden gives the compass to Halle instead of Joel.

D   Mr. Braden falls in the river and loses his glasses.

2. **What can you infer from the fact that Halle and Joel "raced to their father's assistance"?**

A   They are very competitive.

B   They care a lot about their father.

C   They like to run fast.

D   They argue all the time.

3. **Read this sentence from the story.**

> "I can't see without my glasses," Mr. Braden said. "Everything's <u>blurry</u>."

Which word is an antonym for *blurry* as used in the sentence above?

A   clear

B   fuzzy

C   hazy

D   damp

4. **How does the wilderness setting of "A Twist in the Trail" directly affect the events of the plot? Use details and information from the story to support your answer.**

Now answer numbers 1 through 4. Base your answers on the article "The Work of Giants."

1. **This article is mainly about**

   A   the Union Pacific Railroad.
   B   the Central Pacific Railroad.
   C   workers who came from China.
   D   the building of the Transcontinental Railroad.

2. **The map helps the reader to**

   A   find out when the building of the railroad began.
   B   quickly see where the railroad was built.
   C   learn about William Tecumseh Sherman.
   D   find out more about the Union Pacific Railroad.

3. **When did construction of the railroad finally begin?**

   A   1869
   B   1836
   C   1865
   D   1863

4. **General Sherman called the railroad builders "giants" because**

   A   they were unusually strong people.
   B   he admired the work of the builders.
   C   railroads were a large business in the 1800s.
   D   he realized how fast they had to work.

Write on Demand

PROMPT Why was it so difficult to build the Transcontinental Railroad? What were some of the obstacles that had to be overcome? Use details from the article to support your answer. Write for 8 minutes. Write as much as you can for as long as you can.

The Big Question

How can you use your intelligence to outwit others?

Theme Launcher Video

LOG ON

Find out more about using your wits at www.macmillanmh.com.

Your intelligence can be your greatest weapon. People often think that only great strength can combat danger, but more often, our greatest tools for keeping ourselves safe are our wits and our ability to think creatively.

Think about detectives, escape artists, and even scientific researchers! They all keep themselves or others safe because they are smart.

Even in the animal kingdom, certain animals —like the fox—are known for their trickery and cunning—or their ability to outwit stronger and bigger animals.

Learning about using your wits can help you solve problems maturely and creatively.

Research Activities

In this unit, you will learn about using your wits to solve problems. Research a person or group of people who used their intelligence to solve a problem in a creative way.

Keep Track of Ideas

As you read, think about what you are learning about using intelligence to solve problems. Use the **Study Book** to help you organize your ideas. Each week, keep track of what you have learned about using your wits from the characters in your stories.

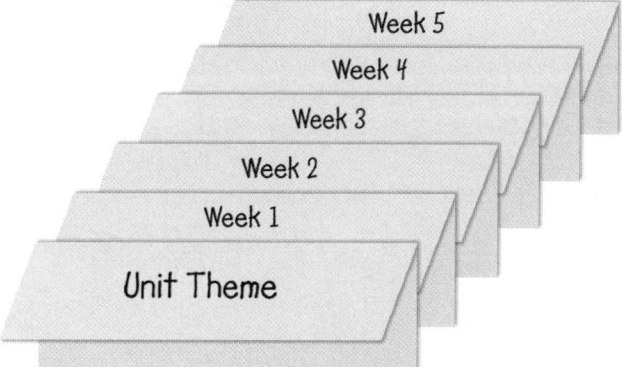

Week 5
Week 4
Week 3
Week 2
Week 1
Unit Theme

Research Toolkit

Conduct Your Unit 3 Research Online with:

Research Roadmap
Follow step-by-step guide to complete your research project.

Online Resources
- Topic Finder and other Research Tools
- Videos and Virtual Fieldtrips
- Photos and Drawings for Presentations
- Related Articles and Web Resources

California Web Site Links

Go to **www.macmillanmh.com** for more information.

California People

Frederick G. Cottrell
Inventor

A member of the National Inventors Hall of Fame, Cottrell invented a device that removed pollution, gases, and particles from smokestacks.

265

TRICKSTERS

CA **Talk About It**

Why do you think the wolf in this picture is wearing a sheep disguise?

LOG ON ▶ Find out more about trickster tales at **www.macmillanmh.com**.

267

ANANSI AND COMMON SENSE

A Stage Play Adapted from a Jamaican Folktale

by Trey Reeves

Characters

ANANSI   **NARRATOR**   **LITTLE GIRL**

Stage is bare except for a tall tree on one side and the edge of a river on the other.

ANANSI (*is sitting by the riverbank thinking.*)

NARRATOR: Anansi the spiderman was greedy for power and wealth. One day he decided he could get these things by gathering all the common sense in the world.

ANANSI: (*snapping his fingers*) That's it! If I have all the common sense, people will come to me with their problems. The **wares** I sell will be bits of advice! I will make so much money that I will need to hire a **treasurer** to be in charge of my finances.

NARRATOR: So Anansi set out to gather every bit of common sense in the world. As he found it, he stuffed it in a large hollow fruit called a calabash. When he thought he had found every bit of common sense, Anansi closed the calabash with dry leaves.

ANANSI: I will hide this stack of precious **merchandise** at the top of the island's tallest tree!

(**LITTLE GIRL** *enters and sits by the riverbank.*)

NARRATOR: Anansi tied a rope to the neck of the calabash. Then he tied the two ends of the rope around his neck. The calabash hung against his stomach.

(**ANANSI** *tries to climb the tree, falls down, tries again.* **LITTLE GIRL** *watches him and laughs.*)

ANANSI: (*whirling around toward the riverbank*) Who's there?

LITTLE GIRL: You need a teacher to **instruct** and **educate** you. Don't you know that heavy **burdens** are best carried on your back?

NARRATOR: Anansi didn't value her helpful tip and showed no **appreciation**.

ANANSI: Useless calabash! (*ripping the calabash from his neck*) The day I filled you was a sad and **unfortunate** day indeed! (*flinging the calabash against the tree, so that it breaks open*)

NARRATOR: When the calabash broke, little pieces of common sense were scattered everywhere. That is why today everyone has at least a little bit of common sense.

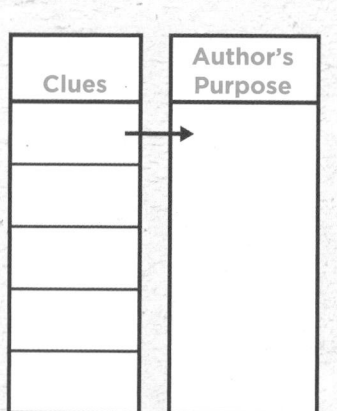

Reread for **Comprehension**

Evaluate
Author's Purpose

An author has a purpose for writing. It may be to entertain, persuade, inform, or explain. An Author's Purpose Chart helps you organize clues in the text so you can figure out the author's purpose. Reread "Anansi and Common Sense" and use your Author's Purpose Chart to find the author's purpose.

Clues	Author's Purpose

Genre

A **Play** is a story told through dialogue that is intended to be performed.

Evaluate

✓ **Author's Purpose**

As you read, fill in your Author's Purpose Chart.

Clues	Author's Purpose

Read to Find Out

What purpose did the author have for writing this play?

THE CATCH OF THE DAY

A TRICKSTER PLAY

Award Winning Author

written by Angela Shelf Medearis
illustrated by Wendy Born Hollander

CHARACTERS

THE GRIOT (STORYTELLER)

GROUP OF CHILDREN

CHILD ONE

CHILD TWO

THE FISHER

THE BASKETMAKER

THE BAKER

THE WOMAN WITH THE FRUIT

THE FARMER WITH SOME YAMS AND CORN

THE MAN WITH THE BAGS OF RICE

The **GRIOT** stands in the center of a **GROUP OF CHILDREN** who are seated on the ground. A **GRIOT** is an African storyteller and keeper of the history of the family and the village. It is early evening and time for the nightly story. It is a common practice in Africa to tell stories in the evening to pass on oral history, carry on traditions, **instruct** and **educate** the village children, and to entertain. The **GRIOT** and the **CHILDREN** are off to one side of the stage. All the action for the play takes place center stage.

GRIOT: *(loudly)* Jambo, children! Hello!

CHILDREN: Jambo!

GRIOT: I am a Griot, the keeper of the history of my West African tribe, a storyteller, and a teacher. I have a special story to share with you about a tricky fisher and a bridge made out of a log. When I am ready to begin, I'll clap my hands once. When you are ready to listen, you'll clap your hands twice. *(The GRIOT claps once.)*

CHILDREN: *(Clap their hands twice.)*

273

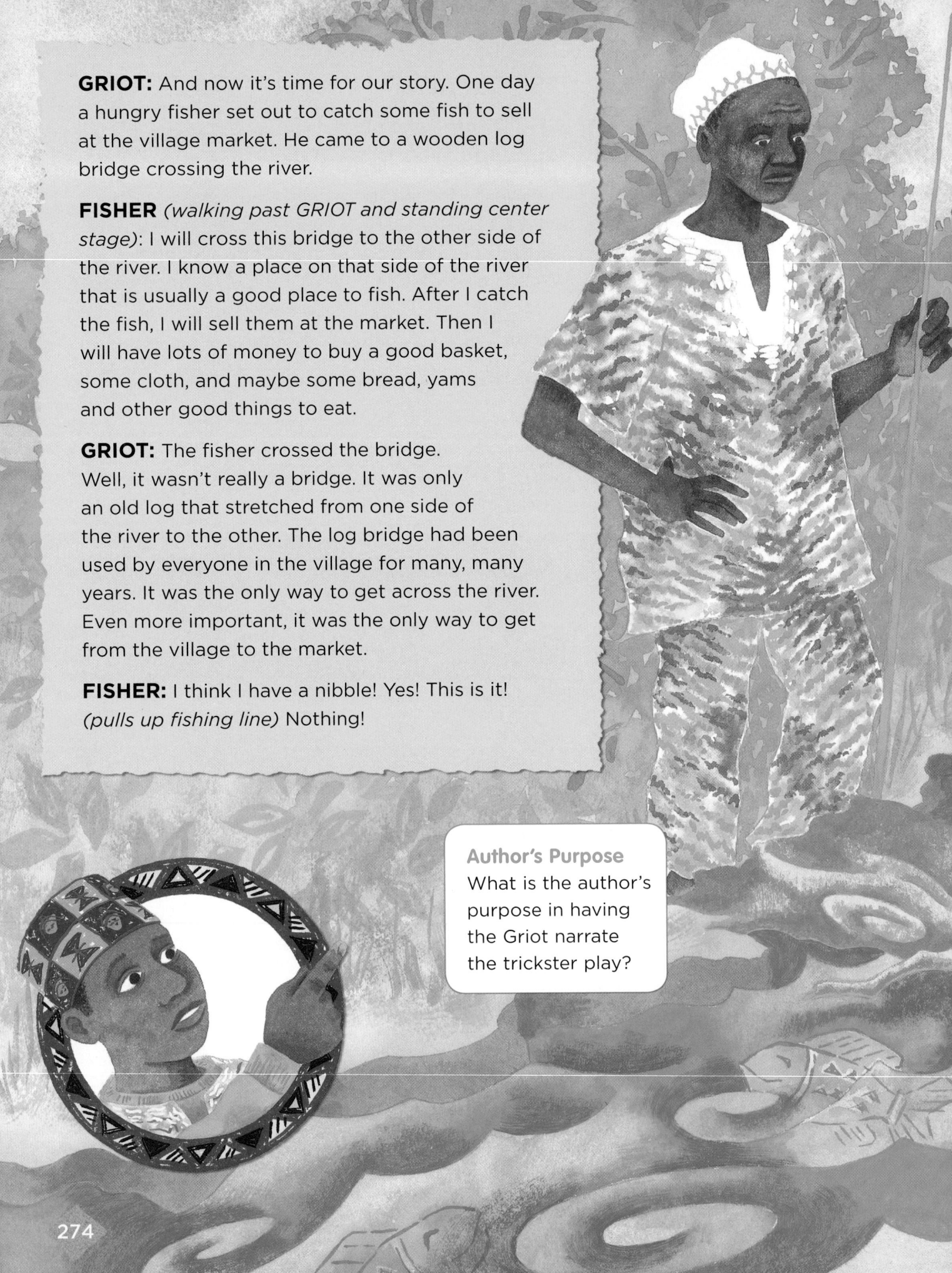

GRIOT: And now it's time for our story. One day a hungry fisher set out to catch some fish to sell at the village market. He came to a wooden log bridge crossing the river.

FISHER (*walking past GRIOT and standing center stage*): I will cross this bridge to the other side of the river. I know a place on that side of the river that is usually a good place to fish. After I catch the fish, I will sell them at the market. Then I will have lots of money to buy a good basket, some cloth, and maybe some bread, yams and other good things to eat.

GRIOT: The fisher crossed the bridge. Well, it wasn't really a bridge. It was only an old log that stretched from one side of the river to the other. The log bridge had been used by everyone in the village for many, many years. It was the only way to get across the river. Even more important, it was the only way to get from the village to the market.

FISHER: I think I have a nibble! Yes! This is it! (*pulls up fishing line*) Nothing!

Author's Purpose
What is the author's purpose in having the Griot narrate the trickster play?

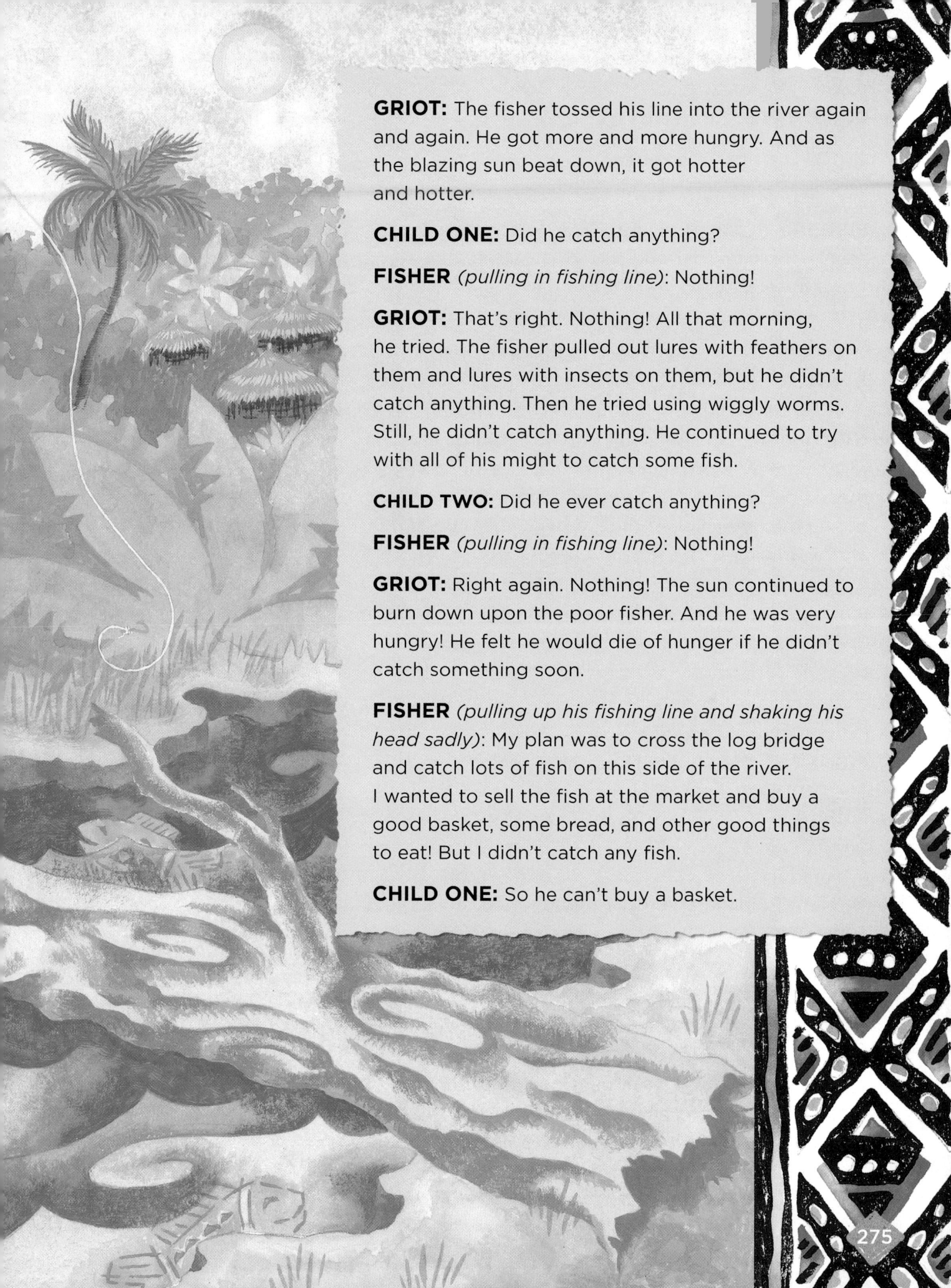

GRIOT: The fisher tossed his line into the river again and again. He got more and more hungry. And as the blazing sun beat down, it got hotter and hotter.

CHILD ONE: Did he catch anything?

FISHER (*pulling in fishing line*): Nothing!

GRIOT: That's right. Nothing! All that morning, he tried. The fisher pulled out lures with feathers on them and lures with insects on them, but he didn't catch anything. Then he tried using wiggly worms. Still, he didn't catch anything. He continued to try with all of his might to catch some fish.

CHILD TWO: Did he ever catch anything?

FISHER (*pulling in fishing line*): Nothing!

GRIOT: Right again. Nothing! The sun continued to burn down upon the poor fisher. And he was very hungry! He felt he would die of hunger if he didn't catch something soon.

FISHER (*pulling up his fishing line and shaking his head sadly*): My plan was to cross the log bridge and catch lots of fish on this side of the river. I wanted to sell the fish at the market and buy a good basket, some bread, and other good things to eat! But I didn't catch any fish.

CHILD ONE: So he can't buy a basket.

CHILD TWO: Or bread.

GRIOT: Or other good things to eat. And he was very, very hungry.

FISHER: I'm hungry, hungry, hungry! I can't believe this turn of events! My great-grandfather was a fisher, and my grandfather and my father before me! My family has fished in this very river for generations. It is how we always have earned a living. If I can't catch any fish, I must think of another way to get the things I need.

GRIOT: The poor fisher was about to return to his home. He had one foot on his side of the log bridge when he saw someone starting out on the other side of the log bridge. It was a basketmaker with a load of baskets.

FISHER (*waving and stepping back onto the riverbank*): Jambo!

BASKETMAKER (*calling to the fisher on the other side of the river*): Jambo! How are you today, Fisher? Did you catch anything?

FISHER (*sadly*): No, I didn't catch a single fish today.

BASKETMAKER: That's too bad. I'm sorry, but I don't have time to talk. I must hurry to the market so that I can sell my baskets.

GRIOT: Suddenly, the fisher thought of a way he could get a basket.

FISHER (*holding up his hands in warning*): Stop! Don't try to cross the bridge.

BASKETMAKER: What is wrong with it?

FISHER: I think the recent rainstorms must have loosened it. If I don't hold this log in place it will fall into the river and no one will be able to get to the market.

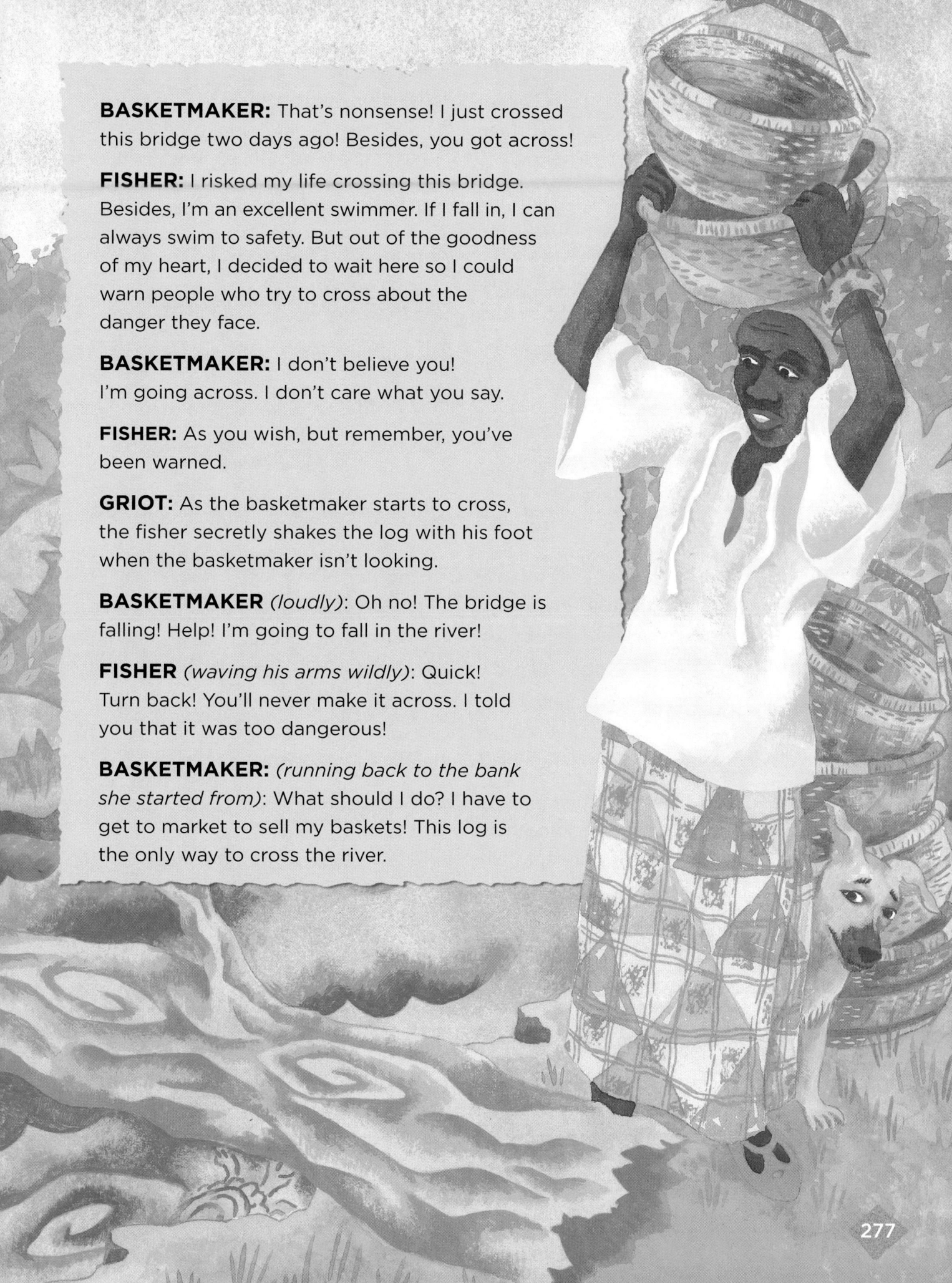

BASKETMAKER: That's nonsense! I just crossed this bridge two days ago! Besides, you got across!

FISHER: I risked my life crossing this bridge. Besides, I'm an excellent swimmer. If I fall in, I can always swim to safety. But out of the goodness of my heart, I decided to wait here so I could warn people who try to cross about the danger they face.

BASKETMAKER: I don't believe you! I'm going across. I don't care what you say.

FISHER: As you wish, but remember, you've been warned.

GRIOT: As the basketmaker starts to cross, the fisher secretly shakes the log with his foot when the basketmaker isn't looking.

BASKETMAKER *(loudly)*: Oh no! The bridge is falling! Help! I'm going to fall in the river!

FISHER *(waving his arms wildly)*: Quick! Turn back! You'll never make it across. I told you that it was too dangerous!

BASKETMAKER: *(running back to the bank she started from)*: What should I do? I have to get to market to sell my baskets! This log is the only way to cross the river.

277

FISHER: I know what you should do! I'll hold on tightly to this end of the log while you cross. But, dear lady, I think that you are carrying too many baskets. You must leave some behind or you will fall into the waters below.

BASKETMAKER: You are right. If I carry all these heavy baskets across the bridge, I might fall into the river. Thank you, my friend! I will leave two baskets on this side of the river for you. Please pick them up when you return here on your way home.

FISHER: Oh, I couldn't do that.

BASKETMAKER: Please, it is a token of my **appreciation**.

FISHER: No, no, no!

BASKETMAKER: Yes, yes, yes!

FISHER: Well, if you want me to have them, how can I refuse? I will hold the log with all of my strength while you cross over. Careful now! Steady! Slowly, slowly, slowly . . . safe!

GRIOT: The basketmaker thanked the fisher and hurried off to market, never realizing that she had been tricked. Two of her nicest baskets were now left behind on the bank for the fisher.

FISHER: Now I have two beautiful baskets. But I'm still hungry, hungry, hungry! I must get something to eat! Wait, I think I hear somebody coming.

GRIOT: It was a weaver with a load of beautiful, multicolored, Kente cloth. The weaver made the Kente cloth especially for the king and it was very valuable.

WEAVER (loudly): Jambo!

FISHER (loudly): Jambo!

GRIOT: It occurred to the fisher that he could get some of the weaver's beautiful Kente cloth in the same way he had gotten baskets.

FISHER *(holding up both hands and calling to the weaver on the other side of the river)*: Stop! Don't try to cross the bridge.

WEAVER: What is wrong with the bridge?

FISHER: I'm holding the log so that it won't fall into the river.

WEAVER: But I've always used this bridge to go to market. I have some Kente cloth I'm going to sell to the king's **treasurer**. I must hurry if I'm going to get to the market in time. You got across safely and so will I.

FISHER: I'm warning you! I barely made it across, and the basketmaker just risked her life crossing the bridge to get to the market.

WEAVER: Oh no! What happened to the basketmaker? Why, there are some baskets on the ground here! Did the basketmaker drop them when she fell into the river?

FISHER *(slowly and sadly with one hand over his heart)*: Well, all I can say is that the basketmaker is no longer here with us.

WEAVER *(sadly)*: How **unfortunate**! The poor, poor woman! But I must get to the market no matter what. I know what I'll do. I will run across the log bridge very quickly! That's how I'll get across safely!

GRIOT: The weaver adjusted the bundle of cloth on his head and tried to run across the bridge. As soon as he reached the middle of the log, the fisher secretly shook it with his foot.

WEAVER *(loudly, swaying back and forth in the middle of the log)*: Help! Help! I'm falling!

FISHER *(gesturing wildly)*: Go back before you fall in! You'll never make it all the way across! It's much too dangerous!

GRIOT: The fisher stopped shaking the log. The weaver ran back to the side of the riverbank where he started his journey, grateful to be alive.

WEAVER: Did you see that? I almost fell in! What am I going to do now? I must get across the bridge so I can get to the market!

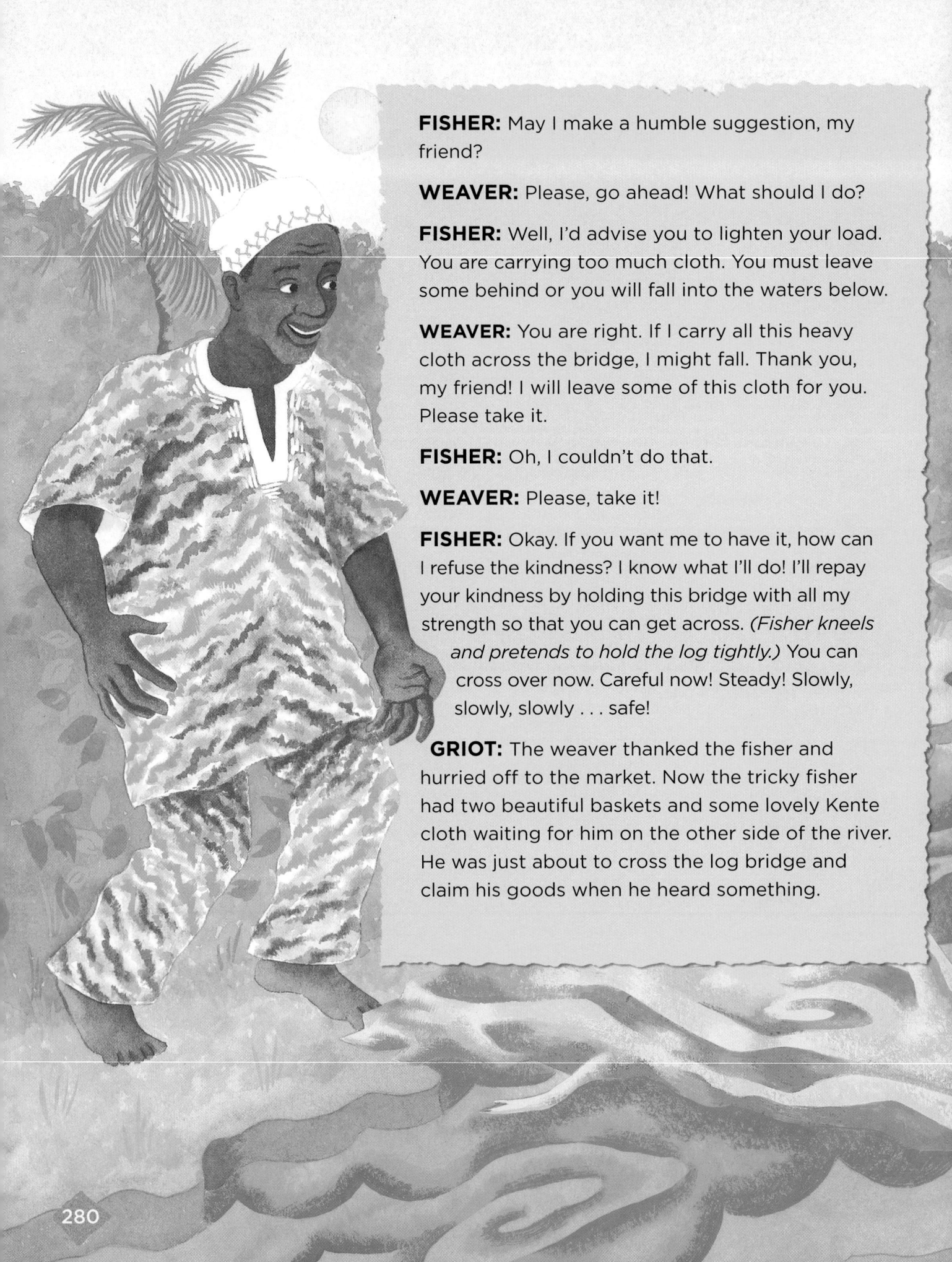

FISHER: May I make a humble suggestion, my friend?

WEAVER: Please, go ahead! What should I do?

FISHER: Well, I'd advise you to lighten your load. You are carrying too much cloth. You must leave some behind or you will fall into the waters below.

WEAVER: You are right. If I carry all this heavy cloth across the bridge, I might fall. Thank you, my friend! I will leave some of this cloth for you. Please take it.

FISHER: Oh, I couldn't do that.

WEAVER: Please, take it!

FISHER: Okay. If you want me to have it, how can I refuse the kindness? I know what I'll do! I'll repay your kindness by holding this bridge with all my strength so that you can get across. *(Fisher kneels and pretends to hold the log tightly.)* You can cross over now. Careful now! Steady! Slowly, slowly, slowly . . . safe!

GRIOT: The weaver thanked the fisher and hurried off to the market. Now the tricky fisher had two beautiful baskets and some lovely Kente cloth waiting for him on the other side of the river. He was just about to cross the log bridge and claim his goods when he heard something.

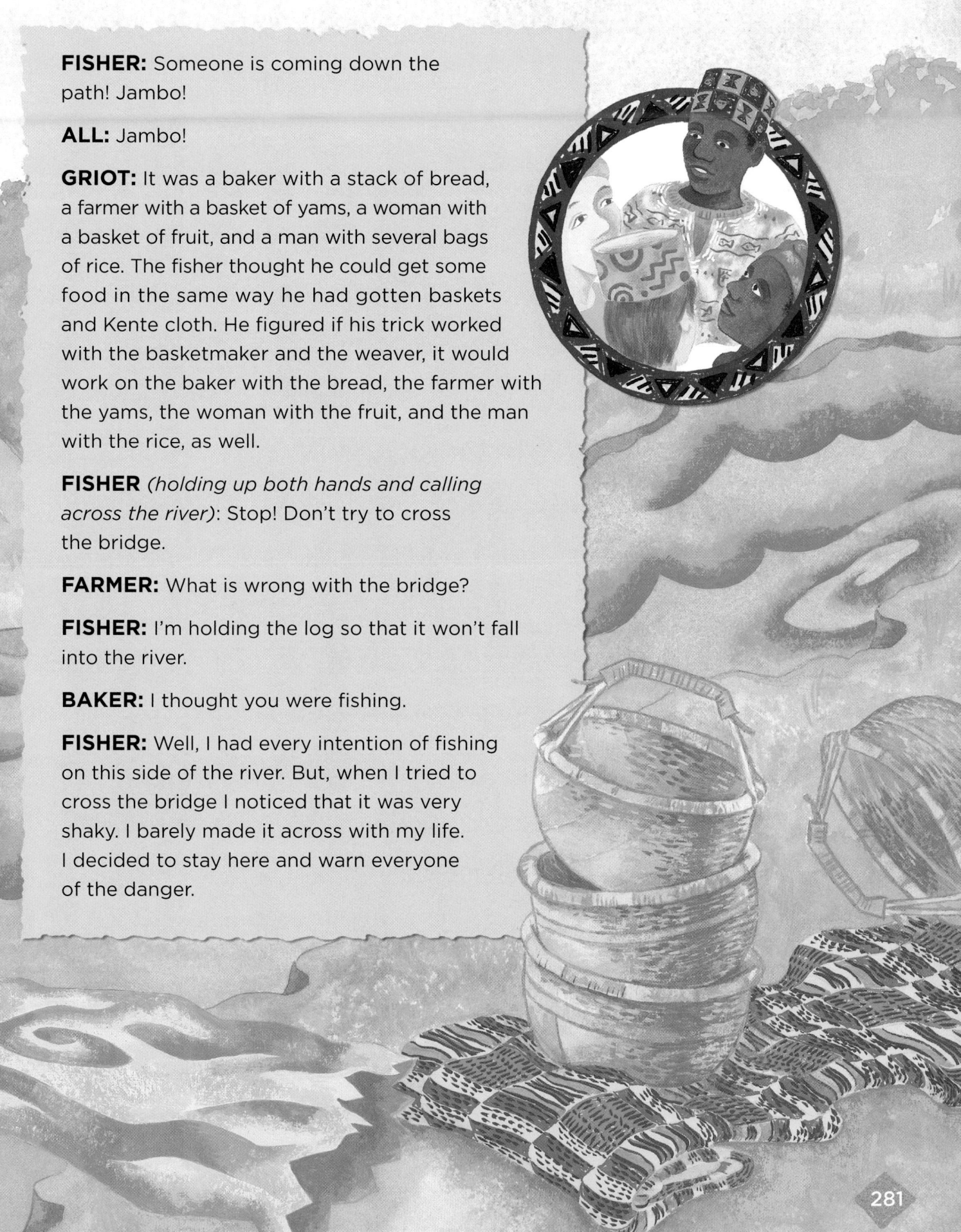

FISHER: Someone is coming down the path! Jambo!

ALL: Jambo!

GRIOT: It was a baker with a stack of bread, a farmer with a basket of yams, a woman with a basket of fruit, and a man with several bags of rice. The fisher thought he could get some food in the same way he had gotten baskets and Kente cloth. He figured if his trick worked with the basketmaker and the weaver, it would work on the baker with the bread, the farmer with the yams, the woman with the fruit, and the man with the rice, as well.

FISHER (*holding up both hands and calling across the river*): Stop! Don't try to cross the bridge.

FARMER: What is wrong with the bridge?

FISHER: I'm holding the log so that it won't fall into the river.

BAKER: I thought you were fishing.

FISHER: Well, I had every intention of fishing on this side of the river. But, when I tried to cross the bridge I noticed that it was very shaky. I barely made it across with my life. I decided to stay here and warn everyone of the danger.

281

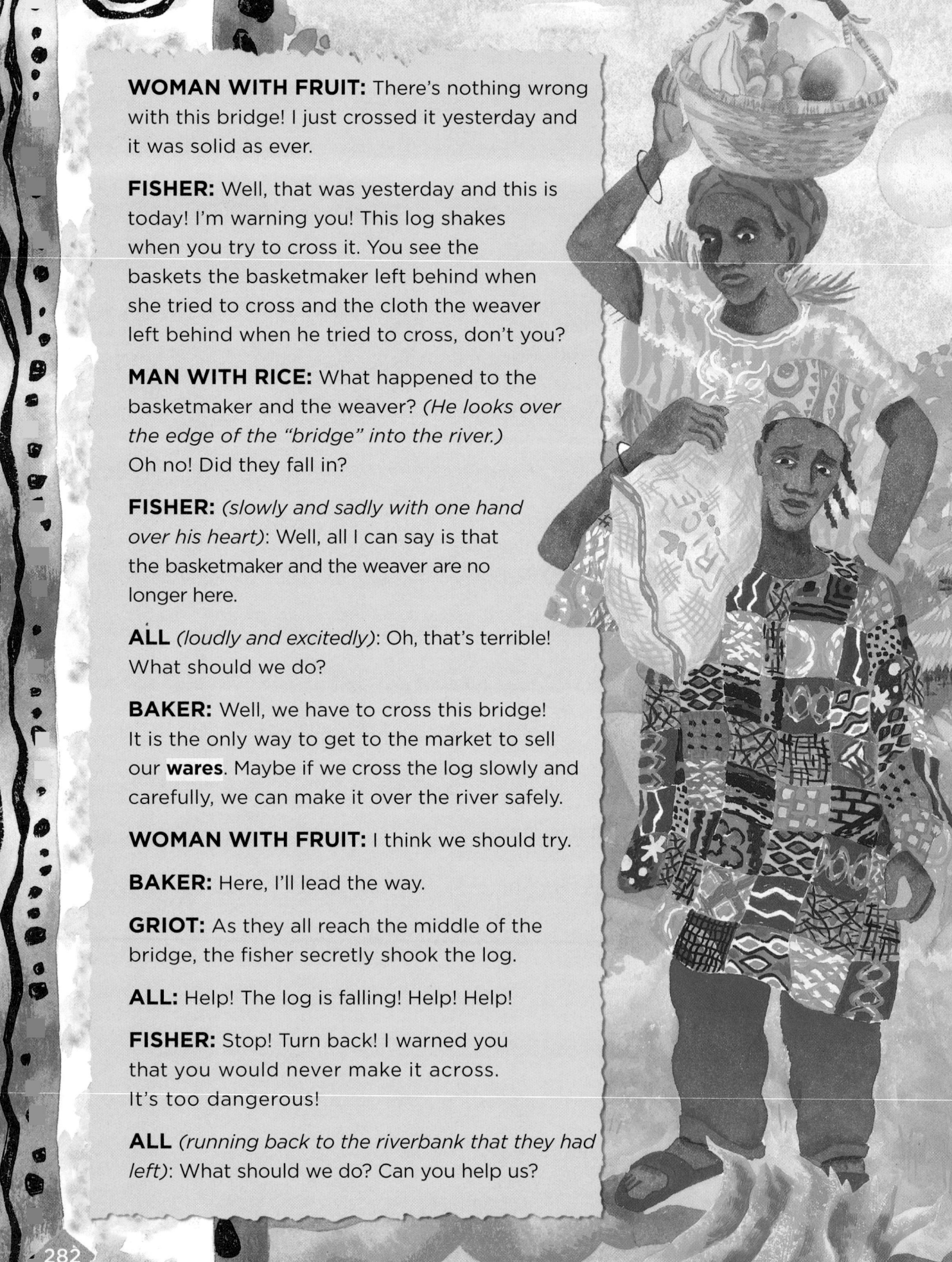

WOMAN WITH FRUIT: There's nothing wrong with this bridge! I just crossed it yesterday and it was solid as ever.

FISHER: Well, that was yesterday and this is today! I'm warning you! This log shakes when you try to cross it. You see the baskets the basketmaker left behind when she tried to cross and the cloth the weaver left behind when he tried to cross, don't you?

MAN WITH RICE: What happened to the basketmaker and the weaver? *(He looks over the edge of the "bridge" into the river.)* Oh no! Did they fall in?

FISHER: *(slowly and sadly with one hand over his heart)*: Well, all I can say is that the basketmaker and the weaver are no longer here.

ALL *(loudly and excitedly)*: Oh, that's terrible! What should we do?

BAKER: Well, we have to cross this bridge! It is the only way to get to the market to sell our **wares**. Maybe if we cross the log slowly and carefully, we can make it over the river safely.

WOMAN WITH FRUIT: I think we should try.

BAKER: Here, I'll lead the way.

GRIOT: As they all reach the middle of the bridge, the fisher secretly shook the log.

ALL: Help! The log is falling! Help! Help!

FISHER: Stop! Turn back! I warned you that you would never make it across. It's too dangerous!

ALL *(running back to the riverbank that they had left)*: What should we do? Can you help us?

FISHER: You are carrying too much food. You must leave some of it behind or you will fall into the waters below. Now, put some of your **merchandise** down and cross the log in single file, one at a time. I will hold this log with all my strength while you go across one by one.

BAKER: Perhaps he is right, my friends. If we carry these heavy **burdens** across the bridge, we might fall into the river. Let's leave some of our food behind so that we can safely reach the other side.

FISHER: Good thinking! Now, come across! I will hold the bridge for all of you. Careful now! Steady! Slowly, slowly, slowly . . . safe!

GRIOT: The baker with the loaves of bread, the farmer with the basket of yams, the woman with the fruit, and the man with the bags of rice all slowly crossed the bridge while the fisher held the log. Once they safely reached the other side, they all thanked the fisher, then hurried off to the market.

The fisher waited until they were down the road and out of sight. Then he danced and skipped across the log bridge. He picked up the bread, the yams, the fruit, the bags of rice and the cloth and put everything into the baskets that the basketmaker had left behind for him.

FISHER: Now I have a beautiful basket, some bread, some lovely Kente cloth, some yams, fruit, and a few bags of rice. I'm going to have a good dinner and I won't be hungry, hungry, hungry anymore.

GRIOT: The fisher danced all the way home, thinking about the sumptuous meal he would enjoy that evening.

CHILD ONE: What a tricky fisher! He made everyone think that the bridge was too dangerous to cross!

CHILD TWO: That's how he tricked them into leaving all the food, the baskets and the cloth.

GRIOT: You're right! But remember, even a trickster gets tricked. When the basketmaker, the weaver, the baker, the farmer, the woman with the fruit, and the man with the rice returned from the market and discovered that there was nothing wrong with the bridge, they decided to teach the fisher a lesson.

CHILD ONE: What did they do?

CHILD TWO: Yes, please tell us!

GRIOT: The very next day the basketmaker, the weaver, and all the other people the fisher had tricked met in the village.

BASKETMAKER (*smiling*): I know how we can play the same trick on the fisher that he played on us.

WOMAN WITH FRUIT: How?

WEAVER: Yes, tell us!

BASKETMAKER: In the next village my brother knows someone who makes his living as a fisher. I will travel there with my horse and cart today, and buy some fish from him. Tomorrow meet me by the river early in the morning. Bring a bucket with you.

MAN WITH RICE: A bucket? Why?

BASKETMAKER: You will see.

GRIOT: And so the basketmaker traveled to the next village and came home later that day with more fish than any one person could eat. The next morning she met the woman with the fruit, the weaver, the baker, the farmer, and the man with the rice on the side of the river closest to the village.

BASKETMAKER:
The fisher crosses to this side of the river every morning to try his luck. Here, each of you put two fish in your bucket, and fill it with water from the river. I have made a fishing pole from this branch. Ah, and just in time. Here comes the fisher now. *(loudly)* Jambo!

ALL: Jambo! Jambo!

FISHER: Jambo, my friends! What are you all doing?

BASKETMAKER: Why, fishing, of course. It's a great day for it! We have each caught more fish than we can eat!

FISHER: Fishing?! But that's my job!

BASKETMAKER: Come now! The fish in the river are for everyone to catch!

WOMAN WITH FRUIT: Yes, and can I help it if these fish are so eager to be caught, they jumped from the river right into my bucket? *(She shows the fisher the fish in her bucket.)*

WEAVER: Mine, too! *(He shows the fisher his bucket.)*

FISHER: I'm coming over there to join you! I didn't catch any fish yesterday.

BASKETMAKER: Wait, Fisher! You remember the bridge is loose. I had better help you to get across, but you shouldn't risk it unless you are a very good swimmer. It may be even more unsteady than it was yesterday.

FISHER: Oh . . . yes. That's very kind of you. I *am* an excellent swimmer and a person with a good sense of balance.

GRIOT: The fisher walked to the edge of the river toward the log bridge. He knew he had to pretend that the log bridge was loose. The basketmaker kneeled down to hold the bridge. As the fisher walked across, the basketmaker began to shake the log with her hand.

FISHER (*excitedly*): What are you doing? I'll fall into the river!

BASKETMAKER (*pretending to be concerned*): Oh, my! The bridge is so loose! I don't think I can control it! Careful now! Steady! Slowly, slowly, slowly . . . Oops!

GRIOT: The basketmaker shook the log so hard that the fisher fell into the river.

BASKETMAKER: Oh, my! I guess the log is even looser than it was yesterday. Sorry, Fisher!

GRIOT: As the fisher floated in the river, a fish swam right by his nose! He was annoyed at the trick played on him but he knew he couldn't say anything. Clearly the others had discovered that the log bridge hadn't been loose and that the fisher had tricked them the day before. Back on the riverbank, the woman with the fruit, the weaver, the farmer, the basketmaker, and the man with the rice just laughed and laughed. And later that day they ate a fine fish dinner!

CHILD ONE: Ha ha! I guess the fisher learned his lesson!

GRIOT: Yes! We will all hope he never tries to trick anyone again! (*He claps his hands once.*) That tricky story was fun! Now my time is done!

Author's Purpose
What is the author's purpose in writing this play? Do any clues indicate a possible second purpose?

287

TELLING STORIES WITH ANGELA SHELF MEDEARIS

ANGELA SHELF MEDEARIS'S father was in the Air Force, so she moved a lot when she was growing up. One of the first things Angela did after moving to a new place was check out the library. She loved reading books, and she loved talking to the librarians. Angela writes because she likes to learn about life and make people laugh. "I enjoy that wonderful feeling you get when you have a great idea and can't wait to get started at it," she says. Angela also writes cookbooks and books about her African-American heritage.

Other books by Angela Shelf Medearis: *The Singing Man* and *Dare to Dream: Coretta Scott King and the Civil Rights Movement*

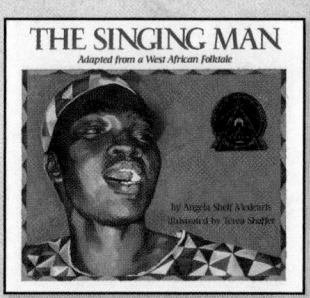

LOG ON ▶ Find out more about Angela Shelf Medearis at **www.macmillanmh.com**.

CA **Author's Purpose**
What features in the text tell you this is a play and that the author intends for it to be performed? Might she have another purpose?

CA Critical Thinking

Summarize

Summarize *The Catch of the Day.* Be sure to present the events in the order in which they happened.

Think and Compare

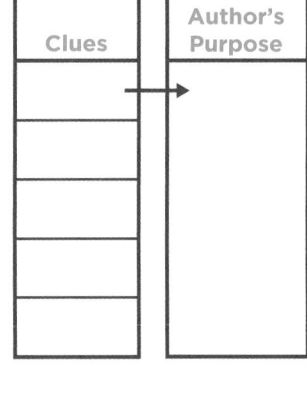

Clues	Author's Purpose

1. What was the **author's purpose** for writing this play? Use details from your Author's Purpose Chart to explain your answer. **Evaluate: Author's Purpose**

2. Reread the Weaver's lines on page 279 and the Fisher's lines that follow. Why didn't the Fisher give specific answers to the Weaver's questions? Use selection details to explain. **Critical**

3. Would you have participated in the trick to get back at the Fisher? Why or why not? **Analyze**

4. Can playing tricks on a trickster, like the Fisher, be an effective way to get them to stop fooling others who are **unfortunate**? Explain your response. **Evaluate**

5. Reread *Anansi and Common Sense* on pages 268–269. Is the author's purpose the same or different in that play as in *The Catch of the Day*? Use examples from the selections. **Reading/Writing Across Texts**

The FOX and the Crow

retold by Mei Kirimoto

A ravenous crow kept a watchful eye on a family eating a picnic lunch.

"I can't believe that they will eat the entire quantity of food," thought the hungry crow.

While waiting for the family to finish, the crow took a dip in the pond to pass the time. The crow loved to admire herself. She was attractive and spent a long time looking at her reflection in the water. In her enthusiasm over her own loveliness, she did not notice that the family had eaten and gone.

However, when her stomach grumbled, she remembered how hungry she was and quickly flew back to the picnic spot. There she found that the family had left behind a big piece of cheese. She clamped the cheese in her beak and flew to a branch in a birch tree to enjoy her snack.

Just then a fox appeared. The fox lifted his long nose and smelled the piece of cheese. "Where could the cheese be?" said the tricky fox to himself. "I must investigate. I'm very hungry today."

He soon spotted the crow with the cheese.

The fox knew the crow quite well. He looked up at her and graciously said, "Why, Miss Crow, don't you look lovely! The sun shines gloriously on your feathers. Your beauty is a ray of sunlight on a gloomy day."

The fox saw that the crow was puffing up with each line of praise, so he continued. "Your feathers are of the finest polished ebony. Ah, if only I could hear your sweet voice. Certainly it's as magnificent as your feathers."

The crow immediately wanted to prove that she did indeed have an impressive voice. She opened her beak and began to sing *Caw, Caw, Caw* with tremendous volume. As she sang, the cheese fell to the ground.

> **This metaphor compares beauty to a ray of sunlight.**

Faster than a blinking eye, the triumphant fox scooped up the cheese and ate it.

"Dear Miss Crow," said the fox as he licked his lips, "your voice may be lovely, but you should think before you act."

MORAL: *Do not trust someone who gives too much praise.*

> **The moral teaches a lesson.**

CA Critical Thinking

1. Give an example of the use of metaphor in the fable. Explain your choice. **Metaphor**

2. What does the fox know about the crow that allows him to trick her? **Analyze**

3. Think about "The Fox and the Crow" and *The Catch of the Day*. How are the fable and the play similar? How are they different? **Reading/Writing Across Texts**

 Find out more about fables at **www.macmillanmh.com**.

Writing

Dialogue and Narration

Good writers use **dialogue** and **narration** to help readers learn about a character's thoughts and feelings from what they say.

Reading and Writing Connection

Read the passage below. Notice how the author Angela Shelf Medearis uses dialogue and narration together in her story.

An excerpt from
The Catch of the Day

The author moves back and forth from dialogue between the weaver and the fisher and narration from the griot. Instead of writing a big section of dialogue and then a big section of narration, the author weaves them together.

Griot: The weaver adjusted the bundle of cloth on his head and tried to run across the bridge. As soon as he reached the middle of the log, the fisher secretly shook it with his foot.

Weaver: *(loudly, swaying back and forth in the middle of the log)*: Help! Help! I'm falling!

Fisher: *(gesturing wildly)*: Go back before you fall in! You'll never make it all the way across! It's much too dangerous!

Griot: The fisher stopped shaking the log. The weaver ran back to the side of the riverbank where he started his journey, grateful to be alive.

THE CATCH OF THE DAY

A TRICKSTER PLAY

written by Angela Shelf Medearis
Illustrated by Wendy Born Hollander

Read and Find

Read Carol's writing below. How did she use dialogue and narration to help you see and hear the moment? Use the checklist below to help you.

Big Trouble

by Carol S.

I saw the look on my mom's face.

"Why do you think I'm standing here?" She asked me. I knew I was in big trouble.

"Ummm . . . because the garbage is still here?" I was still trying to play innocent, but Mom was too smart for that.

"How many times did I tell you to take out this stinky bag of trash?" Her face was like a mask of stone.

See how I mixed dialogue and narration to tell my story.

Writer's Checklist

 Does the writer use dialogue and narration to show what the character said and did?

 Do you feel like you are experiencing what Carol saw and heard?

 Does the writer include about the same amount of **narration** as **dialogue**?

Thinking It Through

CA **Talk About It**

What are some ways people use their wits to get themselves out of tricky situations?

LOG ON ▶ Find out more about folktales at **www.macmillanmh.com**.

Vocabulary

dismiss   seek

intentions   accompany

despair   delicacies

descended   consented

Homophones

Homophones are words that sound the same but have different spellings and meanings. For example, the homophones *bridle* and *bridal* sound alike but have very different meanings.

A Real Princess

by Tonya Schaeffer

Once upon a time there was a prince named Vincent. He was about to turn 30 years old. This was an important age. If he didn't marry a princess by his birthday, the king's advisors would **dismiss** him from the court. They would send the prince away, and he would never be able to become king.

Prince Vincent's **intentions** did not include losing the crown. However, over the years, he had broken the heart of every princess from kingdoms near and far. Now he felt **despair** at finding a real princess to wed. Prince Vincent had lost all hope.

"What will I do?" he asked his mother. "It's not my fault that there are no princesses left."

The queen rolled her eyes. "It's your fault you've treated so many princesses so badly," she snapped back.

Just then a young lady approached the castle. Her bridle had broken. The harness would not go over her horse's nose.

The girl entered the great hall after she **descended** from the great staircase. She introduced herself as Princess Araya from Zelnorm. When Prince Vincent saw her torn and muddy clothes, he sighed. "This cannot be the princess I **seek**," he said to his mother. "In fact, I doubt she's a princess at all," he said.

The queen thought for a moment. "I know how to find out," she said. "However, if it turns out she *is* a princess, you must promise to marry her."

"Done!" Prince Vincent said. He was sure his mother was wrong.

Now the queen had a plan. First, she asked a servant to **accompany** Araya to the dining room. There the princess was fed rare **delicacies** from faraway lands prepared by the royal chef. Then the queen gave orders to get the best room ready.

"I want seven feather-filled mattresses on the bed," she demanded. "Place a small pebble at the bottom of the pile. Only a true princess will be able to feel it."

The next morning the queen asked Araya how she had slept.

"I didn't sleep at all!" Araya said. "I saw a homeless mother and child standing by the castle gate, so I took them two mattresses. When I saw other needy townfolk nearby, I gave away the other mattresses. My father, King Paul, will repay you."

The queen was speechless. Prince Vincent, however, was not. He finally saw the real beauty of Princess Araya and asked her to be his wife. She **consented** to his request, and the two of them became the kindest rulers in all the land.

Reread for **Comprehension**

Summarize

Sequence

Sequence refers to the time order in which events or actions occur. A Sequence Chart helps you summarize information by first listing events or actions in the order they take place. Use your Sequence Chart as you reread the selection to help you summarize events chronologically.

Event

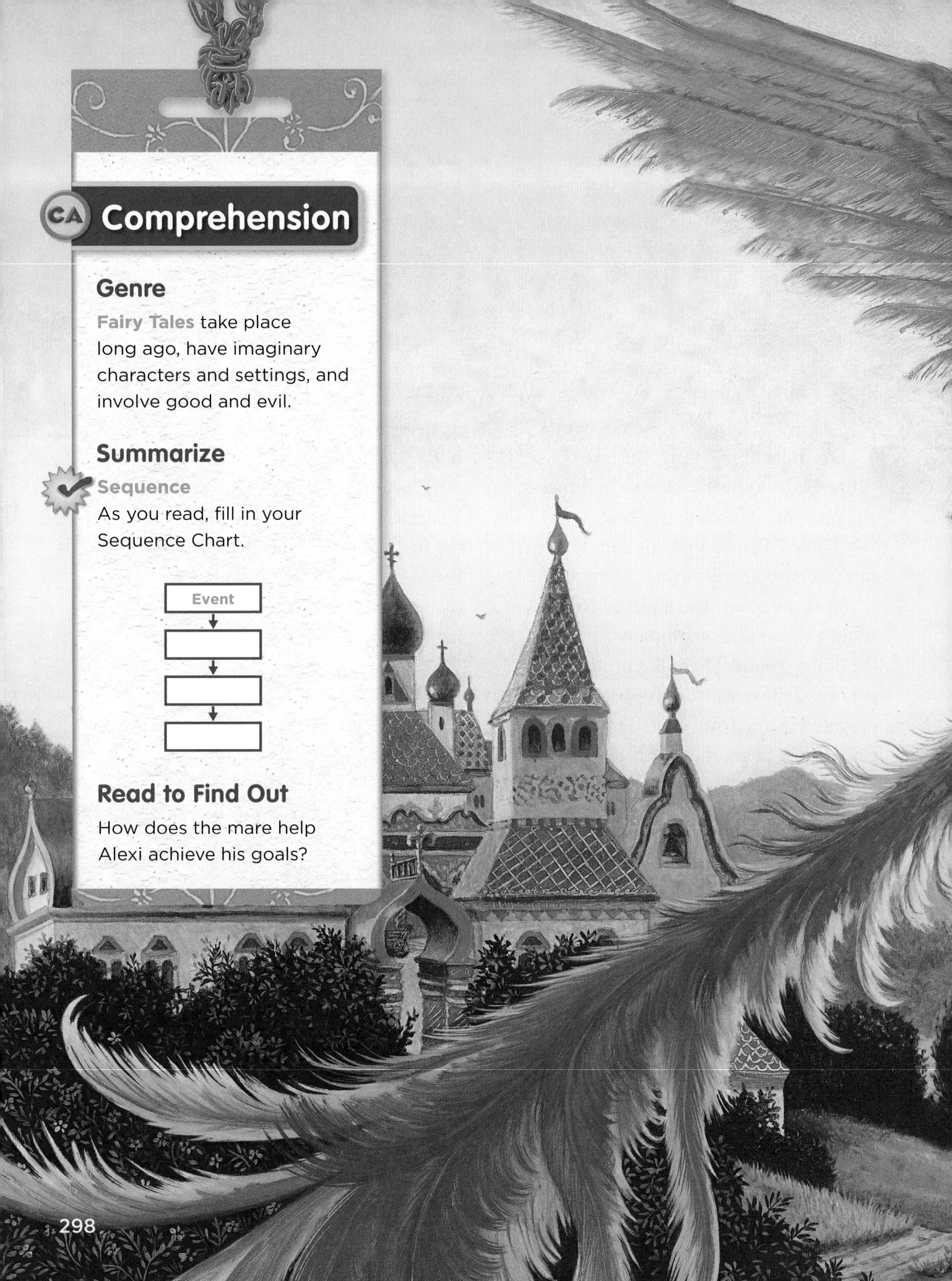

Comprehension

Genre
Fairy Tales take place long ago, have imaginary characters and settings, and involve good and evil.

Summarize
Sequence
As you read, fill in your Sequence Chart.

Event
↓
↓
↓

Read to Find Out
How does the mare help Alexi achieve his goals?

The Golden Mare, the Firebird, and the Magic Ring

by Ruth Sanderson

Award Winning Selection

Once upon a time, in a place where magical beasts still roamed the earth, a young man named Alexi left home to **seek** his fortune and perhaps to find an adventure or two as well.

Alexi was an excellent huntsman, but after traveling for a week he had found neither work nor adventure. One evening, as night **descended** and the moon arose, he made camp at the edge of a glade.

A noise of hoofbeats in the forest startled Alexi. Thinking it a herd of deer or some other game, the lad readied his bow. Yet the young hunter did not loose his arrow, for the beast that appeared in the clearing was too

wondrous to shoot. It was a golden mare with a silvery-white mane that streamed around her and sparkled in the moonlight.

The Golden Mare stood and gazed at the huntsman, who pointed an arrow at her heart.

"Hold, fair sir, do not shoot," said the mare, to the astonishment of the lad. Alexi lowered his bow and slowly approached the remarkable mare.

"I am at your service for sparing my life," she said. "What is your desire?"

Alexi told the mare he sought work and adventure.

"The Tsar of this region could use another huntsman," said the horse. "Tomorrow I will take you to his palace. If he hires you, I promise to serve you well."

The next morning Alexi fashioned a rough bridle with a bit of rope, mounted the Golden Mare, and set off for the palace of the Tsar.

The Tsar hired the young man at once, so impressed was he by Alexi's mount. He offered Alexi a princely sum for the mare.

"Thank you, sire," said Alexi, "but I'm afraid she'll allow no rider but me." Annoyed that his offer was declined, the Tsar ordered a saddle and a real bridle put on the horse, but not one of his men could stay on the Golden Mare's back.

The Tsar glowered at Alexi, for he usually got what he wanted. "I trust that you will serve me *quite* well," he said coldly, not wanting to **dismiss** him in case he turned out to be a good huntsman.

In just a few weeks, Alexi became first among the Tsar's huntsmen, for he was a good shot and the Golden Mare was swift at the chase. As luck would have it, there came a day that Alexi spied no game but rode on and on until it began to grow dark. He was about to turn the mare around when he noticed something glowing brightly on the path ahead. It was a golden feather, bright as a flame, and Alexi knew it must be a feather from the great Firebird.

"I will take this prize to the Tsar," said Alexi. "Then perhaps he will look upon me with favor."

The Golden Mare was protective of her kind master. "If you take the Firebird's feather, you will surely learn the meaning of fear," she warned. But so confident was Alexi that he did not heed her words and presented the feather to the Tsar the very next day.

Sequence
What sequence of events in the story leads Alexi to a position as a huntsman with the Tsar?

As the Tsar greedily took the feather, he saw a way to rid himself of this insolent huntsman, whose horse was a constant reminder of what he could not have.

"You bring me a mere feather!" bellowed the Tsar. "If you are so clever, bring me the whole bird, or I'll have your head brought in on a platter!"

Alexi left the throne room in **despair** and went to the Golden Mare's stall.

"Do not worry," said the Golden Mare. "Ask the Tsar to have a hundred sacks of maize scattered at midnight upon the open field on the hill. I will see to the rest."

The Tsar agreed to Alexi's request, and at midnight his men scattered one hundred sacks of maize on the field. Alexi took the saddle and bridle off the Golden Mare and she wandered loose in the field. Then he hid in the branches of a huge oak tree that stood at the top of the hill. All night they waited.

As the first golden rays of dawn lit the sky, from the eastern edge of the world the Firebird came flying, wings aflame with the reflected light of the sun.

The mighty bird landed in the field and began to eat the maize. As the Golden Mare grazed nearby, she wandered closer and closer to the Firebird. When the bird was close enough, the mare placed a hoof upon its tail, pinning it to the ground. The Firebird tried in vain to fly away, but the mare held fast. Alexi jumped from the tree, tied the struggling bird securely with rope, and placed it carefully in a sack.

The Tsar was amazed to see Alexi bearing the mythical Firebird. He ordered a huge, ornate cage built for the magnificent bird. People came from miles around to see the captive Firebird, and all the neighboring tsars were quite jealous of his prize possession. Alexi, however, felt sorry for the bird and wished he had never seen its feather shining in the forest path.

Alexi remained the Tsar's best huntsman and brought him much profit. But no matter how well Alexi did, he could not please the Tsar, for the Golden Mare still obeyed Alexi alone.

A few weeks later, the Tsar called Alexi to him.

"Since you seem to have a talent for impossible tasks, I have another one for you," said the Tsar. "In a distant eastern land, Yelena the Fair sails in her golden boat upon the Lake of the Sun. Find her and bring her back to be my bride. It will mean your death if you fail."

With a heavy heart, Alexi went to the Golden Mare, certain that this new task was hopeless. "Ask the Tsar for a brocaded tent and all sorts of sweetmeats and **delicacies**," the mare said, "and I will take you to her."

The Tsar supplied Alexi with a beautiful tent and fine foods, which Alexi packed into saddlebags upon the Golden Mare's broad back.

As they set out, it seemed to Alexi that the mare's feet barely touched the ground, so swiftly did she run. For seven days and nights she ran, through green forests, past waterfalls, up and down mountains, until on the eighth morning she stopped.

Silhouetted against the blazing sunrise, the boat of Yelena the Fair sailed upon the Lake of the Sun.

Alexi set up the tent and arranged rugs and cushions inside along with the fancy foods he had brought. Then he sat inside and waited for Yelena the Fair. Before long the boat sailed closer and closer to the shore until finally she lowered sail and landed upon the beach. Stepping out lightly, the maiden approached the regal-looking tent and saw the feast that Alexi had laid out.

Yelena and Alexi had a merry time, eating and talking of many things.

"My master the Tsar is rich and powerful, and famous, too," Alexi boasted. "And he has in his possession the legendary Firebird. Perhaps you would accept the Tsar's invitation to be an honored guest at his palace."

Yelena the Fair was so impressed by Alexi's persuasive words and gracious manner that she agreed to **accompany** him. When Alexi lifted the beautiful young maiden upon the Golden Mare's back, he felt a pang of guilt for not mentioning the old Tsar's true **intentions** to make her his wife.

The Tsar was astonished to see Alexi coming through the palace gates with Yelena the Fair.

"My bride!" he exclaimed.

Yelena the Fair was not pleased and quickly realized that Alexi had brought her there under false pretenses. She looked from the old Tsar to the young huntsman who had trapped her.

"I will marry no man," she said to the Tsar, "without my grandmother's wedding ring. It lies under a stone at the bottom of the Lake of the Sun."

"Well," said the Tsar, gesturing impatiently to Alexi, "what are you waiting for? Go at once and fetch the ring!"

When Alexi was alone with the Golden Mare, he said, "I do not wish to fetch Yelena's wedding ring for the Tsar, for then she, too, would be a captive like the Firebird."

"I will retrieve it then," said the Golden Mare. "Whatever happens, do not worry, for it is a magic ring and can grant its wearer any one wish."

When she reached the Lake of the Sun the mare stamped her hoof three times on the sand. A huge crab crawled out of the water.

"At the bottom of the lake there is a ring under a stone," said the Golden Mare. "Please get it for Yelena the Fair, for she has need of it."

Patiently the Golden Mare waited on the shore while the crab called together all the creatures that crawled on the lake's bottom to search for the ring. After some time he emerged with ring in claw. Delicately the Golden Mare took the ring in her teeth and then fairly flew back to the palace stables, where Alexi awaited.

Alexi presented the ring to the Tsar, who gave it at once to Yelena the Fair.

"You have your ring," he said. "Now let the wedding bells be rung! Let the feast be prepared!"

"Wait," said the shrewd maiden, who saw the remorse in Alexi's eyes. "I cannot marry a man as old as you, for you are surely four times my age."

"But what can I do about that?" asked the Tsar.

"Indeed, you can do something…with my help," said Yelena. "Prepare a cauldron of boiling water, and with my magical power I will turn it into the Water of Youth. If you bathe in it you will become young again."

The Tsar ordered the cauldron prepared, and soon the water bubbled and steamed.

"Let us first test this miracle," said the Tsar slyly. "You, Alexi, will be the first to enter the pot. Guards, seize him!" The Tsar's men held Alexi fast. He remembered the Golden Mare's words about the ring and hoped that they were true, for now he knew the meaning of fear.

Yelena the Fair approached the cauldron and passed her hand several times over the boiling water. Silently, she made a wish and dropped the magic ring into the cauldron.

"It is ready," she said.

At the Tsar's signal, the guards flung Alexi into the boiling liquid. He sank below the surface once, twice, and after the third time he rose like a shot and leaped from the cauldron. He was in perfect health and unharmed by the scalding water. No one but Yelena noticed the golden ring on his little finger.

Hoping to be as young and as strong as his huntsman, the Tsar jumped into the cauldron. At the same instant, Alexi made a wish on the magic ring, for he did not desire the Tsar's death.

Sequence
What key events in the story lead up to the moment when Alexi is flung into the cauldron?

313

To everyone's surprise, Alexi reached into the cauldron and lifted out a little baby, smiling and unharmed. The Tsar was indeed young again!

Since the Tsar was now too young to rule, the people made Alexi the Tsar in his place. And Yelena the Fair **consented** to become his bride. So she did marry the Tsar after all. And as for the baby Tsar, he was given a new name and raised as their own child.

As his first official act as Tsar, Alexi ordered the release of the Firebird, for such a bird did not belong in a cage. In a joyful blaze of light it flew to its home in the eastern sky. The Golden Mare ran free once more, but she continued to advise Alexi until the end of his days.

Once Upon a Time with Ruth Sanderson

Ruth Sanderson could usually be found reading books about horses in the library where her grandmother worked. This led to her second passion: drawing. On Saturday mornings in the fourth grade, Ruth started a class to teach her friends how to draw. It's no surprise that when Ruth grew up, she went to art school and became a writer and illustrator of children's fantasy and fairy tale books. Ruth is married and has two daughters.

Other books by Ruth Sanderson: *Papa Gatto* and *Crystal Mountain*

LOG ON ▶ Find out more about Ruth Sanderson at **www.macmillanmh.com**.

CA **Author's Purpose**
Ruth Sanderson entertains the reader with this fairy tale. What makes the story informative, as well?

# CA Critical Thinking

Summarize

Use your Sequence Chart to summarize *The Golden Mare, the Firebird, and the Magic Ring*. Keeping track of the order of events can help you better understand the story.

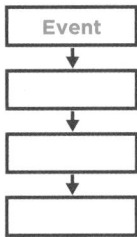

Think and Compare

1. Describe how the story would be different if the author changed the **sequence** of events. Use story details in your description. **Summarize: Sequence**

2. Reread page 309. Why does Alexi feel guilty about persuading Yelena the Fair to visit the Tsar? Use details from the story to explain your answer. **Analyze**

3. If the Golden Mare were to **accompany** you throughout your life, what might you ask her to help you do? Explain. **Synthesize**

4. The Tsar only thinks about himself. How do selfish people create difficult situations? Explain your answer. **Evaluate**

5. Reread "A Real Princess" on pages 296–297. Explain the similarities and differences between Alexi's and Prince Vincent's situations. Use details from both selections in your answer. **Reading/Writing Across Texts**

History/ Social Science

A Tale Told Around the World

by Lateesha Gray

People all over the world enjoy fairy tales. Some fairy tales may be popular in only one country, but others are told around the globe. For example, the story of Cinderella has more than 500 **versions**. In most retellings, a kind young girl is the main character and other characters include a cruel stepmother and her equally cruel daughters, a fairy godmother, and a prince.

The plot is similar in all of the tales. The young girl is forced to do household chores, then someone grants her wish and helps her attend a celebration, such as a ball. At the ball the girl's beauty attracts a powerful man who falls in love at once. The girl's true **identity** is kept secret so the man must search all over the land for her.

318

The French Cinderella

The French writer Charles Perrault wrote the Cinderella tale that most of us know. Cinderella, or Cendrillon, is very beautiful, and her stepsisters are ugly and jealous. Cinderella is forced to do the most difficult chores. One day the prince invites all of the women in the kingdom to a ball. Cinderella almost does not go, until a fairy godmother appears and helps Cinderella. The fairy godmother waves her wand and **transforms** Cinderella's ragged dress into a beautiful gown.

Cinderella also wears glass slippers. The transformation will wear off at midnight so she must be sure to leave before then. As she is leaving the ball, Cinderella loses a slipper and the prince looks all over the kingdom for her. The prince finds her and marries her. At the end of the story, Cinderella forgives her stepmother and stepsisters and asks them to come live with her.

Venn Diagram

Reading a Venn Diagram

In a Venn diagram, differences are written in the left and right ovals. The similarities are written in the center section.

French Version
- Glass slipper
- Fancy ball
- Prince
- Fairy godmother
- Stepmother and stepsisters nice to her later

Cinderella Stories
- A kind young girl is treated badly
- Evil stepmother, stepsisters
- Receives help that transforms her
- Must be home at a certain time
- Loses slipper
- Powerful man searches for unknown girl
- Man marries girl

Chinese Version
- Gold slipper
- Festival
- King
- Talking fish
- Stepmother and stepsister never see her again

The Chinese Cinderella

In the Chinese version, Yeh-Shen also has an evil stepmother and stepsisters. Her only friend is a beautiful fish with golden eyes. Her stepmother later kills the talking fish and cooks it for dinner. However, Yeh-Shen learns that the fish's bones are magical and hides them. The bones later help her dress in fine clothing for a festival. While rushing to leave the festival to be home by a certain time, she loses a gold slipper. A king buys the slipper and searches for its owner. When he meets Yeh-Shen, he is struck by her beauty and falls in love. Yeh-Shen's stepmother and stepsisters are forbidden to see her.

The Egyptian Cinderella

An Egyptian version of *Cinderella* is based on the actual marriage of a slave girl and the pharaoh, or ruler, of ancient Egypt. In this version Rhodopis, a servant girl from Greece, is teased by other servants in the household. Her only friends are the animals along the river. She often sings and dances for them. One evening she loses a slipper, and a falcon snatches it. The falcon flies over the pharaoh's throne and drops the slipper. The pharaoh searches his kingdom for the woman whose foot fits the slipper. When he finds Rhodopis, he falls in love and she becomes his queen.

The Native American Cinderella

Some Native American tales echo many of the **elements** of *Cinderella*. One famous tale tells about a young maiden whose hands and face are burned from tending a fire. Like the European Cinderella, she is usually left out of events and feels as though she does not belong. This story, however, uses the setting and customs of the Algonquian nation to tell this tale. A Zuni version features talking turkeys that help the girl. The setting for that tale is a village in the southwestern United States.

 Critical Thinking

1. Look at the Venn diagram on page 319. What are two details from the French Cinderella story that are different from details in the Chinese version? **Reading a Venn Diagram**

2. Why do you think the story of Cinderella is so popular around the world? **Analyze**

3. Think about *The Golden Mare, the Firebird, and the Magic Ring*. In what ways is the story similar to that of *Cinderella* and *Yeh-Shen*? **Reading/Writing Across Texts**

 History/Social Science Activity

Make a Venn diagram that compares and contrasts a Cinderella tale from another culture to the Cinderella story you know.

 Find out more about Cinderella tales at **www.macmillanmh.com**.

Reading and Writing Connection

✔ **Dialogue and Narration**
Good writers use **dialogue** and **narration** to help readers learn about a character's thoughts and feelings.

Read the passage below. Notice how the author Ruth Sanderson uses dialogue and narration together in her story.

An excerpt from
The Golden Mare, the Firebird, and the Magic Ring

The author uses dialogue and narration. Instead of writing a big section of dialogue and then a big section of narration, the author weaves them together.

Yelena the Fair was not pleased and quickly realized that Alexi had brought her there under false pretenses. She looked from the old Tsar to the young huntsman who had trapped her.

"I will marry no man," she said to the Tsar, "without my grandmother's wedding ring. It lies under a stone at the bottom of the Lake of the Sun."

The Golden Mare,
the Firebird,
and the Magic Ring
by Ruth Sanderson

Read and Find

Read Tom's writing below. How did he use dialogue
and narration to help you see and hear the moment?
Use the checklist below to help you.

In the Spotlight

by Tom M.

The talent show host called my name!
"Oh my gosh! Oh my gosh!" I cried as I
bounded up the stage steps. "Hi Mom! Hi
Dad!" I said into the microphone.

The talent show host laughed. She
put her hand on my shoulder and said, "I
can see you're excited to be here."

Read what I said
and did when I was
chosen for the
talent show.

Writer's Checklist

 Do you feel like you are experiencing what Tom
saw and heard?

Does the writer show you exactly what a character
said and what the character did?

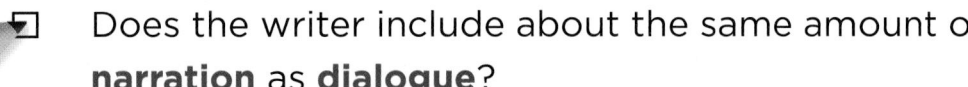 Does the writer include about the same amount of
narration as **dialogue**?

What kinds of stories do you like? How is hearing stories different from reading or watching them?

LOG ON ▶ Find out more about storytelling at www.macmillanmh.com.

Tales

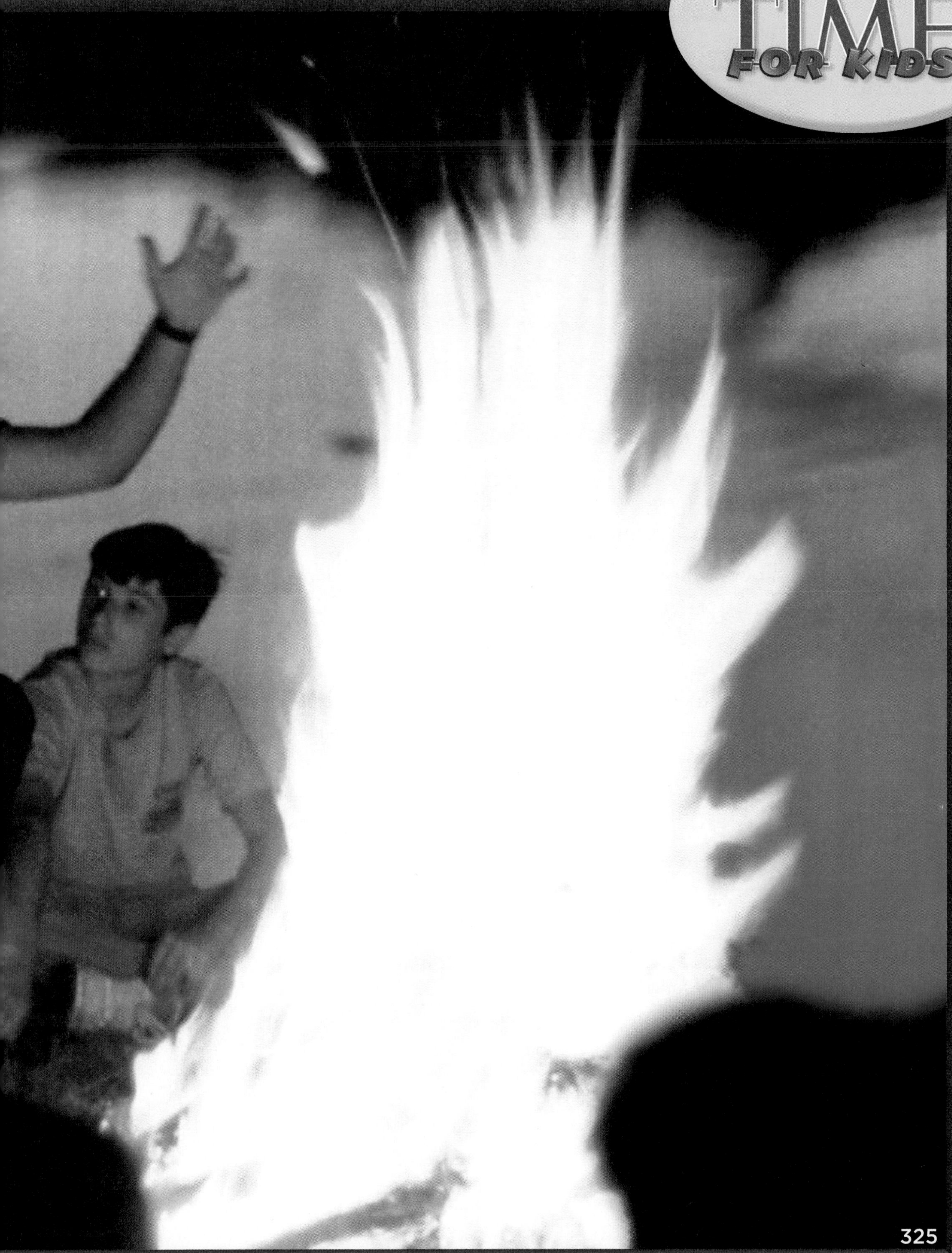

Vocabulary

generations
globe
preserve
reveal
amusing

Tell It Like It Was

The Beyond the Border Festival takes place every year in Wales.

We reach for a book when we want a story. But long before stories were written down, they were passed on through the **generations** by storytellers. These people had to memorize each story carefully. Storytellers used words to take an audience out of their world and into one where heroes and monsters live.

Today a new group of performers are bringing back the tales and skills of the old storytellers. Each year at least 70 storytelling festivals happen around the **globe** in dozens of languages. A major one is Beyond the Border, a three-day story festival in Great Britain. Performers from as far away as Egypt, Japan, and Bangladesh bring their tales to a fresh audience.

Live storytelling may seem outdated in this visual age. But Daniel Morden, a storyteller from Wales, thinks listening to stories brings more enjoyment than watching movies because listeners get to make up their own images. "Every member of an audience makes different pictures in their heads, based on their own experiences [as they listen]," says Morden. "So everyone hears a different story."

Master storyteller Tuup from Guyana at the Beyond the Border Festival.

VOICES OF THE PAST

At the end of the U.S. Civil War, about four million enslaved Africans were freed. More than 130 years later, some of their stories can be heard in their own voices. Twenty-three interviews with freed African Americans appear on the Library of Congress's American Memory Web site.

Between 1932 and 1975, these people were interviewed in nine southern states. The idea was to **preserve** American history. Speaking at least 60 years after their emancipation, the storytellers

Enslaved people during the Civil War.

discuss their experiences in slavery and as free men and women.

Michael Taft, the head of the library's archive of folk culture, says the recordings **reveal** something that written stories cannot. "The power of hearing someone speak is so much greater than reading something from the page," Taft says.

Tale of the Tigers

Los Tigres Del Norte

In 1968 a group of brothers crossed the border from Mexico to San Jose, California. At the border, an immigration official called the boys "little tigers." He didn't know that he was helping to name one of the most successful Latino bands in history. Later the boys formed a band and called it *Los Tigres Del Norte* (The Tigers of the North). This Grammy-winning band has sold millions of CDs, which are packed with *corridos*.

Developed in Mexico in the 1800s, *corridos* are musical tales about everyday life. Through music and lyrics, they describe important events. Whether they are serious or **amusing**, today's *corridos* are usually fictional.

LOG ON ▶ Find out more about *corridos* at www.macmillanmh.com.

327

Tricky Tales

Where does the wind come from? Why is there night? Why does a leopard have spots?

Questions about nature and how the world works have been around forever—and so have the stories that have helped provide answers. Trickster tales were created in the days before science made events like tornadoes and floods understandable. These stories, whose main characters use their wits to get what they want, helped to explain nature and the world around us.

Meet the Trickster

What is a trickster? A trickster is a type of character that appears in many different stories, but doesn't always have the same name or even the same body. Usually a male, he is often an animal with human features, such as a coyote, fox, tortoise, or spider. The name "trickster" can be tricky. He isn't always tricking others—sometimes he is the foolish one being tricked.

A Havasupai storyteller

328

Robert Greygrass

The trickster in Native American stories appears in many different forms. For example, he can be a cunning coyote in a story from the Crow nation or a brave raven in the stories from the Pacific Northwest.

The Way Things Work

Recently, California-born Robert Greygrass, a Native American storyteller, appeared at the Bay Area Storytelling Festival in El Sobrante, California. "He was great," says Patrick Whamond, 10. "He told stories about animals and how things got to be the way they are."

Greygrass uses trickster tales to teach, inspire, and entertain. Some of his stories tell not only the history of Native Americans, but also describe our place in the universe.

Unlike written stories that stay the same on the page, Greygrass's trickster tales can change over time. A storyteller doesn't always memorize a tale word for word like a script. He or she might just remember important story points at the beginning, middle, and end. So the story is never told in exactly the same way twice.

Ongoing Traditions

The Native American tradition of trickster storytelling has a rich history that spans many generations. Nobody knows that better than Tchin (Chin), a Native American who was born in Virginia. As a young boy, he lived with relatives in Rhode Island, where he learned about the culture and traditions of his Narragansett tribe. When Tchin was 15, he moved to New York City. After 10 years in New York, he attended the Rhode Island School of Design, Brown University, and then the Institute of American Arts in New Mexico.

Today Tchin uses stories to entertain audiences across the country. "Native American people, we grow up basically as...[storytellers]," Tchin has said. "We grow up hearing stories all the time. But we don't call them stories, legends, or myths. To us, they are lessons, because they explain the universe." One of Tchin's favorite tales is "Rabbit's Wish for Snow," which reveals an amusing reason for why rabbits have long ears and short legs.

Tchin hasn't stopped looking for new material, and he has studied trickster folktales from around the globe. "I'm studying quite a bit about the Mideast at this time," he has said. "I've studied ancient Greeks, Romans, Egyptians, and what you get out of all that is that you get to understand people more clearly."

Worldwide Tricksters

As Tchin has learned, Native Americans are not alone in telling tales of the trickster. While the character is probably best known in Africa and North America, he is also a familiar figure in myths from all around the world.

The trickster can be found in stories like "The Ungrateful Tiger" in Korea, "The Fish That Were Too Clever" in India, and the Loki tales in Scandinavia. No matter what country he comes from, the trickster is usually a rascal who makes up for a physical weakness with cunning and sharp wit.

Tchin's heritage is Siksika and Narragansett.

A Story for Tomorrow

One of the trickster's most powerful roles is that of creator. For example, a story from the Nez Perce tribe called "The Coyote and the Monster" starts, "A long, long time ago, people did not yet inhabit Earth. A monster walked upon the land, eating all the animals—except Coyote." The coyote is the trickster in this story, and by the time it ends, he has defeated the monster and created Native Americans.

"Trickster stories can pass along jokes, relay instructions on honoring the dead, preserve figures of speech—many things," says Riccardo Salmona, who worked at the American Folk Art Museum in New York City. "But it's the powerful stories like 'The Coyote and the Monster' that almost guarantee trickster tales will be around for a long, long time. They have become part of the fabric of our communities."

The wolf is a trickster in some Native American stories.

CA Critical Thinking

1. How are written stories and oral stories alike? How are they different?

2. According to this article, why were trickster tales first told?

3. Think of an experience you have had. Turn the experience into a trickster tale.

4. Do you think Daniel Morden in "Tell It Like It Was" and Tchin in this article have similar views about storytelling? Why or why not?

CA Show What You Know

Right There

You can put your finger on the answer. Look for key words in the question. Then find those key words in the selection.

Some storytellers wear colorful costumes.

This storyteller has everyone's attention.

Talk About a GREAT STORY

Each year the National Storytelling Festival is held in Jonesboro, Tennessee.

When the festival began about 30 years ago, the art of storytelling seemed to be dying out. "At our first festival we had only 60 people sitting around an old farm wagon," recalls Jimmy Neil Smith, a festival founder. The festival has grown from that one wagon to six huge tents. Why has storytelling become so popular? Perhaps it's because stories help us understand our past—and maybe even our future. "Long ago, when there were no books, no movies, no TV, it was the storyteller's job to unravel the universe, explain why there are stars, why we laugh and cry," says storyteller Brenda Wong Aoki.

"Everyone can be a good storyteller," says Syd Lieberman, a wonderful Chicago storyteller. The trick to telling a good story, Lieberman advises, is to not be afraid of the truth. "Stories aren't always about the smiling moments."

Go on ▶

Directions: Now answer numbers 1 through 5. Base your answers on "Talk About a Great Story."

1. **About how long ago did the National Storytelling Festival begin?**

   A   10 years
   B   30 years
   C   40 years
   D   60 years

Tip
Look for key words.

2. **What is one reason that storytelling has become popular again?**

   A   People are tired of books, movies, and TV.
   B   More people are interested in becoming professional storytellers.
   C   Stories are perfect for people with short attention spans.
   D   Stories help us understand our past and perhaps our future.

3. **According to Syd Lieberman, what is the trick to telling a good story?**

   A   Don't be afraid of the truth.
   B   Always have a happy ending.
   C   Start at the beginning.
   D   Practice storytelling every day.

4. **What information in the article indicates how successful the storytelling festival has become over the years?**

5. **Why do you think people like to listen to stories? Use details and information from the article to help you with your answer.**

Write on Demand

CA A student from a city in the United States is going to Russia to spend the summer with relatives. <u>Write a story</u> about the character's experiences.

Narrative writing tells a story about a personal or fictional experience.

To figure out if a writing prompt asks for narrative writing, look for clue words such as <u>tell about a time</u> or <u>write a story about</u>.

See how one student begins a response to the prompt.

As the bus came to a stop, Tim wasn't so sure about this summer. He felt as if he had landed on Mars, but his name on a sign brought him right back to Earth—in Russia.

The sign was held up by his cousin Alexei. Alexei's English wasn't very good, and Tim's Russian was even worse. Alexei took Tim back to his family's house. Inside there was no computer and the television got only three channels.

Tim started to think up excuses to return home early. Then he heard someone playing a guitar.

The writer uses details to develop the story based on the prompt.

Writing Prompt

Respond in writing to the prompt below. Write for 10 minutes. Write as much as you can, as well as you can. Review the hints below before and after you write.

Think of a place where someone might travel.

Now write a story about someone who travels and does not know the language.

Writing Hints for Prompts

- ☑ Carefully read the prompt.
- ☑ Organize your ideas to plan your writing.
- ☑ Support your ideas by giving reasons or using more details.
- ☑ Write in complete sentences and use a variety of sentence structures.
- ☑ Choose words that help readers understand your ideas.
- ☑ Review your writing and edit as needed.

Challenges

CA **Talk About It**

What challenges might these people face in working together?

LOG ON ▶ Find out more about challenges of different cultures at **www.macmillanmh.com**.

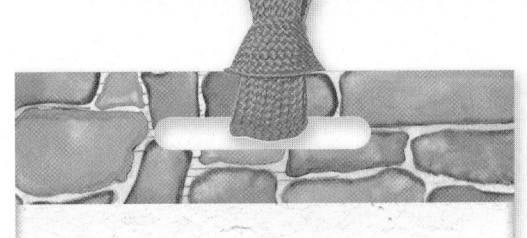

The Party

✓ Vocabulary

tasks	previous
consulted	recover
detected	pursuit
proceeded	urgency

✓ Context Clues

Authors use **Figurative Language** to create more interesting or exciting images with words.

Similes make a comparison using the words *like* or *as*. It is as old as the hills.

Metaphors create a word picture without using *like* or *as: The summer sun is a golden beach ball.*

For months, Charlotte planned her father's special birthday party. When she couldn't sleep, she listed the **tasks** she would need to finish and worked on the invitations.

As the day grew closer, she **consulted** her mother. Just as her smoke alarm always **detected** a fire, Charlotte could always tell when there was a problem. Her mother sighed, "This is such a nice idea. Your father works so hard, and he deserves this. But, I'm afraid we don't have the money." Her mother looked sad as she patted Charlotte's knee and sent her outside.

Charlotte wanted to have the party more than anything, but she was unsure of what to do. Her brother Luke returned from soccer practice and noticed her head hung low. Luke **proceeded** to ask her questions, until she told him the problem.

"Maybe our friends or the neighbors can help us?" Luke suggested.

"In our **previous** neighborhood, they would have. But they aren't very friendly here," Charlotte said.

"And they all seem so busy," Luke added.

Suddenly, Charlotte smiled, and her brother was glad to see her **recover**. She started for the street. Luke was puzzled, but he ran after her in **pursuit**. They stopped at the door of Mr. Romero, the baker.

"Yes?" Mr. Romero grumbled. He looked impatiently from Charlotte to Luke. They could feel the **urgency** in Mr. Romero's voice.

Charlotte exhaled. "We're having a very special party for our father's birthday on Sunday. We're going to have a delicious cake and we hope you can come. All of the other neighbors will be there."

"And balloons and a magician," Luke added.

Mr. Romero's face grew pale. "But where did you get the cake?"

"Well, it's going to be a lovely chocolate cake," Charlotte said. "We know your cakes are the best in the city, but you're very busy."

"But not too busy for this job," Mr. Romero brightened. "I will make the cake, and it will be my gift."

Charlotte and Luke smiled. "Thank you. We'll see you there."

"Great idea!" Luke said to his sister, as they turned the corner. "By making them think there's this great party, we'll actually make the party! And I can be the magician," he winked. "Where to next?"

"To Mrs. Sommberg, the florist," Charlotte grinned.

Reread for Comprehension

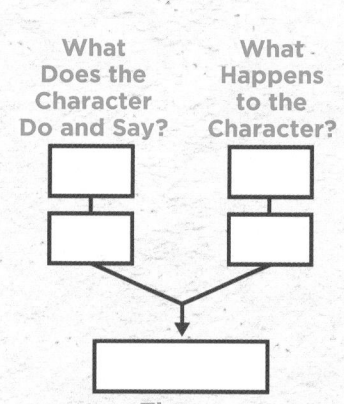

Visualize

Theme

The theme is the main message that the author wants to come across in a story. A Theme Chart can help you find the story's theme. Fill in the Theme Chart as you reread the selection and decide on its theme.

What Does the Character Do and Say?

What Happens to the Character?

Theme

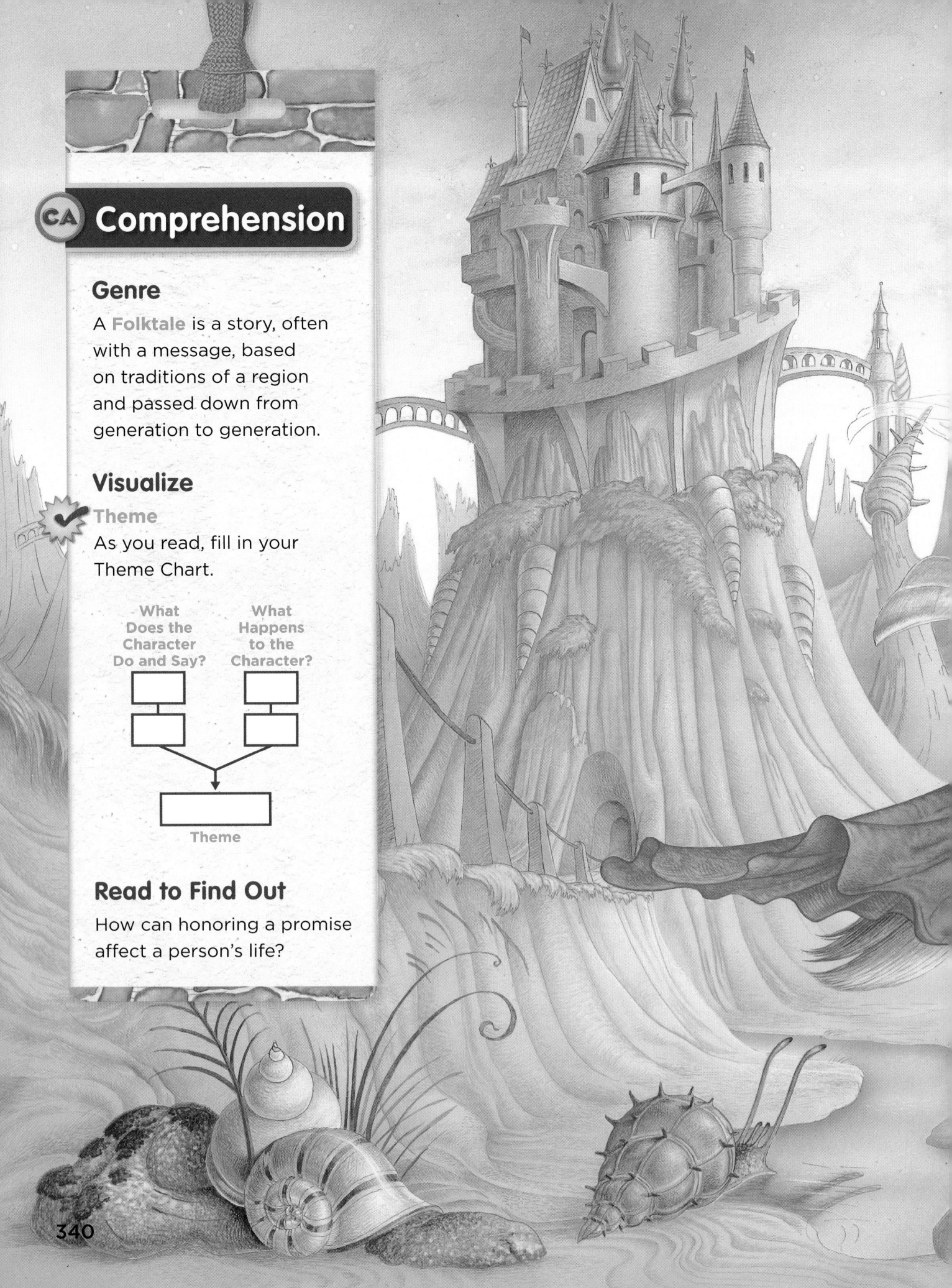

Comprehension

Genre

A **Folktale** is a story, often with a message, based on traditions of a region and passed down from generation to generation.

Visualize

Theme

As you read, fill in your Theme Chart.

What Does the Character Do and Say?	What Happens to the Character?
☐	☐
☐	☐

Theme

Read to Find Out

How can honoring a promise affect a person's life?

Blancaflor

by *Alma Flor Ada*
illustrated by *Valerie Sokolova*

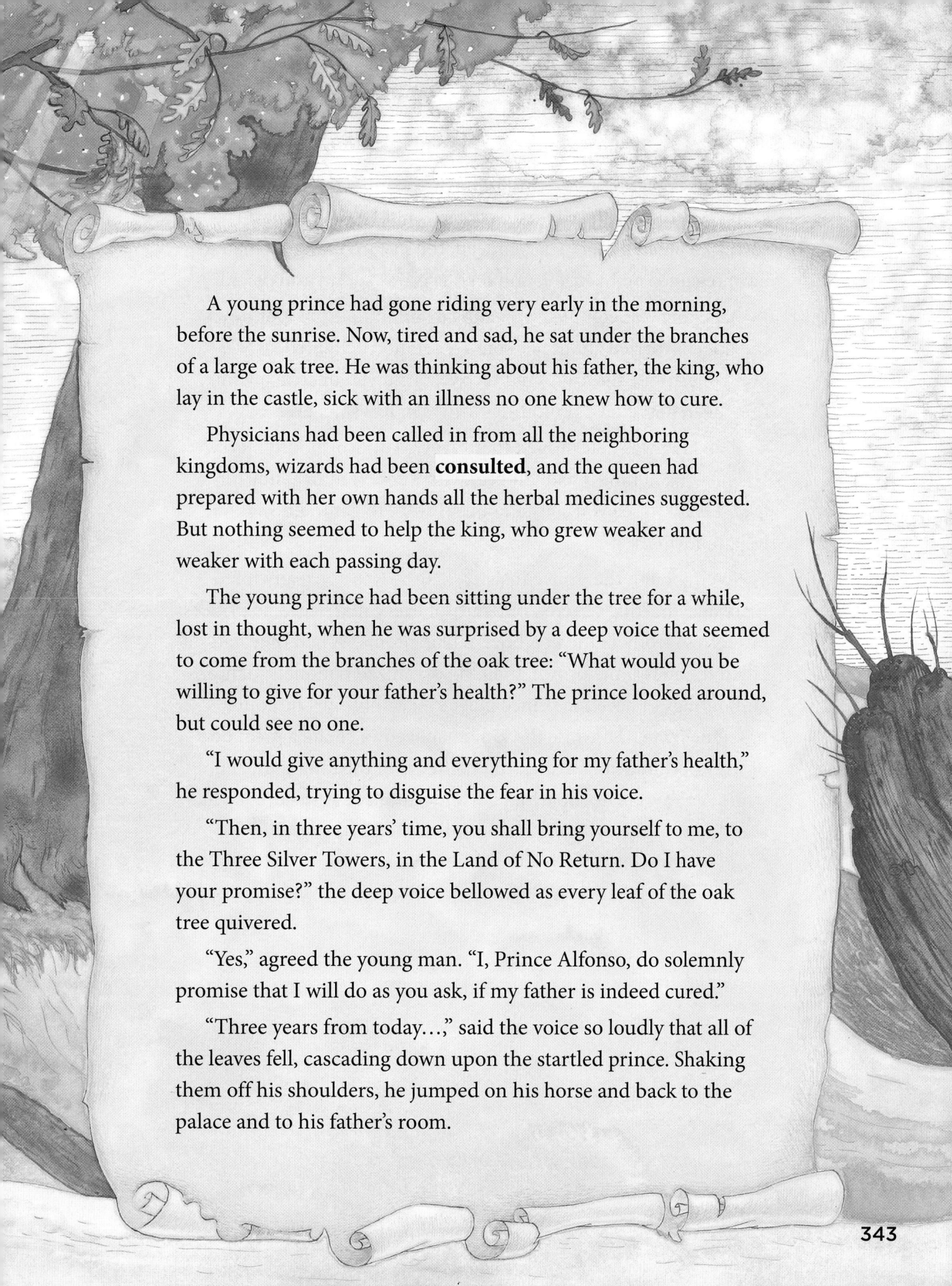

A young prince had gone riding very early in the morning, before the sunrise. Now, tired and sad, he sat under the branches of a large oak tree. He was thinking about his father, the king, who lay in the castle, sick with an illness no one knew how to cure.

Physicians had been called in from all the neighboring kingdoms, wizards had been **consulted**, and the queen had prepared with her own hands all the herbal medicines suggested. But nothing seemed to help the king, who grew weaker and weaker with each passing day.

The young prince had been sitting under the tree for a while, lost in thought, when he was surprised by a deep voice that seemed to come from the branches of the oak tree: "What would you be willing to give for your father's health?" The prince looked around, but could see no one.

"I would give anything and everything for my father's health," he responded, trying to disguise the fear in his voice.

"Then, in three years' time, you shall bring yourself to me, to the Three Silver Towers, in the Land of No Return. Do I have your promise?" the deep voice bellowed as every leaf of the oak tree quivered.

"Yes," agreed the young man. "I, Prince Alfonso, do solemnly promise that I will do as you ask, if my father is indeed cured."

"Three years from today…," said the voice so loudly that all of the leaves fell, cascading down upon the startled prince. Shaking them off his shoulders, he jumped on his horse and back to the palace and to his father's room.

"Son!" His mother greeted him with a smile, the first he had seen on her loving face in many days. "Look at your father! He seems so much better." And, indeed, the sleeping king seemed to have regained all his color, and his sleep was sound and placid.

The king was completely healthy again in no time. But now the queen worried about her son. He seemed delighted, as was everyone, to see the kind king **recover**. And yet, once in a while, the queen **detected** a profound sadness in her son's eyes.

The king was determined that Prince Alfonso should marry. His prolonged illness had left him with a renewed **urgency** for life. "I want to see you start a family. I want to get to know my grandchildren."

Even though the prince insisted that he was not ready for marriage, the king ordered portraits of every marriageable princess brought in from all the neighboring kingdoms. When they had failed to interest the prince, the king organized banquets, dances, and outings to have the prince meet every noble girl he could possibly invite. But while the king managed to create a great deal of work for the seamstresses and coiffeurs of the kingdom, and while many young people had a wonderful time at the events, he could not get the prince to change his mind.

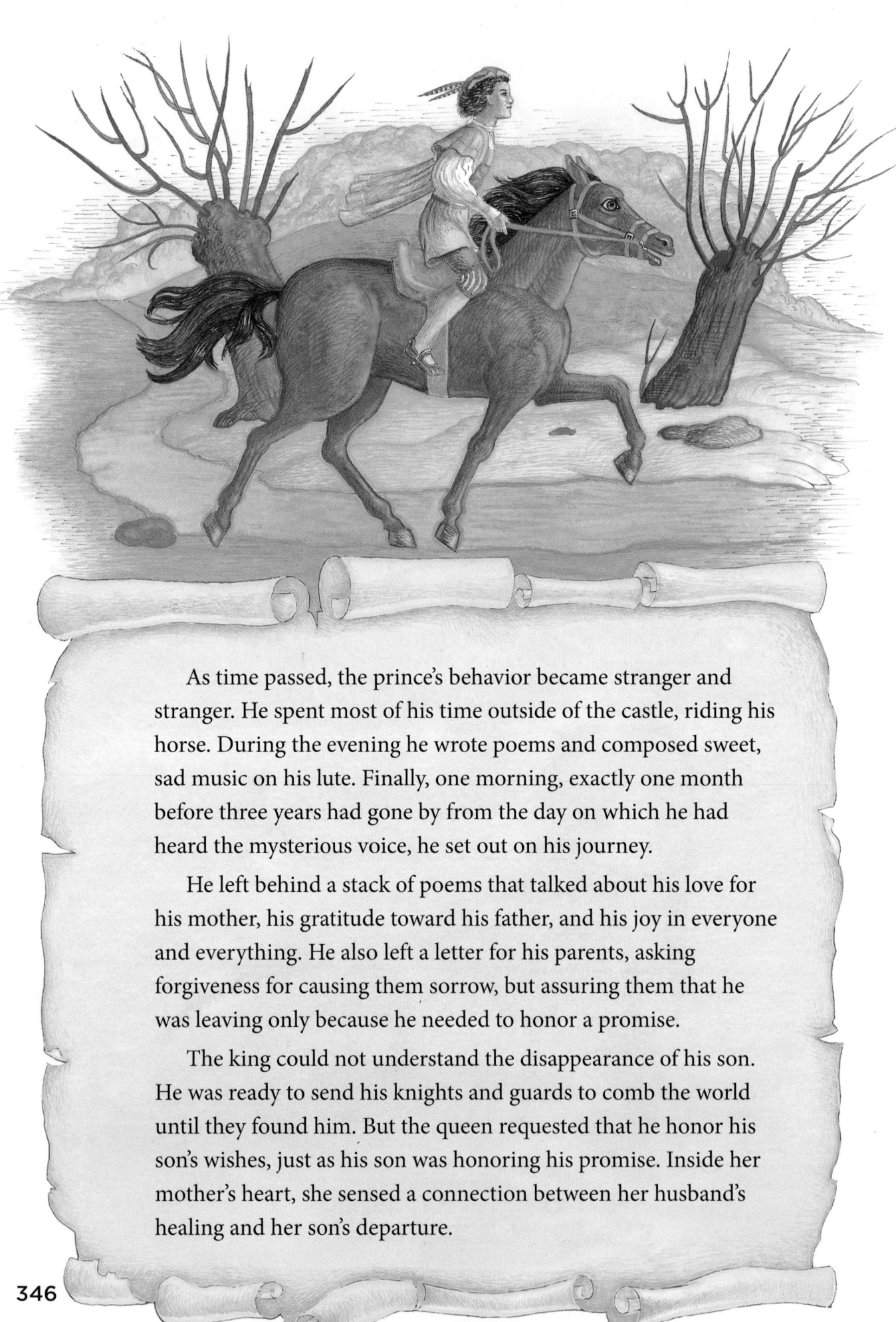

As time passed, the prince's behavior became stranger and stranger. He spent most of his time outside of the castle, riding his horse. During the evening he wrote poems and composed sweet, sad music on his lute. Finally, one morning, exactly one month before three years had gone by from the day on which he had heard the mysterious voice, he set out on his journey.

He left behind a stack of poems that talked about his love for his mother, his gratitude toward his father, and his joy in everyone and everything. He also left a letter for his parents, asking forgiveness for causing them sorrow, but assuring them that he was leaving only because he needed to honor a promise.

The king could not understand the disappearance of his son. He was ready to send his knights and guards to comb the world until they found him. But the queen requested that he honor his son's wishes, just as his son was honoring his promise. Inside her mother's heart, she sensed a connection between her husband's healing and her son's departure.

Young Prince Alfonso rode for many days, eating sparingly of the food he had taken with him. Several times he asked shepherds he met along the way for directions to the Land of No Return. They always pointed in the same direction, toward the setting sun. And when they wondered, "Why should anyone want to go there?" The prince would respond, "To honor my word."

On the seventh day of his journey the prince saw a white dove who seemed to signal him to follow her. And so he did. But after many hours of following the dove, he found himself facing a deep ravine. He stopped, puzzled, knowing well that he could not cross the gorge on horseback or on foot. Then a majestic eagle appeared in front of him and looked piercingly into his eyes.

"Might you carry me to the other side?" he asked the eagle.

"Only if you give me your chain," the eagle responded.

Young Alfonso took off the heavy gold chain that bore the eagle emblem of his kingdom and hung it around the eagle's neck.

"It is only fitting," the prince said. "I have carried your image with me always. Now it should be yours." Then the eagle grasped him firmly by his leather belt and flew across the ravine.

The eagle released the young prince on the other side, where the land was deserted and barren. Basalt and obsidian rocks burned hot under the fierce sun. Far in the distance, high above the steep walls, three towers of silver glittered.

> **Theme**
> What message about honor does the author want readers to understand?

Alfonso had just taken a few steps toward the towers when he was stopped by a thundering voice: "Who dares step on my land?"

"I am here to honor my promise," the young prince answered.

"That is as it should be," the voice replied. "And to reward you, I will give you an opportunity to win your life back. If you fulfill the three **tasks** that I ask of you, you will stay here and marry one of my three daughters. But if you do not complete the tasks, you will be food for my hounds."

Alfonso took a deep breath. Squaring his shoulders and steadying his voice he asked, "What would you like me to do?"

"Take this sack of wheat. Walk up to the valley, plant it, harvest it, and mill it. With the flour, bake some bread and bring it to me tomorrow by eleven o'clock in the morning." To Alfonso's great surprise a small sack of wheat appeared before his eyes.

The young man lifted the sack and began to walk up the path among the rocks. What else could he do? His head hung low and his shoulders drooped because he knew there was no way he could fulfill his task. But he had not walked far when a young girl appeared in front of him.

"What's wrong?" she asked him. "Why are you so sad?"

"I have been asked to do an impossible task. And my life depends on it."

"My father must be up to one of his tricks," she responded. "But do not worry. I will help you. Take this stick and poke the earth with it. Keep walking on a straight line and poke as you walk. I will drop the seeds and all will be well."

That afternoon, after all the wheat had been planted, they watched the sunset together. The young girl said, "My name is Blancaflor. And if you trust me, we will save your life. Now I have to go; otherwise they will miss me at dinner."

After she left, Alfonso went to sleep, resting his back against a large boulder. In the morning the valley was covered with ripe wheat, its golden spikes shining under the early sun.

Alfonso was still rubbing his eyes when Blancaflor appeared.

"It's time to harvest the grain, mill it, and bake bread with the flour," she said. And as she spoke the wheat flew out of its stalks and formed a golden mountain. A mill and an outdoor oven appeared next to the mountain of wheat.

"Keep fetching wood for the oven," Blancaflor told Alfonso. And while he did, the mill ground the wheat, and loaf upon loaf of bread dough appeared ready to be baked. When the smell of the recently baked bread filled the valley, Blancaflor disappeared. "It's better that my father doesn't find me here when he comes for his bread," she told Alfonso before leaving.

Soon a thundering voice was heard: "Either you are a wizard or you have met Blancaflor."

Alfonso kept silent.

"Well, you still have two more tasks!" shouted the voice. "Better get started. Plant these grapevines and have the wine ready for me by eleven o'clock tomorrow morning." And while the loaves of bread moved through the air as if carried by giant hands, Alfonso found one hundred grapevine saplings at his feet.

It was not long before Blancaflor appeared again. And just as the pair had grown the wheat the **previous** day, now they planted the saplings. That evening, as they watched the sunset, Alfonso told Blancaflor about his mother and father and the promise he had made. And once again she asked him to trust her.

The next morning the valley was covered by fully grown grapevines loaded with ripe bunches of grapes. And it took only a few words from Blancaflor for the grapes to be harvested and crushed and for the wine to be stored in huge oak casks.

Just before eleven, after Blancaflor had already departed, the thundering voice was heard again: "Either you are a mighty wizard or you have been talking to Blancaflor."

Alfonso remained silent. But he shivered when he heard the voice laugh.

"Well, let's see how you do with your last task. You need to bring back the ring my great-great-grandmother lost in the ocean. And if you do not have it here by eleven o'clock tomorrow, you will be food for my hounds."

When Blancaflor returned, there were tears in Alfonso's eyes. "I'm not afraid to die. But I hate to break my mother's heart. This task will be impossible," he told her.

"No, it won't be. But you will need to trust me even more," she replied.

Blancaflor led Alfonso to a set of high cliffs next to the ocean.
There the prince spotted the eagle who had carried him across
the gorge.

"The eagle will take us to the middle of the ocean, and then you
must let go of me and let me fall in," Blancaflor instructed.

"But I will not be able to do that," he argued.

"Yes, you will. You must," insisted Blancaflor.

When they were high above the ocean, Blancaflor asked the
prince to let her go. But at the last minute he held on desperately
to her hand. As her fingers slipped from his, he heard a crack. Her
little finger hung broken.

Alfonso felt his heart stop as he saw Blancaflor disappear under the water. His eyes filled with tears as the eagle flapped her wings. Before he knew it, he was standing in the meadow, next to the boulder against which he had slept the last two nights. There, on top of the boulder, was an extraordinary ring in the shape of a dragon with two emeralds for eyes.

He had not admired the ring for very long before he heard the thundering voice. "So you found the ring. Either you are the king of all wizards or you have been helped by Blancaflor."

Alfonso remained silent.

The voice continued, "Follow the path to the castle. Tonight you will meet my three daughters and choose one for your wife!"

When Alfonso reached the Three Silver Towers, the gates were open. He entered, and in the main banquet hall there were three white doves.

"Choose one, right now!" the voice echoed against the thick walls.

Alfonso studied the three doves. They looked identical. But he noticed that one had what looked like a broken wing. He remembered Blancaflor's little finger, hanging twisted from her hand.

"I choose this one," he said, and walked toward the dove with the broken wing. Suddenly Blancaflor stood in front of him surrounded by her sisters, who looked just like her. No one would have been able to tell them apart. But when Alfonso observed Blancaflor's hand, he could see that one of her little fingers had been bandaged.

"Take your wife," ordered the voice. "And let's all go to sleep now. We will celebrate the wedding tomorrow."

Blancaflor guided Alfonso to her bedroom. Once inside, she closed the door and whispered to him, "They will kill us tonight. We must escape." She arranged the covers on the bed to look as if they were both sleeping. She blew on the glass of water next to her bed and led Alfonso outside.

"I will stay here on guard in case my father comes in **pursuit**. You go to the stables to fetch a horse. And bring it here. But mind you, there are two horses there. One is young and strong. His name is Viento, which means 'wind.' The other one is old and thin. His name is Pensamiento, which means 'thought.' Make sure you do not take Viento. Take Pensamiento."

But when Alfonso got to the stable and saw the two horses, he thought, "That old skinny horse will never be able to carry us both." And he **proceeded** to saddle Viento.

While Alfonso was getting the horse, Blancaflor's father was at his daughter's door. He called softly, to see if she was asleep, "Blancaflor?"

And the breath repeated faintly, "Yes, Father?"

But when he called again, a third time, the breath only let out a sigh. He stormed into the room and quickly realized that neither Blancaflor nor the prince was there. And so he set out after them.

Blancaflor was dismayed when Alfonso came to fetch her riding Viento, but seeing that her father was emerging from the castle, she jumped on the horse behind the prince and urged him to go on.

They had galloped across the valley for only a few minutes when they heard Pensamiento, carrying her father, catching up with them.

"If only we had taken Pensamiento instead of Viento," said Blancaflor, "my father would never have been able to keep up with us." Then she took the comb that held her hair and threw it on the road behind them.

The comb turned into a chain of steep mountains that blocked
the way and allowed them to gain a little distance. But very soon
they heard the sound of Pensamiento's hooves approaching again.

Blancaflor took the gold pin that held her shawl and threw it on
the road behind them.

The gold pin turned into a desert of very hot sand, and
that allowed them to gain a little distance. But soon they heard
Pensamiento's hooves again.

"If only we had taken Pensamiento instead of Viento," said
Blancaflor. And she took her blue silk shawl and threw it on the
road behind them.

The blue shawl turned into a large sea with high waves covered
with foam.

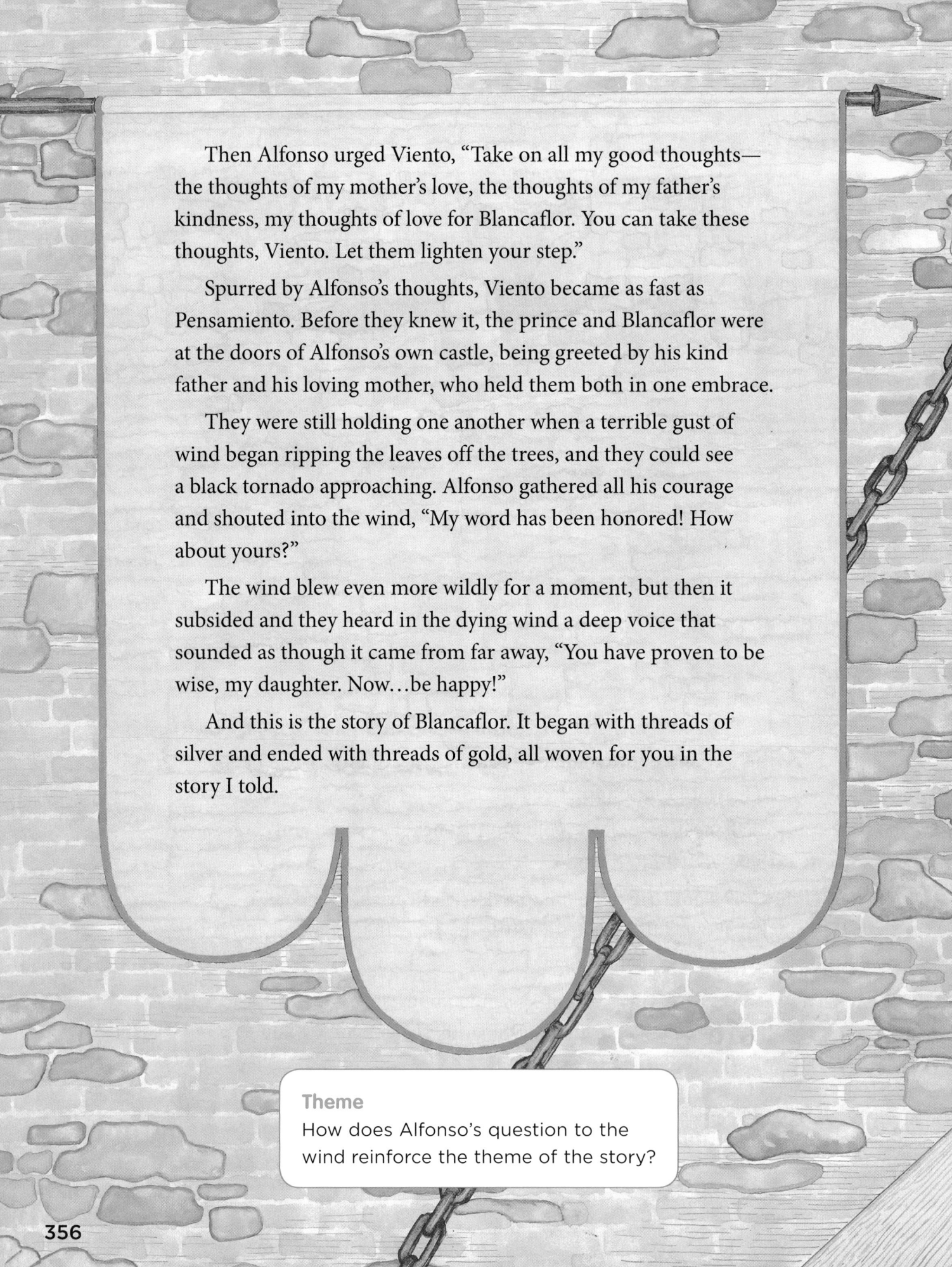

Then Alfonso urged Viento, "Take on all my good thoughts—the thoughts of my mother's love, the thoughts of my father's kindness, my thoughts of love for Blancaflor. You can take these thoughts, Viento. Let them lighten your step."

Spurred by Alfonso's thoughts, Viento became as fast as Pensamiento. Before they knew it, the prince and Blancaflor were at the doors of Alfonso's own castle, being greeted by his kind father and his loving mother, who held them both in one embrace.

They were still holding one another when a terrible gust of wind began ripping the leaves off the trees, and they could see a black tornado approaching. Alfonso gathered all his courage and shouted into the wind, "My word has been honored! How about yours?"

The wind blew even more wildly for a moment, but then it subsided and they heard in the dying wind a deep voice that sounded as though it came from far away, "You have proven to be wise, my daughter. Now…be happy!"

And this is the story of Blancaflor. It began with threads of silver and ended with threads of gold, all woven for you in the story I told.

Theme
How does Alfonso's question to the wind reinforce the theme of the story?

357

Talking with
Alma Flor Ada and Valerie Sokolova

By the time she was in fourth grade, **Alma Flor Ada** knew that she would be a writer someday. "Most of my stories I told aloud before I ever wrote them down," says Alma Flor Ada. "And it was other people listening and other people being interested that gave me a motivation to write them."

Alma Flor Ada grew up in Cuba, but she has also lived in Spain and Peru. Today she makes her home in San Francisco, California. For Ada, knowing two languages has made her world richer. She believes that all children should be given the chance to learn two or more languages.

Valerie Sokolova was born in Lvov, Ukraine, but now makes her home in Brooklyn, New York. She has been an illustrator for 23 years and has illustrated over thirty children's books in Russia and five picture books in the United States.

Other books by Alma Flor Ada.

LOG ON ▶ Find out more about Alma Flor Ada and Valerie Sokolova at **www.macmillanmh.com**.

CA Author's Purpose

What was the author's purpose for writing this story? Do you think Alma Flor Ada wanted to teach a lesson with this story? Why or why not?

CA Critical Thinking

Summarize

Use your Theme Chart to help you summarize how Prince Alfonso succeeds in honoring the promise he made in *Blancaflor*.

What Does the Character Do and Say?

What Happens to the Character?

Theme

Think and Compare

1. Describe the **theme** of the story in one or two sentences. Explain how the author uses the theme to connect the characters and events. **Visualize: Theme**

2. Prince Alfonso successfully finished three difficult **tasks**. But near the end of the story, he makes a mistake. What was his mistake, and how did it almost cost his and Blancaflor's life? **Analyze**

3. Prince Alfonso felt that he had to honor the promise he made to save his father's life. How important do you think it is to keep a promise? **Synthesize**

4. Think of another story that you have read that has a similar theme to *Blancaflor*. Compare and contrast the two stories. **Apply**

5. Reread "The Party" on pages 338–339. How are Charlotte and Blancaflor alike? Use details from both texts to support your answer. **Reading/Writing Across Texts**

History/
Social Science

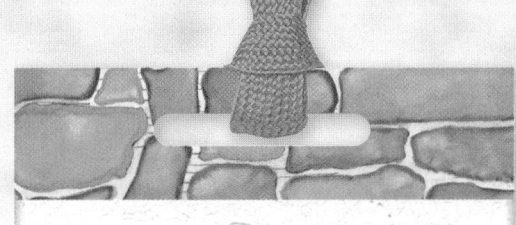

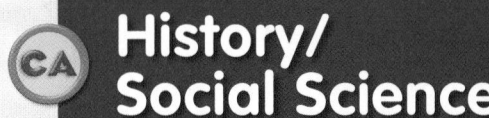

Genre

Nonfiction: A magazine article gives information and facts about a topic.

Text Feature

A **Map** is a drawing of all or part of an area.

Content Vocabulary

rancho	**vaqueros**
missions	**rodeo**

Rancho Life

by Edgar Mera

California was once a land of ***ranchos***, large ranches with workshops, crops, and pasture. Horses came to the Americas with the Spanish, and rancho life depended on horses. Horses were also important characters in many of the folktales of California rancho life.

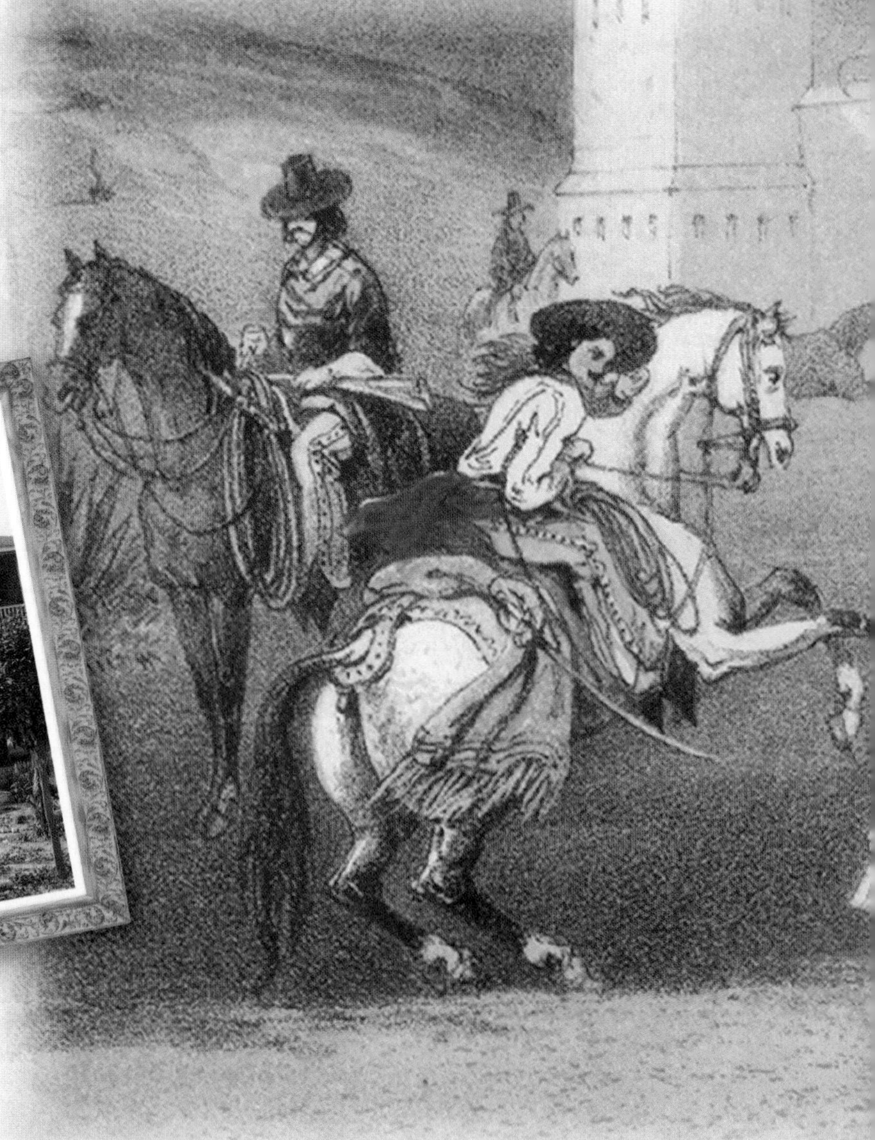

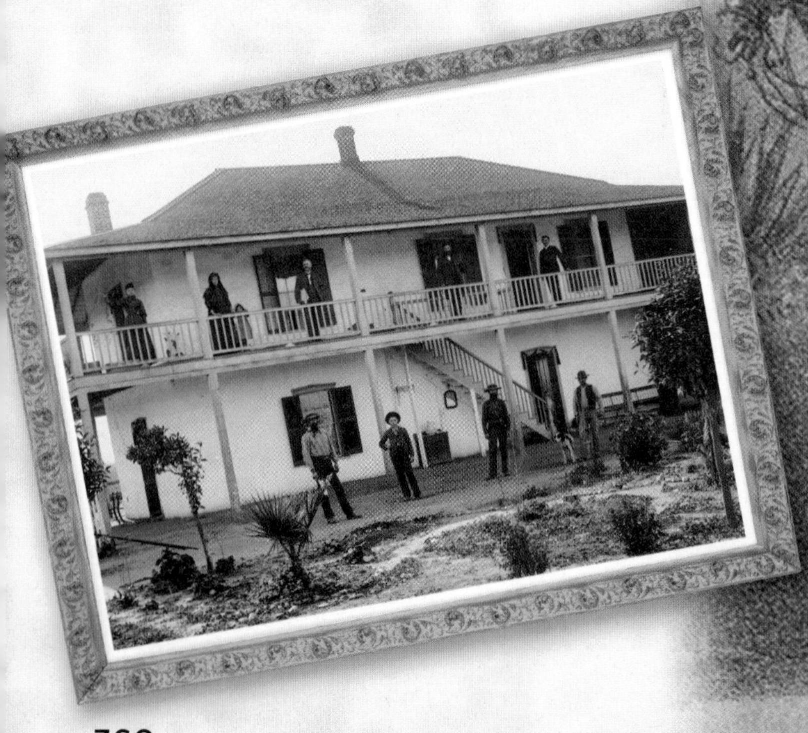

After a long and bloody war, Mexico freed itself from Spanish rule and became an independent country in 1821. The new Mexican government decided to close the **missions** in California and divide the mission lands between the Mexicans and the Native Americans living in California. The *Californios*, as the Mexicans of California were called, turned their lands into ranchos where they could raise animals.

Rancho Customs

The California rancho was a lively place. The *ranchero*, his wife, his children, and other relatives lived there. It took almost one hundred people to run the rancho. Most ranchos were far apart and people had to travel a long way to visit one another. To reward their guests for traveling so far, rancheros and rancheras celebrated with great *fiestas*.

There was great excitement (below) when guests arrived at a rancho. The photo (far left) shows a typical ranchhouse and some of its workers.

Fiestas were a large part of rancho life. Some were held to celebrate weddings and others to celebrate religious holidays. Everyone dressed up in their best colorful clothing, and even the horses' saddles were trimmed in silver. Fiestas provided a chance to take a break from the hard work of the rancho and to have fun.

Work on the Rancho

Much of the hard work on the rancho was done by Native American workers. Many Native Americans were forced to live on the ranchos after the missions were closed. They cooked, cleaned, farmed, and did much of the day-to-day work that made rancho life possible. In exchange for their work, Native Americans received food and a place to live. They had few rights.

Children on a rancho did not go to school. Most of the time, children worked alongside their parents. Girls helped their mothers cook, garden, and sew. Boys worked with their fathers, many of whom were *vaqueros*, or cowhands.

Mexican vaqueros take part in a rodeo, or cattle roundup.

Roundups

For most of the year, cattle roamed across the huge rancho, grazing on the rolling grasslands. Once a year the vaqueros gathered them during the **rodeo**, or roundup. Rodeos also gave vaqueros a chance to show off their riding and roping skills in contests. Modern rodeos are based on the rodeos of rancho days.

Honoring Tradition

Today many parts of California still celebrate the days of fiestas, rodeos, and ranchos. During these celebrations, local residents dress in historical costumes, eat their favorite California/Mexican foods in open-air marketplaces, and enjoy traditional dances, rodeos, and pageants.

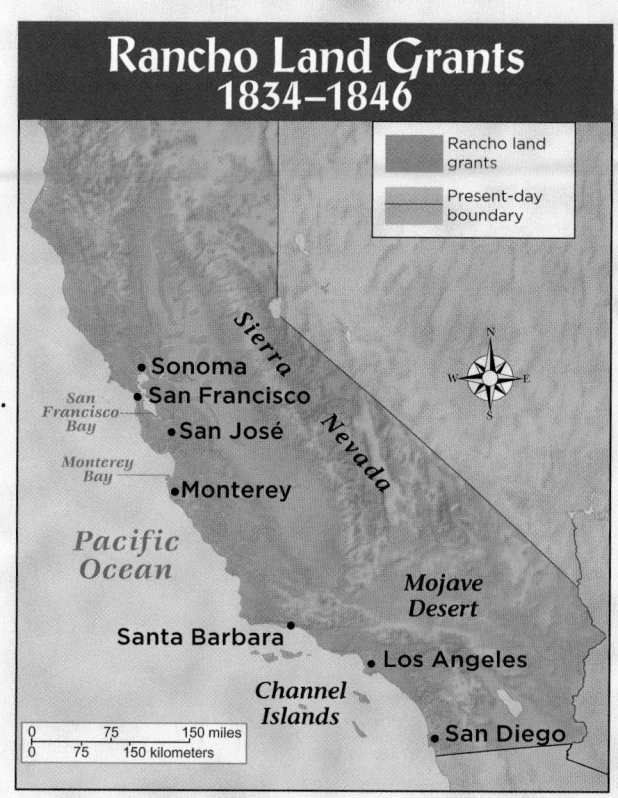

Rancho Land Grants 1834–1846

- Rancho land grants
- Present-day boundary

Sonoma
San Francisco
San José
Monterey
Santa Barbara
Los Angeles
San Diego

San Francisco Bay
Monterey Bay
Pacific Ocean
Sierra Nevada
Mojave Desert
Channel Islands

0   75   150 miles
0   75   150 kilometers

CA Critical Thinking

1. Where were most of the ranchos in California located?
   Reading a Map

2. Compare your daily activities to those of a child living on a rancho. How are the activities similar? How are they different?
   Evaluate

3. What part do horses play in "Rancho Life" and in *Blancaflor*?
   Reading/Writing Across Texts

History/Social Science Activity

Research the history of your town or city. Draw a map that shows how your town looked in its early days.

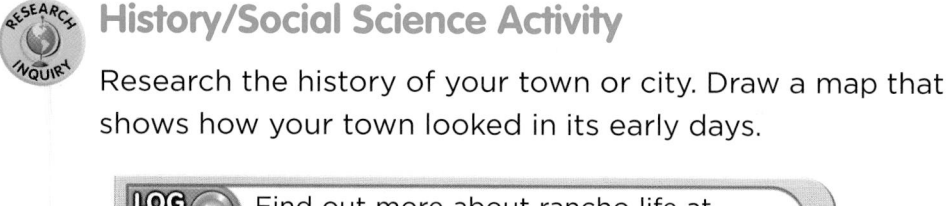

LOG ON ▶ Find out more about rancho life at www.macmillanmh.com.

363

Reading and Writing Connection

✔ Character Development

In a good story, **character development** helps you understand a character. The character's thoughts and actions seem realistic.

Read the passage below. Notice how the author Alma Flor Ada creates a believable character in her story.

An excerpt from
Blancaflor

The author describes the prince's actions in a believable way. If our parents were sick, we would feel sad and lonely, which makes the prince a believable character.

A young prince had gone riding very early in the morning, before the sunrise. Now, tired and sad, he sat under the branches of a large oak tree. He was thinking about his father, the king, who lay in the castle, sick with an illness no one knew how to cure.

Blancaflor
by Alma Flor Ada
illustrated by Valerie Sokolova

Read and Find

Read Derrick's writing below. How did he make his character seem believable? Use the checklist below to help you.

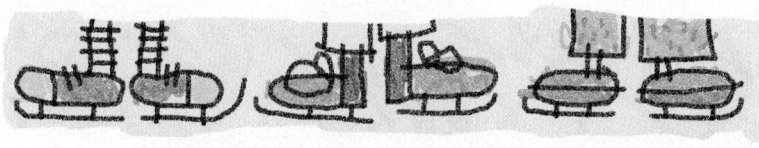

First Skate

by Derrick K.

I laced up my skates. Excitement and nervousness built inside of me making my hands tremble. A puff of breath escaped from my mouth as I took to the ice. My feet wobbled back and forth immediately and I grabbed the side of the rink. This was not going to be easy.

See how I made the character in my story seem believable.

Writer's Checklist

 Does the writer make the character behave in a way that seems familiar to you?

 Are the character's actions consistent? Does he follow through in a way you'd expect?

Does the **character development** seem like someone you might meet in real life?

T·A·L·K·I·N·G

IN C·O·D·E·S

CA **Talk About It**

Name some different kinds of codes. What are some situations in which you might want to talk in code?

LOG ON ▶ Find out more about codes at www.macmillanmh.com.

367

Vocabulary

corridor   invasion
reservation   shield
enlisted   location
transmission   creased

Context Clues

Context Clues are words or phrases that can help you define an unfamiliar word. Clue words can appear in a nearby sentence or somewhere else in the paragraph.

Rita, the Storyteller

by Nina Gabriel

My friend Rita is excited about her new baby sister. She stood in the busy hospital **corridor** watching the baby sleep as people passed by.

Rita's new sister is the newest member of the Meskwaki tribe. Some members of this tribe have never lived on a **reservation**, land set aside for Native Americans by the United States government. Meskwaki are proud of their own traditions, especially storytelling.

The Meskwaki pass on their stories to the very young. Rita loves telling stories. She is very excited to tell her new sister a true story she learned from the elders. It is about the brave Meskwaki code talkers of World War II.

In 1941, twenty-seven men from the Meskwaki tribe **enlisted** in the army because they wanted to fight for their country. From this group eight men were chosen for a secret mission. They became code talkers who used their native language to send secret messages.

Before the code talkers, U.S. troops were not able to move around safely. The enemy was able to understand the messages sent to the troops. The United States turned to the Meskwaki because they had their own language that few outsiders understood. They could send important information in a radio **transmission** without the enemy knowing what was being said.

The group of eight code talkers was sent to North Africa. During an **invasion** some of these code talkers entered enemy territory. The mission took place at night when the **shield** protecting them was darkness. They used walkie-talkies to tell the **location** of the enemy. The position of the enemy was said in code. This information was passed to other code talkers back at camp.

The code was never broken during World War II. The code talkers helped the United States win the war. However, they got little recognition.

When Rita first told me this story, I felt sad. The eight code talkers should be heroes! Rita saw how my shoulders sagged down from my disappointment. My forehead was **creased** as I frowned.

"Don't worry!" she smiled. "In Meskwaki culture we pass down stories about our heroes. The code talkers will never be forgotten."

Reread for **Comprehension**

Generate Questions
Author's Perspective
An Author's Perspective is an author's opinion or point of view toward the subject of the selection. Use your Author's Perspective Chart as you reread the selection to find the author's perspective.

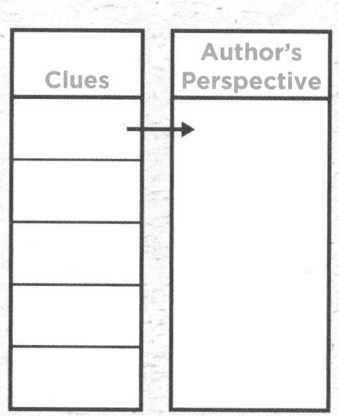

Clues	Author's Perspective

Genre

Historical Fiction tells a story in which fictional characters take part in actual historical events.

Generate Questions

✔ **Author's Perspective**

As you read, fill in your Author's Perspective Chart.

Clues	Author's Perspective
→	

Read to Find Out

How does the author feel about the Navajo language?

The Unbreakable Code

by Sara Hoagland Hunter ◆ illustrated by Julia Miner

Award Winning Selection

John raced up the trail, sending pebbles skidding behind him.
When he reached his favorite hiding place, he fell to the ground out
of breath. Here between the old piñon tree and the towering walls
of the canyon, he felt safe. The river full of late-summer rain looked
like a silver thread winding through his grandfather's farm land.
They would be looking for him now, but he was never coming down.

His mother had married the man from Minnesota. There was
nothing he could do about that. But he was not going with them.
He closed his eyes and rested in the stillness. The faint bleat of a
mountain goat echoed off the canyon walls.

Suddenly a voice boomed above him: "Shouldn't you be packing?"

John's eyes flew open. It was his grandfather on horseback.

"Your stepfather's coming with the pickup in an hour."

"I'm not going," John said.

"You have to go. School's starting soon," said Grandfather, stepping down from his horse. "You'll be back next summer."

John dug his toe deeper into the dirt. "I want to stay with you," he said.

Grandfather's soft, brown eyes disappeared in the wrinkles of a smile. John thought they were the kindest eyes he had ever seen.

"You're going to be all right," Grandfather said. "You have an unbreakable code."

"What's that?" asked John.

Grandfather sat down and began to speak gently in Navajo. The sounds wove up and down, in and out, as warm and familiar as the patterns of one of Grandmother's Navajo blankets. John leaned against his grandfather's knee.

"The unbreakable code is what saved my life in World War II," he said. "It's the Navajo language."

John's shoulders sagged. Navajo couldn't help him. Nobody in his new school spoke Navajo.

"I'll probably forget how to speak Navajo," he whispered.

"Navajo is your language," said his grandfather sternly. "Navajo you must never forget."

The lump in John's throat was close to a sob. "You don't know what it's like there!" he said.

His grandfather continued quietly in Navajo. "I had to go to a government boarding school when I was five. It was the law.

"They gave me an English name and cut my hair off. I wasn't allowed to speak my language. Anyone who spoke Navajo had to chew on squares of soap. Believe me, I chewed a lot of soap during those years. 'Speak English,' they said. But Navajo was my language and Navajo I would never forget.

"Every summer I went home to herd the sheep and help with the crops. I cried when the cottonwoods turned gold and it was time to go back.

"Finally, one night in the tenth grade, I was working in the kitchen when I heard a bulletin on the school radio: 'Navajo needed for special duty to the Marines. Must be between the ages of seventeen and thirty-two, fluent in English and Navajo, and in excellent physical condition.'

"Just before lights out, I snuck past the bunks and out the door towards the open plain. I felt like a wild horse with the lasso finally off its neck. Out in the open, the stars danced above me and the tumbleweeds blew by my feet as I ran. The next day, I enlisted."

"But you weren't seventeen," said John.

"The reservation had no birth records," Grandfather said with a grin. "Two weeks later I was on a bus headed for boot camp with twenty-eight other Navajos. I stared out the window into the darkness. I was going outside of the Four Sacred Mountains for the first time in my life."

"Were you scared?" asked John.

"Of course," said his grandfather. "I didn't know where I was going or what our mission was. Most of all, I didn't know how I would measure up to the people out there I had heard so much about."

"How did you?" asked John, chewing his fingernail.

His grandfather began to laugh. "We were known as the toughest platoon at boot camp. We had done so much marching at boarding school that the drills were no problem. Hiking in the desert of California with a heavy pack was no worse than hauling water in the canyon in midsummer. And I'd done that since I was four years old.

"As for the survival exercises, we had all gone without food for a few days. A Navajo learns to survive.

Author's Perspective
What clues reveal how the author feels about the Navajo platoon?

"One weekend they bused us to a new camp in San Diego. On Monday we were marched to a building with bars on every window. They locked us in a classroom at the end of a long, narrow **corridor**. An officer told us our mission was top secret. We would not even be allowed to tell our families. We were desperately needed for a successful **invasion** of the Pacific Islands. So far the Japanese had been able to intercept and decode all American messages in only minutes. This meant that no information could be passed between American ships, planes, and land forces.

"The government thought the Navajo language might be the secret weapon. Only a few outsiders had ever learned it. Most importantly, the language had never been written down, so there was no alphabet for the Japanese to discover and decode.

"He gave us a list of more than two hundred military terms to code. Everything had to be memorized. No trace of the code could ever be found in writing. It would live or die with us in battle.

"When the officer walked out of the room, I looked at the Navajo next to me and began to laugh. 'All those years they told us to forget Navajo, and now the government needs it to save the country!'

"We were marched every day to that classroom. We were never allowed to leave the building. We couldn't even use the bathroom by ourselves. Each night, an officer locked our notes in a safe.

"The code had to be simple and fast. We would have only one chance to send each message. After that, the Japanese would be tracing our **location** to bomb us or trying to record the code.

"We chose words from nature that would be easy to remember under fire. Since Navajo has no alphabet, we made up our own. 'A' became *wollachee*." "Ant?" asked John in English.

Grandfather nodded.

"'B' was *shush*."

"Bear," said John.

"'C' was *moasi*. 'D', *be*. 'E', *dzeh*." His grandfather continued through the alphabet. Each time he named the Navajo word, John answered with the English.

"We named the aircraft after birds. The dive-bomber was a chicken hawk. The observation plane was an owl. A patrol plane was a crow. Bomber was buzzard.

"At night we would lie in our bunks and test each other. Pretty soon I was dreaming in code.

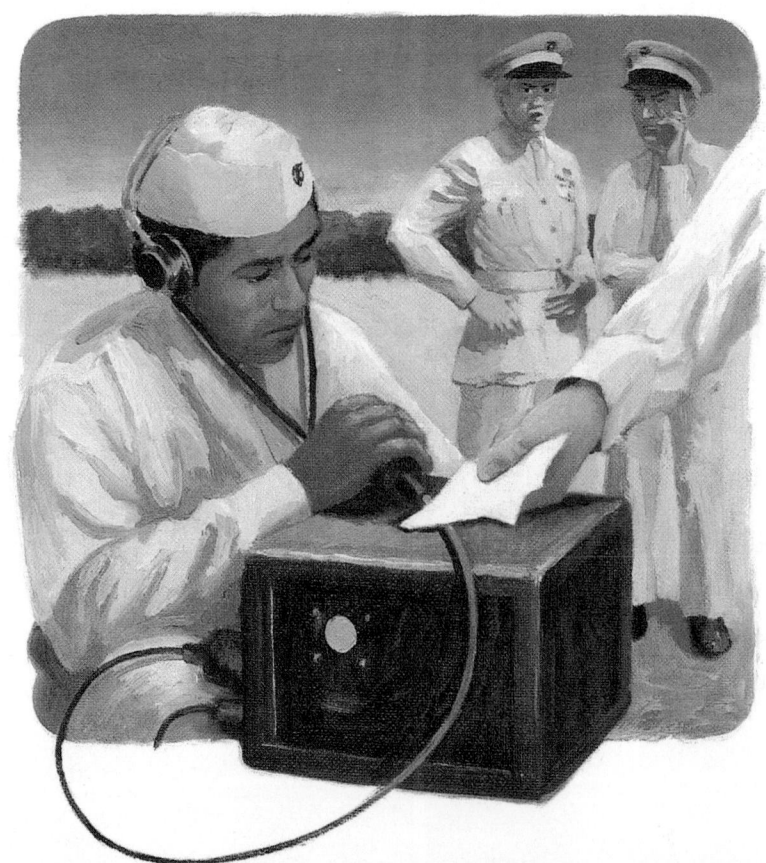

"Since we would be radiomen, we had to learn all kinds of radio operations. We were taught how to take a radio apart and put it together blindfolded. The Japanese fought at night, so we would have to do most of our work in complete darkness. Even the tiniest match flame could be a target.

"When the day came for the code to be tested in front of the top Marine officers, I was terrified. I knelt at one end of a field with our radio ground set. The officers marched towards me. Behind a building at the other end of the field, another code talker sat under military guard waiting for my **transmission**. One officer handed me a written message:

"'Receiving steady machine gun fire. Request reinforcements.'

"It took only seconds for me to speak into the microphone in Navajo code. The officer sent a runner to the end of the field to check the speed and accuracy of the message. The Navajo at the other end handed him the exact message written in English before he even came around the corner of the building! They tested us over and over. Each time, we were successful. The government requested two hundred Navajo recruits immediately. Two of our group stayed behind to train them. The rest of us were on our way."

"Tell me about the fighting!" said John.

Suddenly Grandfather's face looked as **creased** and battered as the canyon walls behind him. After a long pause he said, "What I saw is better left back there. I would not want to touch my home or my family with those pictures.

"Before we invaded, I looked out at that island. It had been flattened and burned. 'Let this never happen to a beautiful island again,' I thought. I just stayed on the deck of the ship thinking about the ceremonies they were doing for me at home. We invaded at dawn.

"I almost drowned in a bomb crater before I even got to shore. I was trying to run through the water and the bullets when I felt myself sinking into a bottomless hole. My eighty-pound radio pack pulled me straight down. I lost my rifle paddling to the surface.

"On the beach, it was all I could do just to survive. I remember lying there with gunfire flying past my ears. A creek that ran to the beach was clear when I first lay there. By noon it was blood red.

"The worst were the fallen soldiers I had to run over to go forward. I couldn't even stop to say I was sorry. I just had to run over them and keep going.

"I had to move through the jungle at night, broadcasting in code from different locations. One unit needed medical supplies. Another needed machine-gun support. I had just begun broadcasting to another code talker. 'Arizona! New Mexico!' I called. The next thing I knew, an American soldier behind me was yelling, 'Do you know what we do to spies?'

"'Don't shoot!' I said. 'I'm American. Look at my uniform.' He didn't believe me. He had just heard the foreign language. He had seen my hair and my eyes. Japanese spies had been known to steal uniforms from fallen soldiers.

"One of my buddies jumped out of the bushes right at that moment and saved my life."

"How did you stay alive the rest of the time?" asked John.

"My belief was my **shield**," Grandfather answered.

He drew a ragged wallet from deep inside of his shirt pocket. "Inside of this, I carried corn pollen from the medicine man. 'Never be afraid,' he said. 'Nothing's going to touch you.' And nothing ever did. More than four hundred code talkers fought in some of the bloodiest battles of World War II. All but a few of us survived.

"The Japanese never did crack the code. When they finally discovered what language it was, they captured and tortured one poor Navajo. He wasn't a code talker and couldn't understand the message they had intercepted. He told them we were talking about what we ate for breakfast. Our code word for bombs was 'eggs'.

"Six months before the war ended, Navajo code talkers passed more than eight hundred messages in two days during the invasion of Iwo Jima.

"When the American flag was raised on top of Iwo Jima's mountain, the victory was announced in code to the American fleet. 'Sheep-Uncle-Ram-Ice-Bear-Ant-Cat-Horse-Itch' came the code."

John tried to spell out the letters.

"Suribachi?" asked John.

"Yes," said Grandfather. "Mount Suribachi.

"When I came home, I walked the twelve miles from the bus station to this spot. There weren't any parades or parties.

"I knew I wasn't allowed to tell anyone about the code. I looked down at that beautiful canyon floor and thought, 'I'm never leaving again.'"

"But why did you leave in the first place?" asked John.

His grandfather lifted him gently onto the horse. "The answer to that is in the code," he said. "The code name for America was 'Our Mother.' You fight for what you love. You fight for what is yours."

He swung his leg behind John and reached around him to hold the reins.

"Keep my wallet," he said. "It will remind you of the unbreakable code that once saved your country."

John clutched the wallet with one hand and held the horse's mane with the other. He wasn't as scared of going to a new place any more. His grandfather had taught him who he was and what he would always have with him. He was the grandson of a Navajo code talker and he had a language that had once helped save his country.

> **Author's Perspective**
> How does the author feel about the Navajo code talkers? How can you tell?

385

Decoding the Facts about Sara Hoagland Hunter and Julia Miner

Sara Hoagland Hunter was a teacher and a journalist before she combined her interests and started her own company. Today she writes and produces books as well as videos, scripts, and albums for children. For this book Sara interviewed the "code talkers." She found them kind and strong, and she felt privileged to be able to tell their story.

Julia Miner became interested in illustrating this book when her college classmate Sara Hoagland Hunter told her about the idea. They made several trips to Arizona to meet with actual code talkers, which helped them capture the spirit of the Navajo code talkers' experience. Besides illustrating children's books, Julia is an architect and writer. Often she travels to different countries for inspiration for her illustrations.

 Find out more about Sara Hoagland Hunter and Julia Miner at **www.macmillanmh.com**.

 Author's Purpose

Why do you think the author wrote *The Unbreakable Code*? What makes the story historical fiction?

386

 Critical Thinking

Summarize

Understanding an author's perspective can help you organize ideas and make judgments about the piece you are reading. Use your Author's Perspective Chart to help you write a summary of *The Unbreakable Code*.

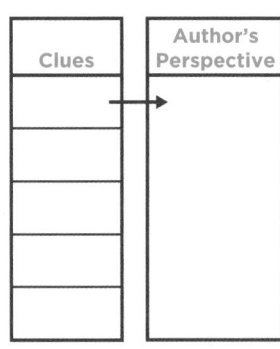

Think and Compare

1. Use details from the Author's Perspective Chart to describe the author's **point of view** about the Navajo code talkers. Explain how the story would change if the author felt differently. **Generate Questions: Author's Point of View**

2. Reread page 382. What is Grandfather's belief? How was it like a **shield** during the war? Use story details to explain. **Analyze**

3. Describe why you would or would not like to have been a Navajo code talker. Explain your answer. **Apply**

4. Grandfather says that "You fight for what you love." Explain why you agree or disagree with his statement. Include examples from your experience in your answer. **Evaluate**

5. Reread "Rita, the Storyteller" on pages 368–369. In what ways are Rita's and John's family histories and traditions similar? In what ways are they different? Use examples from both selections to support your answer. **Reading/Writing Across Texts**

387

Poetry

A **Cinquain** is a five-line poem. The first line has two syllables. The next lines have four, six, eight, and two syllables, respectively.

✔ Literary Elements

Consonance is the repetition of end and intermediate consonant sounds in a series of words.

Symbolism is the use of objects to represent or express ideas, concepts, or qualities.

Navajo Code Talkers
Five Cinquains
by Mary Willie

Uncle
Remembers how
He and fellow fearless
Navajo Code Talkers saved lives
And hope.

Try to
Imagine this:
Dangerous night with stars
Cold stars different from the ones
Back home.

Secrets
We sent kept safe
In this ancient language.
No enemies could understand
Secrets.

The repetition of "t" in *sent* and *kept* is an example of consonance.

This code
Bold invention,
Created for wartime
By brave soldiers, who marched in lines
Like ants.

Soldiers
Guarded the Flag.
The word *America*
Whispered in code as "our mother"
Kept safe.

The words "our mother" symbolize the soldiers' feelings about America.

 **Critical Thinking**

1. Find another example of consonance in one of the cinquains. **Consonance**

2. How does the poet feel about the code talkers? **Analyze**

3. Compare these cinquains to *The Unbreakable Code*. What details from both texts give you clues about how the Navajo felt about fighting in World War II? **Reading/Writing Across Texts**

LOG ON ▶ Find out more about cinquains at **www.macmillanmh.com**.

Reading and Writing Connection

✔ **Character Development**

Good writers use **character development**, to show the character's thoughts and actions and make them realistic or believable.

Read the passage below. Notice how the author Sara Hoagland Hunter develops a believable character in her story.

An excerpt from
The Unbreakable Code

The author describes John's actions in a believable way. Some people hide away when they are upset, which makes John seem realistic.

John raced up the trail, sending pebbles skidding behind him. When he reached his favorite hiding place, he fell to the ground out of breath. Here between the old piñon tree and the towering walls of the canyon, he felt safe. . . . They would be looking for him now, but he was never coming down.

The
Unbreakable Code
by Sara Hoagland Hunter   illustrated by Julia Miner

Read and Find

Read Monique's writing below. How did she make her character seem believable? Use the checklist below to help you.

Test Time

by Monique G.

Patty stared at the test booklet on her desk. A or C? A or C? Both answers seemed right. Her leg began to bounce up and down, and her hands turned cold and clammy. She glanced around the room. A or C? Patty stared at her test miserably, then slowly filled in the bubble next to A.

Read how I developed the character of Patty in my story.

Writer's Checklist

 Does the writer make the character behave in a way that seems familiar to you?

 Does the character seem like someone you might meet in real life?

Is the **character development** believable? Does she behave in ways you would expect?

Review

Theme
Cause and Effect
Draw Conclusions
Context Clues
Metaphor
Time Line

Ben's Bugs Blog

Ben loved insects. Wherever he went, Ben would inspect plants and check under rocks to see what bugs he could find.

Ben used to collect samples in bottles and jars. When an especially scary-looking bark beetle escaped in the house one day, his parents said enough was enough. They told Ben not to pick up or even touch any more bugs. As a compromise, they agreed to buy him a camera so that he could take pictures of them instead.

One day, Ben decided to create a Web site to share his pictures. His parents helped him. Then they created a special e-mail account so that people could comment on Ben's pictures. After thinking up several names, they decided on "Ben's Bugs Blog."

Every day after school, Ben would log on to his Web site and add a new blog entry. His reports included the types of insects, where he saw them, and how many there were.

After six weeks, Ben hadn't received even one e-mail about his blog. He worried that no one was reading it.

Ben decided to make his blog a bit more exciting. "Killer Bugs Attack Local Nursery," Ben wrote for his headline. His story told about a rare kind of beetle that liked to (as he put it) "bite babies."

Within a day, Ben received his first e-mail. "Those poor children!" wrote the local librarian, whom Ben had told about his Web site. Another e-mail came later that day. It was from Professor Kamil at the local college. He wrote that he had been reading "Ben's Bugs Blog" as part of his research on local insect life. He had been surprised by this latest entry and asked if it was true.

Ben admitted that he had stretched the facts, but that parts of the story were true. Insects had killed several young plants at the local tree nursery.

The professor wrote Ben back immediately. He had been tracking a new kind of beetle and wondered where it had come from. Now he knew. The beetles were coming from the trees the nursery was selling.

Ben promised Professor Kamil that he would report exactly what he observed and not make things up again. In return, the professor asked Ben to become a field researcher for the college. With that job title, Ben would have no problem getting people to read his blog!

The Reader
This butterfly
Which on a poppy clings
Opens, shuts
Its book of tiny paper wings.
- *Buson*

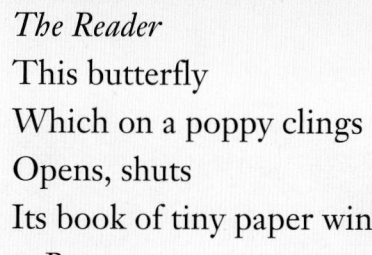

Thomas Alva Edison, INVENTOR

T HE NEXT TIME YOU ENJOY A MOVIE, turn on a light, or use a battery-powered toy you might want to thank Thomas Alva Edison. This famous inventor is responsible for at least 1,000 inventions we use every day.

Edison was born in Ohio in 1847. He began working when he was 12 years old, selling newspapers and food to people on trains headed for Detroit. When he was 15, he saved the son of a man who ran the railroad station. The young boy had wandered onto the train tracks with a train approaching. Edison was able to pull the boy out of the way in the nick of time.

As a reward, the boy's father taught Edison how to use a telegraph. Afterward, Edison began to work for Western Union Telegraph Company. He became fascinated with the telegraph and began working to improve it and other mechanical devices.

Edison's first invention was the stock ticker, which recorded the purchase and sale of stocks. Over the next fifty years, he invented a motion picture camera and made improvements to the electric light bulb. His favorite invention, however, was the phonograph. Edison discovered that he could record sound on cylinders coated with tinfoil. He made a machine that had two needles. One of the needles recorded sound, and the other one played the sound back.

Edison believed in working long hours, and sometimes he worked more than twenty hours a day. He said, "Genius is one percent inspiration and 99 percent perspiration." He set a goal in 1876 to have one major invention every six months, and he came very close to that goal. During his life, Edison applied for and received more than 1,093 patents, the most ever issued to one person. He enjoyed designing new things, but he also wanted people to actually use them.

Not everything Edison worked on was a success. He also had a few failures. He started the Edison Portland Cement Co. in 1899. He wanted to make everything out of cement, including furniture, pianos, and houses. Concrete cost a great deal of money at the time, and the idea never took off. He also worked on machines to process iron ore, which were never successful.

Edison's successes make our everyday lives easier. To honor Edison, President Herbert Hoover ordered all electric lights dimmed for one minute on October 21, 1931, a few days after Edison's death.

Some of Thomas Edison's Inventions

1869	Universal stock ticker
1872	Automatic telegraph system
1877	Phonograph
1879	Incandescent light bulb
1891	Motion-Picture camera
1896	Fluorescent electric lamp
1914	Electric miner's safety lamp

CA Critical Thinking

Now answer questions 1 though 4. Base your answers on the story "Ben's Bugs Blog" and the poem "The Reader."

1. **Which statement is a theme of "Ben's Bugs Blog"?**

   A   People should collect different kinds of bugs.

   B   It's always better to tell the truth rather than make things up.

   C   Lots of people read blogs.

   D   Taking pictures is fun.

2. **Read this sentence from "Ben's Bugs Blog."**

   > Ben would <u>inspect</u> plants and check under rocks to see what bugs he could find.

   What does *inspect* mean?

   A   pick up

   B   leave

   C   smell

   D   examine

3. **In the poem, "The Reader," the poet compares a butterfly to a**

   A   book.

   B   newspaper.

   C   flower.

   D   door.

4. **Why did Ben's parents buy him a camera? Use details and information from the story to support your answer.**

Now answer questions 1 though 4. Base your answers on the article "Thomas Alva Edison, Inventor."

1. **Based on the article, you can conclude that Edison**

   A   believed that the secret to success was hard work.

   B   thought inventions should be fun but not useful.

   C   did not like to set goals for himself.

   D   enjoyed riding the train.

2. **Read the sentence from the article.**

> He became <u>fascinated</u> with the telegraph and began working to improve it and other mechanical devices.

The word *fascinated* means

   A   frustrated.

   B   annoyed.

   C   interested.

   D   bored.

3. **The time line helps the reader to**

   A   find out about Edison's childhood.

   B   quickly locate the year something was invented.

   C   learn how Edison invented the phonograph.

   D   know what year the telephone was invented.

4. **Edison's concrete company failed because**

   A   nobody wanted concrete furniture.

   B   concrete was too expensive.

   C   people did not like Edison's concrete furniture.

   D   concrete furniture was too heavy to move.

Write on Demand

PROMPT What effect did working at the Western Union Telegraph Company have on Edison? How did it help to shape the rest of his life? Use details from the article to support your answer. Write for 10 minutes. Write as much as you can as well as you can.

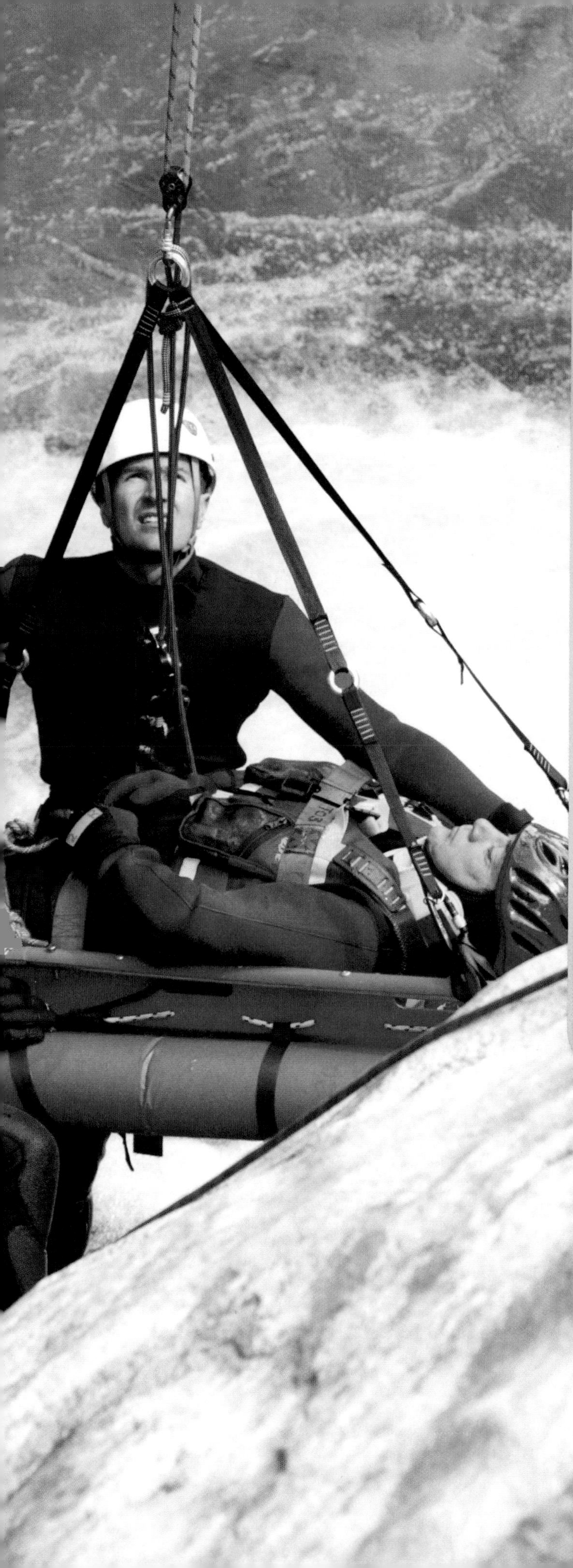

Unit 4
Team Up to Survive

The Big Question

How can teamwork help in a difficult situation?

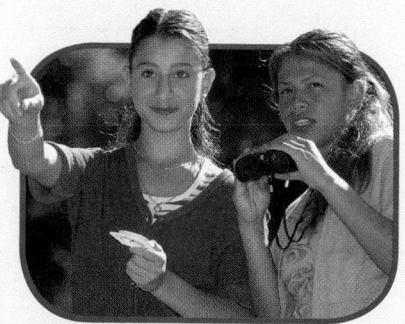

Theme Launcher Video

LOG ON Find out about people working together at **www.macmillanmh.com**.

Did you ever hear the old saying, "There's safety in numbers"? Well, it's true. Young people are much safer in groups of three or more.

So if you are going somewhere at night, make sure you have at least two friends with you. If you're on a hike, make sure there is a group and that everyone has a piece of equipment or a supply—such as a flashlight, a compass, water, a map, a cell phone, blankets—that will help in case you get lost.

Even if you are simply on a trip to a new city or country, be prepared and work as a team with your family or friends. Learning about teaming up to survive will help you better plan your own life and keep safe.

Research Activities

Throughout the unit, you will be gathering information about teaming up to survive. Choose one incident where people had to team up to survive and create a multi-media presentation about it.

Keep Track of Ideas

As you read, keep track of all you are learning about teamwork. Use the Chart Foldable. On the top section, write the Unit Theme: Teaming Up to Survive. In the columns, write facts you learn about teamwork each week.

FOLDABLES®
Study Organizer

Unit Theme	Week 1	Week 2	Week 3	Week 4	Week 5

Research Toolkit

Conduct Your Unit 4 Research Online with:

Research Roadmap
Follow step-by-step guide to complete your research project.

Online Resources
- Topic Finder and other Research Tools
- Videos and Virtual Fieldtrips
- Photos and Drawings for Presentations
- Related Articles and Web Resources

California Web Site Links

Go to **www.macmillanmh.com** for more information.

California People

Richard Stowell, Naturalist

A former independent school administrator, Richard Stowell founded Naturalists at Large to help students build outdoors skills and awareness.

401

EXTREME
CONDITIONS

 **Talk About It**

This man and his dogs work as a team to rescue people. Why is teamwork important in conditions such as extreme cold or heat?

LOG ON ▶ Find out more about surviving extreme conditions at **www.macmillanmh.com**.

ICE and More ICE

by Tamika Washington

People often think of the North and South poles as similar frozen wastelands. They are both places with **frigid** temperatures and few people. However, the North and South poles are not much alike.

The North Pole has no land, only thick sheets of ice. Temperatures rarely go above 32°F, which is the freezing point for water. Most of the time, the thermometer stays below zero. Winter temperatures as low as -30°F are common.

Despite such **treacherous** conditions, people tried for many centuries to reach the North Pole. Then about 100 years ago, two men were able to **triumph** over this tough environment. Robert Peary and Matthew Henson reached the North Pole on March 8, 1909. It was not an easy trip.

There are few things more dangerous than crossing the Arctic on foot. Explorers can face many problems: freezing temperatures, sudden storms, even starvation. Most of the area is **uninhabited** by people. Few people can live in such a harsh place.

One might think that with freezing temperatures for most of the year, the ice pack would be thick and hard. However, this is not true in the Arctic. The movement of ocean currents under the ice causes constant changes on the surface. Sometimes the ice breaks apart, opening lanes of water called "leads." Anyone who falls into a lead can drown or freeze to death in minutes.

Peary, Henson, and the other members of their **expedition** ran into this problem constantly. They learned to move in packs of three or four men, so that if something happened a member of the team would be nearby to help. Henson once slipped into a lead and was rescued just in time by his Eskimo assistant, Ootah.

Another time, four members of Peary's team became trapped on an ice island. The island was formed when leads opened around their igloo in the middle of the night. One of the men woke up just in time, or they would have floated out to sea.

The men built igloos each night to protect themselves from the wind while they slept. An igloo is a small hut made of hard, packed snow. Cutting the blocks in the freezing cold was back-breaking **labor**. Sometimes the wind was very strong, and it **dismantled** the igloos before morning.

Some members of Peary's team gave up and turned back. But Peary and Henson refused to **abandon** their expedition. Their hard work paid off. They became the first people to reach the North Pole!

Reread for **Comprehension**

Generate Questions
Problem and Solution
A Problem and Solution Map helps you identify problems in a selection and the solutions that solve them. Reread the selection and use your Problem and Solution Map to identify problems the writer presents and the actions that are taken to solve them.

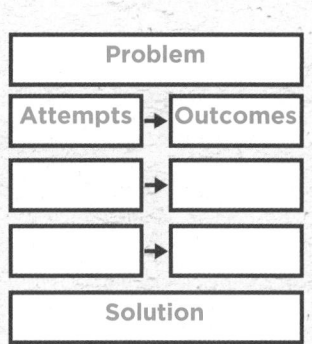

| Problem |
| Attempts → Outcomes |
| → |
| → |
| Solution |

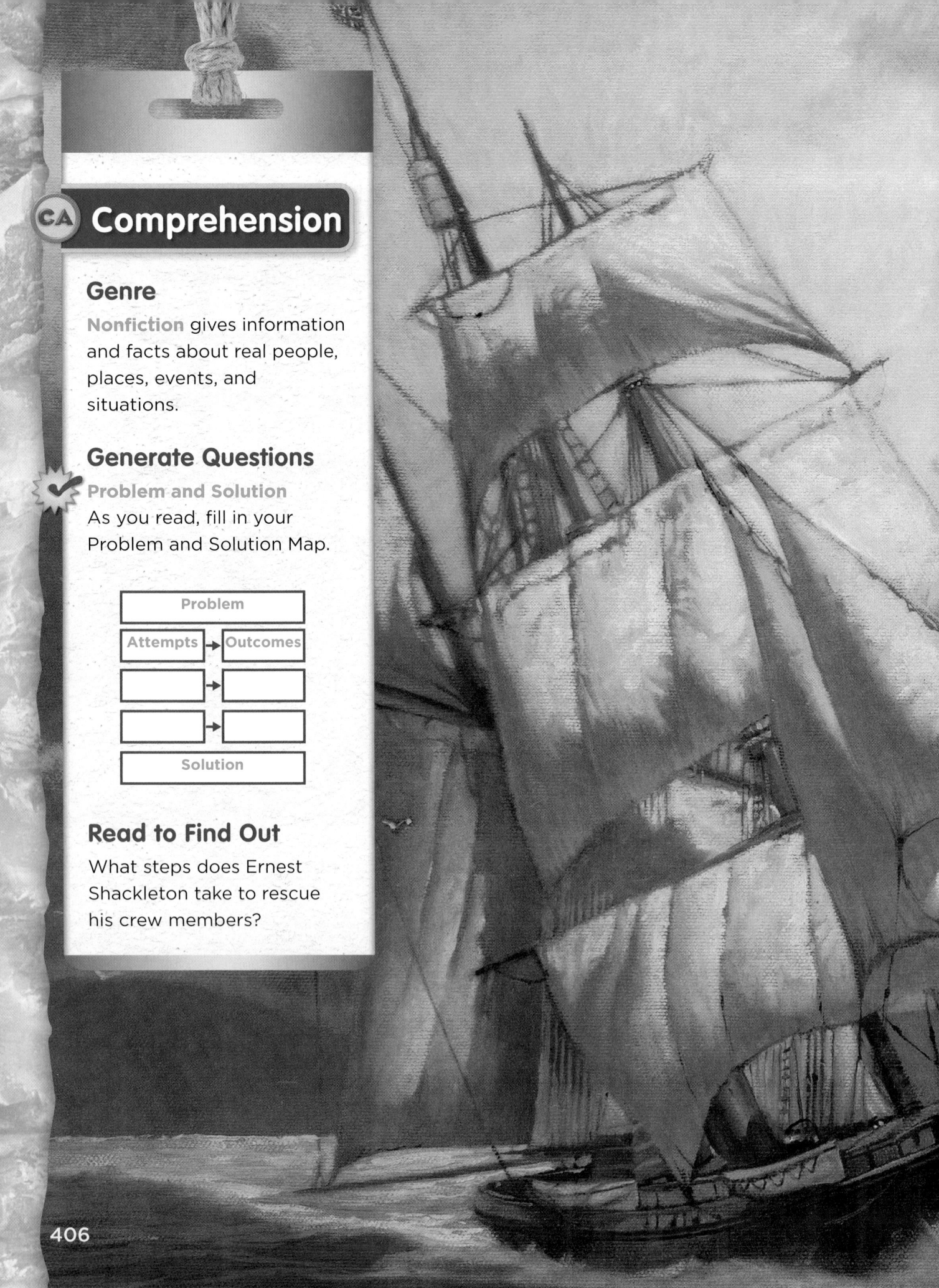

CA Comprehension

Genre

Nonfiction gives information and facts about real people, places, events, and situations.

Generate Questions

Problem and Solution

As you read, fill in your Problem and Solution Map.

Problem

Attempts	→	Outcomes
	→	
	→	

Solution

Read to Find Out

What steps does Ernest Shackleton take to rescue his crew members?

Spirit of Endurance

by Jennifer Armstrong
illustrated by William Maughan

When Ernest Shackleton was young, he fell in love with books and adventure. At 16 he set off to sea to explore the world. His most famous adventure took place in Antarctica in January of 1915. On Shackleton's third expedition to Antarctica, the **frigid** waters on the Wedell Sea that borders Antarctica froze over. Shackleton's ship, the *Endurance*, became stuck in the ice. Shackleton's goal was to be the first explorer to trek 1,500 miles across the **treacherous** continent. Would he and his crew **triumph**? Or would the ice prove to be too much?

The weather outside *Endurance*'s cozy cabins was terrible. Furious winds howled across the ice. Blizzards drove snow into drifts against the sides of the ship. Sometimes the wind was so fierce that it pressed the ice floes against *Endurance*. The ship's wooden timbers squeaked eerily as the pressure grew stronger. The force of the ice was so great that Shackleton began to worry that *Endurance* would be seriously damaged. What if they were forced to **abandon** the ship?

One night in July, at the height of a winter storm, the pressure grew stronger than ever. Shackleton shared his fears with the captain, Frank Worsley.

"If the *Endurance* does have to, well, get left behind, we will manage, somehow," Worsley said to the Boss.

Shackleton replied, "We shall hang on as long as we can. It is hard enough on the men as it is. Without a ship in which to shelter from these blizzards, and in this continuous cold—" He broke off and paced the cabin. He didn't want to think about it. But as commander of the **expedition**, Shackleton had to prepare for the worst.

The members of the Endurance *expedition, photographed as the ship sailed south. Shackleton is in the center, in the hat and buttoned white sweater. Second-in-command Frank Wild is standing behind Shackleton's left shoulder. Next to Wild is the captain of* Endurance, *Frank Worsley (in the white sweater and seaman's cap).*

Frank Hurley (left) and the ship's meteorologist (weatherman), Leonard Hussey, play chess during a night watch.

The ice continued to press against *Endurance* through August and September. On some days, it rammed the ship so sharply that it knocked books and tools and equipment off shelves and made the masts tremble like twigs. The men were becoming frightened and jumpy. Each time the ship let out a squeak or groan from its straining hull, they held their breath.

The crew **dismantled** the dogloos and brought all the animals back on board because they were afraid that the ice would break up under the dogs. One day in October, the ice pressed nonstop against the sides of *Endurance*, pushing the ship over on its port side. Everything that wasn't fastened down crashed onto the decks. For several terrifying minutes, the men thought the ship was done for.

But the pressure stopped, and *Endurance* settled back into place. They were safe—for now.

Then, in the third week of October, the pressure started up again and continued without relief. *Endurance* groaned and creaked as the ice squeezed from all sides. The timbers began to buckle and snap. Water began leaking into the hold.

Endurance photographed at night in August 1915—the depth of the Antarctic winter. The ship is covered with frost, making it white against the inky sky.

The crew took turns at the pumps, trying to keep the water out, but it was no use. On October 27, Shackleton looked around at the ship, which was being crushed like a nut in a nutcracker before his eyes.

"She's going, boys. I think it's time to get off," he said.

Then the crew of *Endurance* abandoned ship—in the middle of the frozen sea.

Luckily, the destruction of *Endurance* happened in slow motion. This gave the crew plenty of time to unload food and equipment. As the ship continued to break up, the pile of gear on the ice grew larger: suitcases, books, clocks, sleeping bags, guns, crates of flour and sugar, clothes, lifeboats, diaries, axes, scrap lumber, toothbrushes, buckets—everything that could be taken off the ship was removed. The crew worked without a break. Their survival would depend on saving everything that might come in handy.

Finally, exhausted, they pitched their tents and crawled inside to sleep. Meanwhile, the timbers and rigging of *Endurance* snapped and crashed onto the deck of the dying ship.

While the rest of the men slept, Shackleton held a conference with his second-in-command, Frank Wild, and with the skipper of *Endurance*, Frank Worsley. With no way to communicate with the outside world, they were completely on their own. If they were going to survive, they would have to rescue themselves.

They came up with a plan: they would drag their three lifeboats, filled with food and equipment, across the ice to Paulet Island. It was 346 miles away. When Shackleton told the men in the morning what lay ahead of them, they reacted calmly. They trusted his leadership. If he said they would walk 346 miles, then that was what they would do.

> **Problem and Solution**
> What kind of plan does Shackleton devise after his crew abandons the *Endurance*? What are the possible outcomes of this plan?

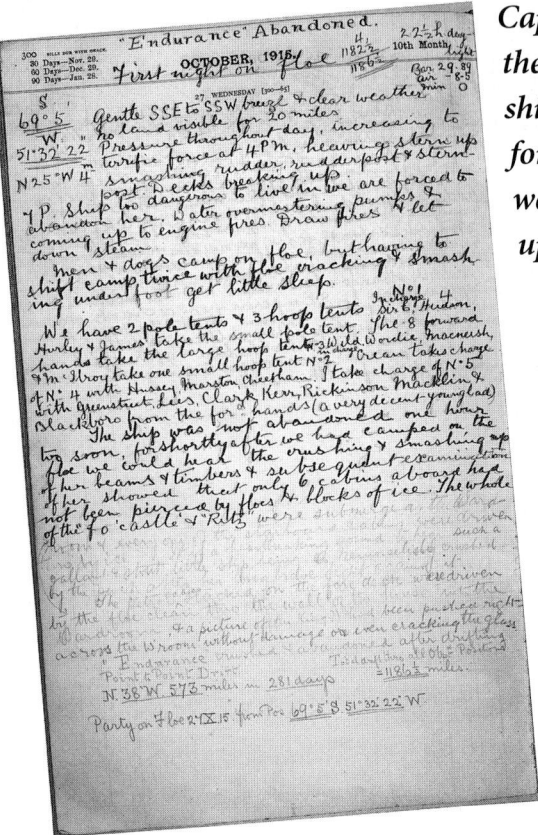

Captain Frank Worsley's logbook describes the day Endurance *was abandoned.* "The ship was not abandoned one hour too soon, for shortly after we had camped on the floe we could hear the crushing and smashing up of her beams and timbers..."

The dogsleds, each loaded with 900 pounds of gear, went in the lead. The drivers struggled to hack a path through the jumbled ice field with axes and shovels. Behind came the three boats, pulled in stages by fifteen men in harness. They dragged one boat forward a quarter of a mile, left it, and returned for the second boat. When the third boat was hauled up to join the other two, they began dragging the first boat again.

But it was torture. The surface of the ice was broken and uneven, and the men sometimes sank to their knees in freezing slush while the snow swirled down onto them. After two hours of backbreaking **labor**, they were only a mile from *Endurance*. At this rate, they would never reach Paulet Island. The floe they were on was solid: they would set up camp and stay put.

Ocean Camp was to be their home for the next two months. They returned to *Endurance* for more equipment and food. With lumber rescued from the ship, they built a cookhouse to hold an oil stove.

Then they settled in to wait. Shackleton knew that the ice they were camped on was drifting north and would carry them to the open ocean. Eventually, they would need to take to the lifeboats. Once the ice drifted into warmer waters, it would not be stable enough to camp on. Their only hope of rescue lay across the water. So the carpenter worked on improving the boats and making them more seaworthy.

The Antarctic spring was under way now, and temperatures sometimes climbed into the thirties, which seemed almost tropical to the men. They continued to hunt, to exercise the dogs, and to keep themselves busy with books and card games and chores. Just keeping their gear dry in slushy Ocean Camp was a steady job.

Slowly, the ice drifted away from Antarctica. Large cracks appeared on their ice floe. The surface became soft. November 21 brought an unforgettable event: the broken, twisted wreck of *Endurance* finally slipped through the ice and sank forever. In December, Shackleton decided they should move again, hoping to narrow the distance between themselves and Paulet Island.

But the going was tough: it still took three days to cover seven miles. After two more days of backbreaking effort, it looked as though they were stuck. The ice was mush and unstable. They couldn't go back. They couldn't go forward. They would have to make another camp.

They called this one Patience Camp, and patience was what they needed. The year 1915 was drawing to a close and the new year was before them.

Dragging one of Endurance's *lifeboats across the ice.*

What lay ahead? Shackleton couldn't be sure. The drift of the ice was haphazard. Sometimes they were carried north, sometimes east or west.

The months of February and March dragged by.

By early April, the ice floe that Patience Camp sat on was alarmingly small, and leads of open sea surrounded them. Killer whales spouted in the water as they hunted seals. The men could feel the rise and fall of the ocean lifting their floe, and some of them began to feel seasick.

On April 8, Shackleton gave the order: "Launch the boats!"

Thousands of birds circled overhead as the crew shoved the boats off the ice. Sitting on their gear and their last crates of food, the men bent to the oars. Waves crashed against icebergs. The three boats picked their way through the maze of ice, pulling north toward the open ocean.

As the light faded, they began looking out for an ice floe to camp on. Shackleton soon spotted one. Luckily, a large seal was sleeping on it, and the men quickly killed it and cooked it for dinner. Then they pitched their tents and tried to get some rest.

Launch the boats! The crew, with their provisions, crowd into three small lifeboats...and set off for Elephant Island...

The next days were filled with danger and hard work. Once they left the shelter of the ice pack, the violence of the open ocean met them like a hurricane. Waves broke over the tiny, crowded lifeboats, and howling winds and sleet lashed the men's faces. The temperature sank. The men could hear ice crackling on their clothes and on the sails that now filled with wind. Sleep was out of the question. They were low on drinking water and short on food. The men were beginning to break.

Shackleton feared that the boats would become separated or that some of the men would die of exhaustion. But ahead of them, somewhere, lay a tiny, rocky islet called Elephant Island. If they could make that, they would be able to rest.

At the limit of their strength, the men saw Elephant Island between tattered rags of mist. They had been in the boats for seven days, climbing giant waves, trying to keep from freezing—seven days with little sleep, little food, no water. When at last they landed, the men fell to their knees on the shore, weeping and laughing.

It was the first time in almost a year and a half that they had stood on solid ground.

Elephant Island was solid ground, but it was also **uninhabited**, and winter was approaching. They would not just wait for a ship to come along and rescue them—it might never happen.

After three days of much needed rest, Shackleton announced that he would take the best boat, the *James Caird*, and sail back to South Georgia Island, over 800 miles away, to get help. He would take Captain Worsley, for his sailing skills; the carpenter, Harry McNeish, in case the boat needed repairs on the way; and three other men. After he reached the whaling station, he would return to rescue the crew.

McNeish reinforced the boat. The men collected fresh water from a glacier on the island. They made the *James Caird* as seaworthy as possible. On April 24, 1916, the *James Caird* shoved off.

For more than two weeks, Shackleton and his five-man crew sailed across the stormiest ocean in the world, facing 100-foot waves, bitter temperatures, and hurricane-force winds. The twenty-two-foot boat was often covered with ice, and the men had to crawl across the decking while the boat heaved and pitched to chop the ice away.

They slept in shifts, crawling into the bow to grab what rest they could. Worsley navigated the best he knew how, although conditions were terrible. In order to calculate their position, he had to be able to see the sun at noon—and with the stormy weather, that was possible only four times. If they lost their way and missed South Georgia Island, they would be headed out into the vast Atlantic Ocean, and that would mean certain death. The men were constantly drenched with salt water and spray as waves broke across the boat. They ached with cold.

Shackleton kept them going with hot meals and drinks—six times a day. Lighting their little camp stove on the bucking boat was tricky, and the moment their cocoa or stew was ready, they put the stove out to save fuel. They learned to eat and drink their meals scalding hot and let the food warm their numbed bodies.

If Shackleton feared they wouldn't make it, he never let on. Day after day he sat at the tiller, scanning the horizon. And with Worsley's almost miraculous skill with compass and sextant, the battered boat and its exhausted crew reached the island on the seventeenth day.

There was just one problem: they had landed on the southwest side of the island, and the whaling station was on the northeast side. The boat was too damaged to risk sailing it around in the stormy waters. But the interior of the island was blocked by a range of jagged mountains and glaciers. They would have to cross it on foot.

Two of the men were completely broken down and a third would have to stay and look after them. That left Shackleton, Worsley, and second officer Tom Crean to make the hike across South Georgia Island.

Problem and Solution
Once the men landed safely on South Georgia Island, what was the next big problem they faced? How did they overcome it?

The voyage of the James Caird. Only twenty-two feet long, the boat has two masts and three small sails and is steered by a rope yoke attached to the rudder. Worsley calculates the Caird's position by sighting the sun through an instrument called a sextant. The cutaway shows the cramped space below, where one man sleeps in the bow and two prepare a meal using a camp stove.

417

Their mountaineering equipment wasn't the best gear they could have wished for on a climb such as this one. They had an ax and fifty feet of rope. They studded the soles of their boots with nails for a better grip on the icy peaks. They rested for several days. Then, with food for three days and a small camping stove, they set out, crossing the first snowfield by moonlight.

Months of poor nutrition and inactivity had left them in no shape for a rugged hike. But as the Boss said long afterward, "The thought of those fellows on Elephant Island kept us going all the time.... If you're a leader, a fellow that other fellows look to, you've got to keep going. That was the thought which sailed us through the hurricane and tugged us up and down those mountains."

South Georgia Island had never been crossed before. There were no trails, no clue which passes led to safety and which ones led to sheer drops. The men rested and cooked quick meals, and pushed on. The Boss didn't dare let them stop to sleep, fearing that they might lose the will to continue. On they trudged, hour after hour, through the first night and a day, then another night. By the next morning, they were haggard, exhausted, and trembling with cold, but they were within sight of the eastern coast.

Faintly, from far below, came the sound of the seven o'clock whistle at the whaling station. They had reached safety at last.

Back on Elephant Island, the rest of the crew had no idea of the Boss's triumph. Once the *James Caird* had disappeared from view, the twenty-two remaining members of the expedition set to work. Frank Wild, in charge, decided on the first task. Antarctic winter was sweeping up from the South Pole, and they would have to shelter themselves from it.

They scavenged the beach for rocks and built a low foundation. Then they took the two remaining boats, the *Dudley Docker* and the *Stancomb Wills,* and turned them upside down over the stones. The tattered canvas sails were lashed across the boats, and the chinks in the walls were stuffed with moss to keep out the wind. They rigged a chimney from some small sheets of metal and installed the blubber stove. When they were done, they had a crude hut to wait out the winter in.

The first storms came quickly. While the winds howled outside their cabin, the men kept each other company. A popular pastime was listing their favorite foods—after a steady diet of seal meat and penguin, the men dreamed of fresh fruit, cakes, and roast beef. The hours passed slowly. The days passed slowly. The weeks passed slowly. Camp Wild was a dreary place.

There were jobs to do: ice had to be chipped off the glaciers and melted for drinking water. There were penguins and seals to hunt.

And there was an operation to be performed. Percy Blackborrow's feet had frozen on the boat journey to Elephant Island, and gangrene had set in. Now the toes on his left foot were dead and black and had to be amputated. There were few medical supplies left. But the expedition's doctors, James McIlroy and Alexander Macklin, performed the surgery by the light of a seal oil lamp.

Outside the hut, the winds screamed over the cliffs of Elephant Island. Sea ice crowded the shore. They knew Shackleton could not return until the winter was over.

Camp Wild. The Dudley Docker *and the* Stancomb Wills *have been overturned and covered with sails to make a hut, where the remaining members of the crew wait for Shackleton to return with a rescue ship.*

419

Rescue! Shackleton returns to Elephant Island to bring home his men. In the background is the Yelcho, *the ship that Shackleton borrowed from the Chilean government for the rescue attempt.*

Wild tried to keep the men optimistic. Every morning, he rolled up his sleeping bag and said to the men, "Get your things ready, boys. The Boss may come today."

But as the months went by, they began to wonder if "today" would ever come.

When Shackleton, Worsley, and Crean walked into the whaling station on May 20, they looked like wild men. They were in rags, their faces black from oily smoke, and their hair and beards long and matted. Dogs barked in alarm as they staggered to the station manager's house.

"Who are you?" asked the manager.

"My name is Shackleton," the Boss replied.

There was stunned silence. No one had expected to see Shackleton alive, let alone see him come walking down from the peaks of South Georgia Island. But when the Boss told their story, they were treated as heroes.

The three weary men were given hot baths and hot food, and allowed to sleep. As soon as they awoke, Shackleton began arranging a rescue party. Worsley set out in a boat with some of the whalers to pick up the men on the other side of the island.

A steamer was outfitted to make for Elephant Island, and Shackleton left at once. But the weather and the ocean were against him. He was forced to turn back for South Georgia Island. Twice more he tried, but the cruel Atlantic winter was too brutal.

June and July went by, and Shackleton was desperate to get his men. At last, in August, he took a Chilean ship called the *Yelcho* and made once more for Elephant Island.

On August 30, George Marston, the expedition artist, was keeping lookout at Camp Wild. On the horizon, he saw the smoke of a ship's funnel. "SHIP HO!" he yelled.

The *Yelcho* steamed into the bay, and a boat was lowered over the side. It was Shackleton. "Are all well?" he shouted as soon as he was near enough.

"YES!"

The men crowded around the Boss as he landed, shaking his hand. "We knew you'd come back," one said to him.

They had all survived. Shackleton had returned to take them home.

ATLANTIC OCEAN

SOUTH GEORGIA ISLAND

Departed South Georgia Island December 5, 1914

Landed May 10, 1916

James Caird *departed April 24, 1916*

Landed April 15, 1916

ELEPHANT ISLAND

Lifeboats launched April 8, 1916

PACK ICE

ANTARCTIC CIRCLE

Endurance *sank November 21, 1915*

Endurance *crushed October 27, 1915*

Entered pack ice December 19, 1914

SOUTH AMERICA

SOUTH GEORGIA ISLAND

DRAKE PASSAGE

WEDDELL SEA

SOUTH POLE

ROSS SEA

ANTARCTICA

Trapped in pack ice January 19, 1915

500 MILES

ANTARCTICA

Exploring with Jennifer Armstrong and William Maughan

JENNIFER ARMSTRONG always felt like a writer, even when she thought about becoming an archaeologist. She says, "I always had a good imagination and loved making up stories. It just seemed natural to me that I would become an author." When she was researching this book, Jennifer went on an unusual field trip to Antarctica. There she saw seals sunbathing, penguins squealing, and Shackleton's winter "house" still standing a century later. Luckily Jennifer ate her own food instead of the canned food left behind by Shackleton. After surviving the South Pole, Jennifer returned to her home in New York.

Another book by Jennifer Armstrong:
Shipwreck at the Bottom of the World

WILLIAM MAUGHAN is both an accomplished artist and teacher. His art has appeared in books and magazines as well as on television and in the movies. When William isn't drawing about Shackleton's heroic trek, he is teaching art to his students—and learning from them at the same time. "Every teacher will admit they learn more from their students than their students learn from them," William says. William lives in California with his wife and seven children.

LOG ON ▶ Find out more about Jennifer Armstrong and William Maughan at **www.macmillanmh.com**.

(CA) Author's Purpose

It is clear that Jennifer Armstrong is informing the reader about Ernest Shackleton's third expedition to Antarctica. The text is full of verifiable facts. Point to examples in the text.

 Critical Thinking

Summarize

Write a summary of *Spirit of Endurance* using your Problem and Solution Map. Be sure to identify the major problems that Shackleton and his men faced, and explain how they solved them.

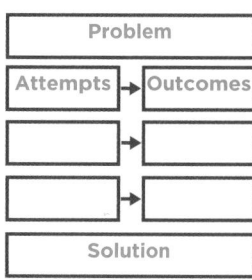

Think and Compare

1. Why did the author choose a **problem** and **solution** structure to tell Shackleton's story? Use details from the selection in your answer. **Generate Questions: Problem and Solution**

2. Think about the problems Shackleton's crew faces. What words would best describe the crew? Use selection details in your answer. **Analyze**

3. What would you name a ship that was about to set out on a long and dangerous **expedition** like Shackleton's? **Apply**

4. Describe the characteristics of a strong leader like Shackleton. Tell why such qualities are important for leaders. **Analyze**

5. Reread "Ice and More Ice" on pages 404–405. Suppose that Shackleton's journey would have taken him to the North Pole instead of to the South Pole. How do you think the search for help for his crew might have been different? Use evidence from both selections to support your answer.
Reading/Writing Across Texts

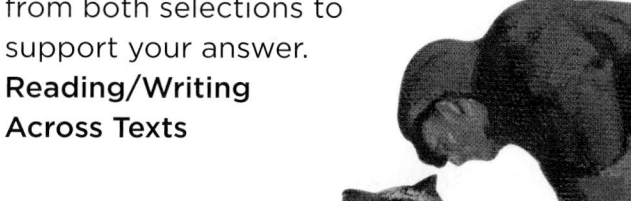

Genre

Nonfiction tells readers about actual people, places, things, or events.

✔ **Text Feature**

A **Primary Source** is information written by someone who actually saw the events described.

Journals and **Letters** are two types of primary sources. Journals are daily records written for a person's own use. Letters communicate information to someone else in writing.

Content Vocabulary

continent

permanent

observations

Exploring the Earth
TOP TO BOTTOM

by Mary Ann Williams

The Top of the World

Explorers have long been interested in the mysteries of the North Pole and its ocean. The Arctic Ocean is the smallest of the world's oceans. It is located at the North Pole and is covered with ice throughout the year. All of the living things in and around the Arctic Ocean must compete for food to survive. Plants, animals, and one-celled organisms, or living things, called protists, are connected in this environment.

The main food chain begins with *phytoplankton*, which are very small, plantlike organisms. These are an important part of the ecosystem of the Arctic. They provide food to *zooplankton*, which are tiny marine animals. Larger animals and fish, such as Arctic cod, then eat the zooplankton. Polar bears are the top predators. They live by eating fish, birds, ringed seals, walruses, and beluga whales.

A World in Sea Ice

The sea ice covering the Arctic Ocean is also an important part of its ecosystem. Sea ice is formed from seawater. It is also where many species of Arctic animals live. Ice algae grow like mold on a damp ceiling. *Melosira*, a green, stringlike form, hangs from the sea ice like moss. The ice algae eventually come loose and fall to the seafloor. Then animals eat the algae. Maintaining this cycle is important.

Researchers who visit the Arctic Ocean see more than most of us might expect. Though far from the rest of the world and covered with ice, it is very active and alive!

PRIMARY SOURCE

This letter shares personal information about an experience in the Arctic.

June 18

Dear Dan,

While you have spent your summer weekends diving off the Florida coast, I've been doing some ocean research of my own. To do my research, though, I have had to cut holes through ice as thick as twelve feet! Yes, I have gone to the Arctic research station I told you about, and the North Pole is like no place I have ever seen.

My job is to check for the effects of climate change on the living things up here. You wouldn't believe how much wildlife we find. Scuba diving is tricky, and not just because of the cold. Polar bears don't like us! We always have to keep our eyes open for them. I don't blame them for wanting to protect their homes. I wish there was a way to tell them that we are here for the same reason.

Stay warm for me!

Randy

The Bottom of the World

It may be hard to believe that any part of today's Earth has gone unexplored. However, the **continent** of Antarctica at the South Pole has held onto many of its secrets. Why is this?

Explorers of Antarctica must face darkness, cold temperatures, and harsh weather. The inner part of the continent, which stays dark, has temperatures of –126°F. High winds and blowing snow can create "whiteouts." In a whiteout, the sky and ground blur together and a person cannot tell which way is up.

PRIMARY SOURCE

This journal provides a daily record of Jennifer Dewey's stay at a South Pole research station.

November 12

For millions of years Antarctica, the fifth largest continent, has been in the grip of an ice age. It is the windiest, coldest, most forbidding region on Earth, and I am heading straight for it.

"Goodbye, America," I whisper as the airplane heaves off the ground with a shuddering roar. "See you later."

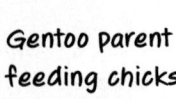

Gentoo parent feeding chicks

November 24th
Palmer Station, Antarctica

- is five and a quarter million square miles; it's larger than Europe.

- has no native human population.

- contains two thirds of the planet's freshwater in the form of glaciers.

- has one hundred million penguins in residence.

- has only one mammal, the Weddell seal (named for an early explorer), that lives there all year long.

- has only two flowering plants: Antarctic hair grass (*Deschampsia antarctica*) and Antarctic pearlwort (*Colobenthos subulatus*).

Research at the South Pole

Despite these challenges, countries have now established **permanent** scientific stations where scientists stay and work on the continent. One such modern-day adventurer is Jennifer Owings Dewey. During a four-month stay, she kept a journal. This daily record of her **observations** and other events can serve to help her remember her experiences. The information may also prove useful for her research later.

Facing obstacles of harsh weather, distance, and darkness, explorers continue to be drawn to Earth's remote places. Their hard work and scientific records help all of us understand more about our planet.

CA Critical Thinking

1. Think about the information Dewey recorded. What is the value of keeping a journal? **Reading a Primary Source**

2. How would you explain to a friend what role the polar bear plays in the ecosystem of the Arctic Ocean? **Apply**

3. In *Spirit of Endurance*, Ernest Shackleton and his crew take a trip to Antarctica. Based on what you know about Antarctica, as well as the Arctic Ocean, what advice would you give someone else planning a polar exploration? **Reading/Writing Across Texts**

Science Activity

Pick one of the world's oceans, not including the Arctic Ocean, and research its ecosystem. Write two paragraphs summarizing your research.

Find out more about the North and South poles at **www.macmillanmh.com**.

Reading and Writing Connection

Read the passage below. Notice how the author Jennifer Armstrong describes the setting.

An excerpt from
Spirit of Endurance

The author describes the harsh setting the crew of the *Endurance* is facing. Notice how she uses sensory detail and strong verbs to help convey the brutal cold so the reader can picture the setting the way Shackleton and his crew experienced it.

The weather outside *Endurance*'s cozy cabins was terrible. Furious winds howled across the ice. Blizzards drove snow into the drifts against the sides of the ship. Sometimes the wind was so fierce that it pressed the ice floes against *Endurance*. The ship's wooden timbers squeaked eerily as the pressure grew stronger. The force of the ice was so great that Shackleton began to worry that *Endurance* would be seriously damaged. What if they were forced to abandon ship?

428

Read and Find

Read Kevin's writing below. How did he use setting to show where the moment took place? Use the Writer's Checklist to help you.

Vacation!

by Kevin C.

The crisp cool breeze ran over me in time to beat the heat. I could hear waves crashing on the beach. My eyes were closed. I kept a towel over them to keep my face cool. The seagulls were squawking for someone to give them some French fries. "Come build a sand castle!" My brother threw a little sand on my feet to get my attention.

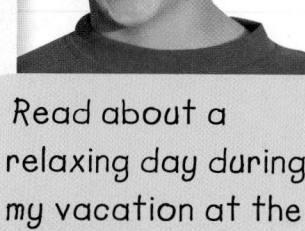

Read about a relaxing day during my vacation at the beach.

Writer's Checklist

 Did the author describe where the story took place?

 Does the author use showing techniques such as strong verbs or sensory details so that you could do more than just "see" the place?

Could you imagine what was around Kevin in this moment?

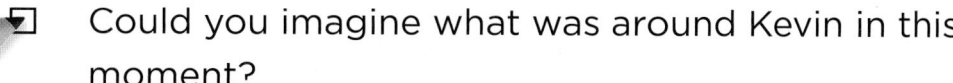

TEAMS ON THE JOB

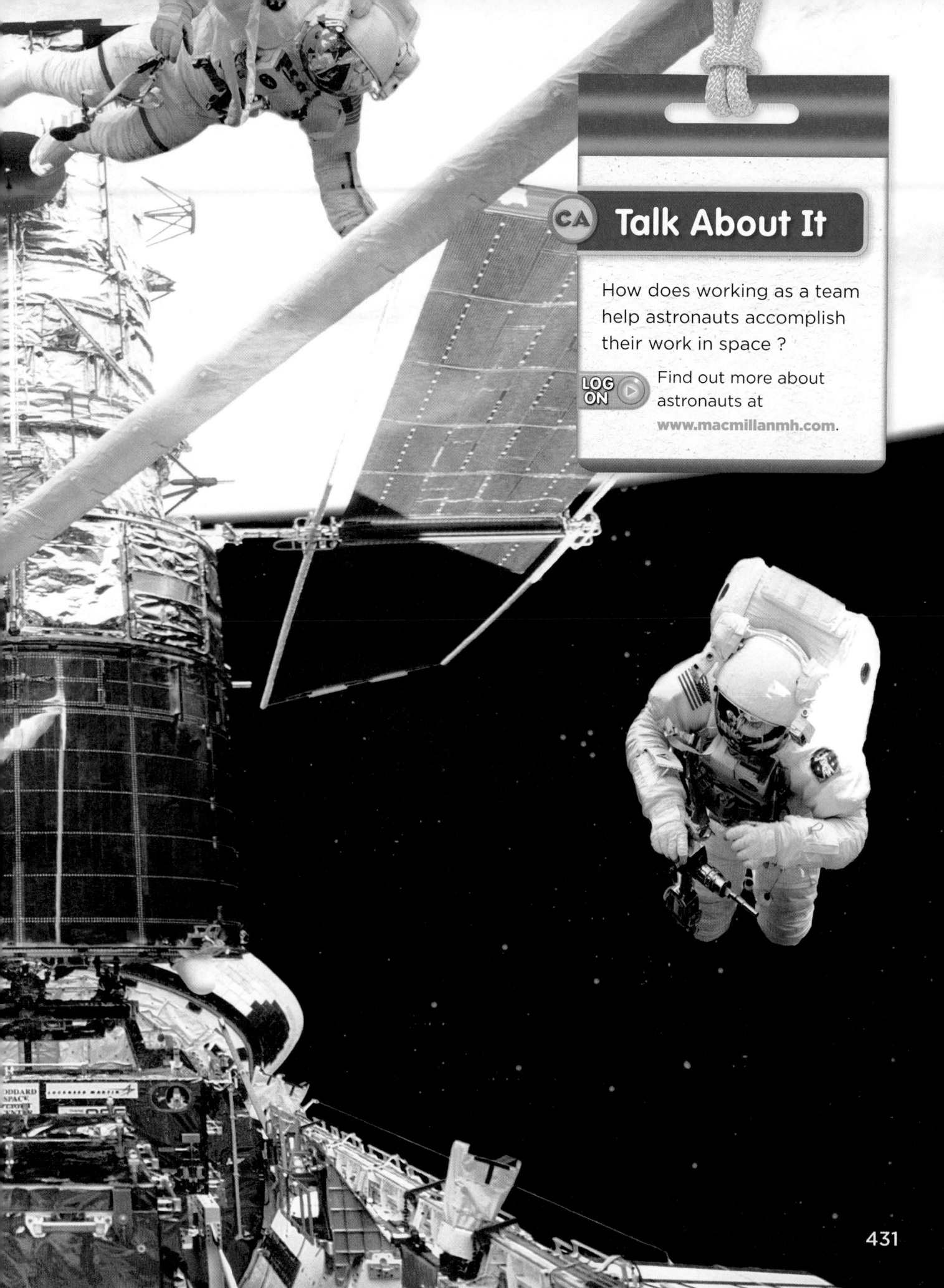

CA **Talk About It**

How does working as a team help astronauts accomplish their work in space ?

LOG ON ▶ Find out more about astronauts at www.macmillanmh.com.

431

JOBS in SPACE

by Latasha Pearson

In the early years of space travel, an astronaut's job was to pilot a spacecraft. Today astronauts do many other types of jobs. These jobs change depending on the goals that must be accomplished on the **mission**.

Astronaut Pilots control and direct the space shuttle. One astronaut pilot is the captain. Captains must make sure the mission is a success. Their job is to keep the crew safe. Captains know that working as a team can prevent **disasters** in space.

Mission Specialists run tests and take care of the equipment on board. The equipment may need to be **adjusted** to fit the task. Sometimes they walk in space or handle the shuttle's robot arm. Astronaut pilots and mission specialists

work for the National Aeronautics and Space Administration (NASA). They learn to live and work in an unusual **environment**. They learn to move in a special **zone** where there is zero **gravity**, the force that pulls things back to Earth. They also figure out how to operate the confusing **maze** of equipment that fills the space shuttle.

Payload Specialists do not work for NASA. These crew members have specific skills and are usually in charge of special projects. They train with the astronauts. Like everyone else getting settled on the shuttle, these specialists have to get used to life in space.

Educator Astronauts are teachers who travel into space. Their job is to encourage students to study science and math. This will help the next generation of astronauts **function** well in space and carry out their jobs successfully.

Reread for **Comprehension**

Generate Questions
Main Idea and Details
The main idea is the most important point an author makes about a topic. The main idea is supported by details that help explain or describe it. Generating, or asking, questions about the information you read can help you identify the main idea. Use your Main Idea and Details Chart as you reread the selection.

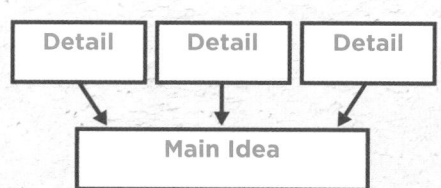

CA Comprehension

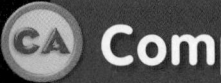

Genre

Nonfiction gives facts about real people, living things, places, or events.

Generate Questions

Main Idea and Details

As you read, fill in your Main Idea and Details Chart.

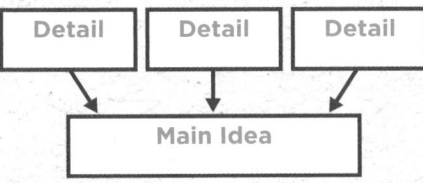

Read to Find Out

How do astronauts prepare for space travel?

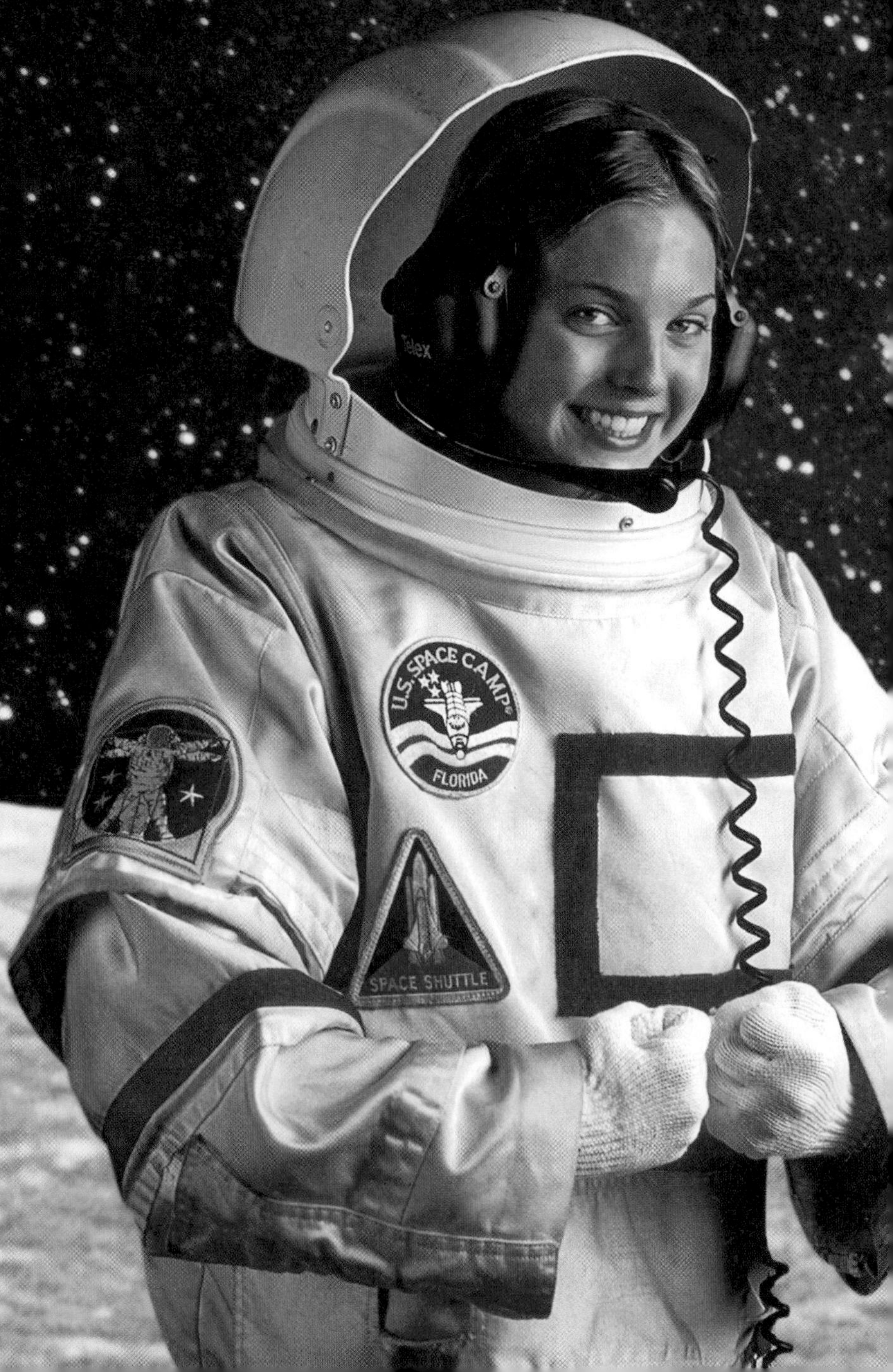

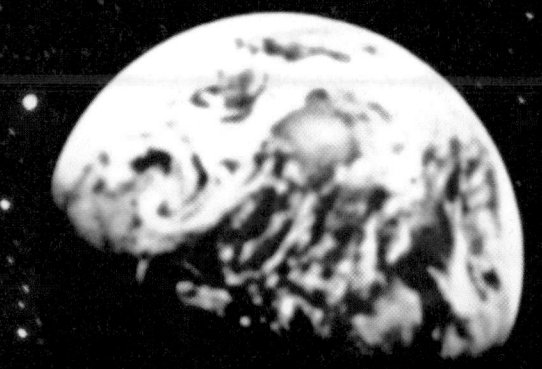

ULTIMATE FIELD TRIP 5

BLASTING OFF TO SPACE ACADEMY

BY
SUSAN E. GOODMAN

PHOTOGRAPHS BY
MICHAEL J. DOOLITTLE

435

Countdown to Adventure

What's the best part of being an astronaut? Is it the thrill of rocketing out of Earth's atmosphere at 25,000 miles per hour? Is it the chance to make new scientific discoveries? Or is it the adventure of leaving the familiar behind and going, as someone once put it, "where no man has gone before"?

Few people actually get to answer these questions by traveling into space. But some kids took the first step by going to U.S. Space Academy at the United States Space and Rocket Center in Huntsville, Alabama.

AMAZING SPACE FACTS

At least half the astronauts experience space sickness at the beginning of their voyage. That's why John Young didn't do Gus Grissom any favor when he smuggled him a corned beef sandwich on the Gemini 3 mission. The story is Grissom threw up; in weightless conditions, that's a difficult cleanup job.

"I can't tell whether this fits or not," said Shane. "Do I look like an astronaut?" Another kid's comment: "If you have to go to the bathroom quick, these flight suits are a bummer."

For almost a week they used the same simulators that real astronauts use and learned how to walk on the Moon and work without **gravity**. They built their own rockets and visited the ones scientists used to launch the Apollo astronauts to the Moon. They tried tasting space food and wearing space suits. They learned how to eat in space, sleep in space, even how to go to the bathroom without any gravity.

During their training they became a team, Team Europa, named after one of Jupiter's seven moons. Then, Europa blasted off on a **mission** of its own. . . .

The Habitat, where kids sleep at Space Academy, was designed as an earthbound space station with stairs and handrails to get from floor to floor. In space, you'd float where you need to go.

On the Training Floor

"**E**uropa, the training center is a dirt-free **zone**," said Paul. "Gum and drinks can create **disasters** here."

Paul, one of Europa's team leaders, led the kids through a **maze** of strange-looking machines. As they walked, the kids peeked at other teams jumping high enough to dunk a basketball and spinning in what looked like a giant gyroscope. Paul explained that astronauts trained for years before going into space. It takes a lot of practice to learn how to **function** in such a different **environment**. On space walks, for example, they must make delicate repairs while floating upside down. In their ships they must learn how to drift rather than walk through the air.

How do they learn these things while anchored by Earth's gravity? To find out, Europa tried some of the simulators that astronauts have used.

The training center is equipped with many simulators.

The ⅙ Gravity Chair

"The Moon has only one-sixth of our gravity," explained Paul. "If you weigh one hundred twenty pounds here, you'd only weigh twenty pounds on the Moon. And you'd have to learn to walk differently because there isn't as much traction."

To practice this movement, the kids used a ⅙ Gravity Chair similar to the Apollo astronauts'. In fact, Europa learned from the astronauts' experiences. The best ways to get around were a slow jog and the bunny hop.

John waited impatiently while Paul **adjusted** the chair to offset five-sixths of his weight.

"Bunny hop for me," said Paul.

"You've got to be kidding," answered John. "I can barely reach the ground."

Soon, however, he was leaping across the training floor.

"This looks like good practice for the high jump," said Stephanie.

"It shouldn't be; you want to jump for distance, not height," said Paul. "Astronaut Charlie Duke of *Apollo 16* tried to set a height record. But his life-support pack changed his center of gravity. He landed on his back and couldn't get up, just like a beetle. If John Young hadn't been around to help him, he could have been stuck there until *Apollo 17!*"

"I felt like I was on a trampoline," said Lindsay, "but I didn't go down—just up!"

Main Idea and Details
What is the main idea of the information on this page? Is it stated or unstated? How do you know?

439

The Multi-Axis Trainer (MAT)

"Remove everything from your pockets," said Bethany, Europa's other team leader. "Take off your necklaces, too, so you don't get whacked in the face."

To get ready for the MAT, some kids took off jewelry; others just took a few deep breaths. The MAT looks like an atom gone wild, with each of its three outer circles spinning separately and you as its whirling nucleus. The Mercury astronauts used it to learn how to regain control of a tumbling spacecraft.

"I couldn't help smiling all the time because it was so much fun," said Lindsay.

The MAT never turns more than twice in the same direction, which is supposed to keep you from feeling sick. That didn't keep a lot of kids from getting nervous. But once they tried it, the glint of silver braces flashed through their smiles.

"It was terrific," said Stacy, "but next time, I'll tie my hair back so it doesn't keep hitting my face."

"It's awesome," Stephanie agreed.

When asked how she'd feel doing it for a ten-minute stretch in a spaceship, Stephanie added, "Your head spins like crazy, but it doesn't feel bad."

The Five Degrees of Freedom (5DF) Chair

On Earth, when you jump up, gravity pulls you back down. In space, you just keep going up. If you push away from a wall, you keep going backward. Bending quickly to grab something could make you do somersaults. To get used to the weightless tumble of space, the Gemini and Apollo astronauts—and the kids at Space Academy—used the 5DF Chair. This chair glided over the floor on a cushion of air like the puck in an air hockey game.

"This is what an EVA, an extravehicular activity, or space walk, feels like," Bethany said, tipping and rolling the chair in all directions to give the kids a taste of the different movements.

Bethany held on to the 5DF Chair to keep it safe. In space, astronauts are tethered to their ship. It's a good thing, too. When astronaut Pete Conrad went on his space walk, he lost hold of *Skylab*. That tether was the only thing that kept him from floating away.

In the 5DF Chair, kids practiced inching their way along a wall. Once Lindsay pushed herself away by accident, she had a hard time getting back.

"Swim, Lindsay, swim!" Courtney called out.

Lindsay tried to breaststroke her way back to the wall—it was hopeless.

"Oh, well," said Charles, "she's *Lost in Space!*"

Space Shot

"This is your last chance to change your mind," said the operator. "Once the generator has been charged, we cannot stop."

In just seconds, the kids were blasting off on the Space Shot. They would rocket skyward with a force of 4 Gs, one more than astronauts experience during their launches. All that force meant that, for a few seconds at the top, before gravity pulled them back, the kids could feel what it was like to be weightless.

Some people call the Space Shot "an elevator with an attitude."

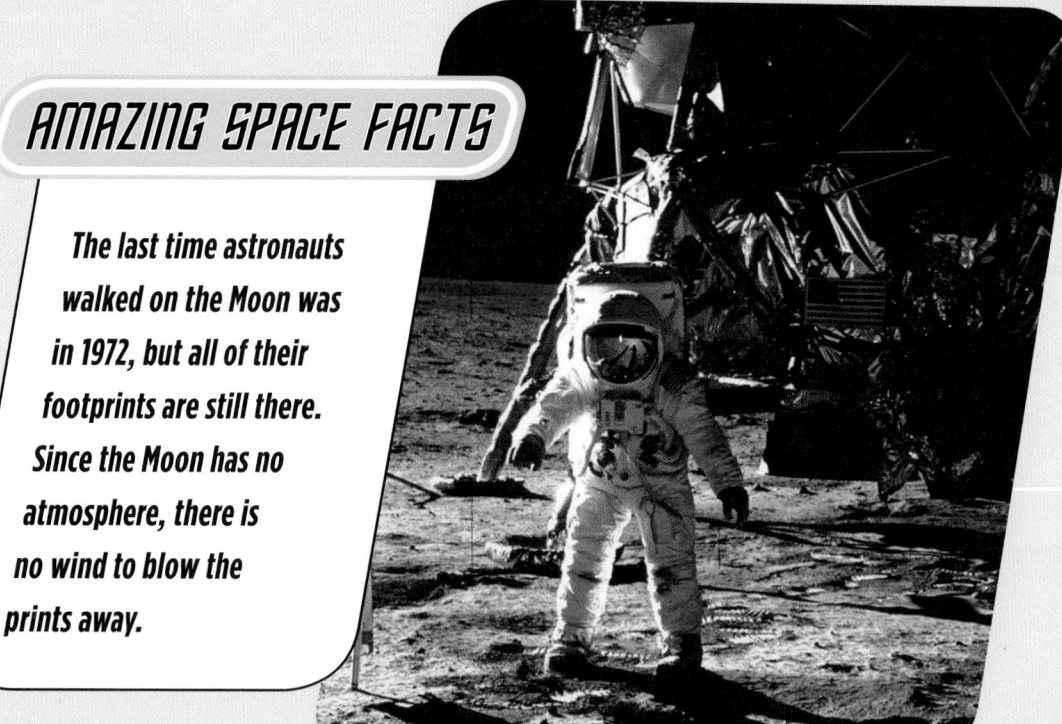

AMAZING SPACE FACTS

The last time astronauts walked on the Moon was in 1972, but all of their footprints are still there. Since the Moon has no atmosphere, there is no wind to blow the prints away.

442

NASA doesn't use the Space Shot to simulate weightlessness; it trains astronauts aboard its KC-135 airplane. The plane climbs sharply and then free-falls straight toward the ground, up again, then down again, and again. For twenty-five seconds, at the top of each roller-coaster ride, the plane's passengers are weightless. But many astronauts have paid a price for this amazing experience. The KC-135 is nicknamed the "Vomit Comet" for good reason.

"I wish I hadn't eaten so much breakfast," said Erin as she waited for her turn on the Space Shot. "I'm going to scream. It helps you not throw up."

Before her second ride, Erin was too excited to feel sick. "I love that feeling of just shooting up there," she said.

"Then you rise up out of your chair and float there for a second," said Stacy. "Weightlessness, I wish it lasted a lot longer."

Main Idea and Details
What is the main idea of the information the author presents under the sub-heading **Space Shot** on pages 442–443?

This is the way Frank and most kids feel going up on the Space Shot . . .

. . . and they feel this way coming down. Devin was amazed that one kid in line thought the experience would cure his fear of heights.

The Pool

Another way the earthbound astronauts simulate working in weightlessness is by going underwater. At Houston's Lyndon B. Johnson Space Center, astronauts practice in a huge water tank holding a full-scale model of the Shuttle's payload bay. At Space Academy, the kids went to a swimming pool.

"Your job is to build a cube underwater as fast as possible," said Bethany. "It takes teamwork, an ability to work in weightlessness, and—something astronauts don't need, I hope—an ability to hold your breath."

Each strut, or tube, belonged in a specific place.

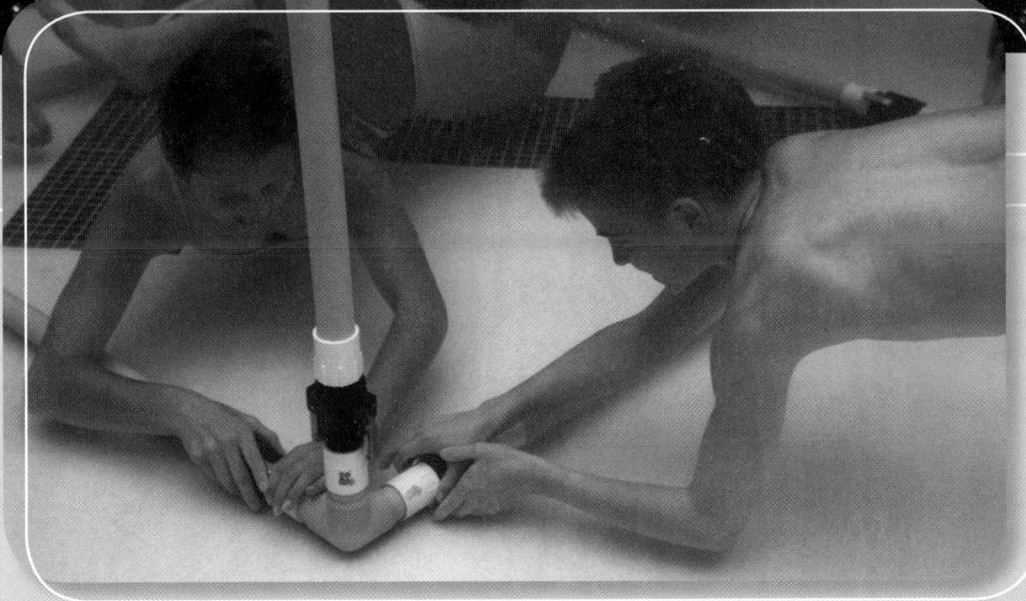

The water started boiling as kids grabbed struts and dove underwater. It kept boiling as they came up for air again and again, slowly realizing they needed a better plan. . . .

"Ten minutes and fifty-six seconds," Bethany said when they finally finished. "Well, every astronaut has to start somewhere. How could you have gone faster?"

"Talk more to each other?" said Isabelle.

"That's right," Bethany agreed. "Communication, letting your leaders lead, and teamwork. It's true in the pool, and it will be even more important when you work to make your own space mission a real success."

Once the kids started working together, the cube was built quickly.

AMAZING SPACE FACTS

Flawed when it went into orbit in 1990, the Hubble Space Telescope was repaired in 1993 during a spectacular mission that required five space walks. Located above our hazy atmosphere, the Hubble sees deep into the universe to reveal black holes, new galaxies, the birth of some stars and the death of others. Its "eagle-eyed vision" is so acute that if the Hubble were on Earth, it could spot a firefly ten thousand miles away!

BLAST OFF WITH SUSAN E. GOODMAN

Susan E. Goodman writes her stories by trying them out first. For this story she actually went to Space Camp at the U.S. Space Academy. There she learned how to do everyday things, like brushing her teeth and "walking" at zero gravity. Experiencing different ways of living helps Susan find the right words when it comes to writing about them. For other stories Susan has stayed in an underwater hotel and even balanced on a girder fifty stories above the ground.

Another book by Susan E. Goodman:
On This Spot: An Expedition Back Through Time

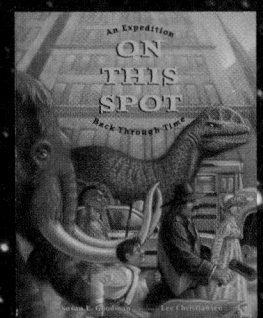

LOG ON ▶ Find out more about Susan E. Goodman at **www.macmillanmh.com**.

CA **Author's Purpose**

Authors of nonfiction often write to inform readers about something. Do you think that is why Susan E. Goodman wrote *Ultimate Field Trip 5*? Explain what clues in the text and captions

Critical Thinking

Summarize

Use your Main Idea and Details Chart to summarize *Ultimate Field Trip 5: Blasting Off to Space Academy*. Your summary should include a main idea from the selection at the beginning of each paragraph.

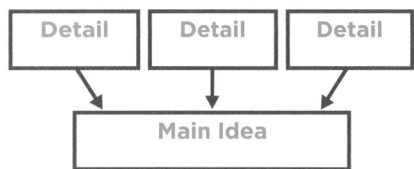

Think and Compare

1. What is the **main idea** on page 440 of *Ultimate Field Trip 5: Blasting Off to Space Academy*? Be sure to include **details** that support the main idea. **Generate Questions: Main Idea and Details**

2. Reread page 439. Why do Team Europa and actual astronauts use a gravity chair? Be sure to include details and information to support your answer. **Analyze**

3. Which activity from space camp would you enjoy most? Explain your answer. **Evaluate**

4. Do you think a future **mission** into space will improve our lives on Earth? **Analyze**

5. Reread "Jobs in Space" on pages 432–433. What aspects of the jobs described aboard a space shuttle would Team Europa be prepared to do? Use details from both stories to explain your answer. **Reading/Writing Across Texts**

The Flight of Icarus

A Greek Myth by Alice Low

CA Language Arts

Genre

Myths are stories that helped people make sense of the world. Myths tell about the life, gods, and heroes of an ancient culture. Some myths explain beliefs, practices, or occurrences in the natural world.

Literary Elements

Symbolism is the use of concrete objects to represent abstract ideas or qualities.

The **Moral** of a narrative is the lesson it illustrates, which the reader can apply to his or her life.

As a form of payment that is due every nine years, Athens must send fourteen young people to King Minos of Crete to be fed alive to the ferocious half-bull, half-man creature called the Minotaur. Young Theseus, son of the king of Athens, volunteers to be one of the fourteen youths in order to kill the Minotaur and put an end to the human sacrifices. Upon seeing Theseus for the first time, King Minos's daughter falls in love with him and helps him plan how to kill the Minotaur and escape from the labyrinth where the Minotaur lives. He succeeds and King Minos is furious.

WHEN KING MINOS heard that Theseus had killed the Minotaur and escaped from the labyrinth, he roared to his soldiers, "Daedalus must have helped Theseus escape, for only he knows the plan of the labyrinth. Take Daedalus and his young son, Icarus, up to the tower and bolt the door. They shall be imprisoned there forever."

But Daedalus, the great architect and inventor who had designed the labyrinth, did not lose hope, though he was locked in the gloomy tower. "The king cannot imprison my mind," he said to Icarus. "I shall think of a way to escape."

"But even if we get out of this tower, King Minos will find us and lock us up again," said Icarus. "We cannot leave Crete by ship, for all ships are searched before they leave. And soldiers patrol the land."

"There is another way open to us," said Daedalus. "The sky! If we could fly, they would never be able to follow us."

"Fly!" said Icarus. "Only birds can fly. No human has ever done so."

Here, birds symbolize freedom.

"But we can learn from the birds," said Daedalus. "Come with me to the roof."

Icarus followed his father, and together they studied the birds flying past the tower.

"If we made wings of feathers, we, too, could fly," said Daedalus. "We must catch the birds and use their feathers to make wings for ourselves."

Soon they had a whole pile of feathers of all colors, for they took only a few from each bird, not wanting to cripple them. Daedalus laid the feathers on the floor, according to size. Then he put the smallest feathers in a row, the middle-sized feathers in another row overlapping the first, and the largest feathers overlapping those.

Icarus watched in wonder as the man-sized wings took shape. "But how will you hold the feathers together?" he asked.

Daedalus pulled out a spool of thread and a large needle from his pocket, which was filled with odds and ends. "An inventor must always have his tools at hand," he said, and he set about sewing the large feathers together.

Next Daedalus pulled out some wax and softened it to hold the smaller feathers to the larger ones. When that was done, he lifted the man-made wings and bent them so that they curved like the wings of a bird. He tied the wings onto his arms. When he moved his arms the wings flapped.

"You are a bird," shouted Icarus. "Now make my wings quickly, Father."

Daedalus constructed a smaller set of wings for Icarus, and at last, early the next morning when everyone was asleep, father and son were ready to test them. "I shall go first," said Daedalus.

He spread his wings, flapped them, and up he rose, above the tower. He soared and glided up and down and around, while Icarus shouted, "Let me fly, too, Father! Let me fly!"

"Come," called Daedalus. "The wings work perfectly, and what a feeling it is to fly."

Icarus spread his wings, and he, too, soared and glided far above the tower, up into the sky. "Come back!" called Daedalus.

But Icarus did not return immediately. It was far too exciting to fly like a bird. When at last he came back, his father was angry. "You must do exactly what I say. We are not ready to leave yet. We must practice every morning until we are skillful enough to make our long trip to the mainland of Greece."

Early each morning, father and son practiced flying, with Icarus venturing farther and farther away, and Daedalus calling him back, speaking to him severely. "You must obey me, for flying is a tricky business. Tomorrow morning we shall set off on our flight of escape, and you must have your wits about you and follow my instructions."

"Oh, flying is easy," said Icarus. "I can even do it without looking."

"Never do that," said Daedalus. "You must steer carefully, taking a middle course. Not too low, near the sea, or your feathers will become damp and useless. And not too high, near the sun, or the wax that holds your feathers together will melt. Do you understand?"

"Of course!" said Icarus. But he was only half listening. He was much too excited about the journey, and, besides, he was tired of hearing his father's advice.

The next morning, Daedalus and Icarus put on their wings. Daedalus made sure his son's wings were fastened on tightly. Then, his voice shaking, he said to Icarus, "Now we must be off. Remember my advice, for you are very dear to me, and I fear for your safety."

They spread their wings, flapped them, and flew up into the air. Far below they saw farmers and shepherds looking up at them in astonishment.

They must think we are gods, thought Icarus, and he did a somersault in the air to show all the world that he was master of his wings. Then he followed his father, up and away, until he was flying over the expanse of blue sea.

Past the island of Delos they flew, on a middle course. But Icarus became impatient with following his father. He wanted to be on his own, flying anywhere he chose. First, he swooped down toward the sea, flying as close to it as possible without dampening his feathers. Again and again he did it. It was like a game, and each time he was the winner.

I shall play the same game with the sun, he thought. He flew upward, higher and higher, nearer to the sun each time. The wax does not melt, he thought. *My father is too cautious.*

I shall fly just a little nearer, he thought, *until I am almost part of the sun. How powerful I shall feel then.*

He flapped his wings harder, until he was even closer to the sun. For an instant he felt radiant, like a god. Then, suddenly, he lost altitude. Down, down he fell, for the wax on his wings had melted with the sun's heat, and his feathers had come apart and scattered in every direction. He plunged into the sea.

When Daedalus looked back, Icarus was no longer following him. "Icarus!" he cried, over and over. "Where are you?" But there was no reply.

Daedalus flew frantically, searching the air, up and down. At last he spotted the feathers tossing about on the waves below, and he knew that his son was lost forever.

Daedalus buried Icarus on an island he called Icaria, in memory of his son. Then he flew sadly to the island of Sicily, where he spent his remaining years.

> **The moral of the myth is implied, not stated.**

 Critical Thinking

1. What does the sun symbolize in this myth? **Symbolism**

2. If you were to write a myth, what would the moral be? Explain your answer. **Synthesize**

3. Think about "The Flight of Icarus" and *Ultimate Field Trip 5: Blasting Off to Space Academy*. How are the children in the text like Icarus? How are they different? **Reading/Writing Across Texts**

 Find out more about symbolism and morals in myths at www.macmillanmh.com.

CA **Writing**

✔ **Setting and Context**
Using strong details can help readers "see" the **setting** of a story.

Reading and Writing Connection

Read the passage below. Notice how the author Susan E. Goodman describes the setting.

An excerpt from
Ultimate Field Trip 5

The author includes setting by showing what the kids see as they enter the space academy. Notice how she describes in detail what the kids see so the reader feels he or she is there with them.

"Europa, the training center is a dirt free zone," said Paul. "Gum and drinks can create disasters here."

Paul, one of Europa's team leaders, led the kids through a maze of strange-looking machines. As they walked, the kids peeked at other teams jumping high enough to dunk a basketball and spinning in what looked like a giant gyroscope.

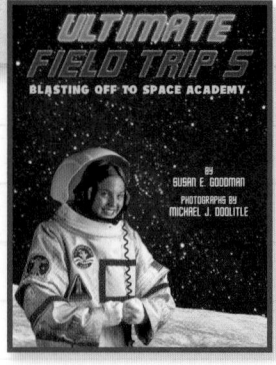

Read and Find

Read Stephanie's writing below. How did she use setting to show where the story took place? Use the Writer's Checklist to help you.

A Trip to the Fair
by Stephanie P.

In the mirrors, I kept seeing myself over and over again. The shifting colored lights made it seem like walls were appearing and disappearing around me. I got a whiff of cotton candy and popcorn. I turned around quickly and bumped my head into the mirrors. I felt my way along the rough, painted-plywood walls. Finally, the glow of a red EXIT sign guided me out.

Read about my experience on a visit to the fair!

Writer's Checklist

✓ Did the author show you how she interacted with the **setting**, as well as what it looked like?

✓ Does the author use showing techniques such as strong verbs or sensory details so that you could do more than just "see" the place?

☑ Could you imagine what was around Stephanie in this moment?

CA **Talk About It**

What are some ways people can help one another?

LOG ON ▶ Find out more about helping others at **www.macmillanmh.com**.

Helping Out

Shark Attack!

Brian Kang knows the importance of surfing with his buddies. This 38-year-old was surfing with friends in Northern California about 200 yards from shore when—BAM!

"Suddenly this giant force hits me....," Brian remembers. The **impact** knocked him off the board. Brian had run into a great white shark. "It had me in its mouth," he says.

Jennifer Savage was surfing with him that day. "Brian was off his board and there was all this churning water, like a **violent** whirlpool," she says. She watched him punch the shark in the snout, a sensitive part of its body.

The 18-foot-long shark released its hold on Brian's hip and legs. Bleeding, he scrambled back on his board. But within seconds the great white was back in his face. Again he punched it on the snout. "At that point it goes underwater," Brian says.

Then, despite the pains, he paddled to shore. Luckily, his friends were waiting. An ambulance rushed Brian to the hospital.

The shark bites had cut a tendon in Brian's left leg. His left hip was sliced to the bone. After three months of healing, however, Brian was back on his surfboard. But without his friends, Brian's story might have had a different ending.

a great white shark

A "Friend" Indeed

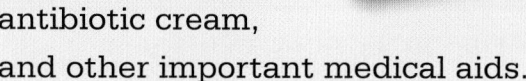

A friend should always be on your "must bring" list when you're planning a hike or going camping. What else should be on that list? Below are things to do and **supplies** to bring for any wilderness trip. To remember them, just think of the acronym **FRIEND**.

FIRST AID KIT: A good kit should include bandages, antibiotic cream, and other important medical aids.

FIRST AID

RESEARCH THE WEATHER: Make sure you're not surprised by weather changes.

INCLUDE SUNBLOCK: Wear sunscreen to avoid a nasty sunburn. In warm climates, walk at dawn and dusk—when the sun is less strong.

EXTRA FOOD: Bring spare snacks— you might be out hiking longer than you think.

NAVIGATION: Don't forget a flashlight, a compass, and a map.

DISCUSS YOUR PLANS: Tell a trusted adult where and when you'll be hiking.

THANKS, BROTHER

In November 2003, Justin and Jeremy Harris went hiking in Chute Canyon, Utah. Justin slipped and broke his leg. Nighttime and freezing temperatures were coming. They needed help.

Jeremy made Justin as comfortable as possible. Then he waved good-bye and set off for their campsite. Jeremy had to wade through pools of freezing water and got lost in the darkness. After 20 hours, he finally reached the campsite and called for help.

Meanwhile, Justin lay in the dark and freezing canyon. It took 36 hours for rescuers to reach him. Then he was strapped to a long sled and lifted 450 feet out of the canyon.

Justin and Jeremy Harris survived that hike for a few reasons. They had the right equipment and knew what to do in an emergency. But the main reason was that they hiked together.

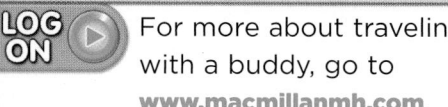

LOG ON For more about traveling with a buddy, go to www.macmillanmh.com.

457

Heroes in Time of Need

How can kids make a difference when natural disasters strike?

In 2005 Mother Nature proved just how powerful she can be. In the United States, one of the worst hurricane seasons pounded coastal areas. Katrina, the strongest hurricane that year, slammed the Gulf Coast. The violent hurricane destroyed parts of Mississippi and Alabama, and it flooded the city of New Orleans.

In South Asia, citizens began the year rebuilding after a tsunami destroyed coastlines from southern India to the island nation of Indonesia. On December 26, 2004, more than 200,000 people were killed in the tsunami, and millions were left in need of help.

Rescue workers search for victims after Hurricane Katrina.

Former Presidents Bill Clinton and George Bush talk to people organizing the rebuilding efforts after the Asian tsunami.

A terrible earthquake shook parts of Afghanistan, India, and Pakistan in 2005. The quake destroyed entire villages and killed about 80,000 people. The quake also left more than 3.3 million people homeless. Those who **survived** this disaster had no shelter.

Teaming Up

What do these three disasters have in common? A wave of generosity followed all three tragedies. Ordinary citizens throughout the world opened their hearts and wallets to people in need. Acting like heroes, people donated time and money to help survivors of these natural disasters.

After Asia's tsunami former presidents George H.W. Bush and Bill Clinton joined up to raise money for relief efforts. These two were former opponents. But they knew they could make a greater impact as a team than alone. They got together again to raise money for Katrina victims.

Shortly after these disasters, rescuers braved dangerous conditions to bring survivors to safety. But adults were not the only ones who stepped up to the plate. Plenty of kids joined grownups to hold fund-raisers in their communities and schools. Some even delivered needed medicines, food, and supplies to the people in need.

Kids Help Out

Layo Obamehinti, 14, from Euless, Texas, is one example of a kid who got **involved** in the rescue efforts. "My school, The North Hills School, is one of many schools in Texas that helped hurricane victims," Layo said. She and her classmates raised money for a charity that supplied many victims with food, water, clothes, and other basic necessities.

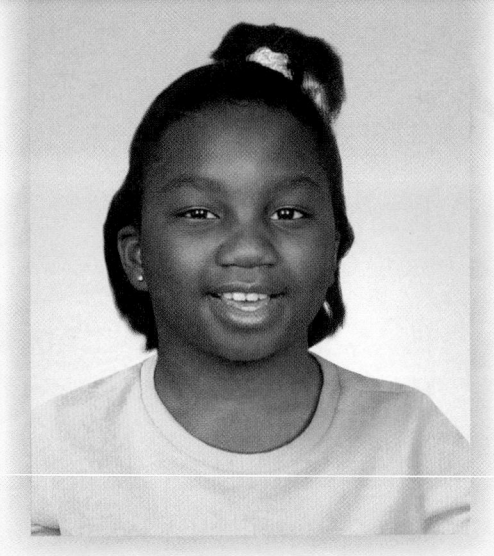

Layo Obamehinti helped people in need.

"Also, our school is hosting three victims of the hurricane," Layo added. "It might not seem like a lot compared to the hundreds some schools are taking in, but at least we are able to make a difference in their lives."

Across the country groups of kids got involved by holding bake sales and setting up drink stands. One of them was Avery Hardy, 12, from Santa Barbara, California. He said, "There were also lots of lemonade stands in Santa Barbara. My friends and I started one at the beach, and we made about fifty dollars."

Avery says he was inspired to act by Santa Barbara's First Responders Fund. This group is made up of Santa Barbara-area firefighters and police officers. They held a fund-raiser to educate locals about Hurricane Katrina. They also collected donations and raised awareness about hurricane victims. The group sent $8.9 million in medicine and medical supplies to Louisiana and Mississippi.

Many young people organized projects to raise money to help Katrina victims.

New Ways to Make a Difference

Bake sales and fund-raisers are great ideas. But many people found new and creative ways to help. In Bethesda, Maryland, a group called Project Backpack filled more than 10,350 backpacks with school supplies for Katrina's youngest survivors. In schools across the United States, kids participated in reading-for-relief fund-raisers to benefit tsunami victims.

The tsunami, the quake, and Hurricane Katrina were tragic events. But we learned what good can come when nations come together to help survivors of disasters. Countries all over the world sent equipment, food, blankets, doctors, tents, medicines, and other resources to help victims recover. As we saw in 2005, Mother Nature's worst often brings out the best in humanity.

 **Critical Thinking**

1. Why did Avery help out the victims of Hurricane Katrina?

2. The article refers to the people who helped the survivors as "heroes." Is this a fact or an opinion? Explain your answer.

3. In what way might you and your classmates help victims of a natural disaster?

4. How is the situation Jeremy faces in "Thanks, Brother" different from the one Layo Obamehinti and her classmates face in this article?

The Kantor sisters started Project Backpack. They show some donated backpacks.

Finch (in the rubble of her home) says the true hero is Steve Rucker. He was the only firefighter to lose his life. "This wasn't even his community," she says.

In October 2003, California's worst wildfires ever swept through the southern part of the state. Twenty-two people died, more than 3,500 homes were destroyed, and 746,000 acres burned. In all the destruction, however, there were stories of heroism.

Carolina Finch is a shining example of such a story. She was one of the more than 15,000 firefighters who battled the wildfires. Finch lives in Cuyamaca, California, an area that was in flames. Her chief placed her on a fire team sent out to protect Finch's neighborhood.

The firefighters "could see the fire up in the hills, blowing over towards my street," Finch says, remembering riding on the fire truck. "As we came around the corner, I saw my house was in flames."

The house next to hers was in better shape. Finch says, "A tree and some brush up against it were on fire, but we thought we could put them out and save my neighbor's house."

Was it a hard decision to help her neighbor's house first? "Sure," Finch says. "You want to rush into your own home and save what you can, but you can't do that." Finch knew she and her team had a job to do. "I was on the hose line putting out the fire by my neighbor's home as I watched mine burn down."

Finch lost family treasures that can never be replaced. "But even though I lost them, it is nice to see my neighbor's home still there," Finch says. "I want to rebuild in the same spot, and I want my neighbors to be there next to me. You try to keep a positive attitude."

Go on ▶

Now answer Numbers 1 through 5. Base your answers on the article "The World's Best Neighbor."

1. Why is Carolina Finch a hero?

- **A** She helped save her neighbors.
- **B** She helped save her neighbor's house.
- **C** She drove a fire truck into a wildfire.
- **D** She saved family treasures from a fire.

2. How did Finch react after the fire in her neighborhood?

- **A** She quickly moved away to another state.
- **B** She decided to quit the fire department.
- **C** She did not want to speak to her neighbor.
- **D** She plans to rebuild her house in the same neighborhood.

3. What advice do you think Finch would give to people recovering from a disaster?

- **A** Always put yourself first.
- **B** Avoid places that have disasters.
- **C** Try to have a positive attitude.
- **D** Think only about what you've lost.

4. Why did the fire team choose to save Finch's neighbor's house?

5. How could the people in Finch's neighborhood reward her for her heroism? Use details from the article in your answer.

Tip

Look for information in more than one place.

 # Write on Demand

All people should know how to help in an emergency.

Think of something you can do to help in an emergency.

Now write to <u>tell how</u> you can help in an emergency.

Expository writing explains, defines, or tells how to do something.

To figure out if a writing prompt asks for expository writing, look for clue words such as <u>explain</u>, <u>tell how</u>, or <u>tell what</u>.

Below see how one student begins a response to the prompt above.

In response to the prompt, the writer included specific details.

One emergency my community faces is wildfires. I have learned that to save our homes from wildfires, we must fight fire with fire. We need to cut all the trees and brush on the edge of our community. This will steal the fire's fuel and, we hope, stop the fire before it reaches our town.

We will also need to set a backfire. This means setting fire to the forest between the wildfire and the fire line we create. The prevailing wind will spread the fire toward us.

Writing Prompt

Respond in writing to the prompt below. Write for
15 minutes. Write as much as you can, as well as you can.
Review the hints below before and after you write.

 There are several ways people can help their community.
Think about how you and your friends can help your
community. Now write to tell how you and your friends
can help your community.

Writing Hints for Prompts

☑ Carefully read the prompt.
☑ Organize your ideas and plan your writing.
☑ Support your ideas by giving reasons and using more details.
☑ Combine sentences to add variety.
☑ Choose words that help readers understand your ideas.
☑ Review your writing and edit as needed.

Family Teams

CA **Talk About It**

In what kinds of situations does a family work together as a team?

LOG ON ▶ Find out more about family teams at **www.macmillanmh.com**.

467

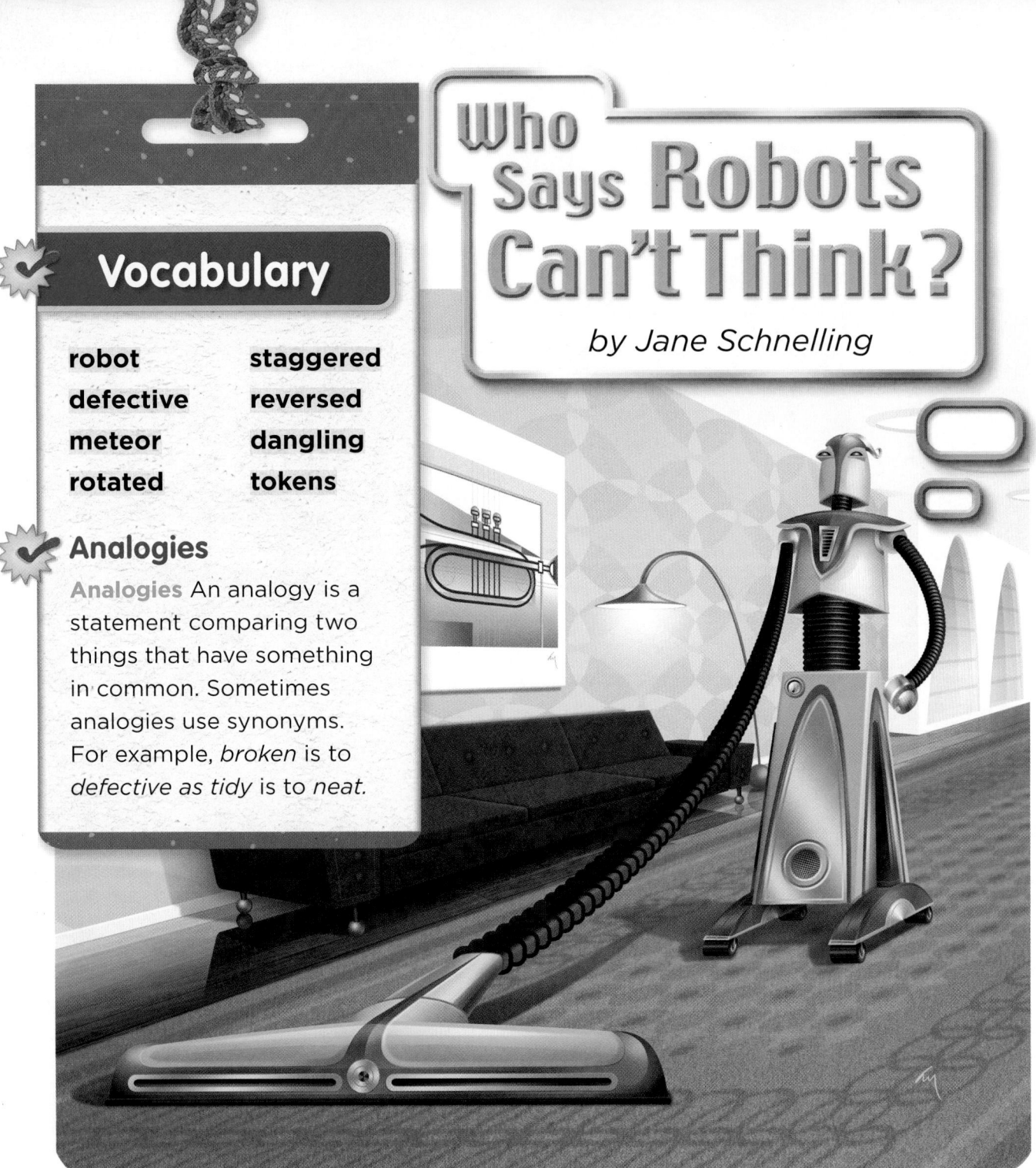

Who Says Robots Can't Think?

by Jane Schnelling

Dad and I are watching the Olympic Games in our media room. The giant screen drops down to cover one wall. I jiggle the lever and my seat turns around, to face the screen. We give our **robot**, Sylvia, our orders for popcorn and fresh lemonade. She is only a machine but she looks like a human and helps with the housework.

468

We are having popcorn for dinner tonight because our oven is **defective**. It is broken and keeps on repeating that it doesn't remember how to cook. Dad thinks the huge **meteor** passing by Earth is messing with its radio waves.

"I did see a shooting star yesterday," I said. "Maybe that's why I had trouble getting Sylvia started this morning. She **rotated** around and around, **staggered** when she tried to take a step, and almost fell backwards. She finally started moving towards me, but then suddenly **reversed**, and went backwards. I thought she was going to crash into a wall. Luckily, she grabbed hold of the wind chimes we have **dangling** from the ceiling, and got her balance."

At last, Sylvia arrives with our popcorn and drinks. I look at the screen and see the Olympic torch burning brightly. Sylvia sees it too. Dad gives her **tokens** from an old board game as a tip. Sylvia thanks him for the pieces and starts to leave the room. Then she reverses direction and comes back to where we are sitting. I hear humming and then some clicking sounds. The sounds mean that she is searching her memory chips for information. "During the Olympics, I should get medals, not tokens," she says.

Dad and I just stare at each other. Sylvia doesn't seem to know that robots aren't supposed to think. Then we burst out laughing and award Sylvia a gold medal.

Reread for **Comprehension**

Make Inferences and Analyze

Draw Conclusions
Making inferences about a story will help you analyze characters and events. You can use your inferences to draw conclusions and come to a new understanding of the story. Fill out your Conclusions Diagram as you reread the selection.

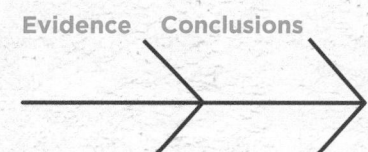

Evidence   Conclusions

Comprehension

Genre

Science Fiction tells a story of imagined events usually set in the future and based on science or technology.

Make Inferences and Analyze

Draw Conclusions
As you read, fill in your Conclusions Diagram.

Evidence → Conclusions →

Read to Find Out

What can you conclude about the relationship of the two brothers at the end of the story?

ZATHURA
A SPACE ADVENTURE

Award Winning Author and Illustrator

written and Illustrated by Chris Van Allsburg

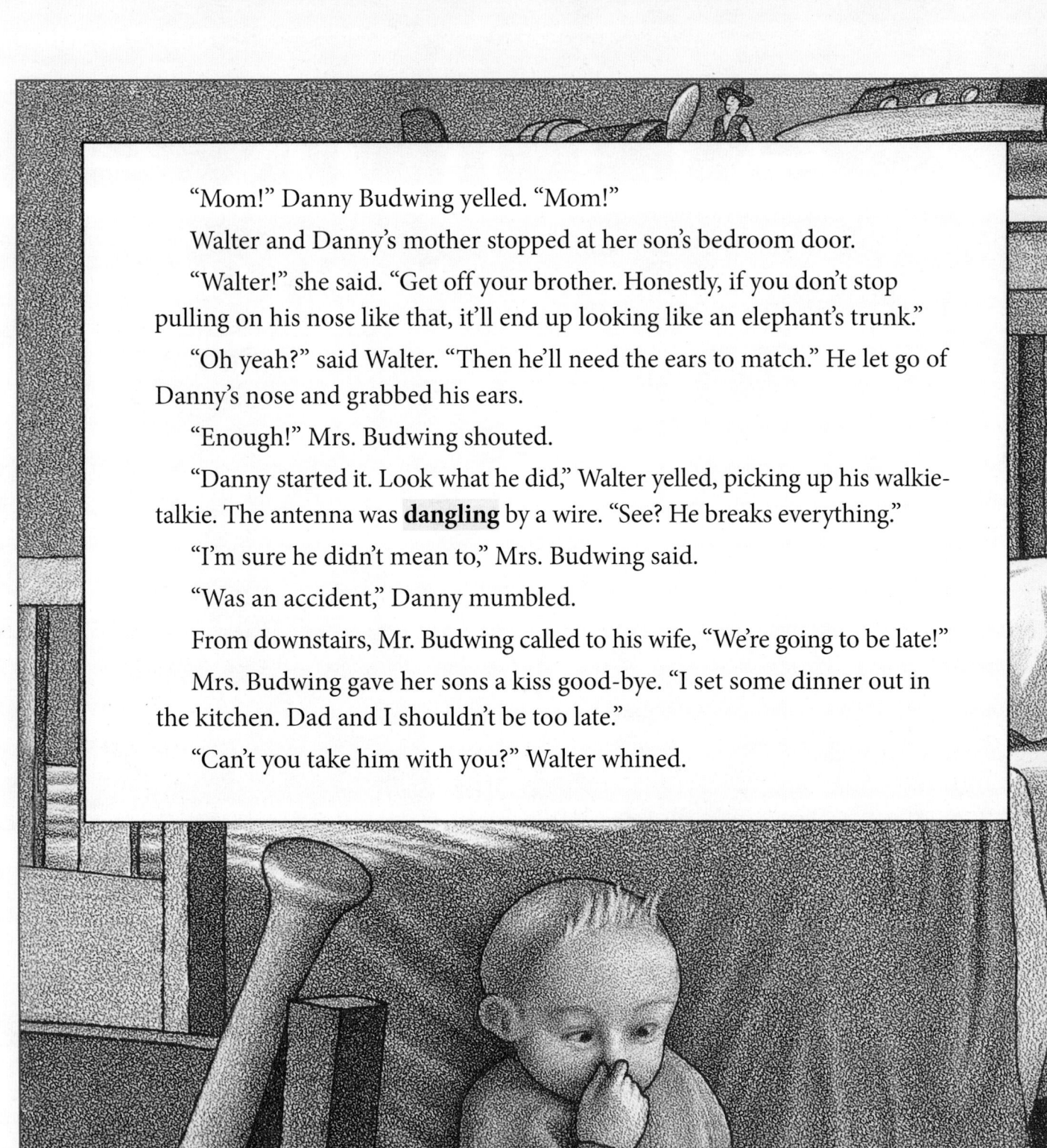

"Mom!" Danny Budwing yelled. "Mom!"

Walter and Danny's mother stopped at her son's bedroom door.

"Walter!" she said. "Get off your brother. Honestly, if you don't stop pulling on his nose like that, it'll end up looking like an elephant's trunk."

"Oh yeah?" said Walter. "Then he'll need the ears to match." He let go of Danny's nose and grabbed his ears.

"Enough!" Mrs. Budwing shouted.

"Danny started it. Look what he did," Walter yelled, picking up his walkie-talkie. The antenna was **dangling** by a wire. "See? He breaks everything."

"I'm sure he didn't mean to," Mrs. Budwing said.

"Was an accident," Danny mumbled.

From downstairs, Mr. Budwing called to his wife, "We're going to be late!"

Mrs. Budwing gave her sons a kiss good-bye. "I set some dinner out in the kitchen. Dad and I shouldn't be too late."

"Can't you take him with you?" Walter whined.

473

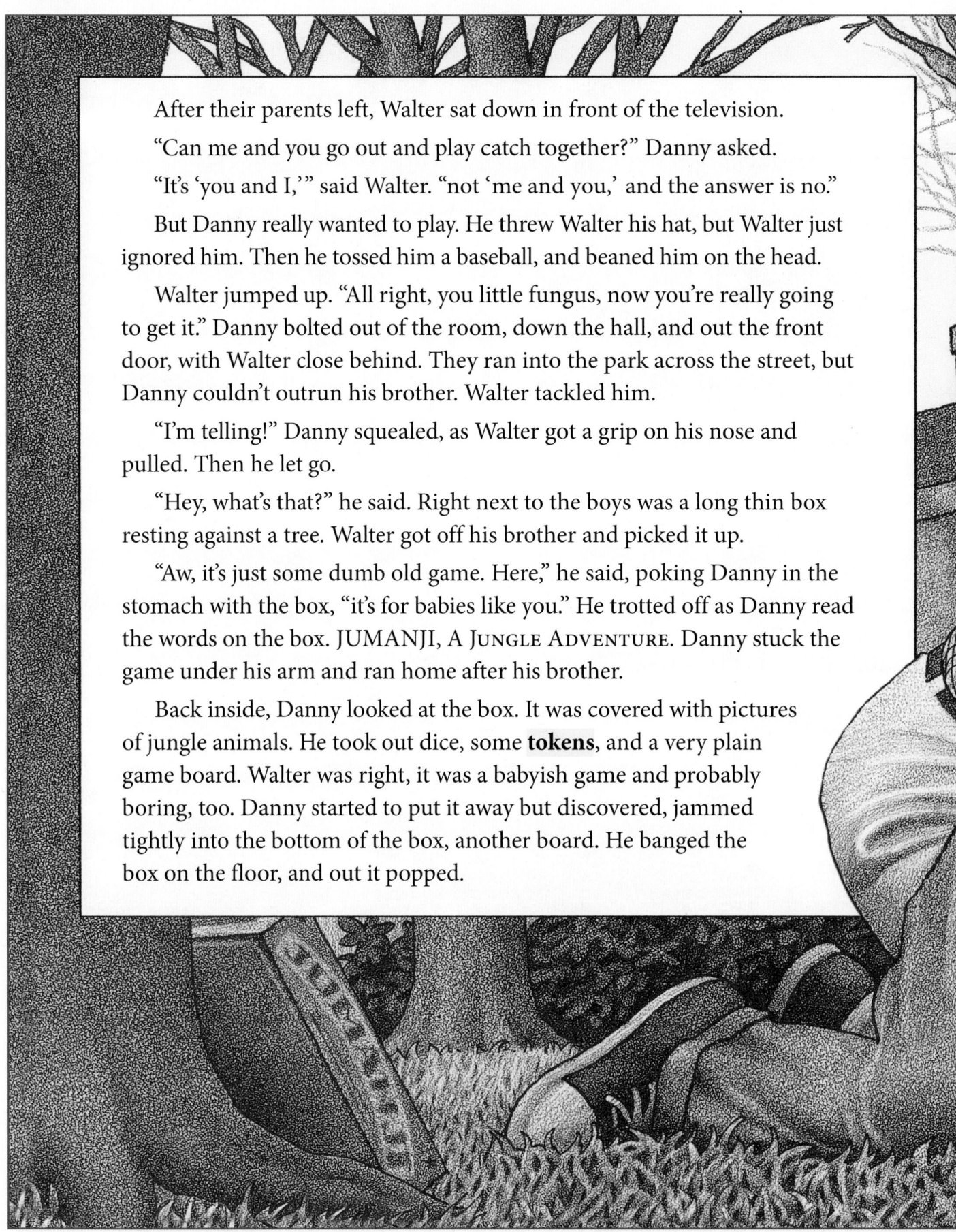

After their parents left, Walter sat down in front of the television.

"Can me and you go out and play catch together?" Danny asked.

"It's 'you and I,'" said Walter. "not 'me and you,' and the answer is no."

But Danny really wanted to play. He threw Walter his hat, but Walter just ignored him. Then he tossed him a baseball, and beaned him on the head.

Walter jumped up. "All right, you little fungus, now you're really going to get it." Danny bolted out of the room, down the hall, and out the front door, with Walter close behind. They ran into the park across the street, but Danny couldn't outrun his brother. Walter tackled him.

"I'm telling!" Danny squealed, as Walter got a grip on his nose and pulled. Then he let go.

"Hey, what's that?" he said. Right next to the boys was a long thin box resting against a tree. Walter got off his brother and picked it up.

"Aw, it's just some dumb old game. Here," he said, poking Danny in the stomach with the box, "it's for babies like you." He trotted off as Danny read the words on the box. JUMANJI, A JUNGLE ADVENTURE. Danny stuck the game under his arm and ran home after his brother.

Back inside, Danny looked at the box. It was covered with pictures of jungle animals. He took out dice, some **tokens**, and a very plain game board. Walter was right, it was a babyish game and probably boring, too. Danny started to put it away but discovered, jammed tightly into the bottom of the box, another board. He banged the box on the floor, and out it popped.

475

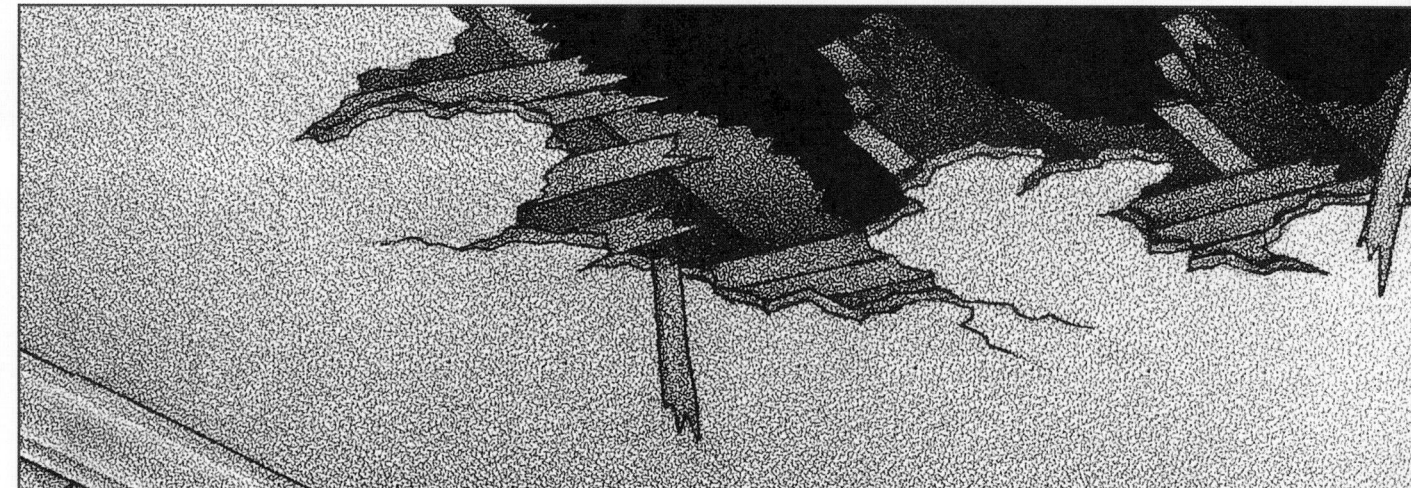

This board was more interesting. It showed flying saucers, rockets, and planets in outer space, with a path of colored squares leading from Earth to a purple planet called Zathura and back to Earth.

Danny put a token on Earth, then rolled the dice. After he'd moved along the path, something surprising happened. A buzzing sound came from the board and, with a click, a small green card popped out of the edge right in front of him. He picked it up and read, "**Meteor** showers, take evasive action."

"Hey, Walter," Danny started to say, "what does eva—" when he was interrupted by a noisy *rat-a-tat-tat* sound coming from the roof.

Walter looked up from the television. "Holy smoke," he said, "must be a hail storm!" "It's not hail!" shouted Danny, holding up the card. "It's meteors."

The noise grew louder, like a thousand golf balls bouncing off the roof. The room got so dark, Walter turned on the lights. Then—KABOOM—a rock the size of a refrigerator fell through the ceiling and crushed the television.

"See," Danny said. "I told you. Meteors."

Walter stared at the hole in the ceiling. "Okay," he agreed, "meteors. But how'd it get so dark so fast?" Through the hole he could see what was left of his parents' bedroom, and beyond that, a black, star-filled sky. "It looks like night up there."

"It's not night," said Danny. "It's outer space."

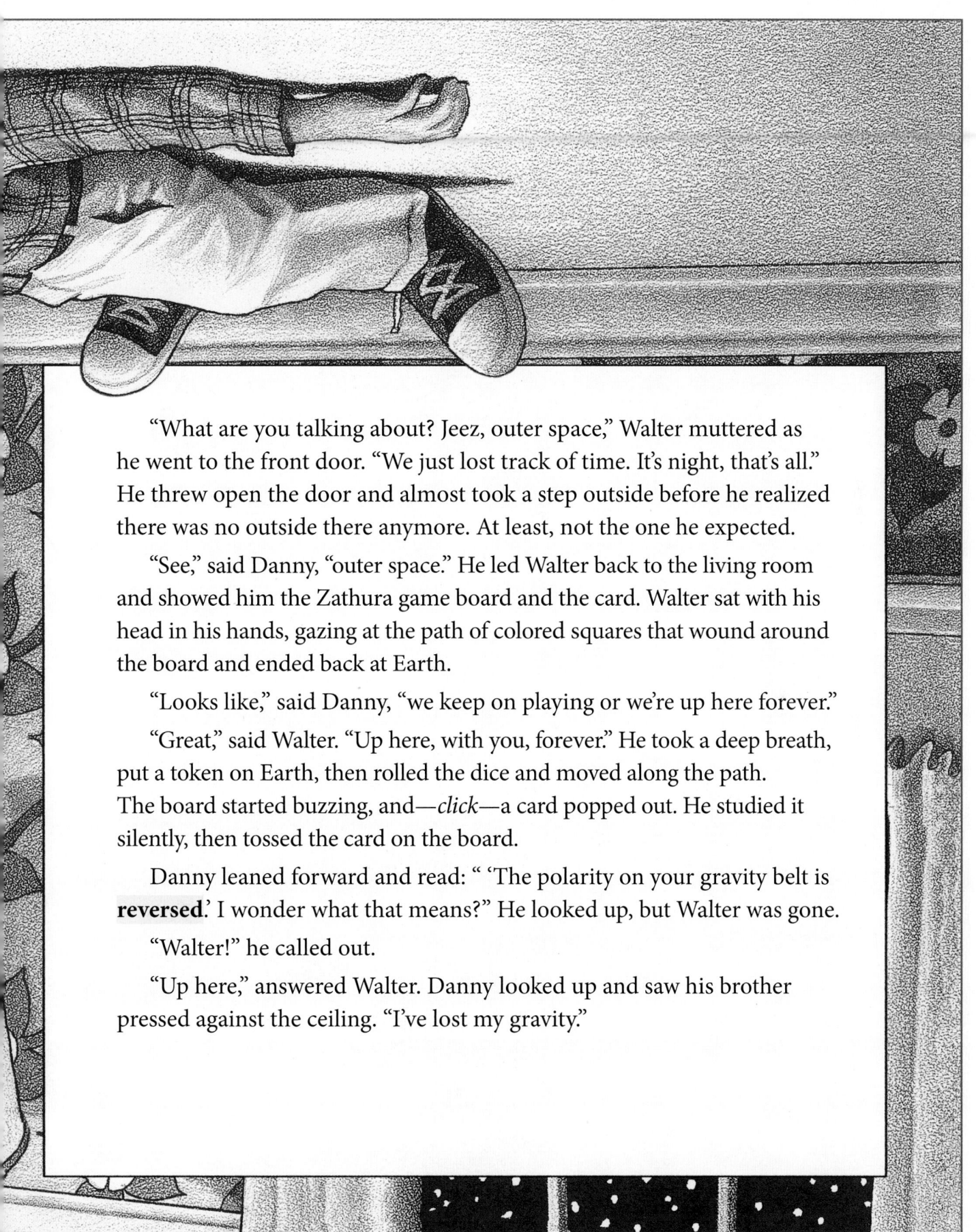

"What are you talking about? Jeez, outer space," Walter muttered as he went to the front door. "We just lost track of time. It's night, that's all." He threw open the door and almost took a step outside before he realized there was no outside there anymore. At least, not the one he expected.

"See," said Danny, "outer space." He led Walter back to the living room and showed him the Zathura game board and the card. Walter sat with his head in his hands, gazing at the path of colored squares that wound around the board and ended back at Earth.

"Looks like," said Danny, "we keep on playing or we're up here forever."

"Great," said Walter. "Up here, with you, forever." He took a deep breath, put a token on Earth, then rolled the dice and moved along the path. The board started buzzing, and—*click*—a card popped out. He studied it silently, then tossed the card on the board.

Danny leaned forward and read: " 'The polarity on your gravity belt is **reversed**.' I wonder what that means?" He looked up, but Walter was gone.

"Walter!" he called out.

"Up here," answered Walter. Danny looked up and saw his brother pressed against the ceiling. "I've lost my gravity."

"That's not all you're going to lose," Danny said nervously, because he could see that Walter was being pulled slowly toward the hole in the ceiling—and a lonely trip into outer space.

Walter realized it too and started clawing at the ceiling, but he couldn't keep himself from moving closer and closer to the hole.

Danny looked around. Lying next to the meteor was the cord from the shattered television. He tossed it to Walter, who knotted it tightly to his belt. Danny grabbed the end of the cord and tied his brother to the sofa.

Danny rolled the dice and moved his token along the path. *Click.* Out popped another card: "Your gyroscope is malfunctioning." Suddenly the house tilted. Everything in the room slid to one side, and Danny got buried under a mountain of furniture. He slowly dug himself out, clutching the game, only to find that Walter was floating back toward the hole in the ceiling.

Draw Conclusions
What is the purpose of a gravity belt?

481

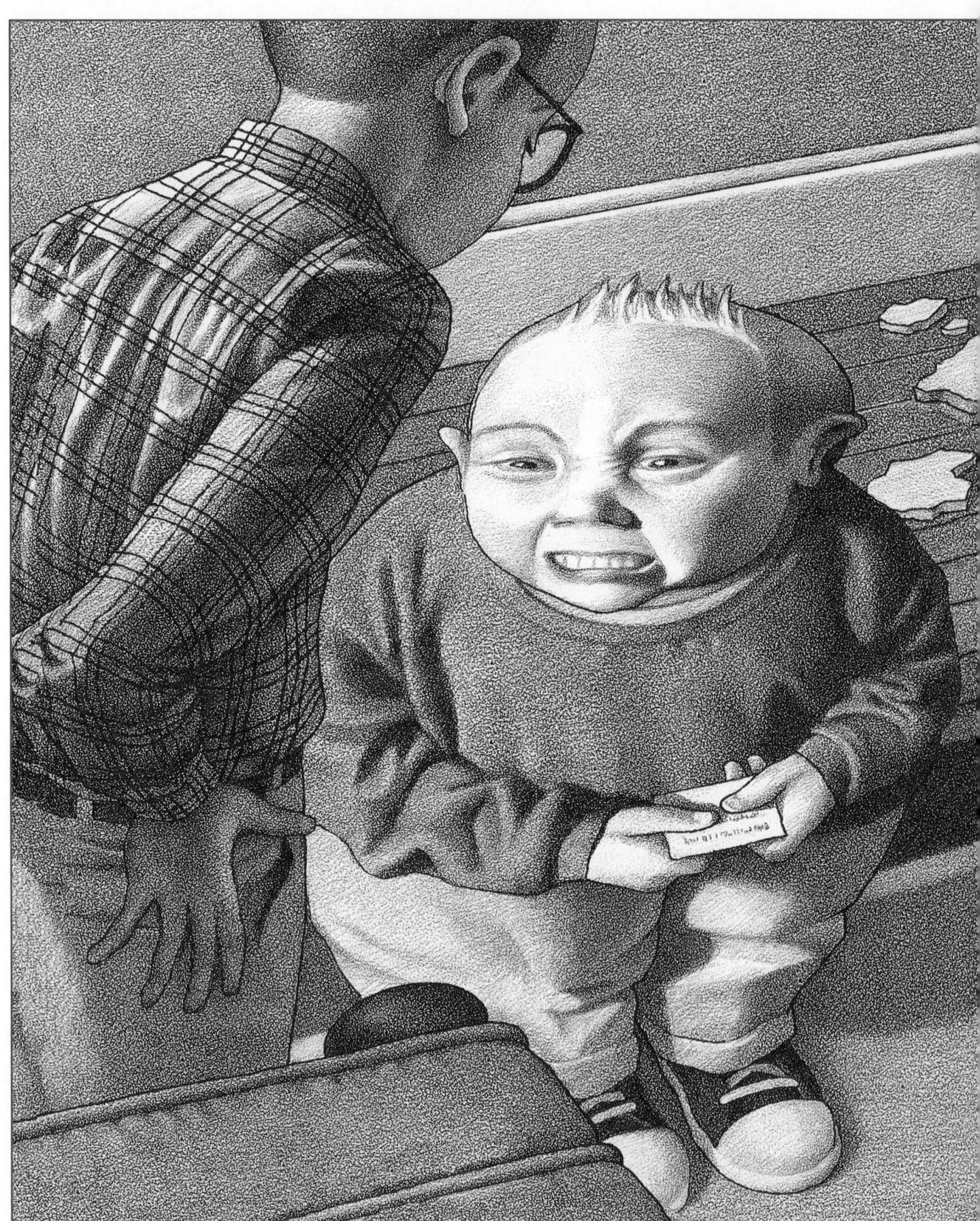

Danny tied him to the sofa again and handed up the dice. Walter rolled and got his gravity back, dropping to the floor with a thud. Danny moved his piece and handed him his card. " 'Your **robot** is **defective**,' " Walter read.

From the hallway came the sound of rattling metal and a steady *clank, clank, clank*. The boys stared at the doorway as a shiny silver robot stepped into view. He was having trouble walking on the tilted floor. His head **rotated** back and forth and seemed to freeze on Walter. The robot's eyes lit up and he spoke in an odd mechanical voice: "Emergency, emergency, alien life form. Must destroy." His clawlike metal hands snapped open and shut.

"Uh-oh," Danny whispered, "I think he's talking about you." Fortunately, when the robot stepped forward he missed the door, banged into the wall, and fell to the floor. He got up and did it again. And then again.

"Better hurry up and roll," said Walter, "before he makes it in here."

Danny rolled the dice and took his card: " 'You pass too close to Tsouris 3, gravity greatly increased.' "

The room began to level out, but something strange was happening to Danny. Walter looked at him. "Holy smoke," he said. Danny was getting shorter, and wider too. Soon he was about the shape and size of a large beach ball.

"Waaalter," he said in a low voice. "I feeeel verrrry heeeavy."

"Destroy alien life forms," the robot repeated from the hall as he picked himself up again. This time he made it through the door and headed for Walter.

Danny yelled to his brother, "Puuush meee!"

"What?" said Walter.

"Puuush meee," Danny yelled again. "Juuust puuush meee."

Walter bent down and gave his brother a shove. Danny rolled across the room and, like a giant bowling ball, knocked the robot over and flattened his legs. "Did I geeet hiiim?" asked Danny, who couldn't see because he'd rolled up against a wall and was upside down.

Walter pushed him back to the game board. "You sure did," he said, patting his brother's head. "You were terrific."

Walter picked up the dice and rolled. He took his card, and his hand trembled as he read, "'Zorgon pirate ship launches photon attack.'"

Through the window, the boys saw a spaceship. Two points of light shot from the ship and headed directly for the Budwing house. The first one hit the chimney and sent bricks falling into the fireplace. The second hit the upstairs bathroom. Water began dripping down from the hole in the ceiling.

Walter handed the dice to Danny, who had a hard time lifting his short, heavy arm. He rolled, and as Walter moved his token for him, he slowly returned to his normal shape. A card popped out. Danny read it silently. "This is bad," he said. "'Zorgon pirate boards your vessel.'"

The room shook as the spaceship banged up against the house. The boys heard footsteps on the roof. Through the opening in the ceiling they saw someone or something climb through the hole in the roof and enter the room above them. Danny and Walter moved to the hallway, standing behind the flattened robot. They held each other, too terrified to move. A humming sound came from their feet. They looked down and saw the robot's eyes light up.

He lifted his head, fixed his eyes on the hole in the ceiling, and spoke: "Alien life form, must destroy." His clawlike hands twitched but he couldn't get up.

Danny and Walter helped him to his feet. He **staggered** forward as the pirate's scaly tail and lizardlike legs swung down from the hole. The robot lifted one of his claws and snapped it sharply around the creature's tail.

The Zorgon howled, jerking himself back through the hole, with the robot still attached. He thrashed and wailed, banging against the walls overhead. Then, minus one arm, the robot dropped down through the hole. The boys heard the Zorgon scramble across the roof and saw the flash of his rockets as his ship sped away.

It seemed hopeless. The robot's eyes were dark again. They'd been playing almost three hours, and their tokens rested a galaxy away from Zathura and twice that far from Earth. "We're never going to make it," said Walter.

"Sure we are," answered Danny. He handed the dice to his brother. "Me and you, together. We can do it."

487

Walter cradled the dice in his hand and sighed. "'You and I,'" he said wearily. "'You and I.'" He looked at his little brother, who was grinning.

"That's right," said Danny. "Together."

Walter rolled the dice, a one and a two. He moved his token to the only black square on the board. The card popped out. "'You have entered a black hole,'" Walter read. "'Go back in time, one hour for each mark on the dice.'"

He jumped up and looked around the room. "You see any black holes?"

His brother pointed to the floor. A black spot was slowly spreading under Walter's feet, like a perfectly round puddle of ink. At first Walter thought he was sinking into it, but it was the hole that was rising. He tried to run but could not feel his feet. Then, as the hole rose higher, he couldn't feel his legs, either. "What's going on?" he cried.

Danny looked below the disklike hole. "Walter," he said, "the bottom part of you is gone." As the hole rose higher and higher, there was less and less of Walter, until only his head remained. Danny tried to pull on the hole to save what was left of his brother, but his hands passed through the blackness as if it were made of smoke. His chin dropped to his chest and he began to sob.

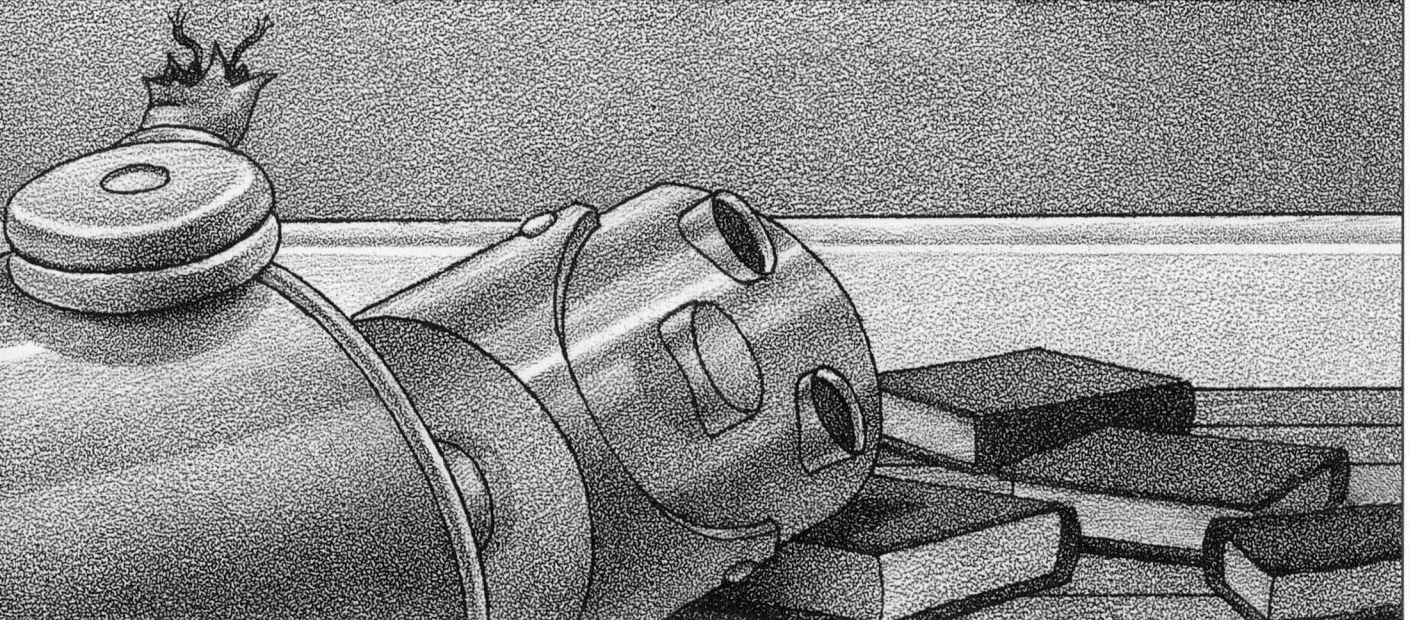

"Danny," Walter called softly. Danny looked up at his brother's floating head. "Danny," he began. "I never told you this, but I . . ." And that was all he got to say, because the hole kept rising, past his mouth, his nose, and finally right over the top of his head.

Walter was completely swallowed up, floating in empty darkness. He closed his eyes as he began to spin, plunging head over heels through pitch-black space. Then, *thud*, he landed hard on his knees. There was something in his arms, something wriggling around.

He opened his eyes and found himself back in the park by his house. He had an arm wrapped tightly around Danny's neck and a hand gripping the boy's nose. "I'm telling," Danny squealed.

Walter let go and fell back on the grass. He was dizzy, very dizzy. Danny jumped up and started to run, but stopped. "Hey," he said, "what's that?" He went to a tree and picked up a box resting against the trunk. He held the box out to Walter. "Look," he said, "it's some kind of game."

Walter grabbed it. "Hey, give it back," said Danny.

His big brother got to his feet. "You don't want to play this," he said. "Trust me, I tried it once." He went over to a trash can and jammed the box deep inside. "Come on," he said, "I've got a better idea. Let's go play catch."

Danny smiled. "You mean together, me and you?"

Walter put his arm around his brother. "Yeah, that's right," he said. "Me and you, together."

> **Draw Conclusions**
> What does Walter realize about the game Danny finds in the park?

Out of This World
with
Chris Van Allsburg

Chris Van Allsburg gets his ideas for stories when he sees a picture of something in his mind. Then he asks "What if…?" What if a boy went on a train that turned into the Polar Express? What if a game about outer space became real? Chris has been drawing since his college days. He calls his work "representational" (which means it's like real life), but he always puts a little mystery into the pictures. Because Chris has so many new ideas, he doesn't like to write sequels. However, kids do. Many of his fans have written sequels to his books.

Other books by Chris Van Allsburg:
Jumanji and *The Polar Express*

CA **Author's Purpose**
A fiction writer usually aims to entertain. Do you believe that is true for Chris Van Allsburg? Why or why not?

LOG ON ▶ Find out more about Chris Van Allsburg at **www.macmillanmh.com**.

CA Critical Thinking

Summarize

Use your Conclusions Diagram to summarize *Zathura.* How does the game change the boys' lives?

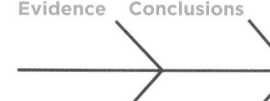

Think and Compare

1. **Draw a conclusion** about what you think Walter would do if Danny brought the game home again. Use evidence from the story to support your conclusion. **Make Inferences and Analyze: Draw Conclusions**

2. Reread page 491. What was Walter going to tell Danny before the black hole swallowed him? Use story details to support your answer. **Analyze**

3. If you were going on a space adventure during which you would be dodging **meteors**, aliens, and robots, would you choose Danny, Walter, or both to go with you? Explain your answer. **Evaluate**

4. This story includes robots and aliens. What other characteristics of science fiction does it have? **Analyze**

5. Reread "Who Says Robots Can't Think?" on pages 468–469. What are the similarities and differences between Sylvia and the robot in *Zathura*? **Reading/Writing Across Texts**

www.example.com

Observing THE Night Sky

By Kyle Seulen

If you have ever seen a starry sky on a clear night, you understand why scientists want to know more about space. Scientists who study stars, planets, and all of space are called **astronomers**. Since ancient times these scientists have spent much time observing the sky. They begin their studies by keeping accurate records of what they see. Afterward they analyze their results and talk to other scientists about their discoveries. Scientists make different kinds of investigations, depending on the questions they want to answer. When exact measurements are not possible, scientists use estimates, or good guesses, based on research.

By observing and keeping records of where objects are in the sky each day, astronomers are able to learn which ones **orbit**, or circle, other objects. They can tell how fast the objects are moving, and even how far away they are.

How did early astronomers study the night sky? Discoveries such as other planets, comets, and stars were first made with the naked eye. Later the **telescope** made distant objects appear larger. As astronomers studied the objects of the universe, they learned more about Earth's place in it. For example, while scientists once believed Earth to be the center of the universe, studies with a telescope showed that Earth in fact moved around the Sun.

A Modern Telescope

Eyepiece lens

Lens

Telescope tube

Tripod stand

Edmond Halley

One important early astronomer was Edmond Halley. In the 1600s he watched a comet in the sky. He took notes about how fast it was moving and what it looked like. He noticed that the comet was similar to one described in the notes of astronomers from the past.

Halley used his notes and calculations to show that the comet was the same one that had been studied by earlier scientists. He proved that the comet could be seen about every 76 years. He was then able to predict, or tell in advance, when the comet would be able to be seen in the sky again. This discovery came to be called Halley's comet.

Astronomy Today

Today's astronomers have high-tech tools that ancient scientists could not have imagined. Scientists now use high-powered telescopes and cameras guided by computers to view space. These tools allow scientists to study such things as planet surfaces, gravity, light, and whether life exists elsewhere in the universe. One thing has not changed from ancient times, however. Astronomers still answer questions about the universe by observing and recording what they see. Then they analyze the results and communicate them to others. That way the scientists learn from each other and the discoveries continue. Using high tech or low, today's astronomers still have a sense of wonder about the night sky.

This photo of Halley's comet was taken through a modern high-powered telescope.

This strip of icons is called a toolbar.

An artist's illustration of Halley's comet from the 1700s

Links related to this topic

Related Articles

▶ Halley's Comet Today

▶ Telescopes

▶ Famous Astronomers

 Critical Thinking

1. If you wanted to read information on the most recent sighting of Halley's comet, which link would you go to? **Understanding Links**

2. What can astronomers learn about objects when they look at them through a telescope? **Apply**

3. What kinds of observations do you think Walter in *Zathura* would record about outer space after playing the board game? What might he tell an astronomer? **Reading/Writing Across Texts**

 Science Activity

Research a tool that is used in astronomy. Write a two-paragraph summary about the history of the tool and how it helps astronomers. Include a sketch of the tool and label it.

 Find out more about astronomy at **www.macmillanmh.com**.

Writing

CA

Setting and Context

The **setting** affects the characters and how they react to the events of the story.

Reading and Writing Connection

Read the passage below. Notice how the author Chris Van Allsburg uses the setting to show how the game is coming to life.

By describing what the characters see around them—the setting—the author shows what is happening to them. The changes in the setting reflect the strange effect of the game.

An excerpt from
Zathura

The noise grew louder, like a thousand golf balls bouncing off the roof. The room got so dark, Walter turned on the lights. Then—KABOOM—a rock the size of a refrigerator fell through the ceiling and crushed the television. . . . Through the hole he could see what was left of his parents' bedroom, and beyond that, a black, star-filled sky.

ZATHURA
A SPACE ADVENTURE

Read and Find

Read Colleen's writing below. How did she show the characters reacting to their setting? Use the Writer's Checklist to help you.

Where Are We?
by Colleen P.

"Colleen?" called my sister Vicky in a tiny voice. "Where are we?" Rubbing the sleep from my eyes, I sat up in the backseat of the car. Instead of the tall trees and low brush that had surrounded us when we'd dozed off, there were a few squat cactus plants and a single ball of tumbleweed. The sky stretched all the way down to the flat, dry horizon line way off in the distance. My nostrils twitched as I breathed in dusty air.

Read about the new place we were about to explore.

Writer's Checklist

 Did the author show you how she interacted with the **setting**, as well as what it looked like?

 Does the author use showing techniques such as strong verbs or sensory details so that you could do more than just "see" the place?

☑ Could you imagine what was around Colleen in this moment?

CA **Talk About It**

Why is teamwork important when you go camping?

 Find out more about camping at **www.macmillanmh.com**.

CAMPING OUT

Vocabulary

guaranteed   ease

supervise   scenery

frustrated   bundle

coordination   fused

Dictionary

A word can have more than one meaning. A **Dictionary** can help you choose the best definition for the words you read. For example, *fused* can mean "made into a liquid by heating" or "blended together by melting."

THE BEST
FOURTH OF JULY

by Lateesha Gilbert

Sunday, July 5

Dear Mom and Dad,

I hope you had a great Fourth of July. You can imagine what a big deal it was here at Camp Freedom. With a name like that, the camp really went all out to celebrate!

For weeks every cabin was working on a Fourth of July skit. Since all the girls in my cabin are super funny, our counselor **guaranteed** the other cabins we would have the funniest skit in camp. At first we were pretty casual about working on it. Then the days went by and no one had come up with a good idea. Our counselor, Jean, started getting worried. Finally, she decided she should **supervise** us and our ideas more closely. She went from cracking jokes with us to being bossy. We all felt **frustrated**. She kept telling us what to do and she would not listen to our ideas. In the end, we did a skit about the founder of the camp, Fannie Freedom. Hardly anyone laughed.

502

After the skits we had a cookout, complete with those yummy chocolate, marshmallow, and cracker things. Arranging everything on sticks involved a lot of **coordination**. The ingredients were sticky and hard to manage. I didn't poke my stick all the way through each marshmallow. As I would **ease** the stick into the fire, the marshmallows would fall off. I am surprised the fire didn't go out from all the marshmallows that fell in.

Later that day the counselors took us to the top of Lookaway Mountain. The **scenery** was amazing from up there. The hard part was we had to carry a large **bundle** of blankets tied together with some string. The big surprise at the end of the day was a fireworks display, which lit up the entire sky. On the way back to camp, Jean apologized to us for not listening to our ideas. We told her that we had fun anyway.

By the way, thank you for the package you sent me. Everything was really great. The jelly beans melted and **fused** together, but don't worry. That didn't affect the taste. My bunkmates and I ate them for a late night snack on July Fourth, and everyone agreed they were still delicious!

Love you all,
Lateesha

Reread for **Comprehension**

Monitor Comprehension
Make Judgments
Making judgments about a character's actions in a story can help you monitor your comprehension while you read. A Judgments Chart helps you judge how wise a character's actions are. Use your Judgments Chart as you reread "The Best Fourth of July" to make judgments about Jean's actions.

Action ➔ Judgment		
	➔	
	➔	
	➔	
	➔	

CA Comprehension

Genre
Realistic Fiction has real-life settings, well-developed characters, and realistic problems and solutions.

Monitor Comprehension

Make Judgments
As you read, fill in your Judgments Chart.

Action ➜ Judgment
➜
➜
➜
➜

Read to Find Out
How does Teddy feel about the camping trip?

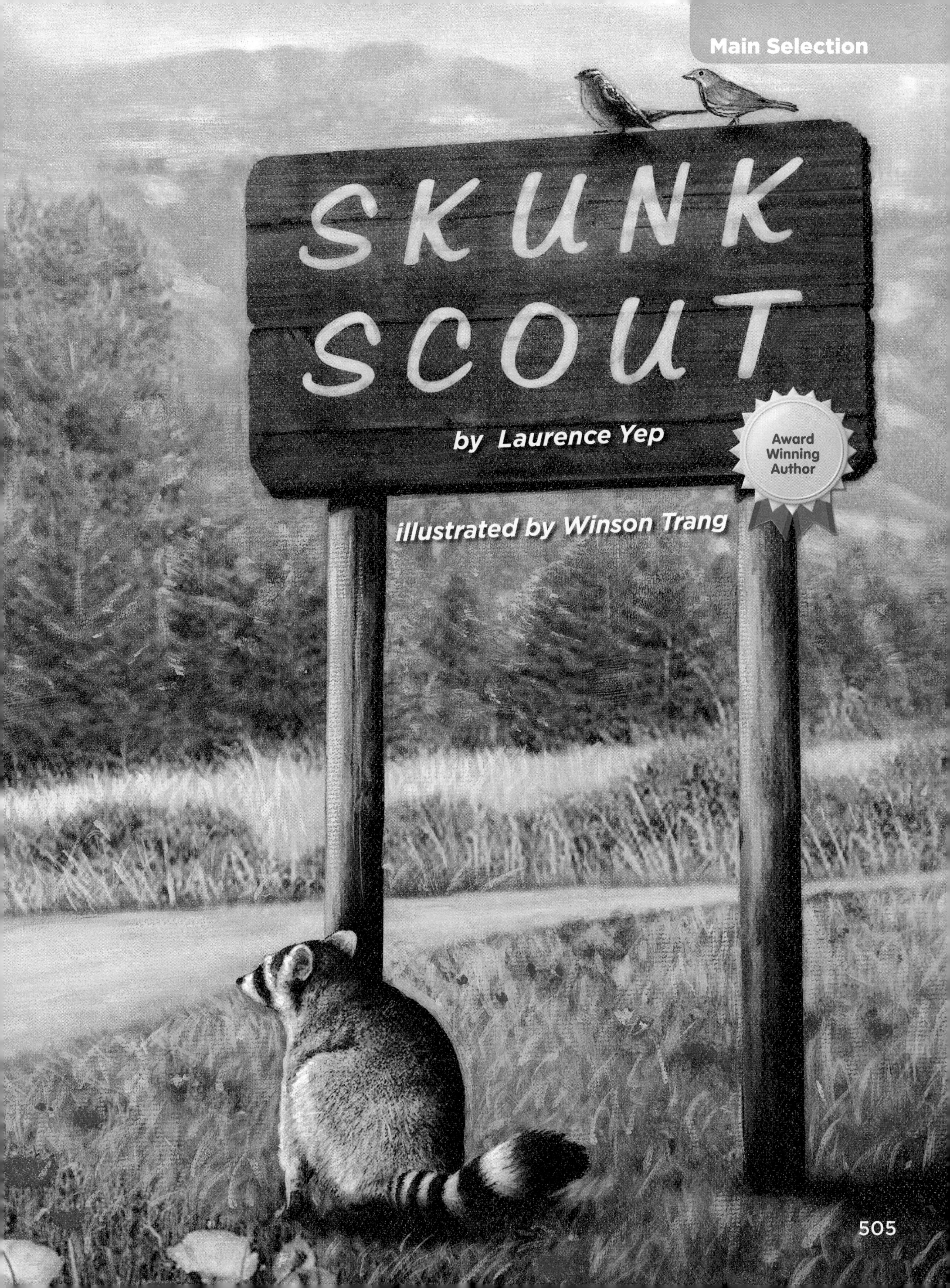

SKUNK SCOUT

by Laurence Yep

illustrated by Winson Trang

Award Winning Author

Teddy lives in San Francisco's Chinatown and loves city life. When Teddy reluctantly accepts an invitation to go camping with his Uncle Curtis and little brother Bobby, he has no idea what adventures Mother Nature has in store for them.

Mount Tamalpais kept growing bigger and bigger as we drove along. I thought some of the skyscrapers in San Francisco had been big, but they were toys compared to it.

You wouldn't think anyone could miss something that huge, but our uncle did. "Look, boys. That hawk's diving!" I thought he had told us everything possible about hawks, but he began spouting more.

"Oh, too bad," Bobby said. "He missed. I wonder what he was going for?"

The hawk wasn't the only one that needed better aim. As we shot past the exit, I leaned over the back of my uncle's seat. "Unh, Uncle Curtis, you should have turned back there."

Bobby rattled his map as he examined it. "Really?"

"Bobby you're supposed to be the navigator," I sighed.

"I'm sorry," Bobby said.

"How could you miss the sign?" I asked. "It's as big as a car."

"Now, now, no harm." Uncle Curtis shrugged. He left the freeway the first chance he got and then reentered the freeway, heading south.

Bobby leaned against his shoulder strap. "We'll get it this time."

But just as we got near the correct exit, Uncle Curtis suddenly twisted in his seat. "There's a rabbit!" he cried, pointing.

"Where?" Bobby asked, craning his neck.

As we shot past, I moaned, "We missed it again."

Uncle Curtis glanced into the rearview mirror. "Man, that came up faster than I thought."

I put a hand on his shoulder. "Okay. This time, no hawks. No rabbits. Just exit signs. Okay?"

Uncle Curtis gave a thumbs-up. "Got you."

"And don't you dare say anything except navigation stuff," I warned Bobby.

This time we got off at the right exit. I began to wonder how Uncle Curtis found his own bathroom at home. Maybe Aunt Ethel put up signs.

> **Make Judgments**
> Do you think Teddy's actions on this page are appropriate? Why or why not?

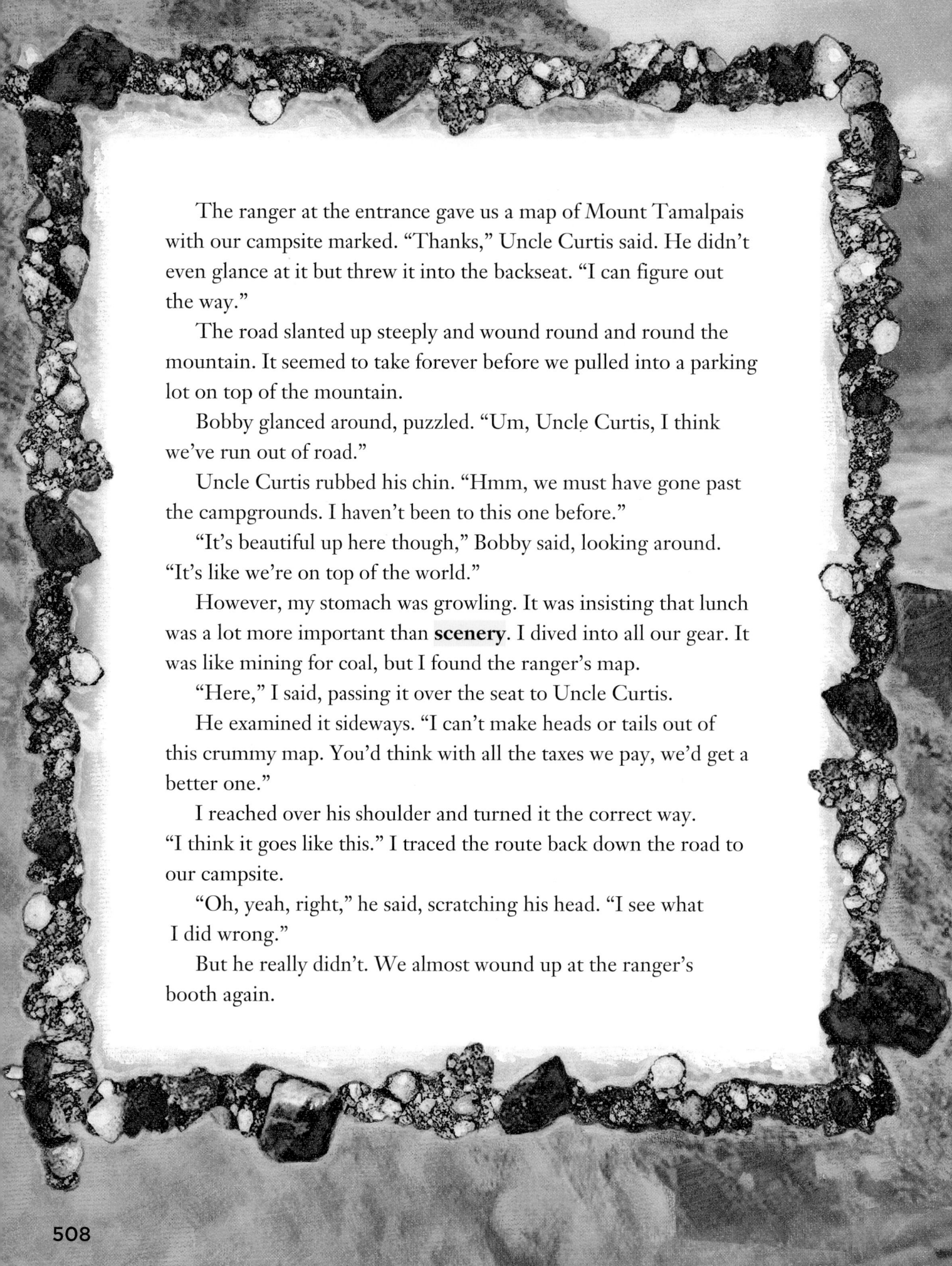

The ranger at the entrance gave us a map of Mount Tamalpais with our campsite marked. "Thanks," Uncle Curtis said. He didn't even glance at it but threw it into the backseat. "I can figure out the way."

The road slanted up steeply and wound round and round the mountain. It seemed to take forever before we pulled into a parking lot on top of the mountain.

Bobby glanced around, puzzled. "Um, Uncle Curtis, I think we've run out of road."

Uncle Curtis rubbed his chin. "Hmm, we must have gone past the campgrounds. I haven't been to this one before."

"It's beautiful up here though," Bobby said, looking around. "It's like we're on top of the world."

However, my stomach was growling. It was insisting that lunch was a lot more important than **scenery**. I dived into all our gear. It was like mining for coal, but I found the ranger's map.

"Here," I said, passing it over the seat to Uncle Curtis.

He examined it sideways. "I can't make heads or tails out of this crummy map. You'd think with all the taxes we pay, we'd get a better one."

I reached over his shoulder and turned it the correct way. "I think it goes like this." I traced the route back down the road to our campsite.

"Oh, yeah, right," he said, scratching his head. "I see what I did wrong."

But he really didn't. We almost wound up at the ranger's booth again.

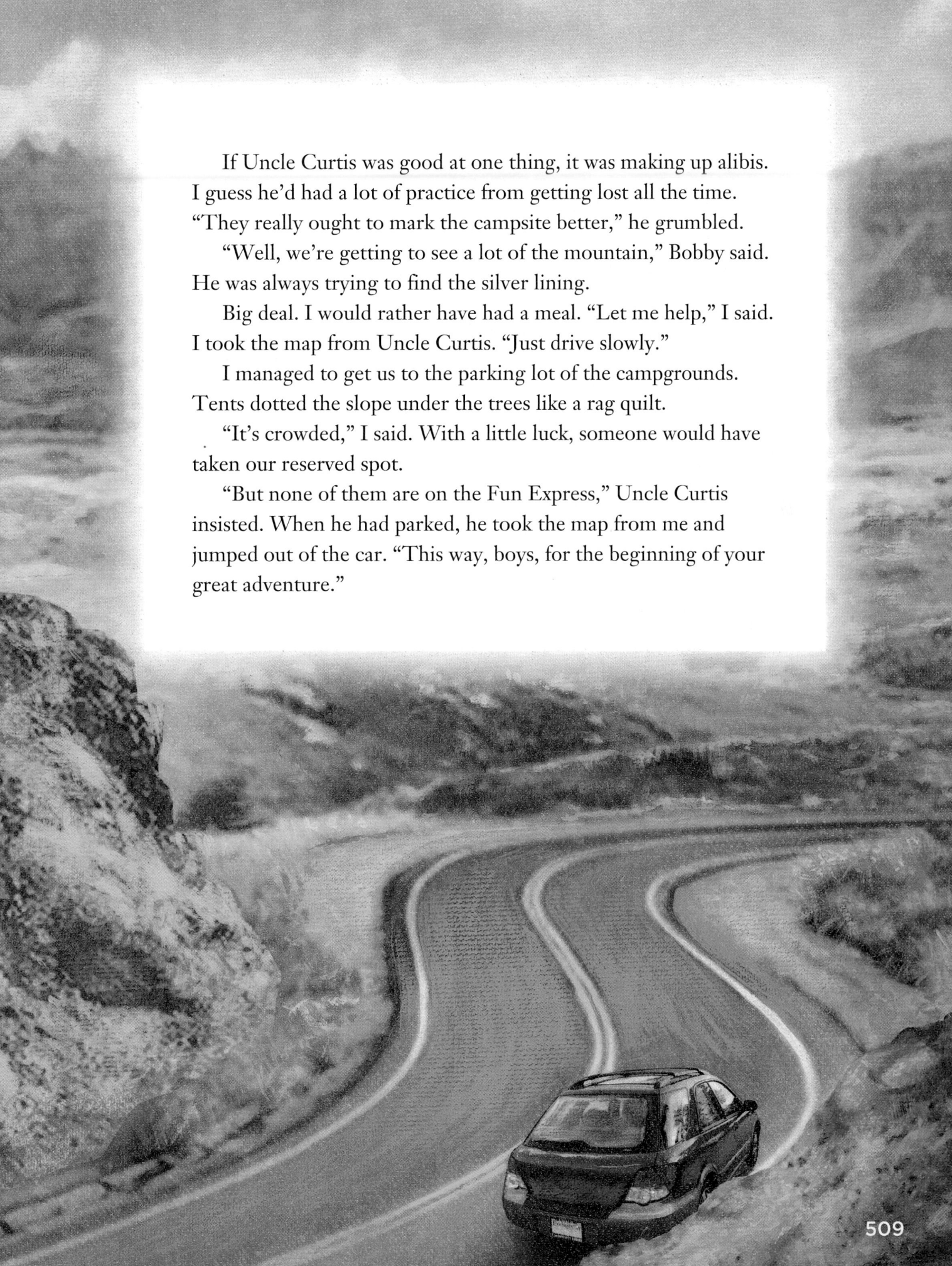

If Uncle Curtis was good at one thing, it was making up alibis. I guess he'd had a lot of practice from getting lost all the time. "They really ought to mark the campsite better," he grumbled.

"Well, we're getting to see a lot of the mountain," Bobby said. He was always trying to find the silver lining.

Big deal. I would rather have had a meal. "Let me help," I said. I took the map from Uncle Curtis. "Just drive slowly."

I managed to get us to the parking lot of the campgrounds. Tents dotted the slope under the trees like a rag quilt.

"It's crowded," I said. With a little luck, someone would have taken our reserved spot.

"But none of them are on the Fun Express," Uncle Curtis insisted. When he had parked, he took the map from me and jumped out of the car. "This way, boys, for the beginning of your great adventure."

We followed him up a dirt trail from the parking lot to a patch by some trees. Uncle Curtis stopped. "This is it," he declared, folding the map into neat little squares. "The great outdoors!"

As I kicked at one of the many rocks on the ground, I didn't see what was so great about it. "Isn't fun supposed to be less lumpy?"

My parents are always scolding me about being so messy. However, they should have seen Mother Nature. There were all these pebbles and leaves littering the dirt. I would have tidied up a little, especially for paying guests.

Satisfied, Uncle Curtis surveyed the site. "All this fresh air! It's **guaranteed** to make you feel so tired, you won't notice any rocks."

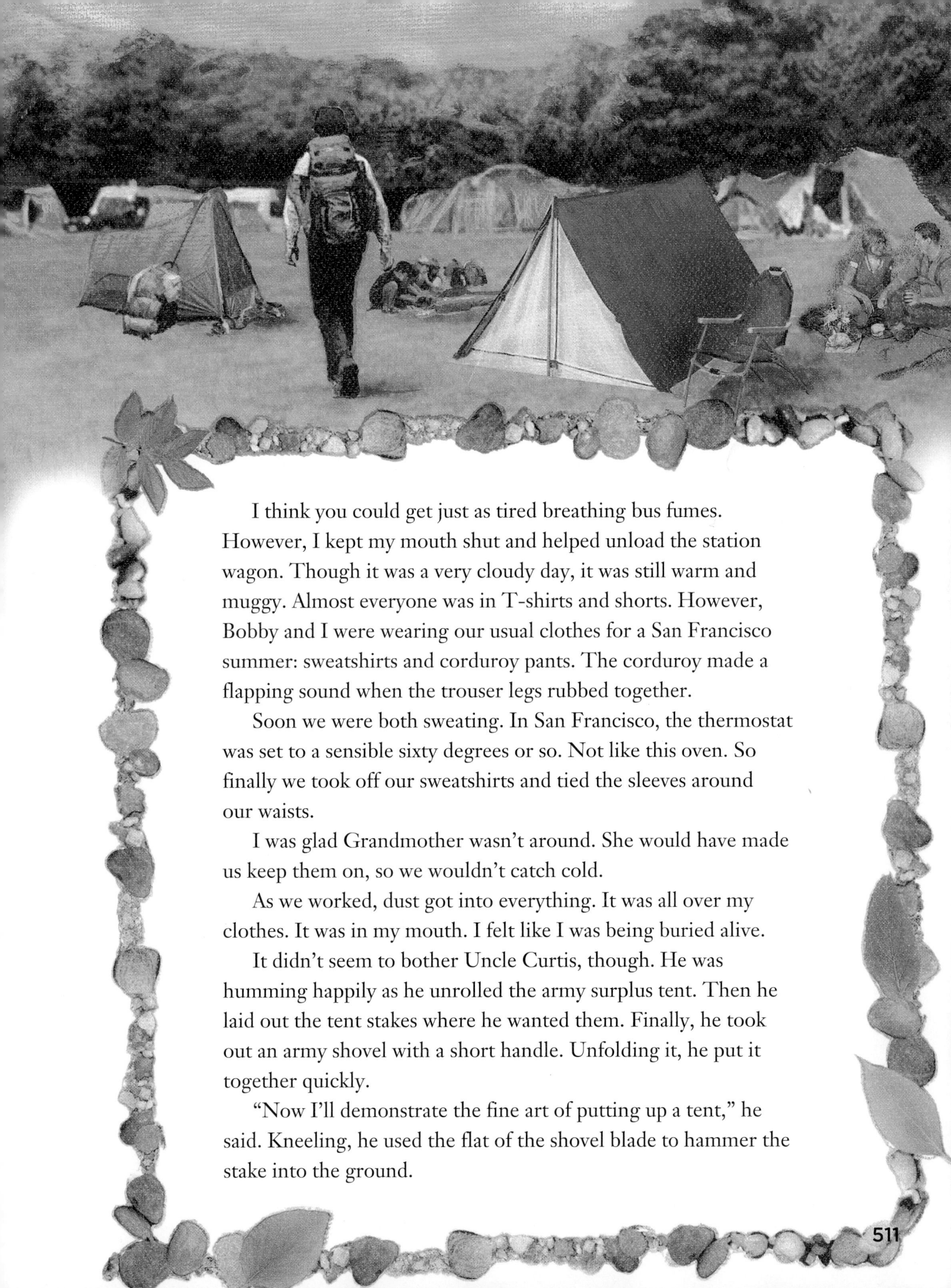

I think you could get just as tired breathing bus fumes. However, I kept my mouth shut and helped unload the station wagon. Though it was a very cloudy day, it was still warm and muggy. Almost everyone was in T-shirts and shorts. However, Bobby and I were wearing our usual clothes for a San Francisco summer: sweatshirts and corduroy pants. The corduroy made a flapping sound when the trouser legs rubbed together.

Soon we were both sweating. In San Francisco, the thermostat was set to a sensible sixty degrees or so. Not like this oven. So finally we took off our sweatshirts and tied the sleeves around our waists.

I was glad Grandmother wasn't around. She would have made us keep them on, so we wouldn't catch cold.

As we worked, dust got into everything. It was all over my clothes. It was in my mouth. I felt like I was being buried alive.

It didn't seem to bother Uncle Curtis, though. He was humming happily as he unrolled the army surplus tent. Then he laid out the tent stakes where he wanted them. Finally, he took out an army shovel with a short handle. Unfolding it, he put it together quickly.

"Now I'll demonstrate the fine art of putting up a tent," he said. Kneeling, he used the flat of the shovel blade to hammer the stake into the ground.

"Me next," Bobby said eagerly.

"You want to try everything, don't you?" Uncle Curtis grinned but he surrendered the shovel.

I knew my little brother, so I stepped back. Bobby thought that energy could always make up for lack of **coordination**. Uncle Curtis, though, made the mistake of staying close to **supervise**. He almost lost a kneecap when Bobby whacked at the tent stake and missed.

"Easy there," Uncle Curtis warned as he stumbled back.

Most of the time I try to get someone else to do all the work. But I saw another chance to prove I was just as good as my little brother.

"Let me have a turn," I said, holding out my hand.

I guess Uncle Curtis figured Bobby could take forever. "Let Teddy do that. You help me get the tent ready."

"But I want to do it," Bobby complained.

Uncle Curtis rubbed his head. "The sooner we set up camp, the sooner I can show you around. Isn't that what's really important?"

Bobby grudgingly handed the shovel to me and helped Uncle Curtis unroll the tent itself.

The ground was a lot harder than it looked. But lifting all those boxes in the store had given me muscles. So I hammered away until I got the stakes in.

It took all three of us to put up the tent. I still thought it leaned a little when we were done.

Uncle Curtis inspected the tent ropes carefully. He acted as though they were the cables holding up the Golden Gate Bridge. Finally, though, he nodded his head in approval. "That looks good."

When we had stowed our gear inside, I said, "I'm hungry. Let's eat."

"We've gotten used to eating Spam," Bobby explained.

"When you ride the Fun Express, you dine first class," Uncle Curtis boasted as he went over to the ice chest in the shadow of a big tree. He squatted down and undid the lid's clasps. "I brought hot dogs and hamburgers. I'll make you boys a feast." When he raised the lid, fog rolled out around him.

Bobby and I jumped back. "What's wrong?" my brother asked.

"It's just the dry ice." I laughed. I was enjoying my moment of triumph.

Uncle Curtis fanned his hand over the chest to help blow away some of the fog. "Boy, Teddy, I know this is one batch of meat that's not going to spoil."

White ribbons crept out of the chest and down the sides while Uncle Curtis carefully lifted out a big parcel wrapped in pink butcher paper.

He lost his grin though. "It's like a glacier."

I poked at the package in his hands. It was cold enough to make my body and hands ache. Through the paper, I traced the shape of hot dogs. "They feel like rocks."

Uncle Curtis lifted out the other package and hefted it over his shoulder like a shot put. "The hamburger's like a lump of coal, too."

I wasn't going to let this ruin my achievement. "Let's set them out," I urged. "Part of one of these packages will thaw out and we can have that."

So Uncle Curtis placed both packages out on a rock. "You boys have to get some firewood anyway. Just pick up the dead wood lying around. We're not allowed to chop down any trees."

"Right away," Bobby said, heading out.

"Wait for me, oh, fearless leader," I muttered, and wandered off after Bobby. "Just how much wood do you need to cook food anyway?" I asked the researcher. "I don't think we can carry back a log."

"The books didn't say," Bobby said, "but on television they always seem to use the wood about this thick." He held his fingers apart about six inches.

In the movies, there's always dead wood lying around, but all we could gather were twigs.

Disgusted, I looked at the handful I had. "This isn't even enough for a broom."

Bobby held up his own. "The other campers must have picked the mountain clean."

When we returned, Uncle Curtis stared at the handful of twigs. "That's okay for kindling. But where are the branches?"

"This is all we could find," I confessed helplessly.

Uncle Curtis rubbed the back of his neck. "I was counting on using firewood."

I saw a column of smoke rising a short distance away. "Maybe someone has spare firewood?"

"I'll borrow some. Nature lovers always share with one another. It's the code of camping," Uncle Curtis said. Suddenly he slapped himself. "Ow. Darn mosquitoes."

Apparently, there were other creatures besides humans having a meal. "I guess it's time to use my birthday gift," I said.

I went back to the tent. Something rustled in the brush nearby, but the bushes were too small for a bear to hide behind. So I went inside and got the mosquito repellent.

I can't say it did much good. Even as I sprayed my arm, a mosquito flew right through the mist to land on it. "This stuff just makes us tastier to the mosquitoes," I said.

I was hot, sweaty, being eaten alive, and hungry. So hungry that even Spam would have tasted good.

I poked each package in disappointment. "They're still like ice."

Bobby turned the packages over on the rock. They each clonked against the stone. "Darn dry ice." **Frustrated**, he picked up the package and dropped it against the rock. It landed with a loud crack. I thought there was a fifty-fifty chance that either the rock or the meat had broken.

Uncle Curtis grabbed a package under either arm. "We'll defrost the meat as we cook it. What's the menu for today, boys? Hot dogs or hamburgers?"

Bobby punched cheerfully at the air. "Hot dogs!"

I guess the dry ice hadn't been such a good idea, after all. Sulking, I jammed my hands in my pockets. "I'll settle for anything that isn't part of the polar ice cap."

Uncle Curtis put the hamburger into the chest and snapped the clasps shut. "You boys bring the buns and mess kits. I'll bring the hot dogs."

The cooking area was an open space. A row of stoves had been built from stones and metal grills.

Uncle Curtis went over to a table where some campers were eating.

He came back with half a bag of charcoal. "Ten dollars for this," he complained. "Fellow lovers of nature, my eye."

"Well, maybe it's the membership fee to the club," I said.

Uncle Curtis shot me a dirty look as he poured charcoal from the bag into the pit beneath the metal grill. Without lighter fluid, it took a little work and a lot of fanning and blowing before the coals caught.

As the coals slowly turned red, we began to set our stuff out on a nearby picnic table.

The previous cooks had not bothered to clean the grill. Uncle Curtis, though, had brought a spatula. He used it to scrape the metal bars.

In the meantime, we unwrapped the paper. The hot dogs were **fused** together into a lump the size of a football. No matter how hard we tried, we could not break them apart.

"Wait." Bobby proudly opened his borrowed mess kit and took out a fork. When he tried to pry a hot dog off, the tines bent.

We still hadn't freed any hot dogs by the time the coals were ready. By now, Uncle Curtis was too impatient to be careful. Lifting the mass of hot dogs, he set the whole fused lump on the grill. "I'll pry them off as they defrost." Water began dripping onto the coals with loud hisses. As steam rose around the hot dogs, Uncle Curtis straightened the tines of the fork. Carefully he worked at one of the hot dogs. "Almost…almost," he muttered.

With a plop, the hot dog fell through the grill and onto the coals. In no time, it was as black as a stick of charcoal. By the time this had happened to three more hot dogs, I tried to use a stick to **ease** them out of the coals.

Uncle Curtis shoved me back. "They're dirty."

"I don't care," I admitted. "I'm hungry."

"And they're half raw, too." He threw them into a trash can.

Make Judgments
Was Uncle Curtis right to throw the hot dogs away?

We were still trying to defrost the hot dogs long after the other campers had left. What wasn't burnt into charcoal was like a Popsicle. "We could get worms from eating raw meat." Uncle Curtis sighed. "And then what would your grandmother say? We'll eat the marshmallows instead."

We took the meat-cicles back with us, expecting them to defrost by dinnertime. "We can put the marshmallows on the sticks you brought back," Uncle Curtis said. "And then we can heat them over the coals."

That cheered me up a little. No meal can be too bad if it's mostly sugar.

"They should be in a paper sack, Teddy," Uncle Curtis said as he put the hot dogs back on the rock.

As I went to the tent, I saw its sides moving. I figured it was just the wind, but when I raised the flap of the tent, a gray furry **bundle** waddled out.

It was about the size of a watermelon, but covered all over with gray fur. On its face it had a black mask. From television, I knew it was a raccoon.

Calmly it licked a sticky paw. His toes looked a lot like little fingers.

"Aren't you supposed to be scared of me?" I asked him. Animals always were, on the nature shows.

I thought I saw him shrug. Then he cleaned the other paw.

"Well, I'm bigger than you," I pointed out to him. "That should count for something."

With a sniff, he strolled away into the brush.

I watched him disappear. Then, curious, I raised the flap on the tent.

Inside it was a mess—even worse than my part of our bedroom at home. The sleeping bags had been tumbled about. Worse, the paper bags had been torn open.

Suddenly I understood why the raccoon had licked his paws. The plastic sack with the marshmallows had been split apart. Only a few marshmallows were left. They lay scattered in the dirt. I whirled around. The brush was still shaking in the distance.

"You rotten little pig. I hope you get cavities," I yelled.

Going Camping with Laurence Yep and Winson Trang

Laurence Yep got bitten by the writing bug at his California high school. A teacher challenged his entire class to send their essays off to a national magazine. Laurence did, and soon after that he sold his first story. He was paid a penny a word! His advice to young writers: "Writing only requires one step to the side and looking at something from a slightly different angle." Laurence still lives in California with his wife.

Other books by Laurence Yep: *Dragonwings* and *Dragon's Gate*

Winson Trang is a book illustrator. He has illustrated many stories, especially those focused on Asian American subjects. This is the second time he has worked with Laurence Yep. The first book they both worked on was *Child of the Owl*. Winson currently lives in Los Angeles with his wife and son.

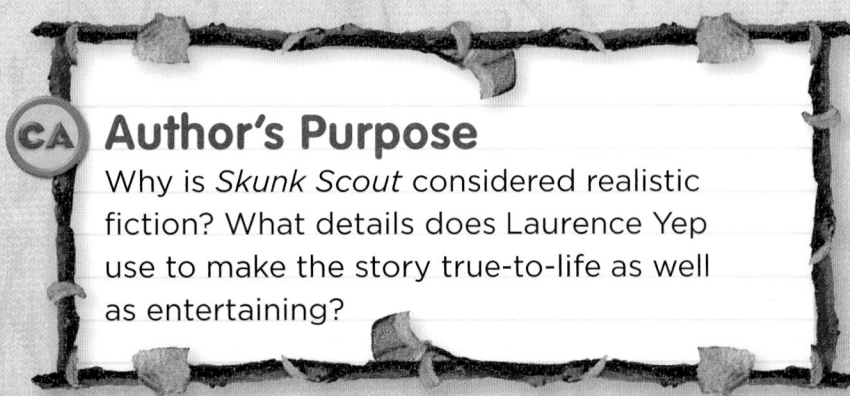

(CA) Author's Purpose

Why is *Skunk Scout* considered realistic fiction? What details does Laurence Yep use to make the story true-to-life as well as entertaining?

LOG ON ► Find out more about Laurence Yep and Winson Trang at **www.macmillanmh.com**.

CA Critical Thinking

Summarize

Use your Judgments Chart to help you summarize the chapter from *Skunk Scout*. The actions of the two brothers and their uncle while they were camping will help you organize your summary.

Action → Judgment
→
→
→
→

Think and Compare

1. Describe how the **judgments** you make about the characters might change if the story were told by Bobby instead of Teddy. **Monitor Comprehension: Make Judgments**

2. Reread pages 510–511. What can you tell about Teddy's life at home? Use details from the story in your answer. **Analyze**

3. Would you enjoy going on a camping trip with Uncle Curtis? Explain why or why not. What kind of **scenery** would you expect to see? **Analyze**

4. Do you think it is important to preserve our national parks? Explain your answer. **Evaluate**

5. Reread "The Best Fourth of July" on pages 502–503. Compare and contrast the camping experiences that Teddy and Lateesha had. Use details from both stories to support your answer. **Reading/Writing Across Texts**

Our National Parks

by Tanya Sumanga

Among the greatest treasures of the United States are its national parks. These parks contain an amazing variety of natural wonders, including plants, wildlife, rock **formations**, and **geysers**, or fountains of hot water. More than 50 national parks attract visitors every year. Some parks are quite large. Big Bend National Park in west Texas encompasses more than 800,000 acres of the Chihuahuan Desert along the United States–Mexico border. Famous for its many different environments, the park offers sharp contrasts in wilderness scenery. The Rio Grande curves through the park in a big bend, creating deep canyons. Rugged mountains, a desert plain, and unusual rock formations make up the park's landscape. Big Bend is noted for its rare forms of animal and plant life, such as roadrunners and prickly pears.

10 Largest National Parks
in the lower 48 States (as of 1997)

1. **Death Valley National Park**
   California
2. **Yellowstone National Park**
   Wyoming
3. **Everglades National Park**
   Florida
4. **Mojave National Preserve**
   California
5. **Grand Canyon National Park**
   Arizona
6. **Glacier National Park**
   Montana
7. **Olympic National Park**
   Washington
8. **Big Bend National Park**
   Texas
9. **Joshua Tree National Park**
   California
10. **Yosemite National Park**
    California

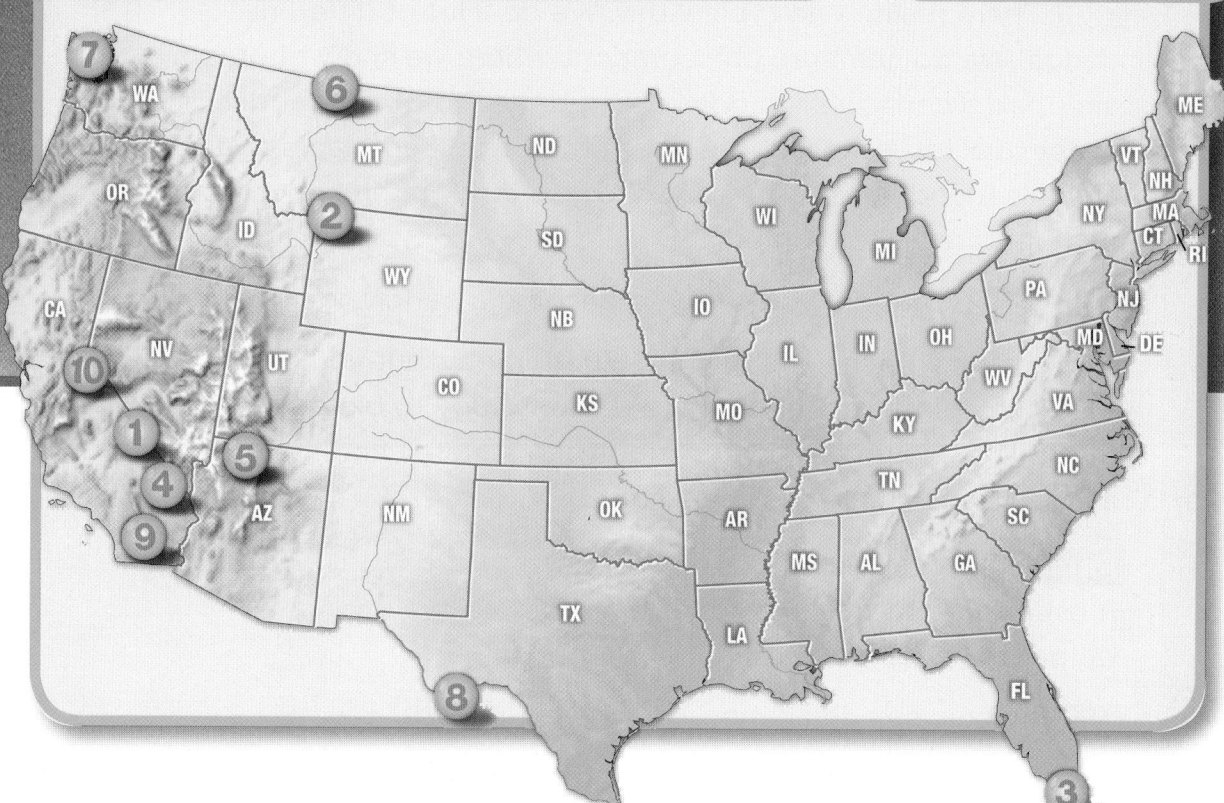

Archaeologists have found and studied pictographs (painted art) and petroglyphs (carved art) on rock walls and artifacts here that are nearly 10,000 years old. They reveal information about early Native American cultures and what life may have been like long ago.

The people who take care of national parks and who guide visitors through the parks are known as park rangers. Park rangers at Big Bend tell visitors how the area has changed over thousands of years.

People who like working outdoors and respect nature often become park rangers. Many park rangers enjoy reading about nature and studying the sciences.

Our reporter interviewed Dan Levitt, a park ranger who works at Big Bend National Park.

Reporter: What are the kinds of things you have to do when you are a park ranger? Do you give talks about the park? What is the typical day for a park ranger like?

Dan: There really is no typical day. We do a lot of different things. We do campfire presentations where we show photos and read a narrative. I'm doing one on the Rio Grande and its water quality. We talk about water, the earth, and plants and animals found here in the park. We also tend to the park trails and operate visitor centers.

Reporter: What did you study to become a park ranger?

Dan: I have a bachelor's degree in geography, but you can study anything from geology to paleontology to biology. I got my start by volunteering at various parks. Here I find that I use all the science courses I've taken.

Reporter: What would be the most important qualities for a ranger to have?

Dan: I would say dedication, understanding your duties, being loyal to the park, and wanting to help visitors.

Park Ranger Dan Levitt

AMAZING NEW BUG SPRAY!

Are you tired of being a breakfast, lunch, and dinner for bugs when you're camping?

Then use 100% natural "Chase Away Bug Spray!" It is guaranteed to work during your ENTIRE camping trip!

Created exclusively for park rangers, this is the first time it is being offered to the public at the low, low price of $19.95.

"'Chase Away Bug Spray' is the only bug spray I trust!" says Junior Park Ranger Charles "Chipper" Cruz.

CA Critical Thinking

1. Reread the interview on page 526. What do you think made Dan Levitt want to become a park ranger? What qualities does he think a park ranger should have? **Reading an Interview**

2. Tell about one way to help preserve national parks. **Analyze**

3. Think about "Our National Parks" and *Skunk Scout*. Do you think either of the boys or Uncle Curtis would make a good park ranger? Use examples from the texts to explain your answer. **Reading/Writing Across Texts**

Science Activity

Research the kinds of science mentioned by Ranger Dan Levitt. Make a chart that tells what the science is and why it would be useful to a national park ranger.

 Find out more about national parks at **www.macmillanmh.com**.

Reading and Writing Connection

✓ Setting and Context

Sometimes the characters in a story react to their **setting** and it causes them to feel or act a certain way.

Read the passage below. Notice how the author Laurence Yep describes the characters' reaction to the setting.

An excerpt from
Skunk Scout

The author shows Teddy's disappointment in his setting. Notice how Teddy kicks the rocks and is upset to see the campground not "tidied up."

Uncle Curtis stopped. "This is it," he declared, folding the map into neat little squares. "The great outdoors!"

As I kicked at one of the many rocks on the ground, I didn't see what was so great about it. "Isn't fun supposed to be less lumpy?"

My parents are always scolding me about being so messy. However, they should have seen Mother Nature. There were all these pebbles and leaves littering the dirt. I would have tidied up a little, especially for paying guests.

528

Read and Find

Read Waldo's writing below. How did he show the characters reacting to their setting? Use the Writer's Checklist to help you.

Dinner Out
by Waldo P.

As we walked into the Chez Molière, I hung back a bit from the rest of my family. There was a sparkling crystal chandelier. Oil paintings hung on the walls. I was suddenly embarrassed by my family's sneakers and T-shirts. I tried to walk as straight as I could as we wove our way to a table covered with shiny silver.

Read about my experience in a fancy restaurant.

Writer's Checklist

 Did the author describe what the character noticed about the setting?

 Does the author have the character do or say something because of the setting?

☑ Do you get an idea of how the character feels about the **setting**?

Review

Problem and Solution
Compare and Contrast
Fact and Opinion
Greek and Latin Roots
Primary Sources

Anansi and the Riddle

A nansi had a good friend named Tacoomah who got into trouble. The king ordered him to be executed. Anansi went to the king and begged for Tacoomah's life. The king said to him, "If he tells me a riddle that I can't answer, I'll spare his life."

Anansi went home and told Tacoomah to fill a hat full of dirt from the garden. Then he told him to get a pair of boots. Anansi put silver coins in the left boot, and gold coins in the right boot. Then he said, "Put on the hat full of dirt and boots full of coins. Go to the king and say:

> 'Under the earth I stood
> and instead silver and gold
> was my tread.'"

Tacoomah did as he was told. The king thought and thought but could not answer the riddle. Tacoomah showed the king his hat full of dirt and explained that he was standing on silver and gold (the coins in his boots). The king laughed and told Tacoomah that he was free to go.

The Riddle of the Sphinx

In Ancient Greece, in order to enter the city of Thebes, a traveler had to pass through a set of enormous bronze gates. One day a terrible creature appeared and took up residence on the dusty road in front of the gates. The creature, a Sphinx, possessed the head of a woman, the body of a lion, the wings of an eagle, and a snake's tail. It never allowed anyone to pass unless they answered a riddle.

If the traveler did not answer the riddle correctly, he or she was devoured by the Sphinx. The road was littered with the bones of unfortunate travelers. The city of Thebes was cut off from contact with the rest of the world as nobody had ever answered the riddle correctly.

One day, a brave young man named Oedipus approached the city.

"Stand your ground and answer my riddle," roared the Sphinx.

Oedipus waited patiently among the bones to hear the riddle.

"What creature moves on four feet in the morning, two feet in the afternoon, and three feet in the evening?"

Oedipus thought and then said, "Why, the creature must be a man. Man crawls on four legs in the morning of his life, walks on two in the afternoon, and in the evening of his life, walks with the help of a stick."

Upon hearing the correct answer, the Sphinx flew into a rage and threw herself off the top of the city walls. Oedipus had freed the city of Thebes.

National Parks:
Our National Treasures

WHERE CAN YOU GO to experience the great outdoors as it was 200 years ago? Fresh air, sparkling lakes, untouched land, and breathtaking scenery are all there for you to enjoy in this country's almost 400 national parks!

Yellowstone National Park

Trappers who had been out West told stories about bubbling mud and steamy springs that gushed hot water and steam. In the East these stories sparked people's interests. Adventurers set out to find the places that inspired such stories. In 1871 a group that included Thomas Moran and William H. Jackson explored the area that would become Yellowstone National Park. Moran was an artist and Jackson was a photographer. They found land formed by a volcano that had erupted more than 640,000 years earlier. Old Faithful and other hot springs amazed the visitors. The stories they had heard seemed to be true!

Moran and Jackson captured the beauty of Yellowstone in paint and on film. Along with Jackson's photographs, Moran's paintings were later used to persuade Congress that Yellowstone needed protection.

President Ulysses S. Grant made Yellowstone the first national park in 1872. This paved the way for the National Park Service, which began in 1916 by an act of Congress.

The Antiquities Act

President Theodore Roosevelt was a great conservationist. More federal land was protected under his administration than under any other President. He said,

The movement for the conservation of wild life and the larger movement for the conservation of all our natural resources are essentially democratic in spirit, purpose, and method.

In 1906 Roosevelt signed the Antiquities Act. This gave the government the power to grant further protection to national parks and other special places because of their beauty or because they are important to history or science. As Stephen T. Mather, the NPS director from 1917 to 1929, said, "The parks do not belong to one state or to one section."

The National Parks and You

When you visit a national park you can do many things. You can see natural waterfalls in Yosemite National Park. You can gaze at the sculpted rock of Grand Canyon National Park. You can learn how animals and plants live together in their natural environment at Joshua Tree National Park. You can explore important events in America's past by visiting Gettysburg National Military Park. At the Clara Barton or Frederick Douglass National Historic Sites, you can learn about people who helped make this country great.

These places, events, and people helped write the American story. By learning about them, you can begin to understand and appreciate your own place in this country's continuing story.

Thomas Moran, *Grand Canyon of the Yellowstone Park*, 1872

Moran became so well known for his watercolors of Yellowstone that people started calling him Thomas "Yellowstone" Moran.

CA Critical Thinking

Now answer numbers 1 through 4. Base your answers on the stories "Anansi and the Riddle" and "The Riddle of the Sphinx."

1. **What is Oedipus's main problem in "The Riddle of the Sphinx"?**

    A   Oedipus is afraid of the Sphinx.

    B   Oedipus must solve the Sphinx's riddle or else he will die.

    C   Oedipus does not want to go to Thebes.

    D   Oedipus is unable to solve the Sphinx's riddle.

2. **Anansi and Oedipus are alike because**

    A   they like to play tricks.

    B   they like to help their friends.

    C   they like to talk to kings.

    D   they are very clever.

3. **Anansi solves Tacoomah's problem by**

    A   having him wear a hat.

    B   having him wear boots.

    C   thinking up a clever riddle.

    D   talking to the king.

4. **How are the two stories "Anansi and the Riddle" and "The Riddle of the Sphinx" alike? Use details and information from the stories to support your answer.**

Now answer numbers 1 through 4. Base your answers on the article "National Parks: Our National Treasures."

1. **Which statement is an opinion?**

A   National parks are the best places to go on vacation.
B   These places, events, and people helped write the American story.
C   Moran and Jackson captured the beauty of Yellowstone.
D   In 1906 Roosevelt signed the Antiquities Act.

2. **Which word below has a Latin root that means *good*?**

A   reflect
B   benefit
C   explore
D   photograph

3. **Which statement comes from a primary source?**

A   Each park is special, and each park has a story.
B   Old Faithful and other hot springs amazed the visitors.
C   The parks do not belong to one state or to one section.
D   The trappers' stories of the West sparked people's interests.

4. **How were President Grant and President Roosevelt alike?**

A   They both tried to preserve and protect land.
B   They both signed the Antiquities Act.
C   They both met Moran and Jackson.
D   They both made Yellowstone a national park.

Write on Demand

PROMPT What role did Moran and Jackson play in helping to protect the land that would become Yellowstone National Park? Use details from the article to support your answer. Write for 15 minutes. Write as much as you can as well as you can.

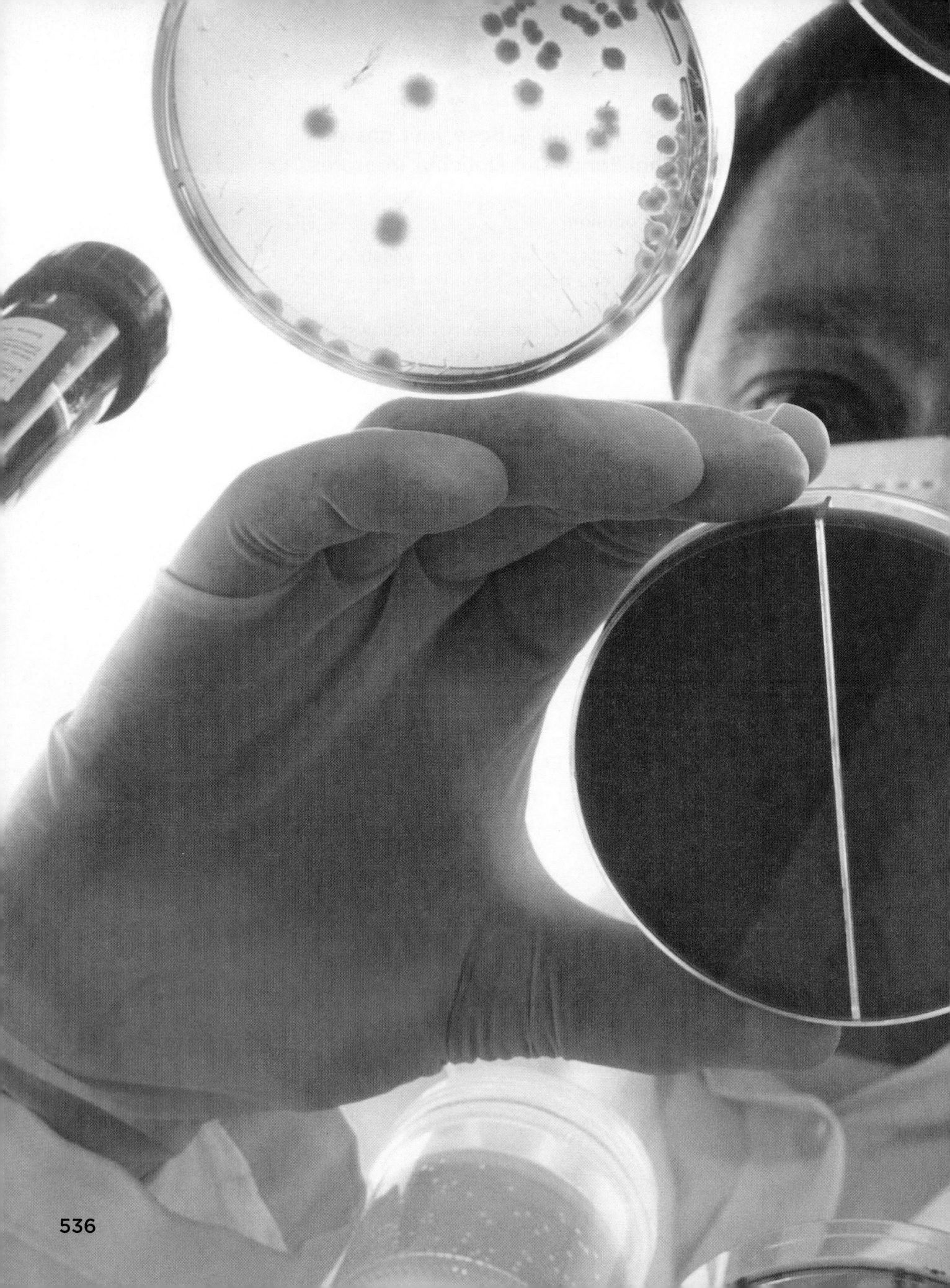

The Big Question

How do scientists learn about the natural world?

Theme Launcher Video

LOG ON Find out more about scientists at **www.macmillanmh.com**.

537

How do scientists learn about the natural world? They begin by being curious. They form a theory. Then they collect samples. They examine their samples, they do research, and then they report their findings.

You are like a scientist every time you go outside. You use your senses to discover nature, to collect flowers or insects and study them, and then to tell people what you have learned.

Learning how scientists study about the natural world can help you. You, too, can be a scientist or just someone who appreciates their work.

Research Activities

Throughout the unit, you will be reading about scientists who study the natural world. Decide which science selection interests you most. Then do research to find out more about the scientists who study this part of the natural world. Find out how people get into this field of science and what their most recent discoveries are.

Keep Track of Ideas

As you read, keep track of all you are learning about scientists who study nature. Use the Accordion Book organizer. On the first section, write the Unit Theme: Investigations. On each layer of the book, write about what you learn each week.

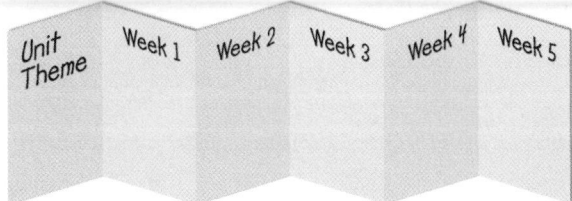

Research Toolkit

Conduct Your Unit 5 Research Online with:

Research Roadmap
Follow step-by-step guide to complete your research project.

Online Resources
- Topic Finder and other Research Tools
- Videos and Virtual Fieldtrips
- Photos and Drawings for Presentations
- Related Articles and Web Resources

California Web Site Links

 Go to **www.macmillanmh.com** for more information.

California People

Dorothea Lange
Photographer
With her photographs, Dorothea Lange would document rural poverty and the hardships and struggles of sharecroppers and migrant workers.

scientists
at work

CA **Talk About It**

If you could be a scientist, what would you study? What do you think the scientist in the photograph is studying?

LOG ON ▶ Find out more about scientists at **www.macmillanmh.com**.

541

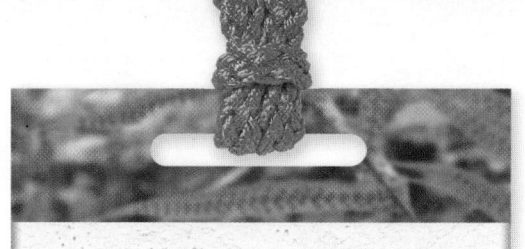

Vocabulary

specimens	**scoured**
murky	**biology**
dormant	**research**
transferred	**observer**

Word Parts

Some words have **Greek** or **Latin Roots**. If you know the meaning of a root, you can figure out a word's definition. For example, *bio-* means "life," so *biology* means "the study of living things."

Dr. Priscilla C. Grew, GEOLOGIST

by Josh Taylor

Dr. Priscilla C. Grew is a well-known scientist in the field of geology, the study of Earth's rocks. As a geologist, Dr. Grew looks at a lot of **specimens** to learn how Earth has changed in the past 4.5 billion years.

A good time and place to look for these changes is after a volcano has erupted. Afterward, the air becomes dark and **murky** from ash. When the ash settles, it blankets the land. Sometimes a volcano can release hot lava as well. When hot lava spills out, the ground becomes an excellent place to study how new rocks and minerals are formed. This is especially true for the ground near a **dormant** volcano because the area surrounding such a volcano has not changed in a very long time.

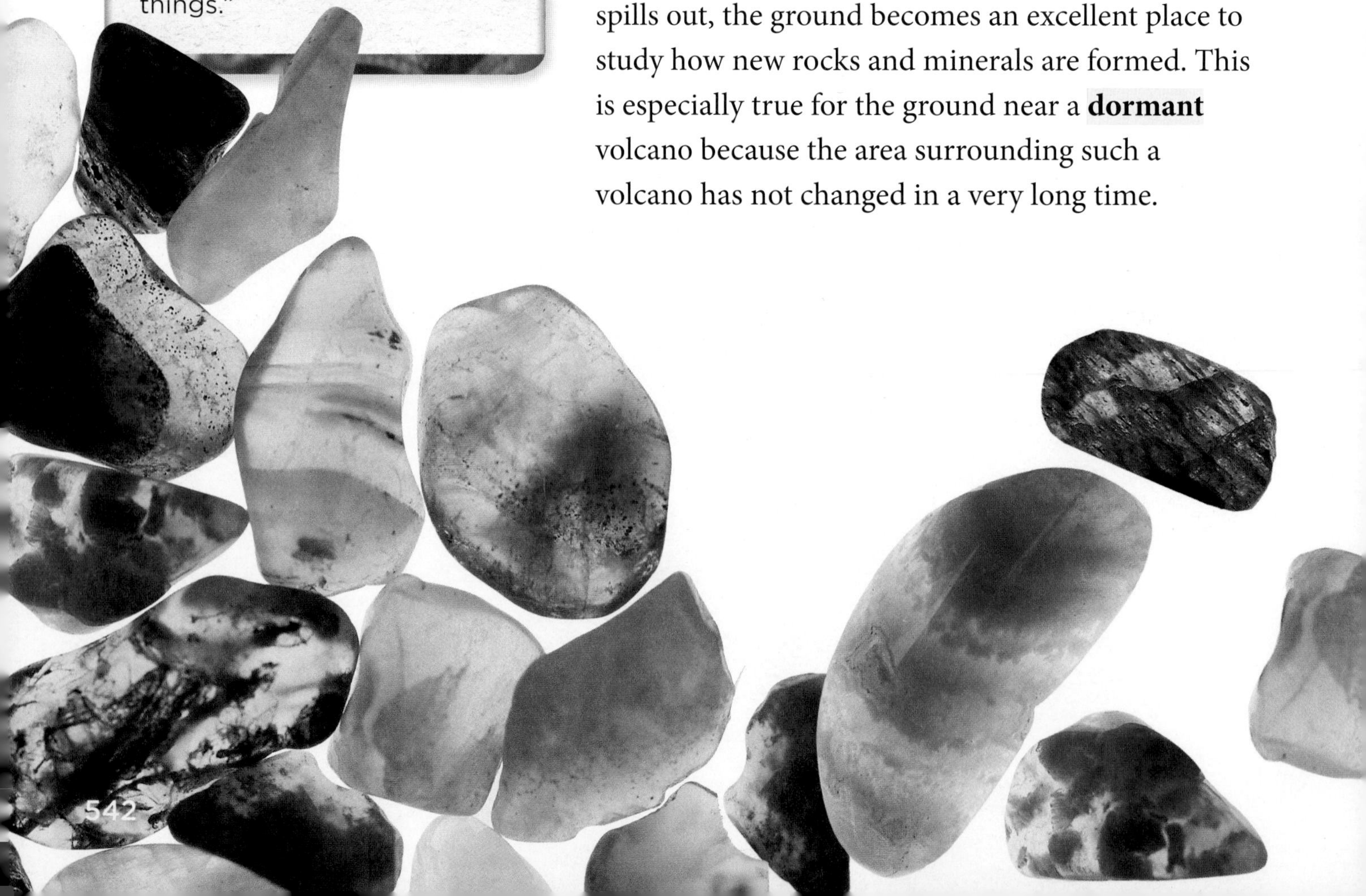

Areas affected by earthquakes are another good place to find a geologist. Early in her career, Dr. Grew **transferred** her interest in geology to help many people in California lower the chances of getting harmed during major earthquakes. Then Dr. Grew moved to Minnesota where she became the first woman to be named state geologist. She and her team searched all over the state for minerals in the soil. Once they were found, they were **scoured** clean and prepared for study.

After leaving Minnesota, Dr. Grew became the first female director of the University of Nebraska State Museum. Visitors to the museum learn about geology, earth science, and **biology**. They enjoy the displays of rocks and fossils.

During her life and career, Dr. Grew has tried to connect the world of rocks and soil to people's needs. By helping people to be safer during earthquakes and looking for important minerals in the soil, Dr. Grew connects her **research** to the real world. All this makes Dr. Grew more than an **observer**. She is a hands-on scientist who is making a difference.

Dr. Priscilla C. Grew

Reread for Comprehension

Summarize
Sequence

A Sequence Chart helps you summarize information by listing events or actions in the order that they take place. Use your Sequence Chart as you reread "Dr. Priscilla C. Grew, Geologist" to figure out the sequence of events in Dr. Grew's career.

Event

543

 Comprehension

Genre

Nonfiction gives information and facts about real people, places, events, and situations.

Summarize

 **Sequence**

Look for clues that indicate the order of events.
As you read, use your Sequence Chart.

Event
↓
↓
↓

Read to Find Out

What events influenced Dennis's career in science?

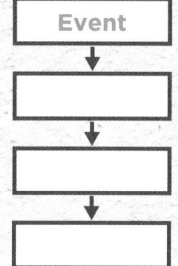

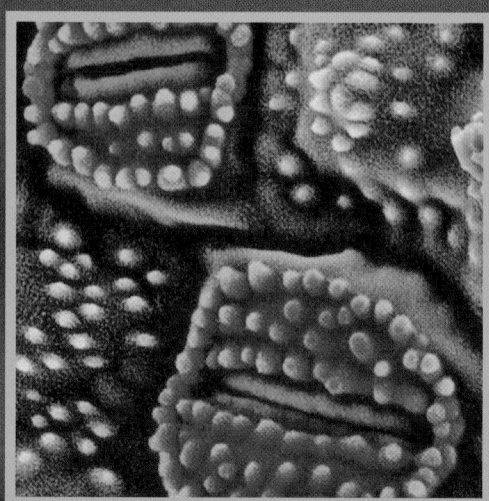

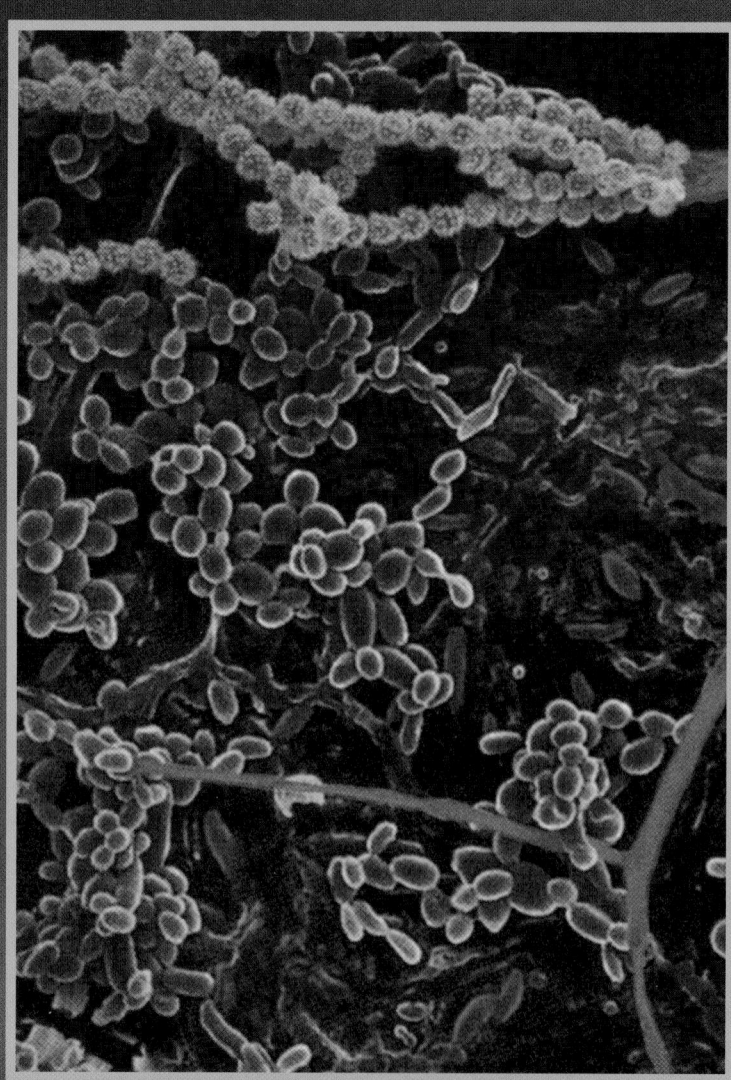

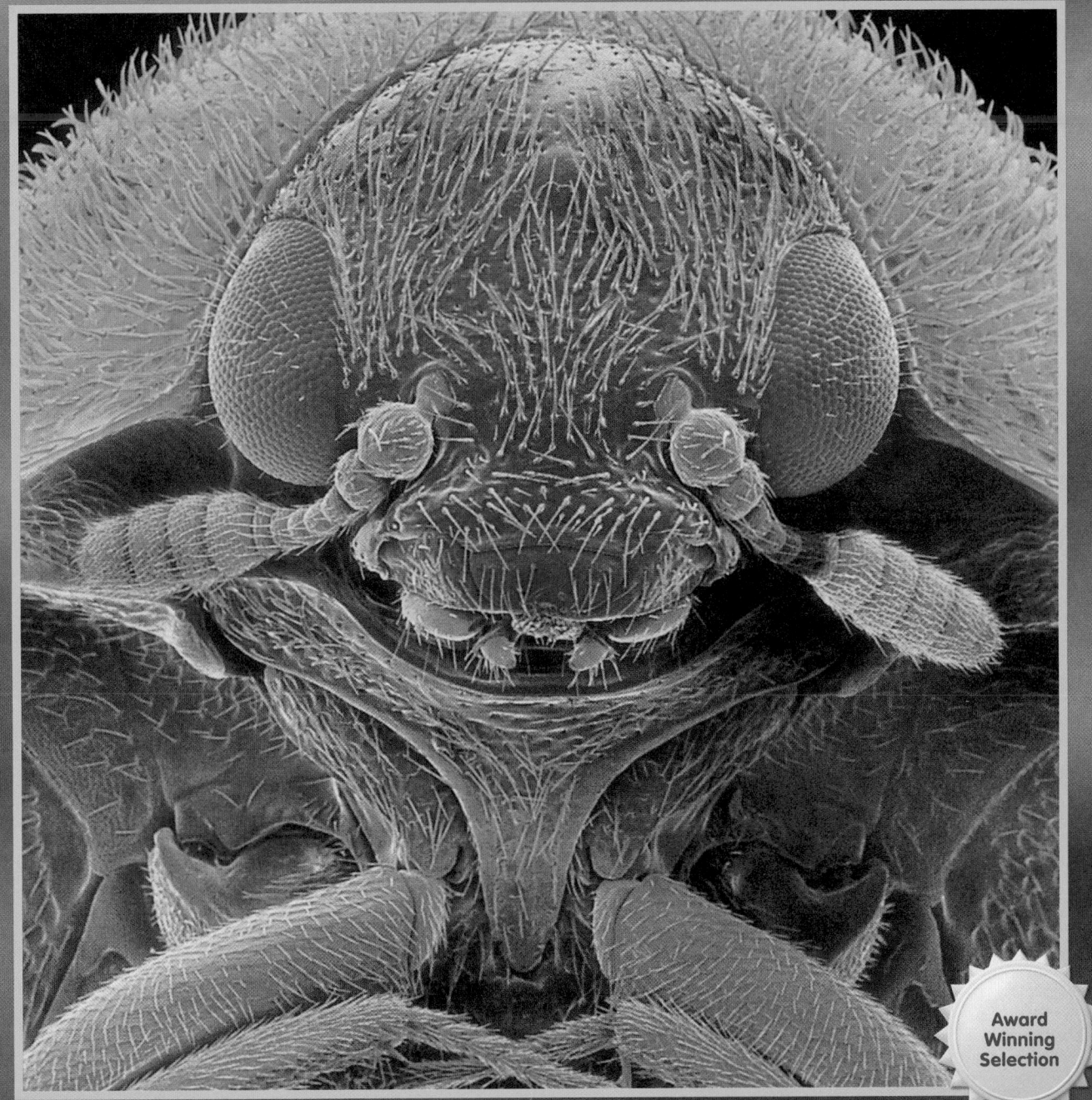

Award Winning Selection

Hidden Worlds

Looking Through a Scientist's Microscope

by Stephen Kramer
photographs by Dennis Kunkel

Becoming a Scientist

Dennis Kunkel grew up in the Iowa countryside, where cornfields stretched for miles in all directions. Dennis helped tend the flowers and vegetables in the family garden. He went on weekend fishing trips with his parents and his sisters, and he took care of the family pets. Dennis loved nature and being outdoors, but he did not know that someday he would become a scientist.

Then Dennis received a gift that changed his life. "When I was ten years old, my parents gave me a microscope for Christmas," he recalls. "It came with a set of prepared slides—things like insect legs, root hairs, and tiny creatures called protozoans. As soon as I unwrapped the microscope, I forgot about my other presents and tried to figure out how to use it."

Dennis working at one of his microscopes

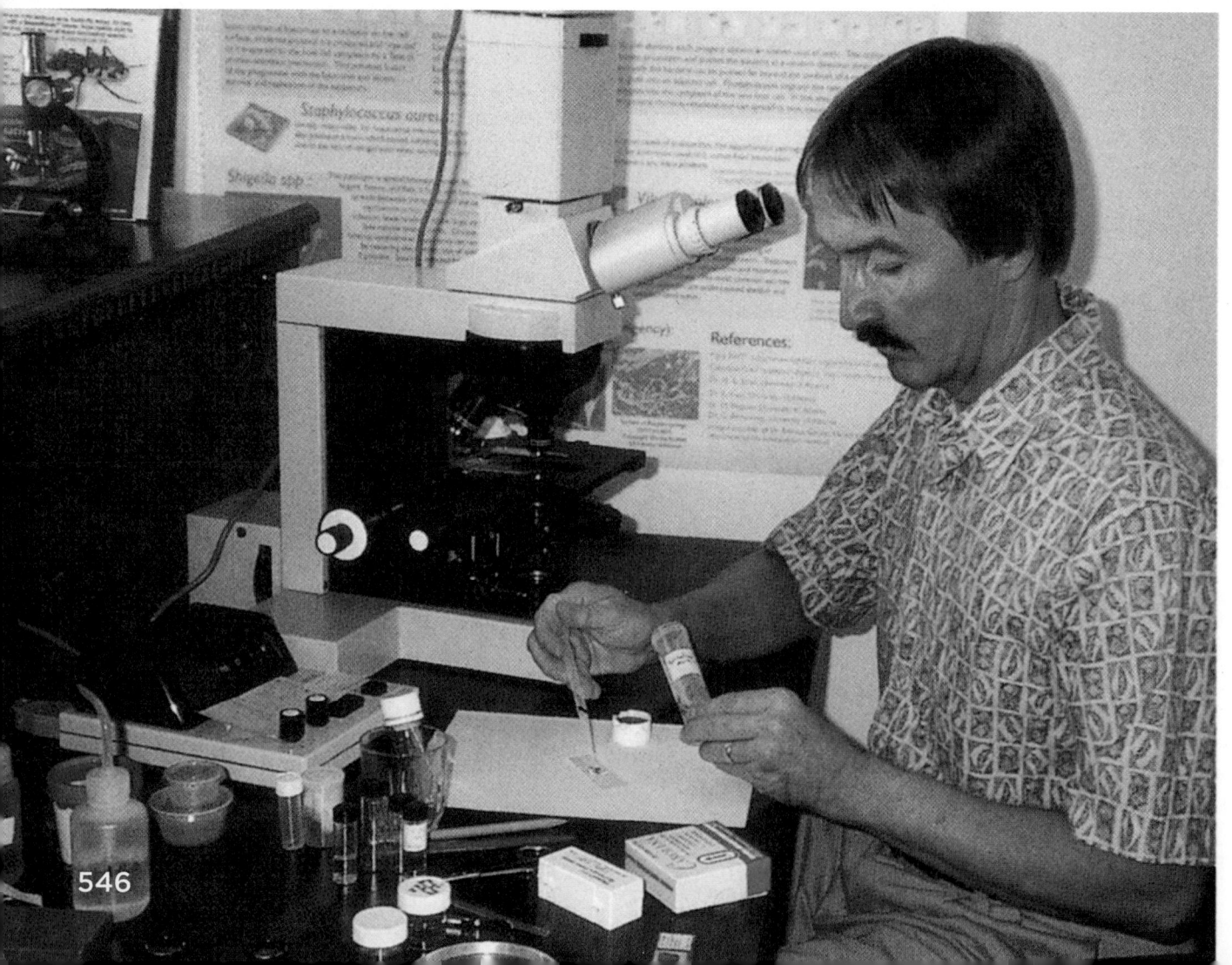

When Dennis looked at pond water with his first microscope, he saw these kinds of simple plants. They are green algae. Above: *Volvox*. Right: *Micrasterias*.

The prepared specimens that came with the microscope were dead. Dennis quickly discovered that it was more fun to observe things that were alive and moving, so he began to take collecting trips. One of Dennis's first trips was to a pond about a mile and a half from his house. "I started hiking down there with my little collecting bottles and bringing back water samples to look at under my microscope," he explains. "I couldn't wait to get home from school in the afternoon so I could go to the pond. Before long I was looking at all kinds of fascinating creatures."

Dennis used his microscope to look at anything he could fit under its lenses. He examined insects, soil samples, and parts of plants. He looked at fur from his pets and seeds from nearby fields. Dennis made drawings of the things he observed, and he spent many hours reading about them.

After Dennis graduated from high school, he enrolled in a junior college in his hometown. A **biology** teacher there encouraged his love of science and microscopes. Dennis often worked in the science lab after school, using microscopes to study the things he collected.

Then Dennis **transferred** to the University of Washington, in Seattle. Finally he could learn and do things he had dreamed about. "I had the chance to work in labs with good microscopes," explains Dennis. "I spent hours speaking with professors and students about science. I had dreamed of exploring and learning about undersea life like Jacques Cousteau, but until I left Iowa I had never even seen the ocean. While I attended the University of Washington, I learned how to scuba dive. It was thrilling to go underwater to observe and collect the plants and animals I wanted to study."

**Dennis examines leaves
with two young scientists.**

Sequence
What clue words does the author use to indicate the time order of events in Dennis Kunkel's life?

548

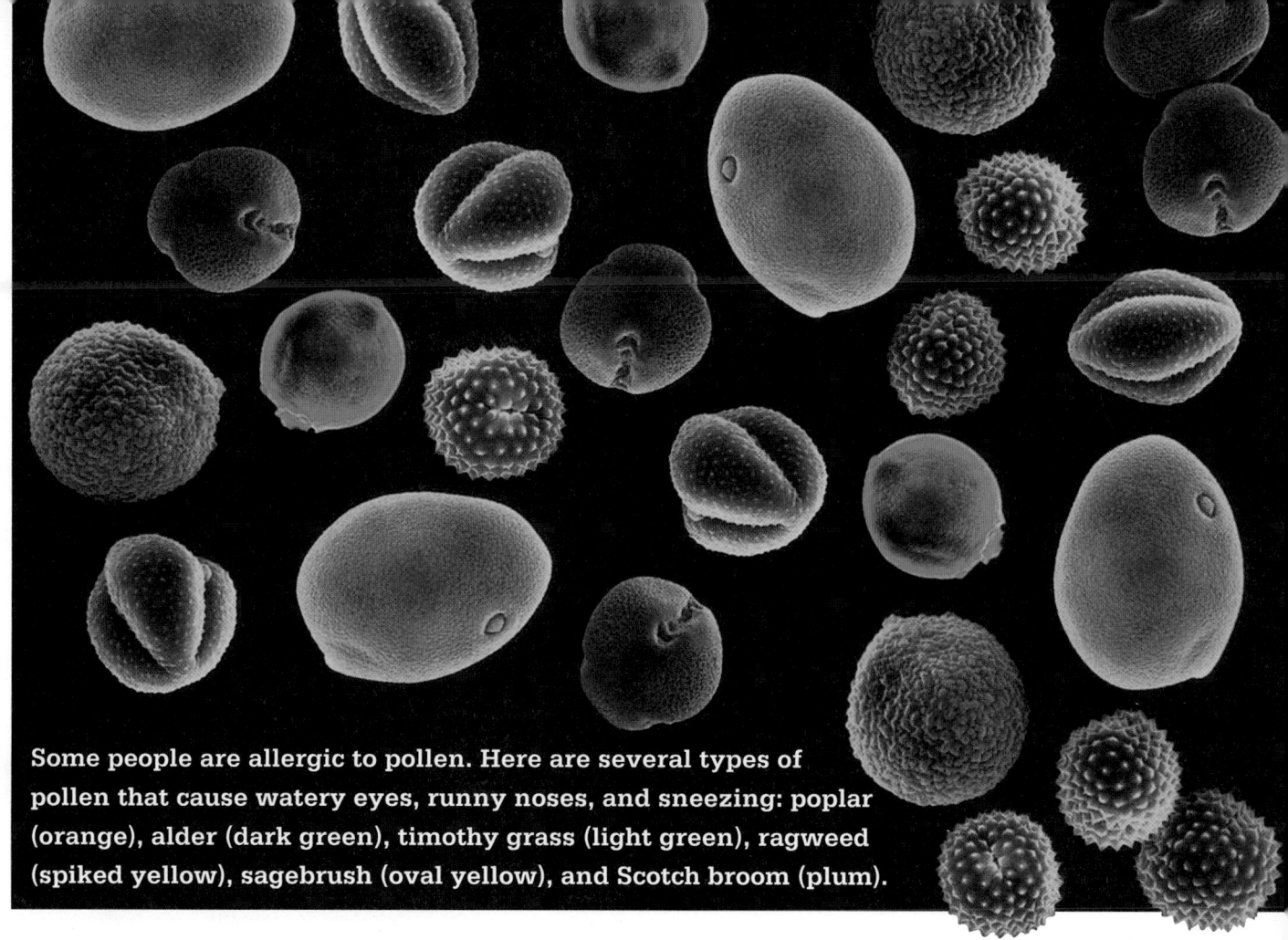

Some people are allergic to pollen. Here are several types of pollen that cause watery eyes, runny noses, and sneezing: poplar (orange), alder (dark green), timothy grass (light green), ragweed (spiked yellow), sagebrush (oval yellow), and Scotch broom (plum).

In graduate school, Dennis began to use the science department's electron microscopes for his own **research**, studying tiny living things called cyanobacteria. But Dennis also used the microscopes to help other scientists. He helped one of his professors study and classify pollen grains from different kinds of flowers. He helped a fellow graduate student examine wood with an electron microscope to learn about how plant cells deposit minerals and create "hard" wood. He helped other students with their studies of algae, fungi, and flowering plants.

After eight years of graduate work—including thousands of hours of research and work with microscopes—Dennis earned a Ph.D. in botany, the study of plants. Although Dennis was finishing his schooling, he was just beginning a lifetime of scientific learning and discovery.

Dennis worked on research projects at the University of Washington and the University of Hawai'i for about twenty-five years. Now he does much of his work in his home on the island of O'ahu, Hawai'i.

Working as a Scientist

Scientists are explorers. They usually make discoveries by asking questions and then trying to answer them. Some scientists find their answers in laboratories, surrounded by equipment and instruments. Others travel to natural areas to find their answers. Dennis's work has taken him to mountains, rainforests, deserts, caves, beaches, and into the sea.

Whenever Dennis goes on field trips, he takes along collecting boxes and bottles. When he returns to the lab, the boxes and bottles are usually full of interesting **specimens**: algae, lichens, mushrooms, seeds, leaves, insects, bark, soil, and flowers. Dennis has explored hidden worlds in places ranging from the blast zone of a volcano to the dust balls underneath people's beds!

The aquatic nymph stage of the mayfly. Adult mayflies are slender flying insects found around streams and ponds.

A butterfly's proboscis, the coiled mouthpart it uses to sip nectar.

Dennis and the scientific team collect water samples.

Mount St. Helens

In 1980, a **dormant** volcano called Mount St. Helens erupted in Washington State. The blast from the eruption flattened huge forests of tall trees. Floods of boiling mud and water from melting snow **scoured** riverbeds. The countryside was covered with a thick layer of ash for miles around.

Some of the first people allowed to visit the blast zone were biologists, scientists who study living things. They were stunned by the destruction. One of the first things they wanted to know was whether any living things had survived.

A team of scientists from the University of Washington made plans to study the lakes and streams of the blast area. Since Dennis was an expert on algae, the simple plants found in lakes and streams, he was invited to help with the study. The scientists traveled to a camp set up on the north side of Mount St. Helens. Twice a day, a helicopter flew them into the blast zone. All they could see, for miles in every direction, were dead trees blanketed by a heavy layer of ash.

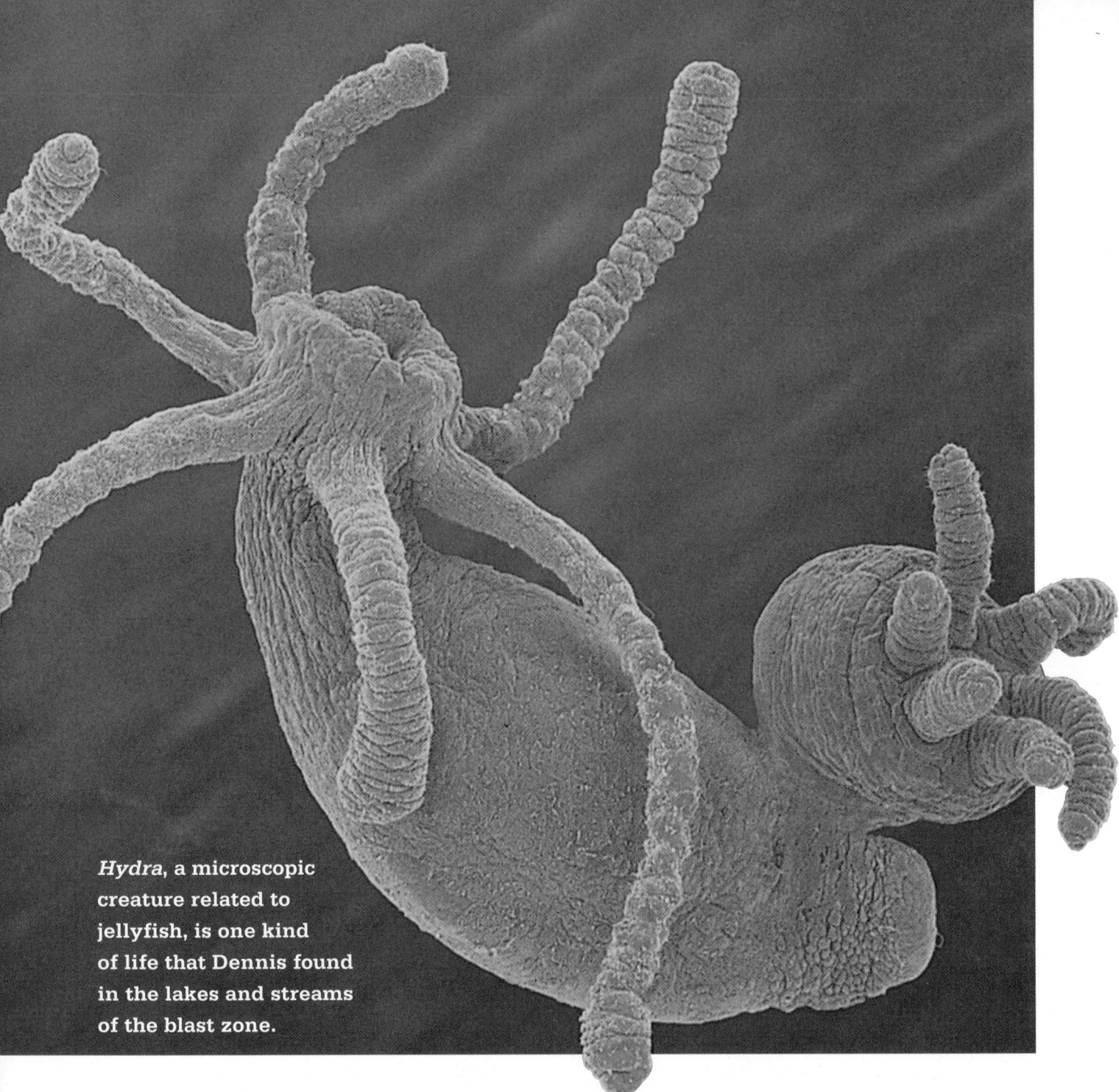

Hydra, a microscopic creature related to jellyfish, is one kind of life that Dennis found in the lakes and streams of the blast zone.

The scientists were thrilled because they had never explored the area around an active volcano so soon after this type of eruption. But no one knew when the mountain might erupt again. In fact, no one even knew for sure whether it was safe to land a helicopter in the blast zone. Some pilots thought the ash stirred up by the whirling helicopter blades might choke the engines. So Dennis and the other scientists weren't allowed to land in the study area on the first few trips. They had to collect their water samples while the helicopter was in the air!

As Dennis and the team crisscrossed the blast zone in the helicopter, they kept their eyes open for water. When they spotted a lake or pond that had survived the blast, the pilot flew the helicopter into position. As the helicopter hovered over the **murky** gray water, Dennis lowered collecting bottles on ropes. The bottles had triggers so Dennis could open them at different depths. This allowed him to collect some water samples from near the surface and others from deep in the lakes.

The first water samples the scientists collected showed that some of the lakes were completely dead. Nothing had survived the heat, gases, and choking ash of the eruption.

Just a few weeks later, Dennis used microscopes to look at new water samples he had collected from the same lakes. He was amazed to see algae, protozoans, and bacteria living in the water. Within several months, small crustaceans—animals that feed on algae and bacteria—began to reappear in some of the lakes.

Dennis and the other scientists kept careful records of the kinds of living things that returned to the lakes and when they reappeared. They identified the kinds of algae, protozoans, bacteria, and crustaceans they found. Later, Dennis and the team also discovered that frogs and fish were returning to some of these lakes, apparently carried in by surrounding streams. Their studies helped other scientists understand what happens to life in lakes when a nearby volcano erupts—and how living things eventually return to areas where all life was destroyed.

Vorticella, **a single-celled protozoan**

Sequence
List the different life forms that developed in the dead lakes near the volcano in the order that they appeared.

How to Become a Scientist

Here is Dennis's advice for students who think they might like to become scientists:

Become an **observer**. One of the most important things you can do to become a good scientist and microscopist is practice being a careful observer. Find a comfortable chair and put it in the middle of your garden, yard, or a park. Sit in the chair for ten minutes or thirty minutes or an hour. Watch the insects that fly past or land on the plants. Look at the shapes of leaves and stems and branches. Listen to the sounds of buzzing bees and chirping crickets. See if you can find a sight or smell or sound that surprises you. Use a loupe or magnifying glass to look closely at interesting objects.

Dennis and a graduate student examine a South African clawed frog.

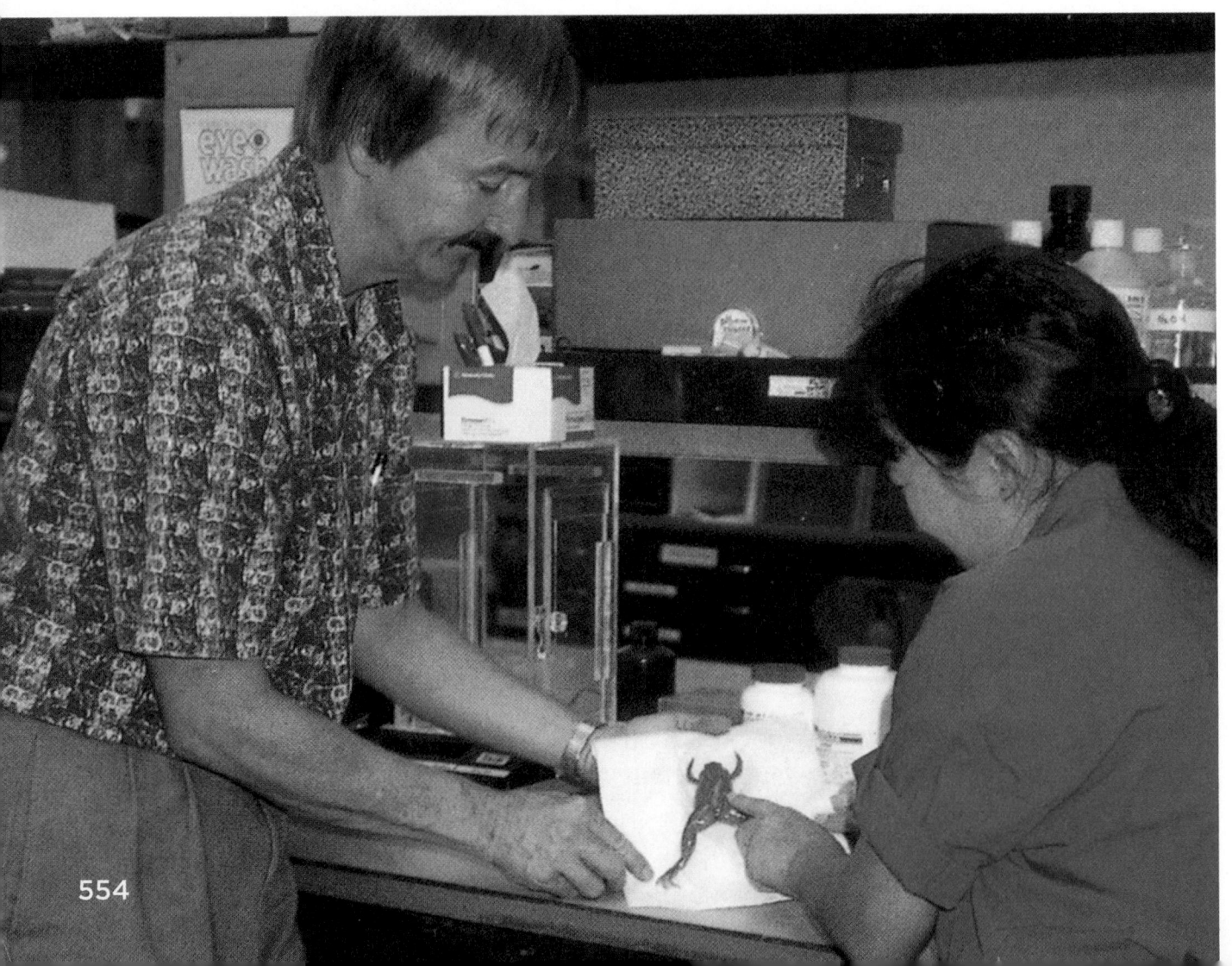

Dennis looking closely at a fern leaf

Learn everything you can about a topic that interests you. Suppose you'd like to explore flowers by using a microscope. Go to the library and check out some flower books. See what you can find on the Internet. Pick some flowers and carefully take them apart. Use a loupe or a magnifying glass to see how everything fits together. The more you know about flowers from reading about them and observing them, the more you'll understand when you begin looking at them with a loupe or a microscope.

Ask for help from a knowledgeable person. After you've learned everything you can on your own, ask someone else to help with questions you still have. Maybe there's someone at a nearby school or museum who knows about insects, spiders, algae, moss, or something else you'd like to learn about. If you don't have a microscope of your own, maybe a teacher would help you look at some specimens with a school microscope.

Find a scientist to talk to or find a place where scientific research is being done. If you still want to learn more, you may be able to find a scientist to talk to at a nearby college, university, or research station. Write a letter or an e-mail message to the scientist, explaining what you're interested in. Ask if you can schedule a time to visit. Most scientists are happy to talk to students who share their passion for science.

Under the Microscope with Stephen Kramer and Dennis Kunkel

Stephen Kramer is an author and teacher. When he is not writing about avalanches or following Dennis Kunkel into a volcano, he is teaching fifth graders. Both of his careers focus on a love of science and teaching. He especially enjoys teaching children different scientific facts about bats, rainforests, or machines. Stephen lives in Vancouver, Washington, with his wife and their two sons.

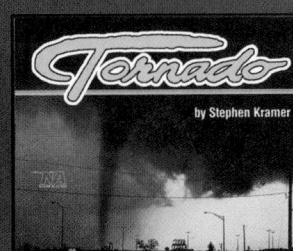

Another book by Stephen Kramer:
Tornado

Dennis Kunkel is often found looking at fleas, bacteria, and blood cells under his microscope. He has made large contributions to the science world with what he has witnessed through his lens. Dennis loves the new information his microscope unveils because he appreciates the beauty of what is missed by the naked eye. Dennis's research and pictures have appeared in magazines, museum exhibits, and even movies.

LOG ON ▶ Find out more about Stephen Kramer and Dennis Kunkel at **www.macmillanmh.com**.

(CA) Author's Purpose

How can readers tell that Stephen Kramer respects scientists greatly? Give examples from the text, headings, or photos.

 **Critical Thinking**

Summarize

Use your Sequence Chart to summarize important information from *Hidden Worlds: Looking Through a Scientist's Microscope*.

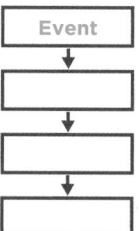

Think and Compare

1. Describe the **sequence** of steps Dennis thinks are important in becoming a better scientist. **Summarize: Sequence**

2. Why do you think Dennis looked for living things after the eruption of Mt. St. Helens? Include facts from the selection in your answer. **Analyze**

3. Explain how you would practice becoming a careful **observer**. Include where you would choose to observe and what you might see, smell, hear, and touch. **Evaluate**

4. What effect do scientists like Dennis Kunkel, Albert Einstein, and others, have on the world? Explain your answer. **Analyze**

5. Reread "Dr. Priscilla C. Grew, Geologist" on pages 542–543. Compare and contrast Dr. Grew's experiences with Dennis Kunkel's career. Use details from both selections in your answer. **Reading/Writing Across Texts**

Our high and mighty termite mound arises far above the ground, and just as deep, grows underground. Our nest is blessed to be immense. It gives us all a firm defense, superior to any fence. It shields us from our enemies. It keeps us cooler, by degrees. From floods and droughts it guarantees. A prize nobody will assign in architectural design, but still our hill suits us just fine.

558

 Critical Thinking

1. How do the rhythm and rhyme scheme help you to read this poem with the appropriate tone? **Rhyme Scheme and Rhythm**

2. How does the shape of this concrete poem tell you more about its subject? **Analyze**

3. Compare the information in "Termites" with *Hidden Worlds: Looking Through a Scientist's Microscope.* How do both selections tell you about nature? **Reading/Writing Across Texts**

 Find out more about poetry at **www.macmillanmh.com**.

559

Writing

CA

✓ Relevant Evidence

Good writers use **relevant evidence** and important details to support their opinions.

Read the passage below. Notice how the author Stephen Kramer includes details to match his opinion that collecting data was very important.

An excerpt from
Hidden Worlds

The author shows that Dennis's team of scientists really wanted to travel to the blast zone but evidence shows they did not have complete access.

The scientists were thrilled because they had never explored the area around an active volcano so soon after this type of eruption. But no one knew when the mountain might erupt again. In fact, no one knew for sure whether it was safe to land a helicopter in the blast zone. . . . So Dennis and the other scientists weren't allowed to land in the study area on the first few trips. They had to collect their water samples while the helicopter was in the air!

Hidden Worlds
Looking Through a Scientist's Microscope
by Stephen Kramer
photographs by Dennis Kunkel

Read and Find

Read Alex's writing. How did he use details to show why other students liked his drawing? Use the Writer's Checklist below to help you.

Corner Drawings
by Alex W.

Eric liked my drawing because it had details and shading. We had to draw a picture of the little things we noticed. I sketched an electric outlet. I looked at the details. I noticed holes that were rectangles and circles. I noticed the screws' angles along the outside. My pencil was sharp and I drew what I saw.

Read about the details I captured in my drawing.

Writer's Checklist

 Did the author use **relevant evidence** or details to show why Eric liked his sketch?

 Did the author stick to one topic?

 Are you able to picture what the drawing looks like?

Slithery Snakes

Talk About It

When you hear the word *snake*, what do you think of? What are some facts that you know about snakes?

LOG ON ▶ Find out more about snakes at **www.macmillanmh.com**.

Poisonous SNAKES

by Thomas Kane

There are about 130 different **species** of snakes found in the United States and Canada. Many people are afraid of snakes because they think they are poisonous. However, only four kinds of poisonous snakes live in the United States. One, the coral snake, is in the cobra family. The other three snakes belong to the pit viper family. A bite from a poisonous snake can kill a person. However, most people bitten by snakes **survive** if they are treated quickly.

All snakes have some characteristics in common. For example, none of them hear well. Instead, they are constantly aware and on **alert** for times when the ground **vibrates**, or shakes slightly. They feel, rather than hear, something coming.

copperhead snake

564

Snakes also have a keen sense of smell. They use their tongues to pick up smells from the air. They sort out these smells to find out whether an animal in their nearby **surroundings** is **prey**. Snakes are **predators** that hunt other animals for food. Snakes usually eat small animals, sometimes swallowing them whole.

Coral Snakes

Coral snakes live in the southern part of the United States. Their shiny red, yellow, and black bands make them easy to spot. A coral snake has a small head. You can see its fangs at the front of its mouth. When a coral snake bites, it shoots poison into its prey. The animal soon stops breathing and dies.

Pit Vipers

A pit viper is named for the two large pits or dents on each side of its head. When both pits feel the same temperature, the pit viper knows it is facing its prey

coral snake

and it springs forward. **Lunging**, the viper digs its fangs into the animal. The poisonous bite causes bleeding and swelling that leads to death.

The three types of pit vipers in the United States are rattlesnakes, copperheads, and cottonmouths. Copperheads and cottonmouths are sometimes called moccasins.

Pit vipers live in the southeastern United States, the West, and the Midwest.

Reread for **Comprehension**

Summarize
Main Idea and Details
The main idea is the most important point that an author makes about a topic. The main idea is supported by details that help to explain or describe it. Use the Main Idea and Details Chart to help you identify and summarize main ideas as you reread the selection.

Main Idea	Details

CA Comprehension

Genre

Nonfiction: A nonfiction article gives information and facts about a topic.

Summarize

✔ **Main Idea and Details**

As you read, fill in your Main Idea and Details Chart.

Main Idea	Details

Read to Find Out

How do rattlesnakes catch their prey?

RATTLERS!

by Ellen Lambeth

Are you rattled by rattlesnakes? Well, don't be. Just sink your teeth into the real truth about these amazing reptiles.

567

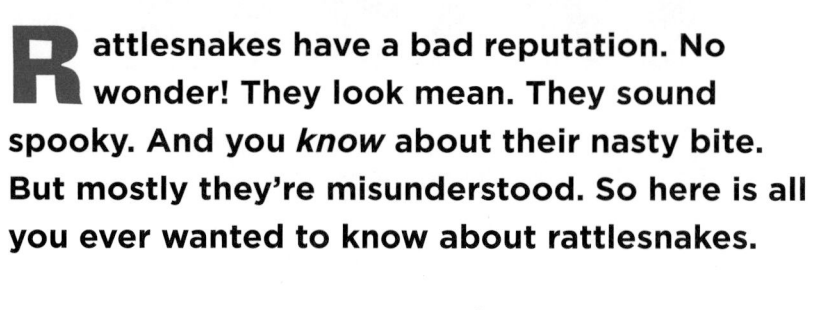

Rattlesnakes have a bad reputation. No wonder! They look mean. They sound spooky. And you *know* about their nasty bite. But mostly they're misunderstood. So here is all you ever wanted to know about rattlesnakes.

What are rattlesnakes?

They're a group of snakes that have what no other snakes have: rattle-tipped tails. They also have thick bodies, wide heads, cat-like eyes, and long, hollow fangs that fold away when they're not needed. Their dull colors and patchy patterns help them blend in with their **surroundings**.

Where do rattlers live?

There are about 30 different **species** (kinds), and you can find at least one kind or another in almost every state. Rattlers also live in southern Canada, Mexico, and Central and South America.

Different rattlers hang out in different habitats. For example, sidewinders are in deserts, and many timber rattlers live in rocky woodlands. Canebrake rattlers can be found in swamps, while prairie rattlers live in grasslands.

> **Main Idea and Details**
> Name two details that support the main idea in the paragraph "Where do rattlers live?"

Are rattlesnakes dangerous?

To their **prey**, they're deadly! To people, their bite is painful . . . and *sometimes* deadly. But it's very unusual for a person to be bitten: People and rattlers aren't often in the same place at the same time.

Even when they are, most rattlers would rather stay hidden or slither away than attack. The prairie rattler in the photo **(see right)** has been surprised by a hiker. Its vibrating rattle is giving the hiker a clear warning: *Don't take another step forward!*

569

What's the rattle made of, and how does it work?

The rattle is a stack of hard sections of skin **(see drawing)**. In other snakes, all of the skin comes off during shedding. In rattlesnakes, some stays attached at the end of the tail.

The beginning of the rattle is called the button. It stays stuck to the end of the tail the very first time a young rattlesnake sheds its skin. The next time the snake sheds, a new section is added underneath the button, and so on.

Each section fits loosely over the one under it. When the snake **vibrates** its tail, the sections rattle against each other and make a buzzing sound.

Can you tell a rattlesnake's age by counting the sections in the rattle?

No. A section is added each time a rattlesnake sheds. But some snakes shed several times a year. Others shed not as often. Also, one or more of the rattle's sections may have broken off.

button

What happens when a rattlesnake bites?

First it strikes by **lunging** toward the prey or enemy. The mouth opens wide, and the fangs swing out **(see above)**. When the snake hits its target, the fangs sink in deep. The rattler may—but doesn't always—pump venom (poison) through each fang. All this happens in about a second.

Can a rattlesnake bite be cured?

Yes, especially if a doctor treats it right away. If the kind of snake is known, the person may be treated with medicine made from the venom of the snake. And how do people get venom to make medicine? By "milking" the snake! **(see right)**

nostril

heat-sensing pit

What do rattlers eat?

Most kinds go for small mammals—such as mice, squirrels, and rabbits—and sometimes birds. Some kinds eat mostly lizards, and others eat mostly frogs.

How does a rattlesnake find its prey?

It picks a good spot and waits. When prey comes along, all the snake's senses are on **alert**. First it may feel vibrations in the ground. Next it looks about and gathers scent molecules on its tongue. It sticks the tip of the tongue into a special smelling organ on the roof of its mouth. Then it uses deep pits on its face to sense body heat coming from the prey. Finally the snake knows exactly where the prey is—and STRIKES!

How does a rattlesnake eat its prey?

It sinks in its fangs and pumps in venom. Then it lets go and waits. If the dying prey crawls away, no problem. The snake can follow the scent trail with its tongue. Then the snake grabs the prey headfirst and swallows it whole. **(see above)**

Do rattlesnakes drink?

Rattlers, like all snakes, get water from the food they eat. But sometimes they suck some in from a puddle or pond, as the western diamondback rattler **(see below)** is doing.

How big are rattlers?

All sizes. The eastern diamondback probably is the biggest. It can get to be 6 feet (1.8 m) long or more. But usually it grows no more than 4 feet (1.2 m) or so. Most of the smallest species, such as the pygmy rattlesnake, are less than 20 inches (50 cm).

Do rattlesnakes have any natural enemies?

Sure. Big animals, such as bison, sometimes crush them underfoot—by mistake or on purpose. And some animals eat rattlesnakes. Red-tailed hawks nab lots of them. And so do other snakes—especially king-snakes **(see black-and-white snake above)**. Other animals, such as coyotes, may gobble up a rattler once in a while.

How can **predators** eat a rattler without getting hurt? Some are quick enough to keep from being bitten. Others don't seem to be bothered by the venom.

Main Idea and Details
Name two details that support the main idea on this page.

574

Are any rattlesnakes endangered?

Two kinds—the New Mexican ridge-nosed and the Aruba Island rattlesnakes—are on the U.S. endangered species list as "threatened." That means they could easily become endangered. So they must be protected by law. Many other kinds also are a lot rarer than they once were. Here's why:

Humans have changed many of the places rattlesnakes live—by plowing under grasslands or draining wetlands, for example. That can make it hard for the rattlesnakes to find food or hiding places.

Humans have also killed way too many rattlers—sometimes for the skin or meat, but more often just for "fun" or out of fear.

Do rattlers lay eggs?

No. They give birth to live young—usually at summer's end. A mother rattlesnake may have only one baby . . . or more than twenty! But the average number is eight.

Each young rattler is inside a thin sac when it comes out of the mother. Soon it wriggles itself free.

Like the newborn timber rattler **(see left)**, the young snakes may stay near their mother for several days or longer. But then they all go their separate ways.

575

Rare Rattler Rescue!

– John Cancalosi

Most people want to know how to protect themselves from rattlesnakes. But one scientist and his family want to help protect rattlesnakes from people.

Hugh McCrystal is a herpetologist (her-pih-TOL-uh-jist). And his two best helpers are his kids, Rachel and James.

The McCrystals are studying the ridge-nosed and rock rattlesnakes. These shy, rare snakes live in the mountains of southeastern Arizona. The more the McCrystals learn about them, the easier it will be to protect them.

But how do you study a dangerous creature up close? Carefully! First Dad catches a rattler and sticks it headfirst into a plastic tube so it can't bite. Then James scans it with a special machine **(below)**. If the McCrystals have caught the snake before, it will have an ID tag that they had put under its skin. The machine works like a store scanner to "read" the tag.

Rachel writes down which snake it is and then records the animal's weight, length, and temperature. (If it's a new snake, they give it a tag and number.) She also jots down other information, such as where the snake was found and what it was doing. After they let the snake go, they hunt for another one.

The family compares the information with other information they've already collected. That way, they can keep track of each rattler and find out more about what it needs to survive.

Rattle Around with ELLen Lambeth

Ellen Lambeth writes for magazines, mostly about animals. Besides meeting monkeys and avoiding snake bites, she talks with scientists, watches videos, and visits zoos. It's a lot of hard work, but the more Ellen learns, the more she wants to know. She has a pet dog and a horse at home. Ellen has taught each of them tricks, but sometimes feels they are the ones teaching her.

 **LOG ON** ▶ Find out more about Ellen Lambeth at **www.macmillanmh.com**.

CA **Author's Purpose**
Ellen Lambeth uses a question-and-answer text structure. How does this information help you to determine her purpose for writing?

Critical Thinking

Summarize

Use your Main Idea and Details Chart to help you summarize "Rattlers!" Be sure to include only the most important information in your summary.

Main Idea	Details

Think and Compare

1. What is the **main idea** of the three passages on page 572? Make a list of **details** from the passages to help you find the main idea. **Summarize: Main Idea and Details**

2. Reread page 568 of "Rattlers!" How does the author feel about rattlesnakes? Include specific examples from the text to support your answer. **Apply**

3. Explain whether you think rattlers and other snakes are misunderstood. Discuss any personal encounters that you may have had with snakes. **Evaluate**

4. Rattlers are on the endangered **species** list. What can be done to help keep these snakes from becoming extinct? **Analyze**

5. Reread "Poisonous Snakes" on pages 564–565. How are coral snakes and rattlesnakes similar? How are they different? Use evidence from both selections to support your answer. **Reading/Writing Across Texts**

How Poison Came Into the World

retold by Paul Sirls

> The plant is the hero in this folktale.

Long ago, when Earth was young, the Choctaw people loved to swim in the cool waters of the bayou. But the Choctaw had to be very careful when swimming because a poisonous plant grew in the heart of the bayou. This plant lived below the surface, so swimmers could not see it until it was too late.

The plant, however, did not want to hurt his friends the Choctaw. As more people fell ill, the poor plant became sadder and sadder. Finally, he decided to give away his poison. The plant called the chiefs of the wasps and snakes to meet with him. He asked them to take his poison.

Wasp shouted out his answer first. "I will put a little poison in my tail. It will help me keep my nest safe." Wasp also promised to make a buzzing sound before he stung anyone.

580

A water moccasin that speaks is an example of **personification**.

Water Moccasin spoke next. "I will put some poison in my mouth to use only if people stomp on me." Water Moccasin promised to open his mouth wide so people could see the white poison and run before he struck anyone.

Finally, Rattlesnake slithered up slowly, shaking his rattle as he spoke. "I will take a lot of your poison. I will rattle my tail loudly before I strike anyone."

And so the plant's poisonous leaves fell off. In their place, beautiful water lilies grew. The waters of the bayou became safe. And that is how poison came into the world.

CA Critical Thinking

1. What are some ways that the author personifies the plant and the animals? **Personification**

2. What is the purpose of this folktale? What does it provide an explanation for? **Analyze**

3. Think about "How Poison Came Into the World" and *Rattlers!* Compare how each author gives information about nature. **Reading/Writing Across Texts**

LOG ON ▶ Find out more about folktales at **www.macmillanmh.com**.

Relevant Evidence

Good writers use details to support the information in their writing.

Reading and Writing Connection

Read the passage below. Notice how the author Ellen Lambeth uses details to explain where rattlesnakes live.

An excerpt from *Rattlers!*

The author uses details about the places where rattlesnakes live so we can imagine how different kinds of rattlesnakes survive in different places.

Where do rattlers live?

There are about 30 different species (kinds) and you can find one kind or another in almost every state. Rattlers also live in southern Canada, Mexico, and Central and South America.

Different rattlers hang out in different habitats. For example, sidewinders are in deserts, and many timber rattlers live in rocky woodlands. Canebrake rattlers can be found in swamps, while prairie rattlers live in grasslands.

RATTLERS!
by Ellen Lambeth

Read and Find

Read Temika's writing. How did she use details or evidence to show us how much she likes to crochet? Use the Writer's Checklist below to help you.

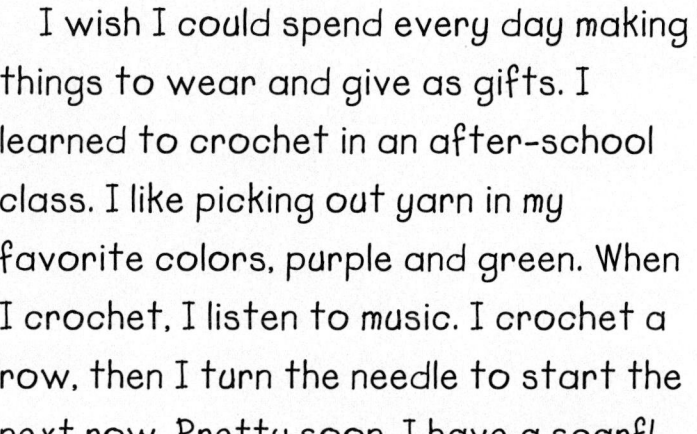

Crocheting
by Temika R.

I wish I could spend every day making things to wear and give as gifts. I learned to crochet in an after-school class. I like picking out yarn in my favorite colors, purple and green. When I crochet, I listen to music. I crochet a row, then I turn the needle to start the next row. Pretty soon, I have a scarf!

Read about why I like to crochet.

Writer's Checklist

 Did the author focus on details that show why she likes to crochet?

 Did the author explain why she likes to choose certain patterns?

Does she give us enough detail so that we believe she likes to crochet? Is there any **evidence** that she offers that does not prove her point?

How have scientific discoveries improved people's lives?

 Find out more about scientific discoveries at **www.macmillanmh.com**.

Scientific Discoveries

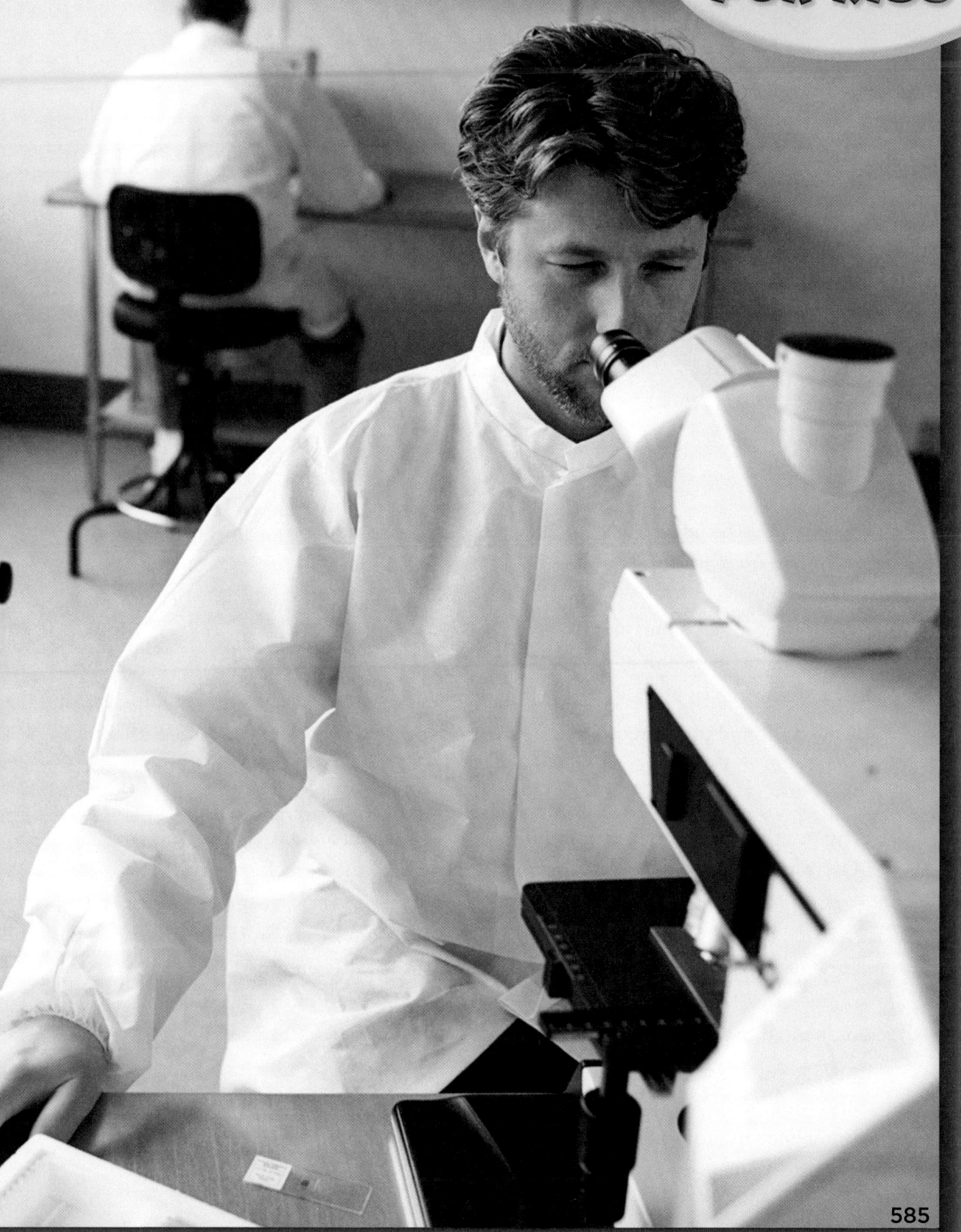

In 1953, Watson (left) and Crick stand next to a DNA model in their lab in England.

The Code Breakers

Their names may be unfamiliar, but 50 years ago these two men changed our lives forever. On February 28, 1953, James Watson of the United States and Francis Crick of England made one of the greatest scientific discoveries in history.

"We have found the secret of life," Crick announced. What the two scientists had found was DNA's structure.

Why was this discovery so important? The DNA molecule carries the recipe for making every living thing. DNA is shaped like a twisted ladder, or double helix. The rungs are made of four chemicals. They are arranged in a different pattern in every kind of living thing.

In 1953, few researchers were **investigating** DNA. "We were probably more interested in exploring DNA than anyone else," Watson says. "It was the only scientific problem I wanted to think about."

Advances in the study of DNA can help us fight disease, increase our life spans, and help in the battle against world hunger. Watson says, "My ambition is to understand the genetic changes that give rise to cancer and to see this information used to treat cancer."

Watson and Crick were awarded the Nobel Prize in 1962 for their work. Watson has advice for kids interested in making their own world-changing discoveries. "Read a great deal," he says. "Have friends who you can learn from."

DNA is in the shape of a twisted ladder. Its rungs are made of four chemicals.

A Lucky Hero?

Was pure luck behind a great scientific discovery? In 1928 Alexander Fleming, a Scottish researcher, was looking for a cure for Staphylococcus, a bacteria that can cause deadly infections. He left a plate smeared with the bacteria in his laboratory during a two-week vacation.

A mold spore landed on the plate during Fleming's vacation. When he returned, he **observed** that Staphylococcus bacteria covered the plate—except around the mold.

Fleming realized that the mold must **inhibit** the bacteria's growth. Fleming called the germ-stopping substance penicillin, after the name of the mold.

Penicillin was the world's most powerful infection-fighting drug. By the 1950s, penicillin was helping to **conquer** bacterial infections.

Fleming's discovery seems like luck. But it took **insight** to understand the importance of the accident.

HEY! WHAT'S THE BIG IDEA?

History is filled with amazing discoveries and inventions. Most take years of investigation and research. See if the items on the timeline inspire you to make your own big discovery.

Around 3800–3600 B.C.	Wheel invented
1543	Copernicus shows that the sun, not Earth, is center of the solar system
1876	Alexander Graham Bell invents the telephone
1903	Wright brothers make first motorized plane
Early 1940s	Atom bomb created
1981	First space shuttle flight
1983	Cell phone invented
1991	Tim Lee-Berners invents World Wide Web
2003	Human genome mapped

LOG ON Find out more about discoveries and inventions at **www.macmillanmh.com**.

These ROBOTS Are Wild!

The latest robots look like insects. How may they help us one day?

I mitating nature has become popular in building machines. This is especially true among those trying to create the next generation of robots. Why? When it comes to solving really difficult design problems, nature has a billion-year head start.

Going Buggy

Most people think that cockroaches are nasty pests. But Roy Ritzmann has observed a lot that he loves about them. "They're fast. They're agile," Ritzmann says.

Comprehension

Genre

Nonfiction: An article in a newspaper or magazine presents facts and information about real people, places, and events.

Monitor Comprehension

Make Generalizations
A generalization is a broad statement that combines facts in a text with the reader's prior knowledge.

In The Swim
Joseph Ayers holds up a lobster. It inspired his invention, RoboLobster, shown half built in tank.

A Bug's Life Quinn (left) and Ritzmann look at
an early version of Robot V. It was based on a roach.

Carefully watching cockroaches is part of Ritzmann's job at
Case Western Reserve University, in Cleveland, Ohio. Ritzmann,
a biologist, is helping other scientists at the school use bugs as
models for robots. They hope that insectlike robots will be able
to operate in places that other robots can't.

Inspecting Insects

"Many engineers now realize that much can be learned from
biology," Roger Quinn says. He's the director of Case Western
Reserve's Biorobotics Laboratory. A growing group of robot
designers wants to copy the physical structures of animals. They
believe that what helps an animal thrive can make a machine
more useful.

Arthropods are very good robot models. They include insects
and crustaceans, such as lobsters and crabs. Arachnids, such as
scorpions and spiders, are also arthropods. Arthropods can travel
quickly over rocky or uneven ground. They also have many sensors
on the outside of their bodies. Antennas and sensitive hairs help
the creatures respond quickly to changes in their environment.

Run, Roach, Run!

Ritzmann has spent time investigating cockroaches. These creepy critters are incredibly good at moving. Ritzmann studies the way they run, jump, and turn. He wants to know what body parts a cockroach uses to check out obstacles in its path. He also wonders how a cockroach's brain uses that information to get around the obstacle. Ritzmann hopes to develop a large vehicle modeled on the insect.

To track how it moves, Ritzmann puts tiny sensors on different parts of the roach's legs. He then takes that information and matches it to the movement of a robot he designs. He wants the robot to walk and climb like a cockroach. For example, the robot's back legs should have the same range of motion as the roach's back legs.

Ritzmann also gets information from wires that are thinner than human hair. They record how the muscles in a cockroach's legs work. Using this information, Ritzmann will make gears that move like a cockroach's muscles. Ritzmann believes that if his robot walks half as well as a cockroach, it will be the best robot in the world.

Creepy, Crawly Robots
Compare these robots to the creatures they look like.

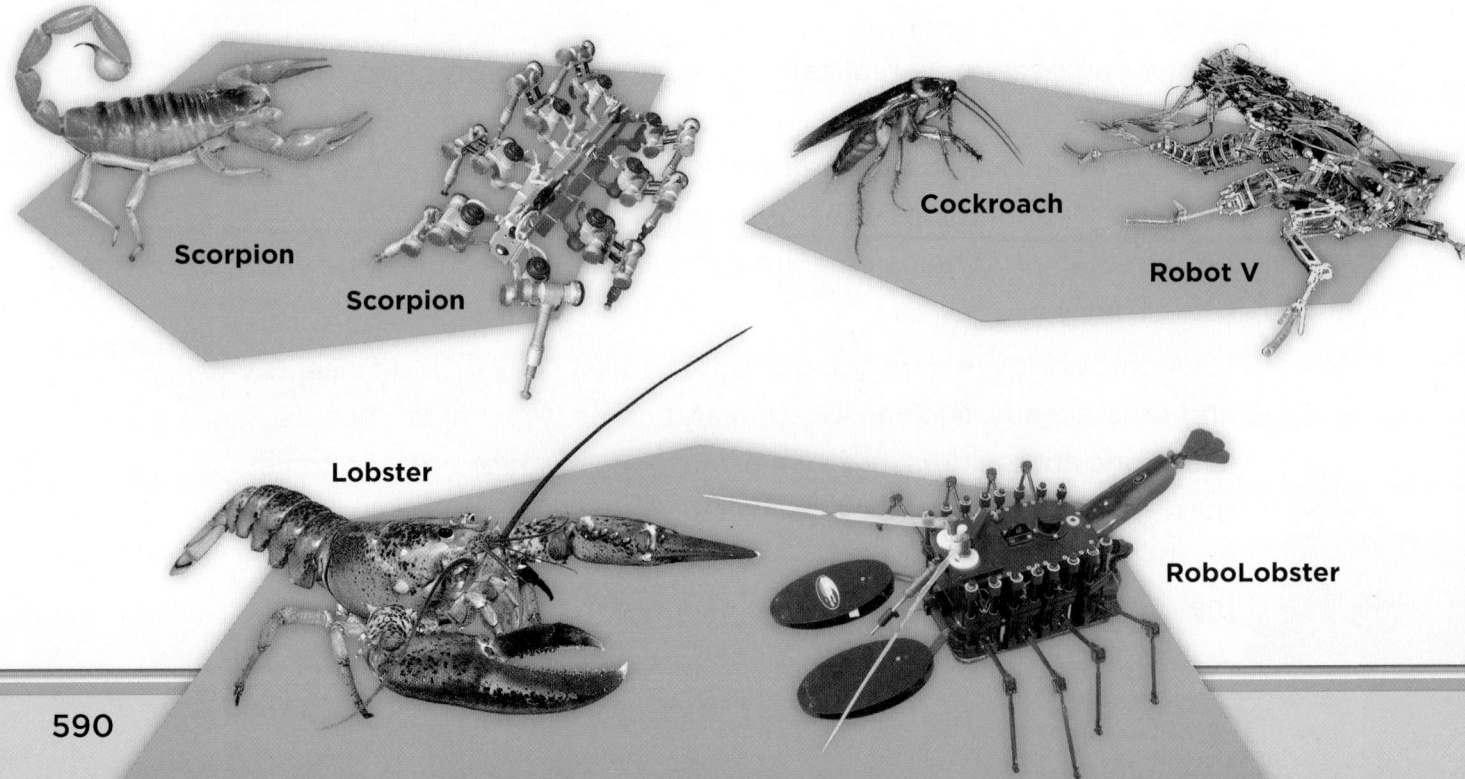

Scorpion

Scorpion

Cockroach

Robot V

Lobster

RoboLobster

One day robots may be able to find earthquake survivors.

Saving the Day

New robots will be able to move through any landscape. They will climb, crawl, or swim into dangerous places. For example, robots could find survivors in collapsed buildings.

Joseph Ayers is a biologist at Northeastern University, in Boston. His robot is based on the lobster. A lobster's sense of smell lets it follow a prey's scent. Scientists are developing electronic sensors that are just as sensitive to smells. Their robot could sniff out explosives underwater.

NASA wants to send multi-legged, insectlike robots to explore planets like Mars. The new robots will travel over big boulders, down steep drops, and into tight spots where today's wheeled rovers cannot go. By behaving like humble bugs, the new generation of robots may help us gain some insight into the mysteries of the universe.

1. What **generalization** can you make about how insects have helped robot designers?

2. What are two types of arthropods?

3. If you were going to design a robot based on an animal, which animal would you choose and why?

4. Fleming worked alone. Scientists work in teams to build robots. Do you think it is better to work alone or in teams? Explain your answer.

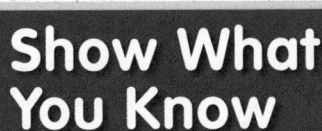

Show What You Know

Right There

You can put your finger on the answer. Look for key words in the question. Then find those key words in the selection.

Preventing Polio

In the early 1950s, summertime was a season of fear for many parents. That's when a disease called polio struck thousands of children. Polio is an illness that damages nerves and muscles. It left many people unable to walk. Those who recovered often had to use crutches or wear leg braces for the rest of their lives.

About one person in every 5,000 people caught the disease—but almost everyone was scared of catching it. News of an outbreak closed public swimming pools and movie theaters. Worried parents kept their children indoors.

Fear of polio ended thanks to the work of a doctor named Jonas Salk. Salk was born in New York City in 1914.

While in medical school, he spent a year studying influenza. Salk wanted to learn if the influenza virus could be used to make a vaccine, a drug that prevents a person from getting a disease.

In the 1950s, Salk began to work on a polio vaccine. His secret was using the dead polio virus. This vaccine also made the body resist the live polio virus. To prove it was safe, Salk injected himself and other scientists with his vaccine. After the government approved the vaccine in 1955, polio began to disappear.

Salk gave away the vaccine's formula for free. His reward for years of work? Making people safe from this terrifying disease.

Go on ▶

CA Standards Practice

Now answer Numbers 1 through 5. Base your answers on the article "Preventing Polio."

1. **Why were people in the early 1950s afraid of polio?**

   A   It left some people unable to talk.
   B   It was easy to cure.
   C   It damaged nerves and muscles.
   D   It struck when children were in school.

2. **Which word means "a drug that prevents a person from getting a disease"?**

   A   polio
   B   outbreak
   C   virus
   D   vaccine

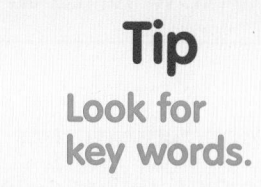

Tip
Look for
key words.

3. **The secret to Salk's polio vaccine was to**

   A   kill the polio virus, and then inject it into a person.
   B   inject a person with a live polio virus.
   C   make a polio vaccine from the virus that causes flu.
   D   have the government do the tests.

4. **How did Salk's research on influenza help him with his polio vaccine?**

5. **Why do you think Salk did not sell the formula for his polio vaccine? Use details from the article to support your answer.**

Write on Demand

Students enjoy different kinds of activities in gym class.

Think of new activities to benefit students in gym class.

Now write to <u>explain why</u> new activities will benefit a gym class.

Expository writing explains, defines, and tells how to do something.

To figure out if a writing prompt asks for expository writing, look for clue words such as <u>explain why</u> or <u>tell what</u>.

Below see how one student concluded a response to the prompt above.

The writer summed up her response to the prompt in the final paragraph.

> The purpose of school is to give our brains and our bodies a workout. Many students find the usual choice of team sports and track and field events boring and uninspiring. Instead of joining the rest of the class, they sit off to the sidelines.
>
> If we added new types of activities such as yoga and aerobics as part of our gym program, more students would be motivated to "get up and GO!" They might start to take the idea of physical fitness more seriously. This could lead to healthful exercise habits that will stay with them for the rest of their lives.

Writing Prompt

Respond to the prompt below. Write for 20 minutes. Write as much as you can, as well as you can. Review the hints before and after you write.

Student groups often do service projects to help others. Think of a service project you and a group could do.

Write about a service project you and a group could do.

Writing Hints for Prompts

- ☑ Read the prompt carefully.
- ☑ Plan your writing by organizing your ideas.
- ☑ Support your ideas by giving reasons or using more details.
- ☑ Use negatives and contractions correctly.
- ☑ Choose words that help others understand what you mean.
- ☑ Review and edit your writing.

BALLOON FLIGHT

CA **Talk About It**

Nowadays people can travel quickly by plane to almost any part of the world. Why do you think people still like to go up in hot-air balloons?

LOG ON ▶ Find out more about balloon flight at **www.macmillanmh.com**.

The Science of Hot-Air Balloons

by Enriquez Mera

Since the first hot-air balloon was **launched** in 1783, few things have changed about how they fly. However, some new differences have made ballooning a safer activity enjoyed by many people world wide.

In the past hot-air balloons were always made out of linen and paper. Today most are made of nylon. Long pieces of nylon, called *gores*, are stitched together to create the balloon. Balloonists use nylon because it is a thin and light material. Also, it cannot be damaged by heat.

Heat is the basic ingredient needed for ballooning. As air becomes hotter, tiny **particles** of matter move faster and faster. As the balloon fills with warmer particles, it begins to rise. This is because the air inside is lighter than the **dense** air surrounding the balloon. It is the warmer air particles that allow the balloon to float above the cooler air.

How the air is heated to **inflate** the hot-air balloon has changed a great deal since the early days of ballooning. Back in 1783 fire from damp straw and wool heated the air as the balloon remained **anchored** to the ground. Usually, a brave man or woman and a **companion** would climb into the basket, cut the line, and soar into the air.

Now balloonists use propane— the same gas used in most outdoor grills—instead of straw. For hot-air balloons, it is piped from a tank to metal tubes. Once there, a small fire heats up the tubes and the propane. When the propane flame is released, it creates hot air that fills the inside of the hot-air balloon.

Besides propane, another gas that could be used is **hydrogen**. Hydrogen is a gas that has no odor, color, or taste and burns very easily. One advantage of hydrogen gas is that it does not need to be heated. However, hydrogen is expensive, so it is mostly used for balloons during **scientific** studies. These are studies designed to gather information that will help scientists.

Whether for science or sport, more people than ever are taking to the air in balloons.

Reread for Comprehension

Monitor Comprehension

Make Generalizations
A generalization is a broad statement, judgment, or conclusion that is made by combining important information from the text with the reader's own prior knowledge or experience.

Use your Generalizations Chart to help you make generalizations about the selection.

Information from Text	
Signal Words	
Prior Knowledge	
Generalization	

599

Genre

Nonfiction gives information and facts about real people, places, events, and situations.

Monitor Comprehension

✔ Make Generalizations

As you read, fill in your Generalizations Chart.

Information from Text	
Signal Words	
Prior Knowledge	
Generalization	

Read to Find Out

How has the invention of ballooning been useful?

Up in the Air:
The Story of Balloon Flight

by Patricia Lauber

Award Winning Author

Saturday promises to be fair, with no high winds, no storms. It's a perfect day for ballooning. Members of the balloonist club turn out early and set to work. Fans blow air into the balloons. Tongues of orange flame shoot out of roaring gas burners, heating air to make the balloons rise. The balloons **inflate** and stand up. Pilots climb into their baskets, the ground crews let go of the ropes, and it's up, up, and away.

A balloon floats along, silent as a cloud, until a pilot turns on the burners to heat air inside and gain altitude. Balloons cannot be steered. They travel only where the winds carry them. By changing altitude, though, a pilot may find a different wind, going in a different direction. A chase crew follows on land to bring balloonists and balloons home at journey's end.

Today thousands of people in many parts of the world belong to balloon clubs. Their sport was invented more than 200 years ago by a handful of people who willingly risked their lives flying the balloons they had built.

As the balloons fill with hot air, they stand upright. They are ready to soar away, carrying pilots and passengers in big baskets called gondolas.

MONTGOLFIER BALLOON. Ascent of a Montgolfier balloon from Paris, c. 1864: engraving from an English newspaper.

The Story of Ballooning

People have always dreamed of soaring like a bird or floating like a cloud. Over several hundred years a few people thought they knew how to do this. They theorized that a certain kind of big balloon might lift them up. The balloon would be lighter than the air around it, and it would float in air as a boat floats in water. But no one managed to make such a balloon until 1783 when two French brothers built and **launched** the world's first hot-air balloon. Their names were Joseph and Etienne Montgolfier.

The World's First Balloon Flight

Hot smoky air rising from a fire had given Joseph Montgolfier an idea. Perhaps such air would make a balloon rise. Using small balloons, Joseph found that it did.

After many experiments the brothers built a balloon that was about 30 feet across and 38 feet tall. It had a wooden frame at the base and was made of linen backed with paper. On June 5, 1783, near the city of Lyons, France, the Montgolfiers built a huge fire of damp straw and wool. Hot air poured into the base of the balloon. As a small crowd watched in amazement, the balloon stirred, swelled, and finally rose upright.

Eight men were holding the balloon down. At a signal they let go. It rose some 6,000 feet into the air and stayed aloft for ten minutes, landing gently in a nearby vineyard. This was the world's first public balloon flight.

The Montgolfiers mistakenly thought smoke, not hot air, made a balloon rise. They used damp fuel to create dense smoke which escaped in flight.

605

Professor Charles' hydrogen balloon came to a bad end when attacked by pitchforks and dragged through the mud.

A Lighter-than-Air Balloon

Meanwhile in Paris, Professor Jacques A. C. Charles had designed a lighter-than-air balloon. He filled his balloon with a newly discovered gas called **hydrogen**, which weighed much less than air.

On August 27, 1783, Professor Charles launched his balloon at 5 P.M. As a crowd watched, it rose 3,000 feet and disappeared into the clouds.

Professor Jacques A. C. Charles

Forty-five minutes later the balloon came down outside a village 15 miles away. The villagers, who had never heard of such a thing as a balloon, thought a monster had fallen out of the sky. As it bounced toward them, they attacked it with pitchforks. When at last the monster lay still, men tied it to a horse's tail and dragged it through the mud to make sure it was dead.

Now there were two ways to send balloons aloft: with hot air and with hydrogen. The fires were messy and dangerous, but hydrogen took a lot of time to make. Nevertheless, most of the early flights were made with hot-air balloons.

> **Make Generalizations**
> The author tells of villagers attacking a balloon as a monster. Make a generalization about the villagers' attitude toward balloons.

The king and queen of France watched the launching of the first balloon passengers.

The First Passenger Balloons

The first passengers to go up in a balloon were a trio of animals—a duck, a rooster, and a lamb. On September 19, 1783, they traveled in a wicker basket, or gondola, attached to a balloon. After a short flight, the air in the balloon cooled and the passengers drifted safely to Earth. Their flight showed that it was possible to breathe while floating a few thousand feet above Earth.

It was now time for humans to risk ballooning. A daring young French chemist was the first. On October 15, 1783, François Pilâtre de Rozier went up 100 feet. He was **anchored** to the ground by a long rope called a tether. His balloon carried a big metal pan under its mouth. A fire in the pan sent hot air into the balloon. The flight was a success. After that de Rozier made many tethered flights to find out how much straw and wool he needed to burn for each hour he stayed in the air.

By November 21, de Rozier was ready to make the first untethered flight. A huge crowd gathered to watch. The giant balloon filled, and at 1:54 P.M., de Rozier and a **companion** were up, up, and away. When the balloon was 200 feet in the air, the pair took off their hats and bowed to those below. Then they sailed off over Paris. The travelers flew for 25 minutes and covered about five miles before landing in a field outside the city.

Spectators watch de Rozier and his companion as they take flight in a hot-air balloon.

Blanchard and Jeffries were saluted by boats near the English and French coasts.

610

Daring Balloonists

Between 1783 and 1785, many men, and some women, went up in balloons. Some went for sport. Others, more daring, wanted to do what no one had done before. Jean-Pierre Blanchard was one of these. Blanchard wanted to cross the English Channel from England to France.

On January 7, 1785, the wind was blowing in the right direction over the cliffs of Dover. Blanchard and his American friend John Jefferies filled their balloon with hydrogen, climbed in, and set off for France.

The first half of the trip went smoothly, but then the balloon began leaking gas. The water came closer and closer. To lighten the load, they threw everything overboard—their bags of sand, food and drink, anchors. They were still sinking. Finally they stripped and threw their clothes overboard, saving only their cork life jackets.

The weather changed. The air grew warmer, heating the gas. The balloon rose, and they sailed over the French coast, landing in a forest where they were soon rescued.

On January 9, 1793, Blanchard made the first flight in North America, taking off from Philadelphia and carrying out **scientific** experiments at 5,000 feet. He brought back sealed bottles of air that showed there was less oxygen at that height than at sea level. He also measured his heartbeat and found it was faster. At sea level it beat 84 times a minute; at 5,000 feet it beat 92.

In the years ahead, daring balloonists would keep setting records, but the chief discoveries were made in 1783, when a handful of people who dreamed of flying up, up, and away, made the dream come true.

On June 4, 1784, Marie Thible, an opera singer, became the first woman to make a balloon flight. She sang an aria while floating over Lyons, France.

> **Make Generalizations**
> Make a generalization about the people who went up in hot-air balloons.

A balloonist uses a gas heater to warm the air.

Why a Balloon Rises and Floats

When you place a block of wood in water, it takes up space, pushing some of the water aside. As the wood pushes against the water, the water pushes back. This upward force is called *buoyancy*. Buoyancy is the force that keeps things afloat.

A hot-air balloon rises and floats in an ocean of air for the same reason that the block of wood floats in water. It has buoyancy.

Like all matter, air is made of tiny **particles** called molecules. When air is heated, its molecules spread out and move faster. When the air inside a balloon is heated, some of the molecules inside the balloon are forced out. The air inside becomes thinner, or less **dense**. It weighs less than before, but it takes up the same amount of space. As a result, the air inside the balloon weighs less than an equal amount of outside air. Buoyancy carries the balloon up.

Some gases are lighter than air because the molecules themselves are less dense. One of these is hydrogen, the lightest gas known. However, it is a dangerous gas that can burn and explode. That is why balloonists today use helium, which is slightly heavier but does not burn or explode. Helium is the gas used in party balloons.

The Science Behind Hot-Air Balloons

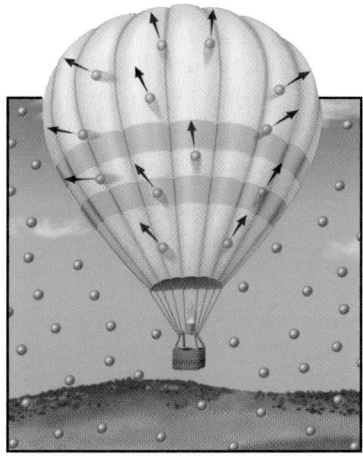

Air inside weighs less than air outside, so the balloon is carried up by buoyancy.

Air is made of tiny particles called molecules.

When air inside a balloon is heated, some of the molecules are forced out.

Balloons Then and Now

In the centuries since 1783, balloons have found many uses in both war and peace. Many balloonists have competed to soar the highest or to make the longest voyage. Here are a few important events.

1860s:

In the Civil War, Union troops, like the French Army before them, used balloons to spy behind enemy lines to see how battles were going.

1900s: The early 1900s brought the dirigible, or blimp. Made of several balloons, it was fitted with motors and propellers that let the pilot steer. A cabin on the underside held more than 100 people on Atlantic crossings.

1875: Three French scientists, exploring the atmosphere, soared to 25,000 feet in a balloon. The men took bottles of oxygen with them, but when the balloon landed only one scientist had survived.

1932:

The man who invented a way to travel safely high into the atmosphere was a Swiss named Auguste Piccard, who built a ball-shaped aluminum gondola. Sealed inside with oxygen tanks, he safely reached a height of 54,000 feet.

1961: Brave men kept going higher and higher. Two U.S. Navy officers, Malcolm D. Ross and Victor Prather, Jr., went up 113,740 feet in an open gondola to test space suits for astronauts.

Present day: Planes have long been the way to travel by air, but you often see a dirigible carrying a TV crew above a football game or other sports event.

1999: Others had crossed the oceans, but Bertrand Piccard (grandson of Auguste) and Brian Jones were the first to balloon non-stop around the world, covering 30,000 miles in 20 days. Their balloon was a cross between a hot-air balloon and a gas balloon.

Every day: Hundreds of small weather balloons explore the atmosphere and transmit their findings to Earth.

Up, Up, and Away with Patricia Lauber

Patricia Lauber says she was probably born wanting to write but had to wait until she had gone to school to learn a few things. She has been writing happily ever since and has produced about 125 books. Many are about things in the natural world, such as volcanoes, dinosaurs, and planets. Patricia loves doing the research for these books because she is always learning something new. Filled with enthusiasm about a new subject, she shares what she has learned by writing books. Patricia Lauber lives in Connecticut with her husband and their two cats, Beemer and Meetoo.

Another book by Patricia Lauber:
Living with Dinosaurs

LOG ON ▶ Find out more about Patricia Lauber at **www.macmillanmh.com**.

CA Author's Purpose
This nonfiction piece informs and explains. Identify text features that offer information.

CA Critical Thinking

Summarize

Making generalizations will help you organize relevant facts and details and summarize them more effectively. Use your Generalizations Chart to help you summarize *Up in the Air*.

Information from Text	
Signal Words	
Prior Knowledge	
Generalization	

Think and Compare

1. Describe a few characteristics of a modern-day balloon ride. What clues in the article help you make these **generalizations**. **Monitor Comprehension: Make Generalizations**

2. Reread page 609. Why do you think the first balloon passengers were animals? Include facts and details from the selection to support your answer. **Analyze**

3. Hot-air balloons transformed life over 200 years ago. Think about a recent **scientific** invention that has affected you. Identify the invention and tell how it has changed your life. **Evaluate**

4. People risked their lives to fly in hot-air balloons. How has their commitment to science contributed to the modern world? **Explain**

5. Reread "The Science of Hot-Air Balloons" on pages 598–599. Compare and contrast the different ways hot-air balloons are able to fly. Use details from each selection in your answer. **Reading/Writing Across Texts**

Poetry

Haiku is an unrhymed form of Japanese poetry that is three lines long. The first line has five syllables; the second line, seven syllables; the third line, five syllables.

✔ Literary Elements

A **Simile** is a comparison of two essentially unlike things that uses the words *like* or *as*.

A **Metaphor** is a comparison of two essentially unlike things that do not use the words *like* or *as*.

Hot-Air Balloon Haiku

by Rita Bristol

What a strange flower!
With petals as white as sheets.
A bee sleeps within.

Balloon, so high up.
A big, bright, bouncing bubble
Too buoyant to burst.

This is an example of a **metaphor**.

What do clouds feel like
Floating above the balloon
As it takes you far?

It floats like freedom
In the hazy August light
Soon, though, it will land.

This is an example of a **simile**.

CA Critical Thinking

1. Find another example of a metaphor in one of the other haiku.
   Metaphor

2. How do these four haiku help readers get a stronger sense of seeing or being in a hot-air balloon? **Analyze**

3. What is the difference between the information in these haiku and the information presented in "Up in the Air"?
   Reading/Writing Across Texts

LOG ON ▶ Find out more about haiku at **www.macmillanmh.com**.

619

✔ **Evidence: Linked to Argument**

Good writers include details in their writing that help the reader understand the writer's feelings or point of view.

Reading and Writing Connection

Read the passage below. Notice how the author Patricia Lauber includes evidence.

An excerpt from
Up in the Air

The author links details to teach us how the first hot air balloon was launched. She shows how it was done and describes the amazed people watching. This helps us see that it was the first time people witnessed such a thing.

Hot smoky air rising from a fire had given Joseph Montgolfier an idea. Perhaps such air would make a balloon rise. Using small balloons Joseph found that it did. . . .

On June 5, 1783, near the city of Lyons, France, the Montgolfiers built a huge fire of damp straw and wool. Hot air poured into the base of the balloon. As a small crowd watched in amazement, the balloon stirred, swelled, and finally rose upright.

Read and Find

Read Luisa's writing. How did she use evidence to show her feelings or point of view? Use the Writer's Checklist below to help you.

Costumes
by Luisa C.

When I put that dress over my head, I felt different. Costumes always make me feel different and weird. Then I thought in a play, everyone looks weird. I looked around and saw other people so I didn't feel so strange anymore. I got into the character more. It was fun pretending to be somebody else. After I took off the dress, I felt like myself again.

Read about how it felt to be in costume.

Writer's Checklist

 Did the author help us see exactly what made her feel different?

 Did the author show us what actually happened to change her perspective?

☑ Do you believe that this author changed her feelings about putting on a costume?

EXTREME WEATHER

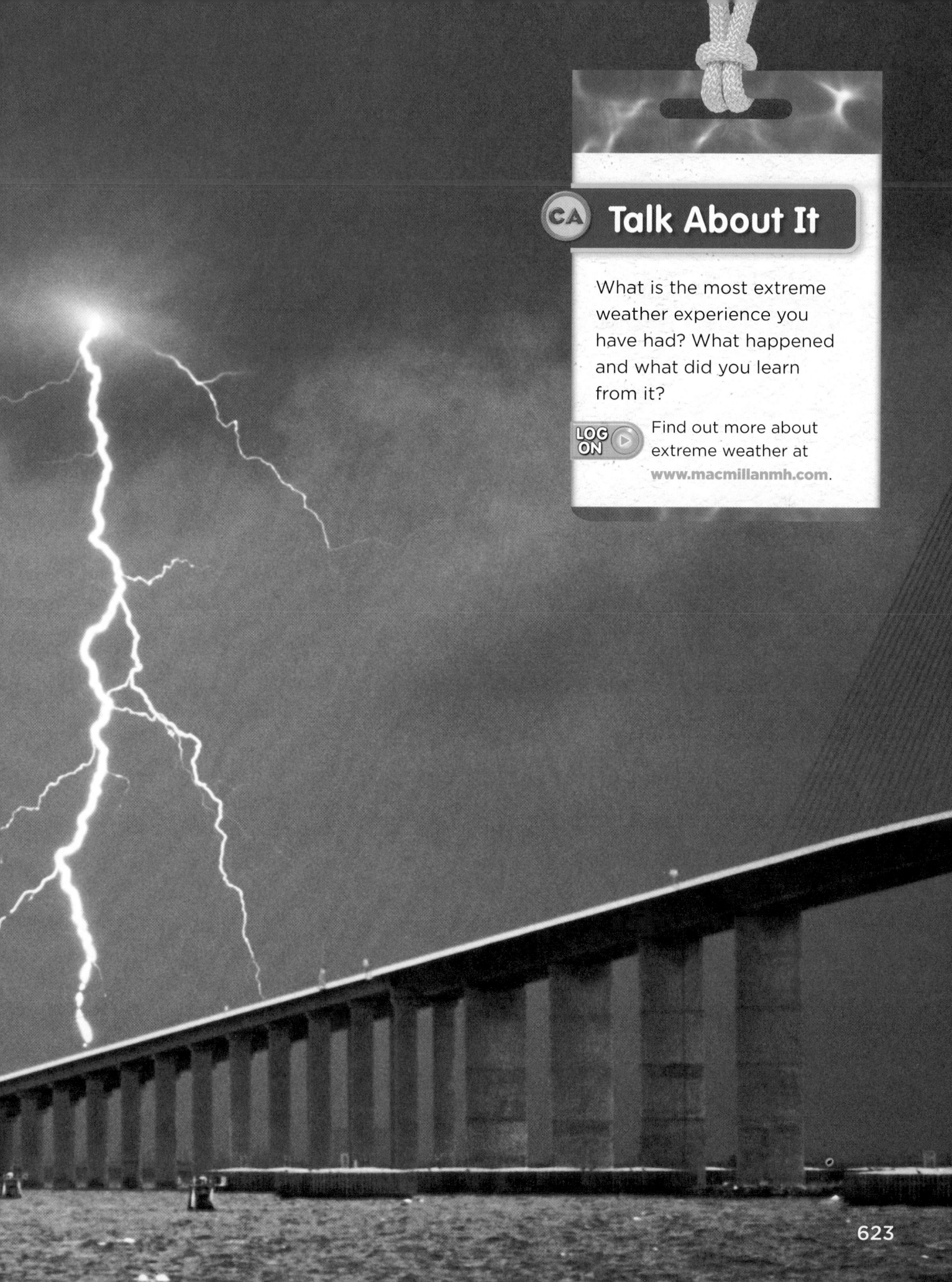

Talk About It

What is the most extreme weather experience you have had? What happened and what did you learn from it?

LOG ON ▶ Find out more about extreme weather at **www.macmillanmh.com**.

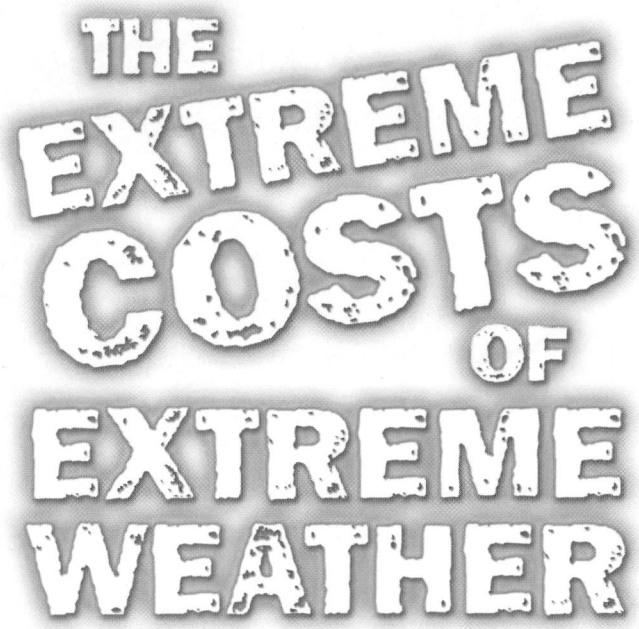

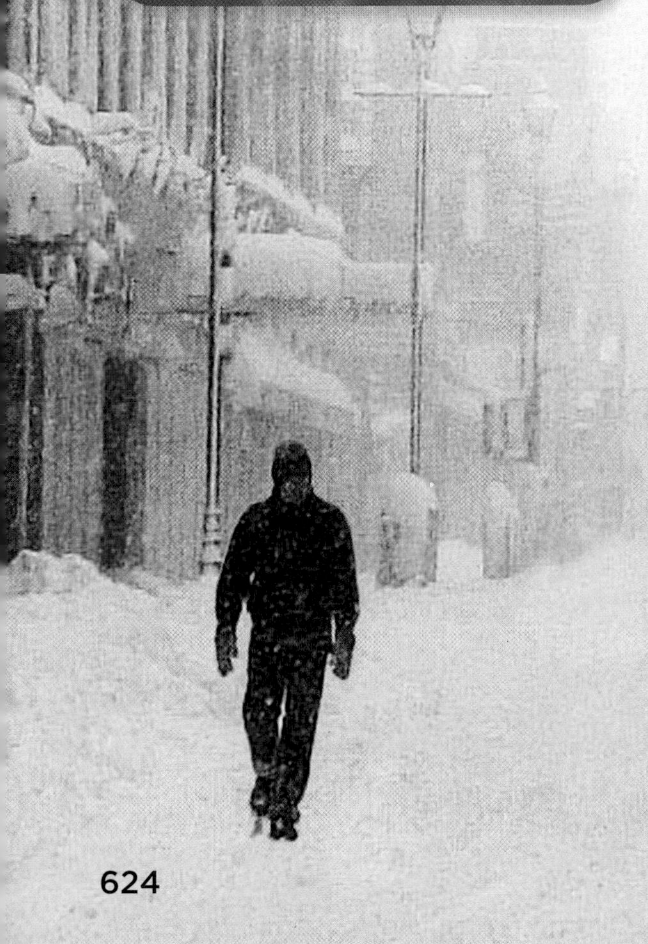

Vocabulary

damages
property
available
contact
atmosphere
destruction
surge

Dictionary

Multiple-Meaning Words are words with several different meanings. If one meaning does not make sense in a sentence look at the other definitions for the word.

THE EXTREME COSTS OF EXTREME WEATHER

by Eliana Rodriguez

Every now and then, nature provides examples of extreme weather. At these times the temperature, wind, water, and air pressure sometimes go wild. The result can be billions of dollars in **damages** to **property**. People's homes and belongings can be destroyed and people are sometimes hurt.

One government agency tracks the cost of extreme weather. Every year it lists each weather event that costs the United States a billion dollars or more. These facts can be obtained readily and are **available** to the public.

From May 1999 to May 2000 many incidents of extreme weather occurred. In May 1999, tornadoes ripped through Oklahoma and Kansas. A tornado is a violently spinning column of air. First, warm air makes **contact** with cool air in the **atmosphere** or surrounding air. Next, the warmer and cooler air stir together, spinning faster and faster. Finally, a tornado is born. The May 1999 tornadoes cut a 1.7 billion dollar path of ruin and **destruction**, killing 55 people.

Hurricanes are storms with heavy rain and strong winds, over 75 miles per hour, that grow stronger over warm oceans. In September 1999 a hurricane called Floyd hit North Carolina. When Hurricane Floyd hit land, its heavy rains lasted for two days. This rain caused a **surge** of water that rushed powerfully along North Carolina's coast. Twelve other states also had flooding. Floyd's price tag was 6.5 billion dollars and 77 people died.

By May of 2000, high temperatures and a drought in the western United States caused raging fires. Nearly 7 million acres burned and losses were more than 2 billion dollars.

Nature sometimes uses snow and ice to create extreme weather conditions. For example, blizzards are costly winter problems. A blizzard occurs when winds blow at 35 miles per hour, the temperature is 20°F or lower, and snow falls. One blizzard called the "Storm of the Century" howled along the east coast of the United States in March 1993. It cost more than 7 billion dollars and caused 270 deaths. Now that's extreme!

Reread for **Comprehension**

Analyze Text Structure

Description

Authors organize or structure information in a nonfiction text in a variety of ways. One way is through description. Signal words such as *first*, *next*, *finally*, or *for example* will alert readers to descriptive facts. A Description Chart will help you understand this text structure. Use the Description Chart as you reread the selection.

Signal Words	Descriptive Facts

Genre

Nonfiction presents facts about real people, things, places, or events.

Analyze Text Structure

Description

As you read, use your Description Chart.

Signal Words	Descriptive Facts
→	

Read to Find Out

How does a tropical storm become a category 5 hurricane?

626

HURRICANES

by SEYMOUR SIMON

Hurricanes are huge spinning storms that develop in warm areas around the equator. Hurricanes bring strong winds, heavy rains, storm surges, flooding, and sometimes even tornadoes. Coastal areas and islands are in the most danger during a hurricane, but even inland areas are at risk.

Hurricane season along the East Coast of the United States begins in June and continues until the end of November. The peak hurricane months are August and September. The East Coast averages about five hurricanes a year. Over other parts of the world, hurricanes happen year-round.

The word *hurricane* comes from people who lived in the Tropics in earlier times. The ancient Mayan people of South and Central America called their storm god Hunraken. An evil god of the Taino people of the Caribbean was called Huracan. Hurricanes are not really evil, but they can cause terrible **destruction** and great loss of life.

Hurricanes are one of three kinds of storms called tropical cyclones. Tropical means that the storms form over the warm waters of the Tropics near the equator. Cyclones are storms spinning around a calm center of low air pressure, which also moves. Cyclones spin counterclockwise in the Northern Hemisphere and clockwise in the Southern Hemisphere.

Tropical depressions are cyclones of clouds and thunderstorms that spin around a central area. They have steady wind speeds of 38 miles per hour or less.

Tropical storms are cyclones of heavy clouds and strong thunderstorms that spin at steady wind speeds of 39 to 73 miles per hour.

Hurricanes are the strongest tropical cyclones. They have steady winds of 74 miles per hour or higher. When these storms form over the North Atlantic, Caribbean Sea, Gulf of Mexico, or the west coast of Mexico, they are called hurricanes. In the North Pacific, these kinds of storms are called typhoons, and in the Indian Ocean they are called cyclones. In Australia, hurricanes are called willy-willies, after the word whirly-whirly.

Hurricanes are the only weather disasters that have been given their own names, such as Andrew, Camille, Floyd, Fran, Hugo, Irene, and Opal. In some ways all hurricanes are alike. But like different people, each hurricane has its own story.

> **Description**
> What characteristics does the author list about hurricanes?

All hurricanes form in the same way. They begin life in the warm, moist **atmosphere** over tropical ocean waters. First, the atmosphere gathers heat energy through **contact** with ocean waters that are above eighty degrees Fahrenheit to a depth of about two hundred feet. Next, moisture evaporating from the warm waters enters the atmosphere and begins to power the infant hurricane.

The growing hurricane forms bands of clouds and winds near the ocean surface that spiral air inward. Thunderstorms form, heating the air further and forcing the winds to rise higher into the atmosphere and the spinning to increase. Because of their power, hurricanes can easily last more than a week and may strike Caribbean islands days before whirling north and east into the United States.

Hurricane forecasts estimate when the eye will pass over a particular location. But even a small hurricane has damaging winds and rains that may arrive many hours before the eye.

One of the worst hurricanes in the United States in terms of **property** damage was Hurricane Andrew. Andrew became a tropical storm in the southern Atlantic Ocean on August 17, 1992. At first, Andrew was a small storm with winds of about 40 miles per hour. But the storm rapidly gained strength over the warm waters, and wind speeds reached 155 miles per hour. Andrew was a category 5 hurricane by the time it passed over the Bahamas and began heading east toward Florida.

> **Description**
> Which signal words in the first paragraph alert you to an upcoming list of descriptive facts?

Andrew hit the coastline of southern Florida on August 24. It was moving quickly and dropped about seven inches of rain across the state. Even more rain would have fallen had it been moving slowly. Storm tides reached seventeen feet along Biscayne Bay.

Wind speeds started to decrease over land, but Andrew quickly reached the warm waters in the Gulf of Mexico, where it regained 120-mile-per-hour winds. Then Andrew turned and slammed into the shoreline of Louisiana on August 26.

Andrew left a path of destruction in its wake. Damages totaled more than $25 billion. Thousands of people had lost their homes. More than a million people had been evacuated. But fewer than fifty-five people died, because of early hurricane warnings.

Weather forecasters at the National Hurricane Center were able to give a twenty-one-hour advance warning of Hurricane Andrew. This made it possible for people to flee dangerous low-lying places along the coast and go to safer spots inland.

Forecasters need to find where a hurricane is developing and how strong it is. At one time this was possible only when people saw the storm from a ship or from land. Nowadays forecasters use satellite images, airplanes, radar, and computers to track a hurricane.

Weather satellites orbit the earth at an altitude of nearly twenty-two thousand miles over the equator. The satellites send back images day and night of bands of clouds and early signs of a tropical storm. To get accurate readings of wind speed and pressure, pilots and scientists fly right through a hurricane into its eye.

633

When a hurricane gets close to the coast, it is pictured on land-based weather radars. Doppler radars show wind speeds and location and quickly detect changes. The National Hurricane Center takes the information from radars and other sources and uses computers to help forecast the path, speed, and strength of hurricanes.

Hurricane and storm warnings are broadcast over radio and television and are also **available** on the Internet. National Oceanic and Atmospheric Administration (NOAA) Weather Radio broadcasts warnings, watches, forecasts, and other weather information twenty-four hours a day. These radio stations cover all the states, coastal waters, Puerto Rico, and United States Pacific territories.

A hurricane or a flood *watch* is usually given within thirty-six hours of an approaching storm. During a watch, it's important to prepare and decide what you and your family are going to do during the storm. A hurricane or a flood *warning* is usually given within twenty-four hours for a particular area. During a warning, listen to local radio or television stations for safety instructions.

National Weather Service (NWS) radios are specially equipped to give you immediate news about tropical hurricanes and floods. Regular NWS programs send out a special tone that turns on these radios in the listening area when there is an emergency. The radios can be connected to lights, computers, even bed shakers so that everyone can get the information.

Because of early warnings, the number of hurricane-related deaths has decreased in the United States in recent years. But hurricanes still remain a danger along the Atlantic coast and the Gulf of Mexico.

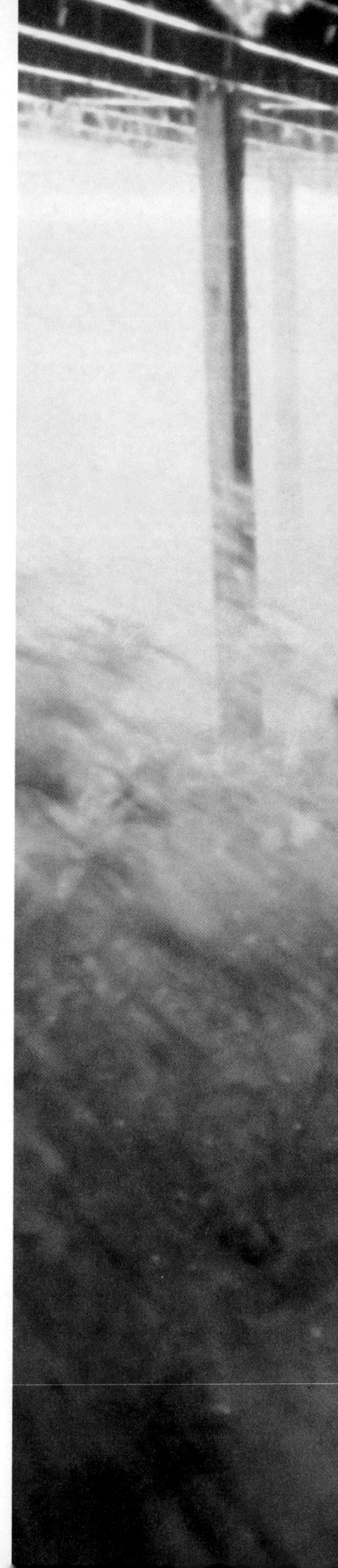

Scientists think that, potentially, the most dangerous place in the United States during a hurricane is New Orleans. That's because a storm **surge** could cover the low-lying city with twenty feet of water. Southwest Florida from Tampa Bay to the Everglades National Park is also dangerous, because the area is also very close to sea level.

If you are ever caught in a hurricane, it's important to know what to do. The first thing to remember is to listen closely to the radio, television, or NOAA Weather Radio for official bulletins. Follow instructions and leave immediately with your family if told to do so.

Only stay in a house if you are not ordered to leave. Stay away from windows and doors during the storm. During the worst of the storm, lie on the floor under a table or another sturdy object. Make sure you have a battery-driven portable radio and keep listening for storm information. Keep on hand at least a three-day supply of water and food that won't spoil.

Even after a hurricane passes by, conditions outside may still be dangerous. Here are some tips for you and your family.

- Keep listening to the radio for updates on flooding and highway conditions. Wait until an area is declared safe before going back into it.

- Stay away from moving water. Rapidly moving water even less than a foot deep can sweep you away. If you see water flowing across a street, turn around and go another way.

- Don't play in flooded areas. They are dangerous. The water may also be electrically charged from downed or underground power lines.

- Use a flashlight for emergency lighting. Don't use a candle or a flame indoors if the power goes off.

- Use bottled or stored water for drinking and cooking. Use tap water only when local officials say it is safe.

- Use the telephone only for emergency calls. If someone needs to be rescued or helped, call the police or local officials.

By preparing ahead and listening to the radio and following instructions, everyone can be much safer during a hurricane.

People are now much more aware of hurricanes than they were twenty-five years ago. When a hurricane threatens the United States, it becomes big news on television and radio. Even people who live in the middle of the country and will never experience a hurricane at home are interested in what's happening during the storm.

Along the East Coast, hurricanes are a fact of life. But nowadays forecasts, combined with timely warnings about hurricane dangers, are saving lives. The more we learn about hurricanes, the better our chances of coming through them safely.

Talking up a storm with Seymour Simon

Seymour Simon has written over 200 books, but he still calls himself a teacher. He started by teaching in a classroom, but now reaches more kids through his books. First, Seymour picks a topic he loved as a child. "Interests don't change," he says. "Kids still love spectacular things." After that, he researches and writes and rewrites the story until the explanations and descriptions are perfectly clear. Seymour wants his books to open up new worlds to the reader, not just answer questions. Then, when the books come out, he is back in the classroom, talking again to students and teachers.

Other books by Seymour Simon: *Storms* and *Volcanoes*

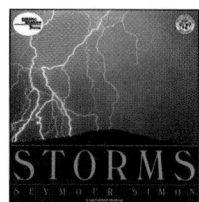 

 Find out more about Seymour Simon at **www.macmillanmh.com**.

CA Author's Purpose

The author's purpose is to inform. The text is informational nonfiction and tells about real weather events. How do the photos contribute?

# CA Critical Thinking

Summarize

Use your Description Chart to help you summarize *Hurricanes.* Be sure to include descriptive facts, characteristics, and important details in your summary.

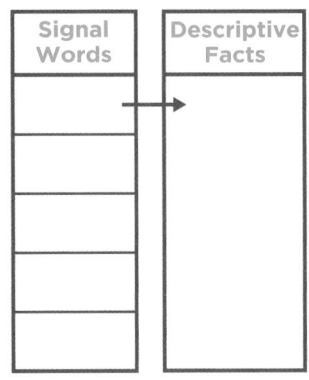

Signal Words	Descriptive Facts

Think and Compare

1. Use the descriptive details on page 629 to describe tropical depressions, tropical storms, and hurricanes. Include facts and characteristics about each kind of storm in your **description**. Analyze Text Structure: Description

2. Reread the tips on page 637. Why should you stay inside until the area is declared safe after a hurricane? **Analyze**

3. Decide why you would or would not like to be a pilot or scientist who flies through the eyes of hurricanes to measure wind speed. Explain your answer. **Analyze**

4. Why are people who will never directly experience a hurricane or storm **surge** interested in these storms? **Evaluate**

5. Reread "The Extreme Costs of Extreme Weather" on pages 624–625. Compare the damage and injury caused by Hurricane Floyd with the damage and injury caused by Hurricane Andrew that is described in *Hurricanes.* **Reading/Writing Across Texts**

Poetry

Free Verse Poems are written without a traditional rhyme scheme or meter.

✓ Literary Elements

Personification is used to give human characteristics to animals, objects, or ideas.

Imagery is the use of descriptions to create vivid pictures in the reader's mind.

Onomatopoeia is a word that sounds like the action or object it describes.

Suspense

by Pat Mora

Wind chases itself
Around our house, flattens
     wild grasses
with one hot breath.
      Clouds boil purple
        and gray, roll
and roil. Scorpions
dart
    under stones. Rabbit eyes peer
From the shelter of mesquite.
      Thorny silence.

> The wind "chases itself" is an example of **personification**.

> The poet uses **imagery** with the words "Clouds boil purple and gray."

My *paisano*, the road runner
    paces, dashes into the rumble,
races from the *plink, plink*
    splatter into his shadow,   leaps
        at the crash   flash
splash,
    sky rivers rushing into arroyos and
Thirsty roots of prickly pears,
        greening cactus.

> "Plink, plink" is an example of **onomatopoeia**.

CA Critical Thinking

1. List another example of imagery from this poem. Describe the picture that this example paints in your mind. **Imagery**

2. What effect does the use of the present tense have in this poem? **Analyze**

3. Compare and contrast the storm in the poem to the information in *Hurricanes.* How are the storms different? How are they the same? Use information in each text to explain your answer. **Reading/Writing Across Texts**

 Find out more about poetry at **www.macmillanmh.com**.

Writing

✔ Evidence: Linked to Argument

Good writers use strong words and details to help support the ideas in their writing.

Reading and Writing Connection

Read the passage below. Notice how Seymour Simon uses names to help us understand the terror of hurricanes.

An excerpt from *Hurricanes*

The author includes the actual words by which people named destructive gods in order to convince us that the word "hurricane" really did come from people's horrible experiences with these storms.

The word *hurricane* comes from people who lived in the Tropics in earlier times. The ancient Mayan people of South and Central America called their storm god Hunraken. An evil god of the Taino people of the Caribbean was called Huracan. Hurricanes are not really evil, but they can cause terrible destruction and great loss of life.

HURRICANES by Seymour Simon

Read and Find

Read Carla's writing. How did she prove that she is not so skilled a player? Use the Writer's Checklist below to help you.

Ultimate Game

 by Carla S.

Catching a flying disk is harder than it looks. I noticed that my backhand was good but not my forehand. I noticed this when I hit Sophie in the thigh with my forehand. The frisbee twisted and turned in the opposite direction. At the end of the game, as I was walking, John threw me a long one. I reached out and caught it with one hand. This was the first time I caught it.

Read about my athletic skills.

Writer's Checklist

✓ Did Carla show us a particular example of when she played badly?

✓ Did Carla show us that some skills are more difficult to learn than others?

 Were you convinced that Carla might get better if she played more?

The HUNGRIEST Dog

There I stood, frozen in thought. I had my story in hand. It was good, and I'd worked hard on it. I'd finished two days early, even. There was no doubt in my mind that I, Jonathan Block, fifth-grader, had a good chance of winning the $200 City-Wide Fifth Grade Story Contest. A very good chance.

So what was this?

I was standing by the wooden bin that read PLACE STORY HERE. I was about to slide mine in the slot when I saw it: a story someone had left by the bin, rumpled and dog-eared. I picked it up. No name. No title. The cover page was torn off. I tried to imagine what might have caused a person to do such a thing. Strange.

Then, at the bottom of the page I saw a handwritten note: *IF SOMEONE CAN USE THIS STORY, TAKE IT. I'm a fourth-grader—not eligible. Good luck, Miss X.*

Ah, so that was it! I tried to picture Miss X, arriving with high hopes. Then she reads the contest rules: fifth-graders only. Darn!

I decided I'd read the thing. Don't ask me why. Just to see if. . . .

It was about a puppy. Fshew! A wave of relief washed over me. It didn't seem likely that some puppy story would be a serious threat, some real competition.

I read on. The story seemed a bit too simple, I thought, but then, toward the end of the second paragraph, it became quite clear. Miss X was on to something. I liked the way she described this pooch, a beagle: The "hungriest dog in America" was her term. This dog was so hungry it opened refrigerators. It unlocked cabinets. It pushed chairs up to the dinner table. It "sang for its supper" like some kooky, half-human canine crooner. It stole a Thanksgiving turkey, a Christmas ham, a. . . .

I caught myself smiling. Silly mutt! Crazy dog!

I kept reading. Now I was laughing out loud. The things this bandit-dog did! It snatched ice-cream cones. It pilfered pizzas, lollipops, cat food, egg salad, everything, anything! It jumped, dived, ran, swam! This dog climbed a tree, for goodness sakes, to get food. A tree!

There was more, a lot more, but suddenly, I had to stop. Not because the story wasn't good. In fact, the opposite: because it was. In fact, there was no denying it: This story was better than my story, my "masterpiece" that I'd worked so hard on.

So what should I do?

Well, first, I might tell you a couple of the things I didn't do, and those included submitting the story under my own name. I also could have destroyed the thing. But I didn't do that, either; I couldn't.

So what did I finally do? I went home. I threw away my "masterpiece." And I sat down to write this, the piece you're reading. It's not as good as Miss X's story. But, hey, if I couldn't use her story, at least I could describe what it was like!

And now if I, Jonathan Block, end up winning, all I can say is this: Miss X, wherever you are, if I get the $200, you get half. I don't care if you are ineligible. You earned it!

Going the DISTANCE

WHAT'S THE FARTHEST DISTANCE you've ever run? A mile? Five miles? Ten miles? Now think what it would be like to run over 26 miles without stopping. That's what happens when runners compete against one another in a marathon.

According to legend, the first marathon ever run wasn't really even a race. The event took place in the year 490 B.C. in ancient Greece. The Greek army fought the much larger Persian army on the plain of Marathon. When the Greeks won the battle, they sent a messenger named Pheidippides (figh-DI-pi-deez) to deliver the news to Athens. Pheidippides ran without stopping for the entire distance, which was almost 25 miles. After telling of the

victory, the young man collapsed from exhaustion and died. His efforts were not forgotten.

The first actual marathon race took place in 1896 when the modern Olympic Games began in Athens, Greece. Runners ran the same 25 miles as Pheidippides from Marathon to Athens. In the 1906 Olympics in

Marathon running became even more popular in the United States after Frank Shorter won a gold medal at the 1972 Olympics.

London, England, organizers changed the distance of the race to about 26.2 miles so that the queen and her children could watch the runners. Most marathons today use that distance as the standard measure.

Throughout its history, the marathon has been a symbol of strength and determination. Many runners see it as the ultimate challenge of their abilities. Thousands of people line up at the starting lines of the most popular races. Many give up before reaching the finish line. Some have even collapsed in their tracks.

Most runners today take precautions to avoid such problems when they run a marathon. Many work with trainers to help build up their strength and endurance for the race. Runners eat wholesome and healthful foods to stay in shape and give their bodies enough energy during the race. They also choose special running shoes and clothing that will help them avoid blisters, cramps, and chills along the course. All of these things have made marathon running safer and more popular than ever before.

Today, the marathon is just one of a growing number of events called endurance sports. These events test the limits of participants in terms of how far they can go and how long they can perform.

However far you go, health experts agree that runners should start with short distances and work their way up to longer routes and times. What if you DID keep running farther and farther every day? How long might it be before YOU win the gold medal in the Olympic marathon?

AVERAGE MARATHON TIMES IN 2005

		1 Hour	2 Hours	3 Hours	4 Hours	5 Hours	6 Hours
Ages 0-19	MALES 5 hrs 4 min 39 sec						
	FEMALES 5 hrs 46 min 58 sec						
Ages 20-24	MALES 4 hrs 22 min 21 sec						
	FEMALES 4 hrs 52 min 38 sec						
Ages 25-29	MALES 4 hrs 24 min 42 sec						
	FEMALES 4 hrs 54 min 45 sec						
Ages 30-34	MALES 4 hrs 25 min 28 sec						
	FEMALES 4 hrs 58 min 18 sec						
Ages 35-39	MALES 4 hrs 22 min 45 sec						
	FEMALES 4 hrs 55 min 37 sec						
Ages 40-44	MALES 4 hrs 21 min 46 sec						
	FEMALES 4 hrs 59 min 01 sec						

CA Critical Thinking

Now answer numbers 1 through 4. Base your answers on the story "The Hungriest Dog."

1. **The author wrote "The Hungriest Dog" to**

   A   entertain readers who like dog stories.

   B   teach a lesson about honesty.

   C   explain how to train a puppy.

   D   write about foods that harm puppies.

2. **What generalization can be made from "The Hungriest Dog"?**

   A   All fifth-graders like to read about dogs.

   B   Jonathan always wanted to win this contest.

   C   The contest should have been open to fourth-graders.

   D   Jonathan knows the identity of Miss X.

3. **Read the following sentence from the story.**

   > The <u>cover</u> page was torn off.

   What is the meaning of the underlined word?

   A   a young official messenger

   B   to locate someone by calling out the name

   C   an important historical event in history

   D   a sheet of paper at the front of a book or other writing

4. **Do you think Jonathan was right not to use Miss X's story? Explain your answer.**

Now answer numbers 1 through 4. Base your answers on the article "Going the Distance."

1. **Which statement is a generalization?**

   A   The first marathon race was not really a race.
   B   Most runners build endurance before a marathon.
   C   The first Olympic marathon was run in 1896.
   D   Pheidippides was exhausted by the race.

2. **Which sentence states the author's purpose in "Going the Distance"?**

   A   The author wants to entertain readers.
   B   The author wants to inform readers.
   C   The author wants to persuade readers.
   D   The author wants to express an opinion.

3. **What is the meaning of the underlined word in this sentence? The first marathon wasn't even a race.**

   A   a group of people who share ancestry and physical characteristics
   B   to take part in a contest of speed
   C   a contest to see which participant is fastest
   D   a group of plants or animals with common characteristics

4. **Which statement about the chart on page 647 is true?**

   A   The fastest marathon races are run by the youngest runners.
   B   The fastest female runners were between the ages of 25 and 29.
   C   The slowest males were under the age of 19.
   D   Male runners always run faster than female runners.

Write on Demand

PROMPT Do you think the Olympic planners were wise to revive the ancient marathon race? Use details from the article to support your answer. Write for 20 minutes. Write as much as you can as well as you can.

649

The Big Question

What events can help you change the way you think ?

Theme Launcher Video

LOG ON ▶ Find out more about changing ideas on **www.macmillanmh.com**.

What events can help you change the way you think?

Sometimes people act like they would never change their minds. Then suddenly something happens and they may even become excited supporters of a new idea. Why? Time changes people's minds. Sometimes new arguments or new experiences lead to new opinions as well.

Less than 100 years ago, women were not allowed to vote in the United States. Little by little and a few at a time, women began to speak out. More and more supporters joined in demonstrations and marches. Eventually, enough Americans became convinced and the Constitution was changed. Today no one thinks it is odd that women vote.

When you learn what makes people change their minds, you can begin to think about your own opinions. Who knows, you may decide on certain topics to change your mind!

Research Activities

Throughout the unit, you will be reading about people who change their point of view about something. Research a person who experienced something that caused him or her to support a new way of thinking.

Write about that person and what caused the change in his or her way of thinking.

Most Valuable Pupil

Darrin Anderson

MVP

AWARD

Keep Track of Ideas

As you read, keep track of the people and characters who change their opinions about something. Use the Layered Book organizer to organize your ideas and information. On the top section, write the Unit Theme: Changes. On each layer of the book, write what you learn each week about changes.

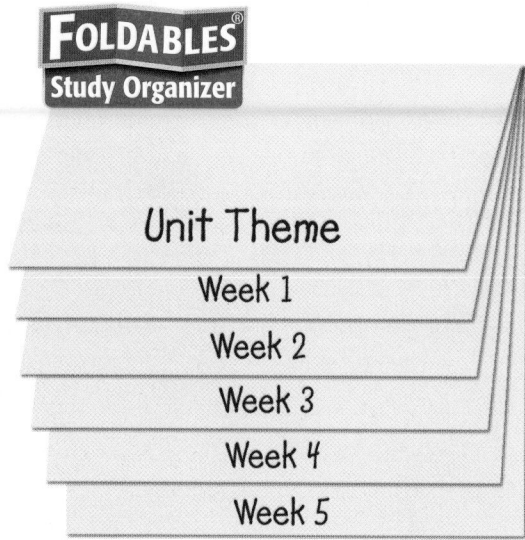

FOLDABLES
Study Organizer

Unit Theme
Week 1
Week 2
Week 3
Week 4
Week 5

Research Toolkit

Conduct Your Unit 6 Research Online with:

Research Roadmap
Follow step-by-step guide to complete your research project.

Online Resources
- Topic Finder and other Research Tools
- Videos and Virtual Fieldtrips
- Photos and Drawings for Presentations
- Related Articles and Web Resources

California Web Site Links

 Go to www.macmillanmh.com for more information.

California People

Earl Warren
Supreme Court Justice
Born in California, Justice Warren was Chief Justice of the Supreme Court during changing times in United States history.

653

Overcoming Obstacles

CA **Talk About It**

What do you do when you are faced with a challenging situation?

LOG ON ▶ Find out more about overcoming obstacles at **www.macmillanmh.com**.

The Talent Contest

by Howard Gabe

As Danny put his lunch tray onto the cafeteria table, milk spilled all over his sandwich. He sat down, hung his head forward, and **slumped** over the food in front of him. Frowning, he began peeling the **soggy** milk-soaked bread from his sandwich. "This is the most ridiculous thing I've ever done!" he said.

"It's not that bad," said his friend Elena, who was sitting across from him. "Just get another sandwich."

"Sandwich? What sandwich? I am talking about the talent contest. It's only two weeks away and I don't know what I'm doing! Everybody will laugh at me. It's inevitable. There's no way to avoid it!"

"Don't be so negative, Danny," said Elena as she rolled her eyes. "You're going to be great. You're very **capable**. You have the skills to do just about anything."

Danny moved his lunch tray to the side and rested his head on the table.

"Sit up Danny," ordered Elena. "I have an idea. Let's brainstorm a list of things you could do. We'll divide the list into **categories** or groups. Let's start with music. You play the piano, right?"

"I stopped taking lessons in third grade," said Danny.

"What about singing a song?" suggested Elena.

Danny shook his head no. "Let's move on to another category."

"What about juggling?" asked Elena, as she twisted thin **strands** of hair around her finger.

"I don't know how to juggle!" Danny almost shouted. "Elena, how did I get myself into this huge, **gigantic** mess?"

"Stop being so…" Elena paused. "That's it, DRAMATIC!" Elena shouted excitedly. "You could do a dramatic

reading. You definitely have the talent for it. Mrs. Pace always calls on you to read aloud in class. You could read a play aloud. Maybe you could even get extra **credit** from Mrs. Pace. She rewards students with points for doing extra reading work."

Danny thought for a minute. Then he smiled. "Elena," Danny said, "you are a great friend!"

Elena smiled back. "I just want to make sure you are a bright, shiny, **luminous** star when you step out onstage."

Reread for Comprehension

Analyze Story Structure

Character and Plot

A Character and Plot Chart helps you figure out a character's personality and how it affects the plot. These traits and events are part of story structure. Use your Character and Plot Chart as you reread "The Talent Contest" to figure out Elena's traits and how her actions affect the plot of the story.

Character	Plot

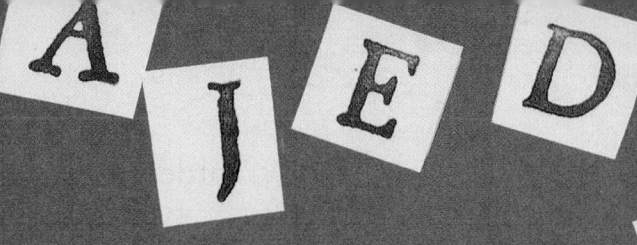

Genre

Realistic Fiction uses settings, characters, and events that could actually exist.

Story Structure

Character and Plot

As you read, use your Character and Plot Chart.

Character	Plot

Read to Find Out

How does the kind of person Sage is affect the plot?

5TH Grade
Room 202
MRS. PAGE

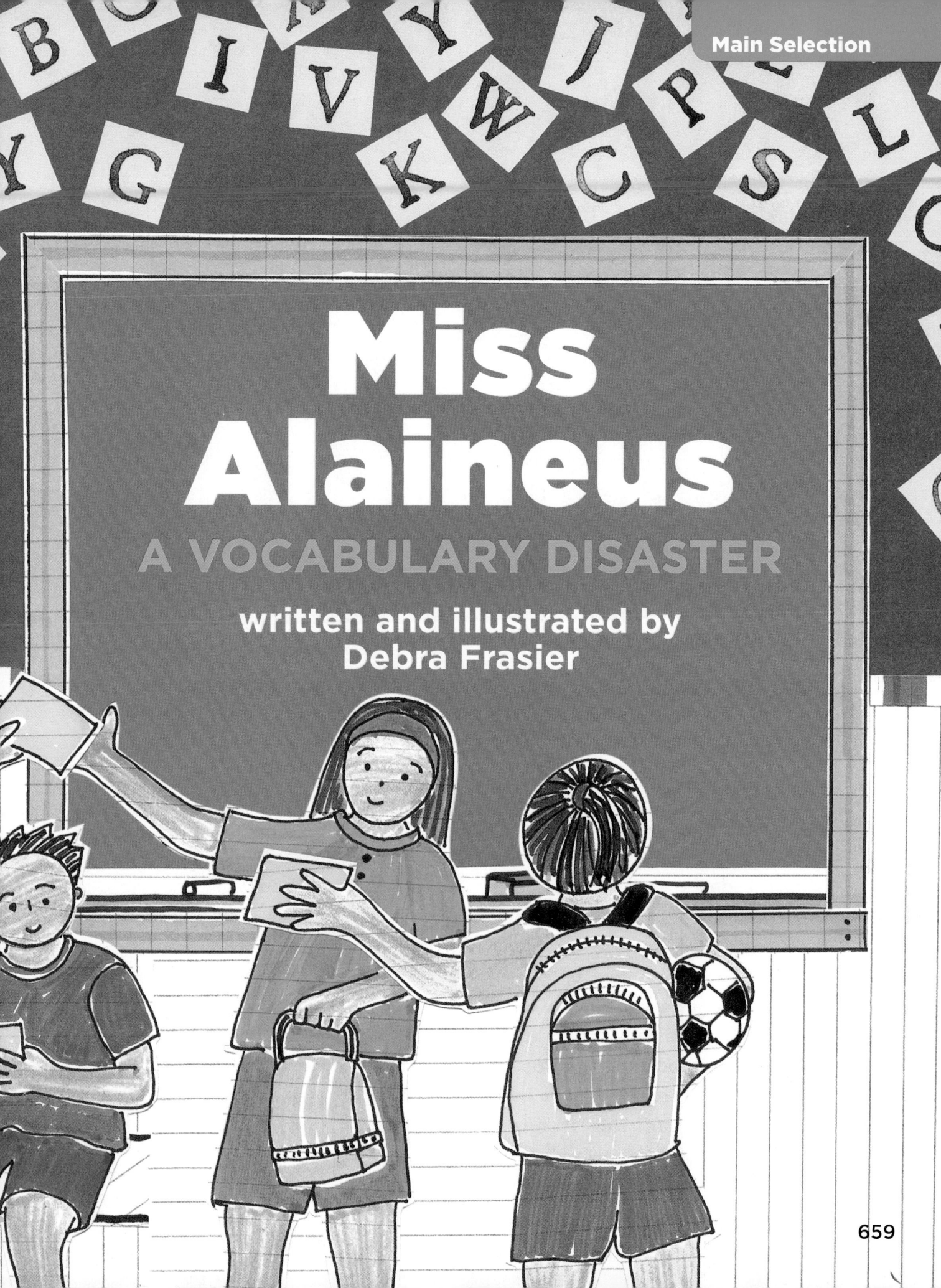

Miss Alaineus

A VOCABULARY DISASTER

**written and illustrated by
Debra Frasier**

None of this would have happened if it wasn't for Forest.
Forest is not a *thicket of trees*. Forest is a boy. A sick boy. A
boy sneezing and coughing all over my desk and pencils.

I caught Forest's cold and had to stay home from school on
Tuesday. Tuesday is Vocabulary Day at Webster School.
Follow my advice: Never get sick on Vocabulary Day.

On Tuesday afternoon I called my best friend, Starr, who is
not *a **luminous** celestial object seen as a point of light in the
sky*, but a very smart girl who listens perfectly on Vocabulary
Day. She was late for baseball practice, so she spelled the first
fourteen vocabulary words as fast as she could.

I had to scribble them quickly because her mom was calling
her to the car. "This last one's 'Miss Alaineus'!" Starr yelled.
"I gotta go. I hope you feel better tomorrow, Sage." And she
hung up the phone with a crash.

I didn't feel much better on Wednesday, so my mom called Mrs. Page, who is not *a single side of a printed sheet of paper usually found bound in a book*. She's my teacher, and actually Mrs. Page is a good name for her because she reads to us every day. My mom told her yes, I had my math problems and vocabulary words, and yes, I would get better soon.

Plot
How do you think Starr's rush to give Sage the vocabulary words will affect what happens next?

VOCABULARY WORDS

1. dinosaur
2. snake
3. museum
4. reptile
5. constrictor
6. herpetologist
7. fossil
8. carnivore
9. herbivore
10. nest
11. species
12. theory
13. hypothesis
14. category
15. Miss Alaineus

Every week Mrs. Page gives us a list of words with a theme, like Story Writing or Musical Performance or Electricity. We're supposed to look up each word in the dictionary, but sometimes I already know the words, so I try to make the definitions sound like I looked them up.

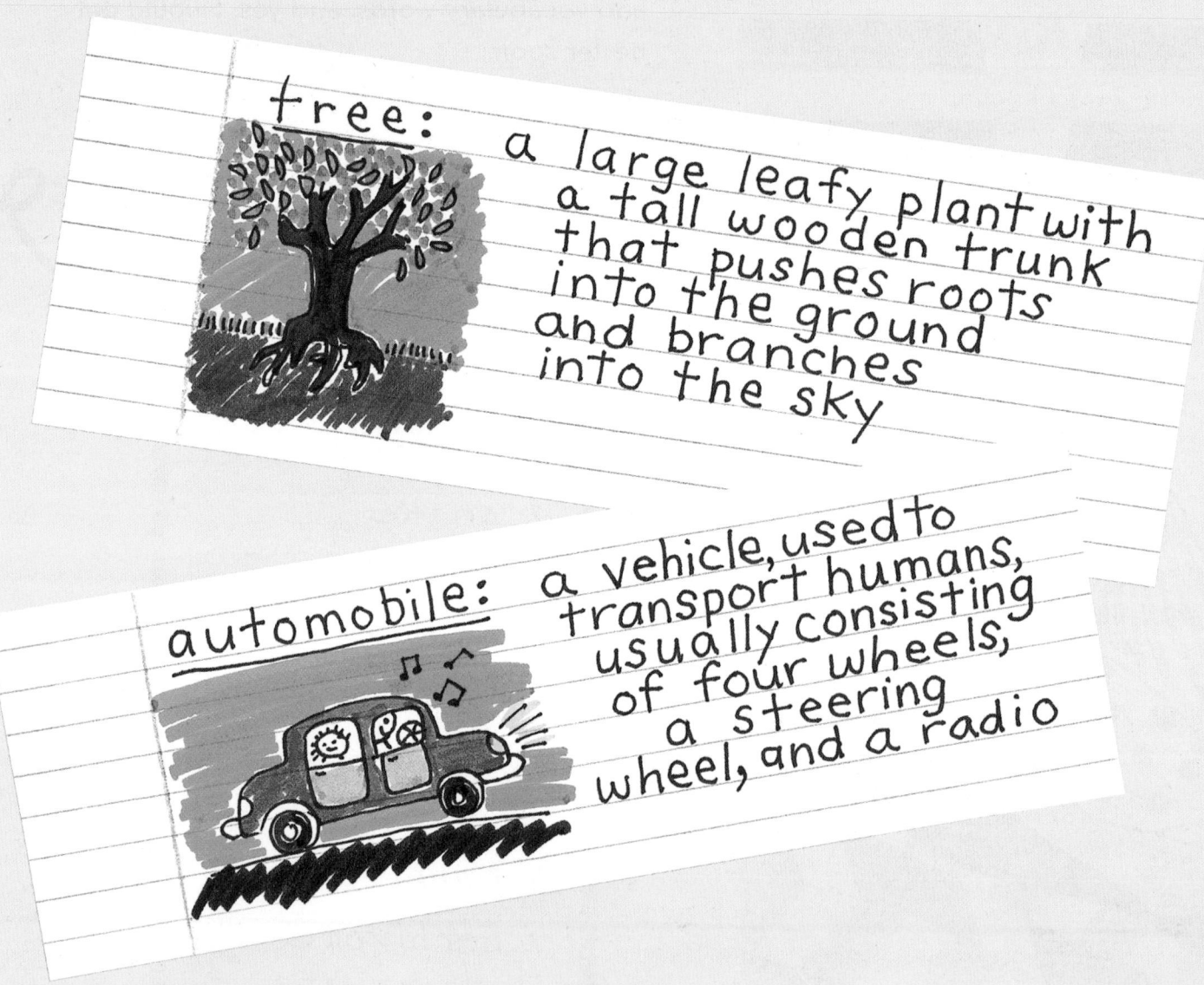

tree: a large leafy plant with a tall wooden trunk that pushes roots into the ground and branches into the sky

automobile: a vehicle, used to transport humans, usually consisting of four wheels, a steering wheel, and a radio

I thought I was pretty good at definitions until this week.

My mom says, "Pride goeth before a fall."

Pride: *an unduly high opinion of oneself.*

Goeth: *Old English for "to go."*

Fall: *what happened on Monday, Vocabulary Test Day.*

By Thursday afternoon my head felt like it was stuffed with cotton and my throat felt swollen shut. I finished defining my vocabulary words while propped up in bed with a box of tissues on one side and a **gigantic** red dictionary on the other. It's hard to look up words in a huge book while you're in bed blowing your nose, so I made my own dictionary language for as many of them as I could.

13. hypothesis: what you guess will happen in your science experiment

14. category: a bunch of things that are alike

15. Miss Alaineus:

The last word seemed a little odd to me because I couldn't figure out what she had to do with snakes or **categories** or theories. Mrs. Page rarely gives us people's names on our vocabulary lists, but we have had a few that turned into words, like Louis Pasteur for **pasteurization** and George Washington for **Washington, D.C.**, so I decided she must have been included for a reason.

You should know that for years I had wondered who Miss Alaineus was. When I was little I figured out that she had something to do with the kitchen, because the Miss Alaineus drawer held the spoons too big to fit anywhere else, the sharp corn holders shaped like tiny cobs, and the spaghetti spork, that weird cross between a spoon and a fork that perfectly lifts slippery spaghetti out of the bowl. I thought maybe she was an **ancestor:** *an ancient relative long dead*, who left us all these odd things in the drawer.

Then just last year my mom and I were at the grocery store and it all fell into place. We were in one of those Very Big Hurries when she said, "You go get some of that long Italian bread and two sticks of butter. I'll get Miss Alaineus' things and meet you here at the cash register."

I found the bread and butter, and my mom came back with spaghetti sauce, a can of Parmesan cheese, a can of corn, and a big green box of spaghetti with a beautiful woman on the front. She was drawn so that her hair tumbled perfectly across the box and ended in a little plastic window, making the spaghetti look just like the ends of the **strands** of her hair.

There she was—Miss Alaineus.

So, propped up on pillows in my bed, with a tissue in one hand and a pencil in the other, I wrote:

15. Miss Alaineus: the woman
    on green spaghetti boxes
    whose hair is the color
    of uncooked pasta

and turns into spaghetti
at the ends

And then I fell asleep.

I finally got better over the weekend and felt great on Monday. I turned in my homework to Mrs. Page and sat down at my desk, glad to be back at school with my friends. I was even glad to see Forest at our morning circle meeting.

"First, I want to remind you of the Tenth Annual Vocabulary Parade on Friday," said Mrs. Page. "I hope you are all working on your word costumes. Second, please remember to bring your bus money and permission slips for our science museum field trip tomorrow. And third, instead of our usual Monday test, we are going to have a Vocabulary Bee today.

"Everyone line up here by the chalkboard, and I'll choose a word from our list. After I pronounce the word, please spell and define it. If you are correct, go to the end of the line. If you miss the word, please sit down at your desk and look it up in the dictionary. Write the word five times and define it once."

Starr was first with **museum**: "M-U-S-E-U-M: *a building for exhibiting objects about art or history or science,*" she said, and went to the back of the line.

Cliff, not *a high, steep face of rock,* but one very tall boy, answered to the word **dinosaur**: "D-I-N-O-S-A-U-R: *a prehistoric, extinct reptile, often huge,*" and he went to the back of the line.

I was tenth, and when Mrs. Page called out my word, I spelled: "Capital **M-I-S-S**, capital **A-L-A-I-N-E-U-S**," and added, *"the woman on green spaghetti boxes whose hair is the color of uncooked pasta and turns into spaghetti at the ends."*

There was a moment of silence in the room. I smiled at Mrs. Page. She waited to see if I would add anything else, and when I didn't, she grinned. Not smiled—**grinned:** *to draw back the lips and bare the teeth, as in a very wide smile*—and the entire class burst into one huge giggling, laughing, falling-down mass of kids. Forest was doubled over. Starr, my best friend, was laughing so hard tears came to her eyes. By now, even Mrs. Page was laughing.

Pride goeth before a fall. I was **Sage:** *one who shows wisdom, experience, judgment.* Why were they laughing? "Wise-girl-with-words" my dad always called me. What had I said? I was beginning to turn red. **Red:** *the color of embarrassment.*

Finally the room quieted. Mrs. Page opened her dictionary and wrote on the chalkboard:

Miscellaneous: *adj. 1. consisting of various kinds or qualities 2. a collection of unrelated objects*

My jaw dropped as I looked at the spelling. My eyes bulged as I read the definition. I didn't bother to tell anyone about my mom and the spaghetti spork and the grocery store. **Humbled:** *aware of my shortcomings, modest, meek,* I dragged back to my seat and wrote **miscellaneous** five times and defined it once. And that's when I remembered I had even drawn a picture of the spaghetti box for extra **credit.** I was **devastated:** *wasted, ravaged.* **Ruined:** *destroyed.* **Finished:** *brought to an end.*

> **Character**
> What does Sage's reaction to her mistake tell you about her character?

They called me Miss Alaineus for the rest of the day. Sometimes a person couldn't even get the words out before bending over with laughter. The day took a week to end. When I got off the bus I **slumped** home—devastated, ruined, finished.

I told my mom the whole story, from the kitchen drawer to the grocery store to the Vocabulary Bee. Even my own mother laughed a little at the part about the drawing for extra credit, but at least she stopped fast and said, "You know what I always say . . . There's gold in every mistake."

Gold? *A bright yellow precious metal of great value?*

Mistake? *Something done, said, or thought in the wrong way?*

"Impossible," I told her. **Impossible:** *not capable of happening.*

I couldn't believe I *ever* had to go back to school. But the next day we went to the science museum, and everyone forgot all about Miss Alaineus at the snake exhibit and the dinosaur bone lab. Then the guide said, "The field of bone archaeology has been influenced by a wide and unusual array of miscellaneous discoveries around the world." The class burst out laughing, and the guide was pleased with herself for entertaining us so easily. And I **knew:** *to apprehend with certainty*, that my mistake was still alive and well, and nothing like gold.

After school I lay on my bed and stared at the wall. How could I have been so stupid?

My mom came in and said it was time to work on my costume for the Vocabulary Parade. We had finished the cape for **Capable**, but I still needed to make the lettering down the back.

"Mom," I said, "I could only be a mistake this year. **Miss Stake.**"

Suddenly I sat up.

I looked at my mom. She looked at me.

I smiled.

She smiled.

"Sweetheart," she said, "let's take another look at that cape."

It took the most courage I've ever had
to walk out on that stage as **Miss Alaineus,**
Queen of All Miscellaneous Things. But
when Mr. Bell read my word and definition,
everyone applauded and laughed **wildly:** *in a*
manner lacking all restraint, and I grinned at
my mom across the auditorium.

Forest came right after me. When he bowed, his **Precipitation** watering-can hat rained on Mr. Bell's new suit, and the entire audience gasped, then cheered when Mr. Bell smiled at his **soggy** clothes.

To my **astonishment:** *great shock and amazement*, I won a gold trophy for The Most Original Use of a Word in the Tenth Annual Vocabulary Parade.

So this time Mom was right. There was gold in this mistake.

And next year I think I'm going to be . . .

Miss Sterious,
Investigator of All Things Mysterious!

A Few Words About Debra Frasier

Debra Frasier's fifth-grade daughter said to her one day, "Mom, today I figured out that *miscellaneous* is not a person." Her daughter's new wisdom gave Debra two gifts: a good laugh and the idea to write *Miss Alaineus*. Debra says her books take a long time because she loves the creative process. Being creative is nothing new for Debra. As a child in Florida, she used to make collages with old wood she found on the beach and miles of tape.

For the illustrations, Debra again turned to her daughter for inspiration. Papers, glue, scissors, and pencils that were crammed in her daughter's desk gave her the idea for the story's school setting. At last Debra had completed a fun adventure about the usually tame world of vocabulary.

Another book by Debra Frasier:
Out of the Ocean

 Author's Purpose

Authors of fiction usually write to entertain, but they may have another purpose. What clues can help you figure out if Debra Frasier had more than one purpose for writing *Miss Alaineus*?

LOG ON ▶ Find out more about Debra Frasier at **www.macmillanmh.com**.

678

Critical Thinking

Summarize

Use your Character and Plot Chart to help you summarize *Miss Alaineus*. Include only the most important events that lead to Sage's creative solution to her problem.

Character	Plot

Think and Compare

1. *Miss Alaineus* is written from Sage's point of view. How does this help you know about her **character**? What words or phrases would you use to describe her? Use story details in your answer. **Story Structure: Character and Plot**

2. Reread page 676. What does Sage mean when she says, "there was gold in this mistake"? Use details from the story to support your answer. **Analyze**

3. Even the most **capable** people make mistakes. How do you feel when you make a mistake? Compare your feelings to Sage's feelings. **Analyze**

4. Why might it be helpful to have a sense of humor when you are trying to solve a problem? **Evaluate**

5. Look back at "The Talent Contest" on pages 656–657. How is Danny's experience similar to Sage's? Use details from each selection. **Reading/Writing Across Texts**

Genre

Nonfiction provides information about real people, places, or events.

Text Feature

Photographs and **Captions** give visual examples that help explain what the text states.

Content Vocabulary

competition

orally

eliminates

The National

by Nicole Lee

Does the word *autochthonous* sound familiar? Luckily, to David Tidmarsh, it did. David correctly spelled *autochthonous* to win the 77th National Spelling Bee. David, from South Bend, Indiana, won the spelling championship at age 14. In the final round of **competition**, David beat Akshay Buddiga, a 13-year-old boy from Colorado.

Welcome to the exciting and intense world of spelling bees. The National Spelling Bee takes place each June in Washington, D.C. The competition has been around for a long time. It began in 1925 with only nine contestants. In 2004 there were 265 contestants ranging in age from 8 to 15. Contestants for the National Spelling Bee come from English-speaking countries all over the world. Students from Jamaica, Puerto Rico, and even Saudi Arabia have competed in the National Spelling Bee.

It takes a lot of hard work and dedication to advance to the National Spelling Bee finals. Students spend a lot of time preparing for competition. The words chosen for the competition are chosen from the dictionary by a panel of word experts. There are more than 470,000 words in the dictionary, and any one of these words could be chosen for the competition. David spent several months preparing for the finals. He spent many hours studying a dictionary, and a list of 10,000 words that he created. Fortunately for David, *autochthonous* was one of the words on his list. After David won he said, "I was just hoping I got a word I studied."

Spelling contestants spend months poring over the dictionary.

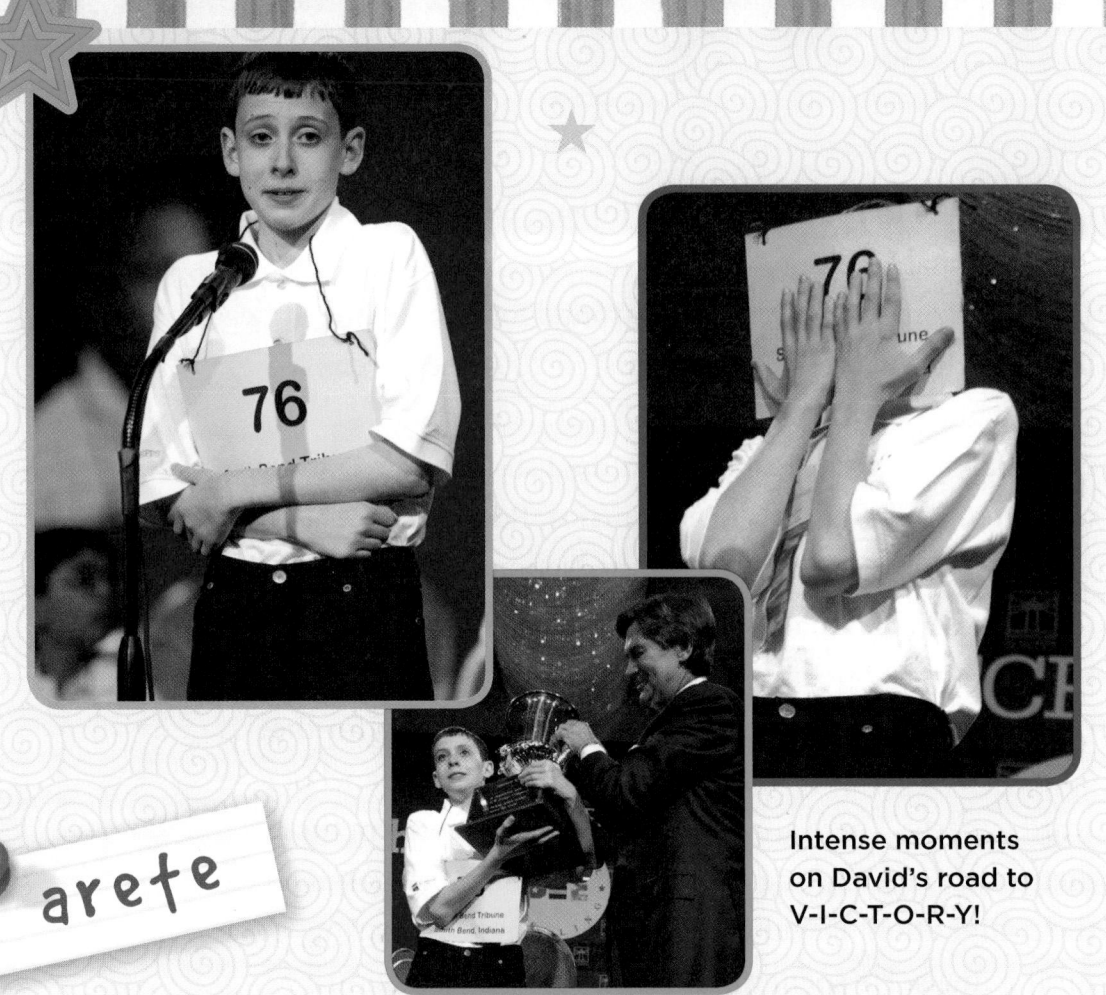

arete

Intense moments on David's road to V-I-C-T-O-R-Y!

The purpose of the National Spelling Bee is to encourage students to improve their spelling, broaden their vocabularies, and develop correct English usage. During round one of the championships, the spellers have to take a 25-word written test. In round two, each student spells a word **orally**. Next, the judges score the students. The top 90 students move on to round three. Any mistake during round three or the later rounds **eliminates** the speller. Some of the words that David had to spell before the 15th and final round were *gaminerie*, *arete*, *balancelle*, and *sumpsimus*.

Akshay (left) and David anxiously await their turns.

Spellers qualify for the finals by winning locally sponsored spelling bees in their home communities. Qualifying for the national competition is a significant accomplishment. Every student who advances to the national competition is awarded a prize. The champion gets $17,000, a set of encyclopedias, an engraved trophy, and several other prizes. When asked what he would do with the prize money, David said, "I might put it in a savings account," and "I'll probably take a little and spend it at the mall."

autochthonous

gaminerie

 Critical Thinking

1. Look at the photo of the spellers sitting on the stage. What feelings do you think the contestants experienced during the competition? **Photographs and Captions**

2. What advice do you think David would give to someone who wanted to enter a spelling bee? **Evaluate**

3. Think about this article and *Miss Alaineus*. Compare how Sage prepared for the vocabulary bee and David prepared for the spelling bee. **Reading and Writing Across Texts**

 Language Arts Activity

Does your state have spelling bees? Research spelling bees in your state and write a paragraph about what you need to do to enter a local spelling bee.

 Find out more about the National Spelling Bee at **www.macmillanmh.com**.

Writing

✓ **Varying Sentence Types**

Writers use **varying sentence types** to make their writing easier to read and more interesting to read.

Reading and Writing Connection

Read the passage below from *Miss Alaineus*. Notice how the author Debra Frasier varies the style of her sentences.

An excerpt from
Miss Alaineus

The author really slows down the pace of the passage with some longer sentences at the end of the piece.

They called me Miss Alaineus for the rest of the day. Sometimes a person couldn't even get the words out before bending over with laughter. The day took a week to end. When I got off the bus I slumped home—devastated, ruined, finished.

I told my mom the whole story, from the kitchen drawer to the grocery store to the Vocabulary Bee. Even my own mother laughed a little at the part about the drawing for extra credit, but at least she stopped fast and said, "You know what I always say . . . There's gold in every mistake."

Miss Alaineus
A VOCABULARY DISASTER
written and illustrated by
Debra Frasier

Read and Find

Read Isabel's writing below. How did Isabel vary sentence types to emphasize her change of heart? Use the Writer's Checklist to help you.

Painting

by Isabel K.

What should I paint about? It all seems so confusing. Then, it hits me. I can paint about my personality and how I am feeling at the moment. I paint different colors in different shapes that show different feelings. I make a border between each to show they are connected but are each different. Then, at the end I paint light brown over all of the colors to show the surface of me. This is a lot of fun.

Read about the interesting topic I chose for my writing.

Writer's Checklist

 Does Isabel include some sentences that are short and some that are much longer?

 When you read it aloud, does it sound like the voice of someone trying to tell you something?

Why might Isabel start and end her writing with short **sentences**?

GROWING UP

We get smarter as we grow up. In what ways do you get smarter as you grow up?

LOG ON ▶ Find out more about growing up at **www.macmillanmh.com**.

687

Nosey and the Porcupine

by Susannah Heil

Nosey knew that she was supposed to stay in the yard, but today the gate was left open. Every time the puppy moved her head to the left, she caught a **glimpse** of the woods up the street. She enjoyed this brief peek at the forest. It reminded her of the time her owners took her there when they went for a jog.

For Nosey there was nothing as wonderful as dashing among the trees and sniffing the flowers. The woods were **secluded**, hardly visited by people from outside the neighborhood. Nosey didn't think it would be a problem if she went exploring for just a little while. After all, she was called Nosey for a reason. Her name described her usual, day-to-day **behavior**.

Today she would have to be especially quiet on this secret outing. Her neighbor, Mr. Garcia, was out fishing at the **source** of the creek. Lucky for Nosey she slipped by her neighbor and headed toward the woods without **arousing** his attention.

688

Soon after Nosey arrived in the woods, a butterfly landed on her nose. She reached for it with her paw, but it flew away. Then Nosey spotted it again on a berry bush. When she was within striking distance, she jumped. The butterfly fluttered out of Nosey's reach once more, but it was too late for the puppy to stop. She landed directly on top of the berry bush with a crash. At first, she was **stunned** by the sudden fall. Then she was shocked to find herself face to face with a sleeping porcupine! The porcupine was **nestled** snugly under the bush.

The arrival of a noisy visitor caused the porcupine to wake up. Nosey wasn't afraid of the small porcupine. However, she *was* curious. She had never seen a porcupine before so she gently sniffed at it with her nose. By this time the porcupine had turned himself around. The quills on his tail were standing up, ready to be released. Suddenly Nosey found herself with a nose full of quills.

Nosey pawed at the quills, but they were firmly stuck. She had no choice but to head for home after this **unpleasant** experience. When Mr. Garcia saw her coming, he began to laugh. "Nosey," he said, "I see once again you've lived up to your reputation. You've had your nose exactly where it doesn't belong."

Reread for **Comprehension**

Evaluate

Author's Purpose

An author writes to inform, persuade, inquire, or entertain. An Author's Purpose Chart helps you evaluate the information in a story to figure out the author's purpose. Use your Author's Purpose Chart as you reread the selection to find the author's purpose.

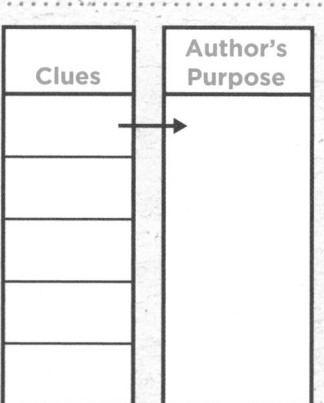

Clues	Author's Purpose

Genre

Realistic Fiction tells an invented story that could have happened in real life.

Evaluate

Author's Purpose

As you read, use your Author's Purpose Chart.

Clues	Author's Purpose
→	

Read to Find Out

What is the author's purpose for writing a story about Carlos?

Carlos
and the
Skunk

Award Winning Selection

written by
Jan Romero Stevens

illustrated by
Jeanne Arnold

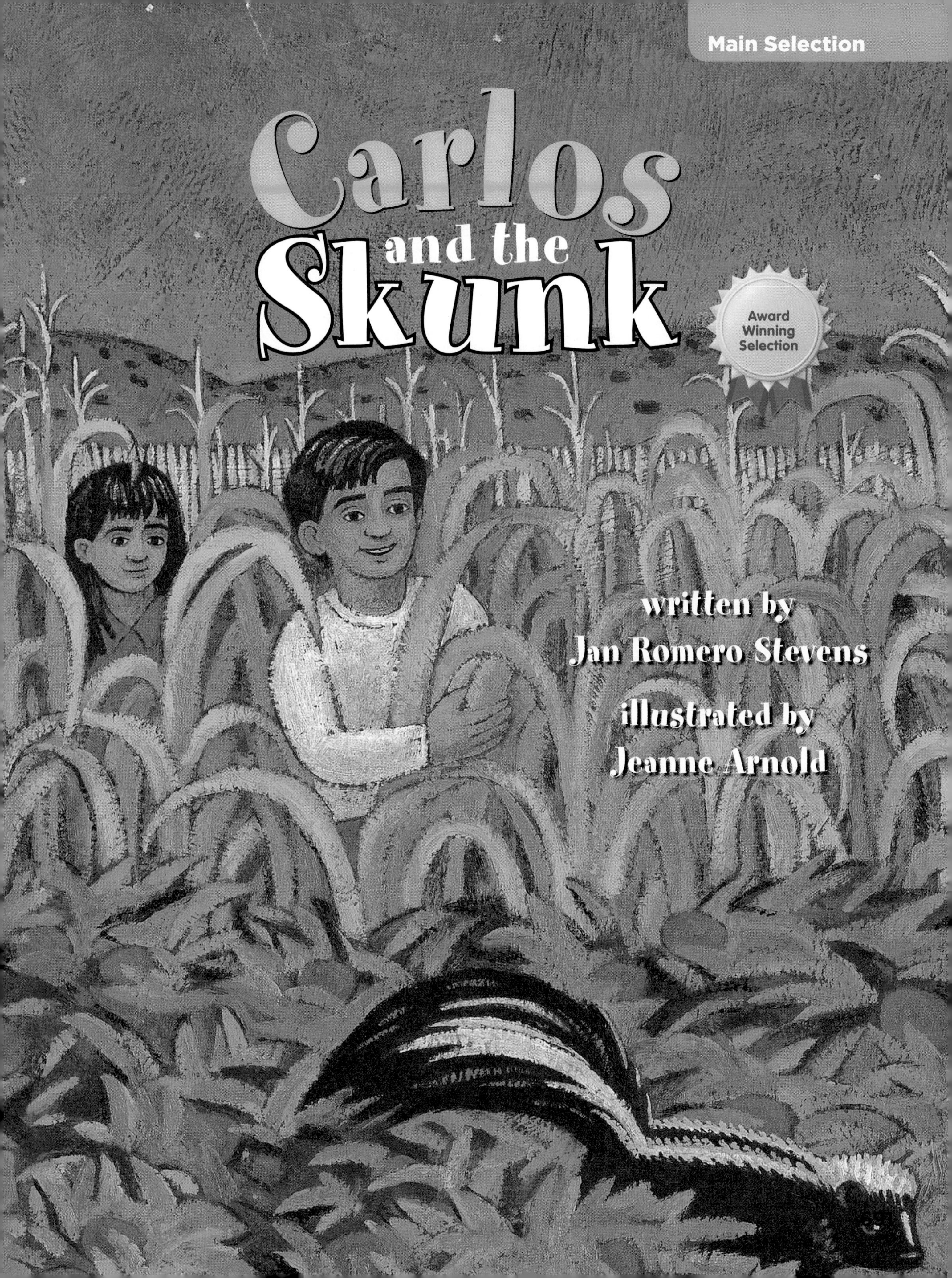

Carlos could not remember how long he and Gloria had been best friends.

When they were little, Gloria's mother would prop them up on old catalogs at the kitchen table while she strung red chiles together or rolled the dough for tortillas. If they were at Carlos's house, his mother would let them play in the garden while she sorted through the shiny green chiles, ripe red tomatoes, and sweet corn.

It seemed as if Carlos and Gloria were always together, but as they grew older, Carlos's feelings toward his friend started to change. He began gazing at himself in the mirror, combing his hair this way and that to see which looked better. He started showing off for Gloria, wanting her to notice how brave and smart he was becoming.

Carlos and Gloria lived in the fertile Española Valley **nestled** in the mountains of northern New Mexico. Their thick-walled adobe homes, with high tin roofs and matching gardens, were within walking distance from one another.

After school each day, Gloria and Carlos did their chores—weeding the garden, feeding the chickens, and doing their homework. After dinner, they were allowed to play.

One fall evening, when they were running through the cornfield playing hide and seek, they caught a **glimpse** of a striped skunk slinking through the shadows of the garden. The children had seen the skunk many times before. It had only two toes on its right front paw, and they had nicknamed it Dos Dedos (Two Toes).

Gloria feared the chance of **arousing** the skunk's anger and kept far away from it. But one afternoon, Carlos, wanting to impress Gloria, moved closer and closer until he could clearly see the narrow, single white stripe running from its head onto its tail.

"Carlos, you'd better be careful," whispered Gloria as Carlos inched along on his stomach toward the skunk.

"Gloria, don't worry. I know just how to catch a skunk," Carlos boasted. "You know what I heard? If you pick a skunk up by its tail, it can't spray you."

Gloria covered her mouth and giggled.

"Oh, Carlos," she said. *"No puedes creer todo lo que te dicen—* you can't believe everything you hear."

"But it's true," Carlos insisted to his doubting friend, and he became more determined than ever to prove himself right. He went to sleep that night still pondering over how to catch the skunk.

> **Author's Purpose**
> What do you think is the author's purpose in writing this scene?

695

The next day, Carlos had planned to take Gloria fishing so he awoke early and got dressed. His mother prepared warm flour tortillas, fried eggs, and fresh salsa for breakfast. Salsa was a family tradition in Carlos's home. Made from tomatoes and green chiles grown in the garden, the salsa was spicy and tasty. Carlos spooned it on just about everything—from breakfast to dinner.

After breakfast, Carlos rushed outside to get his fishing pole and a can for worms. Rounding the corner of his house, he saw Gloria waiting for him by the gate. As they began walking down the road together, they saw Dos Dedos in the garden.

Qué suerte! (What luck!) thought Carlos. "I will catch Dos Dedos this time!"

Carlos gave no thought to what he might do with the skunk if he did catch it, but instead began creeping up behind it. He got closer and closer until he was inches away. For just a moment, Carlos hesitated, then winked at Gloria before he reached out and grabbed the tail. In an instant, the skunk's tail arched, and Carlos was sprayed from head to toe.

With a gasp, Carlos fell backward onto the ground. He was so **stunned** he hardly realized what had happened. He had never smelled such a strong odor. His eyes itched. He coughed and snorted and blew his nose. He did his best not to cry in front of Gloria.

Quite unconcerned, Dos Dedos disappeared down the side of an arroyo. And Carlos ran off to the river—leaving both Gloria and his fishing pole far behind.

Carlos chose a **secluded** spot and pulled off all his clothes as fast as he could. The smell of them was unbearable. He jumped into the stream and washed out his clothing, laying it out on a branch to dry in the sun. By afternoon his shirt and pants were dry, but the strong odor still lingered, especially on his shoes. He dressed and walked the long way home, climbing up and down the sides of the arroyos and stopping to gather piñon nuts. When he finally reached his house, he carefully took off his shoes and left them by the back door.

When his mother came into the kitchen, she noticed a strange smell, but before she could question Carlos, he slipped out the door and into the garden.

Carlos had heard that tomato juice helped to get rid of the smell of skunk, so he picked every ripe tomato he could find and sneaked into the bathroom. He squeezed the tomatoes into the bathtub and all over his hair, scrubbing himself as hard as he could with a washrag.

Beginning to think he smelled better, he crawled into bed and fell asleep quickly after his very **unpleasant** day.

The next morning was Sunday, and Mamá was up early, patting and shaping the dough for tortillas.

Dressed in his best shirt and pants, Carlos sat down at the table.

"Carlos, you look very nice for church this morning," said Mamá as she untied her flowered apron. "Where are your shoes?"

"They're outside, Mamá. I will get them when we leave," said Carlos, feeling uneasy.

Carlos's family walked to the church near their home. When they arrived, they squeezed into a bench near the back. Carlos was pleased that he was able to sit next to Gloria.

But a most peculiar thing happened in church that day.

As the choir began a hymn, some of the singers began to make strange faces and cover their noses with handkerchiefs. The priest, as he walked to the altar, sneezed loudly and cleared his throat.

The people in the first few rows of the congregation turned to each other with puzzled looks. The women began vigorously fanning their faces with their church programs. The children started squirming and pinched their noses. Little by little the strange **behavior** began working its way toward the back of the church.

Carlos couldn't figure out what was going on until he looked down at his feet. He was sitting next to an air vent for the church's heating system. The smell from his shoes, which he had forgotten to clean after being sprayed by Dos Dedos, was spreading through the heating ducts to the entire church.

"Papá, I think we better go home," whispered Carlos, hoping no one would realize he was the **source** of the terrible smell.

Several families began heading for the door. The priest dismissed the service early.

Embarrassed, Carlos pushed his way out of the church. He heard Gloria calling to him, but he bolted through the door, and ran all the way home. He untied his shoes, pulled them off, and left them on the back doorstep. Then he hurried to his room and shut the door.

Troubled over how he might rid himself of the strong-smelling shoes, Carlos stayed in his bedroom until his mother called him for dinner. While they were eating, his parents noticed he was unusually quiet but said nothing to him.

Finally, when dinner was over, Papá turned to Carlos.

"Carlos, I've noticed your shoes are looking a little small," said Papá, with a glance toward Mamá. "Isn't it time for a new pair?"

Carlos nodded, breathing a sigh of relief.

"Oh, *sí, sí,* Papá," he stammered. "My feet are getting too big for those shoes now."

The next day, Carlos and Papá drove to town. After trying on several pairs of shoes, Carlos chose a pair of heeled cowboy boots that made him appear much taller.

A few weeks passed and Carlos forgot about his encounter with the skunk. One evening, after a big dinner of pinto beans, rice, tortillas, and his favorite salsa, he decided to visit Gloria. He put on his new boots and took a good look at his hair in the mirror. As he was getting ready to leave, his father called him outside.

"I need your help," said Papá, and he pointed beneath the bushes alongside the house.

Carlos could just make out the shape of a small, black-and-white animal with three little ones that had made their home under the leaves.

"*Dios mío!*" ("Oh my goodness!") said Carlos. "What will we do?"

"It's no problem, Carlos," said Papá. "You know what I hear? You can catch a skunk if you pick it up by its tail. You go first."

Carlos's nose and eyes began to water just with the thought of it.

"Oh, Papá, *no puedes creer todo lo que te dicen*—you know you can't believe everything you hear," Carlos said, and he drew himself up a little taller, smoothed back his hair, and headed for Gloria's house.

> **Author's Purpose**
> What was the author's purpose in writing this story? Did the author write with a second purpose in mind?

Fresh Tomato Salsa

3 tomatoes, diced

¼ white or yellow onion, diced

2-3 scallions with green tops, chopped

1 medium clove garlic, minced

2 teaspoons vinegar

1 teaspoon vegetable or olive oil

3-4 sprigs of cilantro, chopped

1 roasted green chile or 2 serrano chiles, diced
    (or 2 tablespoons canned green chile)

1 teaspoon salt

¼ teaspoon pepper

Mix all ingredients in a food processor, leaving salsa chunky,
or stir by hand. Chill. Spoon over anything—eggs, beans,
tacos—or use as a dip for tortilla chips.

705

Trading Tales with Jan Romero Stevens and Jeanne Arnold

Jan Romero Stevens said there was nothing better than watching children enjoy her books, in both English and Spanish. Jan loved the Southwest and learned more about her Hispanic heritage by studying Spanish with her kids. To make the Carlos stories realistic, she based them on things that happened to her family and friends. Jan always enjoyed writing. Besides writing the "Carlos" series, Jan worked for newspapers and magazines as a reporter and editor.

Jeanne Arnold is an illustrator and a painter. Her work includes all three books in the "Carlos" series, as well as *When You Were Just a Little Girl* by B.G. Hennessy. Jeanne has spent time backpacking in the Southwest. This helps her capture the regional flavor of the "Carlos" books.

Other books by Jan Romero Stevens and Jeanne Arnold: *Carlos and the Carnival* and *Carlos Digs to China*

CA Author's Purpose

What clues help you to figure out the author's purpose for writing? How well did Jan Romero Stevens succeed in her purpose? Explain.

 **LOG ON** Find out more about Jan Romero Stevens and Jeanne Arnold at **www.macmillanmh.com**.

 # Critical Thinking

Summarize

Summarize the events of *Carlos and the Skunk*. Use your Author's Purpose Chart to help you gather important information from the story.

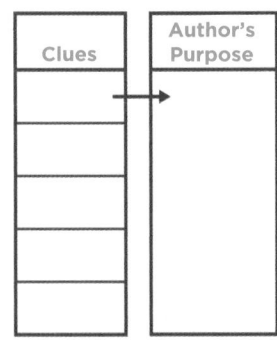

Clues	Author's Purpose

Think and Compare

1. What was the **author's purpose** for choosing a skunk as the animal Carlos wants to catch? Use your Author's Purpose Chart to help explain your answer. **Evaluate: Author's Purpose**

2. Reread page 702 of *Carlos and the Skunk*. Explain why Papá asked Carlos if his shoes were too small. **Analyze**

3. Would showing off for a friend be worth suffering **unpleasant** consequences, such as being sprayed by a skunk? **Explain**

4. Explain why you agree or disagree with the advice, "You can't believe everything you hear." Include specific examples in your answer. **Analyze**

5. Reread "Nosey and the Porcupine" on pages 688–689. What characteristics do Carlos and Nosey share? How are their experiences with animal defenses similar? Support your answer with evidence from each story. **Reading/Writing Across Texts**

Science

Genre

Nonfiction presents facts about real people, animals, things, places, or events.

Text Features

A **Deck** is a short preview of a magazine article designed to grab readers' attention.

Headings are subtitles that break an article into different parts. They help readers organize information so it is easier to understand.

Content Vocabulary

camouflage   **mimicry**

chameleon

Animal Self-Defense

by Elle Wainwright

If you were a wild animal about to become someone's dinner, what would you do? Run? Hide? Fight? Animals may do any of these things when they feel threatened. Nature provides them with special weapons of protection.

Wild animals live dangerous lives. While they hunt for food, they must be careful not to be caught by another animal. To help them stay alive, animals have developed adaptations.

Hide and Seek

Some adaptations help animals hide. If an animal can remain unseen, it will be safe. Of course, an animal cannot really become invisible. However, it can seem to disappear by using **camouflage**. A baby deer can lie perfectly still in a bed of grasses and leaves. With its speckled fur, the little deer is almost invisible. A flounder swimming along the ocean shore is difficult to see. As it passes over sand, it turns a pale sandy color. When it swims over dark rocks, it turns dark. By changing its color, a flounder can avoid attacks by larger fish that would like to eat it. Some animals can hide without even moving! Both the **chameleon** and the octopus can quickly change their skin color and blend into the background.

Another kind of camouflage has to do with an animal's shape. Think of a bird hunting a butterfly for breakfast. The leaf butterfly has wings that resemble leaves. The bird is not looking for leaves to eat, so it will fly right past a leaf butterfly. A thornbug is another animal whose shape protects it from its enemies. Because thornbugs look like prickly thorns, their enemies stay away. There are also animals that change their shapes to hide. One inchworm stiffens up so that it is usually mistaken for a stick.

The octopus (above) and the chameleon (right) change color to blend into their surroundings.

709

What a Stink!

No one can forget the smell of a skunk. Skunks use their odor for self-defense. Have you ever wondered how skunks produce their smell?

These small animals have a physical adaptation that helps them protect themselves. They have two grape-sized sacs under the skin below their tails that hold a strong-smelling liquid. Skunks can shoot this powerful liquid spray and hit a target accurately from up to ten feet away.

How do skunks decide that it's time to get the jets firing? The distance of an enemy plays a big part in the decision. Skunks don't see well. When an enemy comes closer than four feet to a skunk, the skunk finally sees it. Then watch out! First, the skunk freezes. Then, it points its tail straight up as a warning. If the enemy doesn't go away, the skunk's tail bends over until it touches its back. Then the skunk turns around and squirts, stunning its enemy.

Skunks aren't the only animals that spray in self defense. Stinkbugs also spray a smelly liquid when threatened.

Catch Me if You Can!

What happens when a bird is surprised by a person or other animal it considers a threat? The bird flies away. Birds are one of many creatures that avoid danger by moving faster than their enemies. Some animals, such as zebras, travel in herds. If predators appear, the whole herd quickly flees. Most of the herd escapes. Only the slowest zebras get caught.

a herd of zebras

"What is that *smell*? It might be a stinkbug."

Ouch!

Would you touch a black-and-yellow-striped insect? Probably not because you know that yellow jackets can give you a painful sting.

A syrphid fly (left) fools its enemies by looking like a wasp (below).

Animals that eat insects also avoid yellow jackets. They avoid an insect called a syrphid (SUHR-fuhd) fly even though it is harmless. Why? The syrphid fly fools insect eaters because it looks like a stinging wasp. Looking like something else, especially something unpleasant, is called **mimicry.**

Animals have developed many other amazing ways to stay safe. Take a look at the animals you find in your neighborhood, even the insects. How do they defend themselves against other animals that want to attack them?

 ## Critical Thinking

1. How do the headings used in "Animal Self-Defense" engage the reader's attention? **Headings**

2. Of the adaptations you have read about, which kind of adaptation would you choose for yourself and why? **Evaluate**

3. If Carlos in *Carlos and the Skunk* had read the article "Animal Self-Defense," do you think he would have picked up the skunk? Why or why not? Explain your answer.
Reading/Writing Across Texts

 ### Science Activity

Do research on an animal or insect that uses adaptations to survive. Write a magazine article describing how the animal defends itself against its enemies.

LOG ON ▶ Find out more about animal defenses at www.macmillanmh.com.

711

Writing

CA

✔ Varying Sentence Types

Writers can use **varying sentence types** to emphasize a certain point or moment.

Read the passage below from *Carlos and the Skunk*. Notice how the author Jan Romero Stevens varies her sentence structure.

An excerpt from *Carlos and the Skunk*

The author uses longer, compound sentences at the beginning to show Carlos is scheming and creeping.

Carlos gave no thought to what he might do with the skunk if he did catch it, but instead began creeping up behind it. He got closer and closer until he was inches away. For just a moment, Carlos hesitated, then winked at Gloria before he reached out and grabbed the tail. In an instant, the skunk's tail arched, and Carlos was sprayed from head to toe.

With a gasp, Carlos fell backward onto the ground. He was so stunned he hardly realized what had happened. He had never smelled such a strong odor. His eyes itched. He coughed and snorted and blew his nose. He did his best not to cry in front of Gloria.

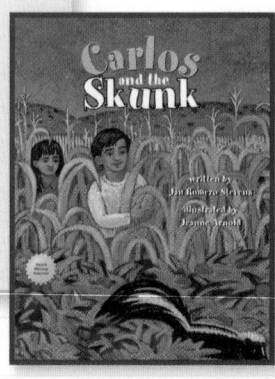

Read and Find

Read Daniel's writing below. How did he use different types of sentences to engage you? Use the Writer's Checklist to help you.

Improvisation

by Daniel J.

Here I am, one person of twelve, and we must all act as one caterpillar. A caterpillar? How? Someone suggests crawling along in pairs. But doesn't this mean that different pairs have to be raised at different times? Someone figures it out and it's not as hard as I thought. The butterfly comes out. I find myself in the left wing. Nobody has to be perfect, and once you learn that, doing this can actually be kind of fun.

Read about my experiment as a caterpillar.

Writer's Checklist

 Do you see sentences that vary in length?

 Does the author use questions to bring the reader through his thought process?

 Does he use compound **sentences** to show when he tries to make logical links?

Talk About It

How can one person's hard work impact the lives of others?

 Find out more about changing lives at **www.macmillanmh.com**.

Improving Lives

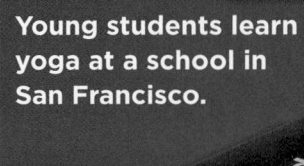

Young students learn yoga at a school in San Francisco.

Vocabulary

elementary

physical

rigid

interact

wheelchair

THE NEW GYM

At Riverside School in Miami, Florida, gym class isn't always held in the gym. In fact, it isn't even always held on land. One option available to kids at Riverside is an **elementary** course in sailing taught on real sailboats on Biscayne Bay.

Thanks to a terrific new **physical** education movement, gym class is no longer just about traditional team sports. The idea is to help kids find activities they'll enjoy so much that they'll stay active for the rest of their lives. The fun activities include yoga, cycling, martial arts, dance, kickboxing, in-line skating, using treadmills, and even sailing and kayaking. The goal is to teach children sports and physical activities that they can enjoy outside of school.

Advocates of the "new" gym class point to studies that show kids are less active than ever before. They believe that children's natural boundless energy isn't being channeled into healthy activities for a lifetime. One in four kids gets no physical education in school at all. Kids' general activity level is at its highest in tenth grade but then slowly declines all the way into adulthood. That's what the new movement is designed to change.

A Miami fourth-grader learns the basics of sailing.

Satellite Guidance for the Blind

Pocket-size GPS guide

Before leaving her apartment, Carmen Fernandez, a blind woman living in Madrid, Spain, used to carefully memorize her route. If she didn't, she would get lost. But a new device using GPS (Global Positioning Satellite) technology frees her from such a **rigid** routine.

Using the gadget's Braille keypad, she punches in her destination. As she walks, the device calls out directions to her. "Now I can walk home by any route," Fernandez says. "I've learned so much about my own neighborhood."

While the current technology cannot guarantee total accuracy, it already grants a new level of freedom for the visually impaired. It allows them to **interact** more directly with their surroundings and their neighbors. "Soon I'll be giving directions to the taxi driver," says Fernandez.

THE SECOND OLYMPICS

Every two years men and women from around the world come to compete at the Olympic Games. However, this is not the only time a gold medal is up for grabs. After the Olympics come the Paralympics.

The Paralympics are just like the Olympics, but these games are for athletes with physical disabilities. A Paralympic athlete may use a **wheelchair** or get around with the help of a guide dog in everyday life. Athletes who share a particular disability compete to win medals and set world records. Paralympians want others to see them as world-class athletes whose disabilities do not hold them back.

Canada's team at the 2002 Winter Paralympic Games

LOG ON Find out more about the Paralympics at **www.macmillanmh.com**.

A Dream Comes True

Why do ALL kids need a place to play?

CA Comprehension

Genre

Nonfiction A nonfiction article in a newspaper or magazine reports on real people, places, and events.

Monitor Comprehension

Persuasion

Persuasion is a method of convincing others that they should believe something or feel a certain way about a subject.

Most kids love recess, but for Hannah Kristan, it was her least favorite part of the school day. "I never got to do anything except sit there," she recalls.

Hannah was born with a disease that kept the bones in her back from forming properly. She uses a **wheelchair**. Sadly, for kids like her, most playground equipment is off limits. In fact, Hannah is one of 5 million kids in the United States who cannot use traditional playground equipment because of some type of disability.

Paint panel

Talk tube

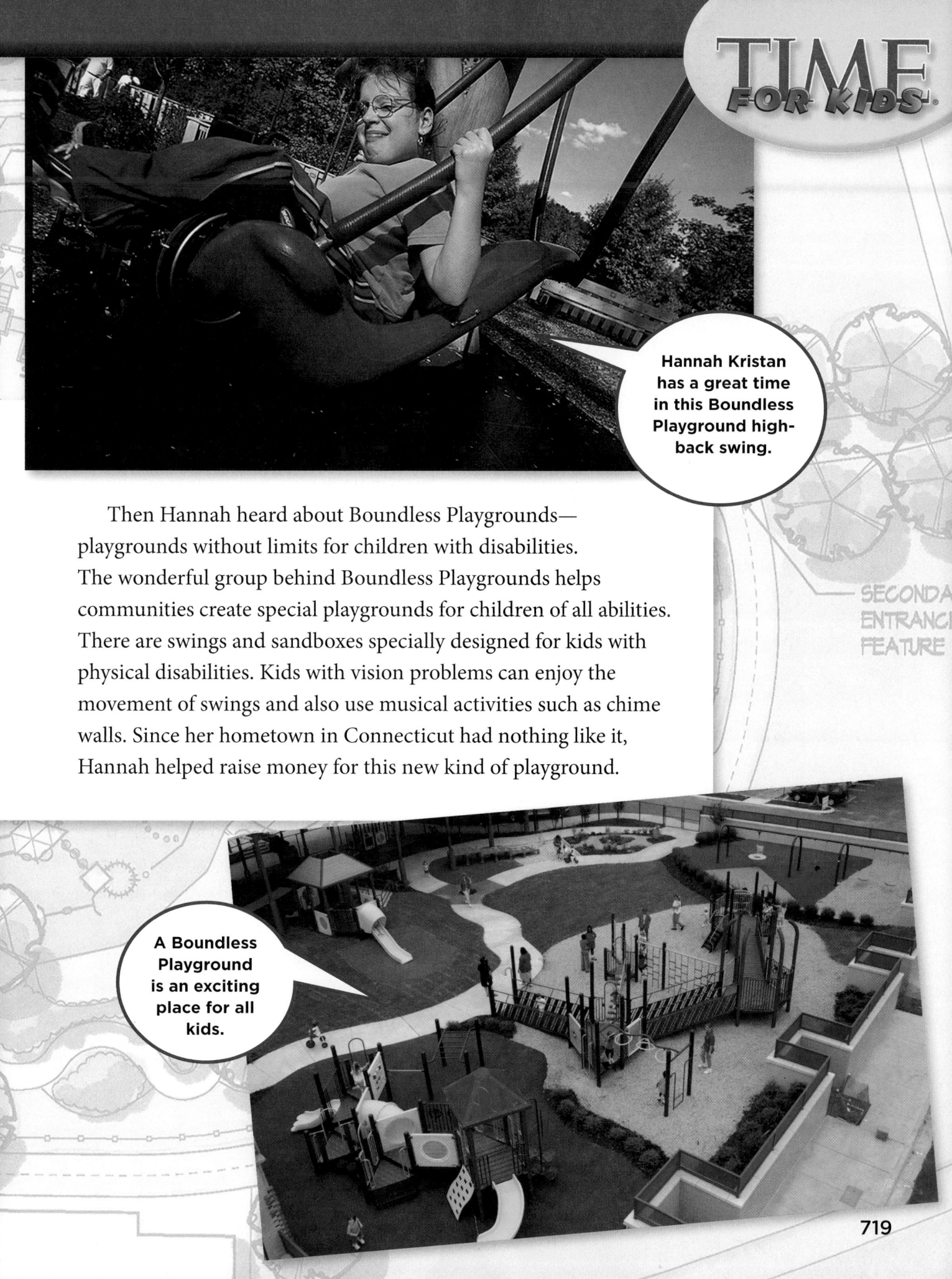

Hannah Kristan has a great time in this Boundless Playground high-back swing.

Then Hannah heard about Boundless Playgrounds—playgrounds without limits for children with disabilities. The wonderful group behind Boundless Playgrounds helps communities create special playgrounds for children of all abilities. There are swings and sandboxes specially designed for kids with physical disabilities. Kids with vision problems can enjoy the movement of swings and also use musical activities such as chime walls. Since her hometown in Connecticut had nothing like it, Hannah helped raise money for this new kind of playground.

A Boundless Playground is an exciting place for all kids.

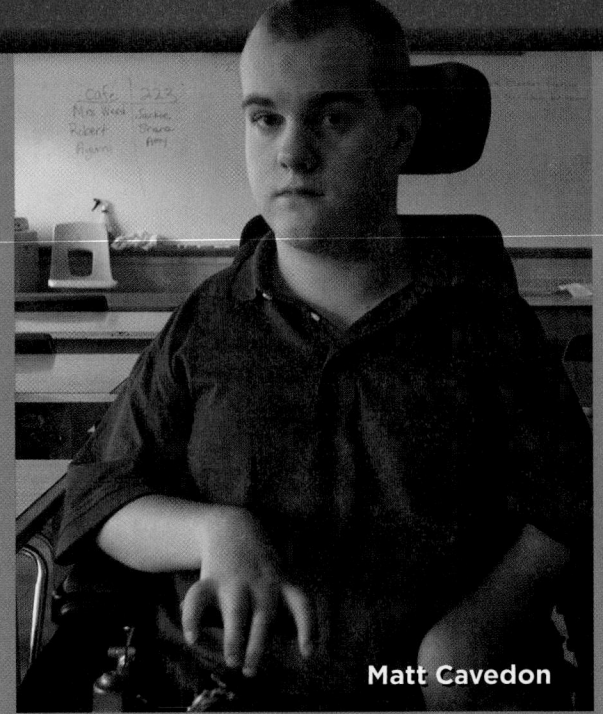

Matt Cavedon

NEW EXPERIENCES

Matt Cavedon designed a swing especially for Boundless Playgrounds, but his commitment didn't stop there. In a speech he gave in 2004, Matt, then 15 years old, described an experience he had at the grand opening of a Boundless Playground in Rhode Island:

"A girl our age [15 years old] was swinging, laughing, and crying all at once. Her mom explained that it was the girl's first time on a swing! Is this a small thing? Not for her! Not for her mom! Not for the kids without disabilities who came up to her to say congratulations! I wonder how many of those kids had just talked to a person with a disability for the first time. I wonder how many will choose to **interact** with people who have different abilities because of that experience."

The inspiration for Boundless Playgrounds was a playground created by Amy Jaffe Barzach. It is named Jonathan's Dream in honor of her son. Jonathan's Dream and many Boundless Playgrounds around the country have a glider swing that can be used by kids who use wheelchairs and their friends. The glider swing at Jonathan's Dream was designed by Matthew Cavedon, who wasn't even 10 years old at the time. Matthew was motivated because he uses a wheelchair himself and wanted to be able to have fun at playgrounds with other kids, regardless of their **physical** abilities or disabilities.

The **elementary** idea behind Boundless Playgrounds is that play is both part of the joy of childhood and an important way for children to learn about the world. Kids who are kept away from playgrounds are denied this enjoyment as well as the learning. Far from being a place of happy excitement, traditional playgrounds are often places of humiliation and isolation for those who can't join in the fun.

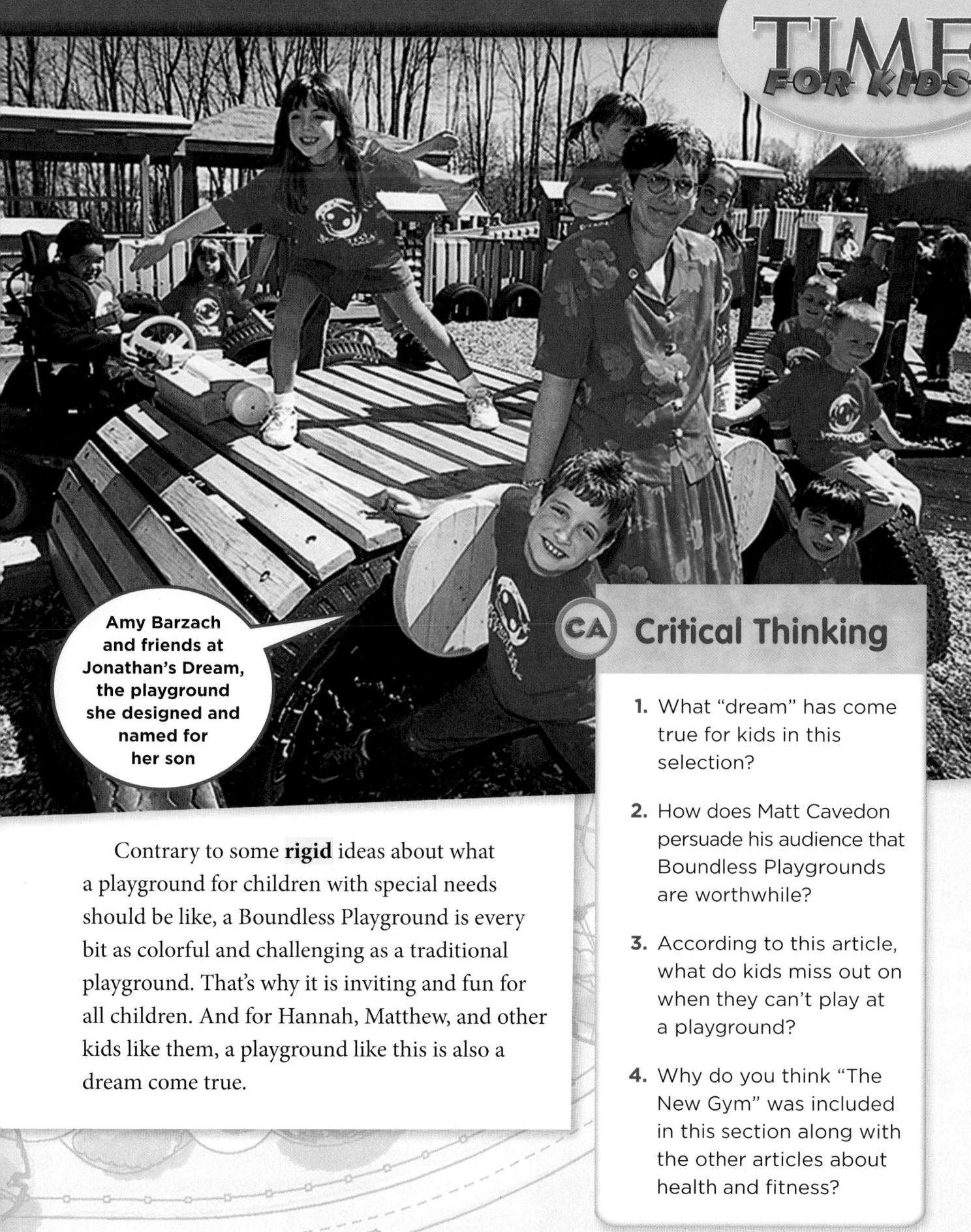

Amy Barzach and friends at Jonathan's Dream, the playground she designed and named for her son

Contrary to some **rigid** ideas about what a playground for children with special needs should be like, a Boundless Playground is every bit as colorful and challenging as a traditional playground. That's why it is inviting and fun for all children. And for Hannah, Matthew, and other kids like them, a playground like this is also a dream come true.

CA Critical Thinking

1. What "dream" has come true for kids in this selection?

2. How does Matt Cavedon persuade his audience that Boundless Playgrounds are worthwhile?

3. According to this article, what do kids miss out on when they can't play at a playground?

4. Why do you think "The New Gym" was included in this section along with the other articles about health and fitness?

721

Show What You Know

Think and Search

Read on to find the answer. Look for information in more than one place.

PROFILE *of a* PARALYMPIAN

Jennifer Howitt may use a wheelchair, but she isn't sitting out life. Since being paralyzed after breaking her back in a hiking accident at age nine, she has developed into one of the country's top young disabled athletes.

Howitt competed in the 1998 World Athletic Championships in track and field and went to the 2000 Sydney Paralympics as the youngest member of the 12-person U.S. women's wheelchair basketball team. Although the team finished in fifth place, "I was on an emotional high," says Howitt. "It was pretty inspirational. If the entire world can come together to celebrate sport and disability, then it is really possible for us, as a planet, to work out all our problems."

Howitt is committed to changing the world in positive ways. She has coached young paraplegic athletes, traveled extensively, and attended Georgetown University in Washington, D.C., where she studied international politics. She hopes "to show young girls with disabilities that they can achieve whatever they want. A disability doesn't get in the way of anything. Maybe you'll have to adapt your goal, but you can always achieve it," Howitt says.

Go on ▶

Now answer numbers 1 through 5. Base your answers on the selection "Profile of a Paralympian."

1. Which of the following best describes Jennifer's attitude?

   A   committed to achieving goals
   B   able only to play basketball
   C   sitting out life
   D   paralyzed

2. What does Jennifer believe about disabilities?

   A   People with disabilities live in Washington, D.C.
   B   Disabilities should not keep a person from achieving his or her goals.
   C   People always need wheelchairs.
   D   You can help the entire world.

3. Jennifer believes that having a disability

   A   is a handicap in many areas of life.
   B   is not an obstacle to achieving one's goals.
   C   can keep someone from traveling.
   D   prevents someone from becoming a good athlete.

4. Other than excelling as an athlete, what are some of Jennifer's other achievements?

5. How would you describe Jennifer's attitude toward her disability and her future? Use details from the article in your response.

 # Write on Demand

CA Suppose a new law will change something in a local park.

Think of a new law that might change a local park.

Now <u>write your opinion</u> of the law that will change a local park.

Persuasive writing tries to convince readers to accept the author's point of view.

To figure out if a writing prompt asks for persuasive writing, look for clue words such as <u>write your opinion</u> or <u>convince readers</u>.

Below, see how one student begins a response to the prompt above.

The writer states his opinion in the introduction.

Dear Mayor,

    We should not allow snowmobiles into Green Place State Park. The park is a beautiful and peaceful place where people can go to relax. With snowmobiles around, being in the park will be like being on the highway—it will be noisy, smelly, and crowded.

    Also, the health of the environment is at stake. If we allow the park to lose its beauty, the park will become unfit as a habitat for wildlife.

               Sincerely,

               John Garcia

Writing Prompt

Respond in writing to the prompt below. Write for 20 minutes. Write as much as you can, as well as you can. Before you write, read the Writing Hints below. Review the hints both before and after you write.

CA Suppose some land becomes available in your community. Think about what would be the best use of the land. Now write your opinion of how best to use available land in your community.

Writing Hints for Prompts

- ☑ Carefully read the prompt.
- ☑ Organize your ideas to plan your writing.
- ☑ Support your ideas by giving reasons or using more details.
- ☑ Use a variety of sentence structures and consistent verb tenses.
- ☑ Choose words that help readers understand your ideas.
- ☑ Review your writing and edit as needed.

CA **Talk About It**

How can you fit in and still be unique?

LOG ON Find more about fitting in at www.macmillanmh.com.

Fitting In

727

shortage   civilization
outcast   traditional
reflected   founding
strategy   complex

✓ **Dictionary**

Use a dictionary when you want to check a **Word Origin**. The definition may include information about the word. For example, the dictionary entry for *strategy* says it comes from two words, *leading* and *army*.

Juanita and the Cornstalk

by Sandra Garcia

Little rain had fallen in the small Mexican village of Tula. Juanita and her mother had planted seeds in the spring. With a **shortage** of rain, nothing grew. "Take the donkey to the market and sell her," Juanita's mother said. "We need the money." Juanita tied a rope to the donkey and led her toward the marketplace.

On the way Juanita met a sad merchant. "It would be a great kindness if you would sell that fine donkey to me," said the merchant. "I need help carrying my goods to the market. Unfortunately, I have only these magic corn seeds to trade. Plant the seeds in the ground. They do not need any water. Soon you will have giant cornstalks in your field." Juanita was happy to help the merchant. She made the trade and hurried home.

728

When Juanita's mother heard her story, she became upset. "How could you have been so foolish?" she yelled. She tossed the corn seeds out the window and went to bed. Juanita felt like an **outcast** even though she was going to sleep in her own house.

The sun that **reflected** off the glass of the window the next morning woke Juanita. She was surprised to find a giant cornstalk outside her window. The stalk reached so high into the sky that Juanita could not see the top.

She decided to climb the stalk to see how high it grew. Soon she developed a **strategy** for climbing and her plan helped her reach the top.

Above the clouds Juanita spotted Quetzalcoatl, the Toltec god of **civilization**. This leader of cultured life was sitting in a **traditional** rocking chair that had been passed down from generation to generation.

Quetzalcoatl welcomed her with a warm smile. "Hello, Juanita. I'm happy to have a visitor after all these years. I'm lonely. I haven't visited Earth since its **founding**."

"I've got an idea, but it's full of detail and quite **complex**," Juanita said. "Why don't you turn yourself into a small creature that I can put in my pocket?"

"Why, little one, that's a brilliant thought! I'll give myself wings so that I can fly back here when I get tired. Let me give you some gold coins for your kindness."

After carrying Quetzalcoatl down to Earth, Juanita hurried home with the gold coins. Juanita hoped that this time her mother might understand how good things can happen when a kind act is repaid.

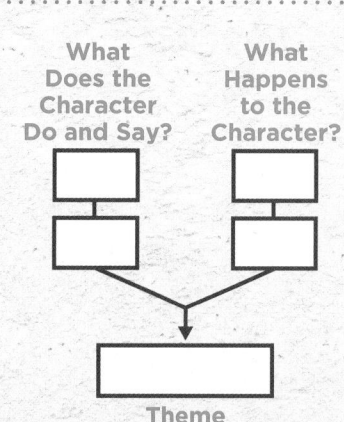

Reread for **Comprehension**

Make Inferences and Analyze
Theme
A Theme Chart helps you make inferences and analyze information so you can determine the overall idea the author wants to tell in a story. Use your Theme Chart as you reread "Juanita and the Cornstalk" to identify the theme in the story.

What Does the Character Do and Say?

What Happens to the Character?

Theme

Weslandia

by Paul Fleischman

illustrated by Kevin Hawkes

Award Winning Selection

"**O**f course he's miserable," moaned Wesley's mother. "He sticks out."

"Like a nose," snapped his father.

Listening through the heating vent, Wesley knew they were right. He was an **outcast** from the **civilization** around him.

He alone in his town disliked pizza and soda, alarming his mother and the school nurse. He found professional football stupid. He'd refused to shave half his head, the hairstyle worn by all the other boys, despite his father's bribe of five dollars.

Passing his neighborhood's two styles of housing—garage on the left and garage on the right—Wesley alone dreamed of more exciting forms of shelter. He had no friends, but plenty of tormentors.

Fleeing them was the only sport he was good at.

Each afternoon his mother asked him what he'd learned in school that day.

"That seeds are carried great distances by the wind," he answered on Wednesday.

"That each civilization has its staple food crop," he answered on Thursday.

"That school's over and I should find a good summer project," he answered on Friday.

As always, his father mumbled, "I'm sure you'll use that knowledge often."

Suddenly, Wesley's thoughts shot sparks. His eyes blazed. His father was right! He could actually *use* what he'd learned that week for a summer project that would top all others. He would grow his own food crop—and found his own civilization!

The next morning he turned over a plot of ground in his yard. That night a wind blew in from the west. It raced through the trees and set his curtains snapping. Wesley lay awake, listening. His land was being planted.

Five days later the first seedlings appeared.

"You'll have mighty bedlam on your hands if you don't get those weeds out," warned his neighbor.

"Actually, that's my crop," replied Wesley. "In this type of garden there are no weeds."

Following ancient tradition, Wesley's fellow gardeners grew tomatoes, beans, Brussels sprouts, and nothing else. Wesley found it thrilling to open his land to chance, to invite the new and unknown.

The plants shot up past his knees, then his waist. They seemed to be all of the same sort. Wesley couldn't find them in any plant book.

"Are those tomatoes, beans, or Brussels sprouts?" asked Wesley's neighbor.

"None of the above," replied Wesley.

Fruit appeared, yellow at first, then blushing to magenta. Wesley picked one and sliced through the rind to the juicy purple center. He took a bite and found the taste an entrancing blend of peach, strawberry, pumpkin pie, and flavors he had no name for.

Theme
What message do you think the author wants to get across in the conversations between Wesley and his neighbor?

Ignoring the shelf of cereals in the kitchen, Wesley took to breakfasting on the fruit. He dried half a rind to serve as a cup, built his own squeezing device, and drank the fruit's juice throughout the day.

Pulling up a plant, he found large tubers on the roots. These he boiled, fried, or roasted on the family barbecue, seasoning them with a pinch of the plant's highly aromatic leaves.

It was hot work tending to his crop. To keep off the sun, Wesley wove himself a hat from strips of the plant's woody bark. His success with the hat inspired him to devise a spinning wheel and loom on which he wove a loose-fitting robe from the stalks' soft inner fibers.

Unlike jeans, which he found scratchy and heavy, the robe was comfortable, **reflected** the sun, and offered myriad opportunities for pockets.

His schoolmates were scornful, then curious. Grudgingly, Wesley allowed them ten minutes apiece at his mortar, crushing the plant's seeds to collect the oil.

This oil had a tangy scent and served him both as suntan lotion and mosquito repellent. He rubbed it on his face each morning and sold small amounts to his former tormentors at the price of ten dollars per bottle.

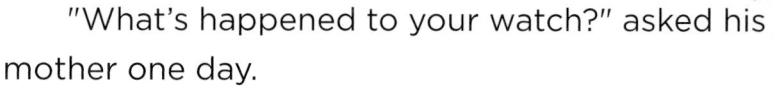

"What's happened to your watch?" asked his mother one day.

Wesley admitted that he no longer wore it. He told time by the stalk that he used as a sundial and had divided the day into eight segments—the number of petals on the plant's flowers.

He'd adopted a new counting system as well, based likewise upon the number eight. His domain, home to many such innovations, he named "Weslandia."

Uninterested in **traditional** sports, Wesley made up his own. These were designed for a single player and used many different parts of the plant. His spectators looked on with envy.

Realizing that more players would offer him more scope, Wesley invented other games that would include his schoolmates, games rich with **strategy** and **complex** scoring systems. He tried to be patient with the other players' blunders.

August was unusually hot. Wesley built himself a platform and took to sleeping in the middle of Weslandia. He passed the evenings playing a flute he'd fashioned from a stalk or gazing up at the sky, renaming the constellations.

> **Theme**
> Wesley uses the plants of Weslandia to make his own clothes and invent his own games. How do these events support the theme of the story?

His parents noted Wesley's improved morale. "It's the first time in years he's looked happy," said his mother.

Wesley gave them a tour of Weslandia.

"What do you call this plant?" asked his father. Not knowing its name, Wesley had begun calling it "swist," from the sound of its leaves rustling in the breeze.

In like manner, he'd named his new fabrics, games, and foods, until he'd created an entire language.

Mixing the plant's oil with soot, Wesley made a passable ink. As the finale to his summer project, he used the ink and his own eighty-letter alphabet to record the history of his civilization's **founding**.

In September Wesley returned to school . . .

He had no **shortage** of friends.

743

Meet Weslandia Creators
Paul Fleischman and Kevin Hawkes

Paul Fleischman, like Wesley, created his own world while he was growing up in California. Paul and his friends invented their own sports, ran a newspaper, and created their own alternative universe. His vivid imagination comes from his father, Sid Fleischman, who also wrote books. Often he would ask Paul to help him with the plot of a story. Words and imagination come naturally to Paul. "They were as much fun to play with as toys," he said.

Other books by Paul Fleischman: *Joyful Noise: Poems for Two Voices* and *Seedfolks*

Kevin Hawkes says he learned how to draw by practicing, practicing, and practicing some more. As a child he drew pictures and used modeling clay to mold sculptures, such as a life-size sculpture of a mountaineer. Today Kevin makes a "dummy" book for each book he illustrates. These first sketches help him create the unique images that bring stories like *Weslandia* to life.

LOG ON Find out more about Paul Fleischman and Kevin Hawkes at **www.macmillanmh.com**.

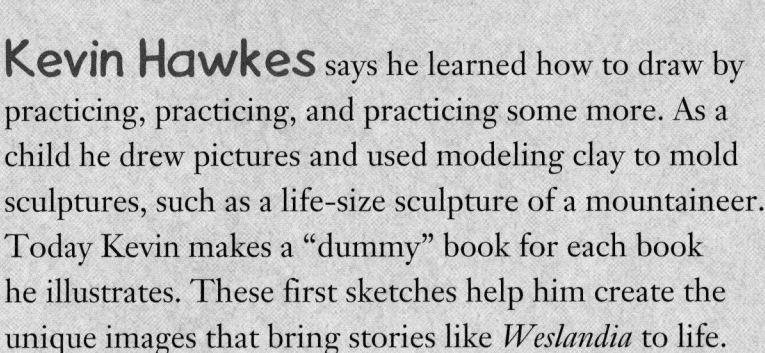

CA Author's Purpose

How is *Weslandia* different from real life? Do you think the author wrote this fantasy story mainly to entertain? Why or why not?

CA Critical Thinking

Summarize

Use your Theme Chart to help you summarize the ways that Wesley's life changes during the summer. Include information about the theme of the story in your summary of *Weslandia.*

What Does the Character Do and Say?	What Happens to the Character?
☐	☐
☐	☐

Theme

Think and Compare

1. Describe the **theme** of this story in one or two sentences. Explain how the author uses theme to connect the characters and events. **Make Inferences and Analyze: Theme**

2. Using evidence from the text on page 740, explain how Wesley uses sports to win over his schoolmates. **Analyze**

3. Wesley names a plant *swist* because of the sound its leaves make in the wind. Rename five items you own on the basis of the sounds they make. Create a dictionary entry for each new word. **Synthesize**

4. Describe some of the elements that make up a **civilization** according to your reading of *Weslandia*. **Apply**

5. Reread "Juanita and the Cornstalk" on pages 728–729. In what ways are Wesley and Juanita alike? How are they different? Use examples from both selections to support your answer. **Reading/Writing Across Texts**

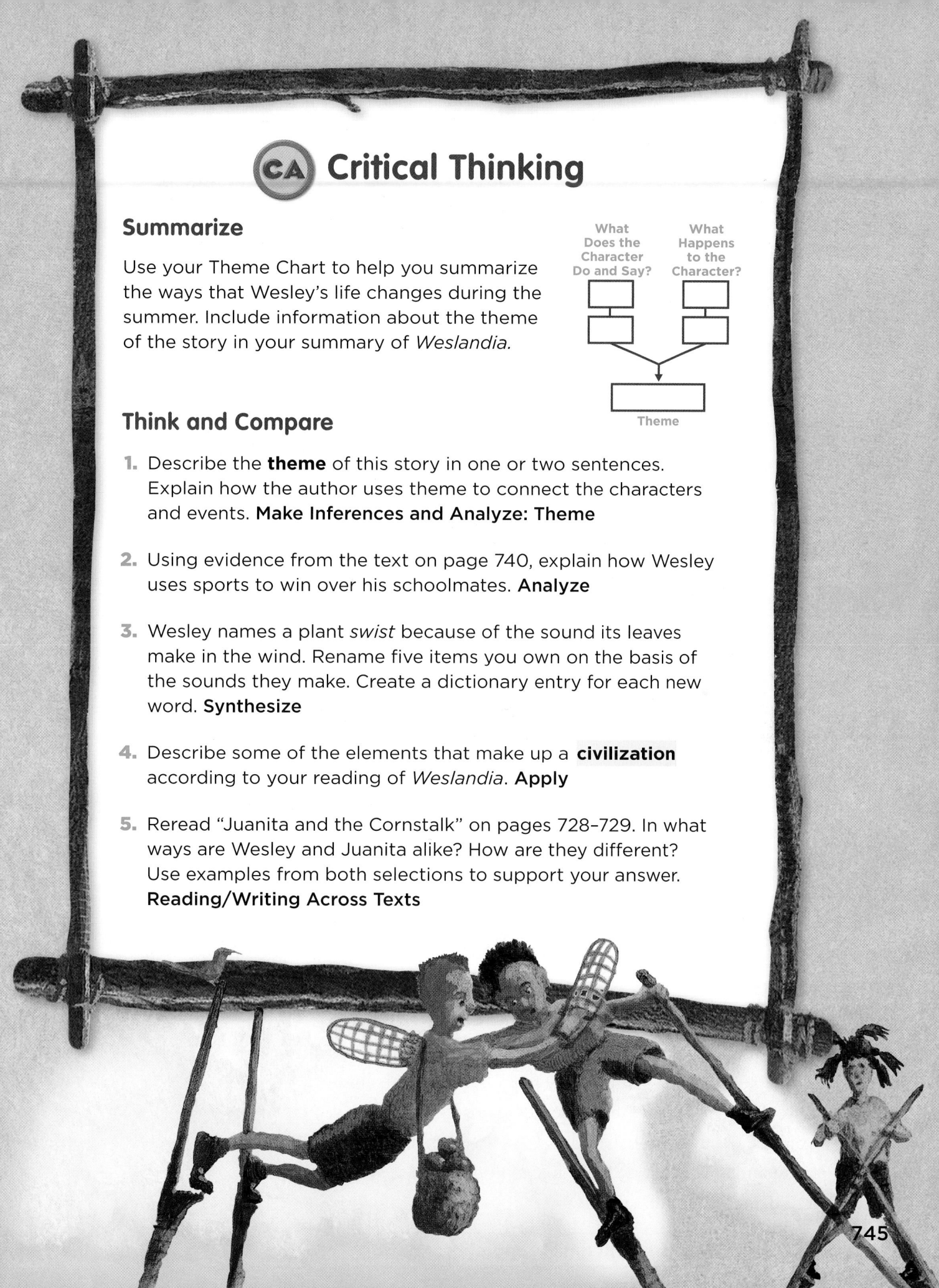

BLUE POTATOES AND SQUARE WATERMELONS

by Omar Naid

Visit the produce section of any large supermarket. You may be astonished by the variety of unusual fruits and vegetables. Square watermelons, blue potatoes, and purple cauliflower attract shoppers' attention. Some plants are unusual because they are grown in special ways. For example, square watermelons grow inside square glass cases. The result is a specially shaped melon that is easy to cut and store in the refrigerator.

Some plants, called **flukes**, result from odd, sudden changes that happen only once. Other plants are "designed" when they are seeds.

Here are two online encyclopedia articles to help you learn more about how these unusual plants come about.

| Address: | ⊚ http://www. example.com | go |

| Home | Browse | Newsletters | Favorites | Search hybrids |

This is a Key Word.

Hybrids

Hybrids are new plants created by scientists. They are a combination of two different "parent" plants that form a whole new kind of plant. Foods from hybrid plants might taste better or stay fresher when they are shipped. For example, a new fruit called the <u>pluot</u> is a cross between a plum and an apricot. It looks like a plum, but it is sweeter and firmer than most plums.

This is a hyperlink to more information.

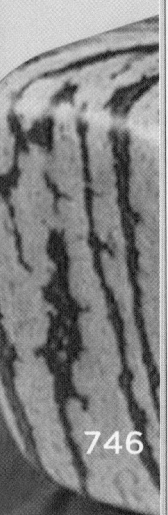

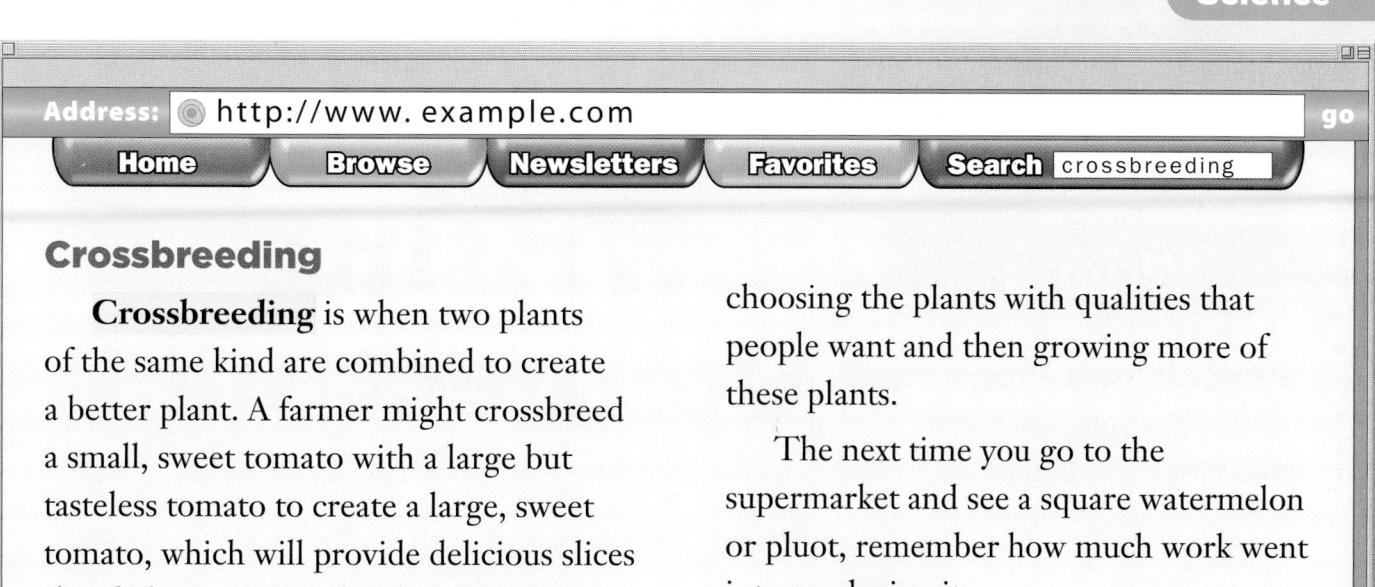

Crossbreeding

Crossbreeding is when two plants of the same kind are combined to create a better plant. A farmer might crossbreed a small, sweet tomato with a large but tasteless tomato to create a large, sweet tomato, which will provide delicious slices that fit better on sandwiches. Farmers must use plant selection, which means choosing the plants with qualities that people want and then growing more of these plants.

The next time you go to the supermarket and see a square watermelon or pluot, remember how much work went into producing it.

TOMATO CROSSBREEDING

CA Critical Thinking

1. How would you find more information about the **pluot**? **Hyperlinks**

2. What type of produce would you like to improve? How could you find out more about how to improve it? **Synthesize**

3. Think about "Blue Potatoes and Square Watermelons" and *Weslandia*. How is the process of growing produce different in each story? **Reading/Writing Across Texts**

Science Activity

Research a plant that is a hybrid. List the traits of this hybrid and compare and contrast it to the two parent plants using a Venn diagram.

 Find out more about new produce at **www.macmillanmh.com**.

Writing

CA

✔ **Subjects and Predicates**

Writers use **subjects** and **predicates** in different ways to emphasize a person or action.

Read the passage below from *Weslandia*. Notice how the author Paul Fleischman repeats the same subject over and over again.

An excerpt from *Weslandia*

The author emphasizes how Wesley is unique by using the simple subject, "he," over and over again to describe what Wesley does that sets him apart from everyone else.

Listening through the heating vent, Wesley knew they were right. He was an outcast from the civilization around him.

He alone in his town disliked pizza and soda, alarming his mother and the school nurse. He found professional football stupid. He'd refused to shave half his head, the hairstyle worn by all the other boys, despite his father's bribe of five dollars.

Passing his neighborhood's two styles of housing—garage on the left and garage on the right—Wesley alone dreamed of more exciting forms of shelter. He had no friends, but plenty of tormentors.

Weslandia
by Paul Fleischman
illustrated by Kevin Hawkes

Read and Find

Read Hannah's writing below. How did Hannah choose subjects that draw our attention to her dislikes and then to her attractions to the castle? Use the Writer's Checklist to help you.

The Castle

by Hannah K.

The lack of space and height are always noticeable in a medieval-style building. The stairs are narrow and make me feel claustrophobic. I feel cramped because there is so little light. While not pretty, small and dark are the special characteristics of the castle. If everything was big and light and airy, then going through a castle would be like everything else.

Read about my visit to a medieval castle.

Writer's Checklist

 Does the author tell different things about the same subject?

 Does the tone of the piece shift when the subject changes?

Does the author use a complex **subject** in order to develop more complex ideas?

CA **Talk About It**

How are the photographers in this photo taking a chance? What do you think they will gain from it?

LOG ON ▶ Find out more about taking a chance at **www.macmillanmh.com**.

Taking a Chance

A Song for Makaio

by Tamira Jackson

Long ago, near the islands now called Hawaii, lived a young girl named Makaio. She loved to swim and listen to the whales sing. The ocean could be dangerous, but Makaio did not mind the challenge. During the winter months, she bravely **ventured** into the water. Every day Makaio would float for hours, listening to the whale songs.

She always looked wiser when she **emerged** from the waves and walked onto the beach.

Though others could see her, Makaio could not see them. She was blind. Her other senses were unusually strong as a result. In fact, Makaio was the only one who could hear the whales sing.

Makaio said she could recognize each whale by his voice. She did not think it was strange or **unreasonable** to spend so much time listening to whales.

Whenever a new whale joined the group, Makaio would know. The newcomer would sing a different song. Gradually over several winters, the other males would start singing the new whale's song. The **attraction** that pulled Makaio towards the whales had to do with how they respected each other and the kindness they showed each other.

Makaio lived a long life. During her lifetime many of her whale friends died. Each time this happened, Makaio would have a sad look in her eyes. The islanders would **inquire** about what had happened. Makaio would answer simply, "One of my whale friends has died. I miss his voice."

She never wanted to have long **discussions** about it.

One night during her eightieth winter, Makaio did not return to the village. The islanders searched the beach. There they found a whale **sprawled** out on the shore. Next to him was Makaio. Her eyes seemed to be **focused** on the whale's long body spread awkwardly on the sand.

When the villagers reached her, Makaio spoke softly. "The voice of my very first whale friend has gone. It is time for me to go now, too. Do not be sad. Remember the whales' lessons: Learn from others. Always accept newcomers." With those words, Makaio died.

To this day people still try to understand the mystery of whale songs. Perhaps Makaio told us their secret many centuries ago.

Reread for **Comprehension**

Generate Questions
Summarize

A Summary Chart helps you answer questions about what happens at the beginning, middle, and end of a story. Use your Summary Chart as you reread "A Song for Makaio" to summarize the important ideas in the selection.

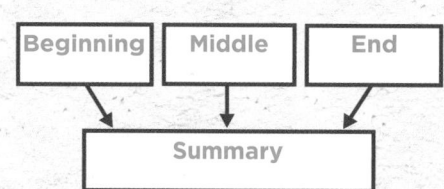

 Comprehension

Genre

Realistic Fiction has real-life settings, well-developed characters, and realistic problems and solutions.

Generate Questions

Summarize
As you read, use your Summary Chart.

Beginning	Middle	End

↓ ↓ ↓

Summary

Read to Find Out

How does Ana Rosa's community come to appreciate her talents?

The Gri Gri Tree
from
The Color of My Words

by Lynn Joseph

illustrated by Marla Baggetta

Award
Winning
Selection

No one had to point out that I was different from everyone else in our village. It was clear from the first day I began climbing the gri gri tree and staying up there for hours.

"What's wrong with your daughter?" neighbors asked Mami.

"She's not right in her head," they answered themselves, when Mami only shrugged her shoulders.

Papi would say, "Nothing wrong with sitting in a tree. It's the same as sitting on a porch except it's higher."

Roberto would climb up with me sometimes but he got bored quickly and swung down, yelling like a monkey. Angela shook her head at me and said I would never be a real *chica*, because *chicas* do not climb trees when they are twelve years old.

Not even Guario understood, although he tried. He asked me once what I did up there. That was more than anyone else had **ventured** to **inquire**.

I told him I looked around.

He asked if I didn't think I was wasting a lot of time, when I could be doing something to prepare for my future such as studying English.

Guario always had his mind on the future. Sometimes I think that he was tormented by all of us who didn't particularly care what tomorrow was going to bring. And really, what was there to know—either it would rain or it would not. But it was definitely going to be hot and Mami was going to cook and Papi was going to sit on the porch and the radio was going to play *merengues* all day. That was for sure.

Besides, I already knew what I wanted to do in my future. I wanted to be a writer, but only Mami knew that. If I told Guario, he would say I was **unreasonable**. If I told anyone else, they would laugh. But in my gri gri tree, I could be anything I wanted to be—even a writer with words for everything I saw from my leafy green hideout.

I could see the ocean glittering silver in the sunlight. I could see people trudging along the dusty road from Sosúa; some balancing buckets of water on their heads. I could see boys playing baseball in the schoolyard with a tree branch bat and a rubber band ball. I could see the river, meandering over rocks, hungry for rain. Far off in Puerto Plata, I could see Mount Isabel de Torres, a green giant with misty white curls dancing 'round her head.

I could see the sleepy lagoon and the sad little homes of the lagoon people. I could see the birds that flew past my gri gri, their ruby-and-gold velvet feathers shimmering on their tiny bodies. I could see the rainbows that glowed in the sea-sky after a rain passed. I could count the sunset roses in Señora Garcia's backyard. I could see my teacher climbing the hill near her house, and I could see Papi sitting on our porch, nodding off to sleep.

Then one day I saw something that I had never seen before and I was so scared that I almost fell out of the tree. There I was looking at the sea when suddenly out of it rose a giant monster, tall and black and covering the sun with its shadow. Before I could scream, the monster fell back into the sea.

I scrambled down the tree quickly and ran toward my house, shouting "Papi, there's a monster in the sea!"

Papi woke from his siesta. "*¿Qué pasa?*"

"A monster," I repeated. "A giant sea monster and it's coming this way!"

I shouted inside the house. "Mami, come quick. There's a monster in the sea. I saw it."

Mami came outside and Angela followed her. They were drying their hands from washing the lunch dishes.

Everyone looked at me as if I were crazy.

"It's true," I said, jumping up and down.

Mami made me sit down and describe exactly what I saw. Before I had finished, Angela shouted my news to her best friend walking by. Then Papi waved over some of his domino-playing *amigos* and told them what I saw from on top of my gri gri tree.

Soon our porch was surrounded with people all asking me to tell my story again.

759

When I had told it for the fourth time, Señor Garcia, the *colmado* owner, began to laugh.

"You must have fallen asleep in the tree and had a bad dream, *cariño*," he said.

"No," I replied, shaking my head. "I saw it."

But his words had relieved everyone's fears of a sea monster. "Yes," they agreed. "You must have imagined it."

"No, you idiots," I wanted to shout. "I didn't imagine anything." But I kept quiet because Mami and Papi would not like it if I shouted at the neighbors and called them idiots. That was for sure.

As everyone sat down on the porch to share a drink and talk about my sea monster, I slipped away and ran to my gri gri tree. I heard Mami calling me, but I pretended I didn't hear and climbed up the tree fast. I needed to find out if what I had seen would come back again.

I sat down on my usual branch and tucked a few leaves away from my eyes. Then I stared at the sea. I looked so hard and for so long that its blueness filled up my eyeballs and I had to blink a lot so I wouldn't go blind.

The afternoon faded into evening and the sea's blueness turned gray. I watched and waited. My stomach made grumbling noises but I covered them with my hand.

Then, just as I began to think that maybe I had imagined it after all, I saw a splash of white water. The splash of water rose up, up until it was high in the air like a magic fountain.

"It's a volcano," I whispered. I remembered that my teacher had told us how many of the Caribbean islands had been formed by volcanoes that rose out of the sea.

I gasped. Maybe I was seeing the beginning of a brand-new island right next to the República Dominicana. As I kept on looking, a black shape **emerged** out of the fountain of water. It rose and turned, as if doing a dance, and that's when I saw the gleaming white throat of the sea monster.

It hovered in between heaven and ocean for a few seconds and then fell back into the water with a splash that sprayed salt drops as high as the pearl-pink clouds.

My heart beat furiously and I steadied myself so I wouldn't fall down from the tree. I was right. I had not imagined anything. There really was a sea monster out there. But this time I didn't rush down to tell anyone.

What would the people do, I wondered. Would they try to find it? Or maybe to kill it? Somehow, although I didn't know why, I could tell that the sea monster was not dangerous. It just wanted to swim and splash and jump out of the sea the same way I jumped over the waves.

I climbed down the tree and went home. The first thing I wanted to do was eat, but people were all over the porch talking wildly. "We saw it, Ana Rosa," they shouted. "We saw that big sea monster of yours."

Mami was passing around a plate of *dulces*, the sweet milk candy that I love. She must have just made them because they were still warm and soft.

Children were carrying huge plates filled with different foods that their mothers had made. Angela was directing them to put the food here or there on our big table. I saw plates piled high with *arroz con pollo*, *plátanos fritos*, and *batatas fritas*.

Señor Garcia apologized over and over to me. About a hundred people were gathered on our porch, in the yard, and along the roadside, talking about the sea monster.

"The tourist high-season is coming," said Señor Rojas, who owned a Jeep that he rented to tourists. "We can't let anyone know we have a sea monster hanging around Sosúa Bay."

"But why not?" asked Señora Perez, who sold paintings on the beach. "It could be a tourist **attraction**. Plenty people may decide to come here just to see it."

Half the folks whispered, "He's right." And the other half said, "She's the one who's right."

> **Summarize**
> Summarize what happened after the narrator went home.

It looked as if we were going to have a big debate on our porch just like the ones that take place when it is a presidential election year. The way everyone was carrying on, soon we would be having people writing *merengues* about the sea monster and there would be sea monster fiestas all over the place just like during elections.

I shook my head and just listened to everyone as I ate a plate heaped high with food. That poor sea monster, I thought.

Then the people began to make a Plan. When Dominicans get together and decide to make a plan, watch out, because there are plans, and then there are Plans, and this was definitely a PLAN!

The first thing the people decided was that someone had to keep watch over this sea monster. Well, everyone looked around to see who would volunteer. That's when we knew the PLAN would not work because no one wanted to do something so stupid as to go down to the sea and watch for the sea monster.

It was Angela who got the bright idea that since I saw it first, I could keep watch over it from my gri gri tree. Everyone turned to me and nodded their heads.

"Finally, a good reason for her to be up there all the time," I heard Señora Garcia whisper.

Papi was looking at me and nodding his head, proud that his daughter was selected for such an important job. I said, Okay, I would do it.

Then the PLAN continued. Half the people wanted to make signs and announce that Sosúa Bay had a new visitor and it was a one-of-a-kind sea monster. The other half of the crowd shook their heads and said, No, it was too obvious.

"We must be subtle about a delicate matter like this," said Señora Perez. "We must make up a wonderful story about this sea monster, give it a name, make it a friendly monster, and then tell the world. Otherwise all we will do is scare everyone away from this side of the island."

She had a point. A story about the sea monster was much better than a big billboard with an arrow pointing "This way to Sea Monster of Sosúa Bay!"

The idea of it all made me giggle. Wait until Guario came home and heard all this. I could hardly wait for him to return from the restaurant.

"Well," said Señor Rojas, "what will we name the sea monster?"

"And who knows how to write a story about it anyway?" asked Señor Garcia.

Señora Perez shrugged her shoulders. "I don't know how to write too good, but we could make up something."

Then Mami, who was usually quiet during these kinds of **discussions**, spoke up loud and clear. "Ana Rosa would be the best person to write a story about the sea monster."

I was shocked. This wasn't the same Mami who worshiped silence.

People began to shake their heads. "A child to do something so important?" they whispered.

"Yes," said Mami. "Let us give her a notebook to write in and she will write us a story about the sea monster. If we don't like it, someone else can try."

The way Mami said it, so definite and firm, made people nod their heads in agreement. "Well it doesn't hurt to let her try," they said.

So Señor Garcia went and brought back a notebook from his *colmado*. Mami gave it to me and her hands were cold like the river.

While the grown-ups stayed up late on the porch talking and drinking and eating, I went inside and began to write a story about the sea monster. First I tried to give him a name. But I couldn't think of a good one. So instead I thought about what he looked like. Then I imagined what he must feel like living all alone in the sea, different from all of the other sea creatures.

The fish and animals in the ocean were probably afraid of his huge size and his big nose and long, swishing tail. And they probably didn't want to play with him. Maybe they whispered about how strange he looked. But the sea monster wanted a friend. Deep down, I understood exactly how the sea monster must feel.

I began to write. I wrote page after page in the notebook the people had given to me. When I was finished, it was almost midnight. I went to the porch. Everyone was still there laughing and talking and some were dancing to the music on the radio.

Children were asleep on their mothers' and fathers' laps. Some of the bigger children were **sprawled** out on a blanket on the floor and the *merengue* music was a background lullaby for them.

> **Summarize**
> What kind of plans do the villagers make to publicize the sea monster, and how do these plans lead to the narrator's story?

When the people saw me, they got quiet. Someone turned off the radio. Some woke the children on their laps. Papi moved from his chair and put his arms around my shoulders. He led me to the front of the porch.

Then everyone watched me and waited. I stood there trembling, holding that notebook with my story close to my heart. I knew right then that this was it. The whole world would find out about me.

I stopped thinking. I just started to read. I did not look at anyone, not Papi, or Mami or Angela. I read and read until I turned to the last page of the story. There the other sea creatures invite the lonely sea monster to a big underwater fiesta, even though there is no one else like him around, and even though he is so big that he knocks over many of them with his big nose and tail.

"And the sea monster is so happy that he leaps out of the ocean, sending sparkling waves all around him in a giant ring of light."

I looked up then and I saw many things at once. I saw Papi sitting on the edge of his chair, strange and silent. I saw Mami with her hands folded and her head bowed as if praying. I saw the neighbors smiling and nodding their heads. Then I saw Guario, who must have walked up to the edge of the porch while I was reading.

It was Guario's face I **focused** on. He was smiling. My big strong brother who worried about our future, my serious Guario who almost never smiled, suddenly let out a loud whoop and grabbed me up. He spun me around and around.

"Little sister, I am buying you a new notebook every month no matter what!" he shouted.

I closed my eyes so I wouldn't start crying there in front of all the neighbors. Guario always kept his promises. I would be able to write down everything now, everything I thought or dreamed or felt or saw or wondered about. I was so happy I thought I would leap as high as the sea monster.

Then, in the background, I heard clapping. The people had stood up from their chairs and were clapping for me.

I heard shouts of how great my story was and people congratulating Papi and kissing Mami's cheeks telling them how lucky it was that I was so smart. I heard Mami saying it had nothing to do with luck. I grinned and went over to her. She put her arms around me and squeezed my shoulders.

"You're going to write many stories, remember, *cara*?" She whispered in my ear. It was the happiest night of my life.

We all forgot about the sea monster until the next day.

Over the radio, a news broadcast announced that one of the humpback whales making its way to Samaná Bay for the annual winter mating season had gotten sidetracked in Sosúa.

"But Samaná Bay is only a two-hour drive from here," said Papi.

"Well, the poor whale doesn't know how to drive," Mami teased.

For two weeks our humpback whale jumped and frolicked about in Sosúa Bay until finally heading east to Samaná to join the other three thousand humpbacks that go there every winter.

But while he was in Sosúa, I watched him every day from my gri gri tree. The beautiful black-and-white sea monster had helped me to make my dream come true. I loved the whale. And I named him Guario.

771

A Whale of a Time with
Lynn Joseph and Marla Baggetta

Lynn Joseph grew up in Trinidad, an island in the West Indies. While growing up Lynn was good with words and loved learning. Today she combines both passions in her two jobs. Besides being an author, Lynn is a lawyer in New York City. Her talent with words comes in handy by allowing her to make her case in court and on paper. Lynn has two sons and a new home in the Dominican Republic.

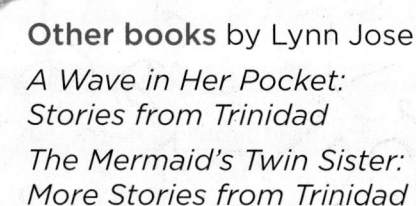

Other books by Lynn Joseph:

A Wave in Her Pocket: Stories from Trinidad

The Mermaid's Twin Sister: More Stories from Trinidad

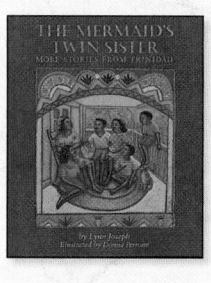

Marla Baggetta is an artist and illustrator whose work has appeared nationally in galleries, books, advertisements, and magazines. She graduated from art school in Pasadena, California. She lives with her husband and two sons in West Linn, Oregon.

LOG ON ▶ Find out more about Lynn Joseph and Marla Baggetta **www.macmillanmh.com**.

CA Author's Purpose

Although the author's main purpose in writing *The Gri Gri Tree* is to entertain, realistic fiction includes true-to-life details. What details here are realistic?

Critical Thinking

Summarize

Use your Summary Chart to help you summarize *The Gri Gri Tree*. When you prepare your summary, be sure to include only important events and details.

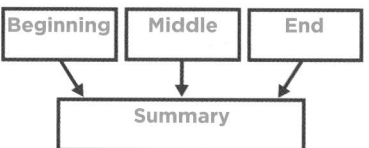

Think and Compare

1. **Summarize** what you know of Ana Rosa's story about the sea monster. Explain why the author did not include Ana Rosa's story within *The Gri Gri Tree*. **Generate Questions: Summarize**

2. Reread the last three paragraphs on page 768. Explain what everyone finds out about Ana Rosa. **Analyze**

3. The gri gri tree is a special place for Ana Rosa. Describe a place that is special to you. Explain what it is about this place that makes it special. **Apply**

4. Ana Rosa's brother is always **focused** on "what tomorrow was going to bring." Do you think people should consider what might await them in the future? Why or why not? **Evaluate**

5. Reread "A Song for Makaio" on pages 752–753. How is Ana Rosa like Makaio? How do others react to each of these characters? Use details from both selections to support your answer. **Reading/Writing Across Texts**

Genre

Nonfiction provides information about real people, living things, places, situations, or events.

Text Feature

Graphs are diagrams that show the relationships among objects. They make it easy to compare different amounts or sizes.

Content Vocabulary

mammals	**organisms**
traits	**carnivores**

The LARGEST Creature on Earth

by Yolanda Robertson

What is the largest animal that ever lived on Earth? Do you think it is a dinosaur? Guess again! It's the blue whale, and it is still on Earth today. A blue whale can grow to be as long as a nine story building turned on its side. The blue whale is so vast that its heart alone weighs about 1,000 pounds and is about the size of a small car.

The blue whale is just one kind of whale. There are many members of the whale family, including porpoises and dolphins. All of these animals belong to the family of sea creatures called Cetaceans. The name *Cetacean* comes from the Latin word *cetus*, meaning large sea animal, and from the Greek word *ketos* meaning sea monster.

Despite living in water, whales are not enormous fish. Like human beings, whales are **mammals**. All mammals share common **traits**, such as using lungs to breathe air and nursing their young. Mammals are warm-blooded, have a heart with four chambers, and have hair. They generally live on land, but whales and manatees are two mammals that spend their entire lives in the water. Unlike humans who use their noses to breathe, whales breathe air through blowholes on top of their heads. There are two main groups of whales— baleen whales and toothed whales. Each has special traits.

Big Whales, Bigger Whales!

Reading a Graph

You can use this graph to compare the weights and lengths of four kinds of whales.

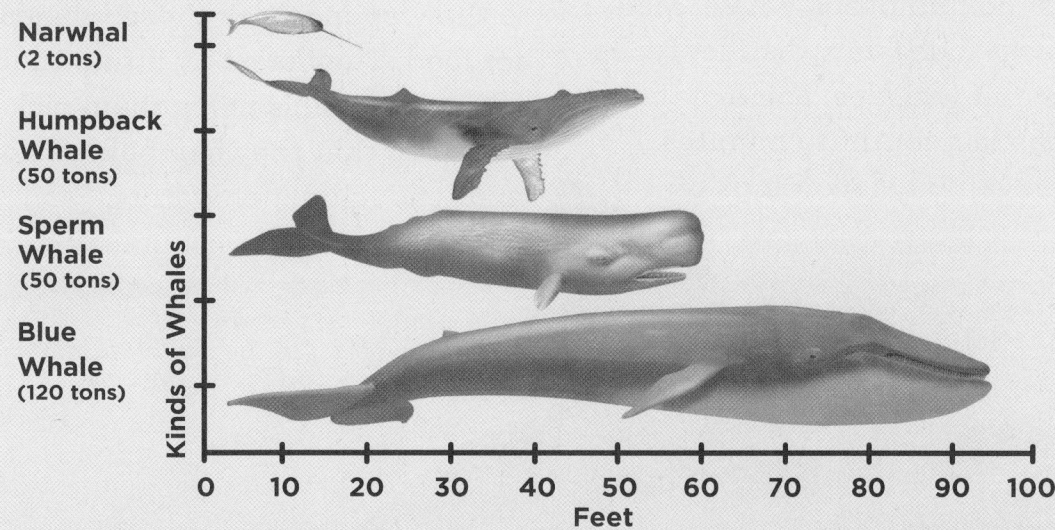

Narwhal (2 tons)
Humpback Whale (50 tons)
Sperm Whale (50 tons)
Blue Whale (120 tons)

Kinds of Whales

0 10 20 30 40 50 60 70 80 90 100
Feet

Baby humpback whale

Baleen Whales

Baleen whales have two blowholes. Instead of teeth they have baleen plates or comb-like structures that strain food from the water. These enormous whales have hundreds of baleen plates. The largest baleen whale is the blue whale. Similar to an enormous vacuum cleaner, a blue whale will suck in and eat up to 8,000 pounds per day of tiny, shrimp-like **organisms** called krill.

Like all other whales, baleen whales live in pods, or small groups. These whales also "sing" to each other. Many whales communicate by singing. The blue whale's songs are the loudest, even louder than a jumbo jet. Scientists think the baleen whale with the most complex songs is the humpback whale. Male humpbacks make very distinct types of clicks and whistles. Some of their songs can last for thirty minutes. You can even buy recordings of humpback whale songs. However, female humpback whales do not sing. One theory scientists have is that males are probably using this whale music to court female humpback whales.

Toothed Whales

A toothed whale has one blowhole and many teeth. The largest of the toothed whales is the sperm whale. Its brain alone weighs up to 20 pounds and is the largest of any animal. Sperm whales are **carnivores**, and they eat about 2,000 pounds of food a day. Their favorite food is the giant squid, but they also eat fish and octopus.

Two other toothed whales that are much smaller than the sperm whale are the porpoise and the dolphin. A quick look at these three creatures makes it difficult to believe that they are related, but a close study will reveal shared traits. One thing that sperm whales, dolphins, and porpoises all do is "fluking." Fluking is the way in which these whales dive for food. They start by lifting their tails into the air. This helps them pick up speed so that they can plunge down and feed in deeper waters.

Fluking tooth whale

Unicorn or Whale?

The strange-looking narwhal is a toothed whale that lives in the Arctic Ocean. The male narwhal is known for its long tooth, called a tusk, which looks like a long, pointed broomstick. The narwhal's special tooth grows out of the front of its head and can be up to ten feet long. Years ago, before they knew about narwhals, some people thought these tusks came from unicorns.

Scientists know about more than 80 kinds of Cetaceans, and they believe that there may be more types of whales that have not yet been discovered. So the next time you are at the ocean, watch for whales. Maybe you'll discover a new breed of Cetaceans!

Male narwhal with tusk

 Critical Thinking

1. Look at the graph on page 775. What are the differences in weight and length between blue and sperm whales? **Reading a Graph**

2. Based on the information in the article, how is the mouth structure of baleen whales suited for their diet of krill? **Analyze**

3. Think about "The Largest Creature on Earth" and *The Gri Gri Tree*. How do you think Ana Rosa would have described a fully grown blue whale? How do you think it would compare to the description given in "The Largest Creature on Earth"? **Reading/Writing Across Texts**

 Science Activity

Research three or four whales not mentioned in the article and make a graph that compares the weights of each type of whale.

 Find out more about whales at **www.macmillanmh.com**.

Writing

✓ **Subjects and Predicates**

Writers sometimes use multiple **subjects** and **predicates** to show readers exactly how something happens.

Reading and Writing Connection

Read the passage below from *The Gri Gri Tree*. Notice how the author Lynn Joseph primarily uses three subjects: Mami, Ana Rosa, and "the people."

An excerpt from
The Gri Gri Tree

The author moves back and forth between the three major subjects and helps us see how they all come to an agreement.

Then Mami, who was usually quiet during these kinds of discussions, spoke up loud and clear. "Ana Rosa would be the best person to write a story about the sea monster."

I was shocked. This wasn't the same Mami who worshiped silence.

People began to shake their heads. "A child to do something so important?" they whispered.

"Yes," said Mami. "Let us give her a notebook to write in and she will write us a story about the sea monster. If we don't like it, someone else can try."

The way Mami said it, so definite and firm, made people nod their heads in agreement. "Well it doesn't hurt to let her try," they said.

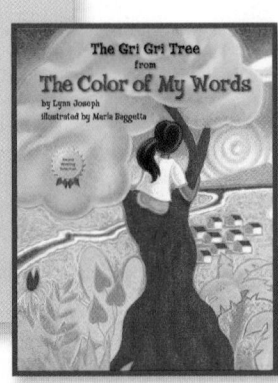

The Gri Gri Tree
from
The Color of My Words
by Lynn Joseph
illustrated by Maria Baggetta

Read and Find

Read Aiden's writing below. How did Aiden help us picture what was happening? Use the Writer's Checklist to assist you.

The Ultimate Game
by Aiden F.

John made a great throw. At that moment, I sprinted out of the crowd. The frisbee was like another person running beside me. Or like a bird flying, continuously flapping its wings to keep pace. I reached the end zone. I cut left. I tried to get my body in front of it but it was too far. I reached. It bounced off my knuckle, idled in the air, and stayed there forever. I reached up and grabbed it with my outstretched hands.

Read about my great catch!

Writer's Checklist

 Does the author seem to use a particular subject for a particular reason?

 When the author repeats the subject, does this repetition focus you on the **right** subject?

☑ Do the **predicates** help us see the **subjects'** actions?

Review

- Persuasion
- Theme
- Sequence
- Synonyms
- Headings

A Welcome Gift

Dario and his mother loved their new apartment. Sunshine streamed through the windows all day long, the walls had been repainted in brilliant colors, and the living room was large enough for their piano. "It sure beats those tiny rooms in our old apartment," Dario said.

That night, the two of them sat side by side at the piano. They played a ragtime song by Scott Joplin to celebrate their new home. The bouncing melody filled the room and left them feeling overjoyed.

The next morning, however, their mood took an unexpected turn. Someone had slipped a note under their door during the night. One of their neighbors had written to complain about the sound of the piano.

Dario's mother was sad and upset. She asked the building superintendent if any of their neighbors had complained to him. He knew nothing about the note. "They're all nice folks," the superintendent said. "I can't imagine any of them being upset."

Later that morning, Dario suggested that they write a letter to their neighbors and apologize for their playing.

"Maybe we could go and visit everyone in person," his mother said.

"What if we invited them to come here instead?" Dario asked.

They both loved the idea. Over the next few days, they sent out invitations and baked desserts for their guests. They decorated the apartment with streamers and party lights.

Finally, the day of the party arrived. Guests began arriving right on time. Some brought housewarming presents. Others brought cards. Some even brought desserts to share. Dario was surprised that they all looked to be his grandparents' age.

One woman, Mrs. Gilbert, presented Dario's mother with a book of piano music by Chopin. "I heard you playing the other night," Mrs. Gilbert said in a strong accent. "The sounds woke me out of bed. I worried that you might play like this every night and keep me awake, so I wrote a short note. I hope you don't think I disliked the playing."

Dario's mother smiled at Mrs. Gilbert. "I think maybe we owe you an apology," she said. "I didn't realize how late it was when we were playing. Maybe if we played quieter music at night. . . ."

"You play, you play!" Mrs. Gilbert said. "I like what you play! Just not so loud at night." She pointed to the book she had given them. "These songs are not such loud music."

"These songs are beautiful music," Dario's mother said. "We will be happy to play them each evening."

"And we won't play so loud or late!" Dario said. He was already looking forward to previewing the new music. More than that, however, he was happy to see the big smile on his mother's face. It made him feel that they were home at last.

781

Community Service Projects

Assisting the Special Olympics

Promoting Recycling

Helping with Homework

Everybody Can Serve

"EVERYBODY CAN BE GREAT, BECAUSE EVERYBODY CAN SERVE," said Martin Luther King, Jr. According to Dr. King, greatness lies in what a person does for other people. Dr. King and others like him spent their lives making the world a better place. He challenged all people to do the same. Think about your skills and the things you enjoy doing. Is there a way you can share these skills and interests with others? A community service project is a great way to learn how to be a leader and to help other people. It will also help you make new friends. Choose an adult to be your advisor. Then invite some friends or family members to plan a project together. Here are a few steps to follow for creating a community service project.

Step 1   Choose the Project

Create a list of community issues that matter to you. It might be helping younger students or working with the Special Olympics. Does your community have a recycling program?

Look over your lists. Are there already groups that do the same thing? Who are the people who might be interested? What materials will you need to do the project?

Choose the project that you think will help your community the most.

Step 2   Plan the Project

Create a schedule for the project. How long will it take to finish? How many days each week will you work? Where will you meet?

Decide what jobs need to be done. Assign each person to a specific job. Mark the completion dates on your schedule.

Contact people or groups that might be able to help. Local librarians can help with research.

Step 3   Begin the Project

After the planning is done, it is time to go to work. No matter what precautions you take, problems may still occur. Let the team members solve the problems as they happen. Make sure everyone's ideas are respected. Most importantly, have fun!

Step 4   Document the Project

As you work on the project, take photographs. Each member of the group can choose one picture and write a journal entry about it. Tell members to describe what is going on in the picture and to tell about their thoughts and feelings at the time.

Step 5   It's Time to Celebrate!

Celebrate the completion of your project. Display the pictures and the journal entries. Invite everyone who helped. Your local newspaper or TV station might cover the event. It's time to celebrate what makes people "great."

CA Critical Thinking

Now answer numbers 1 through 4. Base your answers on the story "A Welcome Gift."

1. **The theme of "A Welcome Gift" is that**

    A all neighbors are good neighbors.

    B people need to be considerate.

    C everybody loves a party.

    D not everyone is nice.

2. **Which event from "A Welcome Gift" happened first?**

    A Dario and his mother gave a party.

    B Dario and his mother played the piano.

    C Dario and his mother moved into a new apartment.

    D Dario and his mother spoke to the building superintendent.

3. **Read the following phrase from the story.**

> . . . the walls had been repainted in <u>brilliant</u> colors. . . .

    What is a synonym for the underlined word?

    A shining or sparkling with light

    B done in an outstanding way

    C having great intelligence

    D rich, vivid, or bright

4. **Why do you think Dario and his mother gave a party? Did their plan work?**

Now answer numbers 1 through 4. Base your answers on the article "Everybody Can Serve."

1. Which statement is an example of persuasion?

   A   A service project is a lot of work.
   B   A service project will help you make friends.
   C   A service project will challenge people.
   D   Martin Luther King liked service projects.

2. What is the purpose of the headings in "Everybody Can Serve?"

   A   to help readers take notes
   B   to make the selection easier to read
   C   to organize the selection's information
   D   to help readers plan a project

3. What is a synonym for the underlined word in this sentence? Create a list and choose a community <u>issue</u>.

   A   an edition of a magazine
   B   a subject for discussion
   C   a result or effect
   D   to send out or give off

4. What should you do last for a community project?

   A   Choose the project.
   B   Plan the project.
   C   Begin the project.
   D   Celebrate the project.

Write on Demand

PROMPT What service project would you like to organize for your community? Write a description of your project. Use words that will persuade others to work with you. Write for 20 minutes. Write as much as you can as well as you can.

Glossary

What Is a Glossary?

A glossary can help you find the **meanings** of words in this book that you may not know. The words in the glossary are listed in **alphabetical order**. **Guide words** at the top of each page tell you the first and last words on the page.

Each word is divided into syllables. The way to pronounce the word is given next. You can understand the pronunciation respelling by using the **pronunciation key**. A shorter key appears at the bottom of every other page. When a word has more than one syllable, a dark accent mark (´) shows which syllable is stressed. In some words, a light accent mark (´) shows which syllable has a less heavy stress. Sometimes an entry includes a second meaning for the word.

maze

robot

Guide Words

First word on the page   Last word on the page

Sample Entry

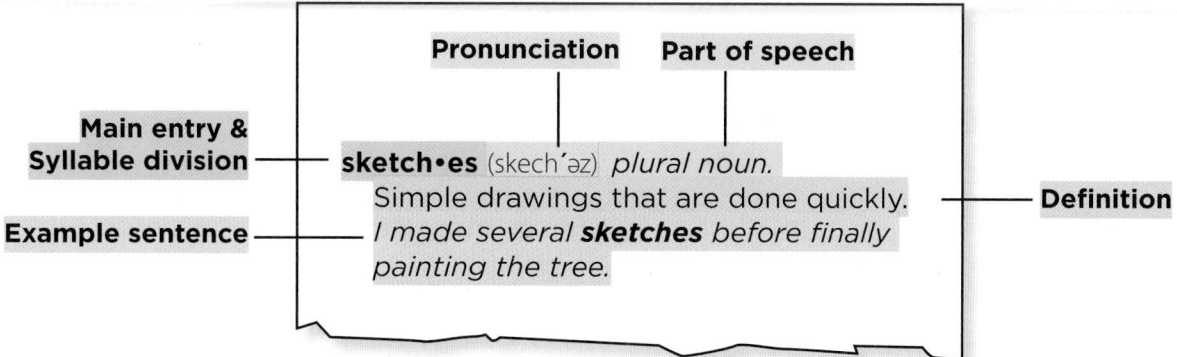

Pronunciation   Part of speech

Main entry &
Syllable division

sketch•es (skech´əz) *plural noun.*
Simple drawings that are done quickly.   Definition
I made several **sketches** *before finally
painting the tree.*

Example sentence

Pronunciation Key

Phonetic Spelling	Examples
a	at, bad, plaid, laugh
ā	ape, pain, day, break
ä	father, calm
âr	care, pair, bear, their, where
e	end, pet, said, heaven, friend
ē	equal, me, feet, team, piece, key
i	it, big, give, hymn
ī	ice, fine, lie, my
îr	ear, deer, here, pierce
o	odd, hot, watch
ō	old, oat, toe, low
ô	coffee, all, taught, law, fought
ôr	order, fork, horse, story, pour
oi	oil, toy
ou	out, now, bough
u	up, mud, love, double
ū	use, mule, cue, feud, few
ü	rule, true, food, fruit
u̇	put, wood, should, look
ûr	burn, hurry, term, bird, word, courage
ə	about, taken, pencil, lemon, circus
b	bat, above, job
ch	chin, such, match

Phonetic Spelling	Examples
d	dear, soda, bad
f	five, defend, leaf, off, cough, elephant
g	game, ago, fog, egg
h	hat, ahead
hw	white, whether, which
j	joke, enjoy, gem, page, edge
k	kite, bakery, seek, tack, cat
l	lid, sailor, feel, ball, allow
m	man, family, dream
n	not, final, pan, knife, gnaw
ng	long, singer
p	pail, repair, soap, happy
r	ride, parent, wear, more, marry
s	sit, aside, pets, cent, pass
sh	shoe, washer, fish, mission, nation
t	tag, pretend, fat, dressed
th	thin, panther, both
th̲	these, mother, smooth
v	very, favor, wave
w	wet, weather, reward
y	yes, onion
z	zoo, lazy, jazz, rose, dogs, houses
zh	vision, treasure, seizure

Aa

a•ban•don (ə banʹdən) *verb.* To leave and not return. *The sailors jumped into the ocean when they were given the order to* **abandon** *the ship.*

ac•com•pa•ny (ə kumʹpə nē) *verb.* To go together with. *My friend decided to* **accompany** *me to the store so that I would have someone to talk to.*

ad•just•ed (ə jusʹtid) *verb.* Changed or arranged to fit a need or demand. *We* **adjusted** *the schedule to include two more singers in the program.*

ad•ver•tise•ment (adʹvər tīzʹmənt) *noun.* A public notice that tells people about a product, an event, or something a person needs. *A successful* **advertisement** *will convince shoppers to buy a product.*

a•lert (ə lûrtʹ) *noun.* A heightened sense of watchfulness for possible danger. *The navy ship was put on* **alert** *after an ice storm was reported in the area.*

a•mend•ment (ə mendʹmənt) *noun.* A change in a law caused by voting of government officials or changes to the Constitution. *Women were given the right to vote in all states by an* **amendment** *to the Constitution.*

a•mus•ing (ə mūʹzing) *adjective.* Causing laughter or enjoyment. *Everyone laughed at Dad's* **amusing** *remark.*

a•nat•o•my (ə natʹə mē) *noun.* The structure of an animal or plant or any of its parts. *Medical students study* **anatomy** *to learn how to treat illnesses in people.*

an•chored (angʹkərd) *verb.* Being held in place by a heavy metal device or object. *The crew is lucky they* **anchored** *the boat to a rock because the sudden storm would have blown them far from shore.*

ap•pre•ci•a•tion (ə prēʹshē āʹshən) *noun.* A feeling of being thankful. *To show his* **appreciation***, Javier gave the boy who found his wallet a small reward.*

ap•proached (ə prōchtʹ) *verb.* Came near in time or space. *We watched as the letter carrier* **approached** *our front door.*

ar•chae•ol•ogists (ärʹkē olʹ ə jists) *noun, plural.* Scientists who study the human past. *The* **archaeologists** *dug in the old cave and found many tools of early people.*

a•rous•ing (ə rouzʹing) *verb.* Stirring up or causing excitement. *The opposing team's fans were* **arousing** *a lot of attention in the bleachers with their cheering.*

ar•ti•facts (ärʹti faktsʹ) *noun, plural.* Anything made or altered by humans, such as tools or objects of daily life. *Historians study* **artifacts** *to learn about daily life in the past.*

as•tron•o•mers (ə stronʹə mərz) *noun, plural.* Students of or experts in astronomy, the science that deals with the planets, stars, and other heavenly bodies. *The* **astronomers** *measured the distance between Earth and the moon.*

at•mos•phere (atʹməs fîrʹ) *noun.* 1. The layer of gases that surrounds Earth. 2. A surrounding mood or environment. *1. We watched on television as the space shuttle entered the* **atmosphere** *after its mission to the moon was over. 2. Our house has a merry* **atmosphere** *during the holiday season.*

at•tor•ney (ə tûrʹnē) *noun.* A lawyer; one who helps with legal matters. *Before arguing your case in court, it may be a good idea to hire an* **attorney***.*

at•trac•tion (ə trakʹshən) *noun.* A person or thing that draws attention. *The new baby elephant was an* **attraction** *that drew a lot of people at the zoo.*

au•to•graph (ô′tə graf′) *noun.* A person's signature written in that person's own handwriting. *My sister got her favorite singer's* **autograph**.

a•vail•a•ble (ə vā′lə bəl) *adjective.* Possible to get. *There were five seats* **available**.

Bb

banned (band) *verb.* Officially forbidden; prohibited. *The teacher* **banned** *books that contained inaccurate information.*

be•hav•ior (bi hāv′yər) *noun.* A way of acting. *The campers were yelled at by the counselor for their mischievous* **behavior**.

bi•ol•o•gy (bī ol′ə jē) *1. adjective. 2. noun.* 1. Characterized by the study of living things. 2. The study of living things. *1. The* **biology** *teacher enjoyed the study of plants.* 2. **Biology** *is my favorite subject in school.*

blurt•ed (blûr′tid) *verb.* Said suddenly or without thinking. *I* **blurted** *out the answer before the teacher finished the question.*

bor•der (bôr′dər) *noun.* The boundary line of a state or country. *We had to show birth certificates when we crossed the* **border** *of our country.*

boy•cott (boi′kot) *noun.* A planned and organized refusal to have anything to do with a person, group, or nation. *The strikers called for a* **boycott** *of the company's products.*

bun•dle (bun′dəl) *noun.* A group of things held together. *The deliveryman left a* **bundle** *of newspapers outside the grocery store.*

bur•dens (bûr′dənz) *noun, plural.* Things that are carried. *The mule carried the* **burdens** *down the trail into the canyon.*

Cc

cam•ou•flage (kam′ə fläzh′) *noun.* Any disguise, appearance, or behavior that serves to conceal or deceive, such as the protective coloring of an animal. *An octopus uses* **camouflage** *to change its skin color and blend into its surroundings.*

ca•pa•ble (kā′pə bəl) *adjective.* Having skill or power; able. *The new planes are* **capable** *of even greater speed.*

car•ni•vores (kär′nə vôrz′) *noun, plural.* Animals or plants such as sharks, eagles, dogs, and Venus's-flytraps that feed chiefly on flesh. *Lions are* **carnivores** *who hunt and feed on smaller animals.*

at; āpe; fär; câre; end; mē; it; īce; pîerce; hot; ōld; sông; fôrk; oil; out; up; ūse; rüle; pull; tûrn; chin; sing; shop; thin; this; hw in white; zh in treasure.

The symbol ə stands for the unstressed vowel sound in about, taken, pencil, lemon, and circus.

cat•e•go•ries (kat′i gôr′ēz) *noun, plural.* Groups or classes of things. *The menu was divided into three* **categories**: *snacks, main courses, and desserts.*

cha•me•le•on (kə mēl′yən) *noun.* Any of various small, slow-moving lizards that can change the color of their skin to match their surroundings. *The* **chameleon** *on the tree bark turned brown.*

civ•il (siv′əl) *adjective.* Of or relating to citizens or a government. *One of our* **civil** *rights is the right to vote.*

civ•i•li•za•tion (siv′ə lə zā′shən) *noun.* A society in which agriculture, trade, government, art, and science are highly developed. *The museum had a number of objects that showed how* **civilization** *has developed over the last 600 years.*

clenched (klencht) *verb.* Grasped or closed tightly. *The boy* **clenched** *his fist when he saw the bully walking angrily toward him.*

colo•nel (kûr′nəl) *noun.* An officer in the U.S. Army, Air Force, or Marine Corps. *The* **colonel** *helped prepare his troops for the difficult battle ahead.*

com•bined (kəm bīnd′) *1. adjective. 2. verb.* 1. Characterized by being joined together or united. 2. Joined together; united. *1. Thanks to the* **combined** *efforts of the voters in our city, the mayor was reelected. 2. The baker* **combined** *eggs, butter, sugar, and flour to make cookie dough.*

com•menced (kə menst′) *verb.* Began or started. *The play* **commenced** *when the audience was seated and quiet.*

com•pan•ion (kəm pan′yən) *noun.* A person or animal who keeps somebody company. *A dog can be a good* **companion** *for a lonely person.*

com•pe•ti•tion (kom′pi tish′ən) *noun.* The act of trying to win or gain something from another person or other people. *We're in* **competition** *with two other teams for the swimming championship.*

com•plex (kəm pleks′) *adjective.* Hard to understand or do. *The math problems were* **complex** *because they involved many steps.*

con•quer (kong′kər) *verb.* To capture or hold by force. *The army was unable to* **conquer** *the enemy city.*

con•sent•ed (kən sen′tid) *verb.* Gave permission or agreed to. *My mom* **consented** *to my sleeping over at Maria's house for her slumber party.*

con•sult•ed (kən sul′tid) *verb.* Having asked for advice or for an opinion. *My parents* **consulted** *a lawyer before they bought our house.*

con•tact (kon′takt) *noun.* A touching or meeting of persons or things. *My uncle burned his arm when it came in* **contact** *with the hot stove.*

con•tam•i•na•tion (kən tam′ə nā′shən) *noun.* The process of spoiling or the state of being spoiled; pollution. *Food should be kept covered to prevent* **contamination**.

con•ti•nent (kon′tə nənt) *noun.* One of the seven large land areas on Earth. *I live in the United States, which is on the* **continent** *of North America.*

co•or•di•na•tion (kō ôr´də nā´shən) *noun.* The act of organizing or working together. *The rescue team needed* **coordination** *in order to cover the entire area.*

cor•ri•dor (kôr´i dər, kor´i dər) *noun.* A long passageway or hallway. *Students walked down the* **corridor** *to the gymnasium.*

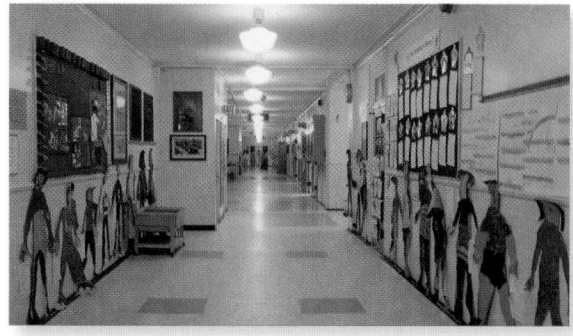

cou•ple (kup´əl) *noun.* Partners; two people working together as a team. *The new* **couple** *came to introduce themselves to my family.*

creased (krēst) *adjective.* Characterized by lines or marked by wrinkling. *My teacher would not accept my* **creased** *book report because it was messy looking.*

cred•it (kred´it) *noun.* 1. Praise or honor; something owed to a person. 2. Trust in a person to pay a debt at a later time. *1. The students who included a visual display with their speeches earned extra* **credit**. *2. The store gave me* **credit** *today so I could buy the shirt and pay for it on Friday.*

cross•breed•ing (krôs´brē´ding) *verb.* Breeding different kinds of plants or animals in order to produce hybrids. *The farmer was* **crossbreeding** *small, sweet peppers with large, tasteless peppers to get large, sweet peppers.*

Dd

dam•ag•es (dam´ij iz) *noun, plural.* Harm that makes things less valuable or useful. ***Damages*** *to the city totaled to millions of dollars after the storm.*

dan•gling (dang´ling) *verb.* Hanging loosely. *The diamonds* **dangling** *from Erin's ears looked pretty in the light.*

de•cen•cy (dē´sən sē) *noun.* The state or quality of good behavior. *She had the* **decency** *to say "thank you" after receiving the gift.*

ded•i•cated (ded´ i kā´ tid) *verb.* Set apart. *The city* **dedicated** *this land for a park.*

de•fec•tive (di fek´tiv) *adjective.* Having a flaw or imperfection. *The* **defective** *radio could play only one station.*

del•i•ca•cies (del´i kə sēs) *noun, plural.* Rare or excellent food. *At the food festival there were* **delicacies** *from around the world.*

de•liv•er•ing (di liv´ə ring) *verb.* Taking or carrying something to a particular place or person. *My job is* **delivering** *groceries to people's homes.*

dense (dens) *adjective.* Packed closely together. *The smoke was* **dense**, *making it difficult for firefighters to see.*

de•picts (di pikts´) *verb.* Represents or describes by pictures or words. *The artist's painting* **depicts** *a field of cows with storm clouds in the sky.*

de•scend•ed (di sen´did) *verb.* Moved from a higher place to a lower one. *The woman* **descended** *the mountain on skis.*

---

at; **ā**pe; f**ä**r; c**â**re; **e**nd; m**ē**; **i**t; **ī**ce; p**î**erce; h**o**t; **ō**ld; s**ô**ng; f**ô**rk; **oi**l; **ou**t; **u**p; **ū**se; r**ü**le; p**ů**ll; t**û**rn; **ch**in; si**ng**; **sh**op; **th**in; **th**is; **hw** in **wh**ite; **zh** in treasure.

The symbol **ə** stands for the unstressed vowel sound in **a**bout, tak**e**n, penc**i**l, lem**o**n, and circ**u**s.

de•spair (di spâr´) *noun.* A complete loss of hope. *The student was filled with* ***despair*** *when he couldn't complete his assignment before the deadline.*

de•struc•tion (di struk´shən) *noun.* Great damage or ruin. *The tornadoes caused a lot of* ***destruction*** *in our neighborhood*

de•tect•ed (di tek´tid) *verb.* Discovered or uncovered something. *The investigators* ***detected*** *a crime and called the police.*

de•test•ed (di tes´tid) *verb.* Hated; disliked intensely. *My dog* ***detested*** *thunder and other loud noise because they frightened him.*

di•ag•nose (dī´əg nōs´) *verb.* To make a ruling as to the nature of an illness. *The doctor can* ***diagnose*** *the patient's illness based on a description of the symptoms.*

dis•as•ters (di zas´tərz) *noun, plural.* Events that cause much suffering, distress, or loss. *Hurricanes are natural* ***disasters***.

dis•cus•sions (di skush´ənz) *noun, plural.* Acts of talking about something or exchanging opinions. *There were many* ***discussions*** *among the voters about the elections.*

dis•man•tled (dis man´təld) *verb.* Took something apart piece by piece. *The workers* ***dismantled*** *the outdoor stage after the concert.*

dis•miss (dis mis´) *verb.* To take away the job of, or fire. *The manager needed to* ***dismiss*** *one of his workers for doing a poor job.*

dis•tinct (di stingkt´) *adjective.* Separate, different from each other. *There were three* ***distinct*** *parts to the musical performance.*

di•verse (di vûrs´, dī vûrs´) *adjective.* Not all the same; varied. *People in my neighborhood come from* ***diverse*** *backgrounds.*

dor•mant (dôr´mənt) *adjective.* Temporarily quiet or not active. *Many tourists visited the* ***dormant*** *volcano because the chance of an eruption was low.*

Word History

Dormant comes from French *dormir,* "to sleep."

Ee

ease (ēz) *verb.* To move slowly or carefully. *I tried to* ***ease*** *the heavy clock off the table without dropping or scratching it.*

ed•u•cate (ej´ə kāt´) *verb.* To teach or train. *It is important to* ***educate*** *the students about dangers in the science lab so that no one gets hurt.*

eld•est (el´ dist) *adjective.* First-born; oldest. *The* ***eldest*** *of the three sisters is two years older than Mary, her next sister in age.*

e•lect•ed (i lek´tid) *verb.* Chosen by voting. *The class* ***elected*** *a representative to discuss the issue with the principal.*

el•e•gant (el´i gənt) *adjective.* Showing richness and good taste; showing grace and dignity. *The* ***elegant*** *dress was trimmed with gold lace.*

el•e•ment•ar•y (el´ə men´tə rē, el´ə men´trē) *adjective.* Dealing with the simple parts or beginnings of something. *We learned* ***elementary*** *facts about life cycles by observing how things change as they grow.*

el•e•ments (el´ə mənts) *noun, plural.* Basic parts from which something is made or formed. *A story should have these basic* ***elements***: *a beginning, middle, and end.*

e•lim•i•nates (i lim´ ə nāts) *verb.* Does away with; gets rid of. *Soap **eliminates** almost all stains and dirt.*

e•merged (i mûrjd´) *verb.* Came out of; appeared from. *When the facts **emerged**, we realized that she had been telling us the truth.*

en•list•ed (en lis´tid) *verb.* Voluntarily joined the military. *Nan's brother **enlisted** in the army after he graduated from high school.*

en•thu•si•asm (en thü´zē az´əm) *noun.* Eager and lively interest. *The audience expressed **enthusiasm** by applauding.*

en•vi•ron•ment (en vī´rən mənt, en vī´ərn mənt) *noun.* The air, water, and soil, and all the other things that surround a person, animal, or plant. *Living things need time to get used to changes in an **environment**.*

e•qual•i•ty (i kwol´i tē) *noun.* The quality or condition of being equal. *The Constitution of the United States provides for the **equality** of all Americans under the law.*

ex•ag•ger•at•ing (eg zaj´ə rā´ting) *verb.* Making something larger or greater than it really is. *Tall tales are always **exaggerating** the powers of their heroes.*

ex•hib•its (eg zib´its) *1. noun. 2. verb.* 1. A public showing. 2. To show or reveal. *1. Many museum **exhibits** are free to the public. 2. The zoo **exhibits** more than one kind of animal.*

ex•pe•di•tion (ek´spi dish´ən) *noun.* A journey with a specific purpose. *The members of the **expedition** had to go back down the mountain because the wind was too strong.*

Ff

fare (fâr) *noun.* The cost of a ride on a bus, train, airplane, ship, or taxi. *My mother paid my **fare** on the bus.*

fea•tures (fē´chərz) *noun, plural.* Parts of the face, such as the nose, or parts of other larger items that make them identifiable. *His **features** were brown eyes, a small nose, and large ears.*

flukes (flüks) *noun, plural.* Chance happenings; unexpected or accidental events, especially lucky ones. *Some discoveries were **flukes** and resulted when scientists were trying to find other things.*

fo•cused (fō´kəst) *verb.* Concentrated or directed attention on. *The basketball player was so **focused** on scoring that he didn't hear the fans roaring.*

for•bid•den (fər bid´ən, fôr bid´ən) *verb.* Ordered not to do something; not allowed. *The children were **forbidden** to play outside after dark.*

fore•cast•er (fôr´ kas tər) *noun.* One who studies and makes predictions about the weather. *The weather **forecaster** on TV predicted a heavy snowfall for the weekend.*

for•ma•tions (fôr mā´ shənz) *noun, plural.* Something shaped, created or formed. *The cloud **formations** looked like giant pillows and teddy bears.*

---

at; āpe; fär; câre; end; mē; it; īce; pîerce; hot; ōld; sông; fôrk; oil; out; up; ūse; rüle; pull; tûrn; chin; sing; shop; thin; <u>th</u>is; hw in white; zh in treasure.

The symbol ə stands for the unstressed vowel sound in about, taken, pencil, lemon, and circus.

found•ing (foun´ ding) *verb.* Establishing; bringing into being. *Everyone in school went to the founding of the new after-school club.*

frac•tures (frak´chərz) *noun, plural.* Cracks, splits, or breaks, as in a bone. *The boy's leg had multiple fractures after the fall.*

frig•id (frij´id) *adjective.* Very cold. *The frigid water was full of ice and snow.*

frus•trat•ed (frus´trā tid) *verb.* Kept from doing something. *Lita was frustrated in trying to light the candle because of the wind.*

func•tion (fungk´shən) *verb.* To work or act; to serve. *Mr. Martinez will function as the principal while Mrs. Arnold is out of town.*

fused (fūzd) *verb.* To blend or unite. *All the crayons in the box were fused together because they were left in the hot sun.*

Gg

gen•er•a•tions (jen´ə rā´ shənz) *noun, plural.* A group of people, especially within one family, born at about the same time. *My grandmother and I belong to two different generations.*

gey•sers (gī´ zərz) *noun, plural.* Natural hot springs from which steam bursts into the air. *Many tourists visit national parks to see the geysers, especially Old Faithful.*

gi•gan•tic (jī gan´tik) *adjective.* Like a giant; huge and powerful. *The airplane looked gigantic when I saw it up close.*

glimpse (glimps) *noun.* A brief look or a passing glance. *I caught a glimpse of the actor as he dashed into the car.*

globe (glōb) *noun.* A sphere that often represents Earth. *My teacher has a globe on his desk.*

gos•siped (gos´ipt) *verb.* Talked or spread rumors, often unfriendly, about matters related to another person. *Kayla gossiped to her friends about Beth because she was jealous of Beth's good grades.*

gov•er•nor (guv´ər nər) *noun.* The person elected to be the head of a state government in the United States, or of a territory. *The governor of my state will sign the new law.*

grav•i•ty (grav´i tē) *noun.* The force that pulls things toward the center of Earth, causing objects to have weight. *Because of gravity, a ball thrown in the air will fall back to the ground.*

guar•an•teed (gar´ən tēd´) *verb.* Made sure or certain. *The salesman guaranteed this was the lowest price for a mountain bike.*

Hh

hes•i•ta•tion (hez´i tā´shən) *noun.* A delay due to fear or doubt. *The talented dancers showed no hesitation on stage.*

ho•ri•zon (hə rī´zən) *noun.* The line where the sky and the earth or sea seem to meet. *We watched as the ship seemed to disappear over the horizon.*

hy•brids (hī´bridz) *noun, plural.* The offspring of two animals or plants of different varieties. *Pluots are hybrids that combine the qualities of plums and apricots.*

Word History

Hybrid comes from Latin *hybrida* or *ibrida*, meaning "mongrel."

Ii

i•den•ti•ty (ī den′ti tē) *noun.* Who or what a person or place is. *The man at the bank used his driver's license as proof of his **identity**.*

ig•nored (ig nôrd′) *verb.* Took no notice of; overlooked. *My mother **ignored** my cousin's rude behavior.*

im•pact (im′ pakt) *noun.* The force of one object hitting another. *The **impact** of the crash broke the windshield of the car.*

im•press (im pres′) *verb.* To have a strong effect on the mind or feelings. *The display of artwork will **impress** the audience.*

in•de•pen•dence (in′di pen′ dəns) *noun.* Freedom; liberty. *In 1776, Americans began a war for their **independence**.*

in•flate (in flāt′) *verb.* To cause to swell by filling with air or gas. *The air pump at the gas station will **inflate** the front tires.*

in•hi•bit (in hib′ it) *verb.* Hold back. *The cold weather will **inhibit** the flowering of the plants in my garden.*

in•ju•ry (in′jə rē) *noun.* Damage or harm done to a person or thing. *Luckily, Roberto's football **injury** was not serious.*

in•quire (in kwīr′) *verb.* To ask questions or seek information. *I will **inquire** at the diner about getting a job as a waitress.*

in•sight (in′ sīt) *noun.* The ability to see into or understand. *The expression on his face gave me an **insight** into what he really wanted to say.*

in•spect (in spekt′) *verb.* Examine closely and carefully. *The detective will **inspect** the crime scene for clues.*

in•still (in stil′) *verb.* To put in or introduce little by little. *Good teachers **instill** a love of learning in their students.*

in•struct (in strukt′) *verb.* To provide with knowledge, information, or skill; to teach. *The dance teacher will **instruct** the students in tap, ballet, and jazz.*

in•ten•tions (in ten′shənz) *noun, plural.* Plans to act in a certain way; purposes. *Franklin hated baseball, so his **intentions** for joining the team were unclear.*

in•ter•act (in′tə rakt′) *verb.* To act on or influence one another. *Band members walked into the audience so they could **interact** with fans.*

in•va•sion (in vā′zhən) *noun.* The entering of an army into a region to conquer it. *When planning an **invasion**, generals must know where the enemy troops are stationed.*

in•ves•ti•gat•ing (in ves′ti gā′ting) *verb.* Carefully, thoroughly examining or searching. *The scientist was **investigating** the crime scene to discover evidence.*

in•volved (in volvd′) *verb.* Included as a necessary part; absorbed. *The solution to the math problem **involved** addition and multiplication.*

ir•re•sist•i•ble (ir′i zis′tə bəl) *adjective.* Not capable of being resisted or opposed. *On a hot day, a cold drink is so tempting that it is **irresistible**.*

---

at; āpe; fär; câre; end; mē; it; īce; pîerce; hot; ōld; sông; fôrk; oil; out; up; ūse; rüle; pull; tûrn; chin; sing; shop; thin; <u>th</u>is; hw in white; zh in treasure.

The symbol ə stands for the unstressed vowel sound in about, taken, pencil, lemon, and circus.

Ll

la•bor (lā′bər) *1. noun. 2. verb.* 1. Hard work; toil. 2. To do hard work. *1. The construction workers were tired from the backbreaking* **labor** *they were hired to do. 2. Tired runners* **labor** *up the hill at the end of a race.*

launched (lôncht) *verb.* Sent off or started in motion. *The science club* **launched** *a rocket into the air.*

lo•ca•tion (lō kā′shən) *noun.* An exact position or place. *The airplane flew by several times before spotting the* **location** *of the lost hikers.*

lu•mi•nous (lü′mə nəs) *adjective.* Bright; shining. *The* **luminous** *glow coming from the windows made the house look warm.*

lung•ing (lun′jing) *verb.* Making a sudden forward movement. *The pitcher was* **lunging** *for the ball when the runner tagged the base.*

Mm

mam•mals (mam′əlz) *noun, plural.* Creatures that are warm-blooded and have a backbone. Female mammals produce milk to feed their young. *Human beings, cattle, bats, and whales are* **mammals***.*

maze (māz) *noun.* A confusing series of paths or passageways through which people may have a hard time finding their way. *There is a* **maze** *in town where people can find their way through tall stalks of corn.*

me•di•a (mē′dē ə) *noun, plural.* Means or forms of communication that reach a large audience; a plural of *medium. Television and newspapers are* **media** *that influence our daily life.*

mer•chan•dise (mûr′chən dīz′, mûr′chən dīs′) *noun.* Things for sale. *A shipment of new* **merchandise** *was delivered to the electronics store last night.*

me•te•or (mē′tē ər) *noun.* A mass of metal or rock that enters Earth's atmosphere from space. *It is rare for a* **meteor** *to strike Earth, but it can happen.*

mim•ic•ry (mi′mi krē) *noun.* The close outward resemblance of one kind of animal to another or to an object in its natural environment. *One type of fly uses* **mimicry** *to fool animals into thinking it is a wasp.*

mis•chie•vous (mis′chə vəs) *adjective.* Full of mischief, or conduct that is often playful but causes harm. *Cal likes to be* **mischievous** *by playing practical jokes.*

mis•sion (mish′ən) *noun.* A special job or task. *My mom sent me on a* **mission** *to find my sister's favorite stuffed bear.*

mis•sions (mish′ənz) *noun, plural.* Churches and their surrounding agricultural lands established by the Spanish in colonial California. *Native Americans lived and worked on Spanish* **missions***, where they also attended church.*

mourn•ful (môrn′fəl) *adjective.* Feeling, expressing, or filled with grief or sorrow. *The* **mournful** *song on the radio made the listeners feel sad.*

murk•y (mûr′kē) *adjective.* Dark or cloudy. *It was scary sitting in the rowboat because there was* **murky** *water all around us.*

Nn

nat•u•ral•ist (nach´ər ə list) *noun.* A person who specializes in the study of things in nature, especially plants and animals. *The **naturalist** spent a lot of time hiking and camping in the woods.*

nav•i•ga•tion (nav´i gā´shən) *noun.* The art or science of figuring out the position and course of boats, ships, and aircraft. *For proper **navigation**, pilots rely on equipment to direct them.*

nes•tled (nes´əld) *verb.* Located in a snug and sheltered spot. *Her desk was **nestled** between piles of books in the back corner of the warehouse.*

no•tion (nō´ shən) *noun.* Idea. *He had no **notion** how to organize the students for their field trip.*

Oo

o•be•di•ence (ō bē´ dē əns) *noun.* The act of carrying out orders for another. *The general expected complete **obedience** from the soldiers during the battle.*

ob•ser•va•tions (ob´zər vā´shənz) *noun, plural.* The act, practice, or power of seeing and noticing. *The detective's careful **observations** helped to solve the crime.*

ob•served (əb zûrvd´) *verb.* Saw; watched. *The boy **observed** the bee collecting pollen from several flowers.*

ob•serv•er (əb zûr´vər) *noun.* A person who watches carefully and with attention. *The nature photographer was a keen **observer** of flowers and insects.*

ob•vi•ous (ob´ vē əs) *adjective.* Easily seen or understood. *He was holding two cookies, so it was **obvious** that he had taken them from the cookie jar.*

or•al•ly (ôr´ə lē) *adverb.* Spoken aloud. *The coach recited the rules **orally** so each student could hear them.*

or•bit (ôr´bit) *noun.* The path of a heavenly body as it revolves in a closed curve around another heavenly body. *Earth makes a full **orbit** of the sun in one year.*

or•gan•isms (ôr´gə niz´əmz) *noun, plural.* Living things. Animals, plants, mushrooms, protozoans, and bacteria are all organisms. *The scientist studied **organisms** that live in ponds.*

o•rig•i•nal (ə rij´ə nəl) *adjective.* Made, done, thought of, or used for the first time. *All of the wood floors in the house are **original**.*

---

at; **ā**pe; **fär**; **câre**; **e**nd; **mē**; **i**t; **īce**; **pîerce**; **ho**t; **ōld**; **sông**; **fôrk**; **oil**; **out**; **up**; **ūse**; **rūle**; **pull**; **tûrn**; **chin**; **sing**; **shop**; **thin**; **this**; **hw** in **wh**ite; **zh** in trea**s**ure.

The symbol **ə** stands for the unstressed vowel sound in **a**bout, tak**e**n, penc**i**l, lem**o**n, and circ**u**s.

out•cast (out´kast´) *noun.* A person rejected by and driven out of a group. *Jason felt like an* **outcast** *when he was thrown off the debating team.*

Pp

par•ti•cles (pär´ti kəlz) *noun, plural.* Small bits or pieces of an element. *Tiny* **particles** *connect together to make up solid objects.*

pa•tri•ots (pā´trē əts) *noun, plural.* People who love and enthusiastically support their country. *American history views Ben Franklin and John Adams as true* **patriots.**

per•mis•sion (pər mish´ən) *noun.* Consent or agreement from someone in authority. *I had to get* **permission** *from my parents before leaving on the school trip.*

phys•i•cal (fiz´i kəl) *adjective.* Having to do with the body. *Doing* **physical** *activities will help you stay in shape.*

poll•ing (pō´ling) *adjective.* The casting and recording of votes in an election. *Voters go to a* **polling** *station to cast their votes.*

Word History

Poll comes from *pol*, meaning "head." To take a poll comes from the phrase "counting heads" of public opinion.

posed (pōzd) *verb.* To hold a particular position. *My parents* **posed** *us carefully for the family photo.*

post•pone (pōst pōn´) *verb.* To put off to a later time. *The officials decided to* **postpone** *the baseball game until tomorrow because of rain.*

pred•a•tors (pred´ə tərz) *noun, plural.* Animals that live by preying on, or hunting and eating, other animals. *Lions and wolves are natural* **predators** *who hunt smaller animals for food.*

pres•ence (prez´əns) *noun.* Something felt to be present in a specific place at a given time. *I could sense my mother's* **presence** *even before I saw her.*

pre•serve (pri zûrv´) *verb.* Protect, maintain. *The club will work to* **preserve** *the wildflower fields near the school.*

pre•vi•ous (prē´ vē əs) *adjective.* Earlier; coming before. *I was the pitcher in the* **previous** *game.*

prey (prā) *noun.* Any animal hunted or killed by another animal for food. *Nature films often show lions hunting their* **prey.**

pro•ceed•ed (prə sē´ dəd) *verb.* Continued; carried on. *The play* **proceeded** *in spite of the audience's chatter.*

pro•jects (proj´ ekts) *noun, plural.* Plans or activities. *The class displayed their science* **projects** *in their classroom.*

prop•er•ty (prop´ər tē) *noun.* A piece of land. *If you're thinking of building a house, the* **property** *next to my house is for sale.*

pur•chased (pûr´chəst) *verb.* Bought. *I* **purchased** *two books with my birthday money.*

pur•suit (pûr süt´) *noun.* Hobby or occupation. *My favorite* **pursuit** *is skiing.*

Qq

qual•i•fy (kwol′ə fī′) *verb.* To make fit, as for a certain job or task. *In order to **qualify** for the Olympics, you must be one of the best athletes in the country.*

Rr

ranch•o (rän′ chō) *noun.* A Spanish farm, which gives us the English word *ranch. A large farm in Spanish California was called a **rancho**.*

ra•vine (rə vēn′) *noun.* A deep, narrow valley, especially one worn by running water. *As you walk along the edge of the road, be careful not to fall into the **ravine**.*

re•bel•lion (ri bel′ yən) *noun.* Armed resistance to a government. *The Battle of Lexington is an example of the **rebellion** against British rule in North America.*

re•cover (ri kuv′ ər) *verb.* Get something back; return to health. *Divers helped to **recover** the treasure from the sunken ship.*

re•flect•ed (ri flek′təd) *verb.* Light, sound, images, or heat that is turned, thrown, or bent back at an angle. *The white tents **reflected** the heat from the hot sun onto the sand.*

re•fuge (ref′ ūj) *noun.* Shelter or place of safety. *Wild birds are protected in a nature **refuge**.*

re•luc•tant (ri luk′tənt) *adjective.* Unwilling or hesitant. *My friend wants to try the high dive, but I am **reluctant** to join him because I'm afraid.*

rep•re•sent•a•tive (rep′ri zen′tə tiv) *noun.* A person who is chosen to represent or stand for another or others. *A **representative** from each district was sent to City Hall to vote for the law.*

re•search (ri sûrch′, rē′sûrch′) *noun.* A careful study to find and learn facts about a subject. *Fawn had to do a lot of **research** at the library before she wrote her paper.*

res•er•va•tion (rez′ər vā′shən) *noun.* 1. Land set aside by a government for a special purpose, such as for Native American tribes to live on. 2. An arrangement to have something kept for another person or persons. 3. Something that causes doubt. *1. Native Americans preserved their culture and traditions on the **reservation** where they lived. 2. We asked the travel agent to make a plane **reservation** for us. 3. Her serious **reservation** about walking home after dark made sense to us.*

---

at; **ā**pe; **fär**; **câre**; **e**nd; **mē**; **i**t; **ī**ce; **pî**erce; **ho**t; **ō**ld; **sông**; **fôr**k; **oi**l; **ou**t; **u**p; **ū**se; **rü**le; **pu̇**ll; **tûr**n; **ch**in; **sing**; **sh**op; **th**in; **th**is; **hw** in **wh**ite; **zh** in trea**s**ure.

The symbol **ə** stands for the unstressed vowel sound in **a**bout, tak**e**n, penc**i**l, lem**o**n, and circ**u**s.

re•veal (ri vēl′) *verb.* Uncover or make known. *The police will **reveal** the name of the suspect after they have arrested him.*

re•versed (ri vûrst′) *verb.* Moved in the opposite direction from what is usual. *We **reversed** our direction when we realized we were going the wrong way.*

rig•id (rij′id) *adjective.* Not changing; fixed. *Our **rigid** schedule did not allow us to make an unplanned stop at the new park.*

ro•bot (rō′bət, rō′bot) *noun.* A machine designed to perform certain human tasks. *The **robot** did a job that was too dangerous for humans to do.*

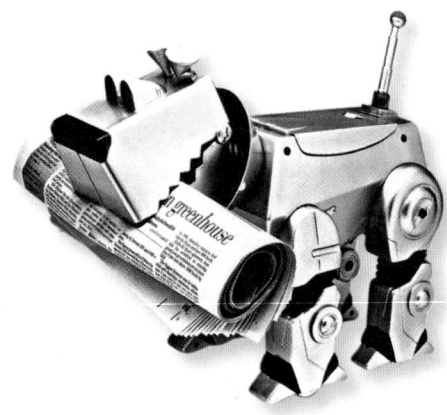

ro•de•o (rō′dē ō′) *noun.* A contest exhibiting cowboy skills. *Calf roping and bronco riding were performed at the **rodeo**.*

ro•tat•ed (rō′tā tid) *verb.* Turned around on an axis. *As the wheels **rotated**, the car moved forward.*

Ss

sat•el•lites (sat′ə līts′) *noun, plural.* Artificial objects placed in orbit around another body in space, such as Earth or the moon. *New weather **satellites** track storms forming all around Earth.*

sat•is•fac•to•ry (sat′is fak′tə rē) *adjective.* Good enough to meet a need or desire. *The work done on the house was **satisfactory**, so the owners could move in.*

saun•tered (sôn′ tərd) *verb.* Strolled. *The happy children **sauntered** along the tree-lined path.*

scald (skôld) *verb.* To burn with hot liquid or steam. *The chef was very careful when pouring out the boiling water, so she would not **scald** herself.*

scen•er•y (sē′nə rē) *noun.* The sights of a place or region. *We admired the beautiful **scenery** while we rode through the mountain range on the train.*

sci•en•tif•ic (sī′ən tif′ik) *adjective.* Having to do with or used in science. *The **scientific** discovery of gravity changed the way people thought about Earth.*

scoured (skourd) *verb.* Cleaned, cleared, or worn away. *We **scoured** the pan with cleanser until it shone.*

se•clud•ed (si klü′did) *adjective.* Shut off from view. *We found a quiet, **secluded** area in the park for our picnic.*

seek (sēk) *verb.* To search for. *Every afternoon, our cats **seek** a sunny spot to nap.*

seg•re•ga•tion (seg′ri gā′shən) *noun.* The practice of separating one racial group, especially African Americans, from the rest of society by making them use different schools and social facilities or making them live in certain areas. ***Segregation** forced African American children to attend schools with poor facilities.*

set•tlers (set′ lərz) *noun, plural.* People who come to live in a new country or territory. *The **settlers** established a small farming town in their new colony.*

shield (shēld) *noun.* A person or thing that protects against danger, injury, or distress. *I used a magazine as a **shield** against the bright sunlight because I forgot my sunglasses.*

short•age (shôr´tij) *noun.* A small amount or lack of supply. *The storm destroyed many farms, so there was a **shortage** of watermelon.*

shrieks (shrēks) *verb.* Makes loud, shrill cries or sounds. *My little sister **shrieks** when I tickle her.*

site (sīt) *noun.* Location. *That post marks the **site** of the farmer's new well.*

slumped (slumpt) *verb.* Sunk or fell heavily. *The tired woman **slumped** down in the back seat.*

sog•gy (sog´ē) *adjective.* Very wet or damp; soaked. *The juicy tomatoes on the sandwich made the bread **soggy**.*

source (sôrs) *noun.* Point of origin for a river or stream. *The **source** of the Amazon is in the Andes.*

spe•cies (spē´shēz) *noun.* A group of animals or plants that have many characteristics in common. *German shepherds belong to one **species**, and wolves belong to another.*

spec•i•mens (spes´ə mənz) *noun, plural.* Items or parts typical of a group. *The scientist collected **specimens** of some germs that could make people sick.*

spec•tac•u•lar (spek tak´yə lər) *adjective.* Very impressive or unusual. *We watched the **spectacular** fireworks display from our backyard.*

sprawled (sprôld) *verb.* Lay or sat with the body stretched out in an awkward or careless manner. *My brother was so tired from swimming that he **sprawled** out on the blanket and left no room for anyone else.*

stag•gered (sta´gərd) *verb.* Moved unsteadily or with a swaying motion. *The tired runners **staggered** to the finish line.*

stark (stärk) *adjective.* Bare. *All of the trees had been cut down so the landscape appeared **stark**.*

strands (strandz) *noun, plural.* Things similar to threads. ***Strands** of spaghetti were wrapped around the fork.*

strat•e•gy (strat´i jē) *noun.* A careful plan for achieving a goal. *Our coach used a new **strategy** that confused the best team in the league.*

stunned (stund) *verb.* Shocked or overwhelmed. *Everyone was **stunned** when I won the essay contest, because I usually needed help with my writing assignments.*

sub•mit (səb mit´) *verb.* 1. To give up; to give in to someone's power. 2. To present. *1. Soldiers may **submit** to the enemy if they are too weak to fight. 2. My teacher asked us to **submit** our reports on Friday.*

at; āpe; fär; câre; end; mē; it; īce; pîerce; hot; ōld; sông; fôrk; oil; out; up; ūse; rüle; pull; tûrn; chin; sing; shop; thin; this; hw in white; zh in treasure.

The symbol ə stands for the unstressed vowel sound in about, taken, pencil, lemon, and circus.

suf•frage (suf′rij) *noun.* The right or privilege of voting. *The women who marched at the rally in Washington, D.C., were fighting for* **suffrage**.

su•per•hu•man (sū′pər hū′ mən) *adjective.* Beyond ordinary human power. *The athlete seemed to have* **superhuman** *strength and skill.*

su•per•vise (sū′pər vīz′) *verb.* To watch over and direct. *It was a huge responsibility to* **supervise** *all the children swimming in the pool.*

supp•lies (sə plīz′) *noun, plural.* Necessary items for ordinary life. *Early settlers brought* **supplies** *such as flour, tools, and seed for crops.*

sur•fing (sûr′ fing) *noun.* A sport in which people ride boards atop ocean waves. *You must be a good swimmer if you plan to take up* **surfing**.

surge (sûrj) *1. verb. 2. noun.* 1. To swell and move with force like a wave. 2. A sudden increase or rise. *1. The waves* **surge** *and toss the ship. 2. There was a* **surge** *in the price of food.*

sur•round•ings (sə roun′ dingz) *noun, plural.* The objects and conditions of a place. *He liked the comfortable* **surroundings** *of his mountain cabin.*

sur•vive (sər vīv′) *verb.* To live and be active through and after an event. *One must know how to find food and shelter to* **survive** *in the woods.*

sur•vived (sər vīvd′) *verb.* Lived longer, or lived through an event. *The people of the city* **survived** *the earthquake and began to rebuild.*

sus•pend•ed (sə spen′dəd) *verb.* Held in place as if attached from above. *The spider was* **suspended** *from the roof by a strand of web.*

swell (swel) *noun.* A tall, unbroken wave. *The little boat was carried along by the ocean's* **swell**.

swerved (swûrvd) *verb.* Turned aside suddenly. *The car* **swerved** *to miss the dog crossing the road.*

sym•pa•thy (sim′pə thē) *noun.* The ability to share the feelings of another or others. *I felt great* **sympathy** *for Jim because I knew what it felt like to have my feelings hurt.*

Tt

tasks (tasks) *noun, plural.* Jobs; chores. *In a fairy tale, the main character often has to complete three* **tasks**.

tel•e•scope (tel′ə skōp′) *noun.* An instrument for making distant objects, such as stars, appear nearer and larger. *Brad used a* **telescope** *to see the craters on the moon.*

ter•ri•tor•y (ter′ i tôr′ē) *noun.* A large area of land without any specific borders. *The Oregon* **Territory** *was made into two American states.*

to•kens (tō′kənz) *noun, plural.* 1. Pieces that mark movement on a board game. 2. Pieces of metal, like coins, used as substitutes for money. *1. Andrea moved her* **tokens** *six spaces ahead and won the game. 2. We put* **tokens** *in the machine to play video games at the mall.*

tra•di•tion•al (trə dish´ən əl) *adjective.* Coming from the knowledge, beliefs, or customs that one generation passes to another. *Our **traditional** Thanksgiving includes eating turkey and watching television.*

traits (trāts) *noun, plural.* Aspects, qualities, or characteristics that a person or thing possesses. *Bravery and honesty are **traits** a person can display.*

trans•ferred (trans´fûrd) *verb.* Moved from place to place. *I **transferred** my school books from my desk to my backpack.*

trans•forms (trans fôrmz´) *verb.* Changes; alters. *Baking **transforms** wheat dough into a loaf of bread.*

trans•mis•sion (trans mish´ən) *noun.* A radio or television broadcast. *Satellites in space can send a television **transmission** anywhere in the world.*

treach•er•ous (trech´ə rəs) *adjective.* Full of danger. *The sharp curves on the **treacherous** road caused many traffic accidents.*

treas•ur•er (tre´zhə rər) *noun.* The person in charge of the money of a business or a group. *The **treasurer** became nervous when he realized money was missing from the company bank account.*

tri•umph (trī´umf) *verb.* To be successful or win. *Everyone is confident that we will **triumph** over the problems we are having due to the weather.*

ty•rant (tī´rənt) *noun.* A person who uses power or authority in a cruel or unjust way. *The king was a **tyrant** because he punished his subjects unfairly.*

Word History

The word **tyrant** comes from Old French *tiran*, which means "despot." The Old French word came from the Latin word *tyrannus*, which means "ruler or despot." *Tyrant* can also be traced to the Greek word *tyrannos*, which means "absolute ruler."

Uu

un•con•sti•tu•tion•al (un´kon sti tü´shə nəl) *adjective.* Not in keeping with the constitution of a country, state, or group, especially the Constitution of the United States. *The Supreme Court in this country decides if a law is **unconstitutional**.*

un•for•tu•nate (un fôr´chə nit) *adjective.* Unlucky. *It was **unfortunate** that it rained on the day we had tickets to the outdoor concert.*

un•in•hab•it•ed (un´in hab´i tid) *adjective.* Not lived in. *The **uninhabited** house had broken windows and a leaky roof.*

un•pleas•ant (un plez´ənt) *adjective.* Not nice; disagreeable. *The newly painted room had an **unpleasant** odor.*

---

at; āpe; fär; câre; end; mē; it; īce; pîerce; hot; ōld; sông; fôrk; oil; out; up; ūse; rüle; pull; tûrn; chin; sing; shop; thin; this; hw in white; zh in treasure.

The symbol ə stands for the unstressed vowel sound in about, taken, pencil, lemon, and circus.

un•rea•son•a•ble (un rē′zə nə bəl) *adjective.* Not showing or using good sense or judgment. *The teacher was being* **unreasonable** *when he punished the whole class for the bad behavior of one student.*

ur•gen•cy (ûr′ jən sē) *noun.* Immediate; of pressing importance. *The gathering storm gave* **urgency** *to people seeking shelter.*

Vv

va•cant (vā′ kənt) *adjective.* Not having anyone or anything in it; empty. *If that seat is* **vacant**, *you can sit in it.*

va•que•ros (vä kâr′ ōz) *noun, plural.* Spanish cowboys. **Vaqueros** *herded cows on the early ranches of Spanish California.*

vast•ness (vast′nis) *noun.* Greatness in size, extent, or number. *The* **vastness** *of the desert made it seem to stretch for miles.*

ven•tured (ven′chərd) *verb.* Went despite risk or danger. *Lucy* **ventured** *out into the storm to look for her dog.*

ver•sions (vûr′zhənz) *noun, plural.* Different or changed forms of an original. *I wrote many* **versions** *of the story before I completed the final draft.*

vet•er•i•nar•i•an (vet′ər ə nâr′ē ən, vet′rə nâr′ē ən) *noun.* A person trained and licensed to give medical or surgical treatment to animals. *I took my dog to the* **veterinarian** *for a checkup.*

vi•brates (vī′brāts) *verb.* Moves back and forth or up and down very fast. *The cell phone* **vibrates** *instead of making a loud ring when someone calls.*

vi•o•lent (vī′ə lənt) *adjective.* Destructive. *A* **violent** *storm destroyed houses and blew down many trees.*

vol•ume (vol′ūm, vol′yəm) *noun.* The amount of space occupied. *Find the* **volume** *of a building block by multiplying its height by its length by its width.*

Ww

wares (wârz) *noun, plural.* Things for sale. *My mother inspects the quality of the* **wares** *at the market before buying anything.*

wheel•chair (hwēl′châr′, wēl′châr′) *noun.* A chair on wheels that is used by someone who cannot walk to get from one place to another. *My grandmother needed to use a* **wheelchair** *after she fell and broke her hip.*

wring (ring) *verb.* To squeeze or twist; to get by force. *I had to* **wring** *out my swimsuit before hanging it in the laundry room.*

Zz

zone (zōn) *noun.* A region or area that has some special quality, condition, or use. *There is a "No Parking"* **zone** *on this street.*

Acknowledgments

The publisher gratefully acknowledges permission to reprint the following copyrighted material:

"Black Cowboy Wild Horses" by Julius Lester, illustrations by Jerry Pinkney. Text copyright © 1998 by Julius Lester. Illustrations copyright © 1998 by Jerry Pinkney. Reprinted by permission of Dial Books, a member of Penguin Putnam Inc.

"Blancaflor" from Tales Our Abuelitas Told: A Hispanic Folktale Collection by F. Isabel Campoy and Alma Flor Ada. Text copyright © by Alma Flor Ada and Isabel F. Campoy. Reprinted by permission of Atheneum Books for Young Readers, an imprint of Simon & Schuster Children's Publishing Division.

"The Bottom of the World" is from ANTARCTIC JOURNAL: FOUR MONTHS AT THE BOTTOM OF THE WORLD by Jennifer Owings Dewey. Copyright © 2001 by Jennifer Owings Dewey. Reprinted by permission of HarperCollins Publishers.

"Carlos and the Skunk" by Jan Romero Stevens, illustrations by Jeanne Arnold. Text copyright © 1997 by Jan Romero Stevens. Illustrations copyright © 1997 by Jeanne Arnold. Reprinted by permission of Rising Moon, Books for Young Readers from Northland Publishing.

"Davy Crockett Saves the World" by Rosalyn Schanzer. Copyright © 2001 by Rosalyn Schanzer. Reprinted by permission of HarperCollins Publishers.

"The Flight of Icarus" by Alice Low is from THE MACMILLAN BOOK OF GREEK GODS AND HEROES. Copyright © 1985 by Macmillan Publishing Company, a division of Macmillan, Inc. Reprinted by permission of the publisher.

"Goin' Someplace Special" by Patricia C. McKissack, illustrations by Jerry Pinkney. Text copyright © 2001 by Patricia C. McKissack. Illustrations copyright © 2001 by Jerry Pinkney. Reprinted by permission of Atheneum Books for Young Readers, an imprint of Simon & Schuster Children's Publishing Division.

"The Golden Mare, the Firebird, and the Magic Ring" by Ruth Sanderson. Copyright © 2001 by Ruth Sanderson. Reprinted by permission of Little, Brown and Company.

"The Gri Gri Tree" is from THE COLOR OF MY WORDS by Lynn Joseph. Copyright © 2000 by Lynn Joseph. Reprinted by permission of HarperCollins Children's Books, a division of HarperCollins Publishers.

"Hidden Worlds: Looking Through a Scientist's Microscope" is from HIDDEN WORLDS: LOOKING THROUGH A SCIENTIST'S MICROSCOPE by Stephen Kramer. Copyright © 2001 by Stephen Kramer. Reprinted by permission of Houghton Mifflin Company.

"Home on the Range" is from I HEAR AMERICA SINGING, FOLK SONGS FOR AMERICAN FAMILIES collected and arranged by Kathleen Krull. Copyright © 1992 by Kathleen Krull. Reprinted by permission of Alfred A. Knopf, an imprint of Random House Children Books.

"Hurricanes" is from HURRICANES by Seymour Simon. Copyright © 2003 by Seymour Simon. Reprinted by permission of HarperCollins Publishers.

"Miss Alaineus" by Debra Frasier. Copyright © 2000 by Debra Frasier. Reprinted by permission of Harcourt, Inc.

"The Night of San Juan" is from SALSA STORIES by Lulu Delacre. Copyright © 2000 by Lulu Delacre. Reprinted by permission of Scholastic Press, a division of Scholastic, Inc.

"Paul Revere's Ride" by Henry Wadsworth Longfellow is from OUR NATION. Copyright © 2003 by Macmillan/McGraw-Hill.

"Rattlers!" by Ellen Lambeth (sidebar by John Cancalosi) is from RANGER RICK. Copyright © 1998 by the National Wildlife Federation. Reprinted by permission of the National Wildlife Federation.

"Shiloh" is from SHILOH by Phyllis Reynolds Naylor. Copyright © 2000 by Phyllis Reynolds Naylor. Reprinted by permission of Aladdin Paperbacks, an imprint of Simon & Schuster Children's Publishing Division.

"Skunk Scout" is from SKUNK SCOUT by Laurence Yep. Copyright © 2003 by Laurence Yep. Reprinted by permission of Hyperion Books for Children.

"Sleds on Boston Common" by Louise Borden, illustrations by Robert Andrew Parker. Text copyright © 2000 by Louise Borden. Illustrations copyright © 2000 by Robert Andrew Parker. Reprinted by permission of Margaret K. McElderry Books, an imprint of Simon & Schuster Children's Publishing Division.

"Spirit of Endurance" by Jennifer Armstrong, illustrations by William Maughan. Text copyright © 2000 by Jennifer Armstrong. Illustrations copyright © 2000 by William Maughan. Reprinted by Crown Publishing, a division of Random House Inc.

"Suffrage for Women" is from OUR NATION. Copyright © 2003 by Macmillan/McGraw-Hill.

"Suspense" is from THE BIG SKY by Pat Mora. Copyright © 1998 by Pat Mora. Reprinted by permission of Scholastic Press, a division of Scholastic, Inc.

"Termites" from "INSECTLOPEDIA: POEMS AND PAINTINGS" by Douglas Florian. Copyright © 1998 by Douglas Florian. Reprinted by permission of Harcourt Brace & Company.

"Through My Eyes" is from THROUGH MY EYES by Ruby Bridges. Copyright © 1999 by Ruby Bridges. Reprinted by permission of Scholastic Press, a division of Scholastic, Inc.

"Ultimate Field Trip 5: Blasting Off to Space Academy" is from ULTIMATE FIELD TRIP 5: BLASTING OFF TO SPACE ACADEMY by Susan E. Goodman. Text copyright © 2001 by Susan E. Goodman. Illustrations copyright © 2001 by Michael J. Doolittle. U.S. Space Camp and U.S. Space Academy are registered trademarks of the U.S. Space Rocket Center. Reprinted by permission of Atheneum Books for Young Readers, an imprint of Simon & Schuster Children's Publishing Division.

"The Unbreakable Code" by Sara Hoagland Hunter, illustrations by Julia Miner. Text copyright © 1996 by Sara Hoagland Hunter. Illustrations copyright © 1996 by Julia Miner. Reprinted by permission of Rising Moon Books for Young Readers from Northland Publishing.

"Valley of the Moon: the Diary of María Rosalia de Milagros" by Sherry Garland. Copyright © 2001 by Sherry Garland. Reprinted by permisson of Scholastic Inc.

"Weslandia" by Paul Fleischman, illustrations by Kevin Hawkes. Text copyright © 1999 by Paul Fleischman. Illustrations copyright © 1999 by Kevin Hawkes. Reprinted by permission of Candlewick Press.

"When Esther Morris Headed West" by Connie Nordhielm Wooldridge, illustrations by Jacqueline Rogers. Text copyright © 2001 by Connie Nordhielm Wooldridge. Illustrations copyright © 2001 by Jacqueline Rogers. Reprinted by permission of Holiday House.

"Zathura" by Chris Van Allsburg. Copyright © 2002 by Chris Van Allsburg. Reprinted by permission of Houghton Mifflin Company.

ILLUSTRATIONS
Cover Illustration: Dan Craig

8: Rick Powell. 10-27: Jerry Pinkney. 38-39: Joel Spector. 41: Joel Spector. 43: Joel Spector. 45: Joel Spector. 47: Joel Spector. 49: Joel Spector. 51-53: Joel Spector. 76-89: Edel Rodriguez. 92: Karen Minot. 99: John Hovell. 101-104: Robert Andrew Parker. 107: Robert Andrew Parker. 109: Robert Andrew Parker. 111: Robert Andrew Parker. 113-119: Robert Andrew Parker. 120-123: Greg Newbold. 123: (t) John Burgoyne. 126-127: Guy Porfirio. 138-139: Deborah Chabrian. 140-141: Kristina Rodanas. 143: Kristina Rodanas. 145: Kristina Rodanas. 147: Kristina Rodanas. 149: Kristina Rodanas. 151: Kristina Rodanas. 152-153: Kristina Rodanas. 155: Kristina Rodanas. 166: David Bowers. 178-195: Jerry Pinkney. 197: Jerry Pinkney. 198-199: Jeff Slemons. 204-205: Jeff Crosby. 206-209: Rosalyn Schanzer. 210-225: Rosalyn Schanzer. 227: Owen Smith. 229: Owen Smith. 236-249: Jacqueline Rogers. 256-257: Joel Spector. 258: W.A. Sharman. 338-339: Diane Greenseid. 340-359: Valerie Sokolova. 391: Mike DiGiorgio. 392-393: Debby Fisher. 406-407: William Maughan. 414: (b) James E. Ransome. 414: (b) William Maughan. 416-417: William Maughan. 419-420: William Maughan. 421: Kailey LeFaiver. 422-423: William Maughan. 446: Courtesy Susan E. Goodman. 448-451: Linda Wingerter. 504-511: Winson Trang. 513-514: Winson Trang. 517: Winson Trang. 519-523: Winson Trang. 525: Joe LeMonnier. 527: John Hovell. 530-531: Ed Gazsi. 541: James Gritz/Getty Images, Inc. 558-559: Doug Martin. 570: Richard Orr. 580-581: Mercedes McDonald. 613: Sharon and Joel Harris. 618-619: Tom Foty. 640-641: Susan Swan. 644-645: Barbara Spurll. 658-679: Debra Frasier. 688-689: Joe LeMonnier. 690-691: Jeanne Arnold. 693: Jeanne Arnold. 718-721: Courtesy of Boundless Playgrounds. 728-729: John Parra. 730-745: Kevin Hawkes. 746-747: Argosy. 752: Donna Perrone. 754-759: Marla Baggetta. 761: Marla Baggetta. 763-764: Marla Baggetta. 767: Marla Baggetta. 769-770: Marla Baggetta. 772-773: Marla Baggetta. 780-781: Guy Porfirio.

PHOTOGRAPHY

All photographs are by Macmillan/McGraw-Hill (MMH) or Ken Karp for MMH except as noted below:

Inside front and back cover: Digital Vision/PunchStock. v: Izzy Schwartz/Getty Images. vi: (bl) Flip Nicklin/Minden Pictures. ix: Richard Hutchings/PhotoEdit. x: (bl) Michael J. Doolittle/The Image Works; (bl) (background) NASA. xi: Michael Newman/PhotoEdit. xii: (cl) Dennis Kunkel Microscopy, Inc.; (bl) Tom McHugh/Photo Researchers. xiii: (tl) Ryan McVay/Getty Images; (cl) Karlheinz Oster/zefa/Corbis; (bl) NASA Johnson Space Center. xv: AP Photo/Petros Karadjias. 2-3: Jason Laurel/The Image Works. 3, 4: David Young-Wolff/PhotoEdit. 5: Courtesy The Bancroft Library, University of California, Berkeley. 6-7: Bettmann/CORBIS. 26: (tl) Courtesy Simon & Schuster; (r) Alan S. Orling. 28: (frame) C Squared Studios/Getty Images; (b) Reproduced by permission of the Norman Rockwell Family Agency, Inc.; Collection of the Norman Rockwell Museum at Stockbridge, Massachusetts. 29, 30: AP Photo. 31: AP Photo/Steven Senne. 33: Amos Morgan/Photodisc/Getty Images. 34-35: Jeff Greenberg/AGE footstock. 36-37: C.W. SCHWARTZ/Animals Animals - Earth Scenes. 37: Eric and David Hosking/CORBIS. 52: Courtesy Simon & Schuster. 54: Frank Lukasseck/Corbis. 54-55: Jack Hollingsworth/Photos.com. 55: Courtesy RaeAnn Meyer/Struve Labs. 56: Joe Munroe/Getty Images. 56-57: Jack Hollingsworth/Photos.com. 59: Tom Le Goff/Digital Vision/Getty Images. 60-61: Izzy Schwartz/Getty Images. 62: (t) AP Photo; (bl) AP Photo/Tom Uhlman. 63: (tl) Joel Rennich/UPI Photo Service/Newscom; (t to b) McDaniel Woolf/Getty Images; Jack Hollingsworth/Corbis; PictureNet/Corbis; Creatas/PunchStock; Adalberto Rios Szalay/Sexto Sol/Getty Images. 64: AP Photo/Gregory Bull. 65: (tl) AP Photo/Dennis Cook; (br) AP Photo/J. Scott Applewhite. 66: AP Photo/Dave Martin. 67: AP Photo/Jay Sailors. 68: AP Photo/Nick Ut. 71: (l) PhotoLink/Getty Images; (c) John Clines/Shutterstock; (r) Stockdisc/PunchStock; (br) Pixtal/PunchStock. 72-73: Michael Pole/CORBIS. 74-75: Theo Allofs/CORBIS. 88: Courtesy Scholastic, Inc. 90: David Fleetham/Alamy. 91: Joe Carini/Pacific Stock. 92-93: Les Walker/NewSport/Corbis. 95: Richard Hutchings/PhotoEdit. 96-97: Art Resource, NY. 98: (frame) C Squared Studios/Getty Images; (tr) Courtesy The Rhode Island Historical Society. 100-101: Kevin Flemming/CORBIS. 118: (tl, r) Courtesy Simon & Schuster. 119: Kevin Fleming/CORBIS. 125: Dynamic Graphics Group/IT Stock Free/Alamy. 128: Classic PIO/Fotosearch. 129: H. Armstrong Roberts/Robertstock. 132-133: Bruno Perousse/AGE footstock. 133: The Art Archive/Bill Manns. 134: Bettmann/CORBIS. 135: Courtesy Oakland Public Library. 136-137: California Historical Society Collection at the University of Southern California. 154: (tl) Courtesy Sherry Garland; (r) Courtesy Kristina Rodanas. 156, 157: Bettmann/CORBIS. 158-159: Library of Congress, Prints & Photographs Division, [LC-USZC4-2634]. 159: (l to r) Library of Congress, Prints & Photographs Division, [LC-USZ62-20214]; Library of Congress, Prints & Photographs Division, [LC-USZ62-10609]; Digital Archive Japan/Alamy; Larry Brownstein/Getty Images; Library of Congress Prints and Photographs Division [LC-USZC4-2915]. 161: Royalty-Free/CORBIS. 162-163: Flip Nicklin/Minden Pictures. 164: Mark A. Philbrick/Brigham Young University. 165: (tl) Joe Andrews; (br) AP Photo/Matthew Cavanaugh. 167: (tr) National Park Service, Independence National Historical Park Archives. Accession #13.161, Peale, Charles Wilson, 1741-1827, painter; (bl) National Park Service, Independence National Historical Park Archives. Accession #13.048, Peale, Charles Wilson, 1741-1827, painter. 168: (tr) Jeremy Woodhouse/Masterfile; (bl) Clark Family Collection, William Clark Papers, Missouri Historical Society, St. Louis. Photographic copy by David Schultz, 1997; NS 21278, © 1997. 169: Jose Azel/Aurora Photos. 170: Mark Karrass/Corbis. 173: (l) PhotoLink/Getty Images; (c) John Clines/Shutterstock; (r) Stockdisc/PunchStock; (br) Ryan McVay/Getty Images. 174-175: Trout Photo, Jess Stahl on Glass Eye, [California] Rodeo, Salinas, 1910 ca., Photographic postcard, 2005.047.8, Photographic Study Collection, National Cowboy & Western Heritage Museum, Oklahoma City, OK. 176-177: Lake County Museum/CORBIS. 177: West Texas room tiles depicting a Cowboy on a Horse (ceramic), Mexican School, (20th century)/Dallas Historical Society, Texas, USA/The Bridgeman Art Library. 196: (tl) Courtesy Julius Lester; (r) Courtesy Simon & Schuster. 201: Richard Hutchings/PhotoEdit. 202-203: Visions of America, LLC/Alamy. 204-205: (frame) C Squared Studios/Getty Images. 224: Courtesy Rosalyn Schanzer. 231: Scott T. Baxter/Photodisc/Getty Images. 232-233: Underwood & Underwood/CORBIS. 234-235: Jeff Hunter/Getty Images. 235: Jeff Greenberg/The Image Works. 235: (tl) Courtesy Terri Jepson; (r) Courtesy Holiday House. 250: (tr) Wisconsin Historical Society; (r, bl) Museum of London/HIP/The Image Works. 251, 252: Bettmann/CORBIS. 253: (t) Bettmann/CORBIS; (inset) Museum of London/Topham-HIP/The Image Works. 255: BananaStock/PictureQuest. 259: W.A. Sharman; Milepost 92 1/2/CORBIS. 262-263: Digital Vision/PunchStock. 263: Stefano Bianchetti/Corbis. 264: Ariel Skelley/CORBIS. 265: Library of Congress, Prints & Photographs Division, [LC-DIG-ggbain-30388]. 266-267: Tim Davis/CORBIS. 288: (tl) Courtesy Angela Shelf Medearis; (cr) Antiochiana Collection, Antioch College. 293: Mediomimages/Alamy. 294-295: Roger-Viollet/The Image Works. 316: Morgan Robinson. 323: Digital Vision Ltd./Getty Images. 335: (cl) Tracy Montana/PhotoLink/Getty Images; (c) John Clines/Shutterstock; (r) PhotoLink/Getty Images; (bl) Stockbyte/PunchStock. 336-337: Charles O. Cecil/Alamy. 358: (tr) Courtesy Alma Flor Ada; (l) Alexander Osipovitch. 360: (frame) C Squared Studios/Getty Images; (bl) Courtesy of University of Southern California, on behalf of the USC Special Collections. 360-361: General Research Division, The New York Public Library, Astor, Lenox and Tilden Foundations. 362: The Art Archive/Bill Manns. 365: Bob Daemmrich/The Image Works. 366-367: CORBIS. 368-369: J. Speer/Tama News-Herald. 386: (l, r) Courtesy Northland Publishing. 388: OFFICIAL U.S. MARINE CORPS PHOTO, USMC/National Archives. 388-389: (border) Christie's Images/CORBIS. 389: Saunder, DEFENSE DEPT. PHOTO (MARINE CORPS)/National Archives. 391: Ryan McVay/Photodisc/Getty Images. 394-395: Stock Montage/Getty Images. 395: (tl) Schenectady Museum; Hall of Electrical History Foundation/CORBIS; (t to b) Time & Life Pictures/Getty Images; Michael Freeman/CORBIS; Bettmann/CORBIS; Schenectady Museum; Hall of Electrical History Foundation/CORBIS; Bettmann/CORBIS; Schenectady Museum; Hall of Electrical History Foundation/CORBIS; Yevgeny Khaldei/CORBIS. 398-399: Mauro Fermariello/Photo Researchers, Inc. 399: David Young-Wolff/PhotoEdit. 400: C Squared Studios/Getty Images. 401: Courtesy Peter Stekel/www.peterstekel.com. 402-403: tom Kidd/Alamy. 404-405: Image Plan/Corbis. 405: Digital Vision/PictureQuest. 408-410: Royal Geographic Society. 412-413: Scott Polar Research Institute. 421: Royal Geographic Society. 422: (tr) Emma Dodge Hanson; (bl) Courtesy William Maughan. 424-427: Digital Vision/PunchStock. 429: Jim Arbogast/Photodisc/Getty Images. 431: Images/Alamy. 432-433: (t) Ian McKinnell/Getty Images; (b) Digital Vision/Getty Images. 434: Michael J. Doolittle/The Image Works. 434-435: StockTrek/Getty Images. 435: Bettmann/CORBIS. 436: Michael J. Doolittle/The Image Works. 436-437: StockTrek/Getty Images. 437, 438: Michael J. Doolittle/The Image Works. 438-439: StockTrek/Getty Images. 439, 440: Michael J. Doolittle/The Image Works. 440-441: StockTrek/Getty Images. 441: Michael J. Doolittle/The Image Works. 442: (l) Michael J. Doolittle/The Image Works; (r) CORBIS SYGMA/CORBIS. 442-443: StockTrek/Getty Images. 443, 444: Michael J. Doolittle/The Image Works. 444-445: StockTrek/Getty Images. 445: (t) Michael J. Doolittle/The Image Works; (br) AP Photo/NASA. 446: (tr) Courtesy Susan E. Goodman; (chair) Michael J. Doolittle/The Image Works. 446-447: StockTrek/Getty Images. 452: (sky) StockTrek/Getty Images; (moon) Bettmann/CORBIS; (girl) Michael J. Doolittle/The Image Works. 453: Richard Hutchings/PhotoEdit. 466-467: Erin Patrice O'Brien/Getty Images. 492: Courtesy Constance Brown. 494: (t) Royalty-Free/CORBIS; (r) Frank Zullo/Photo Researchers, Inc. 495: (tr) The Granger Collection, New York; (bl) Thinkstock/PunchStock. 496: Royalty-Free/CORBIS. 497: The Granger Collection, New York. 499: Dynamic Graphics Group/IT Stock Free/Alamy. 500-501: Thinkstock/PunchStock. 502, 503: Martin Fox/Index Stock Imagery. 522: (tl) Joanne Ryder; (br) Courtesy Winson Trang. 524-525: Masterfile/Masterfile. 526: Sharon Collyer, Courtesy Daniel Levitt. 526-527: Scott T. Smith/CORBIS. 529: Digital Vision Ltd./Getty Images. 532-533: Robert Glusic/Getty Images. 533: Grand Canyon of the Yellowstone Park (oil on canvas), Moran, Thomas (1837-1926)/Private Collection/The Bridgeman Art Library International. 536-537: IFA Bilderteam/AGE footstock. 537: Annie Griffiths Belt/CORBIS. 538: Frans Lanting/Minden Pictures. 539: Library of Congress, Prints & Photographs Division, FSA/OWI Collection, [LC-DIG-fsa-8b27245]. 540-541: Jeff Rotman/Getty Images. 542-543: Royalty-Free/CORBIS. 543: Hasselbalch Imaging. 544-554: Dennis Kunkel Microscopy, Inc. 555: Stephen Kramer. 556: (tr) Joshua Kramer; (c) E.R. Degginger/Animals Animals - Earth Scenes; (bl) Dennis Kunkel Microscopy; (bcl) Courtesy Dennis Kunkel. 557, 560: Dennis Kunkel Microscopy, Inc. 561: Tom & Dee Ann McCarthy/CORBIS. 562-563: Stephen Cooper/Getty Images. 564: Joe McDonald/CORBIS. 565: M. FOGDEN/OSF/Animals Animals - Earth Scenes. 566-567: Tom McHugh/Photo Researchers, Inc. 568: Paul Chesley/Getty Images. 568-569: Will Crocker/Getty Images. 569: Lee Kline. 570: BRECK P. KENT/Animals Animals - Earth Scenes. 571: (t) JOE MC DONALD/Animals Animals - Earth Scenes; (br) John Cancalosi/DRK PHOTO. 572: John Cancalosi. 573: David Boag/Alamy. 574: (t) David A. Northcott/DRK PHOTO; (br) Deborah Allen. 575: (tr) Stephen Cooper/Getty Images; (bl) ZIGMUND LESZCYNSKI/Animals Animals - Earth Scenes. 576-577: Gary McVicker/Index Stock Imagery. 577: John Cancalosi. 578: (tl) Courtesy Ellen Lambeth; (cl) BRECK P. KENT/Animals Animals - Earth Scenes. 578-579: Siede Preis/Getty Images. 582: Tom McHugh/Photo Researchers, Inc. 583: Ariel Skelley/CORBIS. 595: (r) PhotoLink/Getty Images; (bl) The McGraw-Hill Companies Inc./Ken Cavanagh Photographer; (br) Brand X Pictures/PunchStock. 596-597: Andrea Booher/Getty Images. 598-599: Fast Track/Getty Images. 599: Myrleen Ferguson Cate/PhotoEdit. 600-601: Karlheinz Oster/zefa/Corbis. 602-603: George D. Lepp/CORBIS. 604: The Granger Collection, New York. 605: San Diego Aerospace Museum. 606: Bettmann/CORBIS. 607: CORBIS. 608: The Ballooning Experiment at the Chateau de Versailles, 19th September, 1783 (coloured engraving), French School, (18th century)/Musee d'Art et d'Histoire, Meudon, France, Lauros/Giraudon/The Bridgeman Art Library International. 609: The First

LISTENING AND SPEAKING

1.0 Listening and Speaking Strategies Students deliver focused, coherent presentations that convey ideas clearly and relate to the background and interests of the audience. They evaluate the content of oral communication.

Comprehension

1.1 Ask questions that seek information not already discussed.

1.2 Interpret a speaker's verbal and nonverbal messages, purposes, and perspectives.

1.3 Make inferences or draw conclusions based on an oral report.

Organization and Delivery of Oral Communication

1.4 Select a focus, organizational structure, and point of view for an oral presentation.

1.5 Clarify and support spoken ideas with evidence and examples.

1.6 Engage the audience with appropriate verbal cues, facial expressions, and gestures.

Analysis and Evaluation of Oral and Media Communications

1.7 Identify, analyze, and critique persuasive techniques (e.g., promises, dares, flattery, glittering generalities); identify logical fallacies used in oral presentations and media messages.

1.8 Analyze media as sources for information, entertainment, persuasion, interpretation of events, and transmission of culture.

2.0 Speaking Applications (Genres and Their Characteristics) Students deliver well-organized formal presentations employing traditional rhetorical strategies (e.g., narration, exposition, persuasion, description). Student speaking demonstrates a command of standard American English and the organizational and delivery strategies outlined in Listening and Speaking Standard 1.0. Using the speaking strategies of grade five outlined in Listening and Speaking Standard 1.0, students:

2.1 Deliver narrative presentations:
   a. Establish a situation, plot, point of view, and setting with descriptive words and phrases.
   b. Show, rather than tell, the listener what happens.

2.2 Deliver informative presentations about an important idea, issue, or event by the following means:
   a. Frame questions to direct the investigation.
   b. Establish a controlling idea or topic.
   c. Develop the topic with simple facts, details, examples, and explanations.

2.3 Deliver oral responses to literature:
   a. Summarize significant events and details.
   b. Articulate an understanding of several ideas or images communicated by the literary work.
   c. Use examples or textual evidence from the work to support conclusions.

Aerial Voyage by Monsieur Francois Pilatre de Rozier (1754-85) and the Marquis of Arlandes (1742-1809) from Muette to the Windmill at Croule-Barbe, 21st November 1783 (coloured engraving), De Frene (18th century)/Bibliotheque Nationale, Paris, France, Lauros/Giraudon/The Bridgeman Art Library International. 610: Bettmann/CORBIS. 611: Bettmann/CORBIS. 612: Jay Syverson/CORBIS. 614: (tcl) Bettmann/CORBIS; (tr) Hulton-Deutsch Collection/CORBIS; (bl) Hulton Archive/Getty Images; (bcr) Bettmann/CORBIS. 614-615: Don Farrall/Getty Images. 615: (tl) AP Photo; (tr) Tony Ruta/Index Stock Imagery; (bl) AP Photo/Keystone, Fabrice Coffrini; (bcr) David Parker/Photo Researchers, Inc. 616: (tr) Kevin R. Morris/CORBIS; (inset) Russell Frost. 616-617: (bkgd) Don Farrall/Getty Images; (b) Karlheinz Oster/zefa/Corbis. 620: Karlheinz Oster/zefa/Corbis. 621: Image Source/Getty Images. 622-623: Pete Turner/Getty Images. 624-625: Reuters America LLC. 625: James Leynse/CORBIS. 626-627: Weatherstock/Omni-Photo Communications. 628-629: Kjell B. Sandved/Visuals Unlimited. 630-631: Greg Lovett/Palm Beach Post (digitally altered by MMH). 632-633: Science VU/Visuals Unlimited. 634-635: David Lane/Palm Beach Post. 636: Nancy P. Alexander. 638: (tl) Courtesy Seymour Simon; (cl) University Corporation for Atmospheric Research; (cr) U.S. Department of Interior, U.S. Geological Survey, J.D. Griggs. 638-639: StockTrek/Getty Images. 642: Weatherstock/Omni-Photo Communications. 643: Scott T. Baxter/Photodisc/Getty Images. 645: The McGraw-Hill Companies Inc./Ken Cavanagh Photographer. 646: AP Photo/IOPP. 646-647: Sylvain Grandadam/Getty Images. 650-651: Dirk Anschutz/Getty Images. 651: Dex Image/PunchStock. 652: Jeff Greenberg/AGE footstock. 653: Bettmann/CORBIS. 654-655: Digital Vision/Getty Images. 656: (t) Royalty-Free/CORBIS; (bl) SW Productions/Photodisc/Getty Images. 657: Tony Freeman/PhotoEdit. 678: James Henkel. 680: (tr) Steve Cole/Getty Images; (inset) AP Photo/Linda Spillers. 681: Royalty-Free/CORBIS. 682: (tl) Matthew Cavanaugh/Getty Images; (tc, tr, b) AP Photo/Linda Spillers. 685: Paul Edmondson/Getty Images. 686-687: Jean Michel Labat/Ardea. 706: tl, cr) Courtesy Northland Publishing. 708-709: ZIGMUND LESZCZYNSKI/Animals Animals - Earth Scenes. 709: Gloria H. Chomica/Masterfile. 710: Frans Lanting/Minden Pictures. 710-711: Steve Bloom Images/Alamy. 711: (t) Dwight Kuhn; (cr) Fritz Rauschenbach/zefa/Corbis. 713: BananaStock/PictureQuest. 714-715: AP Photo/Petros karadjias. 716: (tr) Elena Dorfman; (bl) Andrew Kaufman/Contact Press Images. 717: (tl) AP Photo/Shizuo Kambayashi; (br) AP Photo/Douglas C. Pizac. 718: (bl, br) Courtesy Boundless Playgrounds. 719: (t) Time & Life Pictures/Getty Images; (b) Courtesy Boundless Playgrounds. 720: AP Photo/Steve Miller. 721: Dwight Carter. 722: Jeaneen Lund. 725: (l) PhotoLink/Getty Images; (r) PhotoLink/Getty Images; (b) John Clines/Shutterstock; (br) Tracy Montana/PhotoLink/Getty Images. 726-727: PhotoAlto/PunchStock. 744: (tr, cl) Courtesy Candlewick Press. 746: USDA. 746-747: Kyodo News. 749: Brand X Pictures/PunchStock. 750-751: Ted Cheeseman/Peter Arnold, Inc. 772: (tr) Ed Scott; (cl) Courtesy Marla Baggetta. 774-775: Kelvin Aitken/AGE footstock. 776: Paul Sutherland Photography. 776-777: Stuart Westmorland/CORBIS. 777: Flip Nicklin/Minden Pictures. 779: Greg Ceo/Getty Images. 782: Jim Corwin/Getty Images. 783: Tony Freeman/PhotoEdit. 786: (l) Royalty-Free/CORBIS; (r) photolibrary.com pty. ltd./Index Stock. 790: Rolf Bruderer/CORBIS. 791: Geostock/Getty Images. 793: BananaStock/Alamy. 796: Royalty-Free/CORBIS. 797: Hartmut Schwarzbach/Peter Arnold. 799: Digital Vision/PunchStock. 800: photolibrary.com pty. ltd./Index Stock. 801: Foodcollection.com/Alamy. 804: PhotoLink/Getty Images. California Standards 1-5: Medioimages/PunchStock.

Reading/Language Arts
CA California Standards
Grade 5

READING

1.0 Word Analysis, Fluency, and Systematic Vocabulary Development

Students use their knowledge of word origins and word relationships, as well as historical and literary context clues, to determine the meaning of specialized vocabulary and to understand the precise meaning of grade-level-appropriate words.

Word Recognition

1.1	Read aloud narrative and expository text fluently and accurately and with appropriate pacing, intonation, and expression.

Vocabulary and Concept Development

1.2	Use word origins to determine the meaning of unknown words.
1.3	Understand and explain frequently used synonyms, antonyms, and homographs.
1.4	Know abstract, derived roots, and affixes from Greek and Latin and use this knowledge to analyze the meaning of complex words (e.g., *controversial*).
1.5	Understand and explain the figurative and metaphorical use of words in context.

2.0 Reading Comprehension (Focus on Informational Materials)

Students read and understand grade-level-appropriate material. They describe and connect the essential ideas, arguments, and perspectives of the text by using their knowledge of text structure, organization, and purpose. The selections in *Recommended Literature, Kindergarten Through Grade Twelve*, illustrate the quality and complexity of the materials to be read by students. In addition, by grade eight, students read one million words annually on their own, including a good representation of grade-level-appropriate narrative and expository text (e.g., classic and contemporary literature, magazines, newspapers, online information). In grade five, students make progress toward this goal.

Structural Features of Informational Materials

2.1	Understand how text features (e.g., format, graphics, sequence, diagrams, illustrations, charts, maps) make information accessible and usable.
2.2	Analyze text that is organized in sequential or chronological order.

READING (continued)

Comprehension and Analysis of Grade-Level-Appropriate Text

2.3 Discern main ideas and concepts presented in texts, identifying and assessing evidence that supports those ideas.

2.4 Draw inferences, conclusions, or generalizations about text and support them with textual evidence and prior knowledge.

Expository Critique

2.5 Distinguish facts, supported inferences, and opinions in text.

3.0 Literary Response and Analysis Students read and respond to historically or culturally significant works of literature. They begin to find ways to clarify the ideas and make connections between literary works. The selections in *Recommended Literature, Kindergarten Through Grade Twelve* illustrate the quality and complexity of the materials to be read by students.

Structural Features of Literature

3.1 Identify and analyze the characteristics of poetry, drama, fiction, and nonfiction and explain the appropriateness of the literary forms chosen by an author for a specific purpose.

Narrative Analysis of Grade-Level-Appropriate Text

3.2 Identify the main problem or conflict of the plot and explain how it is resolved.

3.3 Contrast the actions, motives (e.g., loyalty, selfishness, conscientiousness), and appearances of characters in a work of fiction and discuss the importance of the contrasts to the plot or theme.

3.4 Understand that *theme* refers to the meaning or moral of a selection and recognize themes (whether implied or stated directly) in sample works.

3.5 Describe the function and effect of common literary devices (e.g., imagery, metaphor, symbolism).

Literary Criticism

3.6 Evaluate the meaning of archetypal patterns and symbols that are found in myth and tradition by using literature from different eras and cultures.

3.7 Evaluate the author's use of various techniques (e.g., appeal of characters in a picture book, logic and credibility of plots and settings, use of figurative language) to influence readers' perspectives.

WRITING

1.0 Writing Strategies Students write clear, coherent, and focused essays. The writing exhibits the students' awareness of the audience and purpose. Essays contain formal introductions, supporting evidence, and conclusions. Students progress through the stages of the writing process as needed.

Organization and Focus

1.1 Create multiple-paragraph narrative compositions:
   a. Establish and develop a situation or plot.
   b. Describe the setting.
   c. Present an ending.

1.2 Create multiple-paragraph expository compositions:
   a. Establish a topic, important ideas, or events in sequence or chronological order.
   b. Provide details and transitional expressions that link one paragraph to another in a clear line of thought.
   c. Offer a concluding paragraph that summarizes important ideas and details.

Research and Technology

1.3 Use organizational features of printed text (e.g., citations, end notes, bibliographic references) to locate relevant information.

1.4 Create simple documents by using electronic media and employing organizational features (e.g., passwords, entry and pull-down menus, word searches, a thesaurus, spell checks).

1.5 Use a thesaurus to identify alternative word choices and meanings.

Evaluation and Revision

1.6 Edit and revise manuscripts to improve the meaning and focus of writing by adding, deleting, consolidating, clarifying, and rearranging words and sentences.

2.0 Writing Applications (Genres and Their Characteristics) Students write narrative, expository, persuasive, and descriptive texts of at least 500 to 700 words in each genre. Student writing demonstrates a command of standard American English and the research, organizational, and drafting strategies outlined in Writing Standard 1.0.

Using the writing strategies of grade five outlined in Writing Standard 1.0, students:

2.1 Write narratives:
   a. Establish a plot, point of view, setting, and conflict.
   b. Show, rather than tell, the events of the story.

2.2 Write responses to literature:
   a. Demonstrate an understanding of a literary work.
   b. Support judgments through references to the text and to prior knowledge.
   c. Develop interpretations that exhibit careful reading and understanding.

WRITING (continued)

2.3 Write research reports about important ideas, issues, or events by using the following guidelines:
- **a.** Frame questions that direct the investigation.
- **b.** Establish a controlling idea or topic.
- **c.** Develop the topic with simple facts, details, examples, and explanations.

2.4 Write persuasive letters or compositions:
- **a.** State a clear position in support of a proposal.
- **b.** Support a position with relevant evidence.
- **c.** Follow a simple organizational pattern.
- **d.** Address reader concerns.

WRITTEN AND ORAL ENGLISH LANGUAGE CONVENTIONS

The standards for written and oral English language conventions have been placed between those for writing and for listening and speaking because these conventions are essential to both sets of skills.

1.0 Written and Oral English Language Conventions Students write and speak with a command of standard English conventions appropriate to this grade level.

Sentence Structure

1.1 Identify and correctly use prepositional phrases, appositives, and independent and dependent clauses; use transitions and conjunctions to connect ideas.

Grammar

1.2 Identify and correctly use verbs that are often misused (e.g., *lie/ lay*, *sit/ set*, *rise/ raise*), modifiers, and pronouns.

Punctuation

1.3 Use a colon to separate hours and minutes and to introduce a list; use quotation marks around the exact words of a speaker and titles of poems, songs, short stories, and so forth.

Capitalization

1.4 Use correct capitalization.

Spelling

1.5 Spell roots, suffixes, prefixes, contractions, and syllable constructions correctly.